Mathematical Methods for Management

Mathematical Methods for Management

R. Veerachamy
Senior Faculty
Alliance University, Bangalore
Karnataka
Ex. Professor and Chairman
Department of Economics, Bangalore University
Bangalore, Karnataka

PUBLISHING FOR ONE WORLD
NEW AGE INTERNATIONAL (P) LIMITED, PUBLISHERS
New Delhi • Bangalore • Chennai • Cochin • Guwahati
Hyderabad • Kolkata • Lucknow • Mumbai
Visit us at **www.newagepublishers.com**

Published by New Age International (P) Ltd., Publishers
First Edition: 2012

Branches:

- 37/10, 8th Cross (Near Hanuman Temple), Azad Nagar, Chamarajpet, **Bangalore**-560 018
  Tel.: (080) 26756823, Telefax: 26756820, E-mail: bangalore@newagepublishers.com
- 26, Damodaran Street, T. Nagar, **Chennai**-600 017. Tel.: (044) 24353401, Telefax: 24351463
  E-mail: chennai@newagepublishers.com
- CC-39/1016, Carrier Station Road, Ernakulam South, **Cochin**-682 016. Tel.: (0484) 2377004, Telefax: 4051303
  E-mail: cochin@newagepublishers.com
- Hemsen Complex, Mohd. Shah Road, Paltan Bazar, Near Starline Hotel, **Guwahati**-781 008. Tel.: (0361) 2513881
  Telefax: 2543669, E-mail: guwahati@newagepublishers.com
- 105, 1st Floor, Madhiray Kaveri Tower, 3-2-19, Azam Jahi Road, Nimboliadda, **Hyderabad**-500 027
  Tel.: (040) 24652456, Telefax: 24652457, E-mail:hyderabad@newagepublishers.com
- RDB Chambers (Formerly Lotus Cinema)106A, 1st Floor, S.N. Banerjee Road, **Kolkata**-700 014
  Tel.: (033) 22273773, Telefax: 22275247, E-mail:kolkata@newagepublishers.com
- 16-A, Jopling Road, **Lucknow**-226 001. Tel.: (0522) 2209578, 4045297, Telefax: 2204098
  E-mail: lucknow@newagepublishers.com
- 142C, Victor House, Ground Floor, N.M. Joshi Marg, Lower Parel, **Mumbai**-400 013. Tel.: (022) 24927869
  Telefax: 24915415, E-mail: mumbai@newagepublishers.com
- 22, Golden House, Daryaganj, **New Delhi**-110 002. Tel.: (011) 23262370, 23262368, Telefax: 43551305
  E-mail: sales@newagepublishers.com

ISBN: 978-81-224-3320-3

₹ 275.00

C-11-06-5624

Printed in India at Parmanand Offset, Delhi.
Typeset at In-house, New Delhi.

PUBLISHING FOR ONE WORLD
NEW AGE INTERNATIONAL (P) LIMITED, PUBLISHERS
4835/24, Ansari Road, Daryaganj, New Delhi-110002
Visit us at **www.newagepublishers.com**

Dedication

This book is dedicated to my
beloved Mother
Chellamal
who infused in me determination,
hardworking nature and
warmth of relations.

PREFACE

In modern business continuous decision making is an essential part. To achieve such a task modern management uses several readily available mathematical tools without bothering much about the principals involved in developing such tools. In this book a modest attempt has been to explain all the commonly used mathematical techniques in a wide spectrum of decision making environment.

The book is completely self-contained with all the essential mathematical techniques used in business. Each chapter is designed to be modular, so that the book can very well be tailored to suit the need of a course. The author has taken due care to avoid excessive theatrical description in favor of selective, real-life applications. To provide exposure in every topic, numerous problems from various Indian university question papers are provided.

The text assumes minimal mathematical background but at the same time demonstrates the importance of mathematics with several numerical examples in all the chapters. Keeping the students capability in mind the author has provided few review chapters as well in the beginning of the text. Though several text books are available in the market, some of them overemphasize the mathematics and hence give less importance to the underlying theory; some others give priority the theory and ignore the usefulness of mathematics. Having the drawback of both these approaches in mind, the author has used a balanced approach. Moreover, attempt has been made to provide tool based business applications.

This book could be used as text book for both graduate and post graduate levels in business related courses. In addition this book is designed to the needed prerequisites for competitive examinations like JRF, NET, SLET etc.

Although enough care has been taken to keep the book error free, the author personally takes the sole responsibility for the leftover errors, if any. The author greatly indented to the students community at large, without their support and constructive suggestions this text would not have taken this shape. Critical evaluation and value adding suggestions, that will help the author to enhance the utility of this book in latter editions, would be greatly appreciated. The author also owe his gratitude to the dedicated team of New Age International Publishers Private Limited for their sincere effort in bring this text in time.

R. Veerachamy

CONTENTS

1

Chapter

INTRODUCTION TO MATHEMATICAL METHODS

1.1 The Changing Scenario of Business

Until recently, it was felt that the analysis of events that take place in business needs only a good sense and a sound logical reasoning. However, the complexity of modern business environment makes the process of decision-making more difficult. Thus, the decision-maker cannot completely relay upon the commonsense observations and obtained business experience. Recent trends in the development of business certainly have convinced all of us that there is an urgent need for a better understanding of the subject matter. No doubt, this improved understanding can be brought about only through a scientific approach to the complex real world happenings in business. In the process, one must bring the date old verbal business related theories within the framework of technical competence that makes it possible to use the up-to-date mathematical and statistical techniques. In fact business is basically a quantitative subject in the sense that most of the variables like prices, income, employment, profit etc., that we use in business are always measured and stated in quantitative terms. Business theories often deal with the analysis of relationships between variables. When such relationships are laid down in a specific format they form business theories or otherwise called business principles. For example, the inverse relationship between price charged and the quantity demanded is popularly known as the law of demand in business. Similarly, the relationship between inputs and outputs solely determined by the state of technical knowledge of the vintage concerned is called the production function. In all these relationships the involved variables are measured and stated in quantitative terms. Moreover, to depict the exact form of the said relationships, linear or otherwise, it is handy to use both mathematical and statistical techniques in various combinations.

The scientific management revolution of the early 1900's initiated by Frederic W. Taylor provided the foundation for the use of quantitative methods in business management. The recent development in the use of statistical data in making business decisions has created some new and powerful tools of analysis. The pressure of more complex business problems and large-scale operation of business has stimulated research in the development sophisticated tools. Many fields of knowledge have contributed to this improvement in business decision-making. The use of more objective methods and more accurate information improves the understanding of business problems. The increasing use of statistical methods has provided more and more precise information. In recent years a great deal of experimentation has been carried out to bring out improved method of understanding the business. During World War-II, the methods used by scientists were applied with outstanding success to certain military problems, such as mining the enemy's water, searching out enemy's ship, etc. Two developments that occurred during post war II period led to the growth and use of quantitative methods in non-military applications. Continued research resulted in numerous methodical developments. Probably the most significant development was the discovery of simplex method for solving linear programming problems by Gharge Dantzig in 1947. Subsequently, many methodological developments followed. In 1957 Churchman, Ackoff, and Arnoff published the first book on operation research. Business organizations are now successfully apply these techniques to problems like inventory fluctuations, the product mix that maximizes profit, shipments of goods from origin's to different destinations etc. Mathematics, statistics, physics, economics, and engineering are some of the fields in which operations research methods are used effectively. Since the variables under consideration are expressed in quantities it is often called quantitative technique as well.

1.2 Mathematics and Management Decisions

Nowadays, the branch of knowledge that uses mathematical techniques specially in economic theorizing is popularly known as "Mathematical Economics". In explaining the economic theory the use of mathematics makes the theory not only simple but also more precise and exact. In fact in mathematical economics we transform the economic theory into a compact and precise mathematical form by using appropriate mathematical functional form. For example, the law of demand tells us, that when other thing does not change the price and quantity demanded are inversely related. As a first approximation to this demand law, economists often use linear equations of the type $q = a + bp$; $a > 0$, $b < 0$ to make the analysis simple. Similarly, to represent consumer's preference in the theory of consumption we often use convex indifference curves. Often economic theories are expressed in mathematical terms to obtain their important characteristic results. However, it should be remembered that mathematical economics is certainly not a separate branch of knowledge by itself. In fact, the mathematical approach is common to all fields in economics, like microeconomics, macroeconomics, public finance etc. Hence mathematical economics is considered as a scientific approach, which can be used in almost all branches of economics. The only difference now is that, in mathematical economics we use mathematical language instead of the verbal language in explaining the concerned economic theory. However, it should not be mistaken that in mathematical economics the economic theory is simply transformed into its mathematical form. The very purpose of such a transformation is not only to make the theory easy but also to arrive at certain interesting characteristic results. For example, after transforming both demand and supply functions in its simple linear mathematical form we can easily calculate both the equilibrium price and the quantity. Similarly, we can calculate the appropriate tax rate that gives maximum tax collection to the government. It is important to note that such typical questions can be answered more precisely only by using mathematics. Therefore mathematical economics can always be considered as complementary rather than competitive in economic analysis.

1.3 Advantages of Using Mathematics in Business

1. The mathematical language by nature is concise and precise. Hence, by using mathematics we can restate the business theory in a more compact form like the one

stated above in the case of the demand law. In it the involved relationship is simple and self-explanatory in its mathematical form.

2. The mathematical simplicity enhances the precision of analysis like the calculation of equilibrium price, equilibrium quantity, price elasticity of demand etc.
3. The mathematical approach can have always the advantage of using the ever-growing unlimited amount of tools and theorems in pure mathematics for their advantage. The use of Euler's mathematical theorem in business in explaining the distribution of income among the factors of production is the classical example for such an advantage.
4. Once a certain specific mathematical relationship is obtained, the business manager can deduce more useful new propositions.
5. The biggest advantage of mathematical science is its ability to handle large number of variables at a given point of time. For example, in the theory of consumption especially in indifference curve analysis, at the most we can handle only two commodities, one along the x-axis and one along y-axis. But in reality, our consumption basket contains a large number of commodities. Mathematical science can handle this situation by increasing the commodity space which can accommodate any number of commodities in getting the extended equi-marginal principle.

1.4 Disadvantages of Using Mathematics in Business

1. In certain sections of business, we come across variables like the tastes, preferences etc. Since these variables are qualitative in nature we often find it difficult to use quantitative mathematical techniques.
2. The most common criticism leveled against mathematical interpretation of business problem is about its abstract and unrealistic nature. The abstract and unrealistic results derived by using mathematical methods are mainly due to unrealistic assumptions that have been made in the beginning about the concerned theory. Moreover, such unrealistic and abstract results are often found in non-mathematical theoretical treatment as well. Therefore, wherever the assumptions of the theory are more realistic, less will be the abstract nature of the theory both in mathematical and in non-mathematical presentations.

1.5 Problem Solving and Decision-Making

Decision-making is the term normally associated with the following steps:

- Identify and define the problem.
- Determine the alternative solutions.
- Determine the criterion that will be used to evaluate the alternatives.
- Evaluate the alternatives.
- Choose the best alternative.

Let us consider the following illustrative example for the decision-making process.

Problem defined: Assume that you are in a well-paid job in Weprow, a leading IT industry in Bangalore, and would like to move to some other company. Then you define the alternatives as follows:

- Move to Infosys
- Move to Micro System
- Network Solution
- System Management.

Once the four alternatives are defined, the next job is to define criteria's for selecting one among the four. Let the highest starting pay is the first criterion. Now the job of selection is simply the highest starting paying job. This type of problems is called single criterion problems.

Suppose in addition to the highest starting salary, you also want to have nearest work location and potential for promotional avenues as additional criterions. Now since your problem involves three criterions it is called multi-criterion problem. Evaluating each alternative with added criterions is a difficult job because evaluations are based on subjective factors which are difficult to quantify. Let us rate the added criterions as poor, average, good and excellent. Now let the data relating to our problem are as shown below:

Table 1.1

Alternatives	Starting Salary	Potential Avenues for Promotions	Job Location
1	Rs. 35,000	average	average
2	Rs. 40,000	good	good
3	Rs. 42,000	excellent	excellent
4	Rs. 50,000	average	good

Now with this added scaling information we are better placed in decision-making. Alternative 3 seems to be the best decision under the given circumstances.

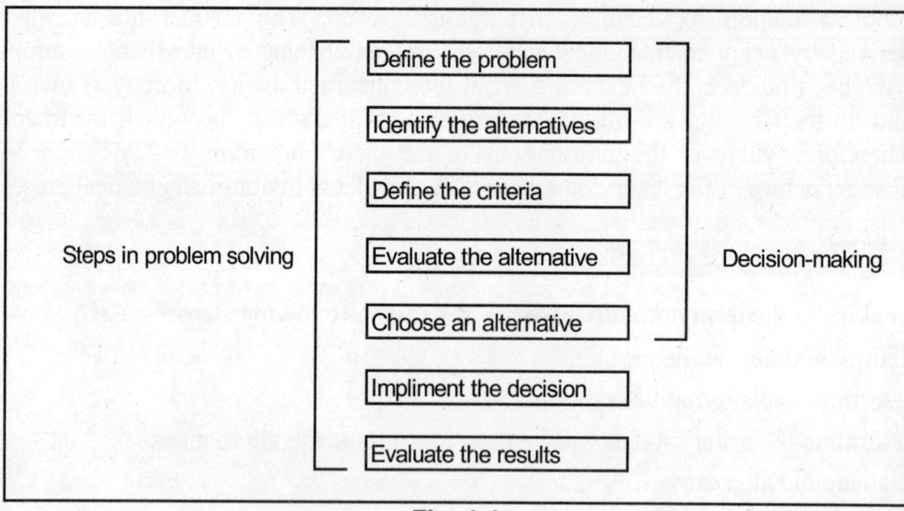

Fig. 1.1

Once the decision is made to go for alternative 3, the decision is implemented and the result is evaluated.

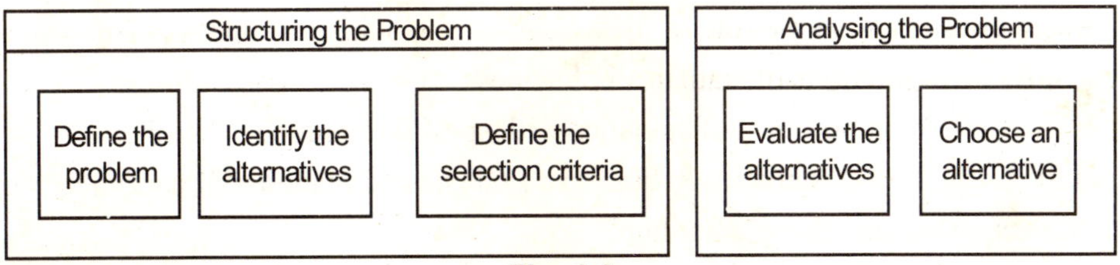

Fig. 1.2

Figure 1.1 shows the analysis phase of the decision-making problem. In any decision making problem one will face the both qualitative and quantitative judgements. The qualitative judgement decision is often based on the value judgement experience of the decision-maker. It normally includes the decision-maker's intuitive "feel" of the problem and hence based on considered as an art rather then science. If the decision-maker is well experienced in the related field, then one must give due respect to the qualitative decision and accept his judgement. Alternatively, if the decision-maker is with little experience in the field and the problem is more complex, then one must opt for quantitative analysis. Under the circumstances, using one or more quantitative methods, the analysts will recommend the appropriate optimum decision.

Although the skill in the qualitative part of the problem is based on experience, the quantitative skill goes beyond one's own comprehension. One can acquire this skill only by learning management science. In fact these two approaches are complementary in optimum decision-making. The following chart [Fig. 1.3] summarises the entire process of decision making.

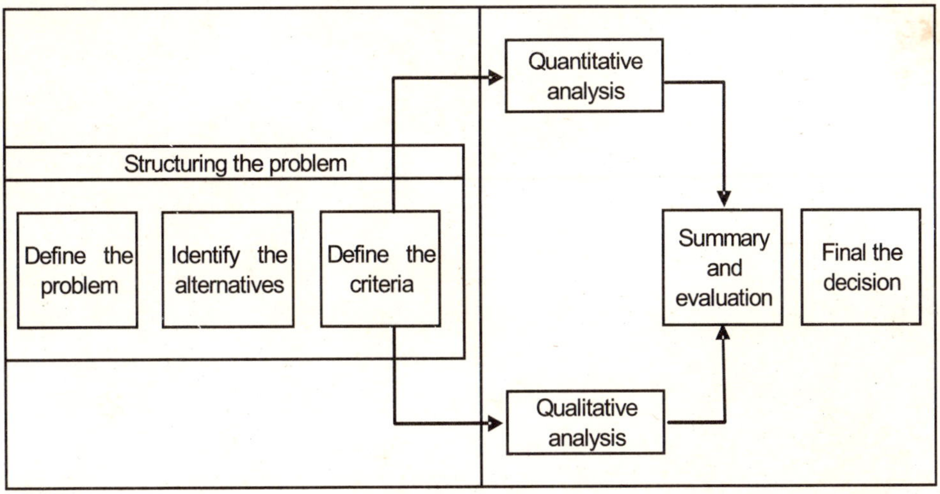

Fig. 1.3

EXERCISES

1. Discuss the importance of quantitative methods in business.
2. Do you think that quantitative techniques have a definite role to play in every future decision-making? Substantiate your answer with suitable illustrations.
3. Discuss fully the limitations of quantitative techniques in business.
4. "Statistics is the straw out of which I, like every other economists, make my bricks". Explain.

5. With illustrations examine the role of mathematical and statistical methods in business.
6. Discuss fully the limitations of statistics in business.
7. Discuss in detail the importance of statistics with special reference to business.
8. Explain the usefulness of statistics in business analysis and planning in particular.
9. "Statistics can prove any thing". Explain.
10. "Statistics are like clay of which you can make either a God or Devil as you please". Give your comment on the above statement.
11. Describe the role of both mathematical and statistical methods in business.
12. "Quantitative analysis has considerable accomplishments to its credits but it is not a panacea, and hence is in occasional danger of living oversold." Discuss.
13. Describe the steps involved in problem formulation and problem solving.

❍ ❍

2

Chapter

THE THEORY OF SETS

2.1 Introduction

In our day-to-day life, we all use the concept 'set' invariably in all walks of life. In all cases by set we simply mean the collection of some well-defined objects like the set of teachers in the college, the set of planets in our solar system, the set of Economics text books in the University library etc. In all these examples, the said objects have been grouped together and viewed as a single entity. This idea of grouping objects together gives rise to a mathematical concept often called the set. Thus, the objects of a given set may be anything, as we please, expect the fact that there should not be any room for doubt as whether the given object belongs to the set under reference or not.

2.2 Definition of a Set

These sets are often denoted by capital letters A, B, C, etc. The elements of a set are written within a pair of braces {}. The following are the set of some well-defined objects.

A = {The set of colours in the Indian National Flag}

B = {Bangalore, Mumbai, Chennai, Delhi}

C = {1, 2, 3, 4, 5, 6, 7}

D = {a, b, c, d, e,}

E = {The set of all even numbers}

In general if 'A' is the set and 'x' is a member of the set, then we simply say that 'x' belongs to the set A. To make the representation simple, we often use the symbol '$\in$' to mean 'belongs to' and write the above statement simply as $x \in A$. If x is not a member of the given set A, then to mean 'does not belongs to' we use the symbol '$\notin$' and write the same as $x \notin A$.

Example 1: If A = {1, 2, 3} then since 2 is a member of the set A we would say that $2 \in A$. Further, since 4 is not a member of the set A we can also say that $4 \notin A$.

The elements of a given set may either be written completely by listing out all its members or by writing some common characteristics to represent them all.

Example 2: A = {saffron, white, green} or

A = {The set of all colours in the Indian National Flag}.

In a set, the order in which the elements are placed does not matter at all. For example, the set A = {1, 2, 3, 4, 5} and the set B = {5, 3, 4, 2, 1} are equal to one another in all respects, though the order of placement of the individual elements are different. Similarly, we do not count a certain given member more than once in a given set though there are repetitions. By this we mean that the sets

A = {1, 2, 3} and B = {1, 2, 2, 3, 3} are equal to one another in all respects.

Finite and Infinite Sets: A set, which has finite number of elements is called a finite set. Similarly, the set that contains infinite number of elements is called an infinite set.

Example 3: A = {a, b, c, d} is called a finite set because it contains four finite number of elements in it.

Example 4: Similarly, the set B = {the set of all positive integers} is called an infinite set because it contains infinite number of positive integers in it.

Notations in Sets: To describe a given set, in general we often use certain specialized type of notations.

Example 5: Let B = {x/x is an integer}. We read this statement as 'B is the set of all x's such that x is an integer'. Alternatively, by this notation we simply mean that B is the set of all integers. i.e., B = {... – 3, – 2, – 1, 0, 1, 2, 3...}. Similarly, if S = $\{x/x^2 - 3x + 2 = 0\}$ then we insists that our set S should contains only the solutions to the given quadratic equation namely 1 and 2. i.e. S = {1, 2}.

Venn Diagram: To make the analysis more comprehensive and easily understandable we often use compact pictorial representations of sets. Such pictorial representations are often called Venn diagrams.

Example 6: If A = {a, b, c} is the set under reference, then the corresponding pictorial Venn diagram is shown below. Here a small ellipse is used to represent the set. Within this ellipse all its members namely a, b and c are accommodated.

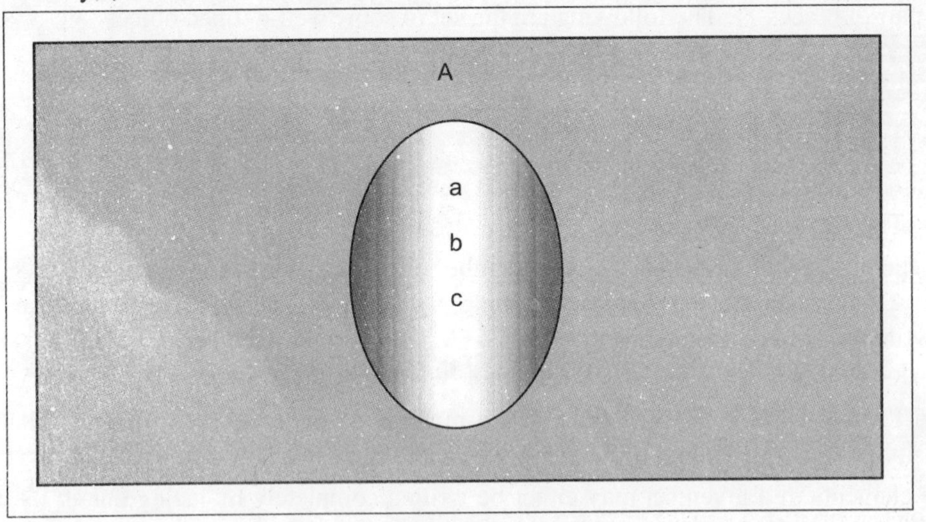

Fig. 2.1

Universal set and sub-sets: The whole of the given set is often called the universal set. The sub-set by definition is simply a portion or a part of the given universal set.

Example 7: If U = {1, 2, 3} is the universal set then, A = {1, 2}; B = {2, 3}; C = {3, 1} are some of the sub-sets of U that one can frame. Further, since sub-sets by definition are partitions or parts of the universal set U, it is quite but natural that they all must contained in U, the universal set. To mean 'contained in' we use the notation '$\subset$'. Hence, in our illustration given above, since A, B and C are sub-sets of the universal set U, we simply write $A \subset U$, $B \subset U$, $C \subset U$ and so on.

Proper and improper sub-sets: A proper sub-set contains at least one element less than the given universal set. In this sense the proper sub-set is really a part and not the whole of the universal set U. An improper sub-set however will have all the members of the universal set U. In other words, the improper sub-set of the given universal set is the universal set itself.

Example 8: If U = {a, b, c, d} stands for the universal set, then A = {a, b}, B = {a, b, c} are some of the examples for the proper sub sets of U.

If D = {a, b, c, d} then D is called the improper sub-set of U because D = U.

Note: A is the proper sub-set of B, then $A \subset B$ and $A \neq B$.

Singleton set: A set that contains only one element in it is often called a singleton set.

Example 9: A = {1}; B = {b}; C = {Bangalore} are some the examples of singleton sets.

Null or Empty set: A set, which contains no element of what so ever, is often called the null or empty set. It is normally denoted by the notation ϕ.

Example 10: If ϕ = {x/x is a human being in the moon} is called the empty set because there are no human beings in the moon as on today. Similarly, if ϕ = {x/x is a real number such that $x^2 + 1 = 0$}, then again the solution set of the quadratic equation is empty because $\pm\sqrt{-1}$ does not belongs to the real number set.

Set of sets: A set whose elements themselves are sets is called a set of sets.

Example 11: If A = [{3, 4}, {a, b,},ϕ], then the set A is called the set of sets because in it the members themselves are sets.

Power set: The collection of all possible proper sub-sets of a given universal set U is called the power set of the universal set U. Here the members themselves are sets of varying size. If the set A has 'n' elements in it then its power set will have altogether 2^n elements.

Example 12: If U = {1, 2, 3} then the set

P = {(1), (2), (3), (1, 2), (1, 3), (2, 3), (1, 2, 3),ϕ} is called the power set of the set A. Here $2^3 = 8$ elements are found in this power set.

2.3 Basic Operations on Sets

Like any other branch of Mathematics, in the theory of sets as well we have some important basic operations.

1. **Differences among sets:** If A and B are the two given sets then the difference set denoted by A – B is obtained by simply removing all the elements of the set B found in A.

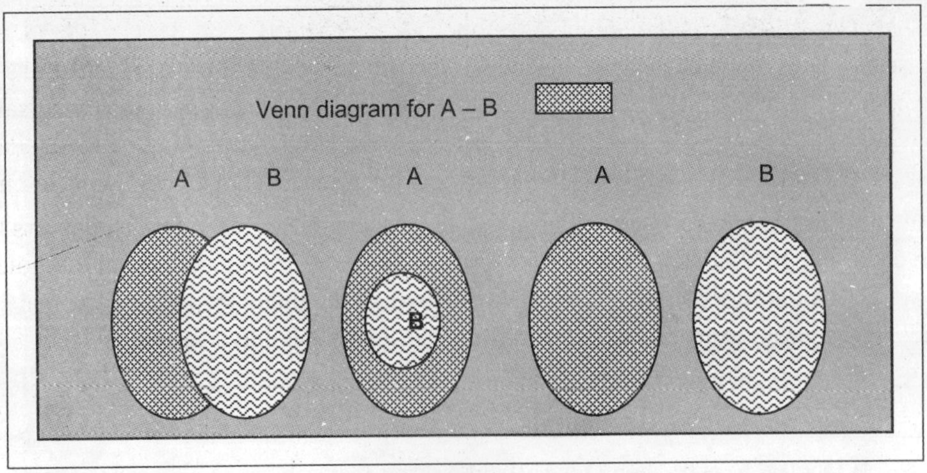

Fig. 2.2

In all these diagrams (Fig. 2.2) the darkly shaded areas give us the needed set A – B.

By similar reasoning we define the set B – A simply by removing all the elements of the set A from the set B.

Example 13: If A = {1, 2, 3, 4} and B = {3, 4, 5, 6} then the set A – B is defined as A – B = {1, 2}. Here the elements 3 and 4 found in B is removed from A.

Example 14: If A = {1, 2, 3, 4} and B = {3, 4, 5, 6} then the set B – A is defined as B – A = {5, 6}.

Note: A – B ≠ B – A, because the set {1, 2} ≠ {5, 6} in our illustration.

Example 15: If A = {a, b} and B = {c, d} then the set A – B = A. Here no element of B is found in A hence removal of elements does not arise.

Difference of sets by using notations

In symbolic form $A - B = \{x/x \in A \text{ but } x \notin B\}$

$$B - A = \{x/x \in B \text{ but } x \notin A\}$$

2. **Intersection of sets:** If A and B are the two sets then the intersection between A and B denoted by $A \cap B$ is defined as a third set having only the common elements of both the sets A and B.

In all these diagrams (Fig. 2.3) the shaded areas, which are common to both A and B, give us the needed set $A \cap B$.

Example 16: If A = {1, 2, 3, 4} and B = {2, 3, 4, 5, 6}, then the set

$$A \cap B = \{2, 3, 4\}.$$

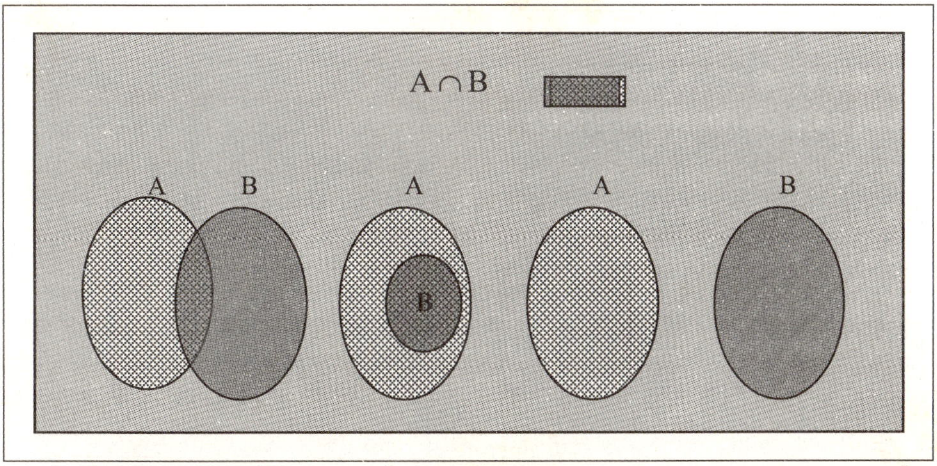

Fig. 2.3

Example 17: If A = {a, b} and B = {c, d, e} then $A \cap B = \phi$, the empty set, since no common elements are found in this case.

Intersection of sets using notations

$A \cap B = \{x/x \in A \text{ and } x \in B\}$

Note: $A \cap B = A$ if $A \subset B$

$A \cap B = B$ if $B \subset A$

$A \cap B = \phi$ when A and B are disjoint sets

Commutative property of intersection: We all know that 4 + 5 = 5 + 4. In other words, this is to say that if two numbers are to be added then it does not matter whether the first number is added to the second or second number is added to the first. This simple property is known as commutative property of addition. Such a property holds good even for the set operation '∩', the intersection. Since the operation '∩' is defined as the collection of all common elements of both A and B, it dose not matter whether the collections are made from A first and then B or vice versa. In other words this is to say that $B \cap A = A \cap B$

Example 18: If A ={1, 2, 3, 4} and B = {3, 4, 5, 6} then $A \cap B = B \cap A = \{3, 4\}$.

Associative property of intersection: It is also true that {7 + 3} + 10 = 7 + {3 + 10} = 20. While grouping of numbers for addition it does not matter whether the first two numbers are grouped for addition and then added to the third or the last two numbers are grouped for addition and then added to the first. In fact, we can group them in any way as we please. This property is known as the associative property of addition. Such a property holds good even for the operation '∩', the intersection.

i.e., $(A \cap B) \cap C = A \cap (B \cap C)$.

Example 19: Let A = {1, 2, 3}, B = {2, 3, 4}, C = {3, 4, 5} then

$$(A \cap B) \cap C = \{2, 3\} \cap \{3, 4, 5\} = \{3\}$$

$$A \cap (B \cap C) = \{1, 2, 3\} \cap \{3, 4\} = \{3\}$$

3. **Union operation in sets:** If A and B are the two sets then the union of A and B, normally written as $A \cup B$, is defined as a unified set containing the elements A alone i.e. $(A - B)$ or B alone i.e. $(B - A)$ or both A and B i.e. $(A \cap B)$. Hence by using the set notation the union of A and B is written as $A \cup B = \{x/x \in A - B \text{ or } x \in B - A \text{ or } x \in A \cap B\}$. Since by definition all the elements of $A \cap B$ is found in both A and B the above statement may also be written as $A \cup B = \{x/x \in A \text{ or } x \in B\}$. Obviously to get the union of two sets A and B we simply collect all the elements found in both A and B without being any repetition.

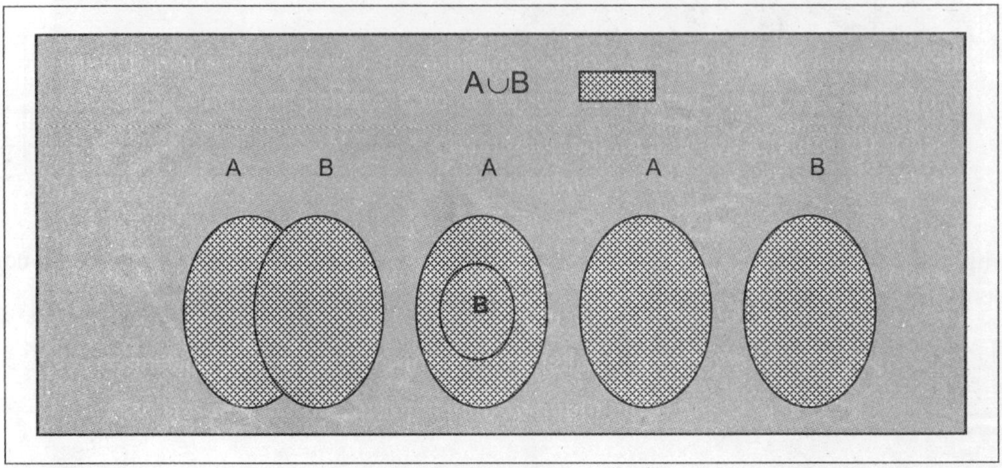

Fig. 2.4

Example 20: Let A = {a, b, c} and B = {c, d, e, f}

Then $A - B = \{a, b\}$;

$B - A = \{d, e, f\}$;

$A \cap B = \{c\}$.

Hence $A \cup B = \{a, b, c, d, e, f\}$.

Example 21: Let A = {1, 2} and B = {3, 4, 5}

Then $A - B = A$;

$B - A = B$;

$A \cap B = \phi$.

Therefore, $A \cup B = \{1, 2, 3, 4, 5\}$

In all these diagrams (Fig. 2.4) the shaded area denotes the needed $A \cup B$.

Note: $A \cup B = A$ when $B \subset A$; $A \cup B = B$ when $A \subset B$.

Commutative law of union: The commutative law stated in the previous section for the operation intersection holds good even in the case of the operation '∪', union.

Example 22: If A = {l, m, n} and B = {n, o, p, q} then from the definition of union it follows that $A \cup B = B \cup A = \{l, m, n, o, p, q\}$.

Associative law of union: Since by definition all the elements of $(A \cup B) \cup C$ are found in $A \cup (B \cup C)$ it follows that $(A \cup B) \cup C = A \cup (B \cup C)$.

Example 23: Let $A = \{1, 2\}$, $B = \{2, 3, 4\}$ and $C = \{4, 5\}$

then $(A \cup B) \cup C = \{1, 2, 3, 4\} \cup \{4, 5\} = \{1, 2, 3, 4, 5\}$

$A \cup (B \cup C) = \{1, 2\} \cup \{2, 3, 4, 5\} = \{1, 2, 3, 4, 5\}$

Disjoint sets: If A and B are two sets such that $A \cap B = \phi$, the empty set, then A and B are said to be disjoint sets.

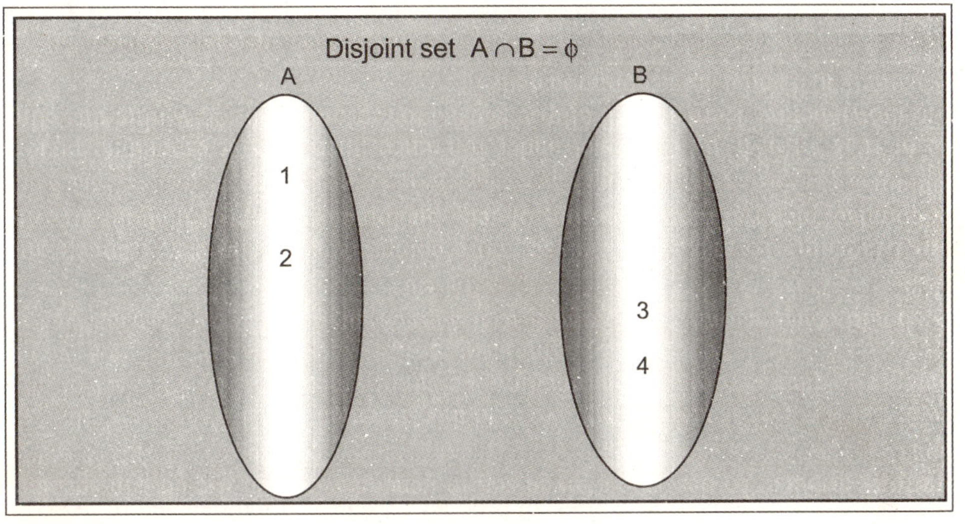

Fig. 2.5

In the above diagram (Fig. 2.5) A and B are disjoint in the sense that there are no common elements.

Complements

Let U = {1, 2, 3, 4, 5, 6} stands for the universal set. Now let A = {1, 2, 3} be a sub-set of U. Now consider the set of elements that do not belong to A i.e. (U – A). i.e. {4, 5, 6}. This set is called the complement of the set A and is denoted by A^c or A'

i.e. $A^c = \{x/x \in U \text{ and } x \notin A\}$

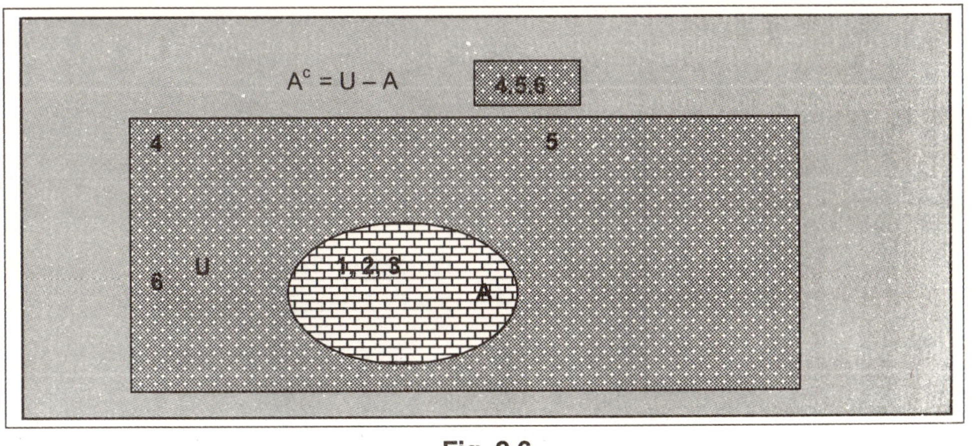

Fig. 2.6

Note: (1) $A \cup A^c = U$, the universal set.

(2) $A^c = U - A$

(3) $A \cap A^c = \phi$.

Number of elements in a given union: Let A and B are two finite sets. Further let n (A), n (B) and n $(A \cap B)$ are the number of elements in A, B and $A \cap B$ respectively. To count the number of element in $A \cup B$ we first count the number of elements in A [i.e. n (A)] and then count the number of elements in B [i.e. n (B)] then add them alltogather. While doing so the elements in $A \cap B$ [i.e. n $(A \cap B)$] is counted twice. So we must subtract the number of elements in $A \cap B$ once from n (A) + n (B) to get at the correct number of members. Thus $n(A \cup B) = n(A) + n(B) - n(A \cap B)$. However, if A and B are disjoint sets then $(A \cap B) = \phi$. So the above result reduces to $n(A \cup B) = n(A) + n(B)$. Similarly, if A, B and C are three finite sets then, $n(A \cup B \cup C) = n(A) + n(B) + n(C) - n(A \cap B) - n(B \cap C) - n(C \cap A) + n(A \cap B \cap C)$.

Ordered pairs: If A = {2, 4, 5} and B = {3, 6, 7} are the two sets then pairs like (2, 3), (2, 6}, (5, 7) etc., formed by taking the first component from the first set A and the second component from the second set B in an orderly manner are called ordered pairs.

2.4 The Cartesian Product Set

If A and B are the two given sets then the set of all possible ordered pairs represented by (x, y) so that $x \in A$ and $y \in B$ is called the Cartesian product set and is often denoted by A×B (read as A cross B).

Example 24: If A = {a, b} and B = {1, 2, 3} then by definition

A×B = {(a, 1), (a, 2), (a, 3), (b, 1), (b, 2), (b, 3)}

Example 25: If A = {1, 2, 3} then

A×A = {(1, 1), (1, 2), (1, 3), (2, 1), (2, 2), (2, 3), (3, 1), (3, 2), (3, 3)}.

Notation for Cartesian product: Using notations the Cartesian product set A×B is normally written as $A \times B = \{(x, y) / x \in A \text{ and } y \in B\}$.

Note: If the set A has n elements and B has m elements then the A × B will have 'm × n' elements. Also note that $A \times B \neq B \times A$.

Example 26: If A = {1, 2} and B = {a, b}

then A × B = {(1, a), (1, b), (2, a), (2, b)}

and B × A = {(a, 1), (a, 2), (b, 1), (b, 2)}

From above it is easy to see that $A \times B \neq B \times A$.

2.5 Relations

Let P = {Raman, Lakshmi, John, Iqbal, Abdul Kadar, Marry, Joseph, Shiva Kumar, Roopa...} be the set of all living persons in a certain city. It is quit possible that some members of this society may be related to some other members of the same society in some way or the other. The following are some of the typical relations that one could find within the set P.

1. Raman is the father of Shiva Kumar.
2. Iqbal is the son of Abdul Kadar.
3. Roopa is the daughter of Lakshmi.

However, one could notice a lot more unspecified relations within the members of this large society. Now let 'R' refers a typical relation to mean 'is the father of'. Suppose in our society Raman, Abdul Kadar and John are the fathers of Shiva Kumar, Iqbal and Joseph respectively. Now one could easily see that (Raman, Shiva Kumar), (Abdul Kadar, Iqbal), (John, Joseph) are some of the ordered pairs of the Cartesian product set P×P having the relation 'R'. It is also true that the relation R = {(Raman, Shiva Kumar), (Abdul Kadar, Iqbal), (John, Joseph). . . . .} is a proper sub-set of the Cartesian product set P× P.

An alternative presentation

Now let us look at the same illustration in a slightly different angle. Let A be the sub-set of the set P representing only the fathers and B be the sub-set representing only the sons and daughters in our typical society.

i.e. A = {Raman, Abdul Kadar, Peter, John,. . . . . . .}

and B = {Shiva Kumar, Roopa, Krishnan, Iqbal, Joseph....... }

Now our relation 'R' to mean 'is the father of' is a sub-set of A × B

i.e. R = {(Raman, Shiva Kumar), (Abdul Kadar, Iqbal), (John, Joseph) . . . .}

Alternatively, R = {(x, y)/ x ∈ A and y ∈ B} so that ^xR_y

Example 27: If A = {1, 2, 3} and B = {1, 2, 4, 5} then

A×B = {(1, 1), (1, 2), (1, 4), (1, 5), **(2, 1)**, (2, 2), (2, 4), (2, 5), **(3, 1)**, **(3, 2)**, (3, 4), (3, 5)}

Now let **'R'** to mean ' **is greater than'** relation from A to B, then

R = {(x, y)/ x > y} = {(2, 1), (3, 1), (3, 2)}

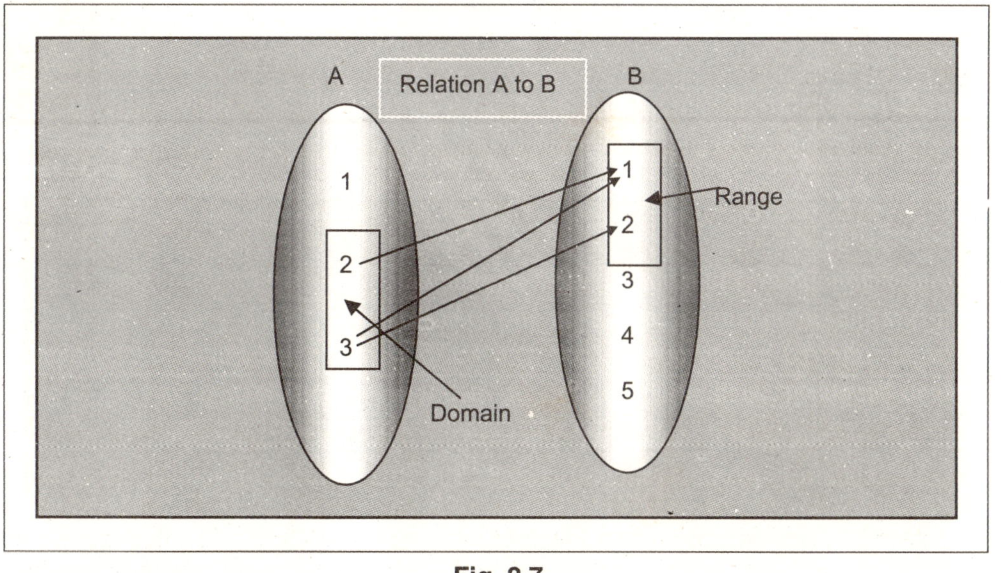

Fig. 2.7

Note 1: Obviously R ⊆ A × B.

Note 2: The set A and B are called the set of departure and set of destination of the relation R respectively.

Note 3: All elements in set A need not necessarily have the relation R with the elements of B. In the example cited above the element 1 in set A do not have the relation R (greater than) with the elements of B.

Note 4: In a similar way some elements of the B set may also do not have relation R with the elements of A. In our illustration the element 4 and 5 are not related by R with A.

Note 5: Some elements in A can have the relation R with more than one element in B. In our illustration the element 3 in particular have the greater than relationship with two elements of B namely 1 and 2.

Domain and range: The domain of the relation R is a set of first components of the ordered pairs in R. Similarly the set of second components of the ordered pairs in R is called the range of the relation R

i.e. Domain of R $= \{x/(x, y) \in R\}$ and

Range of R $= \{y/(x, y) \in R\}$

In our pervious Example 27 the domain of R $= (2, 3)$ and the range of R $= (1, 2)$

Note 1: Domain of R $\subseteq$ A

Note 2: Range of R $\subseteq$ B

Inverse relation: In our earlier discussion the relation 'R' to mean 'is the father of' holds good only from A to B and not certainly from B to A. For example, Raman (in set A) 'is the father of 'Shiva Kumar (in set B) 'as per the relation R and not the other way round. If we want to define the function from B to A then the appropriate relation would be 'is the son of '. Such a relation that holds good from B to A is called the inverse relation of R and is normally denoted by R^{-1} (read as R inverse).

Thus if R = {(Raman, Shiva Kumar) . . .}

$= \{(x, y)/x \in A \;\&\; y \in B$ so that ${}^{x}R_{y}\}$.

Then R^{-1} = {(Shiva Kumar, Raman), . . .} $= \{(y, x)/(x, y)\ \varepsilon\ R\}$

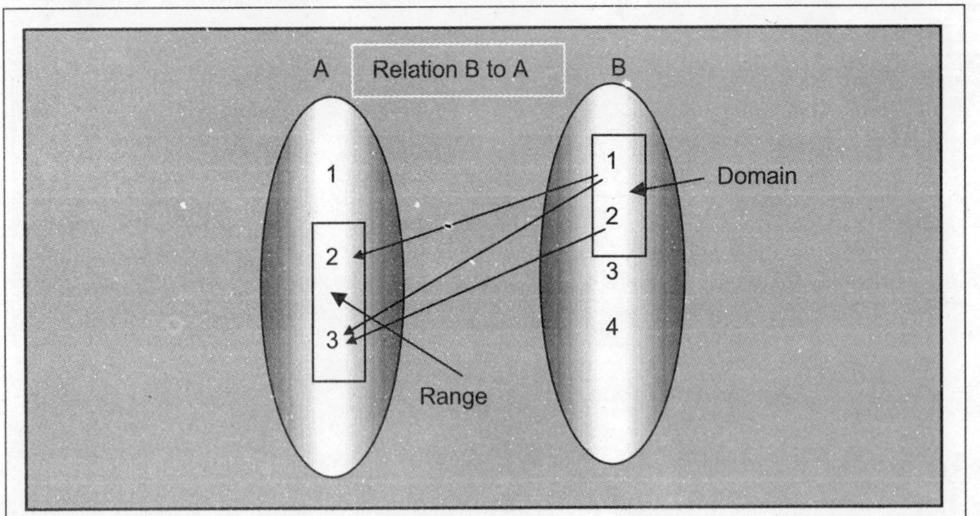

Fig. 2.8

Note 1: If R stands for 'is greater than' relation from A to B then

R^{-1} would necessarily be 'is less than' and is applicable from B to A. In our Example 27 given above $R^{-1} = \{(1,2), (1,3), (2,3)\}$

Note 2: Domain of R = range of R^{-1} and range of R = domain of R^{-1}.

The total number of relations from set A to set B: If set A has n elements and the set B has m elements then the Cartesian product set A×B will have m×n elements. Now we know that P = (A×B), the power set of A×B will have 2^{mn} elements, each one being the proper set of A×B. Since by definition a relation is a sub-set of A×B there must be 2^{mn} distinct relation from A to B.

Symmetric relation: Let R be a sub-set (and hence a relation) of A×A. Now the relation R is said to be symmetric provided ${}^{x}R_{y}$ also implies ${}^{y}R_{x}$. In other words, this is to say that $(x, y) \in R$ implies (y, x) belongs to R^{-1} i.e. $R = R^{-1}$.

Example 28: Let A = (a, b, c). Now let R = {(a, b), (a, c), (b, a), (c, a)} is a sub-set of A×A. Here this relation R is symmetric because $R^{-1} = \{(b, a), (c, a), (a, b), (a, c)\} = R$.

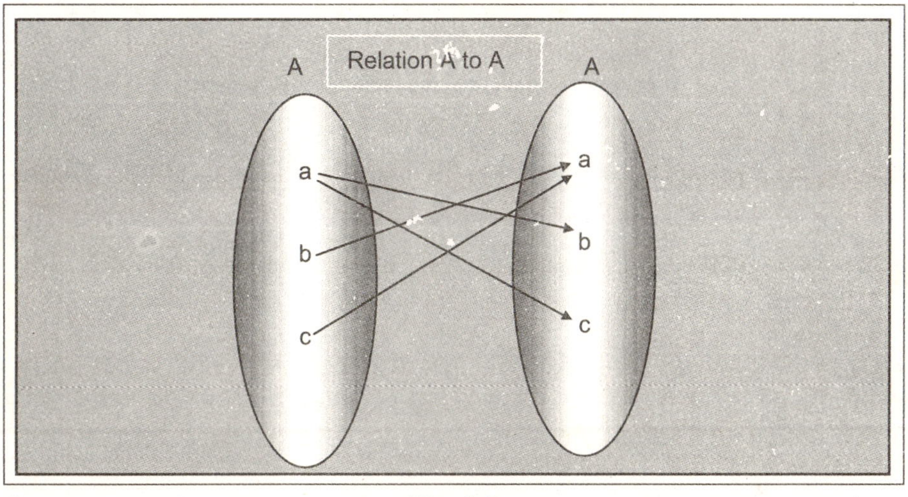

Fig. 2.9

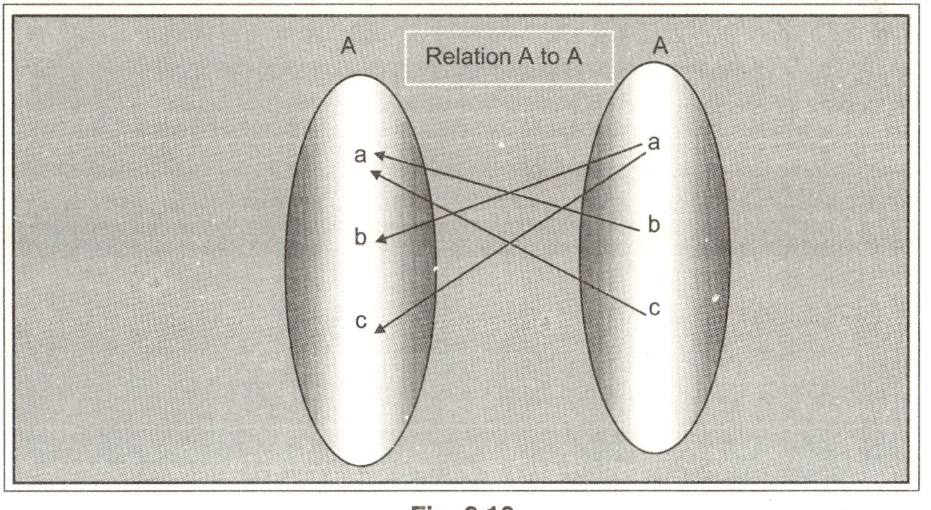

Fig. 2.10

Example 29: Let A = (1, 2, 3) and R = {(1, 2), (2, 3), (1, 3)}. Here the relation R is not symmetric because R^{-1} = {(2, 1), (3, 2), (3, 1)} ≠ R.

Reflexive relation: The relation R in A×A is said to be reflexive provided ^xR_x for every x ∈ A i.e. x is related to itself.

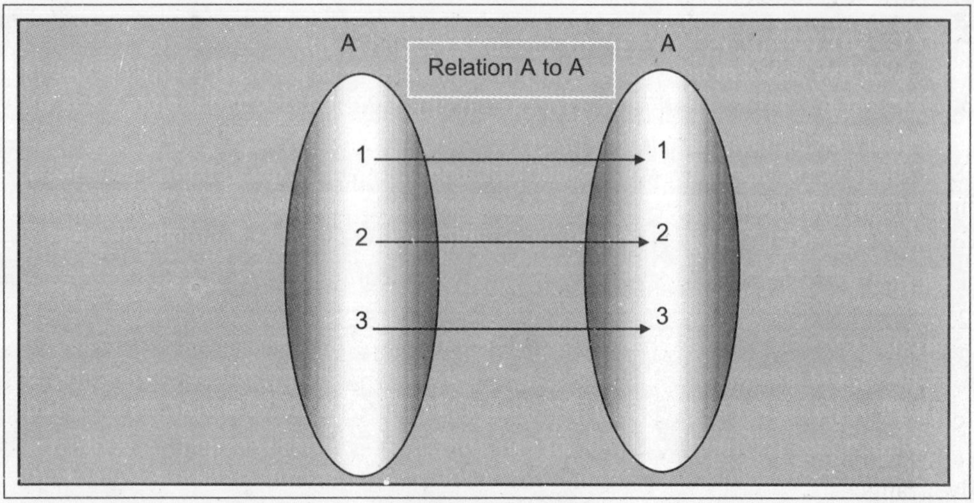

Fig. 2.11

Example 30: Let A is the set of baskets containing various commodities. Let R is the relation to mean 'is preferred to'. Now let x be a basket such that x ∈ A then ^xR_x because x is certainly preferred to itself.

Example 31: Let, A is the set of all male children of a family also let R stands for 'is the brother of '. Now for any x ∈ A, ^xR_x is not true because the individual x cannot be brother to himself.

Transitive relation: The relation R in a set A is said to be transitive provided ^xR_y and ^yR_z implies that ^xR_z.

Example 32: Let again A be the set of baskets containing collection of commodities. Also let R to mean 'preferred to'. Now if the basket x is preferred to the basket y and the basket y is preferred to the basket z then clearly the basket x is preferred to the basket z. Hence, the relation R is transitive.

Example 33: Let A is the set of cricket matches played in a world cup series. Now let the relation R to mean 'has won'. Clearly Indian team has won the Pakistan team and Pakistan team has won the England team need not imply that the Indians have won the England team. Here the relation R is non-transitive.

Equivalence relation: A relation R in set A is said to be equivalence provided R is

1. Reflexive
2. Symmetric
3. Transitive.

Example 34: Let R is a relation on the set A to mean 'is equal to'. Now

R is reflexive because for each and every x ∈ A, x = x is true

R is transitive because x = y and y = z always implies that x = z

R is symmetric because x = y implies y =x

Hence R is an equivalence relation.

Ordering relations: In economics especially in the theory of consumption we often use ordering (ordinal) relations. Let R be an ordering relation to mean 'is preferred to' on the set A.

1. Now R is reflexive because there is nothing wrong in saying x is preferred to x i.e. ${}^{x}R_{x}$.
2. Further, R is transitive because x is preferred to y and y is preferred to z then always x is preferred to z.
3. However, R is non-symmetric because x is preferred to y need not necessarily imply y is preferred to x unless x = y hence the relation R is not an equivalent relation.

Note: Such a relation is often called strong ordering in economics. Samuelson uses the strong ordering in his revealed preference theory of consumption.

Now let R to mean 'is preferred or equivalent to'. Now this relation

1. R is reflexive because x is preferred or equivalent to x itself is true i.e. ${}^{x}R_{x}$ is true.
2. Transitive because ${}^{x}R_{y}$ and ${}^{y}R_{z}$ imply ${}^{x}R_{z}$.
3. Symmetric because ${}^{x}R_{y}$ imply ${}^{y}R_{x}$ also. Therefore this relation R is definitely an equivalence relation. This type of ordering in economics is called weak ordering.

Note: Such an ordering is used by J.R.Hicks in his indifference curve analysis. On an indifference curve all the points are weakly arranged. But between the indifference curves the points are strongly arranged.

2.6 Functions

A function is a special type of relation in which each and every element of the domain set appearing as the first component of the ordered pair of the relation R is paired with a unique member of the B set appearing as the second component of the ordered pair. This special relation normally called function and is denoted by 'f'.

Example 35: Let P = [1, 2, 3] and Q = [10, 20, 30, 40] are the price and quantity sets of a certain commodity then its Cartesian product set P×Q may by written as P×Q = [(1, 10), (1, 20), (1, 30), (1, 40), (2, 10), (2, 20), (2, 30), (2, 40), (3, 10), (3, 20), (3, 30), (3, 40)]

Now let R, S, T, and U are the four relations defined from set P to set Q.

1. Let R: P→ Q so that R = [(1, 10), (2, 20), (3, 30)]

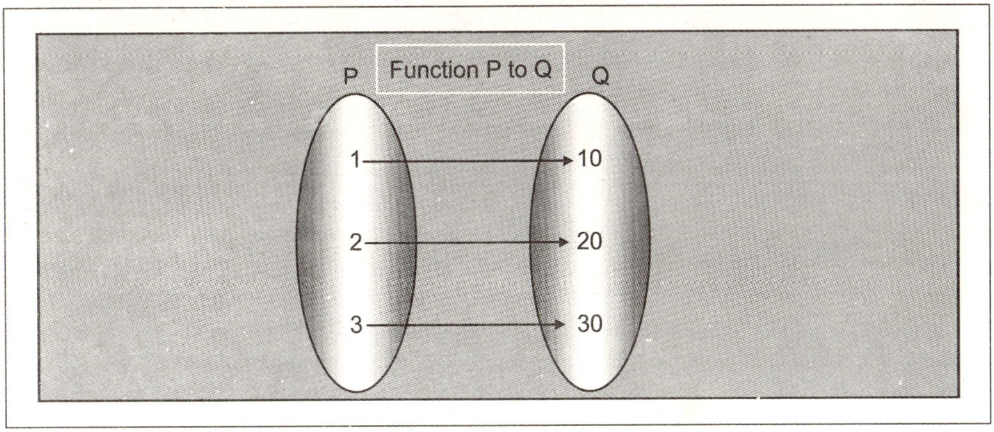

Fig. 2.12

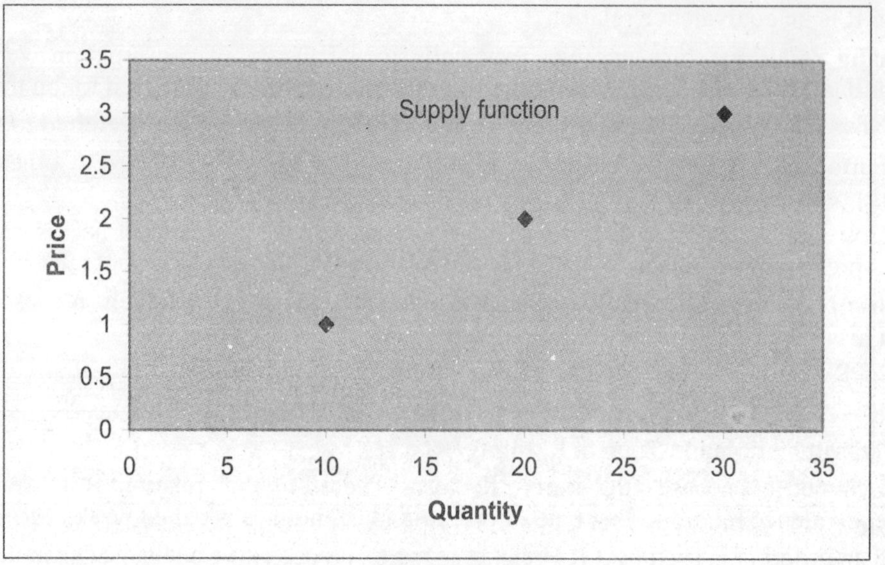

Fig. 2.13

Here the relation R is an upward sloping supply function because in it each and every element of the domain set P is uniquely related to the range set Q.

2. Let S: P → Q so that S = [(1, 10), (2, 10), (3, 10)]

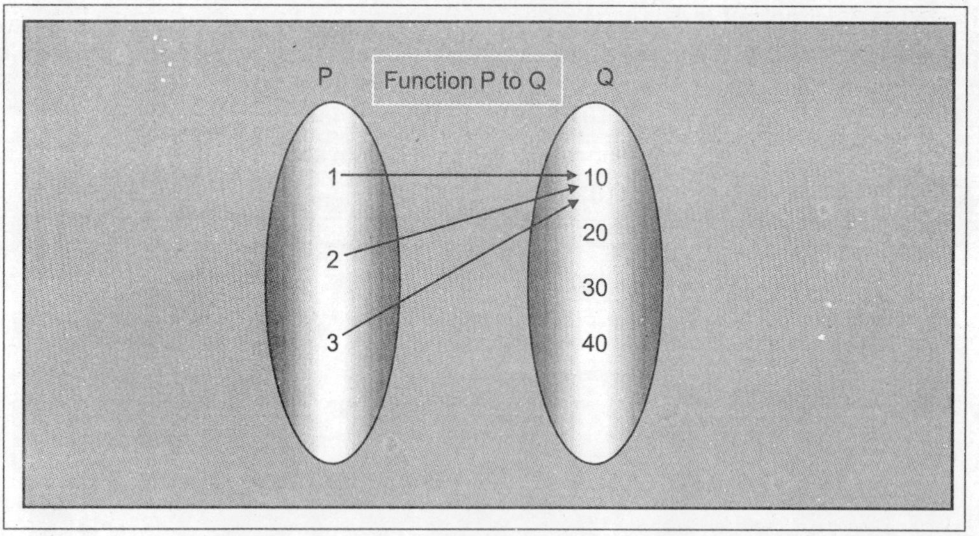

Fig. 2.14

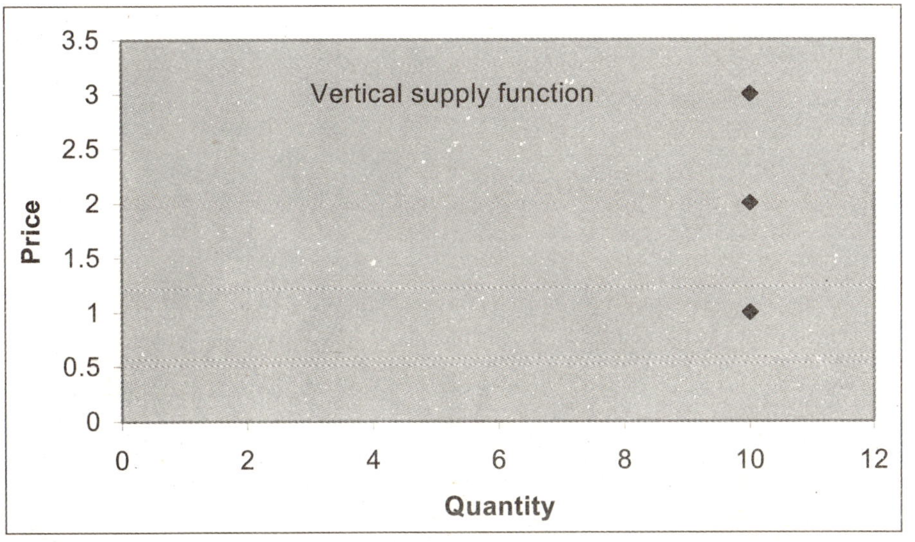

Fig. 2.15

Here again the relation S represents an inelastic vertical supply function because all the first elements of the domain set is uniquely related to a member of the range set Q namely 10.

3. Let T: P→ Q so that T = [(1, 10), (1, 20), (2, 30), (3, 40)]

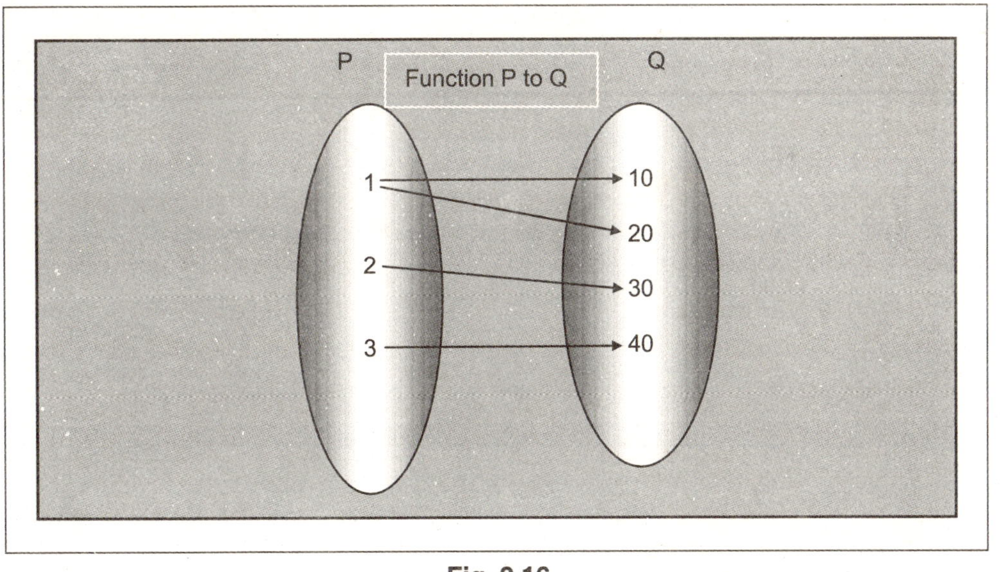

Fig. 2.16

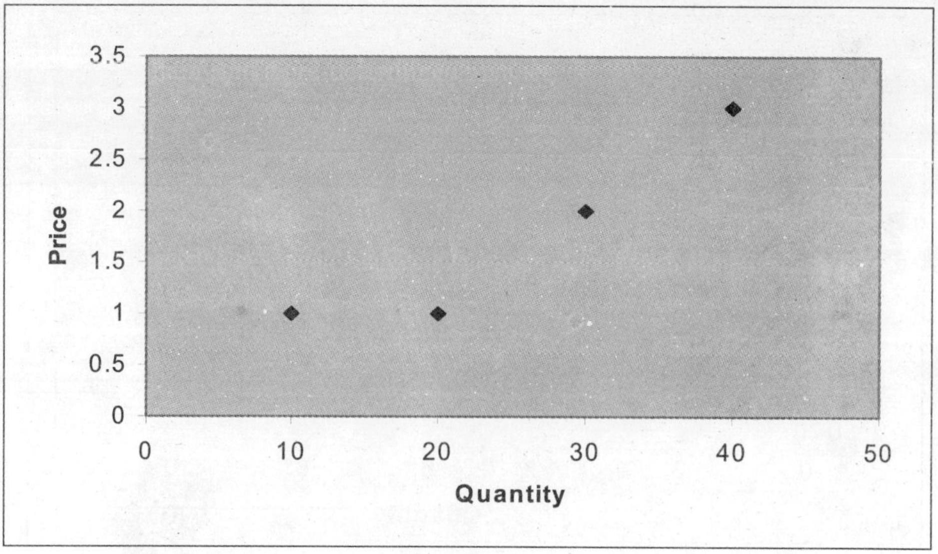

Fig. 2.17

Here the relation T is not a function because the first member of the domain set P namely 1 is related to two members of the Range set Q namely 10 and 20.

4. Let U: P→ Q so that U = [(2, 10), (3, 40)]

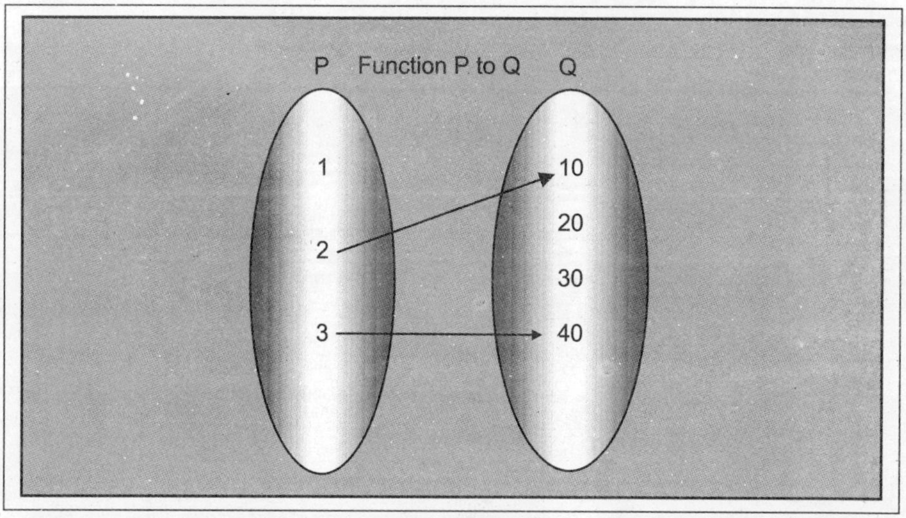

Fig. 2.18

Here the relation U is not a function because the first element of domain set P namely 1 is not having any relation with the range set Q though the other two elements has.

Thus, in general 'f' stands for the function then it is normally written as f : A→ B. Here the set A is often referred as the domain set. The set B is called the range or co-domain of the function f. Further, a function relates each and every element of the domain set with a unique element of the co-domain B in a pre-determined manner.

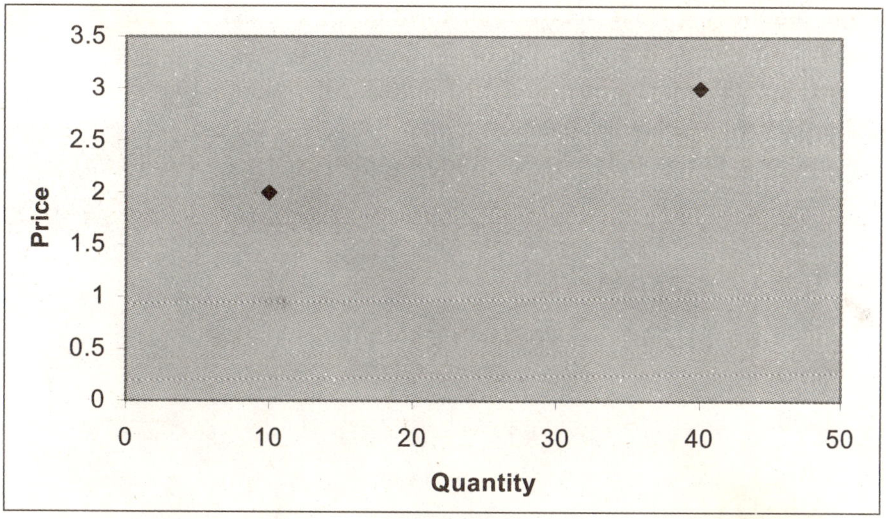

Fig. 2.19

Image: The element of the co-domain, which is having the unique relation with an element of the domain, is called the image of the element under consideration in the domain.

Example 36: Let P = [1, 2, 3] and Q = [10, 20, 30, 40] are the price and quantity sets. Now define f: P→ Q so that f = [(1, 10), (2, 20), (3, 30)]. Here 10, 20, 30, are called images of 1, 2, 3 respectively. In other words, this is to say that f (1) = 10; f (2) = 20; f (3) = 30.

Range: The sub-set of the co-domain having only the images as members is called the range.

Example 37: In our illustration given above f (P) = [10, 20, 30] is called the range set. Here it is important to note that f (P) $\subseteq$ Q.

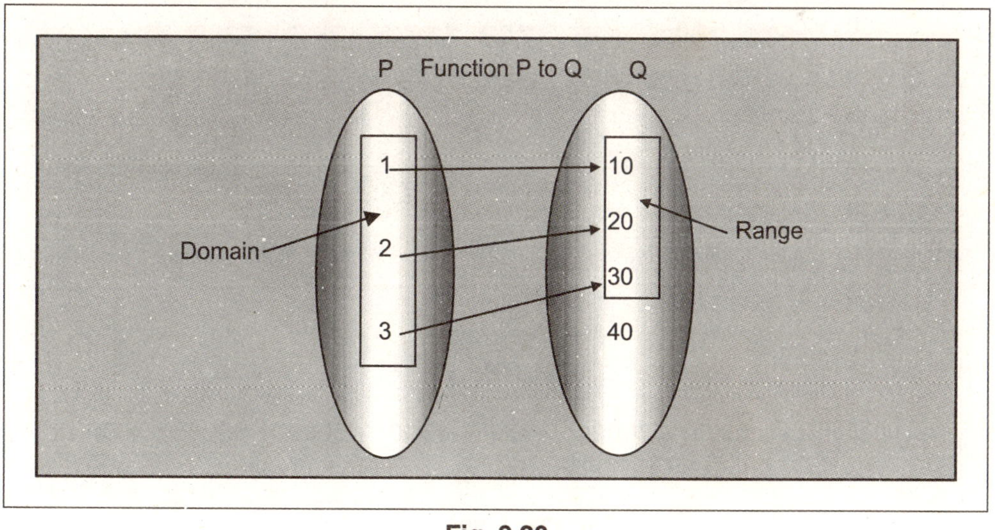

Fig. 2.20

One-to-one function: If each and every element of the domain A has distinct images in the co-domain then the function f: A→B is called a one-to-one function.

Example 38: If C = [500, 1000, 1500] and Y = [1000, 2000, 3000, 4000] are the consumption and income sets respectively then the function

f : C →Y: [(C, Y); C = 0.5 Y] = [(500, 1000), (1000, 2000), (1500, 3000)] is a one-to-one function.

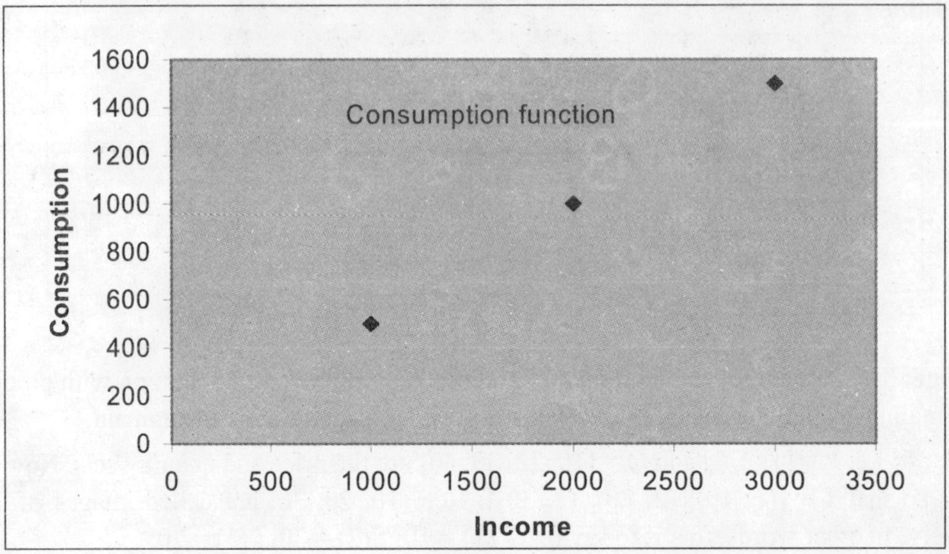

Fig. 2.21

Onto function: If each and every element of the co-domain appears as an image of some element of the domain set under the function f then the function f is called an onto function.

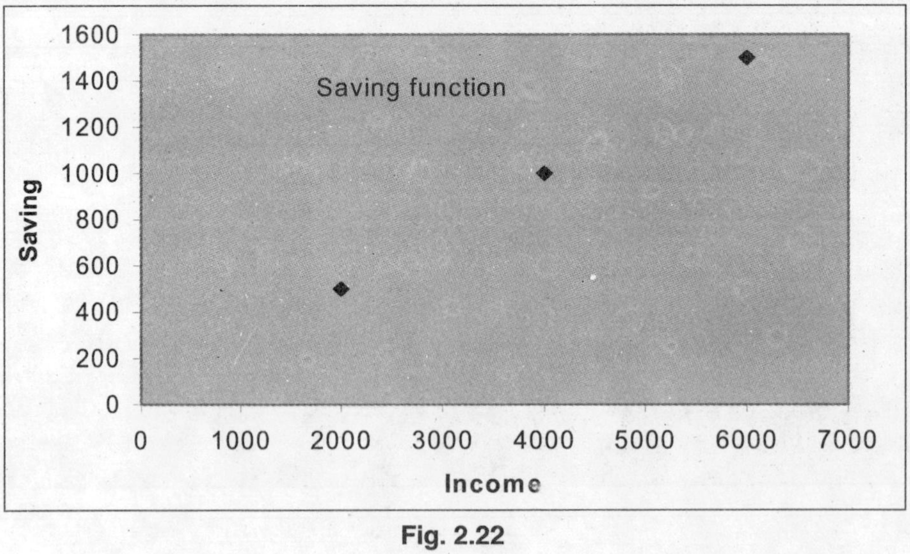

Fig. 2.22

Example 39: If S = [500, 1000, 1500] and Y = [2000, 4000, 6000] are the savings and income sets of a certain economy then the function f: S→ Y = [(S, Y); S = .25 Y] = [(500, 2000), (1000, 4000), (1500, 6000)] is an on to function.

Note: In this case the range of the function is equal to the whole of the co-domain.

One-to-one and onto function: If a function that satisfies both one-to-one and onto characteristics then it is called the one-to-one and onto function.

Example 40: If I = [1000, 2000, 3000] and r = [5%, 10%, 15%] are the investment and interest rate sets respectively then the function

f : I→ r = [(1000, 15%), (2000, 10%), (3000, 5%)] is called the one-to-one and onto function.

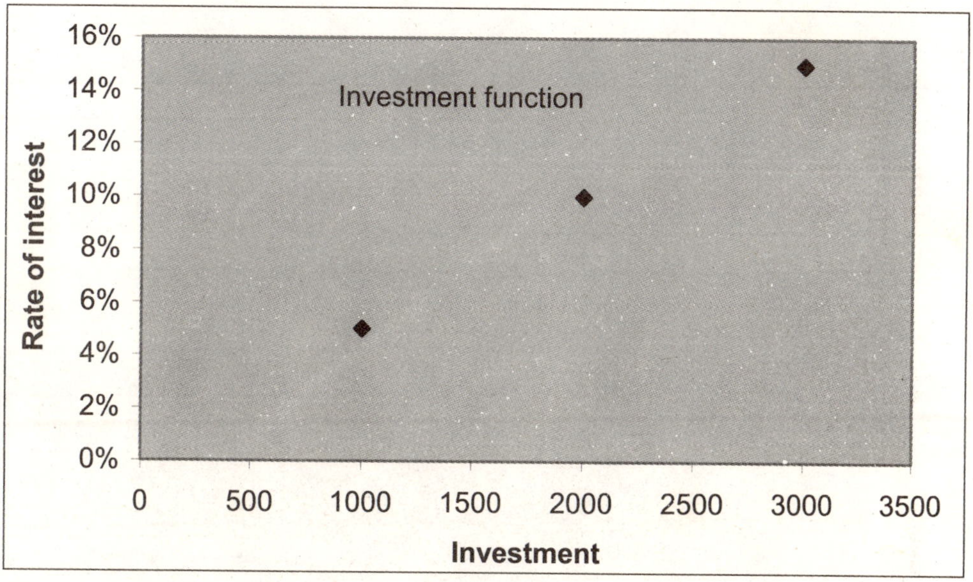

Fig. 2.23

Inverse function: If f: A→B is an one-to-one and onto then the inverse of f denoted by f^{-1} is defined as

$$f^{-1}: B \rightarrow A = [(y, x)/ x, y \in f]$$

Example 41: P = [1, 2, 3] and Q = [10, 20, 30] are the price and quantity set then the Walrasian demand denoted by f is written as

$$f: P \rightarrow Q = [(1, 30), (2, 20), (3, 10)]$$

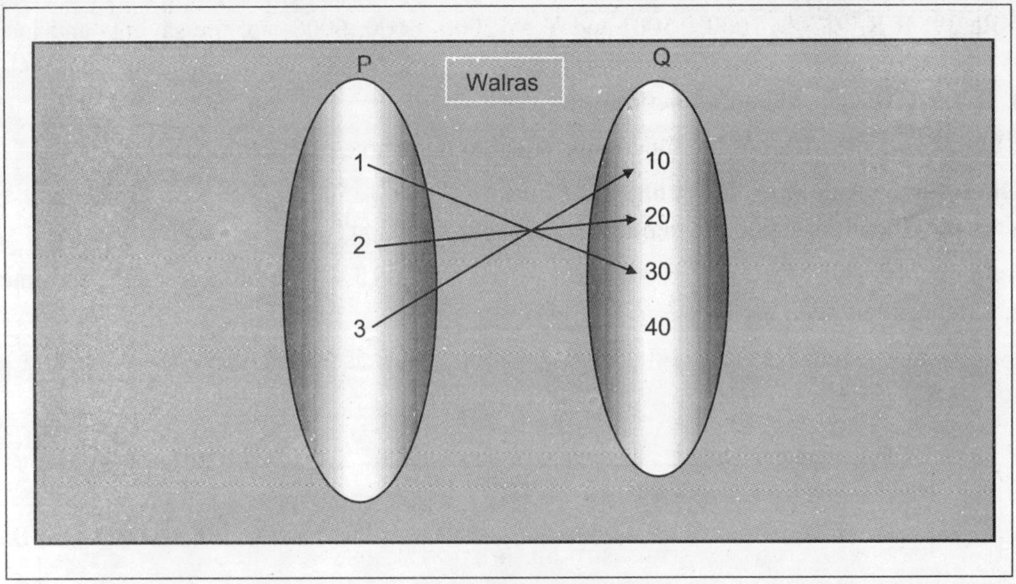

Fig. 2.24

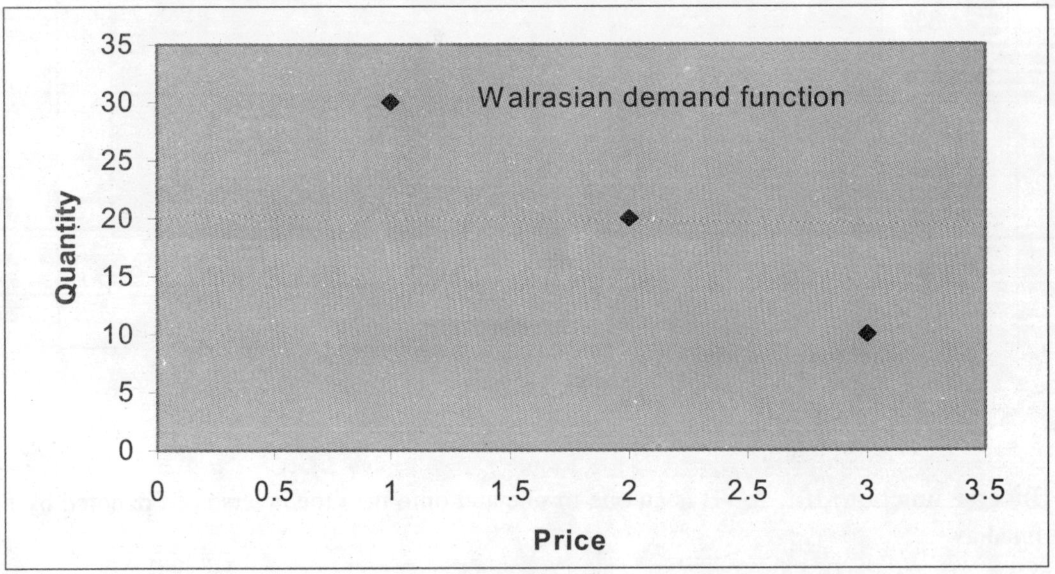

Fig. 2.25

The Marshallian demand denoted by f^{-1} may be written as

$$f^{-1} : Q \rightarrow P = [(10, 3), (20, 2), (30, 1)]$$

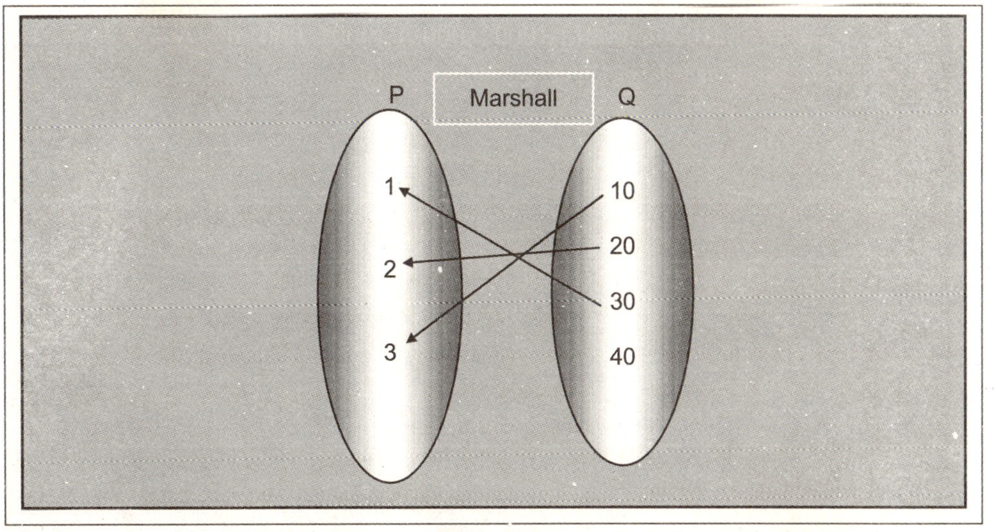

Fig. 2.26

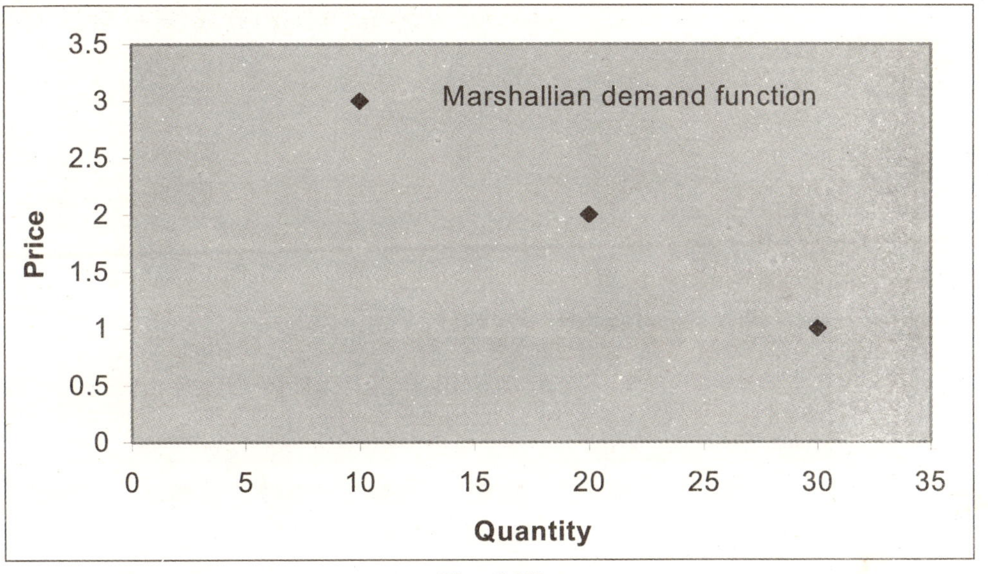

Fig. 2.27

Note: f^{-1} exist if and only if the function f is both one-to-one and onto.

Identity function: The function f: A→ B defined by f (x) = x for every x ∈ A then the function f is called an identity function.

Note: In this case note that $f = f^{-1}$.

Example 42: If A = [1000, 2000, 3000] then

f : A→ A = [(1000, 1000), (2000, 2000), (3000, 3000)]

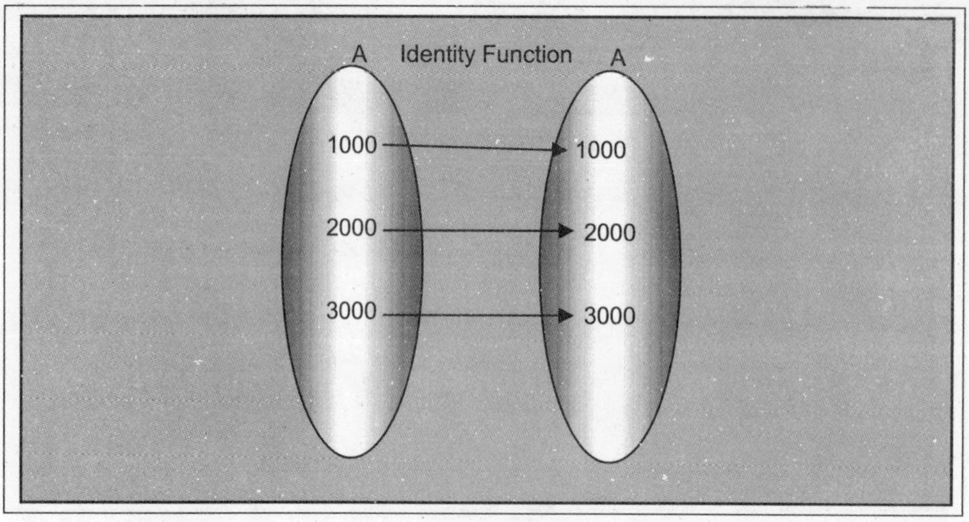

Fig. 2.28

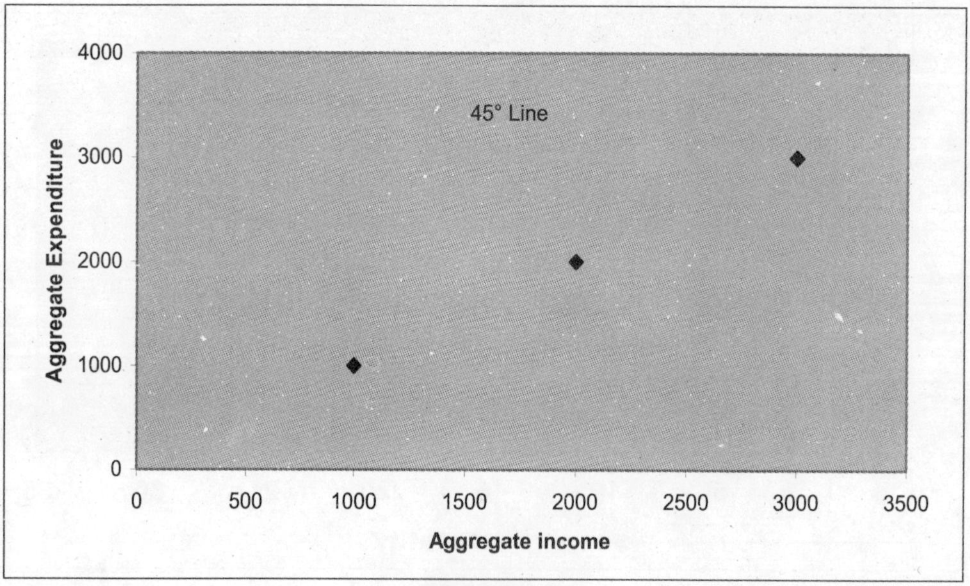

Fig. 2.29

Constant function: The function f: A→B defined such that f (x) = k where k is a constant for every x ∈ A and k ∈ B then f is called a constant function.

Example 43: If Q = [1, 2, 3] and F = [20] are the output and fixed cost of production sets of a firm respectively then the function f: Q → F = [(1, 20), (2, 20), (3, 20)] is a constant function called the total fixed cost.

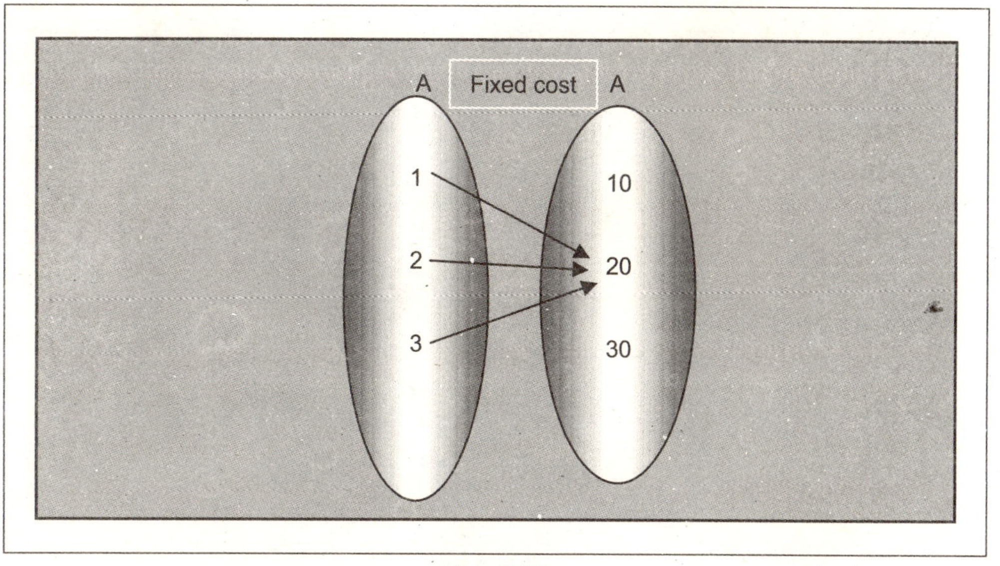

Fig. 2.30

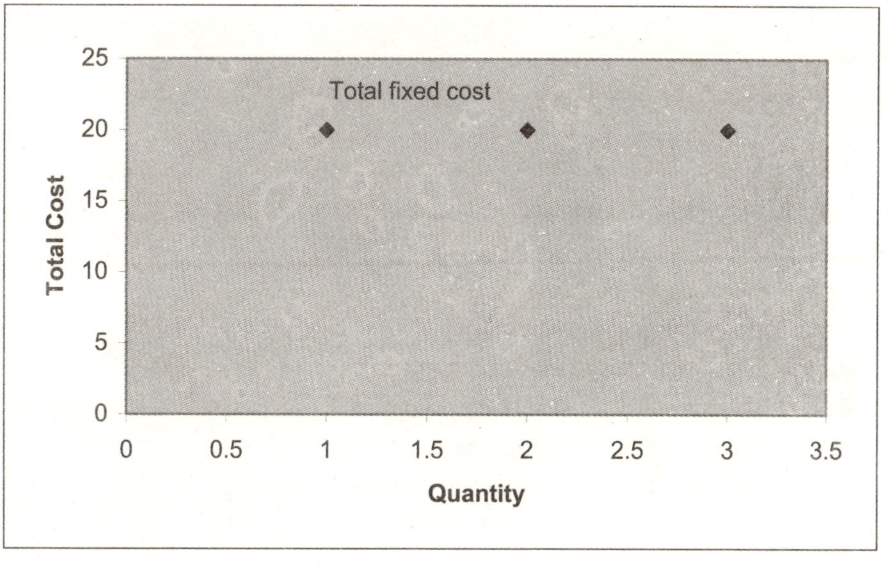

Fig. 2.31

Composite or function of function: If f: A→ B and g: B→ C then the composite function gf is a function defined from A to C such that gf (x) = g [f (x)] for every x ∈ A.

Example 44: If L = [10, 20, 30], Q = [2, 4, 6], R = [200, 400, 600] are the labour, output and revenue set of a production process then

$$f : L \rightarrow Q = [(10, 2), (20, 4), (30, 6)]$$

and $$g : Q \rightarrow R = [(2, 200), (4, 400), (6, 600)].$$

Now gf: L → R = [(10, 200), (20, 400), (30, 600)] is called the composite or function of a function. It gives the revenue corresponding to any given level of the labour input in labour set L.

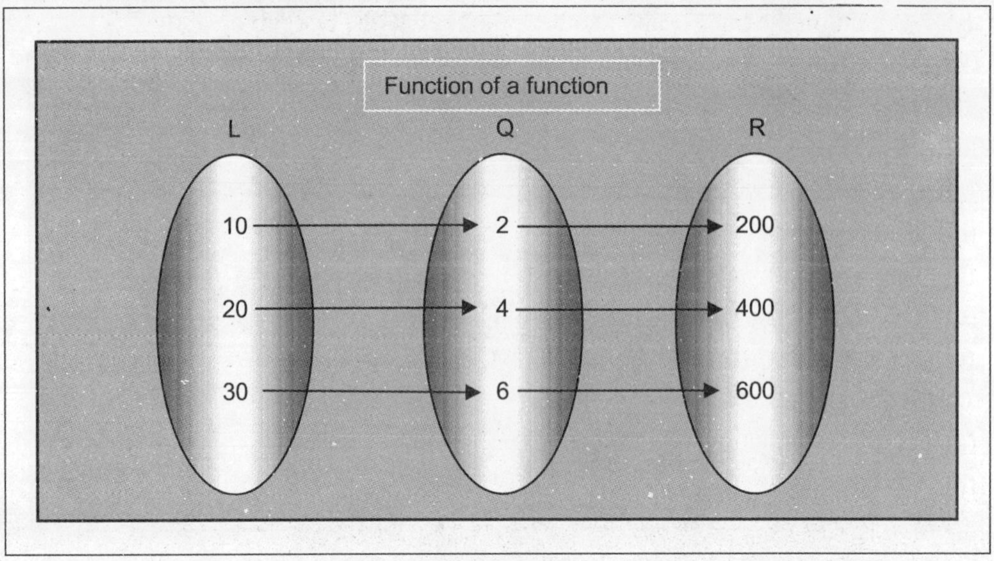

Fig. 2.32

EXERCISES

1. Examine the following statements for (i) symmetry, (ii) asymmetry, (iii) transitivity (iv) reflexivity.

   (i) {(a, a), (a, b)} (ii) {1, 1), (2, 3), (4, 1)} (iii) {1, 3), (2, 4)}

   (iv) {(a, a), (b, b), (c, c)} (v) a is greater than b.
2. Give three real life examples for transitivity.
3. Give three real life examples for non-transitivity.
4. Give three real life examples for reflexivity.
5. Give a real life example for equivalence relation.
6. Give three real life examples for strong ordering.
7. Give three real life examples for weak ordering.
8. Examine the following statements for strong and weak ordering:
   (a) The national income of country A is greater than that of B.
   (b) Individuals A and B are having the same basket of commodities.
   (c) All points on an indifference curve.
   (d) A point on the lower indifference curve and another point on the higher indifference curve.
   (e) Samuelson theory of consumption.
   (f) Hicks-Allen theory of consumption.
   (g) Newmam-Margenston theory of consumption.
   (h) All points on a budget line.
   (i) A point on the lower budget and another point on the higher budget.

(j) A point on the budget and another point below the budget.
(k) A point on the budget and another point above the budget.
(l) Both the points on the same budget.

9. Which of the following functions is (i) one-to-one (ii) on to (iii) one-to-one and on to?
   (a) Upward sloping supply function.
   (b) The downward slopping demand function.
   (c) The horizontal supply function.
   (d) The vertical supply function.
   (e) Autonomous investment functions.
   (f) Induced investment function.
   (g) Total cost function.
   (h) Total fixed cost function.
   (i) Total variable cost function.
10. Give two examples for composite function.
11. Give two examples for identity function.
12. Give two examples for inverse function.

3

Chapter

LINEAR AND NON-LINEAR FUNCTIONS

3.1 Generalized Mathematical Form of a Function

If x stands for a typical member of the domain set A and y stands for the corresponding image of x in the co-domain B then by definition f (x) = y or y = f (x). Such a representation is often called a function. In this format the function f simply tell the value of y in the co-domain set B for a given value of x in the domain set A. Here, since the value of y in the co-domain set depends upon the value of x in the domain, it is often called the dependent variable. Obviously, the choice variable x in the domain set is called the independent variable. It must be noted that function given in this general format is nothing more than the representation to stresses of the relationship between x and y. Instead, if we write $y = 100 + 2x$ to represent a relationship between x and y, for any given x the corresponding y is obtained by merely substituting the x value in the given functional relationship. For example, if $x = 2$ then from the given function $y = 100 + 2 \times 2 = 104$. Further, it is important to note that in this mathematical representation both x and y are continuous variables. In other words, this is to say that both domain and co-domain are infinite sets.

3.2 Types of Functions

The function can be either algebraic or transcendental. The algebraic functions possess the following properties:

If u = f(x) and v = g(x) are two given algebraic functions then we define variety of algebraic functions by using all the four algebraic operations:

1. The sum function u + v is obtained as f(x) + g(x).
2. The difference function u – v is obtained as f(x) – g(x).
3. The product function u .v is obtained as f(x). g(x).
4. The quotient function u/v is obtained as f(x)/g(x).

The following are some of the examples of algebraic functions:

- $y = f(x) = 2x + 4$
- $y = f(x) = 2x^2 + 10x + 5$

The non-algebraic functions are often called transcendental functions. For such functions the algebraic operation cannot be performed. For example functions like $y = e^x$, $y = \log x$, $y = \sin x$ are transcendental functions. To begin with let us discuss the use of algebraic functions first after reserving the transcental function to latter sections.

The algebraic functions

The mathematical forms of this type of functions are further classified into two broad categories depending upon the shapes that these functions create when they are graphed on a graph sheet. If it generates a linear or otherwise called straight-line graphs, then it is called a linear function. Instead, if it generates a non-linear curve shape on a graph sheet, then it is called a non-linear function. The following are some of special types of algebraic functions used in business related studies.

1. Linear functions. 2. Quadratic functions. 3. Cubic functions.
4. Exponential functions. 5. Logarithmic functions.

Now in this section let us explore the utility of all of them one by one and discuss their important characteristics and their business related applications.

3.3 Linear Functions

A linear function always gives rise a straight-line graph when it is graphed on a graph sheet. Whenever we come across situations in which both x and y variables increase or decrease at a constant proportion we often use linear functions of the type $y = mx + c$ to represent such relationships. In this format the variable x is called the independent variable because its choice is ours. The left hand side variable y is called the dependent variable because its value depends upon the choice of x. In this standard form the constant c represents the y- axis intercept when it is graphed on a graph sheet. The other constant 'm' designed to take care of the constant proportionality hypothesis that is being assumed. It is often called the slope of the given straight line. It is normally measured by the ratio of the opposite side to the adjacent side of the right angled triangle formed by the given straight line with x-axis. It gives a definite predetermined inclination to the straight line under consideration on x-axis. If it is positive, then the straight line slopes upwards, if it is negative then it slopes downwards, if it is zero then it is vertical, if it is infinite then it is horizontal. The varying combinations of 'c' and 'm' will generate variety of straight lines. The following table gives the summary of such variety of straight lines.

Table 3.1(a)

Sl No.	m	c	Example	Remark
1	positive	positive	y = 2x +5	upward sloping straight line with positive Y-axis intercept.
2	positive	negative	y = 2x - 5	upward sloping straight line with negative Y-axis intercept.
3	positive	zero	y = 2x	upward sloping straight line with zero Y-axis intercept.
4	negative	positive	y = -2x +5	downward sloping straight line with positive Y-axis intercept.
5	negative	negative	y = -2x - 5	downward sloping straight line with negative Y-axis intercept.
6	negative	zero	y = -2x	upward sloping straight line with zero Y-axis intercept.
7	zero	positive	y = 5	horizontal straight line with positive Y-axis intercept
8	zero	negative	y = -5	horizontal straight line with negative Y-axis intercept
9	zero	zero	y = 0	horizontal straight line zero Y-axis intercept
10	infinity	infinity	5 = x	vertical straight line with 5 units X-axis intercept
11	infinity	infinity	-5 = x	vertical straight line with - 5 units X-axis intercept

Different forms of straight lines

The following table summarizes the relevant formula for a given situation. If we are given with the 'c' and 'm' values then $y = mx + c$ is the relevant formula for getting the straight line. Instead if we are given with one point and the slope coefficient 'm' then the relevant formula is given in equation (2) below. Thirdly, if we know the coordinates of two points then we refer the formula given in (3).

Equation of the straight line when the intercept and slopes are given:

$$y = mx + c \qquad ...(1)$$

Equation of the straight line when one point and the slope coefficient are known:

$$y - y_1 = m(x - x_1) \qquad ...(2)$$

Equation of the straight line when two points are known:

$$y - y_1 = \frac{y_2 - y_1}{x_2 - x_1}(x - x_1) \qquad ...(3)$$

In the following sections we discuss some useful varieties with their respective utilities. To begin with let us introduce ourselves to the method of drafting a given straight line on the graph sheet.

Graphical representation of linear straight line

A function can always be represented by a two-dimensional graph on a graph sheet. To do this trick we divide the two-dimensional graph sheet into four parts called quadrants by inserting one vertical and another horizontal straight line as shown in the following graph. The point of intersection between these two straight lines is our reference point for measurement. It is commonly known as the origin and denoted by O. In this partitioned graph the horizontal straight line is called X-axis. On it we measure the positive x values on the right side and the negative x values on the left side. In a similar way we call the vertical line as Y-axis and measure the positive values of y above origin O and negative values of y below the origin O.

Example 1: Plot the points given in the table below on a graph sheet.

Table 3.1

Plotting of Points		
x	10	–10
y	10	–10

Solution:

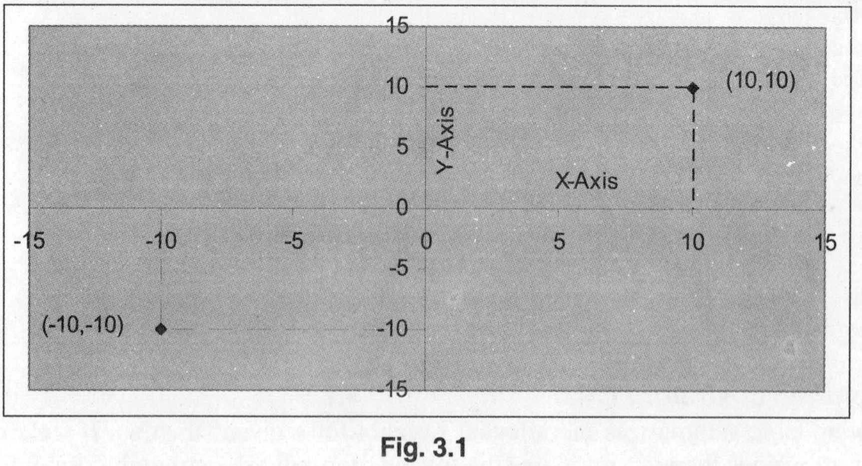

Fig. 3.1

Example 2: Draw the straight line y = 2x + 4 on a graph sheet.

Solution:

To draw the given straight line, first let us calculate few values of the dependent variable y by substituting few arbitrary values of the independent variable x. The following table gives the y values for 5 arbitrary chosen values of x ranging from 0 to 4 for the function y = 2x + 4.

Table 3.2

Straight Line Graph for y = 2x + 4						
x	0	1	2	3	4	5
y	4	6	8	10	12	14

All these five points are plotted on the graph sheet. After such a plot the needed straight line is obtained by connecting them all by a straight line using a scale. Not that it is extendable on either side indefinitely. The extended portions of both the sides will satisfy the given straight line. In this straight line, the Y-axis intercept is c = 4 and the slope of the straight line is m = 2.

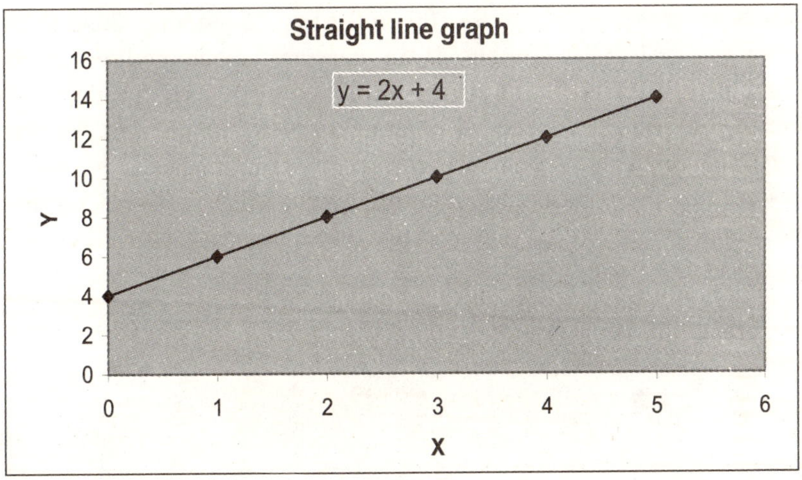

Fig. 3.2

Note: In the above illustrative example we have chosen 5 points to draw the given straight line. In fact, to draw a straight line we need only a bare minimum of two points. Once these two points are plotted on the graph sheet, the needed straight line is obtained by merely connecting these two points by a straight line. The so obtained straight line portion can always be extended on either side to any amount of length depending upon our need as described earlier.

3.4 Application of Linear Functions in Microeconomics

In economics often we use linear straight lines to represent functional relationships between two variables as a first approximation to the theory under reference. For example, to represent the inverse demand we often use downward sloping straight lines. Similarly, we use straight line consumption and investment functions in macroeconomics. The following section illustrates some of the specialized uses of straight line functions in economics.

Use of linear functions in the theory of consumption

The budget equation of the consumer is the typical illustration for the use of linear equations in the theory of consumption. The following example illustrates the method of getting the straight-line budget line.

Example 3: A consumer buys two commodities 1 and 2 in q_1 and q_2 quantities at Rs. 5 and Rs. 10 per unit respectively. If his income is Rs.100 show the straight line budget equation graphically. Also, obtain q_2 value when $q_1 = 10$ from the graph.

Solution:

The budget equation of a consumer in it general form is normally written as $M = p_1q_1 + p_2q_2$. In this general representation M refers the money income of the consumer, p_1 refers the price of the commodity 1 and p_2 refers the price of the commodity 2. Since p_1 = Rs. 5, p_2 = Rs.10 and M = Rs. 100 in our illustration, the concerned budget in its specific numerical form is written as $100 = 5q_1 + 10q_2$.

Now to get the graph of this equation at least we must have two points on this straight line. If our consumer spends his entire income of Rs.100 on the first commodity alone at Rs.5 per unit he will be in a position to buy 100/5 = 20 units. If we measure the commodity 1 on the X-axis then this typical purchase is represented by the point A (20,0) on the X-axis. Similarly, if the consumer spends the whole of Rs. 100 on the second commodity at Rs.10 per unit then he will be in a position to buy 100/10 = 10 units. Since the commodity 2 is measured on the Y-axis, such a purchase is represented by the point B (0,10) on the Y-axis. After plotting A on the X-axis and B on the Y-axis the needed budget line is obtained by connecting these two points by a straight line as shown in the Fig. 3.3.

Table 3.3

Budget Line		
q_1	20	0
q_2	0	10

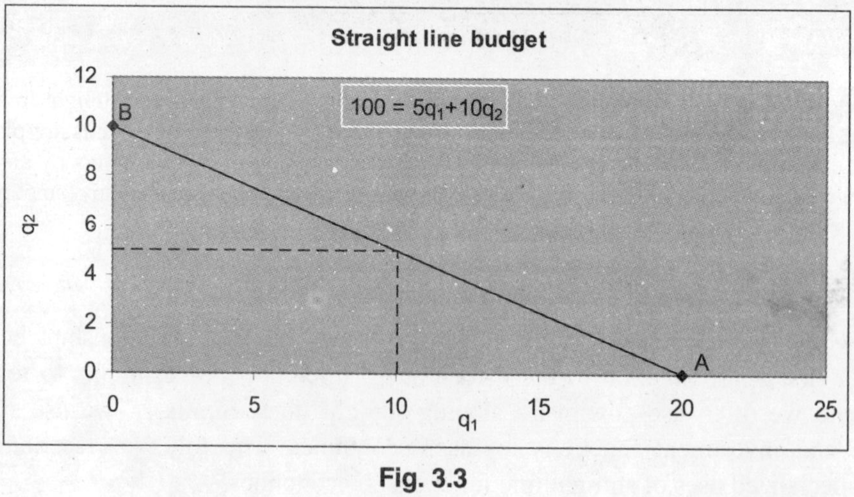

Fig. 3.3

From the figure when $q_1 = 10$, the corresponding value of $q_2 = 5$.

Note: The budget equation given above can always be written in the standard form of a straight-line namely $y = mx + c$ as shown below

$$M = p_1q_1 + p_2q_2$$

$$-p_2q_2 = p_1q_1 - M$$

$$q_2 = \frac{p_1q_1 - M}{-p_2}$$

$$q_2 = \frac{M}{p_2} - \left(\frac{p_1}{p_2}\right)q_1$$

So in standard form the slope coefficient m and intercept coefficient c are obtained as shown below.

$$m = -\frac{p_1}{p_2} \quad \text{and} \quad c = \frac{M}{p_2}$$

Example 4: In Example 3 above if the price of the first commodity alone is reduced from Rs. 5 to Rs. 2 obtain the new budget and compare it with the original line.

Solution:

In this case the price of the first commodity alone is brought down from Rs. 5 to Rs. 2. This means that the price of the second commodity and the income of the consumer remain unaltered. So our new budget line is obtained as

$$100 = 2q_1 + 10q_2$$

If the consumer buys only commodity 1 using his entire income then he will buy 100/2 = 50 units. So the associated point on the X-axis is A′ (50,0). Since no change in the price of the second commodity, the point on the Y-axis will be the same, that is B (0,10). In the graph the straight line A′B is the needed new budget line. Thus, after the first commodity price decrease, the budget line rotates in the anti-clockwise direction as shown in the Fig. 3.4.

Table 3.4

New Budget		
q_1	50	0
q_2	0	10

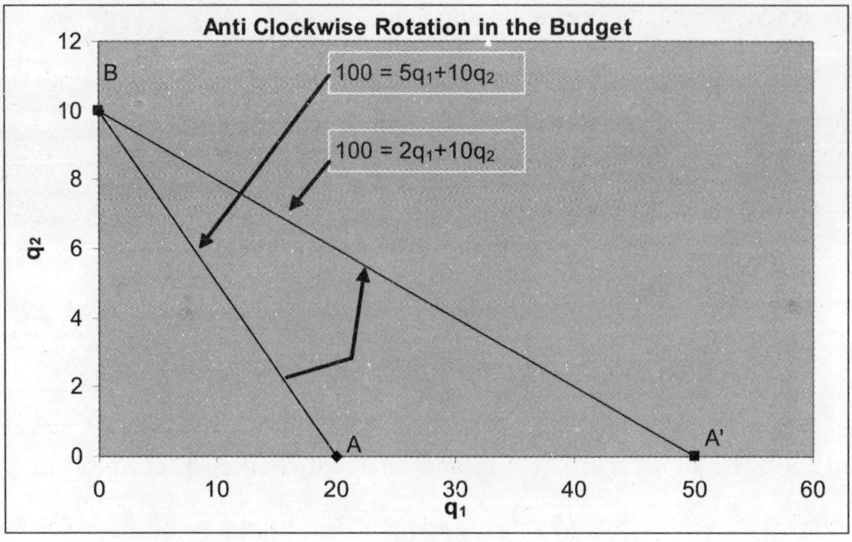

Fig. 3.4

If the consumer buys only commodity 1 using his entire income then he will buy 100/2 = 50 units. So the associated point on the X-axis is A' (50,0). Since no chance in the price of the second commodity, the point on the Y-axis will be the same, that is B (0,10). In the graph the straight line A'B is the needed new budget line. Thus, after the first commodity price decrease, the budget line rotates in the anti-clockwise direction as shown in Fig 3.4.

Example 5: In Example 3 above if the price of the first commodity alone is increased from Rs. 5 to Rs.10 obtain the new budget and compare it with the original line.

Solution:

In this case the price of the first commodity alone is increased from Rs. 5 to Rs. 10. This means that the price of the second commodity and the income of the consumer remain unaltered. So our new budget line is obtained as

$$100 = 10q_1 + 10q_2$$

If the consumer buys only commodity 1 using his entire income then he will buy 100/10 = 10 units. So the associated point on the X-axis is A' (10,0). Since no change in the price of the second commodity, the point on the Y-axis will be the same, that is B (0,10). In the graph the straight line A'B is the needed new budget line. Thus, after the first commodity price increase, the budget line rotates in the clockwise direction as shown in the Fig. 3.5.

Table 3.5

New Budget Line		
q_1	10	0
q_2	0	10

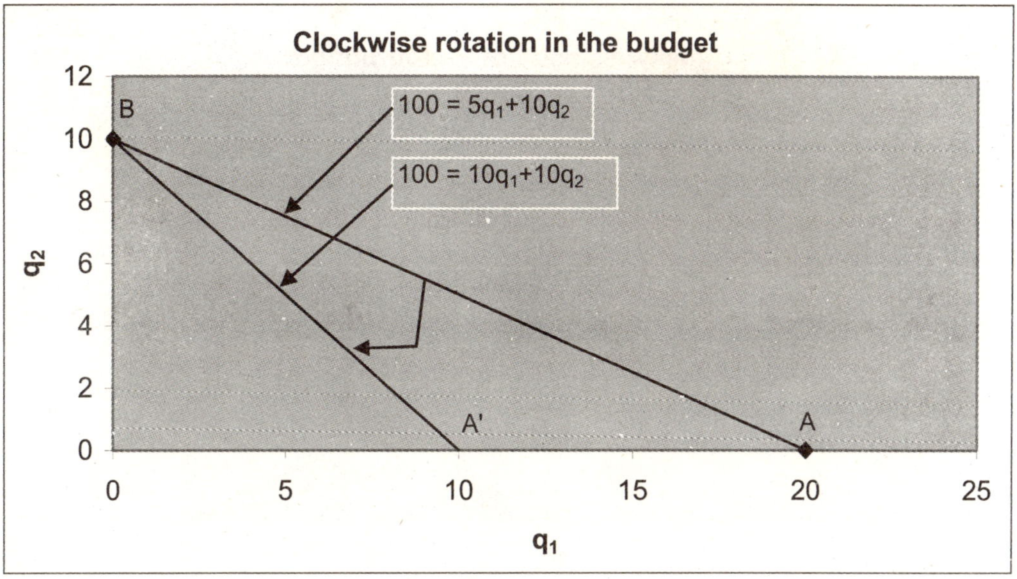

Fig. 3.5

Example 6: In Example 3 above if the price of the second commodity alone is reduced from Rs. 10 to Rs. 5 obtain the new budget and compare it with the original line.

Solution:

In this case the price of the second commodity alone is brought down from Rs.10 to Rs.5. This means that the price of the first commodity and the income of the consumer remain unaltered. So our new budget line is given by

$$100 = 5q_1 + 5q_2$$

If the consumer buys only commodity two using his entire income then he will buy 100/5 = 20 units. So the associated point on the Y-axis is B' (0,20). Since no change in the price of the first commodity the point on the X-axis will be the same, that is A (20,0). In the graph the straight line AB' is the needed new budget. Thus, after the decrease in the price of the second item the budget line rotates in the clockwise direction as shown in the Fig. 3.6.

Table 3.6

Budget Line		
q_1	20	0
q_2	0	20

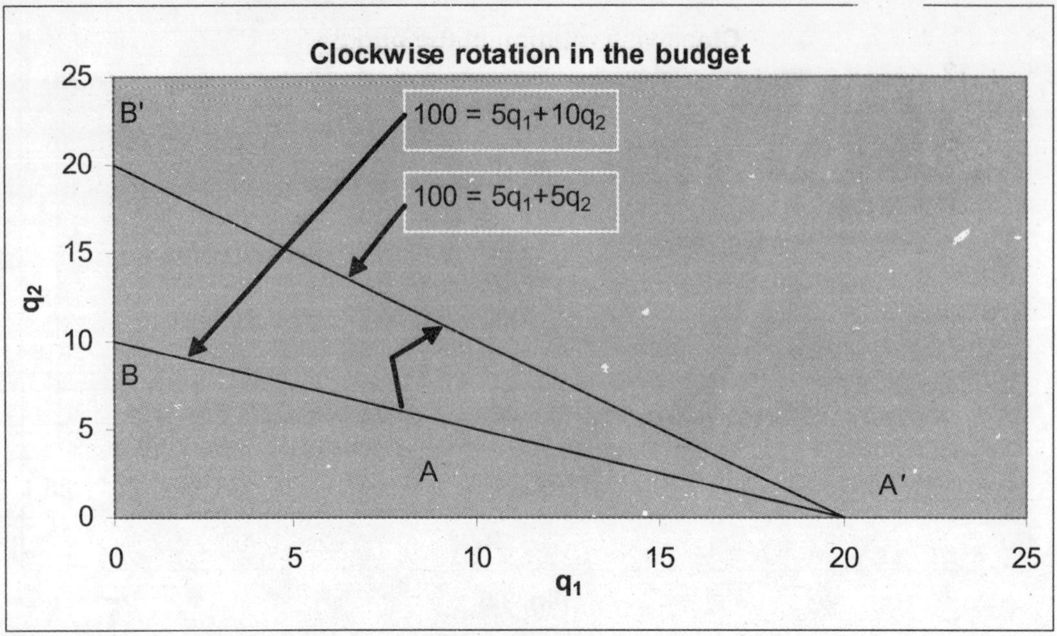

Fig. 3.6

Example 7: In Example 3 above if the price of the second commodity alone is increased from Rs. 10 to Rs. 20 obtain the new budget and compare it with the original line.

Solution:

In this case the price of the second commodity alone is brought down from Rs. 10 to Rs. 5. This means that the price of the first commodity and the income of the consumer remain unaltered. So our new budget line is given by

$$100 = 5q_1 + 20q_2$$

If the consumer buys only commodity two using his entire income then he will buy 100/20 = 5 units. So the associated point on the Y-axis is B' (0,5). Since no change in the price of the first commodity the point on the X-axis will be the same, that is A (20,0). In the graph the straight line AB' is the needed new budget. Thus, after the decrease in the price of the second item the budget line rotates in the anti-clockwise direction as shown in the Fig. 3.7.

Table 3.7

Budget Line		
q_1	20	0
q_2	0	5

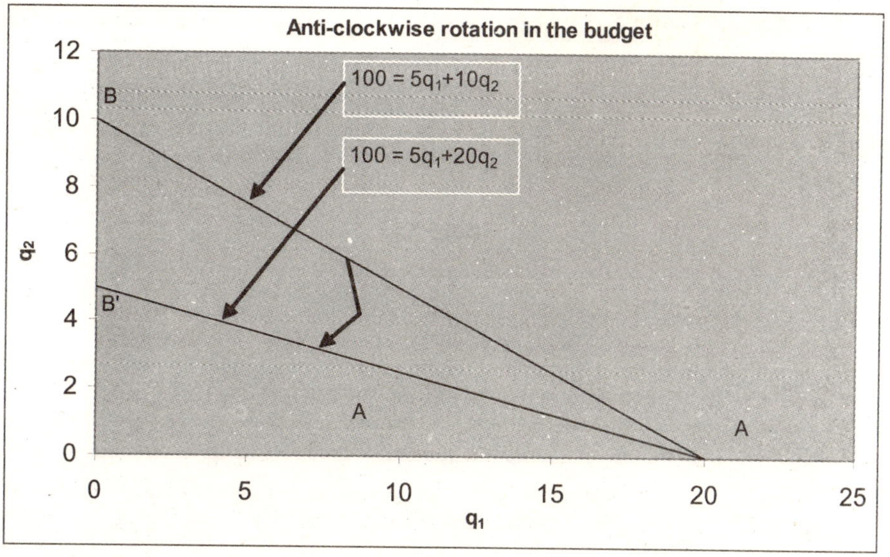

Fig. 3.7

Example 8: In Example 3 above if income alone is doubled, obtain the new budget and compare it with the original.

Solution:

After doubling income alone the new budget is obtained as

$$200 = 5q_1 + 10q_2$$

Table 3.8

Budget Line		
q_1	40	0
q_2	0	20

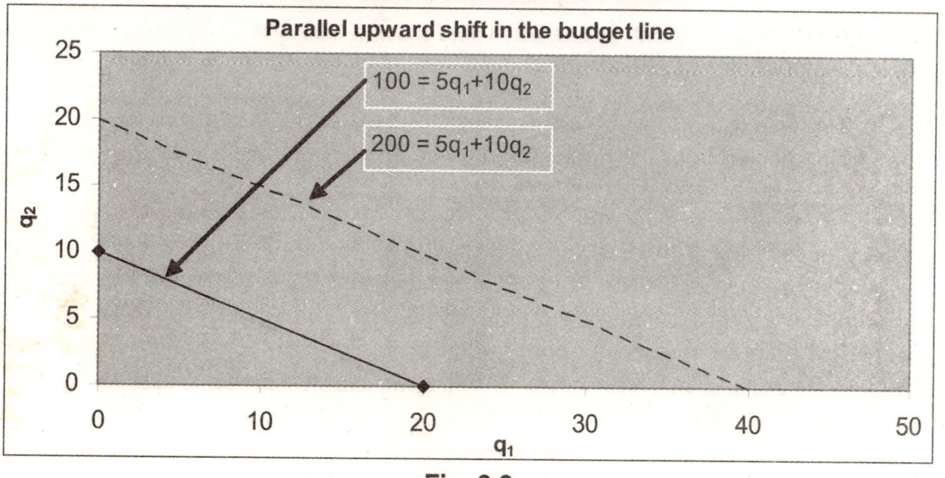

Fig. 3.8

Note: The budget line gets shifted upward by maintaining its slope intact.

Example 9: In Example 3 above if income alone halved, obtain the new budget and compare it with the original.

Solution:

After doubling income alone the new budget is obtained as

$$50 = 5q_1 + 10q_2$$

Table 3.9

Budget Line		
q_1	10	0
q_2	0	5

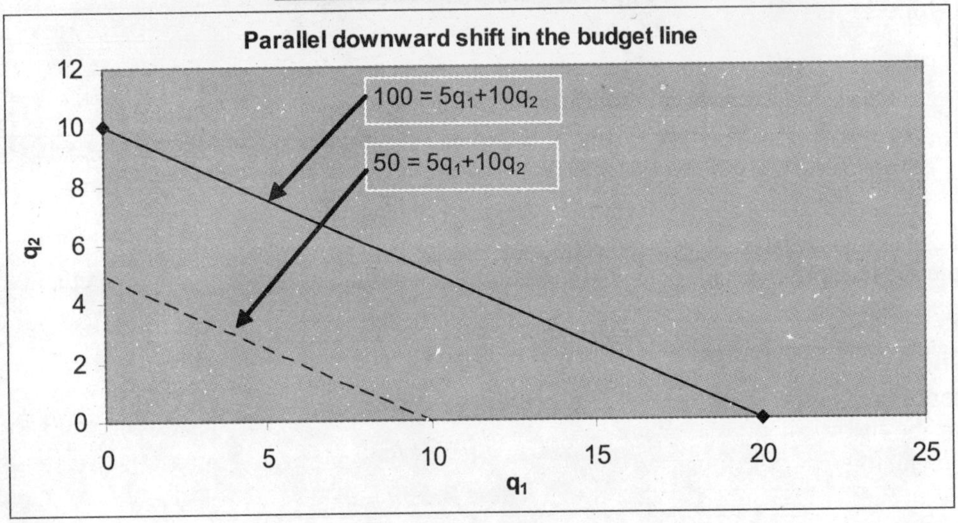

Fig. 3.9

Note: The budget line gets shifted downwards by maintaining its slope intact.

Example10: In Example 3 above if income and prices of both the items are doubled, obtain the new budget and compare it with the original.

Solution:

After doubling income and both the prices the new budget is obtained as

$$200 = 10q_1 + 20q_2$$

If our consumer spends his entire income of Rs. 200 on the first commodity at Rs.10 per unit he will be in a position to buy 200/10 = 20 units. If we measure the commodity 1 on the X-axis then this typical purchase is represented by the point A (20, 0). Similarly, if the consumer spends the whole income of Rs.200 on the second commodity at Rs.20 per unit then he will be in a position to buy 200/20 = 10 units. Since the commodity 2 is measured on the Y-axis such a purchase is represented by the point B (0,10) on the Y- axis. After plotting A on the X-axis and B on the Y-axis the needed budget line is obtained by connecting these two points by a straight line as shown in the Fig. 3.9. Here since A and B are one and the same points before and after both the budget lines wili coincides one over the other as shown in the Fig. 3.10.

Table 3.10

Budget Line		
q_1	20	0
q_2	0	10

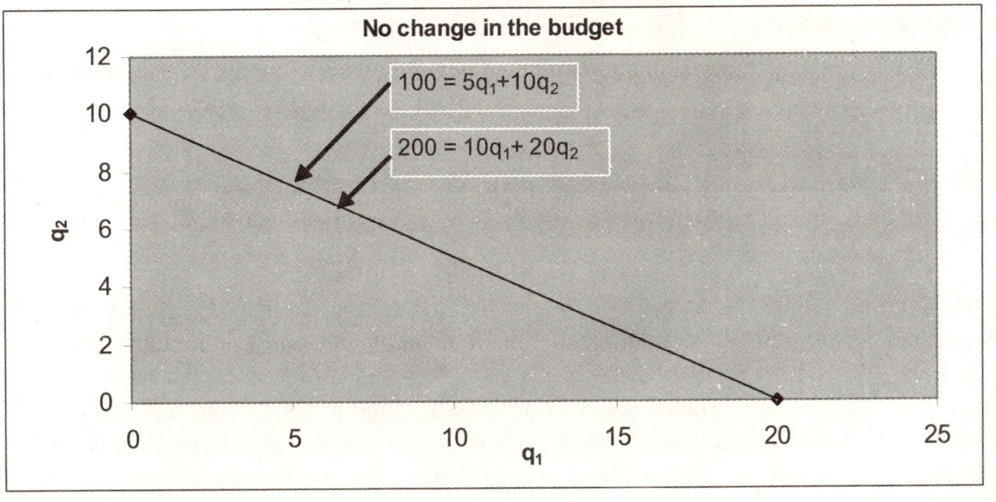

Fig. 3.10

Use of linear functions in the theory of production

Similar to budget equations in the theory of consumption we come across straight linear budget lines in the theory of production as well. In the theory on consumption it represents the budget that is available for consumer. In the theory of production it refers the budget of the producer. The linear budget line in production is normally written in its general form as

$$C = P_L L + P_K K$$

where

$$C = \text{cost of production}$$
$$P_L = \text{price of labour } L$$
$$P_K = \text{price of capital } K$$
$$L = \text{the amount of labour used in the production}$$
$$K = \text{the amount of capital used in the production}$$

Note: The budget equation given above can always be written in the standard form of a straight line namely y = mx + c as shown below

$$C = P_L L + P_K K$$

$$-P_K K = P_L L - C$$

$$K = \frac{P_L L - C}{-P_K}$$

$$K = \frac{C}{P_K} - \left(\frac{P_L}{P_K}\right) L$$

So in its standard form, the slope coefficient m and intercept coefficient c are obtained as shown below.

$$m = -\frac{P_L}{P_K} \quad \text{and} \quad c = \frac{C}{P_K}$$

Numerical illustrations

Example 11: A producer hires L quantity of labour and buys K quantity of capital at Rs. 10 and Rs. 20 per unit respectively. If he has Rs.100 to spend on these two inputs obtain the graphical representation of his budget. Also, find K when L = 5.

Solution:

With the data given in the problem the budget in its numerical form is written as

$$100 = 10L + 20K$$

As we did earlier, let us try to get two points on this budget first. If he spends the whole of Rs. 100 on labour alone then the amount of labour at Rs.10 per unit that he can hire is given by L = 100/10 = 10. If L is measured on the X-axis then this point is represented as A (10, 0). Similarly if he spends the whole of Rs. 100 on capital alone at Rs. 20 per unit then he will buy K = 100/20 = 5. If K is measured on the Y-axis then this point is represented as B (0, 5). After marking both the points we obtain the needed budget line by merely connecting them by a straight line.

Table 3.11

Budget Line		
L	10	0
K	0	5

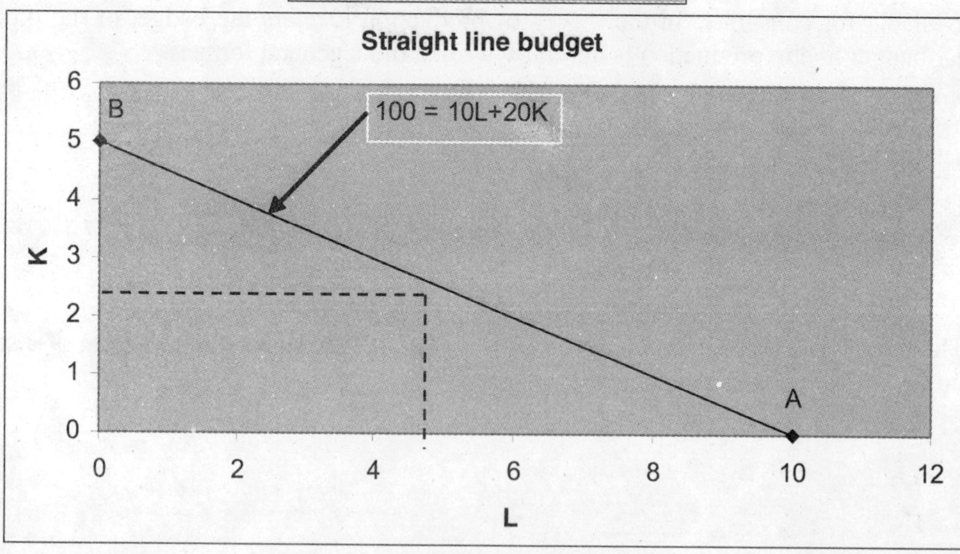

Fig. 3.11

From the figure when L = 5, the corresponding K = 2.5.

Example 12: In Example 11 above if the price of labour alone rises to 20 obtain the new budget and compare it with the original.

Solution:

Here since the price of labour alone rises to Rs. 20 the budget may be rewritten as

$$100 = 20L + 20K$$

Thus the line intersect the X-axis at A' (5, 0) and Y-axis at B (0, 5).

The needed budget is obtained by connection these two points by a straight line as shown in the Fig. 3.12.

Table 3.12

Budget Line		
L	5	0
K	0	5

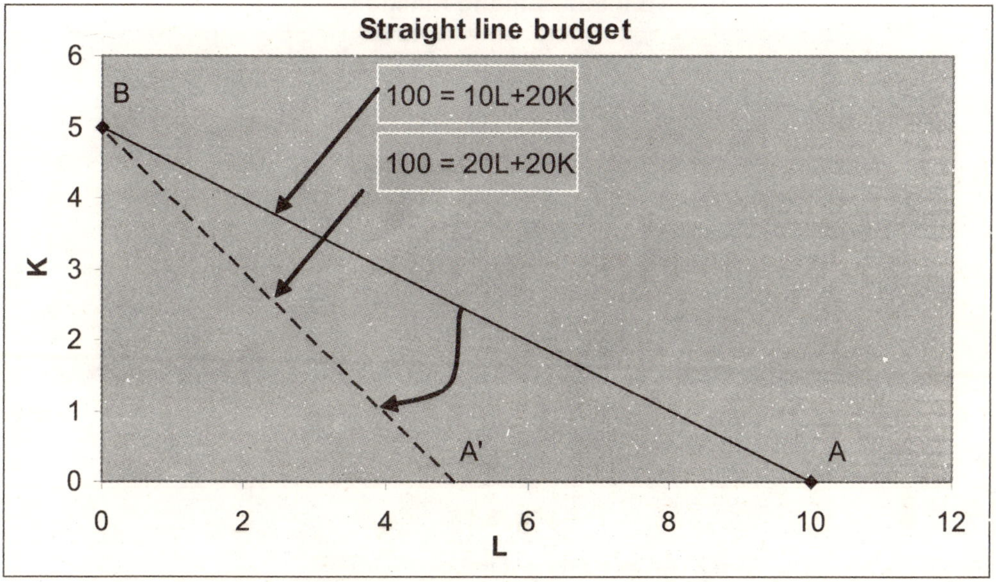

Fig. 3.12

Use of linear equations in the market analysis

Linear Demand Functions: In the market analysis we often use Walrasian demand function. It exhibits negative relationships between the price and the quantity. Moreover, in it price is the independent variable and quantity is the dependent variable. The simple linear demand with price as the independent variable is normally written as $q = a - bp$. In this equation the negative slope of the demand is depicted by $-b$. The constant term 'a' here represents the quantity axis intercept of the said demand function. It simply gives the level of the demand when price for the product is zero.

Note: As Economists, we follow our special convention of measuring the independent variable p on the Y-axis and dependent variable q on the X-axis. This is just the reverse that we normally do in mathematics.

Thus, the reader is advised to take note of this special convention into account while interpreting the concepts like the slope and the intercept.

Example 13: If a = 100 and b = – 2 plot the demand function on a graph sheet. Also predict the demand when the price is Rs. 20.

Solution:

After substituting the given values of a and b in the general form given above the demand equation is written as D = 100 – 2p. Let us get two points on this demand first to draw the needed demand function.

Table 3.13

Demand Function		
p	50	0
D	0	100

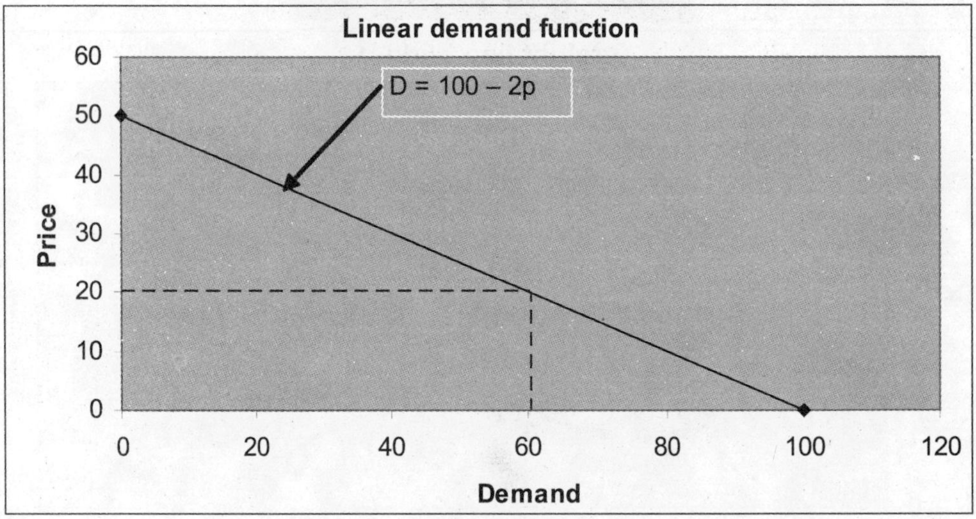

Fig. 3.13

From the graph when p = 20 the corresponding demand is D = 60.

Example 14: When the price of a certain product was Rs. 2 the seller was able to sell 10 units. When its price came down to Re.1 he was able to sell 20 units. Obtain the linear demand for the said product. Also predict the price when the expected sale is 20 units.

Solution:

The standard form of the straight line demand is written as

$$D = a - bp \quad \ldots(1)$$

It is given here that the price of the commodity was Rs. 2 when the demand was 10 units. So let us substitute these values in the demand given in equation (1) above. So it becomes

$$10 = a - 2b \quad \ldots(2)$$

Similarly, on substituting the second set of data given in equation (1) it becomes

$$20 = a - b \quad \ldots(3)$$

Now we are having two equations (2) and (3) in two unknowns 'a' and 'b'.

So let us eliminate 'a' first by merely subtracting (3) from (2).

$$10 - 20 = -2b - (-b)$$
$$-10 = -b$$
$$b = 10$$

Now the value of 'a' is obtained by merely substituting this value of b in equation (2) above.

so
$$10 = a - 2 \times 10$$
$$10 + 20 = a$$
$$a = 30$$

So the needed straight line demand is written as

$$D = 30 - 10p \quad \ldots(4)$$

Now to get the graph of the demand, two points on it are located in the table as usual.

Table 3.14

Demand Function		
p	10	0
D	0	30

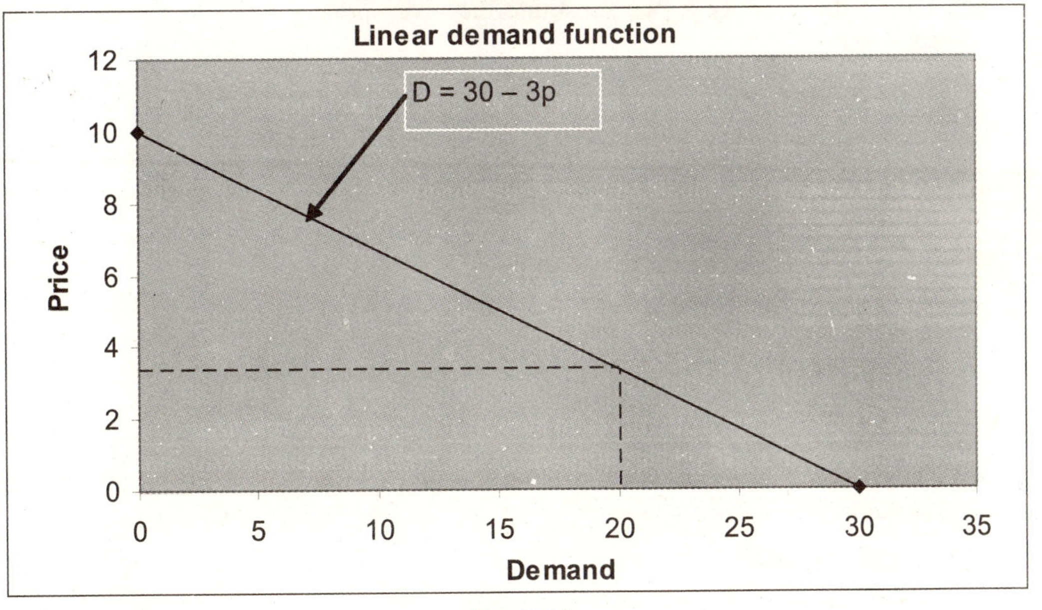

Fig. 3.14

Now when D = 20 the corresponding price is obtained by substituting this value of D in the demand equation (4)

$$20 = 30 - 3p$$
$$20 - 30 = -3p$$
$$-10 = -3p$$
$$p = 3.3333$$

We get the same result from the graph as well. So we conclude that when D = 20 the price for the product would be Rs. 3.33.

Example 15: The demand curve for a commodity is x =10 – y/4, where 'y' represents the price and 'x' represents the quantity demanded.

(a) Find the quantity demanded, if the price is (i) 2, (ii) 25.
(b) Find the price if the quantity demanded is (i) 2, (ii) 9.
(c) What is the highest price at which the demand is zero?
(d) What quantity would be the demand, if the commodity under reference is a free good?
(e) Map the demand curve.

Solution:

(a) (i) To get the quantity x, we substitute the given price y = 4 in the given demand equation.

$$x = 10 - y/4$$
$$x = 10 - 4/4 = 9$$

(ii) To get the quantity x, we substitute the given price y = 25 in the given demand equation

$$x = 10 - y/4$$
$$x = 10 - 25/4 = 15/4 = 3.75$$

(b) (i) To get the price y, we substitute the given quantity x = 2 in the given demand equation.

$$2 = 10 - y/4$$
$$2 = \frac{40 - y}{4}$$
$$8 = 40 - y$$
$$y = 40 - 8 = 32$$

(ii) To get the quantity x, we substitute the given price x = 9 in the given demand equation.

$$9 = 10 - y/4$$
$$9 = \frac{40 - y}{4}$$
$$36 = 40 - y$$
$$y = 40 - 36 = 4$$

(c) To obtain the height price y at which the demand is zero we put x = 0 in the demand and obtain the associated price.

$$0 = 10 - y/4$$

$$0 = \frac{40 - y}{4}$$

$$0 = 40 - y$$

$$y = 40$$

(d) To obtain the quantity x at which the commodity is a free good put y = 0 and obtain the associated quantity.

$$x = 10 - y/4$$

$$x = 10 - 0/4$$

$$x = 10$$

(e) To draw the demand, we need a minimum of two points, one on the X-axis and another on Y-axis.

Table 3.15

x = 10 -y/4	
x	y
0	40
10	0

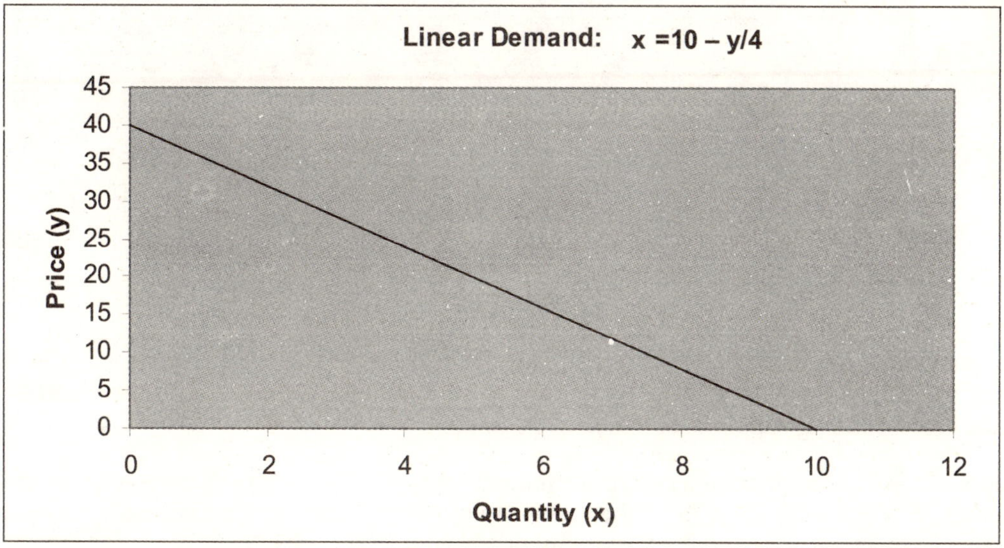

Fig. 3.15

Linear Supply Functions: Under normal conditions, the price offered and the quantity supplied is positively related. In other words, the supply function normally slopes upwards. Such an upward sloping supply function can always be represented by a linear straight line of the form S = a + bp. If b is positive then this equation will exhibit the needed positive relationship between the price and the quantity.

Example 16: If a = 20 and b = 2 obtain the linear supply function. Also plot the supply on a graph sheet and predict the supply when p = 5.

Solution:

The linear supply in its standard form is written as S = a + bp. After substituting the given a and b values the needed supply is written as S = 20 + 2p

Now to plot the linear supply equation we first obtain two points on it as usual.

Table 3.16

Supply Function		
p	0	10
S	20	40

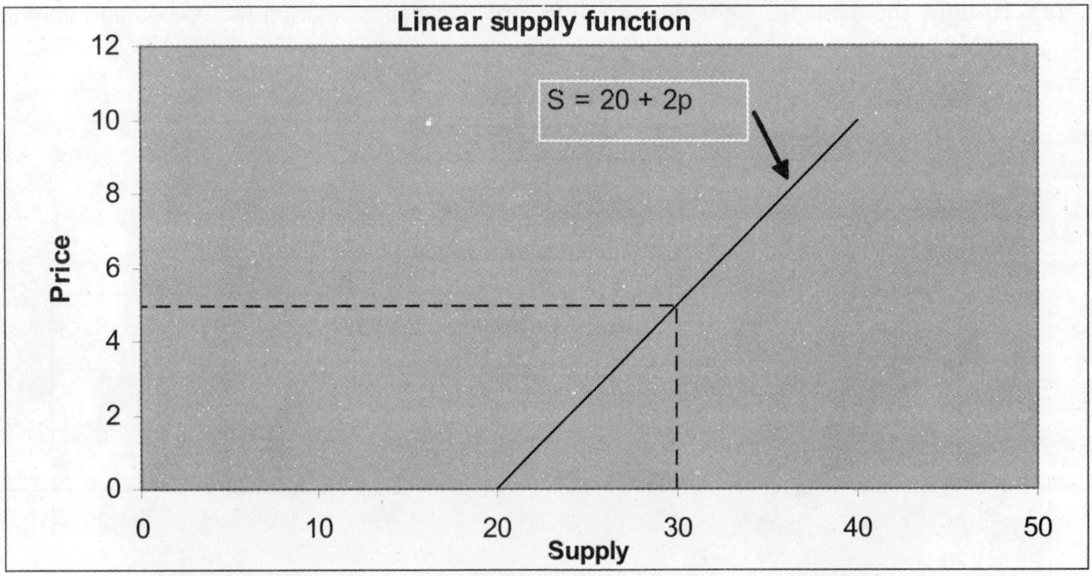

Fig. 3.16

These two points are marked on the graph sheet. Once this is done the needed straight line is obtained by simply connecting these two points as shown in the Fig. 3.15. From the graph when p = 5 the corresponding supply is obtained as 30 units.

Example 17: When the price of a certain commodity was Rs. 2 per unit, 10 units were supplied to the market. When it went up to Rs. 4 the supplier supplied 40 units to the said market. Obtain the linear supply function. Also predict the supply on a future price of Rs. 3.

Solution:

The standard form of a linear supply function is normally written as

$$S = a + bp \qquad \text{...(1)}$$

Now since S = 10 when p = 2 on substituting the above equation becomes

$$10 = a + 2b \qquad \ldots(2)$$

It is also true that S = 40 when p = 4. So once again on substitution in equation (1) becomes

$$40 = a + 4b \qquad \ldots(3)$$

Thus, we are having two equations in two unknowns a and b

Now to eliminate 'a' subtract equation (3) from (2).

$$10 - 40 = 2b - 4b$$
$$-30 = -2b$$
$$b = 15$$

Now the needed 'a' value is obtained by merely substituting this value of b in equation (2) above.

$$10 = a + 2 \times 15$$
$$-a = 30 - 10$$
$$-a = 20$$
$$a = -20$$

Thus the needed supply function is S = – 20 + 15p

Table 3.17

Supply Function		
p	2	4
S	10	40

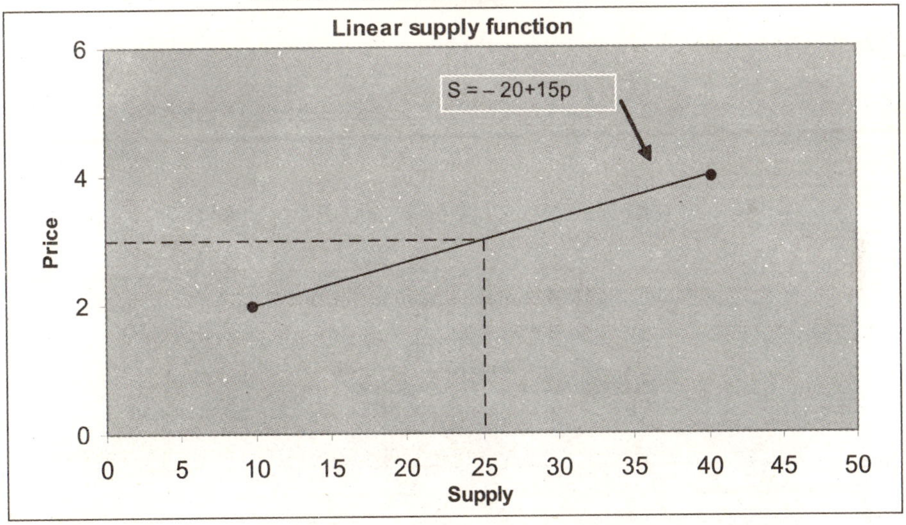

Fig. 3.17

From the graph, when p = 3 the quantity supplied = 25

Example 18: Plot the very short run supply function when S =1000

Solution:

In the very short run the supply is vertical and hence the supply will remain constant irrespective of the price.

Table 3.18

Supply Function		
p	0	10
S	1000	1000

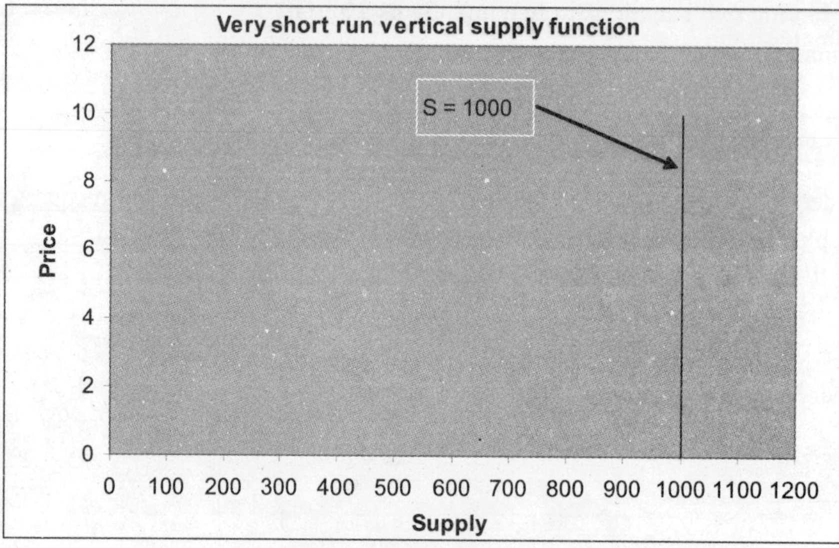

Fig. 3.18

Example 19: When p = Rs.10 always, draw the corresponding supply function.

Table 3.19

Supply Function		
p	10	10
S	0	1000

Solution:

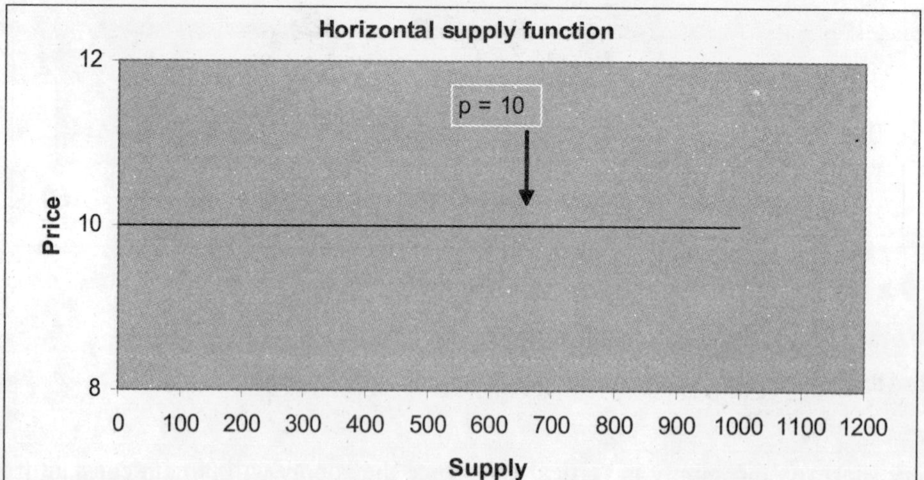

Fig. 3.19

In this case the price remain constant irrespective of the quantity supplied.

Market equilibrium

The market for the said commodity is in equilibrium provided the demand is equal to the supply. In diagrammatic terms this is to say that at the equilibrium the demand and the supply will intersect. The X-coordinate of the point of intersection determines the equilibrium quantity and the Y-coordinate of the equilibrium point determines the equilibrium price.

Example 20: If $D = -50p + 250$ and $S = 25p + 25$ are the demand and the supply functions of a certain product plot both the functions on a graph sheet and obtain the equilibrium price and the quantity from the graph sheet.

Solution:

As usual to plot the demand and supply let us first obtain two pairs of data points for both the demand and the supply.

Table 3.20

Market Equilibrium		
p	0	5
S	25	150
D	250	0

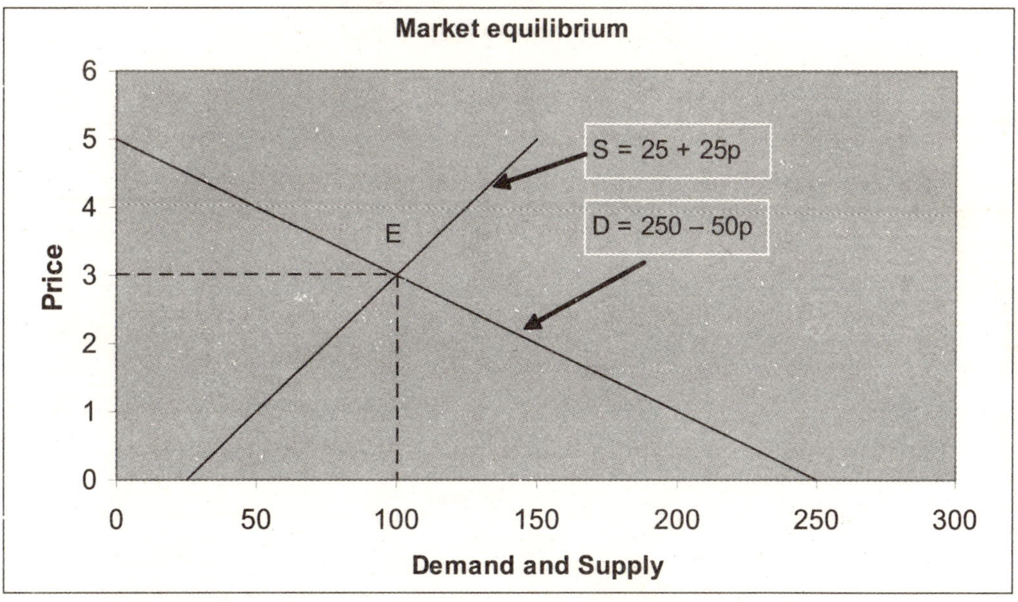

Fig. 3.20

From the graph the equilibrium price = 3 and the equilibrium quantity = 100

3.5 Use of Linear Functions in International Trade

In international trade theories especially in Adam Smith and Ricardian theories we assume constant cost conditions in production. Under such circumstances, the product transformation curves take linear shape as shown below.

Example 21: An economy A produces two commodities Wheat (W) and cloth (C) by using 100 units of its only resource labour (L). Let per unit production of wheat costs 5 units of labour and per unit production of cloth costs 10 units of labour. Write the equation of the production possibility curve. Also obtain its graph.

Solution:

The linear product transformation curve in its general form is written as

$$L = P_W W + P_C C$$

where L = The amount of labour used in the production

P_W = The price of wheat

P_C = The price of cloth

With the given data, the equation of the product transformation curve is written as $100 = 5W + 10C$. To draw the line we obtain two points on it in the usual manner as follows.

Table 3.21

PTC		
C	10	0
W	0	20

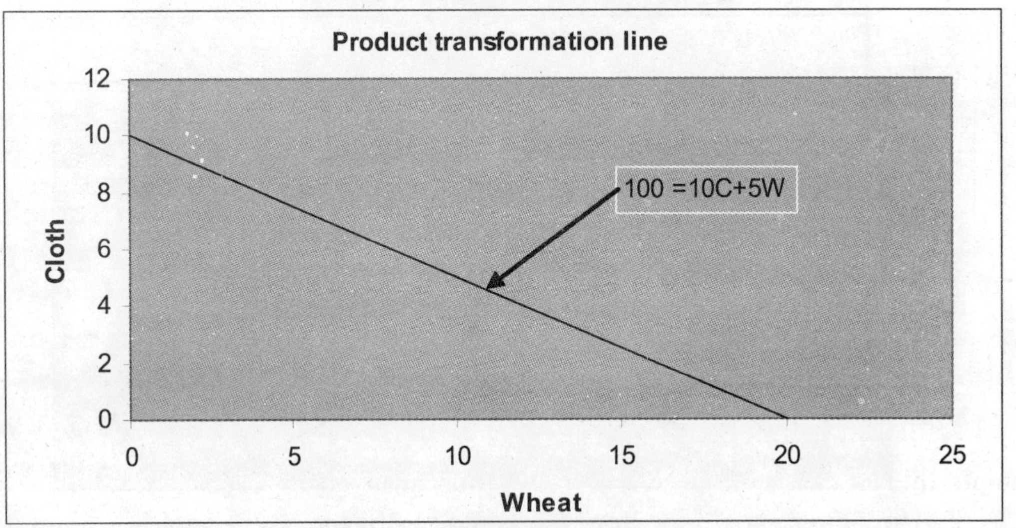

Fig. 3.21

Note: In the above diagram the cost of production is measured in real terms (in units of labour).

3.6 Application of Linear Functions in Macroeconomics

In Macroeconomics too we use linear equations to represent investment, consumption, saving etc. So let us take few illustrations from this field as well for our further discussion.

Linear consumption function

Example 22: Plot the consumption C = 200 + 0.5Y on a graph sheet and predict the level of consumption when the income Y = 800.

Solution:

To plot the needed consumption function let us get two points on the given consumption function first as shown in the table.

Table 3.22

Consumption Function		
Y	0	1400
C	200	900

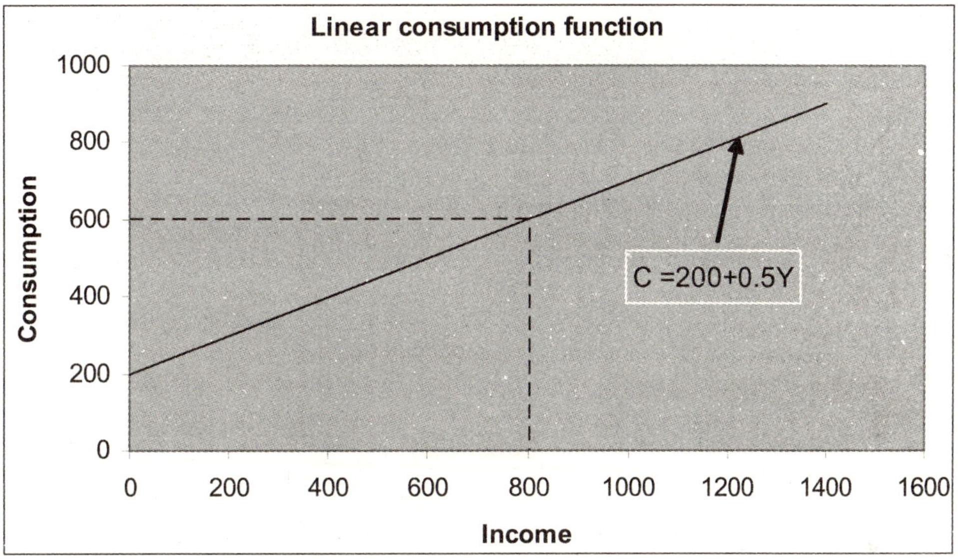

Fig. 3.22

From the graph, when Y equal to 800 the level of consumption is 600.

Linear saving function

Example 23: Plot the saving function S = –200 + 0.5Yon a graph sheet and predict the level of saving when the income Y = 800.

Solution:

To plot the needed savings function let us get points on the given savings function first as shown in the table.

Table 3.23

Saving Function		
Y	0	1400
S	–200	500

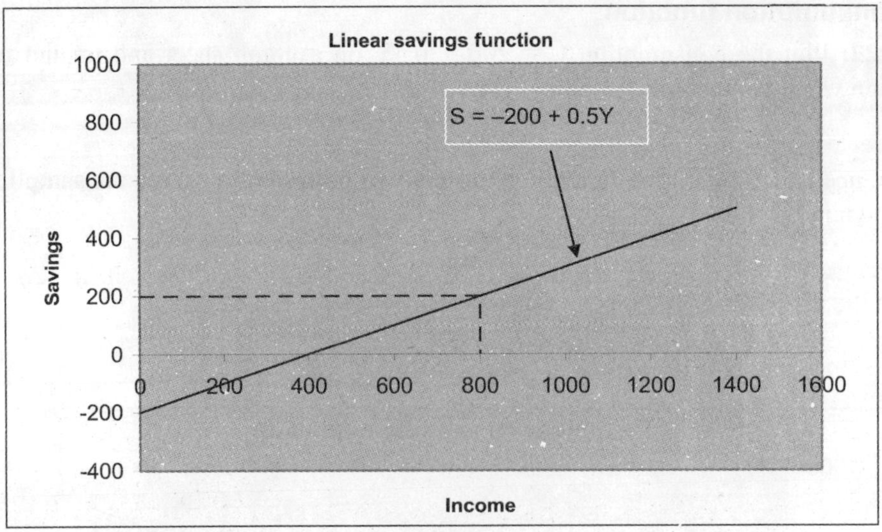

Fig. 3.23

From the graph when Y equal to 800 the level of saving is 200.

Example 24: Plot the saving function S = 0.2Y on a graph sheet and predict the level of saving when the income Y = 5000.

Solution:

To plot the needed savings function let us get two points on the given savings function as shown in the table.

Table 3.24

Saving function		
Y	0	10000
S	0	2000

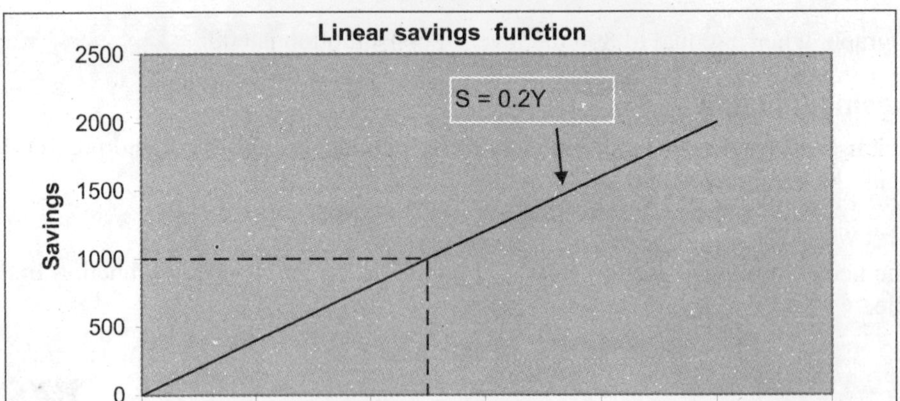

Fig. 3.24

From the graph when Y equal to 5000 the level of saving is 1000.

Note: In this functional form note that the slope 'm' is positive and the intercept 'c' is zero. Also it is important to remember that MPS = APS = 0.2 in this special case.

Example 25: Plot the investment function I = 200 on a graph sheet and predict the level of investment when the income Y = 3000.

Solution:

To plot the needed investment function let us fix two of points on the investment function given as shown in the table.

Table 3.25

Investment Function		
Y	0	4000
I	200	200

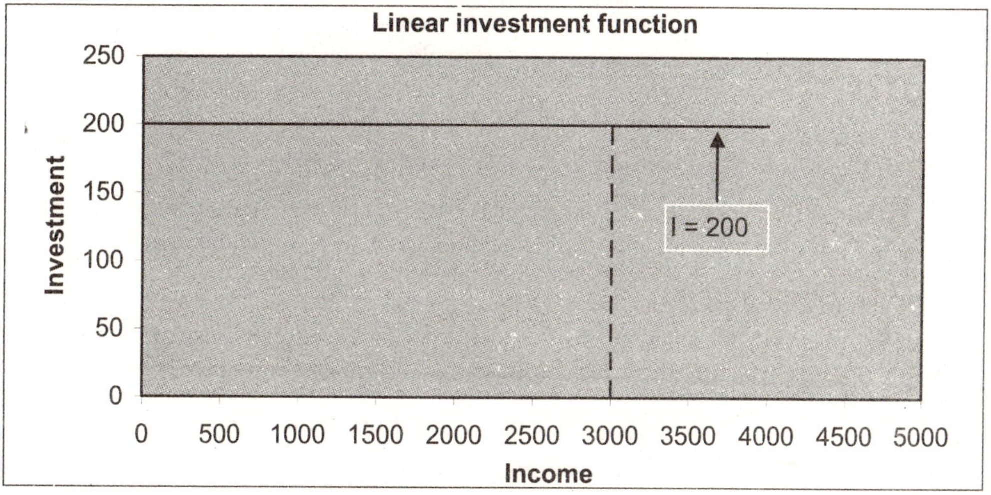

Fig. 3.25

From the graph when Y equal to 3000 the level of investment = 200.

Note: In this functional form note that the slope 'm' is zero and the intercept 'c' is positive. Here the investment I is said to be autonomous in the sense that it remains constant for all levels of income.

Example 26: Plot the investment function I = 2000 + 0.5Y on a graph sheet and predict the level of investment when the income Y = 3000.

Solution:

To plot the needed investment function let us fix two points on it first as shown in the table.

Table 3.26

Investment Function		
Y	0	4000
I	2000	4000

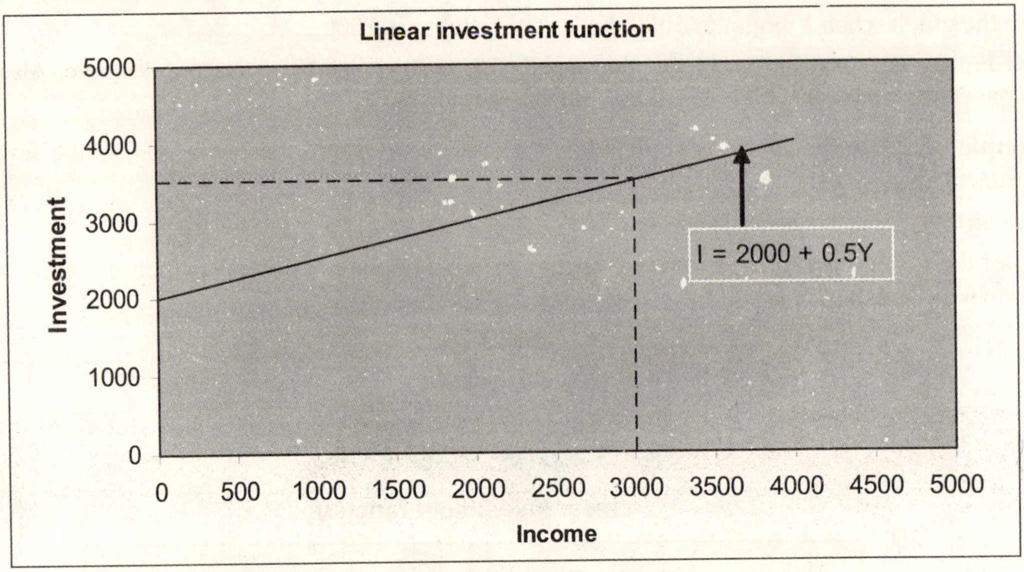

Fig. 3.26

From the graph when Y equal to 3000 the level of investment = 3500.

Note: In this functional form note that the slope 'm' is positive and the intercept 'c' is also positive. Here the investment I is said to be induced in the sense that it increases with the level of income.

Macro-economic equilibrium

The economy as a whole is said to be in equilibrium provided the saving S is equal to the investment I. For diagrammatic illustration consider the following example.

Example 27: If C = 200 + 0.5Y, I = 200 find the equilibrium level of income.

Solution:

Method 1

Under equilibrium we know that aggregate expenditure is equal to aggregate income.

$$Y = C + I$$

$$Y = 200 + 0.5Y + 200$$

$$Y(1 - 0.5) = 400$$

$$0.5Y = 400$$

$$Y = 800$$

Graphical Method:

Table 3.27

Investment Function		
Y	0	1200
I	200	200
C	200	800
C+ I	400	1000

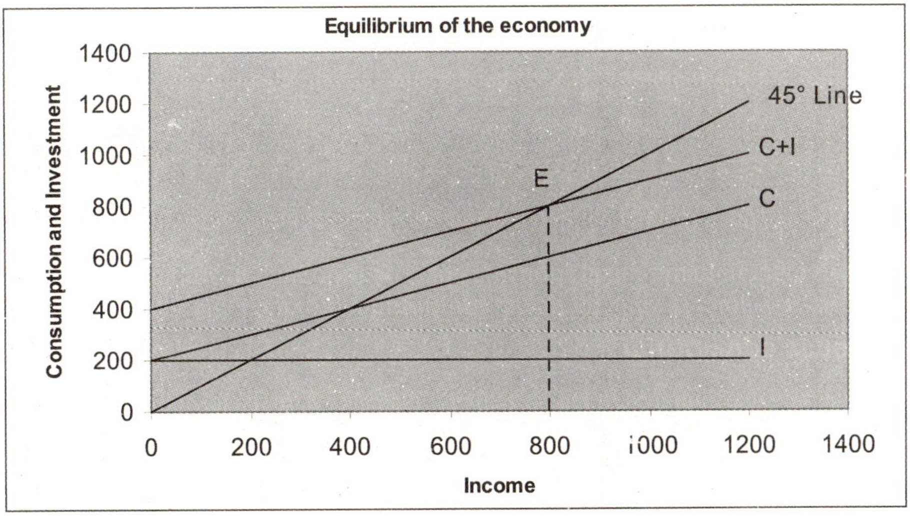

Fig. 3.27

Method 2

Y = C + S is an identity revealing the universal truth all the time. But under equilibrium aggregate expenditure is equal to aggregate income. So we have two conditions

$$Y = C + S$$

$$Y = C + I$$

So by comparing these two conditions we get

S = I as the equilibrium condition

Derivation of S

$$Y = C + S$$

$$\begin{aligned} S &= Y - C \\ &= Y - (200 - 0.5Y) \\ &= -200 + 0.5Y \end{aligned}$$

Example 28: If I = 200 and S = – 200 + 0.5Y are the investment and savings function obtain the equilibrium level of income.

Solution:

To get the equilibrium level of income let us plot both the investment and savings function on a graph sheet first.

Table 3.28

I and S Functions		
Y	0	1000
I	200	200
S	–200	300

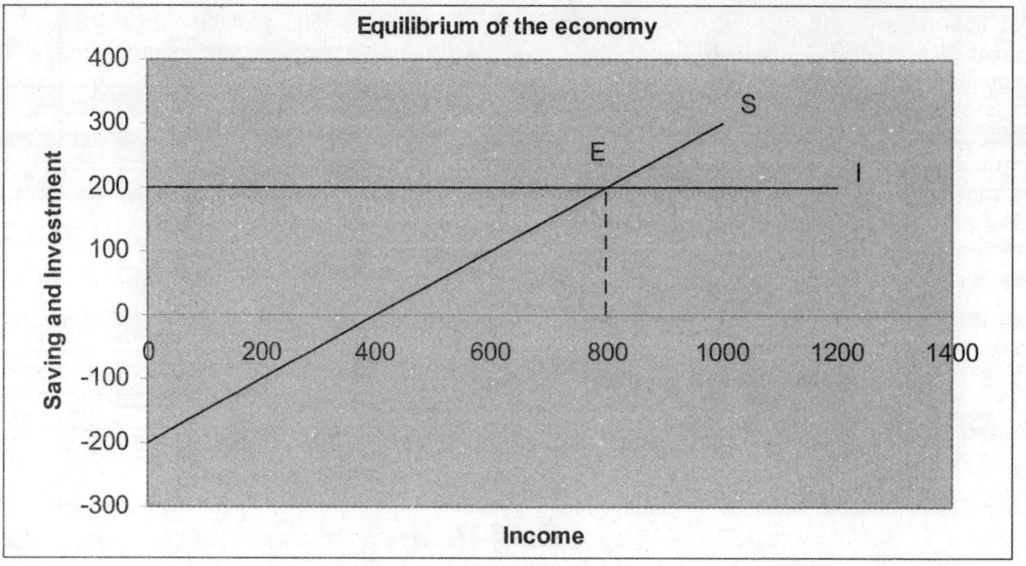

Fig. 3.28

From the graph the equilibrium level of income is 800.

$$\text{Under equilibrium } S = I$$

$$-200 + 0.5Y = 200$$

$$0.5Y = 400$$

$$Y = 800$$

3.7 Linear Equations and their Solutions

Equation: An equation equates to expressions. For example, $4x = 20$ is an equation because it equates the expression $4x$ with 20.

Identity: An identity is a special type of equation that satisfies for all values of the unknown x.

For example, in the expression $(x + 3)^2 = x^2 + 6x + 9$ is true for all possible values of the unknown namely x. For example, if we put $x = 2$ then

$$(2+3)^2 = 2^2 + 2 \times 2 \times 3 + 3^2$$
$$5^2 = 4 + 12 + 9$$
$$25 = 25$$

Similarly, if $x = 3$

$$(3+3)^2 = 3^2 + 2 \times 3 \times 3 + 3^2$$
$$6^2 = 9 + 18 + 9$$
$$36 = 36$$

Hence, the equation of this type is often called an identity. To stress the strongness of the equality we often use a three line equality ($\equiv$) in the place of our familiar two line ($=$) equality.

i.e. $(x + 3)^2 \equiv x^2 + 6x + 9$

Note: In economics often we come across identities in macroeconomics. In the classical theory of full employment we use $S \equiv I$ to represent the full employment equilibrium. Here the identity symbol stresses the equality of S and I under all situations in its expost (realized) sense. However, in Keynesian economics we use only two line equality between saving and investment ($S = I$) to stress its validity only under equilibrium. Thus, this time the equality is true only under equilibrium and not always under all circumstances as in the previous case. However, here anticipated saving is equal to the anticipated investment under equilibrium.

First-degree or linear equations: The nature of an equation is often measured by using a concept called degree. The degree of an equation is defined as the highest power of the unknown 'x' in the given equation. If the highest power of the unknown is one, then it is often called first-degree equation. Sometimes it is also called the linear equation because its functional form plotted on a graph sheet is a straight line.

Example 29: If $4x = 20$ stands for the equation, then the highest power of the unknown 'x' is unity. Hence, this is a first-degree equation.

Solution of a linear equation: The solution of a linear equation is nothing but the value of the unknown 'x' that satisfies the given equation. In other words, by solution we simply mean the value of the unknown 'x' that makes the given equation as a true statement. For example, for the equation $4x = 20$, if we give the value 5 for the unknown x, then the equation becomes $4 \times 5 = 20$. Since this is a true statement we say that $x = 5$ is the solution for the given equation.

Diagrammatic meaning of the solution: To get the corresponding linear function to the given equation we simply transfer 20 to the left-hand side and equate the resultant to zero and rewrite it as $4x - 20 = 0$.

Now to get the corresponding function we replace 0 by the dependent variable y. So the function corresponding to the given linear equation is obtained as $y = 4x - 20$. Now to interpret the solution let us first sketch this straight line on a graph sheet as usual by identifying two points.

Table 3.29

Linear Function		
x	0	10
y	–20	20

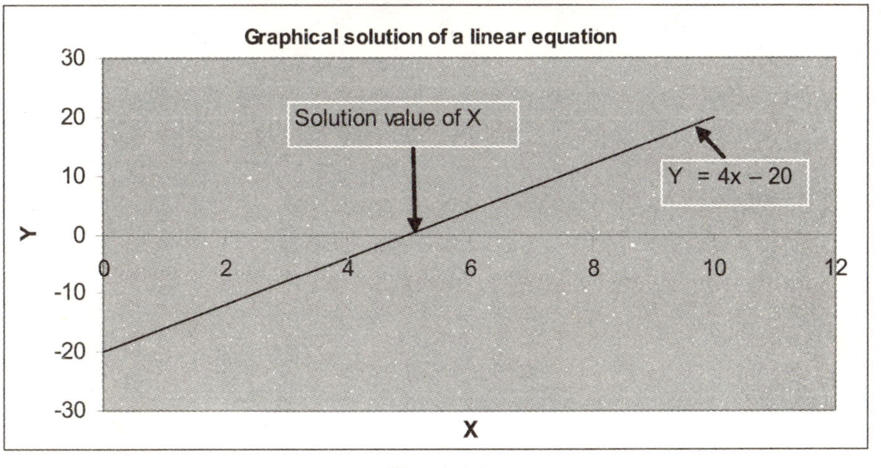

Fig. 3.29

In the graph the solution to the given equation is given by the x-coordinate of the point of intersection of line with x-axis, at which y value is zero.

Note: Since linear function can intersect the X-axis only once the associated linear equation will have only one solution.

Example 30: Find the solution for the first-degree equation

$$4x + 12 = 2x - 6$$

Solution:

As a first step in getting the solution we must arrange all the terms having the unknown 'x' to the left-hand side of the equation leaving the constants on the right side. While doing do not forget to change a plus term into minus and minus term to plus while moving the terms across the equality sign. For example, if we transfer a plus term from RHS to LHS its sign must be changed to a minus.

$$\begin{aligned} 4x + 12 &= 2x - 6 \\ 4x - 2x &= -6 - 12 \\ 2x &= -18 \\ x &= -18/2 \\ x &= -9 \end{aligned}$$

Verification:

The result can always be verified by substituting the obtained solution in the given equation. So let us put x = – 9 in the given equation

$$\begin{aligned} 4x + 12 &= 2x - 6 \\ 4 \times (-9) + 12 &= 2 \times (-9) - 6 \\ -36 + 12 &= -18 - 6 \\ -24 &= -24 \end{aligned}$$

Since the equation is satisfied, the solution for the equation is x = – 9

Example 31: Solve the equation

$$\frac{3x-7}{5} - \frac{3x+7}{4} = \frac{5x-9}{8} - \frac{3x+9}{6}$$

Solution:

Let us take 120 as LCM and rewrite the equation as

$$\frac{24(3x-7) - 30\,(3x+7)}{120} = \frac{15(5x-9) - 20(3x+9)}{120}$$

Now after cross multiplication this equation may be written as

$$\text{i.e.} \quad 72x - 168 - 90x - 210 = 75x - 135 - 60x - 180$$

$$72x - 90x - 75x + 60x = 168 + 210 - 135 - 180$$

$$-33x = 63$$

$$x = \frac{63}{-33}$$

$$x = -1.91$$

3.8 Second Degree or Quadratic Functions

The function y = f (x) is said to be quadratic provided the highest power of x in it is 2. In other words, the degree of the given equation must be equal to 2. The standard form of the quadratic function is written as $y = ax^2 + bx + c$ where a, b and c are constants and $a \neq 0$ If b = 0 and c = 0, then the simplest form of the quadratic function is obtained as $y = ax^2$. This special parabola will have the vertex at the origin and opens upwards when a > 0 as shown in Fig 3.29. When a < 0 then the parabola will have vertex at the origin but opens downwards as in Fig 3.30. For the more general type $y = ax^2 + bx + c$ though the shape remain unaltered its vertex shifted away from the origin as shown in Fig 3.31.

Example 32: Draw the graph for the quadratic function $y = 4x^2$.

Table 3.30

x	y	x	y
-10	400	1	4
-9	324	2	16
-8	256	3	36
-7	196	4	64
-6	144	5	100
-5	100	6	144
-4	64	7	196
-3	36	8	256
-2	16	9	324
-1	4	10	400
0	0	11	484

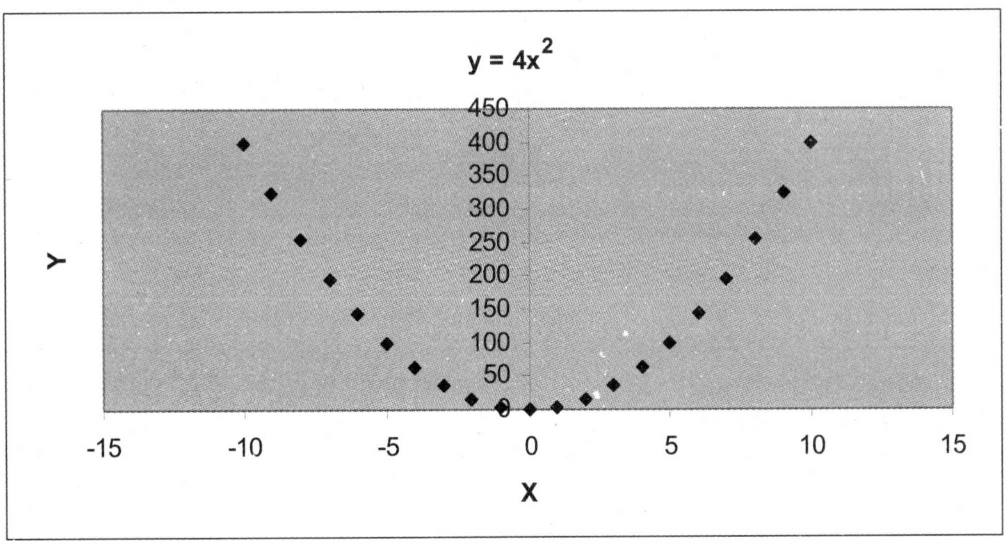

Fig. 3.30

Example 33: Draw the graph for the quadratic function $y = -4x^2$.

Table 3.31

x	y	x	y
-10	-400	1	-4
-9	-324	2	-16
-8	-256	3	-36
-7	-196	4	-64
-6	-144	5	-100
-5	-100	6	-144
-4	-64	7	-196
-3	-36	8	-256
-2	-16	9	-324
-1	-4	10	-400
0	0	11	-484

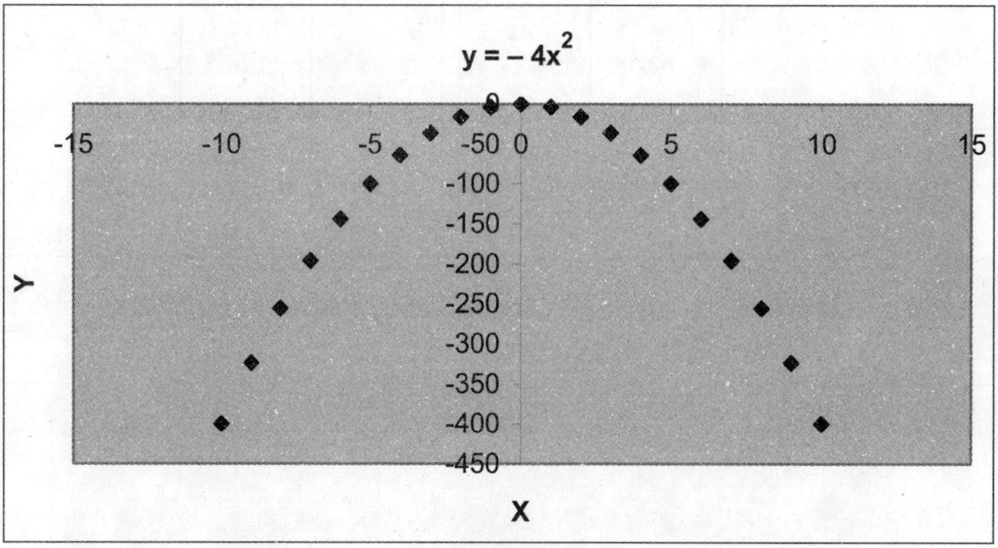

Fig. 3.31

In the two cases mentioned above the curvature turning point is often called vertex of the given parabola. For both the types the vertex points coincide with the origin. This need not be in all the cases. In general for the quadratic functions of the type $y = ax^2+bx+c$, the coordinates of the vertex is obtained by using the following formula. The corresponding graph with other than the origin as vertex is shown in figure 3.32.

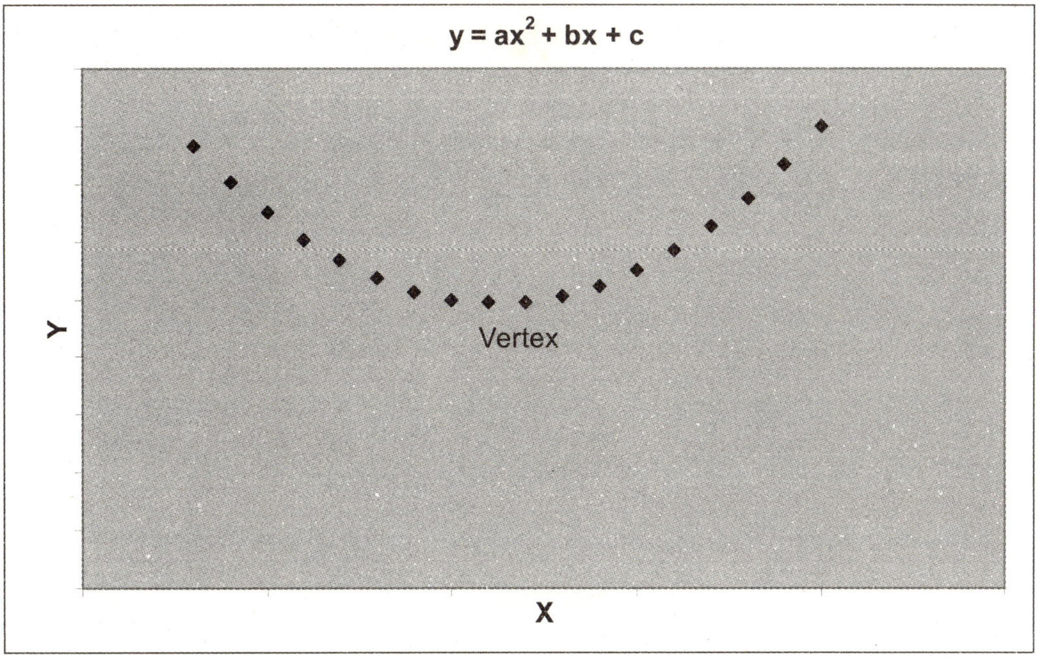

Fig. 3.32

Formula for getting the vertex, $V\left(-\frac{b}{2a}, \frac{4ac-b^2}{4a}\right)$

Remember, vertex gives the maximum point when 'a' is positive and minimum point when 'a' is negative. Hence one could use the vertex formula to get the maximum and minimum points associated to given quadratic function.

Example 34: For the quadratic function, $y = x^2 + 3x - 4$ draw the graph. Also, locate it vertex.

Solution:

The given function is quadratic because the highest power of x in it is 2. Functions of this type are quite often used in economics to describe the 'U' shaped average and marginal cost functions. To draw a smooth quadratic function we must have as many points as possible. In the table given below we obtained 12 points for a smooth graph.

Table 3.32

Quadratic Function												
x	-7	-6	-5	-4	-3	-2	-1	0	1	2	3	4
y	24	14	6	0	-4	-6	-6	-4	0	6	14	24

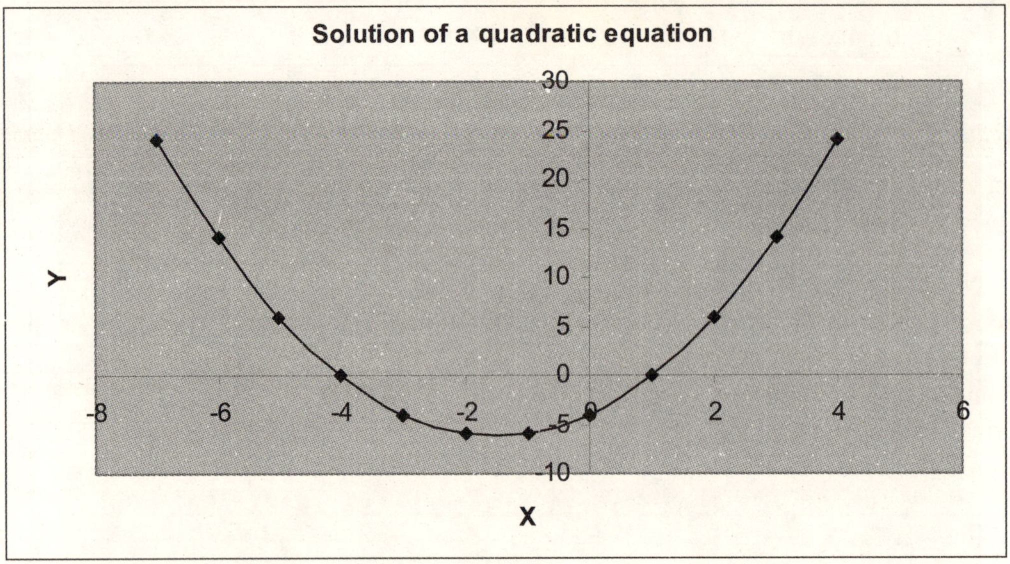

Fig. 3.33

In our problem a =1, b = 3, c = – 4

$$= \left[-\frac{b}{2a}, \frac{4ac - b^2}{4a} \right]$$

$$= \left[-\frac{3}{2 \times 1}, \frac{4 \times 1 \times -4 - (3)^2}{4 \times 1} \right]$$

$$= \left[\frac{-3}{2}, \frac{-25}{4} \right]$$

$$= [-1.5, -6.25]$$

Thus, the coordinates of the vertex is written as V(-1.5, -6.25)

Example 35: The demand function of a form is p = 100-4q. Obtain the revenue function and calculate the Baumol's maximum revenue, the corresponding piece, and the quantity. Also, draw the graph and confirm the result obtained.

Solution:

By definition revenue = price $\times$ quantity sold

$R = p \times q = (100 - 4q)q = 100q - 4q^2$. This is a quadratic function in q with a = – 4, b = 100 and c = 0. Therefore, the maximum revenue point is none other than the vertex to this parabola. The coordinates of the vertex is given by

$$= \left[-\frac{b}{2a}, \frac{4ac - b^2}{4a} \right]$$

$$= \left[-\frac{100}{2 \times -4}, \frac{4 \times -4 \times 0 - (-100)^2}{4 \times -4} \right]$$

$$= \left[\frac{-100}{-8}, \frac{0 - 10000}{-16} \right]$$

$$= [12.5, 625]$$

Thus under equilibrium the maximum revenue R = 625. The corresponding quantity is q = 12.5, the price is obtained by substituting this quantity in the demand law given.

$$p = 100 - 4q = 100 - 4 \times 12.5 = 50$$

Table 3.33

q	p	R		q	p	R
0	100	0		13	48	624
1	96	96		14	44	616
2	92	184		15	40	600
3	88	264		16	36	576
4	84	336		17	32	544
5	80	400		18	28	504
6	76	456		19	24	456
7	72	504		20	20	400
8	68	544		21	16	336
9	64	576		22	12	264
10	60	600		23	8	184
11	56	616		24	4	96
12	52	624		25	0	0

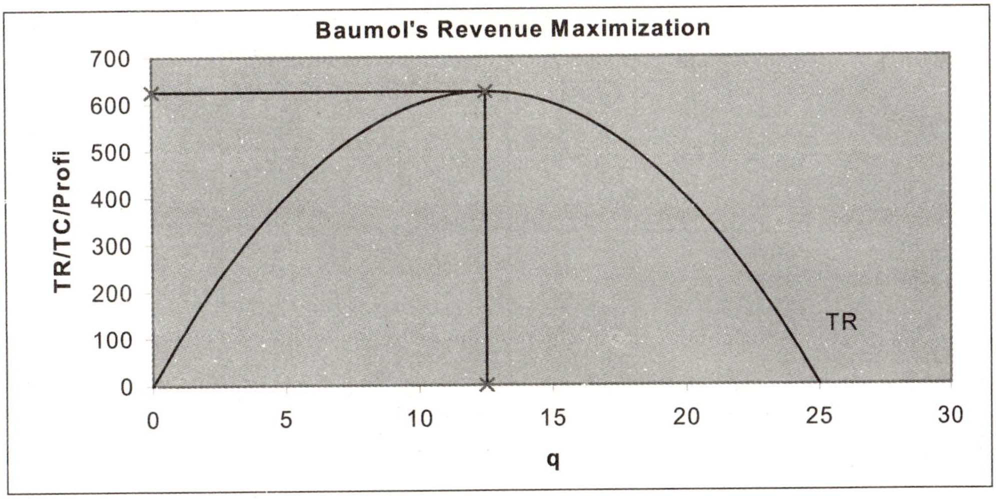

Fig 3.34

Example 36: The demand function of a monopoly p = 100 – 4q. Given his linear cost function C = 50 + 20q obtain the maximum profit, corresponding output and the price.

Solution:

By definition Profit = Revenue – Cost

$$\begin{aligned}\Pi &= R - C\\ &= p \times q - C\\ &= (100-4q)q-(50+20q)\\ &= 100q-4q^2-50-20q\\ &= -4q^2+80q-50\end{aligned}$$

Clearly the profit is a quadratic function in q with a = – 4, b = 80 and c = – 50. Therefore, the maximum revenue point is none other than the vertex to this parabola. The coordinates of the vertex is given by

$$=\left[-\frac{b}{2a}, \frac{4ac-b^2}{4a}\right]$$

$$=\left[-\frac{80}{2\times -4}, \frac{4\times -4\times -50-(80)^2}{4\times -4}\right]$$

$$=\left[\frac{-80}{-8}, \frac{-5600}{-16}\right]$$

$$=[10, 350]$$

Thus the maximum profit = Rs. 350. The equilibrium output = 10 and the corresponding price p = 100 – 4q = 100 – 4(10) = 60

Graphical Solution:

Table 3.34

q	Profit		q	Profit
0	-50		13	314
1	26		14	286
2	94		15	250
3	154		16	206
4	206		17	154
5	250		18	28
6	286		19	24
7	314		20	20
8	334		21	16
9	346		22	12
10	350		23	8
11	346		24	4
12	334		25	0

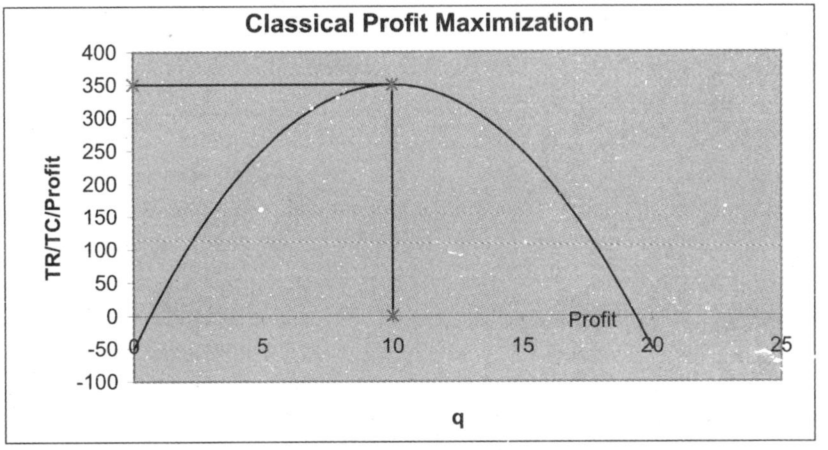

Fig. 3.35

3.9 Second Degree or Quadratic Equations and their Solutions

If $y = x^2 + 3x - 4$ stands for the quadratic function then the equation by putting $y = 0$ often called quadratic equation. For example, the associated quadratic equation is $x^2 + 3x - 4 = 0$.

Solution of the quadratic equation

Since $y = 0$ is the x-axis itself the solution to the given equation is obtained by the x-coordinates of the points of intersection of the given function with the x-axis. From the above Fig. one could read the solutions as $x = -4$ and $x = 1$.

Example 37: For the function $y = x^2 - 15x + 50$ draw the graph and obtain the solutions for the corresponding quadratic equation.

Solution: By graphical method

Table 3.35

Quadratic Function														
y	36	24	14	6	0	-4	-6	-6	-4	0	6	14	24	36
x	1	2	3	4	5	6	7	8	9	10	11	12	13	14

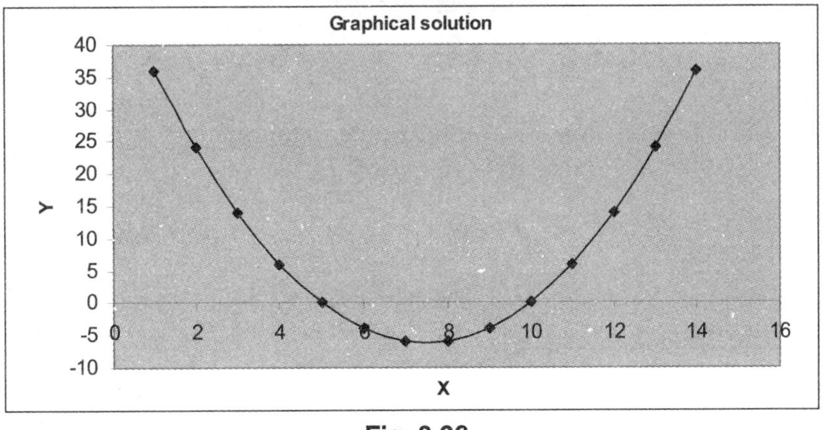

Fig. 3.36

From the graph the two solutions are x = 5 and x = 10.

Solutions of quadratic equations by algebraic method:

The standard form of the quadratic equation is normally written as $ax^2 + bx + c = 0$ where a, b and c are constants. Depending upon the assigned values to these constants we get particular quadratic equations. For example, if a = 2, b = 7, c = 10 then the particular equation may be written as $2x^2 + 7x + 10 = 0$. Every quadratic equation will have two solutions. Using any one of three alternative methods given below we can solve the given quadratic equation.

1. Factorization method.
2. Completing square method.
3. Formula method.

Solution by factorization method:

Example 38: Solve $x^2 - 16x + 48 = 0$ ...(1)

Solution:

In the factorization method we rewrite the given quadratic equation in terms of product of two factors first. If we compare given equation with the standard form the values of the constants are a = 1, b = – 16 and c = 48. Now to factorize the given equation we follow the following stepwise procedure as shown below.

Step 1: Multiply the terms 'a' and 'c' and keep this result in memory for the latter use. In our illustration $a \times c = 1 \times 48 = 48$

Step 2: Split the coefficient x namely 'b' into two parts so that the sum of the bits is once again equal to 'b' but at the same time the product of these two bits equals the product a × c obtained in step 1.

Now to obtain the correct split of 'b' let us consider some of the following splits:

$$-1 \times -15 = 15$$
$$-2 \times -14 = 28$$
$$-3 \times -13 = 39$$
$$-4 \times -12 = 48$$
$$-5 \times -11 = 55$$

and so on.

Among the possible splits shown above the needed split is only

$$-4 \times -12 = 48 = a \times c$$

Hence, the given equation is rewritten as

$$x^2 - 4x - 12x + 48 = 0$$

Now since x can be taken as the common factor between the first two terms and –12 can be taken as the common factor between last two terms.

So the above equation may be rewritten as

$$x(x - 4) - 12(x - 4) = 0$$

i.e. $(x-4)(x-12) = 0$

Now to have two products zero we know that either the first term must be zero or the second term must be zero.

i.e. $x-4 = 0$ i.e. $x = 4$

if $x-12 = 0$ i.e. $x = 12$

Thus, $x = 4$ and $x = 12$ are the two solutions to the given equation.

Solution by completing the square method:

$$\text{Solve } x^2 - 16x + 48 = 0$$

In this method the first two terms of the LHS of the given equation is rearranged into a perfect square by appropriate manipulations.

We know that $(A+B)^2 = A^2 + B^2 + 2AB$

Now let $A = x$ and rewrite the given as

$$x^2 - 16x + 48 = 0$$

$$x^2 - 2.x.8 + 48 = 0$$

Note that in the modified form $A = x$, and $B = 8$

In the above equation since there is no B^2 term let us add and subtract 8^2 to the LHS of the above equation.

$$x^2 - 2.x.8 + 8^2 - 8^2 + 48 = 0$$

$$(x-8)^2 = 8^2 - 48$$

$$= 64 - 48$$

$$= 16$$

So $$(x-8) = \sqrt{16}$$

$$= \pm 4$$

$$x = 8 + 4$$

$$x = 12 \text{ or}$$

$$x = 8 - 4$$

$$x = 4$$

Thus, $x = 4$ and $x = 12$ are the two solutions.

Solution by formula method: Derivation of the formula

To get the formula let us try to solve the standard quadratic equation $ax^2 + bx + c = 0$ by simply applying the technique of completing the square method discussed above. Let the quadratic equation in its standard form be

$$ax^2 + bx + c = 0.$$

Now divide both the sides of this equation by 'a' and make the coefficient of x^2 as unity

$$x^2 + \frac{b}{a}x + \frac{c}{a} = 0$$

Now bx/a must be put in 2AB form

This is accomplished by multiplying and dividing the second term by 2

i.e. $$x^2 + 2x\frac{b}{2a} + \frac{c}{a} = 0$$

Now to make perfect square add and subtract $(b/2a)^2$ in the L.H.S.

i.e. $$x^2 + 2x\frac{b}{2a} + \left(\frac{b}{2a}\right)^2 - \left(\frac{b}{2a}\right)^2 + \frac{c}{a} = 0$$

$$\left(x + \frac{b}{2a}\right)^2 = \frac{b^2}{4a^2} - \frac{c}{a}$$

$$= \frac{b^2 - 4ac}{4a^2}$$

$$\left(x + \frac{b}{2a}\right) = \pm\sqrt{\frac{b^2 - 4ac}{4a^2}}$$

$$= \pm\frac{\sqrt{b^2 - 4ac}}{2a}$$

$$x = \frac{-b}{2a} \pm \frac{\sqrt{b^2 - 4ac}}{2a}$$

$$x = \frac{-b \pm \sqrt{b^2 - 4ac}}{2a}$$

Example 39: Solve $x^2 - 16x + 48 = 0$ by using formula.

Solution:

Comparing this with the standard form, we get a = 1, b = – 16, c = 48

Now $$x = \frac{-b \pm \sqrt{b^2 - 4ac}}{2a}$$

$$x = \frac{-(-16) \pm \sqrt{(-16)^2 - 4(1)(48)}}{2 \times 1}$$

$$= \frac{16 \pm \sqrt{256 - 192}}{2}$$

$$= \frac{16 \pm \sqrt{64}}{2} = \frac{16 \pm 8}{2}$$

$$x = \frac{16 + 8}{2} = 12$$

$$\text{or } x = \frac{16 - 8}{2} = 4$$

So x = 4 and x = 12 are the solutions.

3.10 Use of Cubic Functions

All the second-degree functions will have a unique characteristic shape with only one bend in the entire range as shown above. The cubic functions, on the other hand, will have two bends in its range of operation. Also it will have x^3 term in it. Such types of functions are often used in business to represent total cost function. The cubic equations will have three roots. In other words we would say that the cubic function would cross over the X-axis thrice in its range of operation.

Example 40: Draw the graph of the short run cost function $C = 0.04q^3 - 0.9q^2 + 10q + 100$. Also draw TVC and TFC on the same graph and compare its shapes.

Solution:

Here again to get a smooth curve one must plot good number of points in the relevant range of operation.

Table 3.36

Cost functions

q	TC	TVC	TFC	q	TC	TVC	TFC
0	100	0	100	16	193.44	93.44	100
1	109.14	9.14	100	17	206.42	106.42	100
2	116.72	16.72	100	18	221.68	121.68	100
3	122.98	22.98	100	19	239.46	139.46	100
4	128.16	28.16	100	20	260	160	100
5	132.5	32.5	100	21	283.54	183.54	100
6	136.24	36.24	100	22	310.32	210.32	100
7	139.62	39.62	100	23	340.58	240.58	100
8	142.88	42.88	100	24	374.56	274.56	100
9	146.26	46.26	100	25	412.5	312.5	100
10	150	50	100	26	454.64	354.64	100
11	154.34	54.34	100	27	501.22	401.22	100
12	159.52	59.52	100	28	552.48	452.48	100
13	165.78	65.78	100	29	608.66	508.56	100
14	173.36	73.36	100	30	670	570	100
15	182.5	82.5	100				

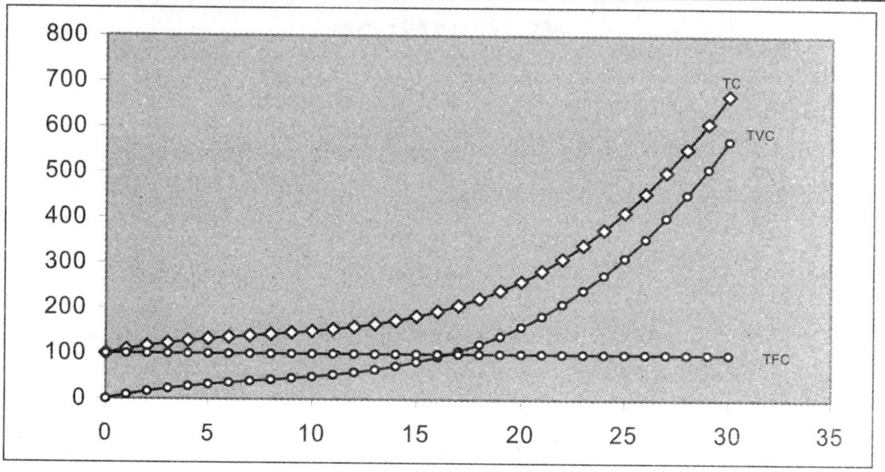

Fig. 3.37

Note: It is important to note that both TVC and TC are not parallel. In fact though they look like parallel in the horizontal range, in relevant vertical range they become closer and closer.

Example 41: For the Short-run cost schedule shown below, draw the graphs for all functions and observe the shapes.

Table 3.37

Short-run Cost Schedule						
q	TFC	TVC	TC	AFC	AVC	AC
0	60	0	60	-	-	
1	60	20	80	60	20	80
2	60	30	90	30	15	45
3	60	45	105	20	15	35
4	60	80	140	15	20	35
5	60	135	195	12	27	39

Solution:

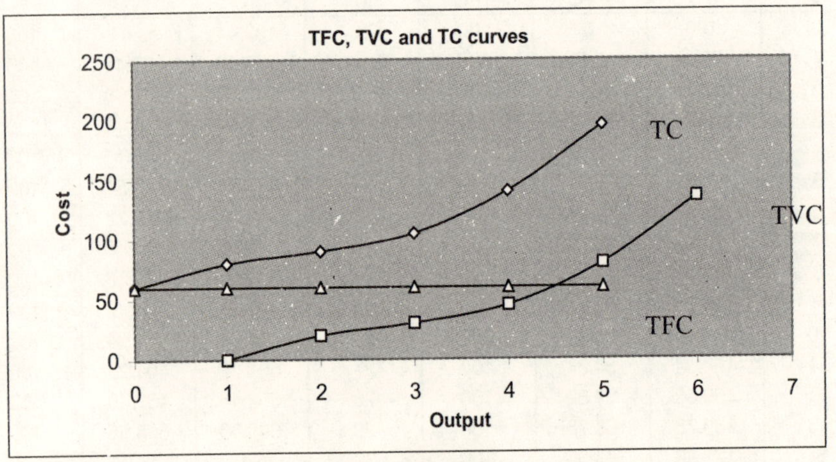

Fig. 3.38 (a)

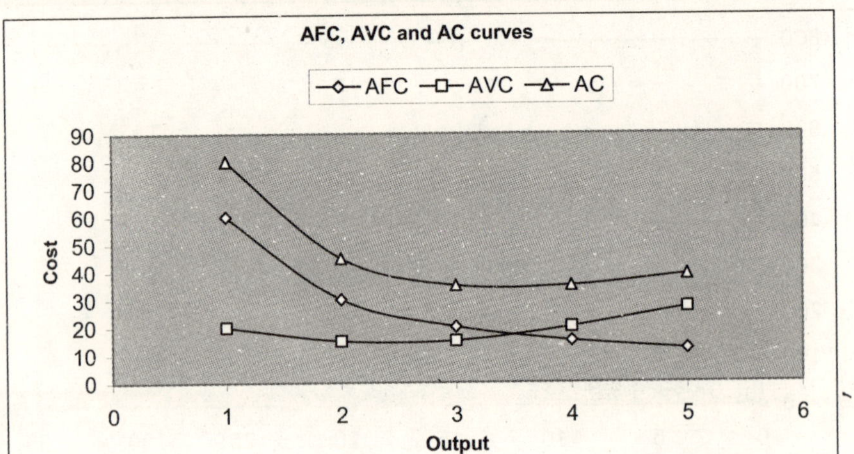

Fig. 3.38 (b)

Note: AVC and AC are not parallel again, they become closer and closer as output increases. Also MC (not shown in this Figure) passes through minimum point of both AC and AVC.

Example 42: The short run cost function of a firm is $C = 0.04q^3 - 0.9q^2 + 10q + 5$. Obtain TFC, TVC, AC, AΓC and AVC.

Solution:

By definition TFC is the cost that does not vary with the output. So from the given cost function

$$TFC = 5.$$
$$TVC = 0.04q^3 - 0.9q^2 + 10q$$
$$AC = C/q = 0.04q^2 - 0.9q + 10 + 5/q$$
$$AFC = 5/q$$
$$AVC = TVC/\,q = 0.04q^2 - 0.9q + 10$$

3.11 Power Functions

In all the functions that we have considered so far the variable x appeared as the base with some constant power. For example, in the equation $y = x^2$ the base x is a variable and the power 2 is a constant. Such functions are called power functions. The table 3.38 and the related graph 3.33 show the progress of the power function $y = x^2$. Remember that the quadratic function discussed in the previous section is none other than the power function of course with power 2.

Table 3.38

	Power Function										
x	0	1	2	3	4	5	6	7	8	9	10
$y = x^2$	0	1	4	9	16	25	36	49	64	81	100

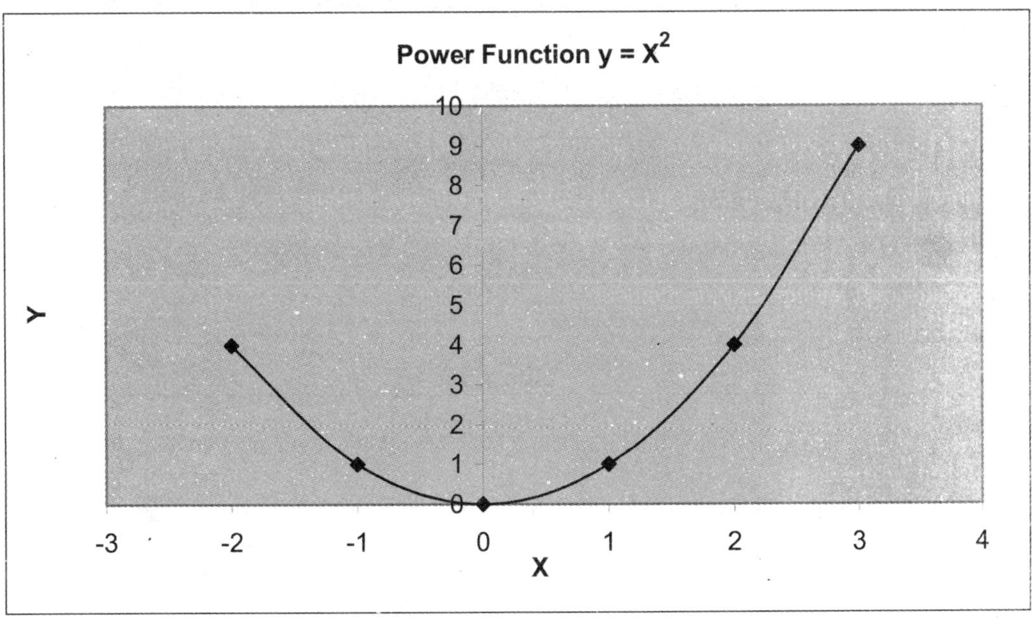

Fig. 3.39

3.12 Exponential Functions

An alternative to power function we define functions with constant base and variable power. For example, in $y = a^x$ the constant 'a' is in the base and the variable 'x' is in the power. Such a representation is called an exponential function. Depending upon the value of 'a' we get variety exponential functions. These types of functions are known for their ability to increase or decrease at a faster rate than the power functions. In particular, if a = 2 then the corresponding exponential function is obtained as $y = 2^x$.

Important characteristics of exponential function

- An exponential function $y = a^x$ is defined only for the positive values of 'a'.
- If a >1 then $y = a^x$ is an increasing function.
- If 0 < a <1 then the function $y = a^x$ is a decreasing function.
- If a = 1 then $y = 1^x$ is a constant function with value 1 all the time.
- The graph of $y = a^x$ and $y = a^{-x}$ are the reflection of each other about Y-axis.

Some important rules of exponents

For a, b, x and y being real numbers and a > 0, b > 0 then

1. $a^x a^y = a^{x+y}$
2. $(a^x)^y = a^{xy}$
3. $(ab)^x = a^x b^x$
4. $\frac{1}{a^x} = a^{-x}$
5. $a^0 = 1$
6. $\frac{a^x}{a^y} = a^{x-y}$

Graph of exponential functions

Depending upon a >1, a = 1 and 0 < a < 1 we get three types of graphs.

Case 1: a > 1 say 2

Example 43: Draw graph for $y = 2^x$.

Table 3.39

Exponential Function													
x	-2	-1	0	1	2	3	4	5	6	7	8	9	10
$y = 2^x$	0.3	0.5	1	2	4	8	16	32	64	128	256	512	1024

Solution:

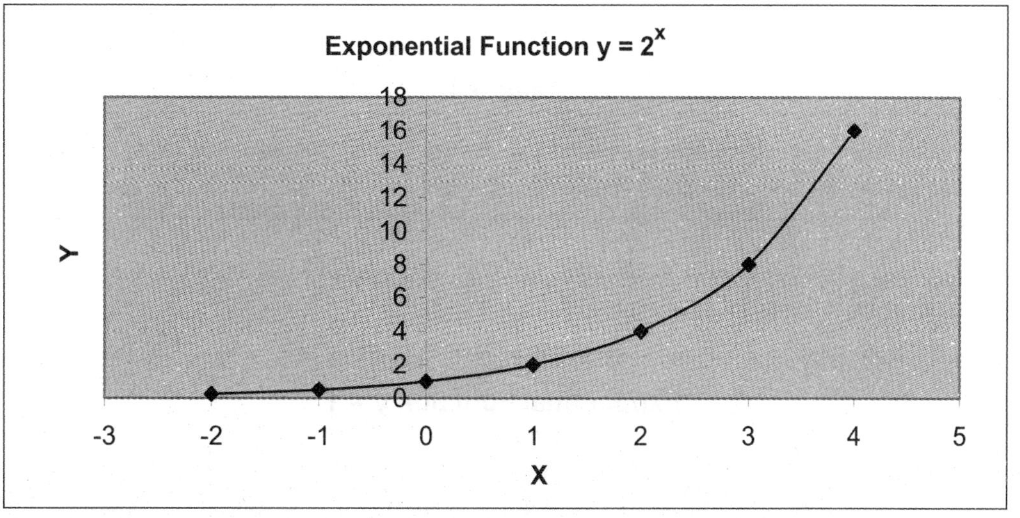

Fig. 3.40

Example 44: Draw the graph for exponential function $y = 2^{-x}$.

Solution:

Table 3.40

Y $=2^{-x}$											
x	-4	-3	-2	-1	0	1	2	3	4	5	6
y $=2^{-x}$	16	8	4	2	1	0.5	0.25	0.125	0.0625	0.0313	0.0156

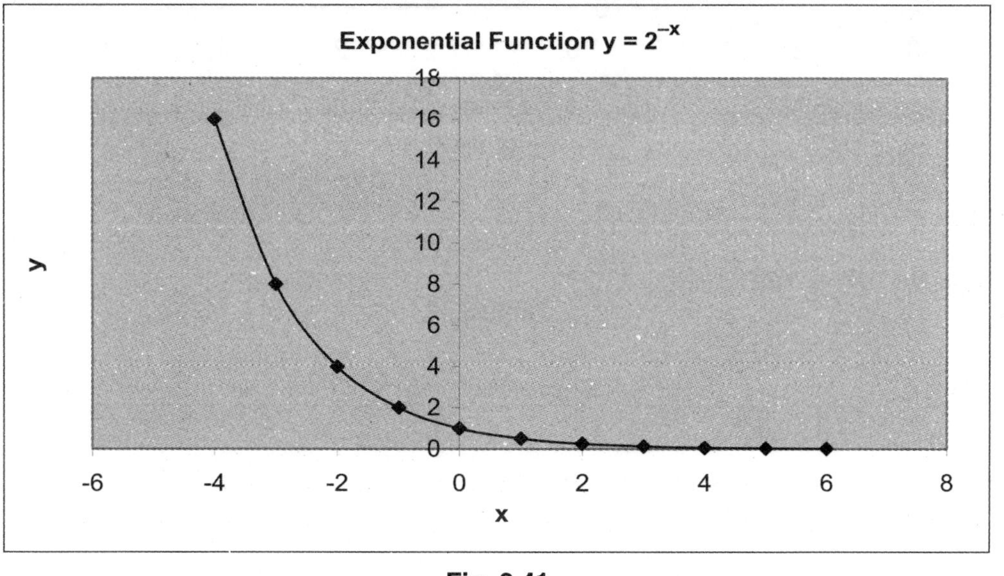

Fig. 3.41

Case 2: a = 1

Example 45: Draw graph for $y = 1^x$.

Solution:

Table 3.41

Exponential Function													
x	-2	-1	0	1	2	3	4	5	6	7	8	9	10
$y = 1^x$	1	1	1	1	1	1	1	1	1	1	1	1	1

In this case each real value of x we have $a^x = 1^x = 1$. Therefore in this case the graph is a straight line passing through the point (1, 0) parallel to X-axis.

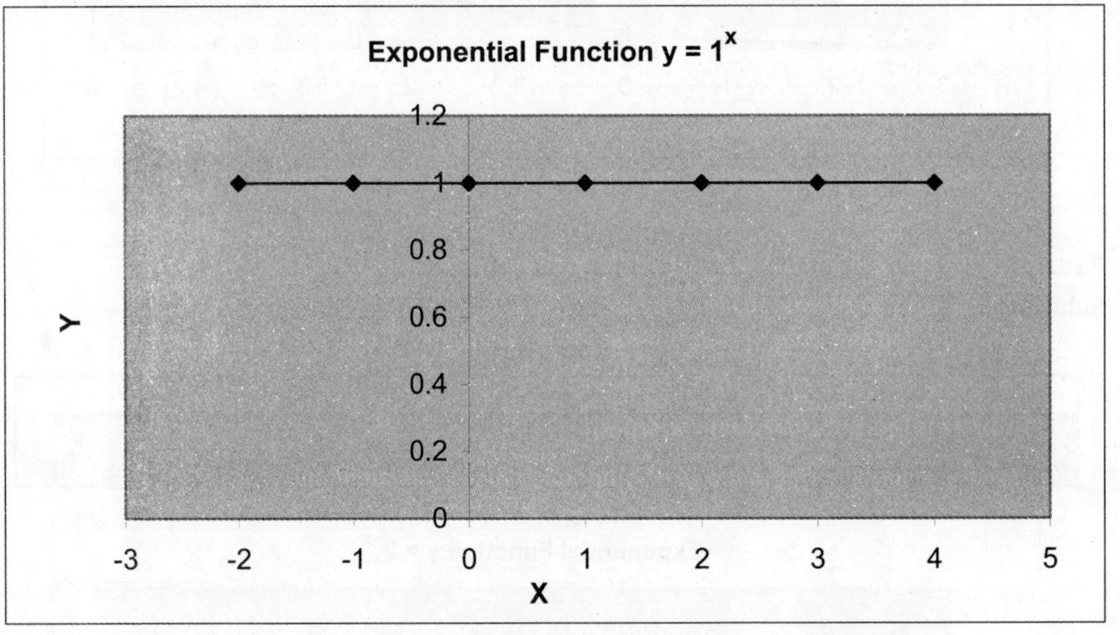

Fig. 3.42

Case 3: 0 < a <1

Example 46: Draw graph for $y = 0.5^x$.

Table 3.42

Exponential Function													
x	-2	-1	0	1	2	3	4	5	6	7	8	9	10
$y = 0.5^x$	4	2	1	0.5	0.3	0.1	0.1	0	0	0	0	0	0

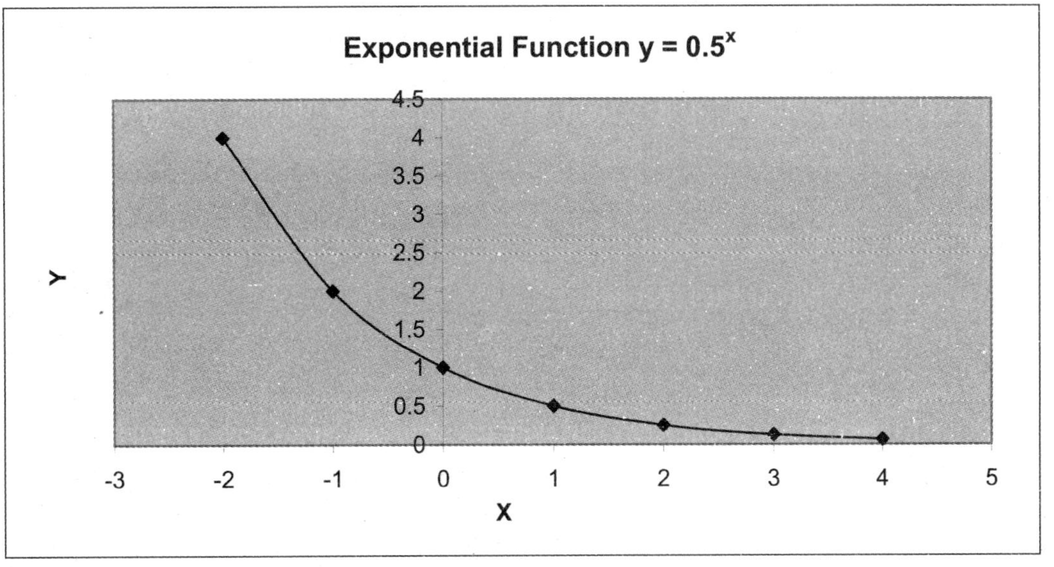

Fig. 3.43

Some important properties of exponential functions:

- Since $a^x > 0$ the entire graph lie above the X-axis.
- At $x = 0$, since $a^0 = 1$ the graph passes through the point (1, 0).
- It is a decreasing function.
- The graph is asymptotic to the X-axis to the right side.
- The parameter 'a' decides the curvature.

Exponential and Power functions: A comparison

Example 47: Draw graph for both $y = x^2$ and $y = 2^x$ and compare their fastness in explaining the change.

Solution:

Table 3.43

	Power and exponential functions										
x	0	1	2	3	4	5	6	7	8	9	10
$y = X^2$	0	1	4	9	16	25	36	49	64	81	100
$y = 2^x$	1	2	4	8	16	32	64	128	256	512	1024

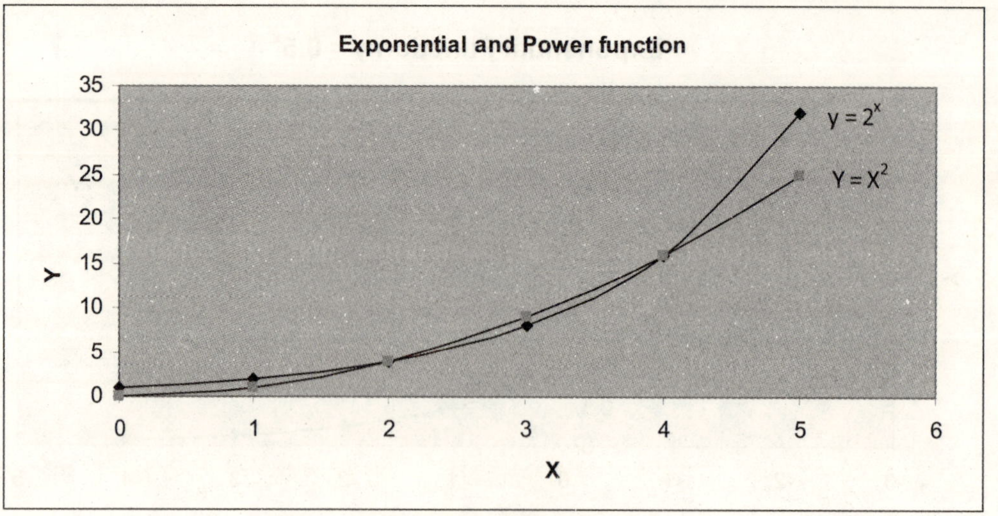

Fig. 3.44

From the table and graph, it is clear that the exponential function grow faster than the corresponding power function. Moreover, this type of functions exhibits constant growth rates of the concerned variables when time is taken as the independent variable. They are used in interest compounding, discounting, and depreciation related problems. These types of functions are very well suited to explain theories of growth and decay.

Special exponential function with base "e"

Often we use some special pre-determined constants as base to get some special and interesting results. The most commonly used base in this context is the number e = 2.71828. This is the summation value of natural series

$$e = 1 + \frac{1}{1!} + \frac{1}{2!} + \frac{1}{3!} + \ldots\ldots \frac{1}{n!}$$

$$= 2.71828$$

This type of functions are normally takes the form $y = e^x$ where e = 2.71828.

Example 48: Draw the graph for the exponential function $y = e^x$ on a graph sheet.

Solution:

The following table and the associated Fig. illustrates this specialized function $y = e^x$.

Table 3.44

	Power and exponential functions										
x	0	1	2	3	4	5	6	7	8	9	10
e^x	1.00	2.72	7.39	20.09	54.60	148.41	403.43	1096.63	2980.96	8103.08	22026.47

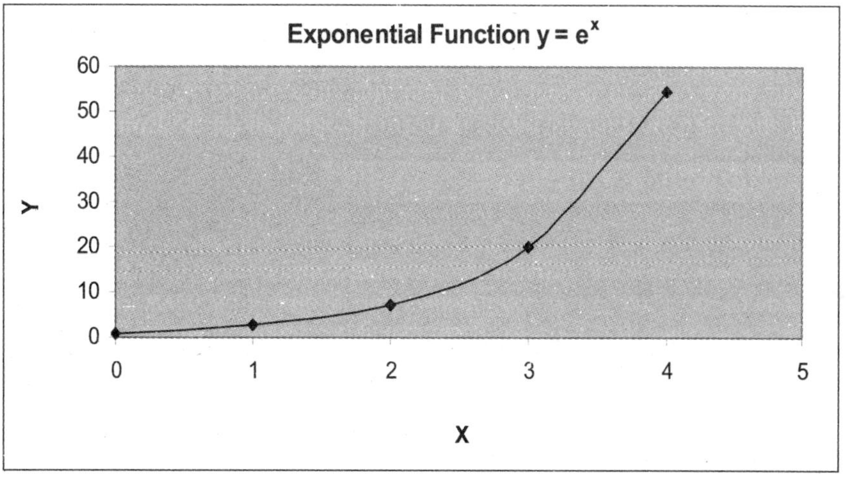

Fig. 3.45

Example 49: Draw the graph for the exponential function $y = e^{-x}$ on a graph sheet.

Solution:

Table 3.45

x	0	1	2	3	4	5	6	7	8	9	10
e^{-x}	1.00	0.37	0.14	0.05	0.02	0.01	0.00	0.00	0.00	0.00	0.00

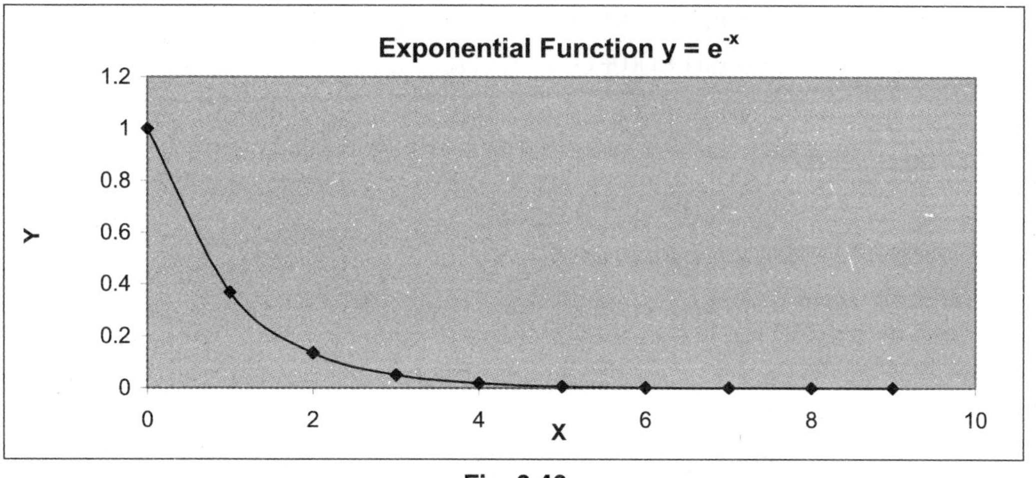

Fig. 3.46

3.13 Use of Exponential Functions in Interest Compounding

Interest is the payment made for the use of money. It may be either simple or compound.

Simple interest

If Rs.P_0 is invested in a Bank at a simple annual interest of r per cent per annum for t years then accrued interest plus the capital at the end of tth year is given by the formula.

$$P_t = \text{Principal} + \text{interest on the principle for t years} = P_0 + P_0rt$$
$$= P_0(1 + rt)$$

Example 50: Calculate the value of an investment of Rs.1000 after 5 years at the simple interest rate of 5% per annum.

Solution:

$$P_t = P_0 + P_0rt$$
$$= P_0(1 + rt)$$
$$= 1000\left(1 + \frac{5}{100} \times 5\right)$$
$$= 1000 \times 1.25 = 1250$$

Compound interest

(a) Annual Compounding

If P_0 stands for the principle amount, r stands for the rate of interest per annum and t stands for number of years then the amount at the end of any given year is calculated as

After one year

$$P_1 = P_0 + P_0r$$
$$= P_0(1 + r)$$

After two years

$$P_2 = P_0(1 + r) + P_0(1 + r)$$
$$= P_0(1 + r)(1 + r)$$
$$= P_0(1 + r)^2$$

After three years

$$P_3 = P_0(1 + r)^2 + P_0(1 + r)^2 r$$
$$= P_0(1 + r)^2(1 + r)$$
$$= P_0(1 + r)^3$$

After n years

$$P_t = P_0(1 + r)^n$$

(b) Quarterly Compounding

If interest is compounded quarterly (4 times in a given year) then the total number of periods for n years = 4n. Similarly if r is the rate of interest per annum then interest per quarter = r/4. So the above formula is modified as

$$P_n = P_0\left(1 + \frac{r}{4}\right)^{4n}$$

(c) Monthly Compounding

If compounding is done 12 times in a year then the total number of periods for n years = 12n. Similarly, if r is the rate of interest per annum then interest per month= r/12. So the above formula is modified as

$$P_n = P_0\left(1+\frac{r}{12}\right)^{12n}$$

(d) Daily Compounding

If compounding is done 365 times in a year then the total number of periods for n years = 365n. Similarly, if r is the rate of interest per annum then interest per day= r/365. So the above formula is modified as

$$P_n = P_0\left(1+\frac{r}{365}\right)^{365n}$$

(e) k time Compounding

If compounding is done k times in a year then the total number of periods for n years = kn. Similarly, if r is the rate of interest per annum then interest per month= r/k. So the above formula is modified as

$$P_n = P_0\left(1+\frac{r}{k}\right)^{kn}$$

(f) Infinite Compounding

In particular if the number of times compounding namely k tends to infinity, amounting to continuous compounding, then the corresponding formula is given by

$$P_n = \underset{k\to\infty}{\text{Lt}}\ P_0\left(1+\frac{r}{k}\right)^{kn} = P_0e^{rn}$$

Here the money grows continuously at exponential rate.

Example 51: Find the value of Rs.1000 at 12% interest rate after 2 years.

(a) Annual compounding.
(b) By- annual compounding.
(c) Quarterly compounding.
(d) Continuous compounding.

Solution:

(a) Compounding annually

$$P_t = P_0(1+r)^t$$

$$P_2 = 1000(1+0.12)^2$$

$$= 1000(1.12)^2$$

$$= 1254.4$$

(b) Compounding bi-annually

$$P_t = P_0(1 + r/n)^{nt}$$

$$P_2 = 1000(1 + 0.12/2)^{2 \times 2}$$

$$= 1000(1 + 0.06)^4$$

$$= 1000(1.06)^4$$

$$= 1262.48$$

(c) Compounding quarterly

$$P_t = P_0(1 + r/4)^{4t}$$

$$P_2 = 1000(1 + 0.12/4)^{4\times2}$$

$$= 1000(1 + 0.03)^8$$

$$= 1000(1.03)^8$$

$$= 1266.77$$

(d) Continuous compounding

$$P_t = P_0 e^{rt}$$

$$= 1000 \times (2.718281828)^{0.12 \times 2}$$

$$= 1271.24915$$

Note: At annual rate, Rs.1000 becomes Rs. 1254.4. If compounding is done biannually then the same amount after two years becomes Rs. 1262.48. If compounding is done quarterly then the said investment after two years becomes Rs. 1266.77. At continuous compounding it becomes Rs. 1271.24915. Thus we notice that the money grow faster and faster when the number of compounding in a given year increases. However, it cannot grow more than Rs.1271.24915 at the given interest rate of 12%.

3.14 Nominal vs. Effective Annual Interest Rates

The interest rate specified on annual basis is normally known as ***nominal interest rate***. If the compounding more than once in a year the actual annualized interest rate would be higher than the specified nominal interest rate and such a rate is called ***effective interest rate.***

Effective interest rate when compounding is done k times in a year

When compounding is done k times in a year then we know that

$$P_n = P_0\left(1 + \frac{r}{k}\right)^{kn} \quad \text{... (i)}$$

If $\dot{r}$ is the effective annualized interest rate then on the basis of annual compounding

$$P_n = P_0(1 + \dot{r})^n \quad \text{...(ii)}$$

Now to obtain the annualized effective interest rate we equate (i) and (ii)

$$P_0(1+\dot{r})^n = P_0\left(1+\frac{r}{k}\right)^{kn}$$

$$(1+\dot{r})^n = \left(1+\frac{r}{k}\right)^{kn}$$

$$(1+\dot{r}) = \left(1+\frac{r}{k}\right)^{k}$$

$$\dot{r} = \left(1+\frac{r}{k}\right)^{k} - 1$$

Example 52: An investment of Rs. 1000 grows at 12% per annum, compounded quarterly. Calculate the maturity value after two years. Also get its effective interest rate.

Solution:

$$P_n = P_0\left(1+\frac{r}{k}\right)^{kn}$$

$$P_2 = 1000\left(1+\frac{0.12}{2}\right)^{2\times 1}$$

$$= 1000(1+0.06)^2$$

$$= 1000(1.06)^2$$

$$= 1123.6$$

Annualized Effective interest rate on the assumption that the compounding is done biannually

$$\dot{r} = \left(1+\frac{r}{k}\right)^{k} - 1$$

$$= \left(1+\frac{0.12}{2}\right)^{2} - 1$$

$$= (1.06)^2 - 1$$

$$= 1.1236 - 1$$

$$\dot{r} = 0.1236$$

Thus, the effective interest rate per annum is $.1236 \times 100 = 12.36\%$

Example 53: An investment of Rs.1000 grows at 12% per annum compounded quarterly. Calculate the maturity value after two years. Also, get its effective interest rate.

Solution:

$$P_n = P_0\left(1+\frac{r}{k}\right)^{kn}$$

$$P_2 = 1000\left(1+\frac{0.12}{4}\right)^{4\times 2}$$
$$= 1000(1+.03)^8$$
$$= 1000(1.03)^8$$
$$= 1266.77$$

The effective interest rate on annual basis is given by

$$\dot{r} = \left(1+\frac{r}{k}\right)^k - 1$$
$$= \left(1+\frac{0.12}{4}\right)^4 - 1$$
$$= (1.03)^4 - 1$$
$$= 1.1255088 - 1$$
$$= 0.1255088$$

Thus, the effective interest rate per annum is $.1255088 \times 100 = 12.55088\%$

To verify the validity of this result let us calculate the maturity value compounded annually at the effective rate $R = 0.1255088$

$$P_n = P_0(1+\dot{r})^n$$
$$P_2 = 1000(1+0.1255088)^2$$
$$= 1000(1.1255088)^2$$
$$= 1266.77$$

Note that both the maturity values are equal.

Example 54: An investment of Rs. 1000 grows at 12% per annum compounded monthly. Calculate the maturity value after two years. Also get its effective interest rate

Solution:

$$P_n = P_0\left(1+\frac{r}{k}\right)^{kn}$$
$$P_2 = 1000\left(1+\frac{0.12}{12}\right)^{12\times 2}$$
$$= 1000(1+.01)^{24}$$
$$= 1000(1.01)^{24}$$
$$= 1269.735$$

The effective interest rate on annual basis is given by

$$\dot{r} = \left(1 + \frac{r}{k}\right)^{k} - 1$$

$$= \left(1 + \frac{0.12}{12}\right)^{12} - 1$$

$$= (1.01)^{12} - 1$$

$$= 1.126825 - 1$$

$$= 0.126825$$

Thus, the effective interest rate per annum is $.126825 \times 100 = 12.6825\%$

Example 55: Investment in NSC deposits grows at 12% per annum compounded quarterly. Calculate the effective interest rate R.

Solution:

$$\dot{r} = \left(1 + \frac{r}{k}\right)^{k} - 1$$

$$= \left(1 + \frac{0.12}{4}\right)^{4} - 1$$

$$= (1.03)^{4} - 1$$

$$= 1.1255088 - 1$$

$$= 0.1255088$$

Thus, the effective interest rate per annum is $.1255088 \times 100 = 12.55088\%$

Annualized effective interest rate when compounding is done continuously

$$P_0(1 + \dot{r})^{n} = P_0 e^{kn}$$

$$(1 + \dot{r})^{t} = e^{kn}$$

$$(1 + \dot{r}) = e^{r}$$

$$\dot{r} = e^{r} - 1$$

Example 56: For the NSC problem given above calculate the Effective interest rate by assuming continuous compounding.

Solution:

$$\dot{r} = e^{r} - 1$$

$$= (2.718281828)^{0.12} - 1$$

$$= 1.1275 - 1$$

$$= 0.1275$$

Thus, the effective interest rate is $.1275 \times 100 = 12.75\%$

3.15 The Time Value of Money (Discounding Principle)

Most financial decisions, such as purchase of assets or procurement of funds, affect the firm's cash flows in different points of time. For example, if fixed assets purchased, it will require an immediate cash outflows. Such outflows invariably generate cash inflows in the form of income in future. Similarly, if the firm brows funds from banks and other individuals, it enjoys cash inflow under the obligation of returning same on future dates with interest. Similarly, when the firm under reference raises funds by issuing equity shares, the firm's cash balance increases immediately. However, at the time of issuing dividend its cash balance automatically decreases. Under the circumstances a sound decision making requires that the cash inflows and outflows must be comparable over a given period of time. In fact, the nominal cash inflows and out flows are not comparable. Cash flows are comparable provided they are adjusted for time and risk.

The recognition of time value of money and risk is extremely important in financial decision making. In the absence of such adjustment mere money comparison in absolute term often proves to be fatal. The firm under reference makes decisions that maximize the wealth of its owner by using the concept called net present value of all the cash flows.

Having Rs.100 right now in hand and getting Rs.112 after one year are equivalent provided the prevailing market rate of interest is 12% per annum. This statement amounts to that one hundred you have right now is invested in a bank it will become 112 after one year at 12% rate of interest per annum. Thus the present discounted value of Rs.112 is equal to Rs.100. Instead of Rs.112 someone is ready to give Rs.120 after one year then clearly the option of Rs.120 after one year is preferable than Rs.100 right now. This phenomenon is often called the time value of money.

DISCOUNTING ON ANNUAL BASIS

If P_0 is the money deposited in a bank in the beginning of the year 0 then the value of the deposit after n year denoted by P_n at interest rate of r per annum is given by the compound interest formula:

$$P_n = P_0(1+r)^n \qquad \text{... (i)}$$

If n = 1 then the above formula reduces to

$$P_1 = P_0(1+r) \qquad \text{... (ii)}$$

Now from (ii) the present value of the income received after one year denoted at the discount rate of r is obtained as

$$P_0 = \frac{P_1}{(1+r)}$$

Similarly, if n = 2 then equation (i) reduces to

$$P_2 = P_0(1+r)^2$$

$$\therefore \quad P_0 = \frac{P_2}{(1+r)^2}$$

Similarly, the present discounted valve of the income receivable at n^{th} years is given by the formula

$$P_0 = \frac{P_n}{(1+r)^n}$$

DISCOUNTING BY k TIMES IN A YEAR

If compounding is done at k times in a given year then we know that

$$P_n = P_0\left(1+\frac{r}{k}\right)^{kn}$$

So the present discounted value is obtained as

$$P_0 = \frac{P_n}{\left(1+\frac{r}{k}\right)^{kn}}$$

CONTINUOUS DISCOUNTING

If k tends to infinity under continuous discounting then we know that:

$$P_n = P_0 e^{rn}$$

So the current discounted value at continuous discounting is obtained as:

$$P_0 = \frac{P_n}{e^{rn}}$$

Example 57: Calculate the present value (PV) for an expected income of Rs. 5000 after 5 years given the market interest rate of 9% per annum.

(a) Under Annual Discounting

(b) Under Quarterly Discounting

(c) Under Continuous Discounting

Solution:

(a) Under Annual Discounting

$$P_0 = \frac{P_n}{(1+r)^n}$$

$$= \frac{5000}{(1+.09)^3}$$

$$= \frac{5000}{1.09^3}$$

$$= 3249.66$$

(b) Under Quarterly Discounting

We know that

$$P_0 = \frac{P_n}{\left(1+\frac{r}{k}\right)^{kn}}$$

$$= \frac{5000}{\left(1+\frac{.09}{4}\right)^{4\times5}}$$

$$= \frac{5000}{1.0225^{20}}$$

$$= 3204.08$$

(c) Under Continuous Discounting

Under continuous compounding we know that

$$P_0 = \frac{P_n}{e^{rn}}$$

$$= \frac{5000}{2.178281828^{.09\times5}}$$

$$= 3188.141$$

1. Present Value (PV) of a stream of income receivable at the end of each year over n future years

If A_1 , A_2 , ...A_n are the stream of income receivable at the end of each year over n years respectively, then at the interest rate of r per annum the current value of all the income streams over n years is obtained as:

$$PV = \frac{A_1}{(1+r)} + \frac{A_2}{(1+r)^2} + \ldots\ldots\ldots\ldots\ldots\ldots + \frac{A_n}{(1+r)^n}.$$

Example 58: In a business the following table gives the stream of income receivable at the end of each year for five years is given. Calculate the current worth of the stream of income at the rate of interest 12% per annum.

Years	1	2	3	4	5
Income	2000	3000	5000	4000	6000

Solution:

$$PV = \frac{A_1}{(1+r)} + \frac{A_2}{(1+r)^2} + \frac{A_3}{(1+r)^3} + \frac{A_4}{(1+r)^4} + \frac{A_5}{(1+r)^5}$$

$$= \frac{2000}{(1+0.12)} + \frac{3000}{(1+0.12)^2} + \frac{5000}{(1+0.12)^3} + \frac{4000}{(1+0.12)^4} + \frac{6000}{(1+0.12)^5}$$

$$= \frac{2000}{(1.12)} + \frac{3000}{(1.12)^2} + \frac{5000}{(1.12)^3} + \frac{4000}{(1.12)^4} + \frac{6000}{(1.12)^5}$$

$$= 1785.741 + 2391.582 + 3558.901 + 2542.072 + 3404.561 = 13682.83$$

2. Present Value (PV) of a stream of income receivable at the beginning of each year over n years

If A_1, A_2, ...A_n are the stream of income receivable at the beginning of each year over n years respectively, then at the interest rate of r per annum the current value of all the income streams over n years is obtained as:

$$PV = A_1 + \frac{A_2}{(1+r)^1} + \dots\dots\dots\dots + \frac{A_n}{(1+r)^{n-1}}$$

Remember, this time income is received in the very beginning on the year under reference. In particular, the very first - year income is received on 1st January itself. We are calculating the present value on the same 1st January. Therefore, the very first year income received and its discounted values are one and the same.

Example 59: In a business the following table gives the stream of income receivable at the beginning of each year for five years is given. Calculate the current worth of the stream of income at the rate of interest 12% per annum.

Months	1	2	3	4	5
Income	2000	3000	5000	4000	6000

Solution:

$$PV = A_1 + \frac{A_2}{(1+r)^1} + \frac{A_3}{(1+r)^2} + \frac{A_4}{(1+r)^3} + \frac{A_5}{(1+r)^4}$$

$$= 2000 + \frac{3000}{(1+0.12)^1} + \frac{5000}{(1+0.12)^2} + \frac{4000}{(1+0.12)^3} + \frac{6000}{(1+0.12)^4}$$

$$= 2000 + \frac{3000}{(1.12)^1} + \frac{5000}{(1.12)^2} + \frac{4000}{(1.12)^3} + \frac{6000}{(1.12)^4}$$

$$= 2000 + 2678.571 + 3985.969 + 2847.121 + 3813.108 = 15324.77$$

3. Present Value (PV) of a stream of income receivable at the end of each quarter over n future quarters

If A_1, A_2, ...A_n are the stream of income receivable at the end of each quarter over n quarters respectively, then at the interest rate of r per annum the current value of all the income streams over n quarters is obtained as:

$$PV = \frac{A_1}{\left(1+\frac{r}{4}\right)} + \frac{A_2}{\left(1+\frac{r}{4}\right)^2} + \dots\dots + \frac{A_n}{\left(1+\frac{r}{4}\right)^n}$$

Example 60: In a business the following table gives the stream of income receivable at the end of each quarter for five quarters is given. Calculate the current worth of the stream of income at the rate of interest 12% per annum.

Quarters	1	2	3	4	5
Income	2000	3000	5000	4000	6000

Solution:

$$PV = \frac{A_1}{\left(1+\frac{r}{4}\right)} + \frac{A_2}{\left(1+\frac{r}{4}\right)^2} + \dots\dots + \frac{A_n}{\left(1+\frac{r}{4}\right)^n}$$

$$= \frac{2000}{\left(1+\frac{0.12}{4}\right)} + \frac{3000}{\left(1+\frac{0.12}{4}\right)^2} + \frac{5000}{\left(1+\frac{0.12}{4}\right)^3} + \frac{4000}{\left(1+\frac{0.12}{4}\right)^4} + \frac{6000}{\left(1+\frac{0.12}{4}\right)^5}$$

$$= \frac{2000}{(1+0.03)} + \frac{3000}{(1+0.03)^2} + \frac{5000}{(1+0.03)^3} + \frac{4000}{(1+0.03)^4} + \frac{6000}{(1+0.03)^5}$$

$$= 1941.748 + 2827.788 + 4575.948 + 3553.948 + 5175.653 = 18074.84$$

4. Present Value (PV) of a stream of income receivable at the beginning of each quarter over n future quarters

If A_1, A_2, ...A_n are the stream of income receivable at the beginning of each quarter over n quarters respectively, then at the interest rate of r per annum the current value of all the income streams over n quarters is obtained as:

$$PV = A_1 + \frac{A_2}{\left(1+\frac{r}{4}\right)^1} + \dots\dots + \frac{A_n}{\left(1+\frac{r}{4}\right)^{n-1}}$$

Example 61: In a business the following table gives the stream of income receivable at the beginning each quarter for five quarters is given. Calculate the current worth of the stream of income at the rate of interest 12% per annum.

Quarters	1	2	3	4	5
Income	2000	3000	5000	4000	6000

Solution:

$$PV = A_1 + \frac{A_2}{\left(1+\frac{r}{4}\right)^1} + \dots\dots + \frac{A_n}{\left(1+\frac{r}{4}\right)^{n-1}}$$

$$= 2000 + \frac{3000}{\left(1+\frac{0.12}{4}\right)^1} + \frac{5000}{\left(1+\frac{0.12}{4}\right)^2} + \frac{4000}{\left(1+\frac{0.12}{4}\right)^3} + \frac{6000}{\left(1+\frac{0.12}{4}\right)^3}$$

$$= 2000 + \frac{3000}{(1+0.03)^1} + \frac{5000}{(1+0.03)^2} + \frac{4000}{(1+0.03)^3} + \frac{6000}{(1+0.03)^3}$$

$$= 2000.00 + 2912.621 + 4712.98 + 3660.567 + 5330.922 = 18617.09$$

5. Present Value (PV) of a stream of income receivable at the end of each month on future on 'n' months.

If A_1 , A_2 , ...A_n are the stream of income receivable at the beginning of each month over n months respectively, then at the interest rate of r per annum the current value of all the income streams over n months is obtained as

$$PV = \frac{A_1}{\left(1+\frac{r}{12}\right)} + \frac{A_2}{\left(1+\frac{r}{12}\right)^2} + \ldots\ldots + \frac{A_n}{\left(1+\frac{r}{12}\right)^n}$$

Example 62: In a business the following table gives stream of income receivable at the end of each month for 5 months. Calculate the current worth of the stream at the rate of interest 12% per annum.

Year	Jan	Feb	Mar	Apr	May
Income	2000	3000	5000	4000	6000

Solution:

$$PV = \frac{A_1}{\left(1+\frac{r}{12}\right)} + \frac{A_2}{\left(1+\frac{r}{12}\right)^2} + \ldots\ldots + \frac{A_n}{\left(1+\frac{r}{12}\right)^n}$$

$$= \frac{2000}{\left(1+\frac{0.12}{12}\right)} + \frac{3000}{\left(1+\frac{0.12}{12}\right)^2} + \frac{5000}{\left(1+\frac{0.12}{12}\right)^3} + \frac{4000}{\left(1+\frac{0.12}{12}\right)^4} + \frac{6000}{\left(1+\frac{0.12}{12}\right)^5}$$

$$= \frac{2000}{(1+0.01)} + \frac{3000}{(1+0.01)^2} + \frac{5000}{(1+0.01)^3} + \frac{4000}{(1+0.01)^4} + \frac{6000}{(1+0.01)^5}$$

$$= 1980.198 + 2840.888 + 48.52.951 + 3843.921 + 5708.794 = 19326.75$$

6. Present Value (PV) of a stream of income receivable at the beginning of each month on future on n months

$$PV = A_1 + \frac{A_2}{\left(1+\frac{r}{12}\right)^1} + \ldots\ldots + \frac{A_n}{\left(1+\frac{r}{12}\right)^{n-1}}$$

Example 63: In a business the following table gives stream of income receivable at the beginning of each month for five months. Calculate the current worth of the stream at the rate of interest 12% per annum.

Year	Jan	Feb	Mar	Apr	May
Income	2000	3000	5000	4000	6000

Solution:

$$PV = A_1 + \frac{A_2}{\left(1+\frac{r}{12}\right)^1} + \dots\dots + \frac{A_n}{\left(1+\frac{r}{12}\right)^{n-1}}$$

$$= 2000 + \frac{3000}{\left(1+\frac{0.12}{12}\right)^1} + \frac{5000}{\left(1+\frac{0.12}{12}\right)^2} + \frac{4000}{\left(1+\frac{0.12}{12}\right)^3} + \frac{6000}{\left(1+\frac{0.12}{12}\right)^4}$$

$$= 2000 + \frac{3000}{(1+0.01)^1} + \frac{5000}{(1+0.01)^2} + \frac{4000}{(1+0.01)^3} + \frac{6000}{(1+0.01)^4}$$

$$= 2000 + 2970.297 + 4901.48 + 3882.361 + 5765.882 = 19520.02$$

7. Present Value (PV) of a stream of income receivable at the end of each day on future on n days

$$PV = \frac{A_1}{\left(1+\frac{r}{365}\right)} + \frac{A_2}{\left(1+\frac{r}{365}\right)^2} + \dots\dots + \frac{A_n}{\left(1+\frac{r}{365}\right)^n}$$

Example 64: In a business the following table gives stream of income receivable at the end of each day for five days. Calculate the current worth of the stream at the rate of interest 12% per annum.

Year	Mon	Tue	Wed	Thu	Fri
Income	2000	3000	5000	4000	6000

Solution:

$$PV = \frac{A_1}{\left(1+\frac{r}{365}\right)} + \frac{A_2}{\left(1+\frac{r}{365}\right)^2} + \dots\dots + \frac{A_n}{\left(1+\frac{r}{365}\right)^n}$$

$$= \frac{2000}{\left(1+\frac{0.12}{365}\right)} + \frac{3000}{\left(1+\frac{0.12}{365}\right)^2} + \frac{5000}{\left(1+\frac{0.12}{365}\right)^3} + \frac{4000}{\left(1+\frac{0.12}{365}\right)^4} + \frac{6000}{\left(1+\frac{0.12}{365}\right)^5}$$

$$= \frac{2000}{(1+0.000329)} + \frac{3000}{(1+0.000329)^2} + \frac{5000}{(1+0.000329)^3} + \frac{4000}{(1+0.000329)^4} + \frac{6000}{(1+0.000329)^5}$$

$$= 1999.343 + 2998.028 + 4995.072 + 3994.744 + 5988.178 = 19975.36$$

8. Present Value (PV) of a stream of income receivable at the beginning of each day on future on n days

$$PV = A_1 + \frac{A_2}{\left(1+\frac{r}{12}\right)^1} + \dots\dots + \frac{A_n}{\left(1+\frac{r}{12}\right)^{n-1}}$$

Example 65: In a business the following table gives stream of income receivable at the beginning of each day for five days. Calculate the current worth of the stream at the rate of interest 12% per annum.

Year	Mon	Tue	Wed	Thu	Fri
Income	2000	3000	5000	4000	6000

Solution:

$$PV = A_1 + \frac{A_2}{\left(1+\frac{r}{365}\right)^1} + \dots\dots + \frac{A_n}{\left(1+\frac{r}{365}\right)^{n-1}}$$

$$= 2000 + \frac{3000}{\left(1+\frac{0.12}{365}\right)^1} + \frac{5000}{\left(1+\frac{0.12}{365}\right)^3} + \frac{4000}{\left(1+\frac{0.12}{365}\right)^3} + \frac{6000}{\left(1+\frac{0.12}{365}\right)^4}$$

$$= 2000 + \frac{3000}{(1+0.000329)^1} + \frac{5000}{(1+0.000329)^2} + \frac{4000}{(1+0.000329)^3} + \frac{6000}{(1+0.000329)^4}$$

$$= 2000 + 2999.014 + 4996.714 + 3996.057 + 5992.116 = 19983.9$$

Computing present value of the stream income receivable on future using excel work sheet

	A	B	C	E	F	G
1						
2	**Rate of interest**					
3	Yearly	0.12				
4	Quarterly	0.03				
5	Monthly	0.01				
6						
7	Period	1	2	3	4	5
8	income recivable	2000	3000	5000	4000	6000
9	**Annual basis**					
10	PV(Receved at the end of the year)	13682.83				
11	PV(Received at the beginning of the year)	15324.77				
12	**Quarterly basis**					
13	PV(Receved at end of the quarter)	18074.84				
14	(PV) Received at the beginning of the quarter	18617.09				
15	**Monthly basis**					
16	PV(Receved at end of the month)	19326.75				
17	(PV) Received at the beginning of the month	19520.02				
18						

Enter the data as shown in the table. In Cell B10 =NPV(B3,B8:G8)

Enter the data as shown in the table. In Cell B10 =B8+NPV(B4,C8:G8)

Enter the data as shown in the table. In Cell B10 =NPV(B4,B8:G8)

Enter the data as shown in the table. In Cell B10 =B8+NPV(B3,C8:G8)

Enter the data as shown in the table. In Cell B10 =NPV(B5,B8:G8)

Enter the data as shown in the table. In Cell B10 =B8+NPV(B5,C8:G8)

3.16 Annuities

An annuity refers to a series of payments of a certain fixed amount of money for a designated period of time at equal intervals. Such periodical payments occur in many practical situations like the installment payments for a TV purchased at home, equated monthly installments (EMI) for the house building loan taken etc,. The time interval between two successive payments is called the *payment interval,* and the time between the first and the last payment is called the *term* of the annuity concerned. On the basis of terms the annuity may be classified as follows

- **Annuity Certain:** When the term of an annuity begins and ends on a certain fixed dates then the referred annuity is called annuity certain.
- **Perpetuity:** The annuity that begins on a particular date but never terminates is called perpetuity. Without touching the principal if interest alone is paid regularly then the said annuity never terminates. It terminates if and only if the whole of the principal is paid back at one installment.
- **Contingent Annuity:** It begins on a particular date as usual but termination is contingent up of certain future happenings. For example, the payment of LIC premium starts on a particular date but ends as soon as the concern person dies.

Annuity can also defined on the basis of the time of payments

- **Ordinary Annuity:** In the case of ordinary annuity the payment is made at the end of each period.
- **Annuity Due:** When the payment is made at the beginning of each period then it is called annuity due.
- **Deferred Annuity:** No doubt the payment takes place at end of each period but the annuity does not begin till some time to come. It begins only after some specified period.

In the present discussion we assume only ordinary annuity unless otherwise specified.

TERMINAL WORTH OF ANNUITY CERTAIN

By amount of an ordinary annuity we mean the terminal value worth of the series of payments starting from the beginning to the end. Let a personal loan is taken from a bank and repayment is made in equated yearly installments starting from the end of the first period. Eventually such installments will have a principal component as well as interest component in it.

Let A = the periodic payment.

n = the number of payments.

r = the rate of interest per period.

Since the first payment is made at the end of the first period, its terminal value is obtained by using the compound interest formula for the remaining n-1 periods. Similarly, since the second installment is paid at the end of the second month, its terminal value is obtained by using the compound interest formula for the remaining n-2 periods. This way we calculate the terminal worth for all the n payments. The total of all such terminal worth values is the needed annuity amount. At this stage note that the last payment would not attract any interest since it is paid at the end of the last period and our terminal worth is calculated on the same day of last installment payment.

If M is terminal worth amount of annuity and A is the installment payment amount then by using the compound interest formula for each payment the annuity amount M is written as

$$M = A(1+r)^{n-1} + A(1+r)^{n-2} + \dots\dots\dots + A(1+r)^2 + A(1+r) + A \quad \dots (1)$$

Now to get the value of M easily we multiply both the sides of above equation (1) by (1+ r) and generate equation (2) as shown below.

$$M(1+r) = A(1+r)^n + A(1+r)^{n-1} + \dots\dots + A(1+r)^3 + A(1+r)^2 + A(1+r) \quad \dots (2)$$

Now let us subtract equation (2) from (1)

$$M(1+r) - M = A(1+r)^n - A$$

$$M + Mr - M = A(1+r)^n - A$$

$$Mr = A(1+r)^n - A$$

$$M = \frac{A\left[(1+r)^n - 1\right]}{r} \quad \dots (3)$$

If (1+ r) = R then the above formula reduces to

$$M = \frac{A\left[(1+r)^n - 1\right]}{(1+r) - 1}$$

$$= A\left[\frac{R^n - 1}{R - 1}\right] \quad \dots (4)$$

Thus the total terminal worth or otherwise called the annuity is obtained simply by multiplying the installment amount A by the term $\frac{R^n - 1}{R - 1}$. This term if often called the amount factor. For easy reference this amount factor is obtained from the readymade table always. The following example illustrates the method of calculating the annuity amount M. This amount is nothing but the effective total money paid by the borrower to the bank.

Example 66: A company wants to establish a sinking (or depreciation) fund for a period of 10 years for replacing Rs. 8,00,000 worth of a machine at the end of 9th year. Calculate the amount that is to be retained out of its profits at the end of every year if the market rate of interest is 8% per annum.

Solution:

Data:

$$M = 8{,}00{,}000,\ r = 0.08 \text{ and } n = 10\ A = ?$$

$$M = \frac{A\left[(1+r)^n - 1\right]}{r}$$

$$800000 = \frac{A\left[(1+0.08)^{10} - 1\right]}{0.08}$$

$$800000 = A\left[\frac{2.156925 - 1}{0.08}\right]$$

$$800000 = A\left[\frac{1.156925}{0.08}\right]$$

$$800000 = A(14.48656)$$

$$A = \frac{800000}{14.48656} = 55223.59$$

Hence an amount of Rs. 55223.59 is to be kept away from the profit at the end of each year.

Example 67: A company wants to establish a sinking (or depreciation) fund for a period of 10 months for replacing Rs. 8,00,000 worth of a machine at the end of 9th month. Calculate the amount that is to be retained out of its profits end of every month if the market rate of interest is 12% per annum.

Solution:

Data:

$$M = 8{,}00{,}000,\ \text{rate of interest per month } r = 0.012/12 = 0.01 \text{ and } n = 10\ A = ?$$

$$M = \frac{A\left[(1+r)^n - 1\right]}{r}$$

$$800000 = \frac{A\left[(1+0.01)^{10} - 1\right]}{0.01}$$

$$800000 = A\left[\frac{1.104622 - 1}{0.01}\right]$$

$$800000 = A\left[\frac{0.104622}{0.01}\right]$$

$$800000 = A(10.46221)$$

$$A = \frac{800000}{10.46221} = 76465.66$$

Hence an amount of Rs.76465.66 is to be kept away from the profit each month.

THE PRESENT VALUE OF THE ANNUITY CERTAIN

For an annuity, the present value is simply the sum total of the present values of all the periodic payments at the end of each period. The present value of the first payment is obtained as $A/(1+r)$.The present value of the second payment would be $A/(1+r)^2$ and so on. If V is the present value of the annuity certain and A is thc installment payment then:

$$\text{Present value (PV)} = \frac{A}{(1+r)} + \frac{A}{(1+r)^2} + \ldots\ldots\ldots\ldots \frac{A}{(1+r)} \quad \ldots(5)$$

Now let us multiply equation (3) by (1+ r) on both the sides

$$PV(1+r) = A + \frac{A}{(1+r)} + \frac{A}{(1+r)^2} + \ldots\ldots\ldots\ldots \frac{A}{(1+r)^{n-1}} \quad \ldots(6)$$

Now let us subtract (6) from (5) and get

$$PV(1+r) - PV = A - \frac{A}{(1+r)^n}$$

$$PV + rPV - PV = A - \frac{A}{(1+r)^n}$$

$$rPV = A\left[1 - \frac{1}{(1+r)^n}\right]$$

$$PV = \frac{A\left[1 - \frac{1}{(1+r)^n}\right]}{r}$$

$$PV = \frac{A\left[1-(1+r)^{-n}\right]}{r} \quad \ldots(7)$$

If R = (1+ r) then the above result is restated as

$$PV = \frac{A\left[1-(1+r)^{-n}\right]}{(1+r)-1}$$

$$PV = A\left[\frac{1-R^{-n}}{R-1}\right] \quad \ldots(8)$$

Thus again the present value of the annuity certain is obtained by merely multiplying the installment payment A by the term $\left[\frac{1-R^{-n}}{R-1}\right]$. This ready to use factor is called the present value factor (PVF). This factor is available in read to usable tabular form for all combinations for ready use.

Example 68: Determine the present value of an annuity certain, given the installment payment of Rs.2000 payable at the end of each year for next 4 years. The market interest rate is 6% per annum.

Solution:

Data A = 2000, r = 0.06 and n = 4, PV=?

$$PV = \frac{A\left[1-\frac{1}{(1+r)^n}\right]}{r}$$

$$= \frac{2000\left[1-\frac{1}{(1+0.06)^4}\right]}{0.06}$$

$$= \frac{2000\left[1-\frac{1}{1.06^4}\right]}{0.06}$$

$$= \frac{2000[1-0.792094]}{0.06}$$

$$PV = 2000(0.207969)/0.06$$

$$= \text{Rs.}6930.2$$

Example 69: Mr. X purchased a colour TV form a ONITA outlet for Rs.12,800. He has made a down payment of Rs.4000 and agreed to pay the balance in an equated monthly payment of 24 installments. If the market rate of interest is 12% compounded monthly, how much Mr. X should pay every month?

Solution:

The present value of the annuity PV = Price of TV – Down payment = 12,800-4,000 = 8,800

Further, the monthly interest r = Annual interest / 12 = 12%/12 = 1% and n = 24 months.

$$PV = \frac{A\left[1-(1+r)^{-n}\right]}{(1+r)-1}$$

$$PV = A\left[\frac{1-R^{-n}}{R-1}\right]$$

$$8{,}800 = A\left[\frac{1-1.01^{-24}}{1.01-1}\right]$$

$$= A(21.2434)$$

$$A = \frac{8{,}800}{21.2434} = 414.25$$

So our customer must pay Rs. 414.25 per installment so that the present value of all the future payments equals to the present due of Rs.8, 800.

Example 70: Mr. X obtained a home Construction loan of Rs. 28, 80,000 from SBM. If fixes the rate of interest at 9% for the first two years and 10% thereafter. The loan will have to be cleared in 228 equated monthly installments. Calculate the EMI for the first two years. Also prepare the annual statement of capital payment and interest payments for availing of the income tax benefit for Mr. X for the first two years. Rescheduled the EMI from third year onwards at 10% rate of interest.

Solution:

Calculation of EMI for the first two years at 9% rate

The present value of the annuity PV= the loan amount = Rs.28, 80,000

Further, the monthly interest r = Annual interest / 12 = 9%/12 = 0.75% and n = 228 months.

$$PV = \frac{A\left[1-(1+r)^{-n}\right]}{(1+r)-1}$$

$$PV = A\left[\frac{1-R^{-n}}{R-1}\right]$$

$$2880000 = A\left[\frac{1-1.0075^{-228}}{1.0075-1}\right]$$

$$= A(109.063531)$$

$$A = \frac{2880000}{109.063531} = 26406.62716$$

Preparation of interest and capital payment for availing the income tax benefit for the first two years

Month	Capital	Interst	Capital	EMI
1	2880000.00	21600.00	4806.63	26406.63
2	2875193.37	21563.95	4842.68	26406.63
3	2870350.70	21527.63	4879.00	26406.63
4	2865471.70	21491.04	4915.59	26406.63
5	2860556.11	21454.17	4952.46	26406.63
6	2855603.65	21417.03	4989.60	26406.63
7	2850614.05	21379.61	5027.02	26406.63
8	2845587.03	21341.90	5064.72	26406.63
9	2840522.31	21303.92	5102.71	26406.63
10	2835419.60	21265.65	5140.98	26406.63
11	2830278.62	21227.09	5179.54	26406.63
12	2825099.08	21188.24	5218.38	26406.63
Total		256760.22	60119.30	316879.53
13	2819880.70	21149.11	5257.52	26406.63
14	2814623.17	21109.67	5296.95	26406.63
15	2809326.22	21069.95	5336.68	26406.63
16	2803989.54	21029.92	5376.71	26406.63
17	2798612.83	20989.60	5417.03	26406.63
18	2793195.80	20948.97	5457.66	26406.63
19	2787738.14	20908.04	5498.59	26406.63
20	2782239.55	20866.80	5539.83	26406.63
21	2776699.72	20825.25	5581.38	26406.63
22	2771118.34	20783.39	5623.24	26406.63
23	2765495.10	20741.21	5665.41	26406.63
24	2759829.69	20698.72	5707.90	26406.63
Total		251120.62	65758.91	316879.53

Resetting the EMI at 10% rate from third year onwards

The monthly interest r = Annual interest / 12 = 10%/12 = and n = 204 months.

$$\text{Loan amount } L = PV = \frac{EMI\left[1-(1+r)^{-n}\right]}{(1+r)-1} \qquad \dots (9)$$

$$Lr = EMI \times \frac{(1+r)^n - 1}{(1+r)^n}$$

$$EMI = Lr \times \frac{(1+r)^n}{(1+r)^n - 1}$$

$$EMI = 2754121.79 \times (0.1/12) \times \frac{(1+(0.1/12))^{204}}{(1+(0.1/12))^{2204} - 1}$$

$$= 28125.38$$

Preparation statement interest and capital component for income tax benefit for another two years

25	2754121.79	22951.01	5174.36	28125.38
26	2748947.42	22907.90	5217.48	28125.38
27	2743729.94	22864.42	5260.96	28125.38
28	2738468.97	22820.57	5304.80	28125.38
29	2733164.17	22776.37	5349.01	28125.38
30	2727815.16	22731.79	5393.59	28125.38
31	2722421.57	22686.85	5438.53	28125.38
32	2716983.04	22641.53	5483.85	28125.38
33	2711499.18	22595.83	5529.55	28125.38
34	2705969.63	22549.75	5575.63	28125.38
35	2700394.00	22503.28	5622.10	28125.38
36	2694771.90	22456.43	5668.95	28125.38
Total		272485.72	65018.83	337504.56
37	2689102.95	22409.19	5716.19	28125.38
38	2683386.76	22361.56	5763.82	28125.38
39	2677622.94	22313.52	5811.86	28125.38
40	2671811.09	22265.09	5860.29	28125.38
41	2665950.80	22216.26	5909.12	28125.38
42	2660041.68	22167.01	5958.37	28125.38
43	2654083.31	22117.36	6008.02	28125.38
44	2648075.29	22067.29	6058.09	28125.38
45	2642017.21	22016.81	6108.57	28125.38
46	2635908.64	21965.91	6159.47	28125.38
47	2629749.16	21914.58	6210.80	28125.38
48	2623538.36	21862.82	6262.56	28125.38
		265677.40	71827.15	337504.56

TERMINAL WORTH OF THE PERPETUITY

We know that in the case of perpetuity though the first payment starts as usual it never ends with n^{th} period payment, the payment goes on and on forever. So there is no concept like terminal worth for perpetuity in such cases.

THE PRESENT VALUE OF THE PERPETUITY

Now from (8) we know that the formula for an annuity certain

$$PV = \frac{A\left[1-(1+r)^{-n}\right]}{(1+r)-1}$$

$$PV = A\left[\frac{1-R^{-n}}{R-1}\right]$$

In the case of perpetuity we know that the payment continue indefinitely. Thus in the above formula n tend to ∞. If n tend to ∞ then the term R^{-n} tend to zero. So the above formula reduces to

$$\underset{n\to\infty}{\text{Lt}}\ PV = \underset{n\to\infty}{\text{Lt}}\ A\left[\frac{1-R^{-n}}{R-1}\right]$$

$$= A\left[\frac{1-0}{1+r-1}\right]$$

$$= \frac{A}{r} \qquad \text{... (10)}$$

Thus, in the case of perpetuity the needed present value factor (PVF) is simply the reciprocal of the interest rate r.

Example 71: A free hold estate was bought for Rs.4,00,000.At what annual rent should it be let so that the owner gets 12% return per annum on the purchase value.

Solution:

Here we will simply find the periodic payment A with the given V = 4, 00,000 and r = 0.12

$$PV = \frac{A}{r}$$

$$4,00,000 = \frac{A}{0.12}$$

$$A = 4,00,000 \times 0.12 = \text{Rs.}48,000 \text{ per annum}$$

Example 72: A free hold estate was bought for Rs.4,00,000.At what rent month should it be let so that the owner gets 12% return per annum on the purchase value.

Solution:

Here we will simply find the periodic payment A with the given V = 4, 00,000 and interest per month r = 0.12/12 = 0.01

$$PV = \frac{A}{r}$$

$$4,00,000 = \frac{A}{0.0.01}$$

$$A = 4,00,000 \times 0.01 = \text{Rs.}4000 \text{ per month}$$

THE PRESENT VALUE OF A DEFERRED ANNUITY

If the annuity begins after p periods from now and continue up to n periods then the present value of the successive payments would be

$$PV = AR^{-(p+1)} + AR^{-(p+2)} + AR^{-(p+3)} \ldots\ldots\ldots\ldots\ldots AR^{-(p+n)} \qquad \text{... (i}$$

To obtain *PV* as usual we multiply both the sides of equation (5) by R first

$$PV \times R = AR^{-(p)} + AR^{-(p+1)} + AR^{-(p+2)} \ldots\ldots\ldots\ldots AR^{-(p+n-1)} \quad \ldots \text{(ii)}$$

Now let us subtract equation (i) from (ii)

$$PV \times R - PV = AR^{-p} - AR^{-(p+n)}$$

$$PV \times (R-1) = AR^{-p} - AR^{-(p+n)}$$

$$PV = \frac{AR^{-p}}{R-1} - \frac{AR^{-(p+n)}}{R-1}$$

$$= A\left[\frac{R^{-p}}{R-1} - \frac{R^{(p+n)}}{R-1}\right]$$

Thus this time the present value factor (PVF) of a deferred annuity is $\left[\frac{R^{-p}}{R-1} - \frac{R^{(p+n)}}{R-1}\right]$ ... (11)

Example 73: The installment of a deferred annuity is Rs.3000 per annum. Its first installment starts 3 years from now. If the current market interest rate is 8% per annum obtain its present value.

Solution:

Data: A = Rs.3000, R = 1+ r = 1+.08, and p = 3

$$PV = \frac{AR^{-p}}{R-1} - \frac{AR^{-(p+n)}}{R-1}$$

$$= \frac{3000 \times 1.08^{-3}}{1.08-1} - \frac{3000 \times 1.08^{-(3+8)}}{1.08-1} = \text{Rs.}9,508.62$$

Example 74: The installment of a deferred annuity is Rs.10,000 per month. Its first installment starts 3 months from now. If the current market interest rate is 12% per annum obtain its present value.

Solution:

Data: A = Rs.10,000, the monthly interest r = 0.12/12 =0.01 R = 1+ r = 1+.01, and p = 3

$$PV = \frac{AR^{-p}}{R-1} - \frac{AR^{-(p+n)}}{R-1}$$

$$= \frac{10000 \times 1.01^{-3}}{1.01-1} - \frac{3000 \times 1.01^{-(3+8)}}{1.01-1}$$

$$= \frac{9705.901}{0.01} - \frac{8963.237}{0.01}$$

$$= 970590.1 - 896323.7$$

$$= \text{Rs.}74266.43$$

THE PRESENT VALUE OF DEFERRED PERPETUITY

If perpetuity is to begin after a certain period from now its present value is obtained by the formula.

Since in the differed annuity formula given above the second term $\frac{AR^{-p-n}}{R-1}$ tends to zero as n tend to infinity the modified present value factor is given by the formula $\frac{R^{-p}}{R-1}$. Thus the present value of a deferred perpetuity is obtained by using the formula

$$\frac{AR^{-p}}{R-1} \qquad \text{... (12)}$$

Example 75: Determine the present value of a perpetuity of Rs.1,000 starting 4 years from now, carrying an interest rate of 5% per annum.

Solution:

$$PV = A\left(\frac{R^{-p}}{R-1}\right) = \frac{1000 \times 1.05^{-4}}{1.05-1} = \text{Rs.}16,454.04$$

Example 76: Determine the present value of a perpetuity of Rs.2,000 starting 4 months from now, carrying an interest rate of 6% per annum.

Solution:

A = 1000, the monthly interest rate r = 0.06/12 = 0.005

$$PV = A\left(\frac{R^{-p}}{R-1}\right) = \frac{2000 \times 1.005^{-4}}{1.005-1} = \text{Rs.}392099.0087$$

3.17 Use of Exponential Function in the Theory of Growth and Decay

The exponential growth can be either discrete or continuous.

(a) Growth at annual compounding

$$P_t = P_0(1+g)^t \qquad \text{... (12)}$$

(b) Growth at multiple compounding

$$P_t = P_0\left(1+\frac{g}{k}\right)^{kt} \qquad \text{... (13)}$$

(c) Growth at continuous compounding

$$P_t = P_0 e^{gt} \qquad \text{... (14)}$$

Note: Here simply the interest rate r is replaced by the growth rate g.

Example 77: Currently the income of a certain factory is Rs.100000 Crores. It was found to grow at 12% annually. Project the level of income after 10 years.

Solution:

Growth at annual rate

$$Y_t = Y_o(1+g)^t$$
$$= 100000(1+0.12)^{10}$$
$$= 100000(1.12)^{10}$$
$$= 310584.8208$$

Excel Calculations:

Cell A2 to A12: enter the time form 0 to 10

Cell B2: Enter the initial income (100000)

Cell B3: Enter the formula: =$B$2*(1+0.12)^A3

Copy this formula up to B12and get the results as highlighted in table 3.46.

Table 3.46

	A	B
1	t	Y_t
2	0	100000
3	1	112000
4	2	125440
5	3	140492.8
6	4	157351.936
7	5	176234.1683
8	6	197382.2685
9	7	221068.1407
10	8	247596.3176
11	9	277307.8757
12	10	310584.8208

Growth calculated at quarterly rate:

$$Y_t = Y_o(1+g/4)^{4t}$$
$$= 100000(1+0.12/4)^{4\times10}$$
$$= 100000(1.03)^{40}$$
$$= 326203.7792$$

The corresponding excel result sheet is shown in table 3.47.

Table 3.47

t	Y_t	t	Y_t	t	Y_t	t	Y_t
0	100000	11	138423.4	21	186029.5	31	250008
1	103000	12	142576.1	22	191610.3	32	257508.3
2	106090	13	146853.4	23	197358.7	33	265233.5
3	109272.7	14	151259	24	203279.4	34	273190.5
4	112550.9	15	155796.7	25	209377.8	35	281386.2
5	115927.4	16	160470.6	26	215659.1	36	289827.8
6	119405.2	17	165284.8	27	222128.9	37	298522.7
7	122987.4	18	170243.3	28	228792.8	38	307478.3
8	126677	19	175350.6	29	235656.6	39	316702.7
9	130477.3	20	180611.1	30	242726.2	40	326203.8
10	134391.6						

Growth at continuous rate:

$$Y_t = Y_o e^{gt}$$

$$= 100000 \times 2.718281828^{0.12\times10}$$

$$= 332011.6923$$

Excel Calculations:

Cell A2 to A12: enter the time form 0 to 10
Cell B2: Enter the initial income (100000)
Cell B3: Enter the formula: =$B$2*EXP(0.12*A3)
Copy this formula up to B12and get the results

Table 3.48

	A	B
1	t	Y_t
2	0	100000
3	1	112749.6852
4	2	127124.915
5	3	143332.9415
6	4	161607.4402
7	5	182211.88
8	6	205443.3211
9	7	231636.6977
10	8	261169.6473
11	9	294467.9551
12	10	332011.6923

Note: The income grows faster at continuous rate than discrete rate.

Calculation of growth rates when the first and the final year values are known:

(a) Annual growth rate at annual compounding:

$$Y_t = Y_o(1+g)^t$$

$$(1+g)^t = \frac{Y_t}{Y_o}$$

$$(1+g) = \left(\frac{Y_t}{Y_o}\right)^{1/t}$$

$$g = \left(\frac{Y_t}{Y_o}\right)^{1/t} - 1$$

(b) Annual growth rate under multiple compounding:

$$Yt = Y_0\left(1+\frac{g}{n}\right)^{nt}$$

$$\therefore \quad \left(1+\frac{g}{n}\right)^{nt} = \frac{Y_t}{Y_0}$$

$$\left(1+\frac{g}{n}\right) = \left(\frac{Y_t}{Y_0}\right)^{1/nt}$$

$$\frac{g}{n} = \left(\frac{Y_t}{Y_0}\right)^{1/nt} - 1$$

$$g = n\left[\left(\frac{Y_t}{Y_0}\right)^{1/nt} - 1\right]$$

(b) Annual growth rate under continuous compounding:

$$Y_t = Y_o e^{gt}$$

$$e^{gt} = \frac{Y_t}{Y_0}$$

$$gt = (\ln Y_t - \ln Y_o)$$

$$g = (\ln Y_t - \ln Y_o)/t$$

Example 78: The income of an economy went up from 10,00,000 Crores to 20,00,000 Crores in about 10 years. Calculate the annual growth rate.

Solution:

(a) Annual growth rate at annual compounding:

$$g = \left(\frac{Y_t}{Y_o}\right)^{1/t} - 1$$

$$= \left(\frac{2000000}{1000000}\right)^{1/10} - 1$$

$$= (2)^{1/10} - 1$$

$$= 1.07177 - 1$$

$$= 0.07177$$

Thus the annual growth rate = $0.07177 \times 100 = 7.18\ \%$

(b) Annual growth rate under quarterly compounding:

$$g = n\left[\left(\frac{Y_t}{Y_0}\right)^{1/nt} - 1\right]$$

$$= 4\left[\left(\frac{2000000}{1000000}\right)^{1/40} - 1\right]$$

$$= 4\left[(2)^{1/40} - 1\right]$$

$$= 0.06992$$

Thus, the annual growth rate = $0.06992 \times 100 = 6.99\%$

(c) Annual growth rate under continuous compounding:

$$g = \left(\ln Y_t - \ln Y_o\right)/t$$

$$= \left(\ln 2000000 - \ln 1000000\right)/10$$

$$= (14.507 - 13.816)/10$$

$$= 0.069315$$

Calculation of Growth rates by using Excel worksheet:

To calculate the compound interest we can always use the Excel worksheet. For the calculation of Annual growth calculations make the following entries in row number 2.

Cell B2: Final year values (Y_t)

Cell C2: Initial value (Y_0)

Cell D2: Number of years (t)

Cell E2: Number of compounding (n)

Cell F2: t×n.

Cell G2: Enter the formula given in Cell H2.

Table 3.49

	A	B	C	D	E	F	G	H
1	Type	Y_t	Y_o	t	n	tn	g	Formula
2	Annual	2000000	1000000	10	1	10	0.071773	=(B2/C2)^(1/F2)-1
3	Quarterly	2000000	1000000	10	4	40	0.069919	=4*(B3/C3)^(1/F3)-1)
4	Continuous	2000000	1000000	10	-	-	0.069315	=LN(B4/C4)/D4

Note: The results given in column G are more or less in conformity with results obtained by manual method:

Example 79: Suppose one set of experts' (A) recommends an investment of Rs.45 Crores in the first year and propose to increase year by year by 6% per annum. The second group of experts' (B) recommends for a little larger investment of Rs.50 Crores in the first year and proposes to increase it by only 4% per annum. Calculate the total investment generated at the end of 10 th year.

Solution:

By using the compound growth formula the Group A's investment pattern is given by the formula.

$$I_A = 45(1+0.06)^t$$

Similarly, the group B's investment pattern over years is given by the formula

$$I_B = 50(1+0.04)^t$$

The calculated growth patterns for both the groups are reported here under.

Using Excel worksheet the results are reported below.

In column A enter the time from 1 to 10.

B2: Enter A's investment 45 Crores in Cell:

C2: Enter B's investment of 50 Crores.

Cell B3: Enter the formula = $B$2*(1+0.06)^A3. Copy this formula up to cell B12.

Cell C3: Enter the formula = $C$2*(1 + 0.04)^A3. Copy this formula up to cell C12. All the needed calculations will appear as shown in table 3.50.

Table 3.50

	A	B	C
1	t	I_A	I_B
2	0	45	50
3	1	47.7	52
4	2	50.562	54.08
5	3	53.59572	56.2432
6	4	56.81146	58.49293
7	5	60.22015	60.83265
8	6	63.83336	63.26595
9	7	67.66336	65.79659
10	8	71.72316	68.42845
11	9	76.02655	71.16559
12	10	80.58815	74.01221

Clearly investment A is more after 10 years.

3.18 Logarithmic Functions

Since 100 can be expressed as $100 = 10^2$, we define log 100 = 2 Thus, in general if $x = 10^y$ then from the definition of common logarithms it follows that $\log_{10} x = y$ $y = \log_{10} x$. Thus, the logarithmic function is simply the inverse of the corresponding exponential function. Both of them convey the same relationship. To show the logarithmic function graphically, we measure x value along the X-axis and the corresponding logarithmic values (log x) along the Y-axis. If we use 10 as the base for all our calculations then the associated logarithm is called the common logarithm. On the other hand if use 'e' as the base then the associated logarithm is called the natural logarithm. For common logarithm, we use the short form 'log'. To distinguish the natural logarithm from the common logarithm we use the notation 'ln' in the place of 'log' notation. The following example and the associated figure illustrates the function $y = \log_{10} x$.

Example 80: Draw the graph for the logarithmic function $y = \log_{10} x$.

Table 3.51

X	y = log X	X	y = log X
1	0.000000	6	0.778151
2	0.301030	7	0.845098
3	0.477121	8	0.903090
4	0.602060	9	0.954243
5	0.698970	10	1.000000

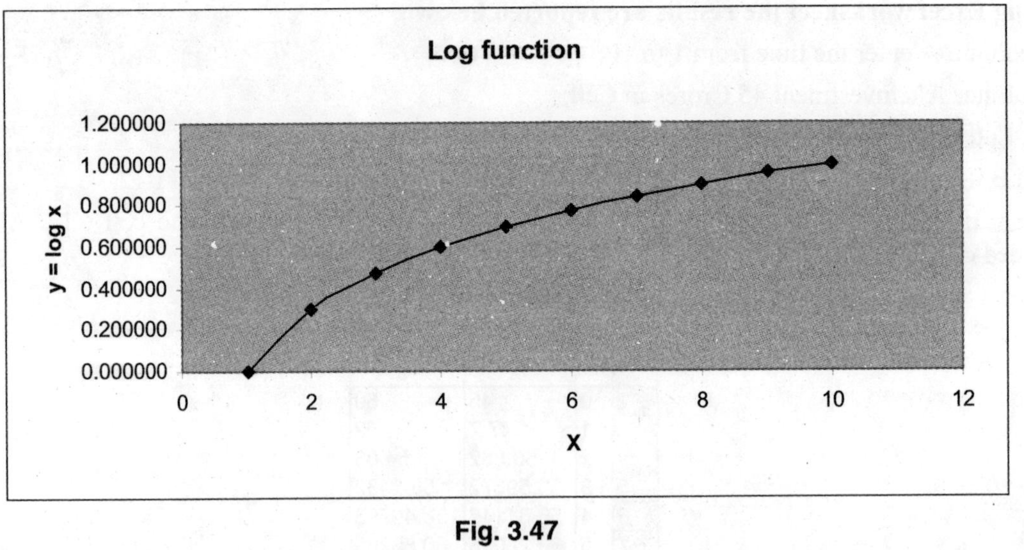

Fig. 3.47

This new function is the inverse of the exponential function discussed above. Further, this graph has a special characteristic shape showing the constant absolute increase in x and a declining growth rate of y. Thus a change in x from 1 to 2 represent a growth of 100%, but a change from 2 to 3 reflect only 50 % growth.

Example 81: Draw the graph for the logarithmic function y = ln x.

Table 3.52

X	y = ln X	X	y = ln X
1	0.000000	6	1.791759
2	0.693147	7	1.945910
3	1.098612	8	2.079442
4	1.386294	9	2.197225
5	1.609438	10	2.302585

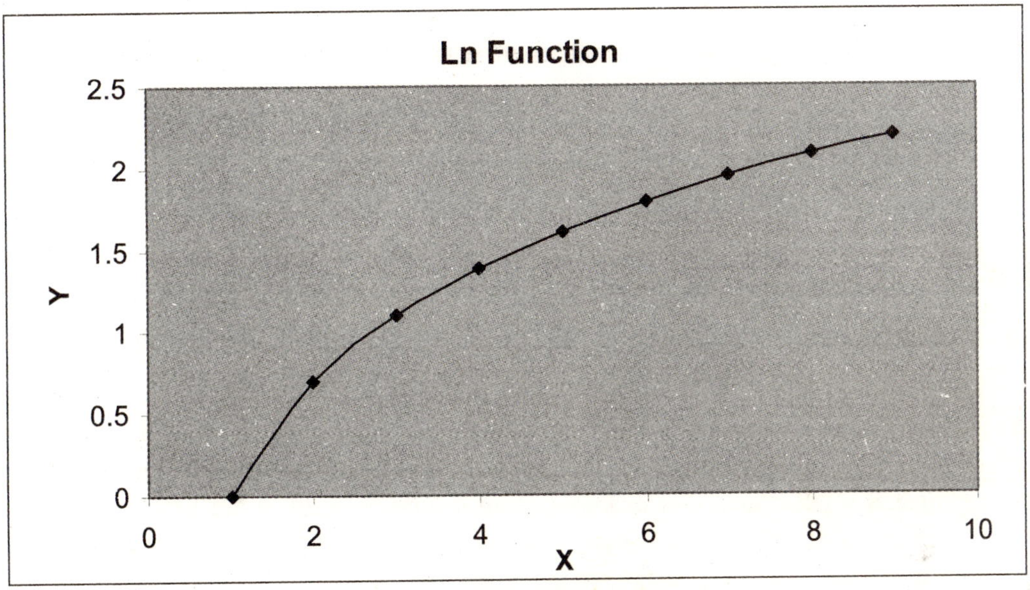

Fig. 3.48

Note: The common log is often used in simplifications of complicated problems. The natural logarithms are having specialized uses in the theory of growth and decay.

Semi log Charts: Logarithmic charts are suitable to portray proportional changes in economic activities.

Example 82: Suppose the two firms are having the following investment pattern for over five years. Draw a semi log chart and explain its utility.

Table 3.53

	1970	1971	1972	1973	1974
Firm A	20	40	80	100	150
Firm B	140	160	200	220	270

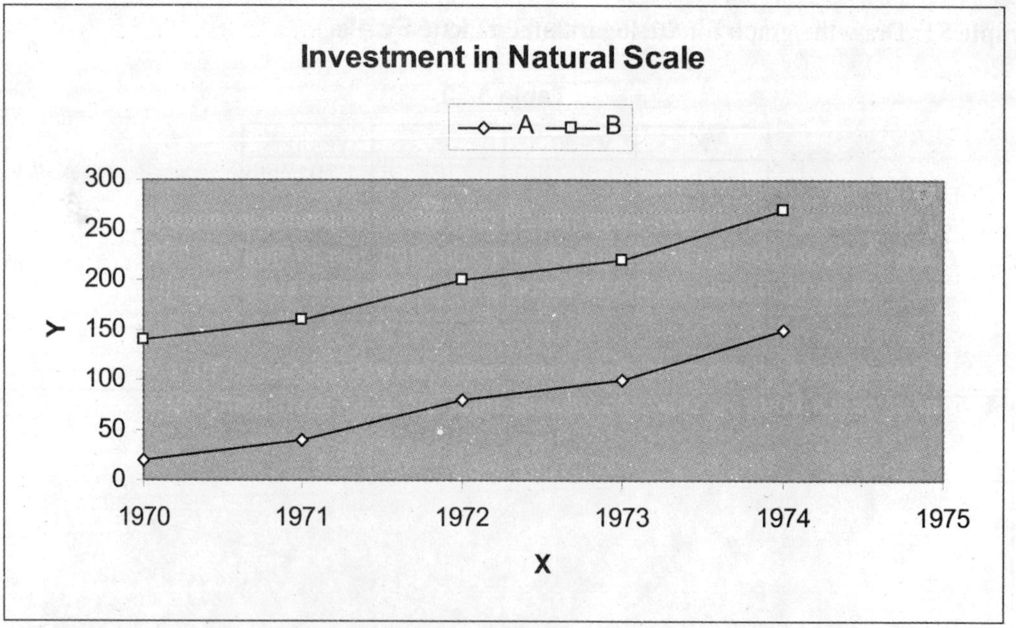

Fig. 3.49

The above diagram shows the investment pattern in absolute term for both the firms.

The absolute increase in investment is same with both the firms; 20 in the first year, 40 in the second year, 20 in the third year, 50 in the fourth year. This pattern is very much clear from the natural graph given. However, such an observation is less interesting. In fact, firm A grow faster than firm B at all stages. For example, from a scratch of 20 in the first year, making an investment of 20 (a 100%) in the second year by firm A is commendable than the firm B's investment effort from 140 to 160 in the second year (only 14%.).

Now to throw light on this issue let us use a semi log graphs rather than the absolute graph in the following section. The following table is obtained by taking the logarithmic values to the original data.

Table 3.54

	1970	1971	1972	1973	1974
Firm A	1.30103	1.60206	1.90309	2.00000	2.17609
Firm B	2.14613	2.20412	2.30103	2.34242	2.43136

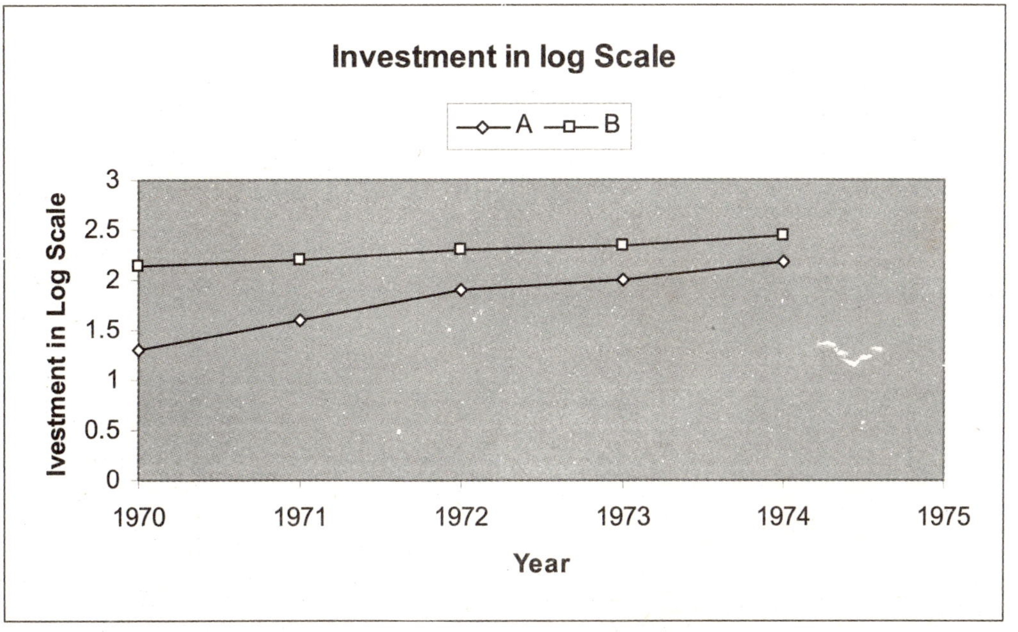

Fig. 3.50

In this graph at every point of time the growth rates are read from their respective slopes. It is appealing to see that for firm A, the slopes are greater at every point of time exhibiting a better relative performance.

Another method to draw semi log graph is to exhibit the very logarithmic scale on the y-axis. Thus, the space between 25 and 50, 50 and 100, and 100 to 200 are equal to reveal equal proportional change. If this is done, then there is no need to change investment figures into log values as we did in the previous case.

EXERCISES

Exercise 1:

Represents the following linear functions graphically on graph sheet:

1. $D = 2p + 5$
2. $S = 2p - 5$
3. $S = 300$
4. $S = 0.8Y$
5. $TFC = 200$
6. $C = 0.6Y + 100$
7. $S = 0.4Y - 100$
8. $200 = 4q_1 + 5q_2$
9. $400 = 5W + 10C$
10. $800 = 20L + 40K$

Exercise 2:

Solve for x

1. $5x + 67 - 3x = 25x + 3$
2. $4x + 3 = 2x + 45$
3. $7(2x + 5) = 4(3 + 2x)$
4. $12x - 4(3x - 5) = 45(2x - 6) + 35$
5. $(x - 2) - 4(x + 3) = 18$

Exercise 3:

Solve the following equations for x.

1. $x^2 + 16x + 48 = 0$
2. $6x^2 - 10x + 4 = 0$
3. $7x^2 + 5x = -3$
4. $(x - 3)^2 + (x - 2)^2 = 1$
5. $4x^2 - 37x - 7 = 0$
6. $x^2 - 6x + 5 = 0$
7. $9x^2 - 105x + 300 = 0$
8. $x^2 - 100x + 24 = 0$
9. $\frac{x-2}{x-1} + \frac{x+2}{x+1} = 0$
10. $\frac{x-3}{x-2} - \frac{x+2}{x} = \frac{3}{2}$
11. $\left(x - \frac{1}{x}\right)^2 + 7\left(x - \frac{1}{x}\right) = \frac{51}{4}$
12. $\frac{1}{x^4} - \frac{11}{5x^2} = -\frac{6}{3}$

Exercise 4:

1. Find the value of Rs.10000 at 15% interest rate after 10 years.
   (a) Compounding annually.
   (b) Compounding biannually.
   (c) Compounding quarterly.
   (d) Infinite compounding.
2. In NSC investment the deposits grow at 9.5% compounded quarterly. Calculate the effective interest rate R.
   (a) Compounding annually.
   (b) Compounding biannually.
   (c) Compounding quarterly.
   (d) Infinite compounding.

3. Calculate the present value for an expected income of Rs.15000 after 5 years given the current interest rate of 10% per annum.
   (a) Under annual compounding.
   (b) Under quarterly compounding.
   (c) Under continuous compounding.
4. Currently the national income of a certain economy is Rs.10000000 Crores. It was found to grow at 8% annually. Project the level of income after 10 years.
   (a) Under annual compounding.
   (b) Under quarterly compounding.
   (c) Under continuous compounding.
5. The income of an economy went up from 10,00,000 Crores to 20,00,000 Crores in about 10 years. Calculate the annual growth rate.
   (a) Under annual compounding.
   (b) Under quarterly compounding.
   (c) Under continuous compounding.
6. 10,000; 20,000; 30,000 are the expected income stream for the next three years, calculate the discounted current value of this income stream at 10% rate of interest.
   (a) Under annual compounding.
   (b) Under quarterly compounding.
   (c) Under continuous compounding.

4

Chapter

AP, GP AND THEIR APPLICATIONS

4.1 Sequence

A sequence is a succession of numbers having written according to some well-defined rules. For example, 1, 3, 5, 7 …is a sequence because the increment between successive terms is a constant namely 2. Similarly, 2, 4, 8, 16, 32… is a sequence because the ratio of the succeeding term to the present term is a constant 2 in this sequence. A sequence is said to be finite provided it has first and the last number. For example, 4, 6, 8, 10 is a finite sequence having only the four terms. A sequence is said to be infinite, provided every term in it has a subsequent term. In fact, it never gets terminated, and there is no last term as such in such. The statement n tends to infinity explains the type on never ending process. For example, 4, 8, 12, 16 … is an infinite sequence.

Thus, in general an infinite sequence $a_1, a_2, a_3...$ is normally denoted by $\{a_n\}$. A sequence $\{a_n\}$ is said to be increasing, provided for each positive integer $a_n < a_{n+1}$. Similarly, a sequence $\{a_n\}$ is said to be decreasing, provided $a_n > a_{n+1}$.

For example,

(1) $1^2, 2^2, 3^2...$ is an increasing sequence because $1 < 4 < 9$.

(2) $1, \frac{1}{2}, \frac{1}{3}, \frac{1}{4}, ...$ is a decreasing sequence because $1 > 1/2 > 1/4$.

(3) $-2, -4, -6, -8, ...$ is a decreasing sequence because $-2 > -4 > -6$

Remember, that all these sequences are infinite sequences having infinite number of terms. The first one clearly tends to $+\infty$ as n tends to infinity. The second one tends to 0 as n tends to infinity. The third one tends to $-\infty$ as n tends to infinity. In addition to the said two types we have a third type of oscillating sequences as well.

For example,

(4) $1, -1, 1, -1...$ oscillate between 1 and -1.

A sequence $\{a_n\}$ is said to have a limit l provided there is an nth term a_n that can be made as close as possible to l by taking n sufficiently large number of terms. This statement in short form may be written as

$$\operatorname*{Lt}_{n\to\infty}(a_n) = l$$

A sequence, which has a limit, is often called a convergent sequence. If it does not have a limit then it could either divergent or oscillatory.

4.2 Arithmetic Progression

An arithmetic progression is a special type of sequence whose successive terms either increase or decrease by a constant amount, often called the common difference. The common difference thus, is obtainable by subtracting each term from its succeeding term.

The series 1, 3, 5, 7... is an AP. In it, we notice that the successive terms are obtained by adding 2 to the preceding term. For example, 5 is the third term in the sequence, so its fourth term is obtained as 5 + 2 = 7. Thus, given the first term and the common difference we can easily generate the entire sequence. To obtain the needed tenth term we continue the sequence starting from 1 as shown below:

1, 3, 5, 7, 9, 11, 13, 15, 17, **19**, 21

The highlighted 19 is the needed tenth term of this AP. Thus, tenth term = ninth term plus the common difference.

Standard form of an AP

a, a + d, a + 2d, a + 3d... a + (n – 1) d,..........is an AP with the first term 'a' and common difference 'd'. This algebraic representation is often called the standard form of an AP.

4.3 The nth term of an AP

From the above standard form, the second term

$$T_2 = (a + d) = a + (2 - 1)d$$

$$T_3 = (a + 2d) = a + (3 - 1)d$$

$$T_4 = a + 3d = a + (4 - 1)d$$

....

....

$$T_n = a + (n - 1)d$$

Thus, in general the nth term is obtained as

$$T_n = a + (n - 1)d \qquad \text{... (1)}$$

Example 1: For the given A.P. 1, 3, 5...obtain the 100th term.

Solution:

One way for getting the 100th term is to continue the sequence of the given AP by adding the common difference d = 2 from the third member till we get the 100 member. This is really a troublesome method for larger values like 1000th term. Luckily, we have the readymade formula given in equation (1) to obtain such terms.

So,

$$T_n = a + (n - 1)d$$

$$T_{100} = 1 + (100 - 1)2$$
$$= 1 + (99 \times 2)$$
$$= 1 + 198$$
$$T_{100} = 199$$

Note 1: That the formula given in equation (1) contains four variables namely T_n, a, n, and d. Thus, given the value of any three of them, we can readily calculate the left over fourth one.

Note 2: Remember, $d = T_2 - T_1 = T_3 - T_2 = \ldots\ldots\ldots\ldots = T_n - T_{n-1}$

Example 2: The nth term of an AP is 4n – 1. Find out the first four terms. Also get the 20th term.

Solution:

$$T_1 = (4 \times 1) - 1 = 3$$
$$T_2 = (4 \times 2) - 1 = 7$$
$$T_3 = (4 \times 3) - 1 = 11$$
$$T_4 = (4 \times 4) - 1 = 15$$
$$T_{20} = (4 \times 20) - 1 = 79$$

Example 3: Which term of the sequence 31, 29, 27… is 3?

Solution:

Let $T_n = 3$, now we have $T_n = 3$, $a = 31$, $d = -2$, $n = ?$

$$T_n = a + (n - 1)d$$
$$3 = 31 + (n - 1) - 2$$
$$3 = 31 - 2n + 2$$
$$3 = 33 - 2n$$
$$-30 = -2n$$
$$n = 15$$

Thus, the 15th term in given sequence will be equal to 3.

Example 4: In an AP the 10th term is one-half of the 24th term. Prove that 72nd term is twice of the 34th term.

Solution:

Let 'a' be the first term and 'd' be the common difference. Now since the 10th term is one-half of 24th term, we have

$$\frac{1}{2}(a + 23d) = (a + 9d)$$
$$(a + 23d) = 2(a + 9d)$$
$$a + 23d = 2a + 18d$$
$$a - 2a = 18d - 23d$$
$$-a = -5d$$
$$a = 5d \qquad \text{... (i)}$$

Now 72nd term $a + 71d = 5d + 71d = 76d$ ... (ii)

Similarly, 34th term $= a + 33d = 5d + 33d = 38d$ ... (iii)

Now clearly, from equation (ii) and (iii) the 72nd term is twice the 34th term.

Example 5: Find three numbers in an AP whose sum = 21 and product = 280.

Solution:

Among the three numbers, let the first term be 'a'. In addition, let the common difference be 'd'.

Thus, the three terms are a, a + d, a+2d.

$$\text{Given } a + (a + d) + (a + 2d) = 21$$

$$3(a + d) = 21$$

$$a + d = 21/3 = 7 \quad \text{... (i)}$$

$$\text{Also given } a \times (a + d) \times (a + 2d) = 280$$

$$a(7) \times (a + 2d) = 280$$

$$(a^2 + 2ad) = 280/7 = 40 \quad \text{... (ii)}$$

Now square equation (i) above on both the sides

$$(a + d)^2 = a^2 + 2ad + d^2 = 49$$

$$40 + d^2 = 49$$

$$d^2 = 49 - 40 = 9$$

$$d = \pm 3$$

If d = 3 then from (1) it follows that a =4 and the associated AP is 4, 7, 10.

If d = – 3 then from (1) it follows that a =10 and the associated AP is 10, 7, 4.

Example 6: Which term of the series 2, 5, 6.......... is 53?

Solution:

We know that the nth term of the series is

$$T_n = a + (n - 1)d$$

$$53 = 2 + (n - 1) \times 3$$

$$53 + 3 - 2 = 3n$$

$$54 = 3n$$

$$n = 18$$

Example 7: The second, thirty first and the last term of a finite AP are 7.75, 0.5, –6.5 respectively. Find the first term and number of terms.

Solution:

$$\text{The second term } = a + d = \frac{31}{4} \quad \text{... (i)}$$

$$\text{The } 31^{st} \text{ term} = a + (31-1)d = \frac{1}{2} \quad \text{... (ii)}$$

$$\text{The } n^{th} \text{ term} = a + (n-1)d = \frac{-29}{4} \quad \text{... (iii)}$$

Now subtracting equation (i) from (ii)

$$29d = \frac{1}{2} - \frac{31}{4} = \frac{2-31}{4} = \frac{-29}{4}$$

$$\text{So, } d = \frac{-29}{4} \times \frac{1}{29} = -\frac{1}{4}$$

Now we can get the value of 'a' by merely substituting this value of d in equation (i)

$$a = \frac{31}{4} - d$$

$$= \frac{31}{4} + \frac{1}{4}$$

$$= \frac{32}{4} = 8$$

Now to get the number of terms in this finite series we simply substitute the obtained values of 'a' and d in equation (iii)

$$a + (n-1)d = -\frac{13}{2}$$

$$8 + (n-1)(-\frac{1}{4}) = \frac{-13}{2}$$

$$-\frac{1}{4}n = -\frac{13}{2} - \frac{1}{4} - 8$$

$$= \frac{-26-1-32}{4}$$

$$= -\frac{59}{4}$$

$$\text{So } n = 59$$

4.4 Sum of the First n Terms of a Given AP

$$\text{Let } S_n = a + (a+d) + (a+2d) + (a+3d) + \ldots\ldots + l \qquad \text{where } l = a + (n-1)d$$

$$S_n = l + (l-d) + (l-2d) + \ldots\ldots + a$$

$$2S_n = n(a+l)$$

$$S_n = \frac{n(a+l)}{2} = \frac{n[a+a+(n-1)d]}{2} = \frac{n}{2}[2a+(n-1)d] \quad \text{... (2)}$$

$$S_n = \frac{\text{Number of terms to be summed up}}{2}(\text{the first term} + \text{the last term}) \qquad \ldots (3)$$

Example 8: Consider the AP = 1, 3, 5, 7, 9, 11, 13..............

In this sequence, the sum of the first 4 terms by observation is 1+3+5+7 = 16.

By using the formula (3)

$$S_4 = \frac{\text{Number of terms to be summed up}}{2}(\text{the first term} + \text{the last term})$$

$$= \frac{4}{2}(1+7) = 16$$

From the formula (2)

$$S_4 = \frac{n[2a+(n-1)d]}{2}$$

$$= \frac{4[2\times 1+(4-1)2]}{2}$$

$$= 2[2+6] = 16$$

Example 9: Find the sum of the first 10 terms of an AP: 1, 4, 7, 10,............

Solution:

The given sequence can be extended easily up to 10 terms as AP: 1, 4, 7, 10, 13, 16, 19, 22, 25, 28....

Therefore, the needed sum up to ten terms

$$\text{Sum} = \frac{n}{2}(\text{First term} + \text{Last term})$$

$$= \frac{10}{2}(1+28)$$

$$= 5 \times 29 = 145$$

Alternatively, one can use the formula as well to get the needed sum.

Given a = 1, d = 3 and n = 10

$$S_n = \frac{n[2a+(n-1)d]}{2}$$

$$= \frac{10[2\times 1+(10-1)3]}{2}$$

$$= 5[2+27] = 145$$

Example 10: Show that 1+3+5+...............to n terms = n^2.

Solution:

Given a = 1, d = 2 and n = n

$$S_n = \frac{n[2a+(n-1)d]}{2}$$

$$= \frac{n[2\times1+(n-1)2]}{2}$$

$$= \frac{n}{2}[2+(2n-2)]$$

$$= \frac{n}{2}\times 2n = n^2$$

Example 11: Find the 40th term of the AP: 3, 7, 11, 15… Hence, obtain the sum of these 40 terms.

Solution:

Given a = 3, d = 4 and n = 40

The 40 term is obtained as

$$T_n = a+(n-1)d$$

$$T_{40} = 3+(40-1)4$$

$$= 3+39\times 4$$

$$= 3+156$$

$$= 159$$

$$S_n = \frac{n}{2}[\text{First term} + \text{Last term}]$$

$$= \frac{40}{2}[3+159]$$

$$= 20[162]$$

$$= 3240$$

Example 12: Find the sum of n terms of the progression 3, 7, 11…

Solution:

$$S_n = \frac{n}{2}[2a+(n-1)d]$$

$$= \frac{n}{2}[2\times3+(n-1)\times4]$$

$$= \frac{n}{2}[6+4n-4]$$

$$= 3n+2n^2-2n$$

$$= n + 2n^2$$
$$= n(2n + 1)$$

4.5 Food Grain Production and AP

In Malthusian theory of population food is assumed to grow in AP. To highlight this type of growth consider the following illustration:

Example 13: A farm produces 550 tons of wheat in the every first year. The sum total of production at the end of 5th year is 3000 tons. If the given production sequence is an AP find the value of annual increase in production. Also find the 10th year production and sum total up to 10th year.

Solution:

We know that

$$S_n = \frac{n}{2}[2a + (n-1)d]$$

$$3000 = \frac{5}{2}[2 \times 550 + (5-1)d]$$

$$6000 = 5[1100 + 4d]$$

$$1200 = 1100 + 4d$$

$$d = 25 \text{ tons}$$

Thus, the entire sequence of production is written as 550, 575, 600, 625...

Now the 10th year output is given by

$$T_n = a + (n-1)d$$

$$T_{10} = 550 + (10-1)25$$

$$= 550 + 9 \times 25$$

$$= 775 \text{ tons}$$

Now the sum for 10 years is given by

$$S_n = \frac{n}{2}(a + l)$$

$$S_{10} = \frac{10}{2}(550 + 775) = 6625 \text{ tons}$$

4.6 Important Characteristic of an AP

In an arithmetic progression, the middle term is the average of the preceding and succeeding terms.

Example 14: Consider the AP: 1, 3, 5, 7, 9.

In this AP, the second term 3 is simply the arithmetic mean of 1 an 5, the first term and the third term respectively. Similarly, 5 is the mean of 3 and 7 and so on.

Example 15: In an AP prove that the middle term is the arithmetic mean of the preceding and succeeding term.

Solution

Let a, A, b are three consequent terms of an AP show that A is the arithmetic mean of the adjacent terms a and b.

Now we now that

$$A - a = b - A = d \text{ (the common difference)}$$

$$2A = a + b$$

$$A = \frac{a+b}{2}$$

Example 16: Given the first term as 3 and last term as 23 in an AP, insert members in between 3 and 23.

Solution:

Let A_1, A_2, A_3, and A_4 are the proposed four terms of the AP in the said interval. So our AP containing 6 terms may be written as 3, A_1, A_2 ,A_3, A_4, 23. Let d be the common difference.

$$T_6 = a + (n-1)d = 23$$

$$= 3 + 5d = 23$$

$$5d = 23 - 3 = 20$$

$$d = 4$$

$$A_1 = a + d = 3 + 4 = 7$$

$$A_2 = a + 2d = 3 + 2 \times 4 = 11$$

$$A_3 = a + 3d = 3 + 3 \times 4 = 15$$

$$A_4 = a + 4d = 3 + 4 \times 4 = 19$$

4.7 Geometric Progression

A geometric progression is a sequence whose term increases or decreases by a constant ratio. In such sequence, the ratio of the any term to the preceding term is constant. For example, 1, 2, 4, 8, 16... is a geometric progression. In it, 2/1 = 4/2 = 8/4= 16/8 = 2 is the common ratio.

Standard form of a GP

If 'a' is the first term and r is the common ratio then the associated GP in it general form is written as a, ar , ar^2, ar^3... ,ar^{n-1}.........

In particular, if a = 1 and r = 2 then the geometric progression is obtained as:

$$1, 1 \times 2, 1 \times 2^2, 1 \times 2^4 \ldots\ldots\ldots\ldots\ldots\ldots$$

$$1, 2, 4, 8, 16 \ldots\ldots\ldots\ldots\ldots\ldots\ldots\ldots$$

4.8 The nth term of the GP

Let a, ar , ar^2, ar^3... ,ar^{n-1}........ be a geometric progression with the first term a and the common ratio r

$$T_1 = a = ar^{1-1}$$
$$T_2 = ar = ar^{2-1}$$
$$T_3 = ar^2 = ar^{3-1}$$
$$T_4 = ar^3 = ar^{4-1}$$
$$\dots \quad \dots \quad \dots$$
$$T_n = ar^{n-1}$$

The nth term of the GP is obtained as $T_n = ar^{n-1}$ ... (4)

Example 17: For the GP 1, 2, 4, 8, 16..., obtain the 20th term.

$$T_n = ar^{n-1}$$
$$T_{20} = 1 \times 2^{20-1}$$
$$= 1 \times 2^{19}$$
$$= 524288$$

Example 18: Find (i) the sixth and (ii) the nth term of the GP 2, 6, 18, ...

Solution:

Here $a = 2$, and $r = 6/2 = 3$, $n = 6$

$$T_n = ar^{n-1}$$
$$T_6 = 2 \times 3^{6-1}$$
$$= 2 \times 3^5$$
$$= 486$$
$$T_n = 2 \times 3^{n-1}$$

Example 19: Write the GP whose 4th term is 54 and the 7th term is 1458.

Solution:

$$T_n = ar^{n-1}$$
$$T_4 = ar^3 = 54 \quad \text{...(i)}$$
$$T_7 = ar^6 = 1458 \quad \text{...(ii)}$$
$$\frac{T_7}{T_4} = \frac{ar^6}{ar^3} = r^3 = \frac{1458}{54} = 27$$
$$\Rightarrow \quad r = 3$$

From (i)

$$ar^3 = 54$$
$$\Rightarrow \quad a(3)^3 = 54$$
$$\Rightarrow \quad a = 2$$

Having known 'a' and 'r' the needed GP is written as

$$a, ar, ar^2, ar^3 \ldots$$

$$2, 6, 18, 54 \ldots$$

4.9 Convenient Method for Representing Consecutive Terms of a GP

The following are some convenient ways of representing consecutive terms

If three numbers are in GP then they are conveniently represented as $\frac{a}{r}, a, ar$

If four numbers are in GP then they are conveniently represented as $\frac{a}{r}, a, ar, ar^2$

If five numbers are in GP then they are conveniently represented as $\frac{a}{r^2}, \frac{a}{r}, a, ar, ar^2$

Example: 20 Insert 4 GP terms between 1 and 243.

Let T_2, T_3, T_4, T_5 be the needed GP terms to be inserted

Given that 1, T_2, T_3, T_4, T_5, and 243 are in GP

Therefore

$$T_6 = ar^5$$

$$243 = 1 \times r^5$$

$$r^5 = 3^5$$

$$r = 3$$

If $a = 1$ and $r = 3$ then

$$T_2 = ar = 1 \times 3 = 3$$

$$T_3 = ar^2 = 1 \times 3^2 = 9$$

$$T_4 = ar^3 = 1 \times 3^3 = 27$$

$$T_5 = ar^4 = 1 \times 3^4 = 81$$

Example 21: The third and the seventh terms of a GP are 3/4 and 4/27 respectively. Find the fourth term.

Solution:

Let a be the first term and r be the common ratio.

Now by definition

$$T_3 = ar^2 = 3/4 \quad \ldots \text{(i)}$$

$$T_7 = ar^6 = 4/27 \quad \ldots \text{(ii)}$$

$$\frac{T_7}{T_3} = \frac{ar^6}{ar^2} = \frac{4/27}{3/4}$$

$$r^4 = \frac{4}{27} \times \frac{4}{3} = \frac{16}{81}$$

$$r^4 = \left(\frac{2}{3}\right)^4$$

$$r = \frac{2}{3}$$

Now the 'a' value is obtained by substituting r in equation (i)

$$ar^2 = \frac{3}{4}$$

$$\Rightarrow \qquad a = \frac{3}{4r^2} = \frac{3}{4\left(\frac{2}{3}\right)^2} = \frac{3}{4\left(\frac{4}{9}\right)} = \frac{3 \times 9}{16} = \frac{27}{16}$$

Now the fourth term $T_4 = ar^3 = \frac{27}{16} \times \left(\frac{2}{3}\right)^3$

$$= \frac{27 \times 8}{16 \times 27} = \frac{1}{2}$$

4.10 Important Characteristic of a GP

In a GP of three consecutive terms, the middle number is the geometric mean of the preceding and succeeding numbers.

Proof: Let a, G, b are in geometric progression

Now we know that

$$\frac{G}{a} = \frac{b}{G}$$

$$G^2 = ab$$

$$G = \sqrt{ab}$$

Example 22: Insert 4 GP terms between 1 and 243.

Solution:

Let G_1 ,G_2 , G_3 ,G_4 are the proposed four members of the GP.

Thus, the GP is written as 1, G_1, G_2, G_3, G_4, 243…

$$G_6 = 1r^5 = 243$$

$$r = 3$$

$$G_1 = ar = 1 \times 3 = 3$$

$$G_2 = ar^2 = 1 \times 3^2 = 9$$

$$G_3 = ar^3 = 1 \times 3^3 = 27$$

$$G_4 = ar^4 = 1 \times 3^4 = 81$$

Sum of first n terms in a finite GP

$$S_n = a + ar + ar^2 + ar^3 + \dots\dots\dots\dots + ar^{n-1}$$

$$rS_n = ar + ar^2 + ar^3 + \dots\dots\dots\dots + ar^n$$

On subtracting

$$S_n(1-r) = a - ar^n$$

$$S_n = \frac{a(1-r^n)}{1-r} \quad \text{when} \quad r < 1 \qquad \dots (5)$$

$$S_n = \frac{a(r^n-1)}{r-1} \quad \text{when } r > 1 \qquad \dots (6)$$

Sum of all the terms in an infinite GP

$$S_\infty = \frac{a(1-r^n)}{1-r} \quad \text{when } r < 1$$

$$S_\infty = \frac{a}{1-r} - \frac{ar^n}{1-r}$$

$$\underset{n\to\infty}{\text{Lt}}\, S_\infty = \frac{a}{1-r} - \underset{n\to\infty}{\text{Lt}} \frac{ar^n}{1-r}$$

$$S_\infty = \frac{a}{1-r} - 0 \text{ as } r^n \to 0 \qquad \dots (7)$$

$$S_\infty = \frac{a(r^n-1)}{r-1} \quad \text{when } r > 1$$

$$S_\infty = \frac{ar^n}{r-1} - \frac{a}{r-1}$$

$$S_\infty = \underset{n\to\infty}{\text{Lt}} \frac{ar^n}{r-1} - \frac{a}{r-1}$$

$$S_\infty = \infty \quad \text{as } r^n \to \infty \qquad \dots (8)$$

Example 23: Find the sum of 10 terms of the GP 2, – 4, 8, ...

Solution:

Here $a = 2$, $r = -2$.

$$S_n = \frac{a(1-r^n)}{1-r} \quad \text{when} \quad r < 1$$

$$S_{10} = \frac{2\left[1-(-2)^{10}\right]}{1-(-2)}$$

$$= \frac{2[1-1024]}{1+2}$$

$$= \frac{-2046}{3}$$

$$= -682$$

Example 24: How many terms of a GP 4, 2, 1…adds to $\frac{127}{16}$?

Solution:

Given a = 4, $r = \frac{2}{4} = \frac{1}{2}$

$$S_n = \frac{a(1-r^n)}{1-r}$$

$$\frac{127}{16} = 4\left[\frac{1-\left(\frac{1}{2}\right)^n}{1-\frac{1}{2}}\right]$$

$$\frac{127}{16} = 8\left[1-\left(\frac{1}{2}\right)^n\right]$$

$$\frac{127}{128} = 1-\left(\frac{1}{2}\right)^n$$

$$\left(\frac{1}{2}\right)^n = 1-\left(\frac{127}{128}\right) = \frac{1}{128} = \left(\frac{1}{2}\right)^7$$

So n = 7

Thus, the sum of seven terms makes the total of $\frac{127}{18}$.

Example 25: Find the sum of the infinite GP $5, \frac{5}{6}, \frac{5}{36} \ldots$

Solution:

Here a = 5 and r = 1/6

$$S_\infty = \frac{a}{1-r} = \frac{5}{1-\frac{1}{6}} = \frac{5}{\frac{5}{6}} = \frac{5}{1} \times \frac{6}{5} = 6$$

4.11 Population Growth and GP

Let P_0 be the initial population of a certain town. Now if it grows at the rate g then after one year it will be

$$P_1 = P_0(1+g)$$
$$P_2 = P_0(1+g)(1+g) = P_0(1+g)^2$$
$$P_3 = P_0(1+g)^3$$
$$\dots\dots\dots\dots\dots\dots\dots\dots$$
$$P_n = P_0(1+g)^n$$

Thus $P_0 + P_0(1+g) + P_0(1+g)^2 + P_0(1+g)^3 + \dots\dots\dots\dots + P_0(1+g)^n$ is a geometric progression with initial value P_0 and common ratio (1+r).

Example 26: Currently, the population of a certain city is 100000. It was found to grow at 12% annually at compound rate. Project the level of population after 10 years.

Solution: Growth at annual rate:

$$\begin{aligned} Y_t &= Y_0(1+g)^t \\ &= 100000(1+0.12)^{10} \\ &= 100000(1.12)^{10} \\ &= 310584.8208 \end{aligned}$$

4.12 Multiplier and GP

Let the Marginal propensity to consume MPC = 0.5. Now let an additional investment of Rs.100 Crores is made in a construction industry. This will increase the income for the inputs used in the construction industry. In turn these income receivers like mason, steel supplier, cement supplier will spend Rs.50 Crores (50%) and save Rs.50 Crores (50%). In the next round out of Rs.50 Crores (50%) Rs.25 will be spent (Rs.25 Crores will be saved). This process will continue as shown in table 4.1.

Table 4.1

Rounds	New Income	New consumption	New Saving
1	100.0000	50.0000	50.0000
2	50.0000	25.0000	25.0000
3	25.0000	12.5000	12.5000
4	12.5000	6.2500	6.2500
5	6.2500	3.1250	3.1250
6	3.1250	1.5625	1.5625
7	1.5625	0.7813	0.7813
8	0.7813	0.3906	0.3906
9	0.3906	0.1953	0.1953
10	0.1953	0.0977	0.0977
11	0.0977	0.0488	0.0488
12	0.0488	0.0244	0.0244
13	0.0244	0.0122	0.0122
14	0.0122	0.0061	0.0061
15	0.0061	0.0031	0.0031
16	0.0031	0.0015	0.0015
17	0.0015	0.0008	0.0008
18	0.0008	0.0004	0.0004
19	0.0004	0.0002	0.0002
20	0.0002	0.0001	0.0001
21	0.0001	0.0000	0.0000
	199.9999	100.0000	100.0000

The above sequence can be represented by

$$100 + 100(.5) + 100(.5)^2 + 100(.5)^3 + \dots\dots$$

$$100(1 + 1 \times 0.5 + 1 \times 0.5^2 + 1 \times 0.5^3 \dots\dots \infty)$$

The term inside the bracket is a geometric progression with unit as the starting term and 0.5 as the common ratio. So the sum of the terms inside the bracket income is obtained from the formula

$$S = \frac{a}{1-r} = \frac{1}{1-MPC} = \frac{1}{1-0.5} = 2$$

So $\Delta Y = k \times \Delta I = 2 \times 100 = 200$

Thus $k = \frac{1}{1-MPC} = \frac{1}{MPS}$ is the needed multiplying factor called multiplier in Economics.

The table 4.1 and the associated fig.4.1 show the sequence of income generation

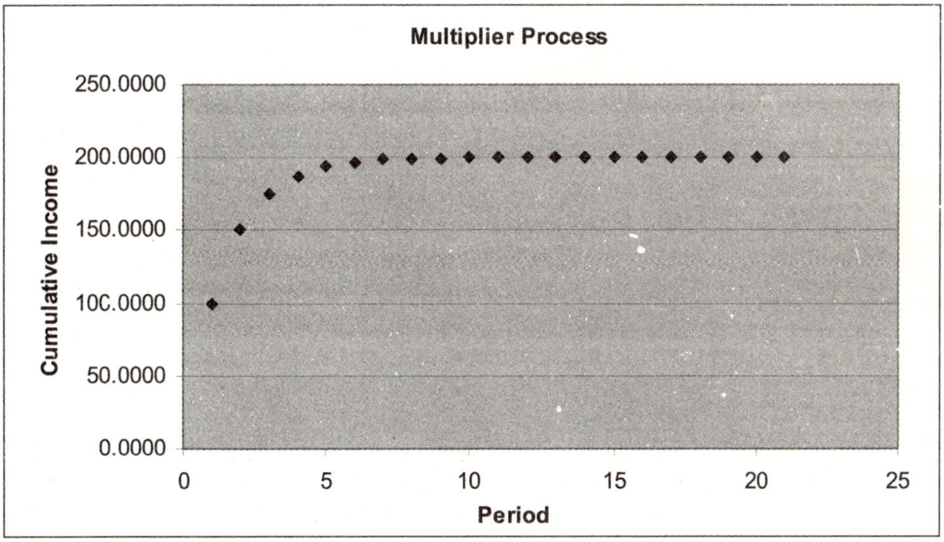

Fig. 4.1

4.13 Cournot Model and GP

Example 27: Two duopolists draw q_1 and q_2 quantities of certain spring water from a common spring with zero cost of production. If $p = 60 - 0.5(q_1 + q_2)$ is market demand for the spring water. Show the duopolist share the water output equally.

Solution:

In the diagram, the demand curve cuts the X-axis at 120 units level. This is simply the output level at zero price follows from the given demand equation. Now let the first duopolist enters the market first and as per Counot behaviorist pattern, assumes himself as follower and supplies one-half of 120 that maximizes the total revenue collection. Now the second duopolist enters later assumes the first duopolist as leader and thus leaves the first duopolist sale of 60 unaltered. He hopes to supply only the residual market namely 120 – 60 = 60. But once again only half of 60 fetch him more revenue, he will supply only 30 units to the market. Now 60 + 30 = 90 is the total by both. The expected market price at this stage is p = 60 – 0.5 (60 + 30) =30 as shown in the diagram. This is not the end of the story. Now in the second round, the first duopolist readjust his output by assuming the second duopolist as business leader as per Cournot. The readjusted output level for the first duopolist is obtained as = (120 – 30)/2 = 45. This is shown in the second row first column in the table 4.2. Once this readjustment is carried over by the first duopolist the second duopolist react to this reaction as follower and readjust his output by using the same formula, p = (120 – 45)/2 = 37.5. The so adjusted new output level is shown the second row third column in the table. This type of adjustment and readjustment continue until the final equilibrium is achieved as shown in the table. In round 11 and there after the output stabilizes at 40 units each and become time independent equilibrium value. In the corresponding diagram, we show only the first and the final rounds.

Table 4.2

Period	Duopolist I	Dupolist II	Total
1	60.0000	30.0000	90.0000
2	45.0000	37.5000	82.5000
3	41.2500	39.3750	80.6250
4	40.3125	39.8438	80.1563
5	40.0781	39.9609	80.0391
6	40.0195	39.9902	80.0098
7	40.0049	39.9976	80.0024
8	40.0012	39.9994	80.0006
9	40.0003	39.9998	80.0002
10	40.0001	40.0000	80.0000
11	40.0000	40.0000	80.0000
12	40.0000	40.0000	80.0000
13	40.0000	40.0000	80.0000
14	40.0000	40.0000	80.0000

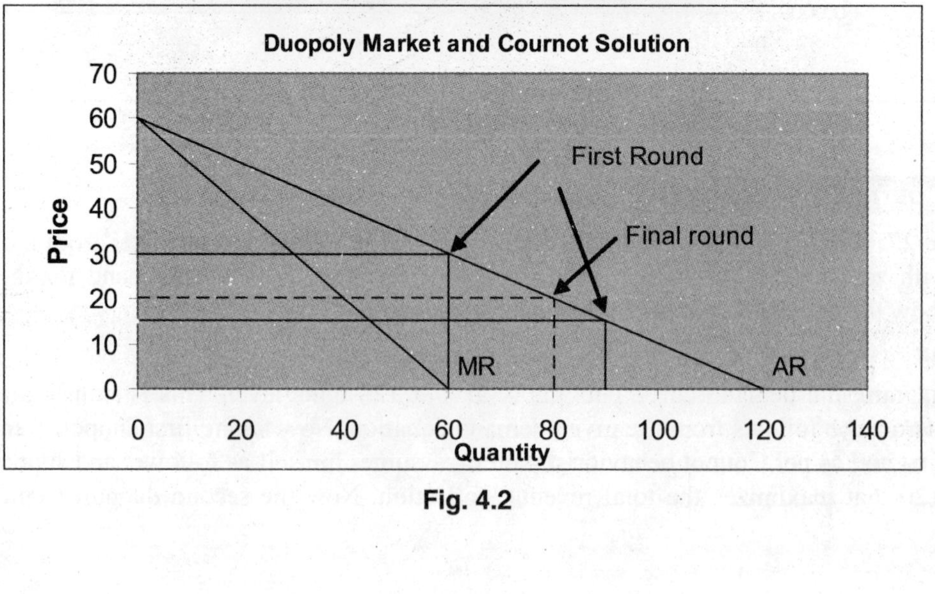

Fig. 4.2

$$\text{A's output} = 120\left[\frac{1}{2}-\frac{1}{8}-\frac{1}{32}-\frac{1}{128}-\ldots\ldots\right]$$

$$= 120\left\{\frac{1}{2}-\left[\frac{1}{8}+\frac{1}{8}\left(\frac{1}{4}\right)+\frac{1}{8}\left(\frac{1}{4}\right)^2+\frac{1}{8}\left(\frac{1}{4}\right)^3+\ldots\ldots\right]\right\}$$

The term inside the square bracket is a GP with 1/8 as the starting term and 1/4 as the common ratio. So the summation in the square bracket is obtained by using the well-known G.P. summation formula

$$\text{So summation of the square bracket } S = \frac{a}{1-r} = \frac{1/8}{1-1/4} = \frac{1}{8}\times\frac{4}{3} = \frac{1}{6}$$

$$\text{A's output} = 120\left\{\frac{1}{2}-\frac{1}{6}\right\} = 120\left\{\frac{3-1}{6}\right\} = 40$$

Similarly,

$$\text{B's output} = 120\left[\frac{1}{4}+\frac{1}{16}+\frac{1}{64}+\frac{1}{256}+\ldots\ldots\right]$$

$$= 120\left\{\frac{1}{4}+\frac{1}{4}\left(\frac{1}{4}\right)+\frac{1}{4}\left(\frac{1}{4}\right)^2+\frac{1}{4}\left(\frac{1}{4}\right)^3+\ldots\ldots\right\}$$

Again, the term inside the square bracket is a GP with 1/4 as the starting term and 1/4 as the common ratio. So the summation in the square bracket is obtained by using the well known G.P. summation formula.

$$\text{So summation of the square bracket } S = \frac{a}{1-r} = \frac{1/4}{1-1/4} = \frac{1}{4}\times\frac{4}{3} = \frac{1}{3}$$

$$\text{B's output} = 120\left\{\frac{1}{3}\right\} = 40$$

Thus the total output = 40+40 = 80. This is exactly 2/3rd of the market observing capacity of 120 units.

EXERCISES

1. Find the 50th term of the sequence 4, 8, 16…
2. Find three numbers in AP whose sum is 9 and product is – 165
3. Find the four members in AP so that their sum is 20 and the sum of their squares is 120
4. Mr.A draws Rs. 550 as basic during the fifth year and Rs. 800 as basic during the 15th year of his service. Find his starting salary and the rate of annual increment. Also, obtain the total basic drawn after 20 years.
5. Currently a certain machine costs Rs.2200. At the end of 6th year, the value of the machine was found to be Rs.400. At constant rate, find the annual depreciation.

6. Two duopolists draw q_1 and q_2 quantities of certain spring water from a common spring with zero cost. If $p = 100 - 0.5(q_1 + q_2)$ is market demand for the spring water, show the duopolist share the water out put equally. Also, show that each one of them will supply only one third of the market capacity.
7. If MPS = 0.2 obtain the sequence of income generation when the initial investment is Rs.200 Crores using Excel worksheet. Also, draw the diagram for the income generation.

5

Chapter

METRIC ALGEBRA AND ITS APPLICATIONS

5.1 Definition of a Matrix

A matrix is an array of numbers arranged in columns and rows within a rectangular space enclosed by a square bracket.

Example 1:

$$A = \begin{bmatrix} 4 & 6 \\ 2 & 1 \end{bmatrix}$$

$$B = \begin{bmatrix} 2 & 3 & 6 \\ 1 & 3 & 7 \\ 5 & 2 & 1 \end{bmatrix}$$

Example 2:

$$C = \begin{bmatrix} a_{11} & a_{12} & a_{13} \\ a_{21} & a_{22} & a_{23} \\ a_{31} & a_{32} & a_{33} \end{bmatrix}$$

In Example (2) above we represent the matrix in its general form. In it the subscripts represents the placement of the elements in the matrix. Between the two subscripts the first subscript shows the row placement and the second subscript refers the column placement of the element under reference. Thus a_{11} is the first row first column element and a_{32} is the third row second column element and so on. In general a_{ij} refers the ith row and j^{th} column element in the given matrix.

The Order of a matrix: The number of rows and columns determines the size of the given matrix. It is often called the order of the matrix. For example, if the matrix contains three rows and four columns then it is called a three by four matrix and is denoted by 3×4.

Vectors: A vector is another special type of matrix in which there is only one row or one column. If it contains one column then it is called a column vector. On the other hand, if it contains only one row then it is called a row vector.

Example 3:

$$\text{Column vector: } A = \begin{bmatrix} 3 \\ 4 \\ 6 \end{bmatrix}$$

$$\text{Row vector: } B = \begin{bmatrix} 2 & 3 & 7 \end{bmatrix}$$

Vector addition: The sum of two vectors of the same type is a third vector whose elements are the sums of the corresponding elements of the given individual vectors.

Example 4:

If $A = \begin{bmatrix} 2 & 3 & 4 \end{bmatrix}$ and $B = \begin{bmatrix} 1 & 3 & 6 \end{bmatrix}$ then

$$A + B = \begin{bmatrix} (2+1) & (3+3) & (4+6) \end{bmatrix} = \begin{bmatrix} 3 & 6 & 10 \end{bmatrix}$$

Example 5:

If $$A = \begin{bmatrix} 1 \\ 2 \\ 3 \end{bmatrix} \text{ and } B = \begin{bmatrix} 3 \\ 4 \\ 5 \end{bmatrix}$$

then $$A + B = \begin{bmatrix} 1+3 \\ 2+4 \\ 3+5 \end{bmatrix} = \begin{bmatrix} 4 \\ 6 \\ 8 \end{bmatrix}$$

Scalar multiplication: If we want to multiply a vector by a scalar (like 2) we simply multiply each and every element of the vector by that scalar number.

Example 6:

If $B = \begin{bmatrix} 2 & 3 & 5 \end{bmatrix}$ then

$$2 \times B = \begin{bmatrix} 4 & 6 & 10 \end{bmatrix}$$

Multiplication of a vector by another vector: A column vector can always be multiplied by a row vector provided both of them have the same number of elements.

Example 7:

If $$A = \begin{bmatrix} 2 & 4 & 6 \end{bmatrix} \text{ and } B = \begin{bmatrix} 1 \\ 2 \\ 4 \end{bmatrix} \text{ then}$$

$$A \times B = \begin{bmatrix} (2 \times 1) + (4 \times 2) + (6 \times 4) \end{bmatrix} = \begin{bmatrix} 2 + 8 + 24 \end{bmatrix} = 34$$

Thus if we multiply a row vector by another column vector the result is a scalar.

5.2 Elementary Operations in Matrices

Addition of two matrices: The sum of two matrices of same order is a third matrix whose elements are the sums of the corresponding elements of the given matrices.

Example 8:

If $A = \begin{bmatrix} 2 & 3 \\ 4 & 5 \end{bmatrix}$ and $B = \begin{bmatrix} 1 & 3 \\ 2 & 1 \end{bmatrix}$ then

$$A + B = \begin{bmatrix} (2+1) & (3+3) \\ (4+2) & (5+1) \end{bmatrix} = \begin{bmatrix} 3 & 6 \\ 6 & 6 \end{bmatrix}$$

Here it is worth to note the following laws of addition.

- **Associative Law Addition:** When we add two matrices it does not matter in what order the two matrices are added together.
  i.e. $A + B = B + A$
- **Commutative Law Addition:** When we add three or more matrices it does not matter in which order they are grouped together for addition.
  i.e. $A + (B + C) = (A + B) + C$

Scalar multiplication of a matrix: When we want to multiply a matrix by a scalar, then each and every element of the matrix gets multiplied by that scalar.

Example 9:

If $A = \begin{bmatrix} 1 & 3 & 5 \\ 3 & 4 & 6 \\ 4 & 3 & 1 \end{bmatrix}$ then

$$4 \times A = 4 \begin{bmatrix} 1 & 3 & 5 \\ 3 & 4 & 6 \\ 4 & 3 & 1 \end{bmatrix} = \begin{bmatrix} 4 & 12 & 20 \\ 12 & 16 & 24 \\ 16 & 12 & 4 \end{bmatrix}$$

Multiplication of a matrix by another matrix: Suppose A and B are the two matrices such that the number of columns (say n) of A is equal to the number of rows of B. Now to get the multiplied matrix denoted by A × B, we multiply the corresponding elements of the first row in A with the corresponding elements of the first column in B and add them all together to get the first column first row element of the resulting matrix. In a similar way we get the first row second column element by multiplying the first row elements of A with the corresponding second column B and add them all together. Thus, in general the ij th element of A × B is obtained by multiplying and adding corresponding elements of the i th row of A with corresponding j th column elements of B.

Example 10:

If $A = \begin{bmatrix} 1 & 2 & 3 \\ 2 & 3 & 4 \end{bmatrix}$ and $B = \begin{bmatrix} 1 & 2 \\ 3 & 1 \\ 2 & 4 \end{bmatrix}$

then $A \times B = \begin{bmatrix} (1\times 1)+(2\times 3)+(3\times 2) & (1\times 2)+(2\times 1)+(3\times 4) \\ (2\times 1)+(3\times 3)+(4\times 2) & (2\times 2)+(3\times 1)+(4\times 4) \end{bmatrix}$

$$= \begin{bmatrix} 13 & 16 \\ 19 & 23 \end{bmatrix}$$

Note 1: If A is a 2 × 3 matrix and B is a 3 × 2 matrix then after multiplication the resulting matrix will be a 2 × 2 matrix as given in the above illustration.

Note 2: If A is to be multiplied with B then the essential condition for the multiplication is that the number of columns in A must be exactly equal to the number of rows in B or vice versa. Thus, wherever the number of columns in A differ from number of rows in B then A×B does not exists.

Example 11: (2 × 5) (5 × 4) = (2 × 4)

Example 12: (5 × 7) (6 × 5) = not defined

(a) Associative law of multiplication: The associative law of multiplication is no longer true for the matrix multiplication. This is to say that A × B ≠ B × A. In deed it quite possible that one of the products is defined but the other is not. Even if both of them are defined they necessarily need not be equal.

$$A \times B = \begin{bmatrix} 1 & 2 & 3 \\ 2 & 3 & 4 \end{bmatrix} \begin{bmatrix} 1 & 2 \\ 3 & 1 \\ 2 & 4 \end{bmatrix} = \begin{bmatrix} 13 & 16 \\ 19 & 23 \end{bmatrix}$$

$$B \times A = \begin{bmatrix} 1 & 2 \\ 3 & 1 \\ 2 & 4 \end{bmatrix} \times \begin{bmatrix} 1 & 2 & 3 \\ 2 & 3 & 4 \end{bmatrix} = \begin{bmatrix} 5 & 8 & 11 \\ 9 & 9 & 13 \\ 10 & 16 & 22 \end{bmatrix}$$

Clearly A × B is not equal to B × A.

(b) Commutative law of multiplication: However, the commutative law of multiplication holds good provided the related products are defined.

Example 13:

If $A = \begin{bmatrix} 2 & 5 \\ 0 & 1 \end{bmatrix}$; $B = \begin{bmatrix} 1 & 2 & 1 \\ 2 & 0 & 0 \end{bmatrix}$; $C = \begin{bmatrix} 2 & 2 \\ 0 & 1 \\ 5 & 0 \end{bmatrix}$ are the three matrices calculate A × (B × C) and (A × B) × C and show that they are equal

$$B \times C = \begin{bmatrix} 1 & 2 & 1 \\ 2 & 0 & 0 \end{bmatrix} \begin{bmatrix} 2 & 2 \\ 0 & 1 \\ 5 & 0 \end{bmatrix} = \begin{bmatrix} 7 & 4 \\ 4 & 4 \end{bmatrix}$$

$$A \times (B \times C) = \begin{bmatrix} 2 & 5 \\ 0 & 1 \end{bmatrix} \begin{bmatrix} 7 & 4 \\ 4 & 4 \end{bmatrix} = \begin{bmatrix} 34 & 28 \\ 4 & 4 \end{bmatrix}$$

$$A \times B = \begin{bmatrix} 2 & 5 \\ 0 & 1 \end{bmatrix} \begin{bmatrix} 1 & 2 & 1 \\ 2 & 0 & 0 \end{bmatrix} = \begin{bmatrix} 12 & 4 & 2 \\ 2 & 0 & 0 \end{bmatrix}$$

$$(A \times B) \times C = \begin{bmatrix} 12 & 4 & 2 \\ 2 & 0 & 0 \end{bmatrix} \begin{bmatrix} 2 & 2 \\ 0 & 1 \\ 5 & 0 \end{bmatrix} = \begin{bmatrix} 34 & 28 \\ 4 & 4 \end{bmatrix}$$

$$A \times (B \times C) = (A \times B) \times C = \begin{bmatrix} 34 & 28 \\ 4 & 4 \end{bmatrix}$$

5.3 Types of Matrices

1. **Square Matrix:** A square matrix is special matrix in which the number of columns will always be equal the number of rows.

Example 14:

$$A = \begin{bmatrix} 2 & 3 \\ 5 & 4 \end{bmatrix}$$

Example 15:

$$A = \begin{bmatrix} 1 & 2 & 3 \\ 4 & 5 & 6 \\ 7 & 8 & 9 \end{bmatrix}$$

2. **Zero Matrix:** A matrix with 'zero' elements everywhere is called the zero matrix. It will act like a 'Zero' in the addition and multiplication of ordinary arithmetic.

Example 16:

If $B = \begin{bmatrix} 0 & 0 \\ 0 & 0 \end{bmatrix}$ and $C = \begin{bmatrix} 1 & 2 \\ 3 & 4 \end{bmatrix}$

then $B + C = C$

also $B \times C = \begin{bmatrix} 0 & 0 \\ 0 & 0 \end{bmatrix}$

3. **Identity or Unit Matrix:** A unit matrix is a square matrix containing unity along the main diagonal and zero's in other places. The unit matrix will act like unity in ordinary arithmetic operations like addition and multiplication. This is to say that the multiplication by a unit matrix leaves the original matrix unaltered.

Example 17:

If $$A = \begin{bmatrix} 1 & 0 & 0 \\ 0 & 1 & 0 \\ 0 & 0 & 1 \end{bmatrix} \text{ and } B = \begin{bmatrix} 1 & 3 & 7 \\ 9 & 4 & 6 \\ 5 & 3 & 8 \end{bmatrix}$$

Hence $$A \times B = B = \begin{bmatrix} 1 & 3 & 7 \\ 9 & 4 & 6 \\ 5 & 3 & 8 \end{bmatrix}$$

4. **Diagonal Matrix:** A matrix with all elements zeros other than the main or principal diagonal is called the diagonal matrix.

Example 18:

$$A = \begin{bmatrix} 5 & 0 & 0 \\ 0 & 5 & 0 \\ 0 & 0 & 7 \end{bmatrix}$$

5. **The Transpose of a Matrix:** If we interchange the rows and columns of an m × n matrix A we get a new n × m matrix. This newly obtained matrix is called the transpose of the matrix A. It is normally denoted by A′.

Example 19:

If $$A = \begin{bmatrix} 2 & 4 & 5 \\ 3 & 4 & 7 \end{bmatrix} \text{ then } A' = \begin{bmatrix} 2 & 3 \\ 4 & 4 \\ 5 & 7 \end{bmatrix}$$

6. **Determinant of a Matrix:** If A stands for the square matrix then the associated determinant is defined and denoted by $|A|$.

Example 20:

If $$A = \begin{bmatrix} 1 & 3 & 7 \\ 4 & 5 & 8 \\ 3 & 5 & 1 \end{bmatrix} \text{ then } |A| = \begin{vmatrix} 1 & 3 & 7 \\ 4 & 5 & 8 \\ 3 & 5 & 1 \end{vmatrix}$$

Value of a (2×2) determinant:

$$|B| = \begin{vmatrix} a_{11} & a_{12} \\ a_{21} & a_{22} \end{vmatrix} = (a_{11} \times a_{22}) - (a_{21} \times a_{12})$$

Example 21:

$$|B| = \begin{vmatrix} 1 & 2 \\ 3 & 4 \end{vmatrix} = (1 \times 4) - (3 \times 2) = -2$$

Value of a (3 × 3) determinant: Rule for sign attachment: The value of 3 × 3 determinant is obtained in six possible ways. It can be through either 1st or 2nd or 3rd row or through 1st or 2nd or 3rd column. For this purpose we must attach relevant signs for each and every element in accordance with their respective placement in the given determinant.

Rule for sign attachment: Add the subscripts that refer the placement of the given number and attach a plus provided the result is even. On the other hand if the said sum is odd then attach a minus.

Example 22:

For first row and first column element namely a_{11} we attach a + sign because 1 + 1 = 2. If it is second row third column element (i.e., a_{23}) then we must attach a – sign because 2 + 3 = 5. In a similar way we attach a plus or a minus depending upon their respective positions in the given determinant as shown below.

$$|A| = \begin{vmatrix} + & - & + \\ - & + & - \\ + & - & + \end{vmatrix}$$

Expansion of a 3 × 3 determinant: The 3 × 3 matrix can be expanded in six possible ways

(a) Through first row

(b) Through second row

(c) Through third row

(d) Through first column

(e) Through second column

(f) Through third column

The following example illustrates the both the first row and the first column methods of expansion

Example 23: Find the value of $|A| = \begin{vmatrix} 1 & 3 & -2 \\ 4 & 1 & 2 \\ 2 & -3 & 0 \end{vmatrix}$

Solution:

(i) Through first row:

$$|A| = \begin{vmatrix} 1 & 3 & -2 \\ 4 & 1 & 2 \\ 2 & -3 & 0 \end{vmatrix} = 1\begin{vmatrix} 1 & 2 \\ -3 & 0 \end{vmatrix} - 3\begin{vmatrix} 4 & 2 \\ 2 & 0 \end{vmatrix} - 2\begin{vmatrix} 4 & 1 \\ 2 & -3 \end{vmatrix}$$

$$= 1[(1 \times 0) - (-3 \times 2)] - 3[(4 \times 0) - (2 \times 2)] - 2[(4 \times -3) - (2 \times 1)]$$

$$= 1[0 + 6] - 3[0 - 4] - 2[-12 - 2]$$

$$= 6 + 12 + 28 = 46$$

(ii) Through first column:

$$|A| = \begin{vmatrix} 1 & 3 & -2 \\ 4 & 1 & 2 \\ 2 & -3 & 0 \end{vmatrix} = 1\begin{vmatrix} 1 & 2 \\ -3 & 0 \end{vmatrix} - 4\begin{vmatrix} 3 & -2 \\ -3 & 0 \end{vmatrix} + 2\begin{vmatrix} 3 & -2 \\ 1 & 2 \end{vmatrix}$$

$$= 1[(1\times 0)-(-3\times 2)] - 4[(3\times 0)-(-3\times -2)] + 2[(3\times 2)-(1\times -2)]$$

$$= 1[0+6] - 4[0-6] + 2[6+2]$$

$$= 6 + 24 + 16 = 46$$

Example 24:

Find the value of $|A| = \begin{vmatrix} a_{11} & a_{12} & a_{13} \\ a_{21} & a_{22} & a_{23} \\ a_{31} & a_{32} & a_{33} \end{vmatrix}$

Solution:

$$|A| = \begin{vmatrix} a_{11} & a_{12} & a_{13} \\ a_{21} & a_{22} & a_{23} \\ a_{31} & a_{32} & a_{33} \end{vmatrix} = a_{11}\begin{vmatrix} a_{22} & a_{23} \\ a_{32} & a_{33} \end{vmatrix} - a_{12}\begin{vmatrix} a_{21} & a_{23} \\ a_{31} & a_{33} \end{vmatrix} + a_{13}\begin{vmatrix} a_{21} & a_{22} \\ a_{31} & a_{32} \end{vmatrix}$$

$$= a_{11}(a_{22}a_{33} - a_{32}a_{23}) - a_{12}(a_{21}a_{33} - a_{31}a_{23}) + a_{13}(a_{21}a_{32} - a_{31}a_{22})$$

Excel Worksheet Method

To get the answer for a 3×3 determinant type the formula as shown below in cell F3

	A	B	C	D	E	F
1						
2		1	3	-2		
3		4	1	2		=B2*((C3*D4)-(C4*D3))-C2*((B3*D4)-(B4*D3))+D2*((B3*C4)-(B4*C3))
4		2	-3	0		
5						

The resulting result is displayed in the following table

	A	B	C	D	E	F
1						
2		1	3	-2		
3		4	1	2	=	46
4		2	-3	0		
5						

7. **Singular and Non-Singular Matrices:** The square matrix A is said to be a singular matrix provided its associated determinant is $|A| = 0$. On the other hand if $|A|$ is not equal to zero then the associated matrix is called non-singular.

Example 25:

If $$A = \begin{bmatrix} 2 & 4 \\ 1 & 2 \end{bmatrix} \text{ then } |A| = 4 - 4 = 0$$

So the matrix A is singular.

Example 26:

If $$A = \begin{bmatrix} 2 & 4 \\ 1 & 3 \end{bmatrix} \text{ then } |A| = 6 - 4 = 2 \neq 0$$

So the matrix A is non-singular.

8. **Co-factors:** The co-factor of an element is nothing but the sign attached left out elements of the given matrix after deleting the row and the column in which the said element occurs.

If $$A = \begin{bmatrix} a_{11} & a_{12} & a_{13} \\ a_{21} & a_{22} & a_{23} \\ a_{31} & a_{32} & a_{33} \end{bmatrix}$$

then the co-factors of the element a_{11}, a_{12} and a_{13} are

$$A_{11} = \begin{bmatrix} a_{22} & a_{23} \\ a_{32} & a_{33} \end{bmatrix} \; ; A_{12} = -\begin{bmatrix} a_{21} & a_{23} \\ a_{31} & a_{33} \end{bmatrix} \; ; A_{13} = \begin{bmatrix} a_{21} & a_{22} \\ a_{31} & a_{32} \end{bmatrix}$$

Co-factor Matrix

$$\text{Co-factor matrix of } A = \begin{bmatrix} A_{11} & A_{12} & A_{13} \\ A_{21} & A_{22} & A_{23} \\ A_{31} & A_{32} & A_{33} \end{bmatrix}$$

9. **Adjoint Matrix:** The Adjoint matrix of A is obtained by replacing the elements of A by its respective co-factors and then transposing it.

If $$A = \begin{bmatrix} a_{11} & a_{12} & a_{13} \\ a_{21} & a_{22} & a_{23} \\ a_{31} & a_{32} & a_{33} \end{bmatrix}$$

then its adj $$= \begin{bmatrix} A_{11} & A_{21} & A_{31} \\ A_{12} & A_{22} & A_{32} \\ A_{13} & A_{23} & A_{33} \end{bmatrix}$$

10. **Inverse of a Square Matrix:** In ordinary algebra it is a known fact that $a^{-1} \times a = (1/a)\, a = 1$. Here $(1/a) = a^{-1}$ is called the inverse of a. Multiplication of a number by its inverse thus always equals to unity.

Example 27:

$$(1/4) \times 4 = 1$$

In a similar way if A is a square matrix there must be a matrix called

A^{-1} so that $A^{-1} A = I$. Here the matrix A^{-1} is called inverse of A.

Method of Getting the Inverse Matrix: Though there are several methods of getting inverse matrix, in this section we shall get it using the Adjoint matrix discussed in the previous section. According to this method

$$A^{-1} = \frac{\text{adj} A}{|A|}$$

Example 28:

If $$A = \begin{bmatrix} 2 & 3 & 4 \\ 4 & 3 & 1 \\ 1 & 2 & 4 \end{bmatrix} \text{ calculate } A^{-1}.$$

Solution:

Calculation of the co-factor matrix:

$$\text{The co-factor matrix of } A = \begin{bmatrix} A_{11} & A_{12} & A_{13} \\ A_{21} & A_{22} & A_{23} \\ A_{31} & A_{32} & A_{33} \end{bmatrix}$$

$$= \begin{bmatrix} +\begin{vmatrix} 3 & 1 \\ 2 & 4 \end{vmatrix} & -\begin{vmatrix} 4 & 1 \\ 1 & 4 \end{vmatrix} & +\begin{vmatrix} 4 & 3 \\ 1 & 2 \end{vmatrix} \\ -\begin{vmatrix} 3 & 4 \\ 2 & 4 \end{vmatrix} & +\begin{vmatrix} 2 & 4 \\ 1 & 4 \end{vmatrix} & -\begin{vmatrix} 2 & 3 \\ 1 & 2 \end{vmatrix} \\ +\begin{vmatrix} 3 & 4 \\ 3 & 1 \end{vmatrix} & -\begin{vmatrix} 2 & 4 \\ 4 & 1 \end{vmatrix} & +\begin{vmatrix} 2 & 3 \\ 4 & 3 \end{vmatrix} \end{bmatrix} = \begin{bmatrix} 10 & -15 & 5 \\ -4 & 4 & -1 \\ -9 & 14 & -6 \end{bmatrix}$$

Now let us take transpose of this co-factor matrix to get the adj A.

i.e. $$\text{adj } A = \begin{bmatrix} 10 & -4 & -9 \\ -15 & 4 & 14 \\ 5 & -1 & -6 \end{bmatrix}$$

Now $|A| = 2\,(10) - 3\,(15) + 4\,(5)$
$= 20 - 45 + 20$
$= -5$

So $A^{-1} = (\text{adj } A) / |A| = \text{adj } A / -5$

$$= -\frac{1}{5}\begin{bmatrix} 10 & -4 & -9 \\ -15 & 4 & 14 \\ 5 & -1 & -6 \end{bmatrix} = \begin{bmatrix} -2 & 0.8 & 1.8 \\ 3 & -0.8 & -2.8 \\ -1 & 0.2 & 1.2 \end{bmatrix}$$

Verification:

$$AA^{-1} = \begin{vmatrix} 2 & 3 & 4 \\ 4 & 3 & 1 \\ 1 & 2 & 4 \end{vmatrix} \times \begin{vmatrix} -2 & 0.8 & 1.8 \\ 3 & -0.8 & -2.8 \\ -1 & +0.2 & 1.2 \end{vmatrix}$$

$$= \begin{vmatrix} -4+9-4 & 1.6-2.4+.8 & 3.6-8.4+4.8 \\ -8+9-1 & 3.2-2.4+0.2 & 7.2-8.4+1.2 \\ -2+6-4 & 0.8-1.6+0.8 & 1.8-5.6+4.8 \end{vmatrix}$$

$$= \begin{vmatrix} 1 & 0 & 0 \\ 0 & 1 & 0 \\ 0 & 0 & 1 \end{vmatrix}$$

Calculation of A^{-1} using Excel Worksheet

Type the following formulas as shown in the table in the respective cells

	A	B	C	D	E	F	G	H
1								
2			[	2	3	4	]	
3		A =		4	3	1		
4				1	2	4		
5								
6								
7	Cofactor of A =		[	=(E3*F4)-(E4*F3)	=-1*((D3*F4)-(D4*F3))	=(D3*E4)-(D4*E3)	]	
8				=-1*((E2*F4)-(E4*F2))	=(D2*F4)-(D4*F2)	=-1*((D2*E4)-(D4*E2))		
9				=(E2*F3)-(E3*F2)	=-1*((D2*F3)-(D3*F2))	=(D2*E3)-(D3*E2)		
10								
11								
12		adj of A =	[	=D7	=D8	=D9	]	
13				=E7	=E8	=E9		
14				=F7	=F8	=F9		
15								
16		Determinant A =			=D2*D7+E2*E7+F2*F7			
17								
18			[	=D12/$E$16	=E12/$E$16	=F12/$E$16	]	
19		A^{-1}=		=D13/$E$16	=E13/$E$16	=F13/$E$16		
20				=D14/$E$16	=E14/$E$16	=F14/$E$16		
21								

The resulting result display is shown in the following table.

$$A = \begin{bmatrix} 2 & 3 & 4 \\ 4 & 3 & 1 \\ 1 & 2 & 4 \end{bmatrix}$$

$$\text{Co-factor of } A = \begin{bmatrix} 10 & -15 & 5 \\ -4 & 4 & -1 \\ -9 & 14 & -6 \end{bmatrix}$$

$$\text{adj of } A = \begin{bmatrix} 10 & -4 & -9 \\ -15 & 4 & 14 \\ 5 & -1 & -6 \end{bmatrix}$$

$$\text{Determinant } A = -5$$

$$A^{-1} = \begin{bmatrix} -2 & 0.8 & 1.8 \\ 3 & -0.8 & -2.8 \\ -1 & 0.2 & 1.2 \end{bmatrix}$$

5.4 Linear Equations in Matrix Form

In the simultaneous equation system given, if the number of independent equations is equal to number of unknowns then we can always represent the system in matrix form. For example, consider the following two equations and two unknowns system.

$$a_{11}x_1 + a_{12}x_2 = c_1$$

$$a_{21}x_1 + a_{22}x_2 = c_2$$

In matrix notation this system can be rewritten as

$$\begin{bmatrix} a_{11} & a_{12} \\ a_{21} & a_{22} \end{bmatrix} \times \begin{bmatrix} x_1 \\ x_2 \end{bmatrix} = \begin{bmatrix} c_1 \\ c_2 \end{bmatrix}$$

i.e. $AX = C$

In more general form, a system of 'm' equations in 'n' unknowns $x_1, x_2, \ldots, x_n$ is normally written as

$$a_{11}x_1 + a_{12}x_2 + \ldots\ldots\ldots + a_{1n}x_n = b_1$$

$$a_{21}x_1 + a_{22}x_2 + \ldots\ldots\ldots + a_{2n}x_n = b_2$$

$$\ldots\ldots\ldots\ldots\ldots\ldots\ldots\ldots$$

$$\ldots\ldots\ldots\ldots\ldots\ldots\ldots\ldots$$

$$a_{m1}x_1 + a_{m2}x_2 + \ldots\ldots\ldots + a_{mn}x_n = b_m$$

In order to make such a system compact, we often use the following matrix form.

$$\begin{pmatrix} a_{11} & a_{12} & \cdots\cdots & a_{1n} \\ a_{21} & a_{22} & \cdots\cdots & a_{2n} \\ \cdot & \cdot & \cdots\cdots & \cdot \\ a_{m1} & a_{m2} & \cdots\cdots & a_{mn} \end{pmatrix} \begin{pmatrix} x_1 \\ x_2 \\ \cdot \\ x_n \end{pmatrix} = \begin{pmatrix} b_1 \\ b_2 \\ \cdot \\ b_m \end{pmatrix}$$

$$AX = C$$

Solution of linear equations: A solution is nothing but the typical values of x_1, x_2 ,……, x_n that satisfy all the given m equations. Such a solution does not change by the following three operations.

- Multiply both the sides of an equation by a non-zero constant.
- Add a multiple of one equation to another.
- Interchange two equations.

The idea behind this technique is to reduce the given system to a simple one for which the solution is almost obvious.

5.5 Gaussian Elimination Method

In this method the variables are eliminated in a systematic manner to arrive at a final solution by backward substitution. In the name of the German mathematician Carl Friedrich Gauss this method is popularly known as Gaussian elimination method. The following example illustrates this method.

Example 29: Consider the following system of three equations in three unknowns

$$x_1 + x_2 + x_3 = 6 \quad \text{...(1)}$$

$$2x_1 + 4x_2 + x_3 = 5 \quad \text{...(2)}$$

$$2x_1 + 3x_2 + x_3 = 6 \quad \text{...(3)}$$

Step 1: Now as a first step let us eliminate x_1 in equation (2) by simply subtracting two times of (1) from (2).

$$(2x_1 + 4x_2 + x_3) - (2x_1 + 2x_2 + 2x_3) = 5 - 12$$

$$2x_2 - x_3 = -7$$

$$x_2 - 0.5x_3 = -3.5 \quad \text{...(2')}$$

Now let us replace (2) by (2') and rewrite the system as

$$x_1 + x_2 + x_3 = 6 \quad \text{...(1)}$$

$$x_2 - 0.5x_3 = -3.5 \quad \text{...(2')}$$

$$2x_1 + 3x_2 + x_3 = 6 \quad \text{...(3)}$$

Remember, since this system is obtained from the original system the solution to the new system will be the same as that of the original.

Step 2: Now as a second step let us eliminate x_1 in equation (3) by simply subtracting two times of (1) from (3).

$$(2x_1 + 3x_2 + x_3) - (2x_1 + 2x_2 + 2x_3) = 6 - 12$$

$$x_2 - x_3 = -6 \quad \text{...(3')}$$

Now let us replace (3) by (3') and rewrite system as

$$x_1 + x_2 + x_3 = 6 \quad \text{...(1)}$$

$$x_2 - 0.5x_3 = -3.5 \quad \text{...(2')}$$

$$x_2 - x_3 = -6 \quad \text{...(3')}$$

Step 3: Now to eliminate x_2 in (3') subtract (2') from (3')

$$(x_2 - x_3) - (x_2 - 0.5x_3) = -6 + 3.5 = -2.5$$

$$-0.5x_3 = -2.5 \quad \text{... (3'')}$$

$$x_3 = 5$$

Now let us replace (3') by (3") and rewrite the system as

$$x_1 + x_2 + x_3 = 6 \quad \text{... (1)}$$

$$x_2 - 0.5x_3 = -3.5 \quad \text{...(2')}$$

$$x_3 = 5 \quad \text{...(3'')}$$

This reduced system is so simple in the sense that the solutions for all the three variables are obtained by backward substitution starting from (3")

By substituting $x_3 = 5$ in (2') it yields

$$x_2 - 0.5x_3 = -3.5$$

$$x_2 - 0.5(5) = -3.5$$

$$x_2 = -1$$

Now substitute $x_3 = 5$ and $x_2 = -1$ in (1) it yields

$$x_1 + (-1) + (5) = 6$$

$$x_1 = 2$$

So the final solutions are $x_1 = 2$, $x_2 = -1$, $x_3 = 5$

Note: The matrix form of the last step in the previous form:

$$\begin{bmatrix} 1 & 1 & 1 \\ 0 & 1 & -0.5 \\ 0 & 0 & 1 \end{bmatrix} \begin{bmatrix} x_1 \\ x_2 \\ x_3 \end{bmatrix} = \begin{bmatrix} 6 \\ -3.5 \\ 5 \end{bmatrix}$$

Thus, in the final step all the elements below the diagonal are reduced to zero.

5.6 Augmented Matrix Method

In this method we carry out the above said row operations in a compact form only with coefficients. Let us write our problem in matrix form as follows:

If Ax = b is our system, where

$$A = \begin{pmatrix} 1 & 1 & 1 \\ 2 & 4 & 1 \\ 2 & 3 & 1 \end{pmatrix} \quad ; \quad b = \begin{pmatrix} 6 \\ 5 \\ 6 \end{pmatrix}$$

then, $$A = \left\langle \begin{array}{ccc|c} 1 & 1 & 1 & 6 \\ 2 & 4 & 1 & 5 \\ 2 & 3 & 1 & 6 \end{array} \right\rangle$$ is called the augmented matrix of the system under reference.

Now we make all the elements of the left side matrix below the diagonal to zero by appropriate row operations.

$$= \left\langle \begin{array}{ccc|c} 1 & 1 & 1 & 6 \\ 2 & 4 & 1 & 5 \\ 2 & 3 & 1 & 6 \end{array} \right\rangle$$

Step 1: Now as a first step let us make the second row first column element in left side matrix to zero {eliminate x_1 in equation (2)} by simply subtracting two times of row 1 from row two.

$$= \left\langle \begin{array}{ccc|c} 1 & 1 & 1 & 6 \\ 0 & 2 & -1 & -7 \\ 2 & 3 & 1 & 6 \end{array} \right\rangle$$

Step 2: Now as a second step let us make the third row first column element to zero {eliminate x_1 in equation (3)} by simply subtracting two times of row one from row 3

$$= \left\langle \begin{array}{ccc|c} 1 & 1 & 1 & 6 \\ 0 & 1 & -0.5 & -3.5 \\ 0 & 1 & -1 & -6 \end{array} \right\rangle$$

Step 3: Now to make the third row second column element to zero, we subtracts row two from row three {eliminate x_2 in (3')}

$$= \left\langle \begin{array}{ccc|c} 1 & 1 & 1 & 6 \\ 0 & 1 & -0.5 & -3.5 \\ 0 & 0 & -0.5 & -2.5 \end{array} \right\rangle$$

Step 4: To make the third row third column element unity multiply the third row by – 0.5

$$\left(\begin{array}{ccc|c} 1 & 1 & 1 & 6 \\ 0 & -1 & -0.5 & -3.5 \\ 0 & 0 & 1 & 5 \end{array}\right)$$

The final step in the augmented matrix represents the given system in a special modified form amenable for simple backward substitution.

$$x_1 + x_2 + x_3 = 6 \qquad ...(1)$$

$$x_2 - 0.5x_3 = -3.5 \qquad ...(2')$$

$$x_3 = 5 \qquad ...(3'')$$

So the final solutions are $x_1 = 2$, $x_2 = -1$, $x_3 = 5$

5.7 The Echelon Form

The last stage of the augmented matrix is often called echelon form of the given problem.

$$\left(\begin{array}{cccccc|c} 1 & * & * & * & * & * & * \\ 0 & 1 & * & * & * & * & * \\ 0 & 0 & 1 & * & * & * & * \\ . & . & . & . & . & . & . \\ . & . & . & . & . & . & . \\ 0 & 0 & 0 & 0 & 0 & 0 & 0 \end{array}\right)$$

In this general form we have the following important characteristics

- The first non-zero entry in each row is 1.
- The position of the leading 1 move to the right as we move down and down the row.
- Any rows, which contain entirely zeros, are pushed to the bottom of the matrix.

However, in this chapter we concentrate only on the special case of the echelon form

$$\left(\begin{array}{cccccc|c} 1 & * & * & * & * & * & * \\ 0 & 1 & * & * & * & * & * \\ 0 & 0 & 1 & * & * & * & * \\ . & . & . & . & . & . & . \\ . & . & . & . & . & . & . \\ 0 & 0 & 0 & 0 & 0 & 1 & * \end{array}\right)$$

In this special form no row contains all zeros. Further the leading 1 move one step to the right as we go down the rows as shown above.

Example 30: Suppose that we have the following system of linear equations in three equations with three unknowns. Obtain the echelon form and get its solution.

$$x_1 + 2x_2 + x_3 = 1 \quad ...(1)$$
$$2x_1 + 2x_2 + 0x_3 = 2 \quad ...(2)$$
$$3x_1 + 5x_2 + 4x_3 = 1 \quad ...(3)$$

Solution:

$$\left\langle \begin{array}{ccc|c} 1 & 2 & 1 & 1 \\ 2 & 2 & 0 & 2 \\ 3 & 5 & 4 & 1 \end{array} \right\rangle \rightarrow \left\langle \begin{array}{ccc|c} 1 & 2 & 1 & 2 \\ 0 & -2 & -2 & 0 \\ 0 & -1 & 1 & -2 \end{array} \right\rangle$$

$$\rightarrow \left\langle \begin{array}{ccc|c} 1 & 2 & 1 & 1 \\ 0 & 1 & 1 & 0 \\ 1 & -1 & 1 & -2 \end{array} \right\rangle \rightarrow \left\langle \begin{array}{ccc|c} 1 & 2 & 1 & 1 \\ 0 & 1 & 1 & 0 \\ 0 & 0 & 2 & -2 \end{array} \right\rangle$$

$$\rightarrow \left\langle \begin{array}{ccc|c} 1 & 2 & 1 & 1 \\ 0 & 1 & 1 & 0 \\ 0 & 0 & 1 & -1 \end{array} \right\rangle$$

Therefore the following system will have the solutions equivalent to that of initial system given.

$$x_1 + 2x_2 + x_3 = 1 \quad ...(1)$$
$$x_2 + x_3 = 0 \quad ...(2)$$
$$x_3 = -1 \quad ...(3)$$

By backward substitution the solutions are $x_1 = 0$, $x_2 = 1$, and $x_3 = -1$

Example 31: The supply function of a commodity in its general form is given by

$S(p) = ap^2 + bp + c$, where a, b, c are constants. When $p = 1$ the quantity supplied is 5; when $p = 2$, the quantity supplied is 12; when $p = 3$, the quantity supplied is 23. Obtain the supply function.

Solution:

By substituting the data in given supply equation we get

$$a(1)^2 + b(1) + c = 5$$
$$a(2)^2 + b(2) + c = 12$$
$$a(3)^2 + b(3) + c = 23$$

So we have the following system of linear equations.

$$a + b + c = 5$$
$$4a + 2b + c = 12$$
$$9a + 3b + c = 23$$

$$\begin{pmatrix} 1 & 1 & 1 & 5 \\ 4 & 2 & 1 & 12 \\ 9 & 3 & 1 & 23 \end{pmatrix} \rightarrow \begin{pmatrix} 1 & 1 & 1 & 5 \\ 0 & -2 & -3 & -8 \\ 0 & -6 & -8 & -22 \end{pmatrix}$$

$$\rightarrow \begin{pmatrix} 1 & 1 & 1 & 5 \\ 0 & -2 & -3 & -8 \\ 0 & 0 & -1 & -2 \end{pmatrix} \rightarrow \begin{pmatrix} 1 & 1 & 1 & 5 \\ 0 & 1 & 1.5 & 4 \\ 0 & 0 & 1 & 2 \end{pmatrix}$$

$$a + b + c = 5$$
$$b + 1.5c = 4$$
$$c = 2$$

By backward substitution a = 2, b = 1, c = 2. So the supply equation is obtained as

$$S(p) = 2p^2 + 1p + 2$$

5.8 Consistent and Inconsistent Linear Systems

In all our illustrations till now we had only one solution. This is due the special form of the echelon result obtained by augmented matrix method. But interestingly, one can have a system with no solution at all. Similarly, we can have systems with infinite number of solutions as well. The echelon form of the system explains all the three possibilities.

- Unique solution.
- No solution.
- Infinite solution.

Example 32: Consider the following system:

$$x_1 + 2x_2 + x_3 = 1 \quad \text{...(1)}$$
$$2x_1 + 2x_2 + 0x_3 = 2 \quad \text{...(2)}$$
$$3x_1 + 4x_2 + x_3 = 3 \quad \text{...(3)}$$

Solution:
As usual let us get the echelon form first by appropriate row operation.

$$\begin{pmatrix} 1 & 2 & 1 & 1 \\ 2 & 2 & 0 & 2 \\ 3 & 4 & 1 & 3 \end{pmatrix} \rightarrow \begin{pmatrix} 1 & 2 & 1 & 1 \\ 0 & -2 & -2 & 0 \\ 0 & -2 & -2 & 0 \end{pmatrix}$$

$$\rightarrow \begin{pmatrix} 1 & 2 & 1 & 1 \\ 0 & 1 & 1 & 0 \\ 0 & -2 & -2 & 0 \end{pmatrix} \rightarrow \begin{pmatrix} 1 & 2 & 1 & 1 \\ 0 & 1 & 1 & 0 \\ 0 & 0 & 2 & -2 \end{pmatrix}$$

$$\rightarrow \begin{pmatrix} 1 & 2 & 1 & 1 \\ 0 & 1 & 1 & 0 \\ 0 & 0 & 0 & 0 \end{pmatrix}$$

So the final matrix yields the new system equivalent to the old one.

$$x_1 + 2x_2 + x_3 = 1 \quad ...(1)$$
$$x_2 + x_3 = 0 \quad ...(2')$$
$$0x_1 + 0x_2 + 0x_3 = 0 \quad ...(3')$$

Among the three equations the third one convey no additional information at all. It simply says $0 = 0$. So after leaving this useless equation we have only two useful equations.

$$x_1 + 2x_2 + x_3 = 1 \quad ...(1)$$
$$x_2 + x_3 = 0 \quad ...(2')$$

From (2') $x_2 = -x_3$. Substituting this in (1) it becomes

$x_1 = 1 - 2x_2 - x_3 = 1 - 2(-x_3) - x_3 = 1 + x_3$. So both x_1 and x_2 are determined by x_3. If $x_3 = k$, any real number then

$x_1 = 1 + k$, $x_2 = -k$, $x_3 = k$. is a solution to this system. So depending upon the value of k we have infinite number of solution to this system.

Example 33: Consider the following system:

$$x_1 + 2x_2 + x_3 = 1 \quad ...(1)$$
$$2x_1 + 2x_2 + 0x_3 = 2 \quad ...(2)$$
$$3x_1 + 4x_2 + x_3 = 2 \quad ...(3)$$

Solution:

As usual let us get the echelon form first by appropriate row operation.

$$\left\langle\begin{array}{ccc|c} 1 & 2 & 1 & 1 \\ 2 & 2 & 0 & 2 \\ 3 & 4 & 1 & 2 \end{array}\right\rangle \rightarrow \left\langle\begin{array}{ccc|c} 1 & 2 & 1 & 1 \\ 0 & -2 & -2 & 0 \\ 0 & -2 & -2 & -1 \end{array}\right\rangle$$

$$\rightarrow \left\langle\begin{array}{ccc|c} 1 & 2 & 1 & 1 \\ 0 & 1 & 1 & 0 \\ 0 & -2 & -2 & -1 \end{array}\right\rangle \rightarrow \left\langle\begin{array}{ccc|c} 1 & 2 & 1 & 1 \\ 0 & 1 & 1 & 0 \\ 0 & 0 & 0 & -1 \end{array}\right\rangle$$

Thus, our original system is equivalent to

$$1x_1 + 2x_2 + x_3 = 1 \quad ...(1)$$
$$1x_2 + 1x_3 = 2 \quad ...(2')$$
$$0x_1 + 0x_2 + 0x_3 = -1 \quad ...(3')$$

This system has no solution since no values of x_1, x_2, x_3 satisfy the last equation. It simply tell us a wrong statement $0 = -1$. Thus the presence of a row of the type (0 0 0....../a) in its echelon form indicates the non-existence of a solution. Thus, clearly the absence of (0 0 0....../a) or (0 0 0......./0) type of rows indicate the presence of a unique solution to the system under reference.

5.9 The Rank of the System

The rank of the given system is nothing but the number of non-zero rows in the corresponding echelon form. Suppose the rank r is less than the number of unknowns' n then the system in echelon form, and hence the original system, does not provide enough information to specify the values of these n given variables.

Example 34: Suppose the echelon form of a given equation is

$$\left(\begin{array}{cccccc|c} 1 & 3 & -2 & 0 & 2 & 0 & 0 \\ 0 & 0 & 1 & 2 & 0 & 3 & 1 \\ 0 & 0` & 0 & 0 & 0 & 1 & 5 \\ 0 & 0 & 0 & 0 & 0 & 0 & 0 \end{array}\right)$$

Clearly, the rank r = 3 (equivalent to the non-zero rows) in this system. This is less than the number of unknowns namely 6 in this case. The corresponding system is

$$x_1 + 3x_2 - 2x_3 + 2x_5 = 0$$
$$x_3 + 2x_4 + 3x_6 = 1$$
$$x_6 = 5$$

These equations are rearranged as.

$$x_1 = -3x_2 + 2x_3 - 2x_5$$
$$x_3 = 1 - 2x_4 - 3x_6$$
$$x_6 = 5$$

Now by backward substitution

$$x_6 = 5$$
$$x_3 = -14 - 2x_4$$
$$x_1 = -28 - 3x_2 - 4x_4 - 2x_5$$

Now if $x_2 = s$, $x_4 = t$, and $x_5 = u$ then the solutions are

$$x_1 = -28 - 3s - 4t - 2u$$
$$x_2 = s$$
$$x_3 = -14 - 2t$$
$$x_4 = t$$
$$x_5 = u$$
$$x_6 = 5$$

Clearly, for specific values of s, t, u we get infinite number of solutions.

5.10 Unit Matrix Method

In this method by using row operations we reduce the given augmented matrix even beyond echelon form till we get unit matrix in which the leading 1's alone will be there along the diagonal. The advantage of this method lies in it straightforward solution yielding capability without any backward substitution as in the case of echelon method. The following example illustrates the procedure.

Example 35: Solve the following system for x_1 and x_2:

$$9x_1 + 2x_2 = 42$$

$$2x_1 + 3x_2 = 17$$

For this method the augmented matrix may be written as

$$\left[\begin{array}{cc|c} 9 & 2 & 42 \\ 2 & 3 & 17 \end{array}\right]$$

Now our purpose is to make the left side partitioned matrix as a unitary matrix by appropriate row operations.

Step 1: To make the first row first column element unity, let us divide the first row throughout by 9.

$$\left[\begin{array}{cc|c} 1 & 2/9 & 42/9 \\ 2 & 3 & 17 \end{array}\right]$$

Step 2: Now to make the second row first column element zero, subtract twice row 1 from row 2.

$$\left[\begin{array}{cc|c} 1 & 2/9 & 42/9 \\ 0 & 23/9 & 69/9 \end{array}\right]$$

Step 3: Now to make second row second column element unity, multiplies the second row throughout by 9/23.

$$\left[\begin{array}{cc|c} 1 & 2/9 & 42/9 \\ 0 & 1 & 3 \end{array}\right]$$

Step 4: Now to make the first row second column element zero, subtract 2/9 times of row 2 from row 1.

$$\left[\begin{array}{cc|c} 1 & 0 & 4 \\ 0 & 1 & 3 \end{array}\right]$$

We now have the solutions for the set of equations i.e., $x_1 = 4$ and $x_2 = 3$.

5.11 The Square Linear System and Inverse Matrix Solution

In this section we consider only the square linear system with exactly the number of equations equal to the number of unknowns (n = m). In such cases we will always have a unique solution set. Since the number of column equal to number of unknowns we can represent the system in its matrix form as follows:

Let AX = C stands for the system in matrix form. Now let us pre multiply the above equation by A^{-1}

i.e., $A^{-1}AX = A^{-1}C$

i.e., $X = A^{-1}C$

Thus to solve this type of simultaneous system we must find A^{-1} first and then calculate $A^{-1}C$.

Example 36: Solve the following simultaneous system using matrices:

$$2x_1 + 3x_2 = 9$$

$$3x_1 + 5x_2 = 12$$

In matrix notation the above system may be written as

i.e. AX = C

i.e., $\begin{bmatrix} 2 & 3 \\ 3 & 5 \end{bmatrix} \times \begin{bmatrix} x_1 \\ x_2 \end{bmatrix} = \begin{bmatrix} 9 \\ 12 \end{bmatrix}$

Now to solve this system we must get A^{-1} first.

Calculation of the co-factor matrix:

The co-factor matrix of $A = \begin{bmatrix} A_{11} & A_{12} \\ A_{21} & A_{22} \end{bmatrix} = \begin{bmatrix} 5 & -3 \\ -3 & 2 \end{bmatrix}$

Now by definition adj A = Transpose of the co-factor matrix

$$\text{adj } A = \begin{bmatrix} 5 & -3 \\ -3 & 2 \end{bmatrix}$$

By definition $A^{-1} = \text{adj } A/|A|$

$$= \frac{\begin{bmatrix} 5 & -3 \\ -3 & 2 \end{bmatrix}}{10-9} = \begin{bmatrix} 5 & -3 \\ -3 & 2 \end{bmatrix}$$

Since $X = A^{-1}C$,

$$= \begin{bmatrix} 5 & -3 \\ -3 & 2 \end{bmatrix} \times \begin{bmatrix} 9 \\ 12 \end{bmatrix}$$

$$= \begin{bmatrix} (5 \times 9) + (-3 \times 12) \\ (-3 \times 9) + (2 \times 12) \end{bmatrix} = \begin{bmatrix} 9 \\ -3 \end{bmatrix}$$

$$x_1 = 9 \text{ and } x_2 = -3$$

Excel Solution:

$$A = \begin{bmatrix} 2 & 3 \\ 3 & 5 \end{bmatrix}$$

$$C = \begin{bmatrix} 9 \\ 12 \end{bmatrix}$$

$$\text{Co-factor of } A = \begin{bmatrix} 5 & -3 \\ -3 & 2 \end{bmatrix}$$

$$\text{adj of } A = \begin{bmatrix} 5 & -3 \\ -3 & 2 \end{bmatrix}$$

$$\text{Determinant } A = 1$$

$$A^{-1} = \begin{bmatrix} 5 & -3 \\ -3 & 2 \end{bmatrix}$$

$$\begin{bmatrix} X_1 \\ X_2 \end{bmatrix} = \begin{bmatrix} 5 & -3 \\ -3 & 2 \end{bmatrix} \times \begin{bmatrix} 9 \\ 12 \end{bmatrix} = \begin{bmatrix} 9 \\ -3 \end{bmatrix}$$

Example 37:

Demand and supply functions of a certain product are D = 25 – 2p; S = – 5 + 3p. Find the equilibrium price and quantity.

Solution:

The demand and the supply may be rewritten as

$$D + 2p = 25$$
$$S - 3p = -5$$

Under equilibrium we know that D = S

$$D + 2p = 25$$
$$D - 3p = -5$$

In matrix notation the above system may be written as
i.e. Ax = C

i.e.,
$$\begin{bmatrix} 1 & 2 \\ 1 & -3 \end{bmatrix} \times \begin{bmatrix} D \\ p \end{bmatrix} = \begin{bmatrix} 25 \\ -5 \end{bmatrix}$$

Co-factor of
$$A = \begin{bmatrix} -3 & -1 \\ -2 & 1 \end{bmatrix}$$

$$\text{Adj of } A = \begin{bmatrix} -3 & -2 \\ -1 & 1 \end{bmatrix}$$

Determinant A = (1) × (– 3) – (1) × (2) = – 5

$$A^{-1} = \frac{\text{adj}A}{|A|} = \frac{\begin{bmatrix} -3 & -2 \\ -1 & 1 \end{bmatrix}}{-5} = \begin{bmatrix} 0.6 & 0.4 \\ 0.2 & -0.2 \end{bmatrix}$$

Since $X = A^{-1} C$,

$$\begin{bmatrix} D \\ p \end{bmatrix} = \begin{bmatrix} 0.6 & 0.4 \\ 0.2 & -0.2 \end{bmatrix} \times \begin{bmatrix} 25 \\ -5 \end{bmatrix}$$

$$\begin{bmatrix} D \\ p \end{bmatrix} = \begin{bmatrix} (0.6 \times 25) + (0.4 \times -5) \\ (0.2 \times 25) + (-0.2 \times -5) \end{bmatrix} = \begin{bmatrix} 13 \\ 6 \end{bmatrix}$$

S = D = 13, P = 6 under equilibrium

Excel Solution:

$$A = \begin{bmatrix} 1 & 2 \\ 1 & -3 \end{bmatrix}$$

$$C = \begin{bmatrix} 25 \\ -5 \end{bmatrix}$$

$$\text{Cofactor of } A = \begin{bmatrix} -3 & -1 \\ -2 & 1 \end{bmatrix}$$

$$\text{adj of } A = \begin{bmatrix} -3 & -2 \\ -1 & 1 \end{bmatrix}$$

Determinant A = -5

$$A^{-1} = \begin{bmatrix} 0.6 & 0.4 \\ 0.2 & -0.2 \end{bmatrix}$$

$$\begin{bmatrix} X_1 \\ X_2 \end{bmatrix} = \begin{bmatrix} 0.6 & 0.4 \\ 0.2 & -0.2 \end{bmatrix} x \begin{bmatrix} 25 \\ -5 \end{bmatrix} = \begin{bmatrix} 13 \\ 6 \end{bmatrix}$$

Example 38: Solve the system

$$2x_1 - 4x_2 + 3x_3 = 3$$

$$4x_1 - 6x_2 + 5x_3 = 2$$

$$-2x_1 + x_2 - x_3 = 1$$

In matrix notation this system is written as

$$\begin{bmatrix} 2 & -4 & 3 \\ 4 & -6 & 5 \\ -2 & 1 & -1 \end{bmatrix} \times \begin{bmatrix} x_1 \\ x_2 \\ x_3 \end{bmatrix} = \begin{bmatrix} 3 \\ 2 \\ 1 \end{bmatrix}$$

i.e., $AX = C$

$$A^{-1} A X = A^{-1} C$$

i.e., $X = A^{-1} C$

Here $$A^{-1} = \begin{bmatrix} 0.5 & -0.5 & -1 \\ -3 & 2 & 1 \\ -4 & 3 & 2 \end{bmatrix}$$

So $$X = \begin{bmatrix} 0.5 & -0.5 & -1 \\ -3 & 2 & 1 \\ -4 & 3 & 2 \end{bmatrix} \times \begin{bmatrix} 3 \\ 2 \\ 1 \end{bmatrix}$$

$$\begin{bmatrix} x_1 \\ x_2 \\ x_3 \end{bmatrix} = \begin{bmatrix} -0.5 \\ -4 \\ -4 \end{bmatrix}$$

i.e., $x_1 = -0.5$ $x_2 = -4$ $x_3 = -4$

Excel Solution:

$$A = \begin{bmatrix} 2 & -4 & 3 \\ 4 & -6 & 5 \\ -2 & 1 & -1 \end{bmatrix}$$

$$C = \begin{bmatrix} 3 \\ 2 \\ 1 \end{bmatrix}$$

$$\text{Cofactor of } A = \begin{bmatrix} 1 & -6 & -8 \\ -1 & 4 & 6 \\ -2 & 2 & 4 \end{bmatrix}$$

$$\text{adj of } A = \begin{bmatrix} 1 & -1 & -2 \\ -6 & 4 & 2 \\ -8 & 6 & 4 \end{bmatrix}$$

Determinant A = 2

$$A^{-1} = \begin{bmatrix} 0.5 & -0.5 & -1 \\ -3 & 2 & 1 \\ -4 & 3 & 2 \end{bmatrix}$$

Contd…

$$\begin{bmatrix} X_1 \\ X_2 \\ X_3 \end{bmatrix} = \begin{bmatrix} 0.5 & -0.5 & -1 \\ -3 & 2 & 1 \\ -4 & 3 & 2 \end{bmatrix} \times \begin{bmatrix} 3 \\ 2 \\ 1 \end{bmatrix} = \begin{bmatrix} -0.5 \\ -4 \\ -4 \end{bmatrix}$$

Calculation of inverse by using augmented matrix

Example 39: For the matrix given below obtain the inverse by augmented matrix method

$$\begin{pmatrix} -2 & 1 & 3 \\ 0 & -1 & 1 \\ 1 & 2 & 0 \end{pmatrix}$$

We set the augmented matrix as follows $\left(\begin{array}{ccc|ccc} -2 & 1 & 3 & 1 & 0 & 0 \\ 0 & -1 & 1 & 0 & 1 & 0 \\ 1 & 2 & 0 & 0 & 0 & 1 \end{array}\right)$

Now conduct row operations as usual, including the right hand side, till we get a unit matrix in the left-hand side. The right hand side result is our needed inverse matrix.

$$\left(\begin{array}{ccc|ccc} -2 & 1 & 3 & 1 & 0 & 0 \\ 0 & -1 & 1 & 0 & 1 & 0 \\ 1 & 2 & 0 & 0 & 0 & 1 \end{array}\right) \rightarrow \left(\begin{array}{ccc|ccc} -2 & 1 & 3 & 1 & 0 & 0 \\ 0 & -1 & 1 & 0 & 1 & 0 \\ 0 & 5/2 & 3/2 & 1/2 & 0 & 1 \end{array}\right)$$

$$\rightarrow \left(\begin{array}{ccc|ccc} -2 & 1 & 3 & 1 & 0 & 0 \\ 0 & -1 & 1 & 0 & 1 & 0 \\ 0 & 0 & 4 & 1/2 & 5/2 & 1 \end{array}\right)$$

$$\rightarrow \left(\begin{array}{ccc|ccc} 1 & -1/2 & -3/2 & -1/2 & 0 & 0 \\ 0 & -1 & -1 & 0 & -1 & 0 \\ 0 & 0 & 1 & 1/8 & 5/8 & 1/4 \end{array}\right)$$

$$\rightarrow \left(\begin{array}{ccc|ccc} 1 & -1/2 & -3/2 & -1/2 & 0 & 0 \\ 0 & 1 & 0 & 1/8 & -3/8 & 1/4 \\ 0 & 0 & 1 & 1/8 & 5/8 & 1/4 \end{array}\right)$$

$$\rightarrow \left(\begin{array}{ccc|ccc} 1 & 0 & 0 & -1/4 & 3/4 & 1/2 \\ 0 & 1 & 0 & 1/8 & -3/8 & 1/4 \\ 0 & 0 & 1 & 1/8 & 5/8 & 1/4 \end{array}\right)$$

So the needed inverse is

$$\begin{pmatrix} -1/4 & 3/4 & 1/2 \\ 1/8 & -3/8 & 1/4 \\ 1/8 & 5/8 & 1/4 \end{pmatrix}$$

$$= \frac{1}{8}\begin{pmatrix} -2 & 6 & 4 \\ 1 & -3 & 2 \\ 1 & 5 & 2 \end{pmatrix}$$

EXERCISES

1. By performing elementary row operations on the augmented matrix, solve the following system of equations.

$$2x_1 + x_2 + x_3 = 7$$
$$2x_1 + 2x_3 = 7$$
$$2x_1 + 2x_2 - x_3 = 4$$

2. By performing elementary row operations on the augmented matrix, solve the following system of equations.

$$x_1 + 2x_2 + 2x_3 = 7$$
$$4x_1 + 5x_2 + x_3 = 11$$
$$7x_1 - 4x_2 - x_3 = 1$$

3. By performing elementary row operations on the augmented matrix, solve the following system of equations.

$$4x_1 + 2x_2 + 3x_3 = 7$$
$$2x_1 + 3x_2 + 4x_3 = 2$$
$$3x_1 + 4x_2 + 2x_3 = 1$$

4. The supply function of a commodity in its general form is given by $S(p) = ap^3 + bp^2 + c$, where a, b, c are constants. When $p = 1$ the quantity supplied is 5; when $p = 2$, the quantity supplied is 11; when $p = 3$, the quantity supplied is 35. Obtain the supply function.

5. The demand function of a commodity in its general form is given by $D(p) = a + bp + c/p$, where a, b, c are constants. When $p = 1$ the quantity demanded is 60; when $p = 2$, the quantity demanded is 40; when $p = 3$, the quantity demanded is 20. Obtain the demand function.

6. Find the rank and hence the general solution of the following system

$$x_1 - x_2 + 5x_3 = 80$$
$$3x_1 + 2x_2 - x_3 = 25$$
$$5x_1 + 9x_2 + 2x_3 = 185$$

7. Reduce the following system into echelon form, determine its rank, and obtain the general solution:

$$5x_1 + 3x_2 + 2x_3 + x_4 = 66$$
$$x_1 + 3x_2 + 4x_3 + 2x_4 = 48$$

$$-x_1 + x_2 + 2x_3 + x_4 = 1\,85$$
$$2x_1 + 2x_2 + 2x_3 + 4x_4 = 38$$

8. Determine the solutions for the following system (if any).

$$2x_1 + 10x_2 + 9x_3 + 14x_4 = 14$$
$$x_1 + 3x_2 - 2x_3 + x_4 = 1$$
$$x_1 + 5x_2 + 3x_3 + 7x_4 = 8$$
$$x_1 + 7x_2 + 5x_3 + 13x_4 = 12$$

9. When the supply and the demand functions are D = –50p + 250 and S = 25p + 25 obtain the equilibrium price and the quantity by using inverse matrix.

10. By using elementary row operation obtain the inverse

$$\begin{pmatrix} 3 & 2 & -1 \\ 1 & 7 & 5 \\ -1 & 0 & 1 \end{pmatrix}$$

11. By using elementary row operation obtain the inverse and check the result by working AA^{-1}

$$A = \begin{pmatrix} 1 & 4 & 3 \\ 1 & 5 & 5 \\ 2 & 11 & 13 \end{pmatrix}$$

12. Show that the following matrix is not inevitable:

$$A = \begin{pmatrix} 1 & -1 & 2 \\ 3 & 5 & -7 \\ 1 & 7 & 11 \end{pmatrix}$$

13. Obtain the solution by using inverse matrix

$$2x_1 + x_2 + x_3 = 7$$
$$2x_1 + 2x_3 = 7$$
$$2x_1 + 2x_2 - x_3 = 4$$

14. Obtain the solution by using inverse matrix

$$x_1 + 2x_2 + 2x_3 = 7$$
$$4x_1 + 5x_2 + x_3 = 11$$
$$7x_1 - 4x_2 - x_3 = 1$$

15. Obtain the solution by using inverse matrix

$$4x_1 + 2x_2 + 3x_3 = 7$$
$$2x_1 + 3x_2 + 4x_3 = 2$$
$$3x_1 + 4x_2 + 2x_3 = 1$$

OO

6

Chapter

DETERMINANTS AND ITS APPLICATIONS

6.1 Definition of a Determinant

Each and every square matrix will have a determinant associated with it. Such determinants on expansion will always give a single scalar value. To distinguish the determinant from the corresponding associated matrix we use two vertical lines on either side as shown below in the place of the square bracket.

Determinant of matrix: If A stands for the square matrix then the associated determinant is denoted by | A |.

Example 1:

If $A = \begin{bmatrix} 1 & 2 & 4 \\ 3 & 4 & 3 \\ 6 & 2 & 1 \end{bmatrix}$ then $|A| = \begin{vmatrix} 1 & 2 & 4 \\ 3 & 4 & 3 \\ 6 & 2 & 1 \end{vmatrix}$ is called the associated determinant of the matrix A.

Minors of a given determinant:

$|A| = \begin{vmatrix} 1 & 2 & 4 \\ 3 & 4 & 3 \\ 6 & 2 & 1 \end{vmatrix}$ then $\alpha_{11} = \begin{vmatrix} 4 & 3 \\ 2 & 1 \end{vmatrix}$; $\alpha_{12} = \begin{vmatrix} 3 & 3 \\ 6 & 1 \end{vmatrix}$ are called the minors. The minor of the first row first column element namely 1, denoted by α_{11} is obtained by deleting the first row and the first column of the given determinant. Thus in general the minor of the ith row and the jth column element is obtained by deleting i^{th} row and the jth column in the given determinant.

Co-factors: The minor of an element, with its correct sign assigned in accordance with the alternative sign rule stated in the previous section is called the co-factor of the element under reference. If A_{ij} refers the co-factor of the ith row and j^{th} column element then by the alternating sign rule, the sign to be attached is given by the expression $(-1)^{i+j}$.

Example 2:

$$A_{11} = (-1)^{1+1}\alpha_{11} = (-1)^2\alpha_{11} = +\alpha_{11}$$

$$A_{32} = (-1)^{3+2}\alpha_{32} = (-1)^5\alpha_{32} = -\alpha_{32}$$

6.2 Some Important Properties of Determinants

1. **The value of a determinant remains unaltered when the corresponding rows and columns are interchanged.**

Example 3:

Let $$|A| = \begin{vmatrix} 2 & 4 \\ 3 & 5 \end{vmatrix} = 10 - 12 = -2$$

Now let us interchange the rows into columns.

$$|B| = \begin{vmatrix} 2 & 3 \\ 4 & 5 \end{vmatrix} = 10 - 12 = -2$$

2. **The value of the determinant is zero if any two of its columns (or rows) are identical.**

Example 4:

Let $$|A| = \begin{vmatrix} 2 & 2 \\ 3 & 3 \end{vmatrix} = 6 - 6 = 0$$

3. **The sign of the determinant is changed if any two of its rows (or columns) is interchanged.**

Let $$|A| = \begin{vmatrix} 2 & 4 \\ 3 & 5 \end{vmatrix} = 10 - 12 = -2$$

Now let us interchange the first and second column

$$|B| = \begin{vmatrix} 4 & 2 \\ 5 & 3 \end{vmatrix} = 12 - 10 = 2$$

4. **Multiplication of all the elements in any one row or column by some scalar results in the value of the determinant being multiplied by that scalar.**

Example 5:

$$|B| = \begin{vmatrix} 4 & 2 \\ 5 & 3 \end{vmatrix} = 12 - 10 = 2$$

Now let us multiply the first row elements completely by the scalar 2 then

$|C| = \begin{vmatrix} 8 & 4 \\ 5 & 3 \end{vmatrix} = 24 - 20 = 4$ This is exactly twice the value of the original determinant.

6.3 Cramer's Rule

The system of simultaneous equation in two unknowns is in its general form is normally written as

$$a_{11}\ x + a_{12}\ y\ = c_1 \ldots \qquad \ldots(1)$$

$$a_{21}\ x + a_{22}\ y\ = c_2 \ldots \qquad \ldots(2)$$

Now before explaining the Cramer's rule let us try to solve the system by the method of elimination. The system described in (1) and (2) can be solved by either eliminating x or y first.

Let us try to eliminate x first from the system. To eliminate x subtract a_{11} times of equation (2) from a_{21} times of equation (1)

$$(1) \times a_{21} \quad ; \quad a_{21}\, a_{11}\, x + a_{21}\, a_{12}\, y = a_{21}\, c_1 \qquad \ldots(3)$$

$$(2) \times a_{11} \quad ; \quad a_{21}\, a_{11}\, x + a_{22}\, a_{11}\, y = a_{11}\, c_2 \qquad \ldots(4)$$

$$(3) - (4) \quad ; \quad y(a_{21}\, a_{12} - a_{11}\, a_{22}) = a_{21}\, c_1 - a_{11}\, c_2$$

$$y = \frac{a_{21}c_1 - a_{11}c_2}{a_{21}a_{12} - a_{11}a_{22}} = \frac{a_{11}c_2 - a_{21}c_1}{a_{11}a_{22} - a_{21}a_{12}}$$

This final answer in term of determinants may be written as

$$y = \frac{\begin{vmatrix} a_{11} & c_1 \\ a_{21} & c_2 \end{vmatrix}}{\begin{vmatrix} a_{11} & a_{12} \\ a_{21} & a_{22} \end{vmatrix}}$$

Here the denominator determinant is simply coefficients of x and y in the given system that too in the given order. The numerator determinant is obtained by replacing the column corresponding to the variable under consideration by the right hand side constants. Since we are solving for y the corresponding second column is replaced by the right hand side constants. However, the first column of the numerator determinant is undisturbed during this operation. What is stated above in the determinant form is exactly the Cramer's rule specification. Once the y value is obtained the corresponding x is obtained by substituting the y in any one of the given equation. However, since we are familiar now with Cramer's rule we can get the value of x straight away by using the rule once again. But this time, since we are solving for x, the numerator determinant is obtained by replacing the first column by the right hand side constants. Obviously, the second column remains undisturbed.

$$x = \frac{\begin{vmatrix} c_1 & a_{12} \\ c_2 & a_{22} \end{vmatrix}}{\begin{vmatrix} a_{11} & a_{12} \\ a_{21} & a_{22} \end{vmatrix}}$$

Example 6: Solve for x and y

$$4x + y = 11$$

$$3x + 5y = 21$$

Now as per Cramer's Rule

$$x = \frac{\begin{vmatrix} 11 & 1 \\ 21 & 5 \end{vmatrix}}{\begin{vmatrix} 4 & 1 \\ 3 & 5 \end{vmatrix}} = \frac{55 - 21}{20 - 3} = \frac{34}{17} = 2$$

$$y = \frac{\begin{vmatrix} 4 & 11 \\ 3 & 21 \end{vmatrix}}{\begin{vmatrix} 4 & 1 \\ 3 & 5 \end{vmatrix}} = \frac{84-33}{20-3} = \frac{51}{17} = 3$$

Example 7: Solve the following system of equations for x, y, z:

$$3x + 2y + 4z = 19$$
$$6x + 2y + z = 37$$
$$x + 2y + 3z = 10$$

Now as per Cramer's Rule:

$$x = \frac{\begin{vmatrix} 19 & 2 & 4 \\ 37 & 2 & 1 \\ 10 & 2 & 3 \end{vmatrix}}{\begin{vmatrix} 3 & 2 & 4 \\ 6 & 2 & 1 \\ 1 & 2 & 3 \end{vmatrix}} = \frac{19\begin{vmatrix} 2 & 1 \\ 2 & 3 \end{vmatrix} - 2\begin{vmatrix} 37 & 1 \\ 10 & 3 \end{vmatrix} + 4\begin{vmatrix} 37 & 2 \\ 10 & 2 \end{vmatrix}}{3\begin{vmatrix} 2 & 1 \\ 2 & 3 \end{vmatrix} - 2\begin{vmatrix} 6 & 1 \\ 1 & 3 \end{vmatrix} + 4\begin{vmatrix} 6 & 2 \\ 1 & 2 \end{vmatrix}}$$

$$= \frac{19(6-2) - 2(111-10) + 4(74-20)}{3(6-2) - 2(18-1) + 4(12-2)}$$

$$= \frac{19(4) - 2(101) + 4(54)}{3(4) - 2(17) + 4(10)}$$

$$= \frac{76 - 202 + 216}{12 - 34 + 40} = \frac{90}{18} = 5$$

$$y = \frac{\begin{vmatrix} 3 & 19 & 4 \\ 6 & 37 & 1 \\ 1 & 10 & 3 \end{vmatrix}}{18} = \frac{3\begin{vmatrix} 37 & 1 \\ 10 & 3 \end{vmatrix} - 19\begin{vmatrix} 6 & 1 \\ 1 & 3 \end{vmatrix} + 4\begin{vmatrix} 6 & 37 \\ 1 & 10 \end{vmatrix}}{18}$$

$$= \frac{3(101) - 19(17) + 4(23)}{18}$$

$$= \frac{303 - 323 + 92}{18} = \frac{72}{18} = 4$$

$$z = \frac{\begin{vmatrix} 3 & 2 & 19 \\ 6 & 2 & 37 \\ 1 & 2 & 10 \end{vmatrix}}{18} = \frac{3(-54) - 2(23) + 19(10)}{18} = \frac{-18}{18} = -1$$

$\therefore$ $x = 5$; $y = 4$; $z = -1$.

Excel solution to two variables case

$$A = \begin{vmatrix} 4 & 1 \\ 3 & 5 \end{vmatrix} = 17$$

$4X + 1Y = 11$
$3X + 5Y = 21$

$$A1 = \begin{vmatrix} 11 & 1 \\ 21 & 5 \end{vmatrix} = 34 \qquad X = 2$$

$$A2 = \begin{vmatrix} 4 & 11 \\ 3 & 21 \end{vmatrix} = 51 \qquad Y = 3$$

Excel solution to three variables case

$$A = \begin{vmatrix} 3 & 2 & 4 \\ 6 & 2 & 1 \\ 1 & 2 & 3 \end{vmatrix} = 18 \qquad X = 5$$

$3X + 2Y + 4Z = 19$
$6X + 2Y + 1Z = 37$
$1X + 2Y + 3Z = 10$

$$A1 = \begin{vmatrix} 19 & 2 & 4 \\ 37 & 2 & 1 \\ 10 & 2 & 3 \end{vmatrix} = 90 \qquad Y = 5$$

$$A2 = \begin{vmatrix} 3 & 19 & 4 \\ 6 & 37 & 1 \\ 1 & 10 & 3 \end{vmatrix} = 72 \qquad Z = 4$$

$$A3 = \begin{vmatrix} 3 & 2 & 19 \\ 6 & 2 & 37 \\ 1 & 2 & 10 \end{vmatrix} = -18 \qquad Z = -1$$

EXERCISES

1. The demand and the supply functions for two related markets are $D_1 = 10 - 2p_1 + p_2$ and $D_2 = 15 + p_1 + p_2$. The corresponding supply functions are $S_1 = -1 + 3p_1$ and $S_2 = -1 + 2p_2$. Find the pair of equilibrium prices and quantities.
2. For the macro model

$$Y = C + I + G$$
$$C = a + bY$$
$$I = I_0$$
$$G = G_0$$

Calculate the equilibrium level of income.

3. For the macro model

$$Y = C + I + G$$
$$C = a + bY_d \quad (Y_d = \text{disposable income})$$
$$T = T_0 + tY$$
$$I = I_0$$
$$G = G_0$$

Calculate the equilibrium level of income and also find $\partial Y/\partial t$, the tax multiplier.

4. The national income model is given by

$$Y = A + C + G$$
$$C = a\,(Y - T)$$
$$T = T_0 + t_1 Y$$

Find the equilibrium level of income when $A = 10$, $G = 10$, $a = 0.7$, $T_0 = 20$, $t_1 = 0.4$

5. In the above problem, is the economy at a budgetary deficit or surplus at this equilibrium? How much a change in tax rate is required to produce a balance budget?
6. Suppose that: $C = 50 + 0.6\,(Y - T)$; $T_0 = 20$; $I_0 = 10$; $G_0 = 0$. Calculate the equilibrium level of income.
7. Solve the following equation systems using Cramer's rule

a. $$3x + 4y = 5$$ $$x - 2y = 6$$

b. $$2x - 5y = 11$$ $$3x - 4y = 2$$

c. $$3x - 4y = 2$$ $$3x + y = 13$$

d. $$x/8 + y/3 = 15$$ $$x/4 - y/5 = 4$$

e.
$$3/x + 2/y = 8$$
$$2/x - 4/y = 7$$

f.
$$2x + 3y - 2z = 12$$
$$-4x + 3y + z = 5$$
$$5x + 3y + 2z = 27$$

g.
$$2x + 3y + 5z = 11$$
$$5x + 2y - 7z = 15$$
$$4x + 3y - z = 10$$

h.
$$3x + 2y + 5z = 32$$
$$2x + 5y + 3z = 31$$
$$2x + 3y - 2z = 15$$

i.
$$1/x + 3/y - 1/z = 5$$
$$2/x + 4/y - 1/z = 7$$
$$2/x + 4/y - 3/z = 6$$

j.
$$x/2 + y/6 - z/4 = 5$$
$$x/4 - y/6 + z/3 = 10$$
$$x/3 + y/3 + z/6 = 16$$

k.
$$4x + 3y = 10$$
$$3y - 4z = 8$$
$$3x + 5z = 4$$

7

Chapter

LIMITS AND CONTINUITY

7.1 Introduction

In day-to-day life we all use the concept limit in different context. A teacher warns his students not exceed the limit in the classroom. The business ethics tell the businessmen not to exceed a certain maximum profit. Quran, the Holy Book of Islam, fixes the rate of interest as zero for lending money to others. In all these illustrations we take about two types of limits, the maximum in certain cases and the minimum in others.

7.2 The Concept Limit

Before we define the concept limit precisely, let us take some illustrations to throw some more light on this important concept. Let the area of the circle given in Fig. 7.1 be equal to A. Now let us insert an equilateral triangle with in this circle so that the circle becomes the outer circle of this triangle. Let the area of this triangle be B. Clearly, the area of the triangle is less than the area of

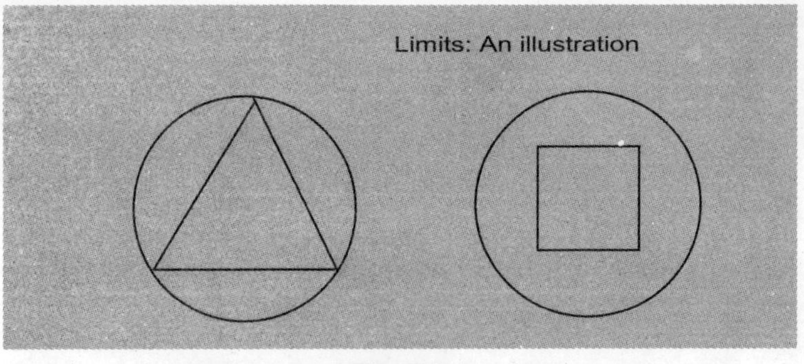

Fig. 7.1

the given circle. Now, in step 2 we increase the side of the triangle by one more and make the triangle into a square. Clearly area of this square is more than the area of the triangle but still less than the area of the circle. In a similar way if we keep on increasing the sides of the inner Fig. 1 to 5, and then to 6 and so on till infinity. In the final stage one could visualize a situation in which the inner Fig. approach the circle in area but never become exactly equal to the area of the circle. In this context, the idea of approaching a point or a value very close but still never reaching it is really appealing. Here the area of the circle is defined as the maximum limit of the inner Fig. 7.2

as n, the number of sides of the inner Fig., tends to infinity. In mathematical terminology this concept is written as

$$\operatorname*{Lt}_{n \to \infty} B = A$$

Example 1: As an another illustration let us consider a numerical illustration.

Let $y = \frac{x^2 - 4}{x - 2}$ is a function. This function is well defined for all values of x except the point x = 2. For example, if x = 2 then the function will yield $y = \frac{2^2 - 4}{2 - 2} = \frac{0}{0}$. Thus this function is not defined at the point x = 2. This observation often leads to the conclusion that when x = 2 the function y does not exists. In fact this is not true. Now instead of putting x = 2 in the function straightaway let us look at the problem from a different perspective. In this alternative approach x can approach the typical value in two ways.

(a) From values less than 2 as shown in Table No 7.1.

or

(b) From values more than 2 as shown in Table No 7.2.

Table 7.1

x	1.9	1.99	1.999	1.9999	……
y	3.9	3.99	3.999	3.9999	……

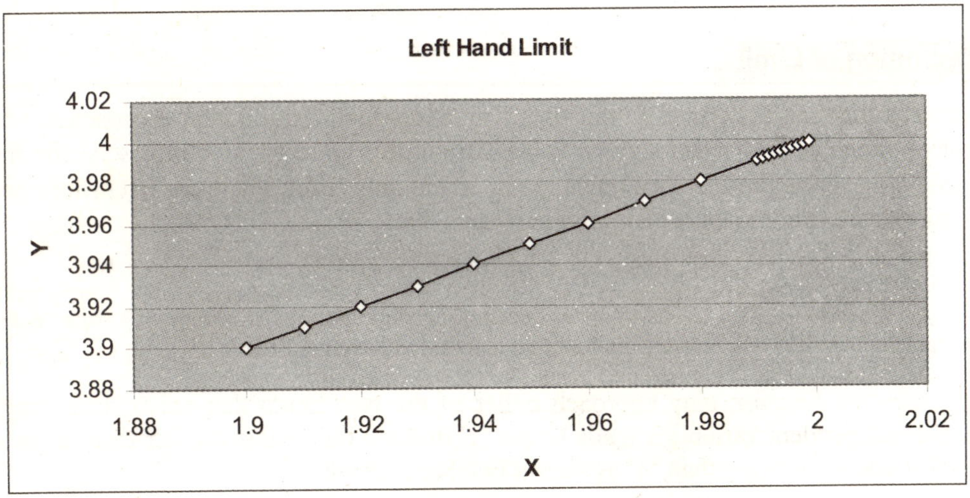

Fig. 7.2

Table 7.2

x	2.01	2.001	2.0001	2.00001	…….
y	4.01	4.001	4.0001	4.00001	…….

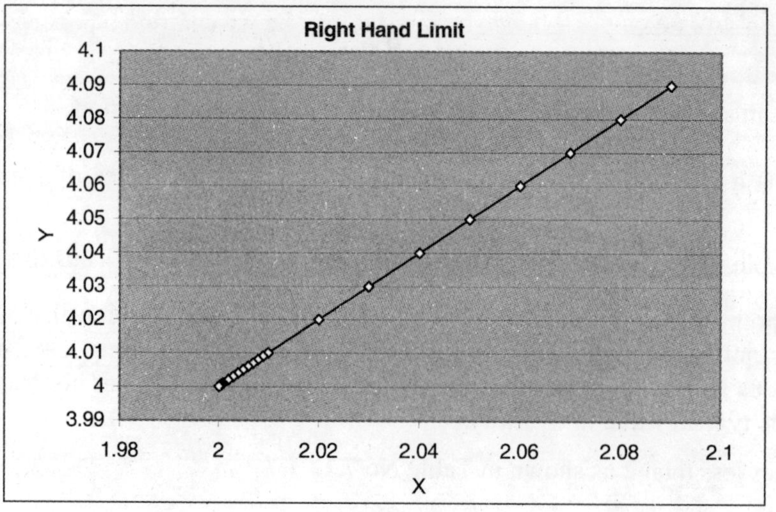

Fig. 7.3

From the table entries shown above we notice that the function approaches 4 as x tends to 2 from either side. Such a behaviour of the function is normally referred as the limit of the function and is denoted as

$$\underset{x \to 2}{\text{Lt}} \left(\frac{x^2 - 4}{x - 2} \right) = 4$$

7.3 Definition of Limit

The limit of a function is defined as the fixed value to which the function approaches when the independent variable approaches a given value. To put this concept more precisely, the function f (x) is said to have the limit '*l*' as x tends to '*a*' if and only if for any given ε (epsilon) however small it may be we can find a positive number δ such that

$$|f(x) - l| < \varepsilon \text{ when } 0 < |x - a| < \delta$$

Note: The existence of '*l*' for f (x) as x → '*a*' does not depend upon the existence of f (*a*) or not. In our example stated above f (a) = 0, but still the function is found to have the limit 4.

In some cases the function may approach either of the two limits that exists depending upon whether the independent variable x tends to the '*a*' through the values smaller than '*a*' as shown in the table 1 above or larger than '*a*' as shown in table 2 above.

7.4 Left Hand Limit

If f (x) approaches a fixed value '*l*' when the independent variable x approaches a fixed value '*a*' starting from less than '*a*' itself as in table 1 above then the fixed value '*l*' is called the left hand limit of the given function. Formally this denoted by

$$\underset{x \to \bar{a}}{\text{Lt}} = f(\bar{a}) = l$$

To put it more precisely, the number '*l*' is said to be the left hand limit of the function f (x) as x → '*a*' provided for any given ϵ > 0 however small it may be we can find a positive number δ such that

$$|f(x) - 1| < \varepsilon \text{ when } 0 < a - x < \delta$$

7.5 Right Hand Limit

If the function f (x) approaches a fixed number '*l*' when the independent variable approaches a fixed number '*a*' starting from a value greater than '*a*' itself then the fixed number '*l*' is called the right hand limit of the given function. This is denoted by

$$\underset{x \to a^+}{\text{Lt}} = f(\overset{+}{a}) = 1$$

To put it more precisely, the number '*l*' is said to be the right hand limit of the function f (x) at x → '*a*' provided for a given ε > 0 however small it may be, we can find a positive number δ such that

$$|f(x) - 1| < \varepsilon \quad \text{when} \quad 0 < x - a < \delta$$

If the left hand and the right hand limits are equal to one another the as in our illustration given above then '*l*' is said to be the limit of the function f (x) as x → '*a*'.

7.6 Working Rule for Getting the Limit

(i) If x = *a* – h and h > 0 then clearly x < *a*. Hence in our new terminology h → 0 is same as x → *a* from the left. Therefore, to find the left hand limit to given function we simply put x = *a* – h in f (x) for x and evaluate it value as h → 0

i.e.
$$f(\bar{a}) = \underset{x \to \bar{a}}{\text{Lt}} f(x) = \underset{h \to 0}{\text{Lt}} f(a - h)$$

(ii) If x = *a* + h and h > 0 then clearly x > *a*. Therefore, h → 0 is the other way of telling x approaches ' *a* ' from the right. Hence to find the right hand limit we simply put x = *a* + h for x in f (x) and evaluate its value as h→0

i.e.
$$f(\overset{+}{a}) = \underset{x \to a^+}{\text{Lt}} f(x) = \underset{h \to 0}{\text{Lt}} f(a + h)$$

Example 2: Evaluate the limit for the function

$$y = \frac{x^2 - 9}{x - 3} \text{as } x \to 3$$

Solution:

Left hand limit

Now
$$\underset{h \to 0}{\text{Lt}} f(a–h) = \underset{h \to 0}{\text{Lt}} \left[\frac{(3-h)^2 - 9}{(3-h) - 3} \right]$$

$$= \underset{h\to 0}{\text{Lt}} \frac{h^2 - 6h}{-h} = \underset{h\to 0}{\text{Lt}} (6-h) = 6 \qquad ...(1)$$

Right hand limit

Now $\underset{h\to 0}{\text{Lt}}\ f(a+h) = \underset{h\to 0}{\text{Lt}} \left[\frac{(3+h)^2 - 9}{(3+h) - 3}\right]$

$$= \underset{h\to 0}{\text{Lt}} \frac{h^2 + 6h}{h} = \underset{h\to 0}{\text{Lt}} (6+h) = 6 \qquad ...(2)$$

Now from (1) and (2) above L.H.L. = R.H.L. = 6

Therefore $\underset{x\to 3}{\text{Lt}} \frac{x^2 - 9}{x - 3} = 6.$

7.7 Theorems on Limit

(1) If u = f (x) and v = g (x) then

$$\underset{x\to a}{\text{Lt}} [f(x) \pm g(x)] = \underset{x\to a}{\text{Lt}}\ f(x) \pm \underset{x\to a}{\text{Lt}}\ g(x)$$

In other words, this is to say that the limit of sum or differences of two or more functions is equal to the sum or differences of their individual limits.

(2) If u = f (x) and v = g (x) then

$$\underset{x\to a}{\text{Lt}} [f(x) \cdot g(x)] = \underset{x\to a}{\text{Lt}}\ f(x) \cdot \underset{x\to a}{\text{Lt}}\ g(x)$$

The limit of the product of two or more functions is equal to the product of their respective individual limits.

(3) If u = f (x) and v = g (x) then

$$\underset{x\to a}{\text{Lt}} \left[\frac{f(x)}{g(x)}\right] = \frac{\underset{x\to a}{\text{Lt}}\ f(x)}{\underset{x\to a}{\text{Lt}}\ g(x)}$$

The limit of the quotient of two functions is equal to the quotient of their individual limits provided the limit exists for the denominator function.

(4) If u = f (x) and k is a constant then

$$\underset{x\to a}{\text{Lt}}\ k.f(x) = k \underset{x\to a}{\text{Lt}}\ f(x)$$

The limit of a function multiplied by a constant is equal to the constant times the individual limit of the said function.

(5) If f (x) = k where k is a constant then

$$\underset{x\to a}{\text{Lt}}\ f(x) = \underset{x\to a}{\text{Lt}}\ (k) = k$$

· The limit of a constant function is the constant itself.

(6) If u = f (x) then

$$\underset{x \to a}{\text{Lt}} \sqrt[n]{f(x)} = \sqrt[n]{\underset{x \to a}{\text{Lt}} f(x)}$$

The limit of the nth root of a function is equal to the nth root of the individual limit of the given function.

Example 3: Find the value of $\underset{x \to 1}{\text{Lt}} (x^2 + 4x - 3)$.

Solution:

$$\underset{x \to 1}{\text{Lt}} (x^2 + 4x - 3) = \underset{x \to 1}{\text{Lt}}\, x^2 + \underset{x \to 1}{\text{Lt}}\, 4x - \underset{x \to 1}{\text{Lt}}\, 3$$

$$= 1 + 4 - 3 = 2$$

Example 4: Find the value of $\underset{x \to 1}{\text{Lt}} (2x + 3)(4x + 1)$

Solution:

$$\underset{x \to 2}{\text{Lt}} (2x + 3)(4x + 1) = \underset{x \to 2}{\text{Lt}} (2x + 3) . \underset{x \to 2}{\text{Lt}} (4x + 1)$$

$$= \left[\underset{x \to 2}{\text{Lt}}\, 2x + \underset{x \to 2}{\text{Lt}}\, 3\right] . \left[\underset{x \to 2}{\text{Lt}}\, 4x + \underset{x \to 2}{\text{Lt}}\, 1\right]$$

$$= (4 + 3).(8 + 1) = 63$$

Example 5: Find limit of $\underset{x \to 0}{\text{Lt}} \left(\frac{x^2 + 8}{x^3 - 4}\right)$.

Solution:

$$\underset{x \to 0}{\text{Lt}} \left(\frac{x^2 + 8}{x^3 - 4}\right) = \frac{\underset{x \to 0}{\text{Lt}}\, x^2 + \underset{x \to 0}{\text{Lt}}\, 8}{\underset{x \to 0}{\text{Lt}}\, x^3 - \underset{x \to 0}{\text{Lt}}\, 4} = \frac{0 + 8}{0 - 4} = -2$$

Example 6: Find the value of $\underset{x \to 1}{\text{Lt}}\, 4x^2$.

Solution:

$$\underset{x \to 1}{\text{Lt}}\, 4x^2 = 4 \underset{x \to 1}{\text{Lt}}\, x^2 = 4 \times 1 = 4$$

Example 7: Find the value of $\underset{x \to 3}{\text{Lt}} \sqrt{25 - x^2}$.

Solution:

$$\underset{x \to 3}{\text{Lt}} \sqrt{25 - x^2} = \sqrt{\underset{x \to 3}{\text{Lt}} (25 - x^2)} = \sqrt{25 - 9} = \sqrt{16} = 4$$

7.8 Continuity of Functions

In simple terms a given function is said to be continuous provided its graph is an unbroken curve. The concept of limit developed in the previous section will enable us to study this important property of the given function. The continuity of the function is normally defined in two ways.

(1) The continuity at a point

(2) The continuity in an interval

The continuity at a point

The function f(x) is said to be continuous at the point x = a if $\underset{x \to a}{\text{Lt}} f(x) = f(a)$. In the definition given above we presume three important points.

1. The function is defined at the point x = a i.e. f (a) is a definite (finite) number.
2. The limit of f (x) as x → a exists, i.e. both right and left limits exists and they are equal to one another.
3. The limit f (x) as x → a is equal to f (a)

If one or more conditions are violated then f (x) is said to be discontinuous at the point x = a and the point x = a is called the point of discontinuity. More precisely the function f (x) is said to be continuous at the point x = a if and only if for any given ε > 0, however small it may be, we can find a positive number δ such that

$$|f(x) - f(a)| < \varepsilon \text{ when } 0 < |x - a| < \delta$$

The Continuity in an interval

The function f (x) is said to be continuous in a given interval provided it is continuous at all points in the said interval.

Properties of a continuous function

If u = f (x) and v = g (x) are two continuous functions then

(i) u ± v = f (u) ± f (v) is continuous

(ii) u × v = f (u) × f (v) is continuous

(iii) u/v = f (u) / f(v) is continuous provided g (x) ≠ 0

Therefore, the sum, the product and the quotient of two continuous functions are themselves continuous, unless the function taken for the divisor is zero.

Example 8: Prove that the function $y = x^2$ is continuous at the point x = 2

Solution:

The function f(x) is continuous at x = 2 provided the function satisfy the following three conditions

(i) f (a) must be finite number

(ii) $\underset{x \to 2}{\text{Lt}} f(x)$ must exist

(iii) $\underset{x \to 2}{\text{Lt}} f(x) = f(a)$

Now

$$f(2) = 2^2 = 4 \qquad ...(1)$$

$$\underset{x \to 2}{\text{Lt}}\ x^2 = 4 \qquad ...(2)$$

From (1) and (2) $\underset{x \to 2}{\text{Lt}}\ x^2 = f(2) = 4$

Thus, the function f (x) is continuous at the point x = 2.

Example 9: For the function $y = \dfrac{x^2 - 4}{x - 2}$ find both left and right hand limits. Also verify that whether the function is continuous or not at x = 2.

Solution:

The function f (x) is continuous at x = 2 provided the function satisfy the following three conditions

(i) f (a) must be finite number

(ii) $\underset{x \to 2}{\text{Lt}}\ f(x)$ must exist

(iii) $\underset{x \to 2}{\text{Lt}}\ f(x) = f(a)$

(i) Now

$$f(a) = f(2) = \frac{x^2 - 4}{x - 2} = \frac{4 - 4}{2 - 2} = 0 \qquad ...(1)$$

Thus f (2) does not exist

(ii) Left hand limit

Now

$$\underset{h \to 0}{\text{Lt}}\ f(a-h) = \underset{h \to 0}{\text{Lt}}\left[\frac{(2-h)^2 - 4}{(2-h) - 2}\right] = \underset{h \to 0}{\text{Lt}}\left[\frac{4 - 4h + h^2 - 4}{2 - h - 2}\right]$$

$$= \underset{h \to 0}{\text{Lt}}\left[\frac{h^2 - 4h}{-h}\right] = \underset{h \to 0}{\text{Lt}}\ (4 - h) = 4 \qquad ...(2)$$

(iii) Right hand limit

Now

$$\underset{h \to 0}{\text{Lt}}\ f(a+h) = \underset{h \to 0}{\text{Lt}}\left[\frac{(2+h)^2 - 4}{(2+h) - 2}\right] = \underset{h \to 0}{\text{Lt}}\left[\frac{4 + 4h + h^2 - 4}{2 + h - 2}\right]$$

$$= \underset{h \to 0}{\text{Lt}}\left[\frac{h^2 + 4h}{h}\right] = \underset{h \to 0}{\text{Lt}}\ (4 + h) = 4 \qquad ...(3)$$

Since condition (1) is not satisfied, though it has both left and right hand limit, the function is not continuous at the point x = 2.

EXERCISES

I. Prove the following results

1. $\underset{x\to 2}{\text{Lt}}\ x^2 = 4$

2. $\underset{x\to 0}{\text{Lt}}\ (7 - x - x^2) = 7$

3. $\underset{x\to 1}{\text{Lt}}\ \dfrac{x^2 - 4x + 3}{x^2 + 2x - 3} = -\dfrac{1}{2}$

4. $\underset{x\to\infty}{\text{Lt}}\ \dfrac{a + bx}{x^2}$

5. $\underset{r\to 2}{\text{Lt}}\ \dfrac{r^2 - 5}{2r^3 + 6} = \dfrac{-1}{22}$

6. $\underset{h\to 0}{\text{Lt}}\ \dfrac{(x - h)^3 - x^3}{h} = 3x^2$

II. Evaluate the limits if exists

1. $\underset{x\to 1}{\text{Lt}}\ \dfrac{x^2}{x - 1}$

2. $\underset{x\to 2}{\text{Lt}}\ \dfrac{3x - 7}{x^3 - 4}$

3. $\underset{x\to 1}{\text{Lt}}\ \dfrac{10}{x}$

4. $\underset{x\to 1}{\text{Lt}}\ \dfrac{x^2 - x}{x - 1}$

5. $\underset{x\to -1}{\text{Lt}}\ \dfrac{6x^3 - 4x^2 + 6}{x^2 - x}$

III. Verify the continuity of the functions if exist

1. $y = \dfrac{x^2 - 16}{x - 4}$ at $x = 4$

2. $y = x^4$ at $x = 4$

3. $y = \dfrac{x^2 - 9}{x - 3}$ at $x = 3$

OO

8

Chapter

DIFFERENTIAL CALCULUS

8.1 Introduction

Calculus is a special and important branch of mathematics. Differentiation and integration are the two important branches in calculus having wider applications in all branches of business. Incrementalism or otherwise called marginalism plays a crucial role both in micro and macroeconomics. Differential calculus, being concerned with the determination of the rate of change in the dependent variable for given small change in the independent variable, is found to have greater applicability in marginal analysis.

8.2 The Derivative or the Differential Coefficient

Let the function y = f (x) is a continuous production function in a given interval. Further let 'x' be the amount of fertilizer used and y be the amount of wheat yielded in our simple illustration. The legitimate question that one would encounter in this context is: What happens to wheat yield 'y' when the fertilizer application x is increased by small amount? If y also increases with x is the answer for the first encounter then the next question that follows is: At what rate does this increase occurs? The differential calculus provides a quantitative answer to both these questions.

Let the independent variable x be increased by a small amount say Δx. Also let Δy be the corresponding increment in the dependent variable y. Hence $y + \Delta y = f(x + \Delta x)$ is the new relation now. From this relation let us calculate the wheat increment Δy first as follows

$$\begin{aligned}\Delta y &= f(x+\Delta x) - y \\ &= f(x+\Delta x) - f(x) \quad \{y = f(x)\}\end{aligned}$$

Now to obtain the rate of change of y per unit change in x we simply divide the above equation both the sides by Δx.

i.e.,
$$\frac{\Delta y}{\Delta x} = \frac{f(x+\Delta x) - f(x)}{\Delta x}$$

Now to make Δx, the increment in x, as small as possible let us take the limit on either side as $\Delta x \to 0$

$$\operatorname*{Lt}_{\Delta x \to 0} \frac{\Delta y}{\Delta x} = \operatorname*{Lt}_{\Delta x \to 0} \frac{f(x+\Delta x) - f(x)}{\Delta x}$$

The so obtained limit value of the given function is called the derivative or the differential coefficient of the given function and normally denoted by dy/dx.

i.e. $$\frac{dy}{dx} = \underset{\Delta x \to 0}{Lt} \frac{\Delta y}{\Delta x} = \underset{\Delta x \to 0}{Lt} \frac{f(x+\Delta x)-f(x)}{\Delta x}$$

The process of differentiation: An illustration

Example 1: If $y = x^2$ then find dy/dx, the first derivative of y with respect to x.

Solution:

$y = x^2$ is the exact functional form of the relation between x and y. Now let Δx stands for the small increment in x and Δy stands for the corresponding increment in y. Now after replacing x by $(x + \Delta x)$ and y by $(y + \Delta y)$ in the given function the new relation is obtained as

$$y + \Delta y = (x + \Delta x)^2$$

$$\Delta y = (x + \Delta x)^2 - y \quad [(A+B)^2 \text{ formula is used for the expansion}]$$

$$= x^2 + 2.x.\Delta x + (\Delta x)^2 - x^2 \quad (y = x^2)$$

$$= 2.x.\Delta x + (\Delta x)^2$$

Now to get the needed incremental ratio we divide both the sides of the above equation by Δx

$$\frac{\Delta y}{\Delta x} = \frac{2.x.\Delta x + (\Delta x)^2}{\Delta x} = 2x + \Delta x$$

Now since by definition the derivative

$$\frac{dy}{dx} = \underset{\Delta x \to 0}{Lt} \frac{\Delta y}{\Delta x}$$

So let us take the limit as $\Delta x \to 0$ on either side of the above equation

i.e. $$\frac{dy}{dx} = \underset{\Delta x \to 0}{Lt} \frac{\Delta y}{\Delta x} = \underset{\Delta x \to 0}{Lt} (2x + \Delta x)$$

$$= \underset{\Delta x \to 0}{Lt} 2x + \underset{\Delta x \to 0}{Lt} \Delta x = 2x + 0 = 2x.$$

8.3 The Meaning of the Concept Derivative: A Diagrammatic Illustration

In the Fig. given below the curve PQ'Q represents the function y = f (x). The independent variable x is measured on the horizontal axis and the dependent variable y is measured on the vertical axis. Let P represents the point (x, y) as shown in the Fig.. Now let the independent variable x is increased from x to $x + \Delta x$. This change in x increases y to $y + \Delta y$. The new point is represented by Q in the graph. Now by connecting P and Q draw a chord QT. Also complete the triangle PQR as shown in the Fig.. In the triangle PQR the opposite side for the angle $Q\hat{P}R$ is $QR = \Delta y$ and the adjacent side $PR = \Delta x$. So our incremental ratio $\Delta y/\Delta x$ is simply ratio of the opposite side to that of the adjacent side of the angle $Q\hat{P}R$. In other words, this is to say that $\Delta y/\Delta x$ is the slope of the chord PQ to the horizontal axis. Now since by definition $\frac{dy}{dx} = \underset{\Delta x \to 0}{Lt} \frac{\Delta y}{\Delta x}$ let us try to make Δx as small as possible step by step. Now let $\Delta x'$ be a smaller increment so that $\Delta x' = \Delta x/2$. This small change will move the point Q to Q' on the given curve as shown in the Fig. 8.1. Now PQ'R' will be the new triangle. In it Q'R' = Δy' and PR' = Δx'. Now since the angle $Q'\hat{P}R'$ is greater than the angle $Q\hat{P}R$, $\Delta y'/\Delta x' > \Delta y/\Delta x$. In other words, this is to say that our new incremental ratio is greater than old one. Thus, the associated chord Q' T' is steeper than the old chord QT.

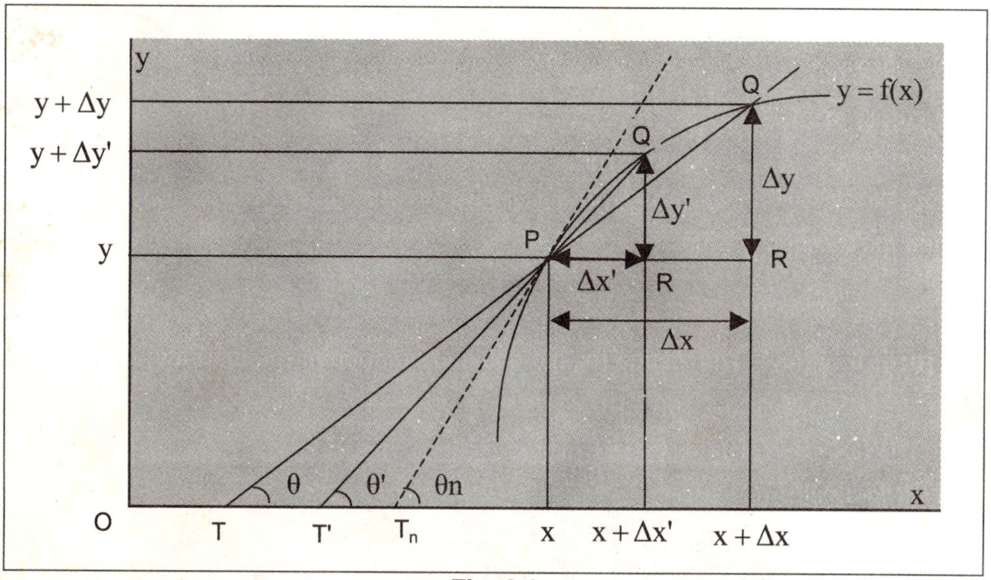

Fig. 8.1

Now let us repeat this process many more times and make Δx as small as we please. At the nth stage when $\Delta x \to 0$, the triangle PQR disappears and all the three points P, Q and R coincide at P. Also notice that our chord PQ will become a tangent at the point P as shown in the Fig. 8.1. Hence the derivative dy/dx at a given point like P is simply the slope of the tangent at P. Also note that, since dy/dx measures the rate of change in y for a given very small unit change in x, in economic terminology it measures the marginal productivity of fertilizer. In the place of production function if we take the cost function C = f(q) then the derivative dC/dq give us the marginal cost. Similarly, if we differentiate the revenue function with respect to the output then what we get is called the marginal revenue and so on.

8.4 Diagrammatic Meaning of the Concept Derivative

In the Fig. 8.2 given above we represent the total cost C as a function of the output q by using a cubic equation. To obtain the marginal cost corresponding to a given point we simply draw a tangent at that point and measure its slope as the ratio of the opposite side to that of the adjacent side of the right angled triangle.

In Fig. 8.2 marginal cost is to the slope of the tangent at P. So MC = $\frac{60}{40} = 1.5$.

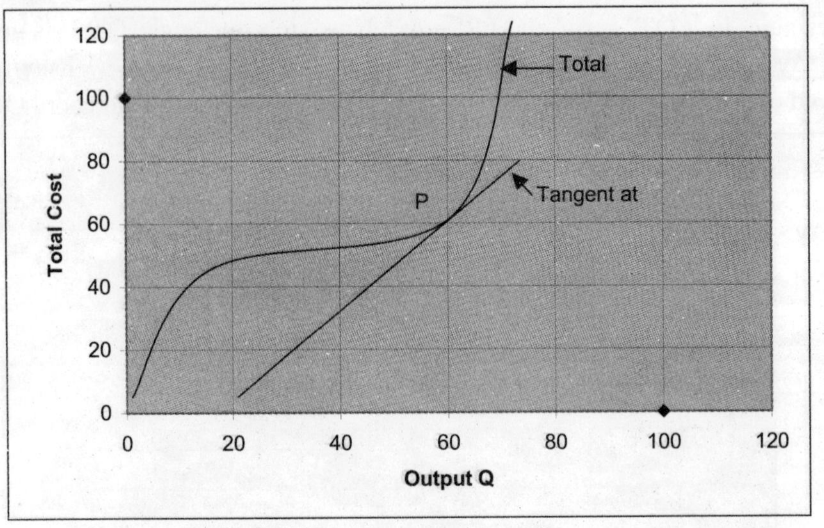

Fig. 8.2

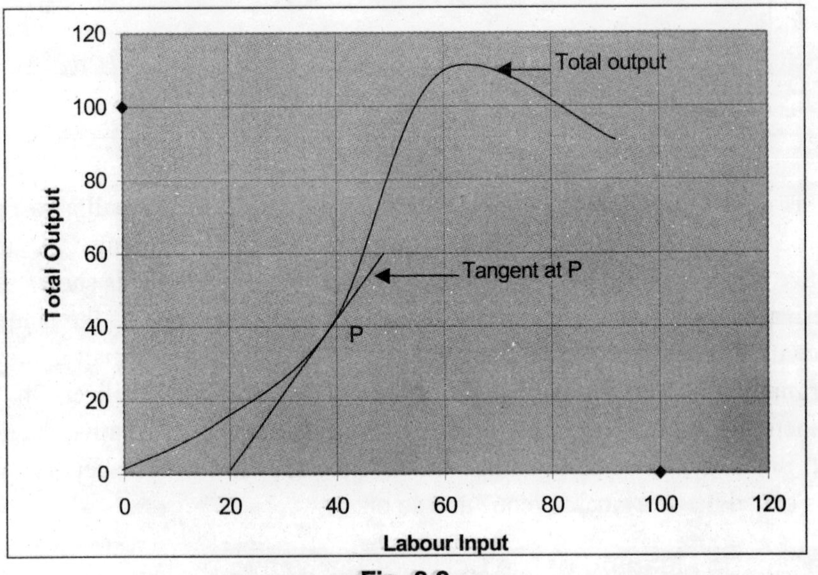

Fig. 8.3

In Fig. 8.3 marginal productivity of labour is obtained as the slope of the tangent at P. So $MP_L = \frac{40}{20} = 2$

8.5 Rules for Obtaining the Derivatives

Rule No.1: Power function rule:

If $y = x^n$

then $\frac{dy}{dx} = n.x^{n-1}$

Example 2:

1. If $y = x^4$

then $\frac{dy}{dx} = 4.x^{4-1} = 4x^3$

2. If $y = x^{10}$

then $\frac{dy}{dx} = 10x^9$

3. If $y = 1/x = x^{-1}$

then $\frac{dy}{dx} = -1x^{-1-1} = -x^{-2} = -1/x^2$

4. If $y = x$

then $\frac{dy}{dx} = 1 \times x^{1-1} = x^0 = 1 \quad (x^0 = 1)$

Rule No. 2: Derivative of a constant:

If y = k where k is constant, then $\frac{dy}{dx} = 0$

Example 3:

1. If y = 18 since 18 is a constant, then $\frac{dy}{dx} = 0$

2 If y = c where c is a constant, then $\frac{dy}{dx} = 0$

Rule No. 3: Derivative of a function when it is pre multiplied by a constant:

If $y = c.x^n$ where c is a constant, then $\frac{dy}{dx} = c.nx^{n-1}$

Here since the given power function is pre multiplied by the constant c the derivative of the function is also pre multiplied by the same constant as shown above.

Example 4:

1. If $y = 5x^7$ then $\frac{dy}{dx} = 5.\,7.\,x^6 = 35x^6$

2. If $y = 20\,x^{10}$ then $\frac{dy}{dx} = 200x^9$

Rule No. 4: Derivative of sum or differences of two or more functions:

If u = f (x) and v = g (x) are the given two functions then

$$\frac{d}{dx}(u \pm v) = \frac{du}{dx} \pm \frac{dv}{dx}$$

Example 5:

1. If $u = x^2$ and $v = x^5$, then $\frac{d}{dx}(u+v) = \frac{d}{dx}(x^2 + x^5) = 2x + 5x^4$

2. If $y = 10\,x^7 + x^6 - 10$, then $\frac{dy}{dx} = 70x^6 + 6x^5 - 0$

3. If $y = x^9 - 4x^6 + 100$, then $\frac{dy}{dx} = 9x^8 - 24x^5 + 0$

Rule No. 5: Product rule:

If $u = f(x)$ and $v = g(x)$ are the given two functions then, $\frac{d(u.v)}{dx} = u\frac{dv}{dx} + v\frac{du}{dx}$

Example 6:

1. If $u = x^3$ and $v = x^7$, then $\frac{d}{dx}(x^3 \times x^7) = x^3 \times 7x^6 + x^7 \times 3x^2 = 7x^9 + 3x^9 = 10x^9$

2. If $y = (2x^2 + 5)(x^4 - 10)$, then $\frac{dy}{dx} = [(2x^2 + 5) \times 4x^3] + [(x^4 - 10) \times 4x]$

$$= 8x^5 + 20x^3 + 4x^5 - 40x$$

$$\frac{dy}{dx} = 12x^5 + 20x^3 - 40x$$

Rule No. 6: Quotient rule:

If $u = f(x)$ and $v = g(x)$

then $\frac{d}{dx}\left(\frac{u}{v}\right) = \frac{v.\frac{du}{dx} - u.\frac{dv}{dx}}{v^2}$

Example 7:

1. If $u = 4x^2$ and $v = (x^3 + 5)$

then

$$\frac{d}{dx}\left(\frac{u}{v}\right) = \frac{[(x^3+5)\times 8x] - [4x^2 \times 3x^2]}{(x^3+5)^2}$$

$$= \frac{8x^4 + 40x - 12x^4}{(x^3+5)^2} = \frac{-4x^4 + 40x}{(x^3+5)^2}$$

2. If $y = x^5/x^2$

then $\frac{dy}{dx} = \frac{x^2 \times 5x^4 - x^5 \times 2x}{x^4} = \frac{5x^6 - 2x^6}{x^4} = \frac{3x^6}{x^4} = 3x^2$

Rule No. 7: Chain or function of a function rule:

If $y = f(z)$ and $z = g(x)$ then $y = f[g(x)]$ is called the function of a function. Further, since y is a function of z and z is a function of x it is also called function of a function. If such is the type of relation then the derivative is obtained as the product of the derivative of the first function with respect to z and the derivative of the second function with respective to x.

$$\frac{dy}{dx} = \frac{dy}{dz} \times \frac{dz}{dx}$$

Example 8:

1. If $y = z^3 + 10$ and $z = x^7$

then $\frac{dy}{dx} = \frac{dy}{dz} \times \frac{dz}{dx}$

$$\frac{dy}{dx} = 3z^2 \times 7x^6 = 3 \times (x^7)^2 \times 7\,x^6 = 21x^{20}$$

2. If $y = z^{10}$ and $z = x^2$

$$\frac{dy}{dx} = \frac{dy}{dz} \times \frac{dz}{dx}$$

then $\frac{dy}{dx} = 10\,z^9 \times 2x = 10\,x^{18} \times 2x = 20x^{19}$

Rule No. 8: Implicit function rule:

The functions of the type $y = x^2$ is called explicit because in it the value of the dependent variable y is explicitly stated in terms of the independent variable x. Very often we come across functions in a mixed form like $x^2 + y^2 - 4 = 0$. Such functions are called implicit functions. In this section for unknown explicit functions we propose to get the derivatives from their known implicit counterpart. To get dy/dx, we differentiate the given implicit function term by term with respect to x first. The so obtained result is solved for dy/dx algebraically to get the needed dy/dx.

Example 9:

1. If $y = x^2 + y^2 - 4 = 0$

$$\frac{d}{dx}(x^2 + y^2 - 4) = \frac{d}{dx}(0)$$

$$\frac{d}{dx}(x^2) + \frac{d}{dx}(y^2) - \frac{d}{dx}(4) = 0$$

$$2x + 2y\frac{dy}{dx} - 0 = 0$$

$$\frac{dy}{dx} = \frac{-2x}{2y} = \frac{-x}{y}$$

2. If $x^2 + 2xy + y^2 = 0$ then

$$\frac{d}{dx}(x^2) + \frac{d}{dx}(2xy) + \frac{d}{dx}(y^2) = \frac{d}{dx}(0)$$

$$2x + 2(x \cdot \frac{dy}{dx} + y) + 2y \cdot \frac{dy}{dx} = 0$$

$$(2x + 2y)\frac{dy}{dx} = -2x - 2y$$

$$= \frac{-2x - 2y}{2x + 2y} = \frac{-2(x+y)}{2(x+y)} = -1$$

Rule No. 9: Inverse function rule:

If $y = x^2$ is the given function then the function $x = \sqrt{y}$ is called the inverse function of the given function. In the inverse function y is the independent variable and x is the dependent variable. In this section given the inverse function we try to find the derivative for the unknown original function. If $x = f(y)$ is the given inverse function then

The Rule: $\dfrac{dy}{dx} = \dfrac{1}{\dfrac{dx}{dy}}$

Example 10: If $x = \sqrt{y}$ then

$$\frac{dx}{dy} = \frac{d}{dx}\left(y^{\frac{1}{2}}\right) = \frac{1}{2}y^{\frac{1}{2}-1} = \frac{1}{2}y^{\frac{-1}{2}} = \frac{1}{2y^{\frac{1}{2}}} = \frac{1}{2x}$$

$$\frac{dy}{dx} = \frac{1}{1/2x} = 2x$$

Note: For $x = \sqrt{y}$ the original function is $y = x^2$. Hence $dy/dx = 2x$. This is same as the result that we got from its inverse shown above.

Rule No. 10: Logarithmic function rule:

If $y = \ln x$ (natural log)

then $\dfrac{dy}{dx} = 1/x$

Example 11: If $y = \ln x^3$ then the derivative is obtained by using the chain rule. First let us rewrite the given function after substituting $z = x^3$.

Now the given function may be written as

$y = \ln z$

Where $z = x^3$

So from the chain rule

$$\frac{dy}{dx} = \frac{dy}{dz} \times \frac{dz}{dx}$$

$$= \frac{1}{z} \times 3x^2 = \frac{1}{x^3} \times 3x^2 = \frac{3}{x}$$

Rule No. 11: Exponential function rule:

Example 12: If $y = e^x$

then $\frac{dy}{dx} = e^x$

Example 13: If $y = e^{x^2}$ obtain its derivative

The derivative is obtained by using the chain rule. So put $z = x^2$ in the given function. Now our problem is rewritten as $y = e^z$ where $z = x^2$. Now from the chain rule

$$\frac{dy}{dx} = \frac{dy}{dz} \times \frac{dz}{dx}$$

$$= e^z \times 2x = e^{x^2} 2x$$

Rule No. 12: Derivative of a derivative or the higher order derivative:

If $y = f(x)$ then $\frac{dy}{dx}$ is called the first order derivative. If we differentiate the so obtained first order derivative once again with respect to x then what we get is called the second order derivative. If we differentiate it again with respect to x then we get the third order derivative and so on.

Thus $\frac{d}{dx}\left(\frac{dy}{dx}\right) = \frac{d^2y}{dx^2}$ is called the second order derivative.

$\frac{d}{dx}\left(\frac{d^2y}{dx^2}\right) = \frac{d^3y}{dx^3}$ is called the third order derivative.

Example 14: If $y = x^3 + 2x + 10$ then

$$\frac{dy}{dx} = 3x^2 + 2 \text{ (First derivative)}$$

$$\frac{d}{dx}\left(\frac{d^2y}{dx^2}\right) = \frac{d^3y}{dx^3} = 6x \text{ (Second derivative)}$$

$$\frac{d}{dx}\left(\frac{d^2y}{dx^2}\right) = \frac{d^3y}{dx^3} = 6 \text{ (Third derivative)}$$

8.6 Application of Derivatives in Economics

Since the derivative is nothing but the slope of the tangent at a given point and hence represents marginal, it is having wider applications in economics. In particular, if we differentiate the total cost with respect to the output then, we get the marginal cost. Similarly if we differentiate the production function with respect to an input then what we get is called the marginal productivity of that input and so on.

Example 15: If $C = q^3 - 5q^2 + 10q + 100$ stands for the short-run cost function of a representative firm in an industry find the marginal cost when its output is $q = 10$.

Solution:

The cost function of the firm is $C = q^3 - 5q^2 + 10q + 100$

Now by definition $MC = \frac{dC}{dq}$. So from the above equation

$$MC = \frac{dC}{dq} = \frac{d}{dq}(q^3 - 5q^2 + 10q + 100)$$
$$= 3q^2 - 10q + 10$$

Now the specific value of the MC at $q = 10$ is obtained by simply substituting this value q in the MC function obtained.

$$(MC)_{q=10} = 310^2 - 10 \times 10 + 10$$
$$= 300 - 100 + 10 = 210$$

Example 16: If $p = 200 - 10q$ stands for the demand law obtain the marginal revenue when the sale $q = 5$

Solution:

By definition the revenue $R = pq$

$$= (200 - 10q)q$$
$$= 200q - 10q^2$$

$$\text{Now } MR = \frac{dR}{dq} = \frac{d}{dq}(200q - 10q^2)$$
$$= 200 - 20q$$

Hence $(MR)_{q=5} = 200 - 20 \times 5 = 200 - 100 = 100$.

Example 17: If $C = 400 + 0.5Y$ stands for the Keynesian consumption function calculate the MPC, the marginal propensity to consume.

Solution:

$$\text{By definition } MPC = \frac{dC}{dY} = \frac{d}{dY}(400 + 0.5Y) = 0.5$$

Example 18: If $S = -400 + 0.5Y$ stands for the Keynesian savings function calculate the MPS, the marginal propensity to save.

Solution:

$$\text{By definition } MPS = \frac{dS}{dY} = \frac{d}{dY}(-400 + 0.5Y) = 0.5$$

Example 19: The production function of the firm is $Q = 100L^2 - 10L^3$. Find the marginal productivity of the labour input L when $L = 5$.

Solution:

By definition MP_L

$$= \frac{dQ}{dL} = \frac{d}{dL}(100L^2 - 10L^3) = 2 \times 100 \times L - 3 \times 10 \times L^2$$

$$(MP_L)_{L=5} = 200 \times 5 - 30 \times 5^2$$

$$= 1000 - 750 = 250$$

8.7 Partial Derivatives: Functions of Several Variables

In economics often we come across functional relations with several independent variables. For example, in the theory of consumption the amount of utility derived by a consumer depends upon variety of commodities that the consumer consumes. Similarly, in the theory of production a given output is produced by using variety of inputs like labour, capital, land, and natural resources etc. Under such circumstances the marginal concept, obtain as the derivative, is always associated to the variable under consideration. In such circumstances, we differentiate the dependent variable with respect to only one independent variable at a time by treating all other independent variables as constants. For example, the marginal productivity of the input labour is defined as the output obtainable by using an additional one unit increase in the labour input by keeping all other inputs at a given constant level. Since such a treatment is partial, the derivative so obtained is often referred as the partial derivative. Further, to distinguish such partial derivatives from the total derivative discussed in the previous section we use a new notation '∂' instead of 'd' in all our partial derivative operations.

The relevant function with two independent variables is normally written as z = f (x, y). Since there are two independent variables in this illustration at the most we can differentiate z with respect to either x or y at a time. If we differentiate with respect to x then y must be treated as constant. If we differentiate with respect to y then x must be treated as constant. Since the operation is partial in either case, the so obtained derivative is called the partial derivative. Hence, $\frac{\partial z}{\partial x}$ is called the partial derivative of z with respect to x and $\frac{\partial z}{\partial y}$ is called the partial derivative of z with respect to y.

Rules for finding the partial derivatives:

To find the partial derivative of a function with respect to an independent variable we use all our derivative rules developed in the previous section by simply treating all other independent variables as constants except the one we are interested.

Example 20:

If $z = 2x^3 + 10\,xy + 5y^2$ then

$$\frac{\partial z}{\partial x} = 6x^2 + 10y + 0$$

$$\frac{\partial z}{\partial y} = 0 + 10x + 10y$$

Higher order partial derivatives:

If z = f (x, y) then $\frac{\partial z}{\partial x}$ is called first order partial derivative of z with respect to x. If we differentiate the so obtained first order derivative once again with respect to x then what we get is called the second order partial derivative.

Example 21:

If $$10x^3 - 4x^2y + 3xy^2 + y^4$$

then $$\frac{\partial z}{\partial x} = 30x^2 - 8xy + 3y^2$$

Now $$\frac{\partial}{\partial x}\left(\frac{\partial z}{\partial x}\right) = \frac{\partial^2 z}{\partial x^2} = 60x - 8y$$

Similarly $$\frac{\partial z}{\partial y} = -4x^2 + 6xy + 4y^3$$

$$\frac{\partial}{\partial y}\left(\frac{\partial z}{\partial y}\right) = \frac{\partial^2 z}{\partial y^2} = 6x + 12y^2$$

Cross partial derivatives:

If z = f (x, y) is once differentiated with respect to x and another time with respect to y then, the so obtained second order derivative is often called the cross partial derivative.

Example 22: If $z = 5x^2y + 4xy^2$

then $$\frac{\partial z}{\partial x} = 10xy + 4y^2$$

$$\frac{\partial^2 z}{\partial x \partial y} = \frac{\partial}{\partial y}\left(10xy + 4y^2\right) = 10x + 8y$$

$$\frac{\partial z}{\partial y} = 5x^2 + 8xy$$

$$\frac{\partial^2 z}{\partial y \partial x} = \frac{\partial}{\partial x}\left(5x^2 + 8xy\right) = 10x + 8y$$

Note: In the above illustration it is important to note that

$$\frac{\partial^2 z}{\partial x \partial y} = \frac{\partial^2 z}{\partial y \partial x} = 10x + 8y$$

In other words, this is to say that while getting the second order cross partial derivative it does not matter the order in which the derivatives are obtained. We can do it first with respective x and then with respective to y or vice versa. This property can be taken as a rule for all the problems.

Type of derivatives:

For clear understanding of the notations, let us summarize the normal and alternative short notations as follows.

Notation	Alternative Notation	Example x^2y+2xy^2
$\frac{\partial z}{\partial x}$	f_x	$2xy+2y^2$
$\frac{\partial z}{\partial y}$	f_y	x^2+4xy
$\frac{\partial z}{\partial x^2}$	f_{xx}	$2y$
$\frac{\partial^2 z}{\partial y^2}$	f_{yy}	$4x$
$\frac{\partial^2 z}{\partial x\partial y}$	f_{xy}	$2x+4y$
$\frac{\partial^2 z}{\partial y\partial x}$	f_{yx}	$2x+4y$

8.8 Use of Partial Derivatives in Economics

If Q = f (L, K) stands for the production function with two inputs L and K then the marginal productivity of the input L is defined as the additional output obtainable by using one more unit of L by keeping the input K as constant. In mathematical terms this is simply the partial derivative of Q with respect to L. Thus in general the marginal productivity of an input is obtained by differentiating the given production function with respect to the input under consideration by keeping all other inputs as constants.

Example 23: For the Cobb-Douglas production function $Q = AL^{\alpha}K^{\beta}$ find both MP_L and MP_K. Further prove that both MP_L and MP_K are downward slopping.

$$MP_L = \frac{\partial Q}{\partial L} = \frac{\partial}{\partial L}\left(AL^{\alpha}K^{\beta}\right) = A\alpha L^{\alpha-1}K^{\beta}$$

$$= A\,\alpha\,L^{\alpha}L^{-1}K^{\beta}$$

$$= \frac{\alpha Q}{L}$$

$$MP_K = \frac{\partial Q}{\partial K} = \frac{\partial}{\partial K}\left(AL^{\alpha}K^{\beta}\right) = AL^{\alpha}\beta K^{\beta-1}$$

$$= AL^{\alpha}\beta K^{\beta}K^{-1}$$

$$= \frac{\beta Q}{K}$$

Now to get at the slope of MP_L and MP_K we derive f_{LL} and f_{KK}

By definition $f_{LL} = \frac{\partial}{\partial L}(f_L) = \frac{\partial}{\partial L}\left(A\alpha\, L^{\alpha-1}K^{\beta}\right)$

$$= A\alpha(\alpha-1)L^{\alpha-2}K^{\beta}$$

In the above expression since α is positive fraction the term $(\alpha - 1)$ is negative. Hence the MP_L function will slope downwards in its entire range of its operation. In other words, this function will have only stage II among the three familiar stages of production. Hence, the Cobb-Douglas production is often called the well-behaved production function. Similarly,

$$f_{KK} = \frac{\partial}{\partial K}(f_K) = \frac{\partial}{\partial K}\left(AL^{\alpha}\beta\, K^{\beta-1}\right)$$

$$= A\, L^{\alpha}\beta\,(\beta-1)K^{\beta-2}$$

Here again since β is a positive fraction the term $(\beta - 1)$ is negative. Hence MP_K is also downward slopping in its entire range of operation as expected.

Example 24: For the CES production function $Q = A\left[\alpha L^{-\rho} + \beta K^{-\rho}\right]^{-1/\rho}$ obtain the partial derivatives f_L, and f_K.

Solution:

The production function of the firm is

$$Q = A\left[\alpha L^{-\rho} + \beta K^{-\rho}\right]^{-1/\rho}$$

Now by definition

$$MP_L = \frac{\partial Q}{\partial L} = f_L = A\left(-\tfrac{1}{\rho}\right)\left[\alpha L^{-\rho} + \beta K^{-\rho}\right]^{-\frac{1}{\rho}-1} \times \alpha(-\rho)L^{-\rho-1}$$

$$= A\left[\alpha L^{-\rho} + \beta K^{-\rho}\right]^{-\frac{1}{\rho}}\left[\alpha L^{-\rho} + \beta K^{-\rho}\right]^{-1} \times \alpha L^{-\rho-1}$$

$$= \frac{\alpha Q}{\left[\alpha L^{-\rho} + \beta K^{-\rho}\right]L^{\rho+1}}$$

$$MP_K = \frac{\partial Q}{\partial K} = f_K = A\left(-\tfrac{1}{\rho}\right)\left[\alpha L^{-\rho} + \beta K^{-\rho}\right]^{-\frac{1}{\rho}-1} \times \beta(-\rho)K^{-\rho-1}$$

$$= A\left[\alpha L^{-\rho} + \beta K^{-\rho}\right]^{-\frac{1}{\rho}}\left[\alpha L^{-\rho} + \beta K^{-\rho}\right]^{-1} \times \beta K^{-\rho-1}$$

$$= \frac{\beta Q}{\left[\alpha L^{-\rho} + \beta K^{-\rho}\right]K^{\rho+1}}$$

8.9 Total Derivative

If $\quad z = f[x, y] \quad$ ...(1)

$\quad x = g(t) \quad$ ...(2)

$$y = h\,(t) \qquad \ldots(3)$$

Then by substituting (2) and (3) in (1), it is rewritten as

$$z = [g\,(t), h\,(t)] \qquad \ldots(4)$$

In (4) above z is a function of 't' alone. However, the rate of change of z for a given small change in t can have two partial effects, one through x another through y. Now the total effect due to both these effects is given by the formula

$$\frac{dz}{dt} = \frac{\partial z}{\partial x}\frac{dx}{dt} + \frac{\partial z}{\partial y}\frac{dy}{dt} \quad \text{or}$$

$$\frac{dz}{dt} = f_x\frac{dx}{dt} + f_y\frac{dy}{dt}$$

Here since two partial effects are summed up, the so obtained derivative is called the total derivative.

Second order total derivative

$$\frac{d^2z}{dt^2} = \frac{d}{dt}\left(\frac{dz}{dt}\right) = \frac{d}{dt}\left(f_x\frac{dx}{dt} + f_y\frac{dy}{dt}\right)$$

$$= \frac{\partial}{\partial x}\left(f_x\frac{dx}{dt} + f_y\frac{dy}{dt}\right)\frac{dx}{dt} + \frac{\partial}{\partial y}\left(f_x\frac{dx}{dt} + f_y\frac{dy}{dt}\right)\frac{dy}{dt}$$

$$= f_{xx}\left(\frac{dx}{dt}\right)^2 + f_{yx}\left(\frac{dx}{dt}\right)\left(\frac{dy}{dt}\right) + f_{xy}\left(\frac{dx}{dt}\right)\left(\frac{dy}{dt}\right) + f_{yy}\left(\frac{dy}{dt}\right)^2$$

$$= f_{xx}\left(\frac{dx}{dt}\right)^2 + 2f_{xy}\left(\frac{dx}{dt}\right)\left(\frac{dy}{dt}\right) + f_{yy}\left(\frac{dy}{dt}\right)^2$$

Special case: If t = x in the above general case we get a special case mostly used in economics.

If

$$z = f\,[x, y] \qquad \ldots(1)$$

$$x = g\,(x) \qquad \ldots(2)$$

$$y = h\,(x) \qquad \ldots(3)$$

Here since the second equation adds no additional information it may by omitted. Now in equation (1) x and y are not independent. In fact they are related by equation (3) above. Under such circumstances the needed total derivative is obtained by simply replacing t by x in our general case discussed above.

$$\frac{dz}{dx} = f_x + f_y\frac{dy}{dx}$$

$$\frac{d^2z}{dx} = f_{xx}\left(\frac{dx}{dx}\right)^2 + 2f_{xy}\left(\frac{dx}{dx}\right)\left(\frac{dy}{dx}\right) + f_{yy}\left(\frac{dy}{dx}\right)^2$$

$$\frac{d^2z}{dx} = f_{xx} + 2f_{xy}\left(\frac{dy}{dx}\right) + f_{yy}\left(\frac{dy}{dx}\right)^2$$

8.10 Use of Total Derivative in Economics

Example 25: If $U = f(q_1, q_2)$ stands for the utility function and $M = p_1q_1 + p_2q_2$ stands for the budget equation find the total derivatives dU/dq_1 and d^2U/dq_1^2.

Solution:

The utility function of the consumer is

$$U = f(q_1, q_2) \quad \text{...(1)}$$

The budget equation of the consumer is

$$M = p_1q_1 + p_2q_2 \quad \text{...(2)}$$

Here in equation (1) above the utility, though depends upon both q_1 and q_2 the choice of both q_1 and q_2 are not independent. With the given money income the consumer has no choice of buying both the commodities in unlimited quantities. Once certain amount of q_1 is bought already the choice of q_2 is constraint by the money left over with the consumer after the purchase of the first commodity q_1. In mathematical term this is to say that q_1 is independent and q_2 is dependent. So equation (2) may be rewritten as

$$-p_2q_2 = p_1q_1 - M$$

$$q_2 = \frac{p_1q_1 - M}{-p_2}$$

$$q_2 = \frac{M}{p_2} - \frac{p_1}{p_2}q_1 \quad \text{...(3)}$$

Now from the total derivative rule $\frac{dU}{dq_1} = f_1 + f_2\left(\frac{dq_2}{dq_1}\right)$

From equation (3)

$$\frac{dq_2}{dq_1} = -\frac{p_1}{p_2}$$

so
$$\frac{dU}{dq_1} = f_1 + f_2\left(-\frac{p_1}{p_2}\right)$$

Note: we can treat q_2 as independent and q_1 as dependent and calculate dU/dq_2 also.

The second order total derivative

As usual the second order derivative is obtained by taking one more derivative to the first order derivative already obtained.

$$\frac{d^2}{dq_1^2}(U) = \frac{d}{dq_1}\left(\frac{dU}{dq_1}\right) = \frac{d}{dq_1}\left[f_1 + f_2\left(\frac{dq_2}{dq_1}\right)\right]$$

$$= \frac{\partial}{\partial q_1}\left[f_1 + f_2\left(\frac{dq_2}{dq_1}\right)\right] + \frac{\partial}{\partial q_2}\left[f_1 + f_2\left(\frac{dq_2}{dq_1}\right)\right]\left(\frac{dq_2}{dq_1}\right)$$

$$= f_{11} + f_{21}\left(\frac{dq_2}{dq_1}\right) + f_{12}\left(\frac{dq_2}{dq_1}\right) + f_{22}\left(\frac{dq_2}{dq_1}\right)^2$$

$$= f_{11} + 2f_{12}\left(\frac{dq_2}{dq_1}\right) + f_{22}\left(\frac{dq_2}{dq_1}\right)^2$$

Now since $\frac{dq_2}{dq_1} = -\frac{p_1}{p_2}$ from the budget equation, the above condition may be written as

$$\frac{d^2U}{dq_1^2} = f_{11} + 2f_{12}\left(\frac{-p_1}{p_2}\right) + f_{22}\left(\frac{-p_1}{p_2}\right)^2$$

8.11 Total Differentials

If $z = f(x, y)$ then the first order total differential is written as $dz = f_x dx + f_y dy$.

Total second order differentials:

Whenever the functional relationship is linear, as most of the cases in economics, the second order differential may be written as

$$d^2z = f_{xx} + 2\, f_{xy}\, dx\, dy + f_{yy}(dy)^2$$

EXERCISES

Differentiate the following functions with respect to x.

1. $y = x^{-10}$
2. $y = 10/x$
3. $y = x$
4. $y = x^{3/2}$
5. $y = x^{-10}$
6. $y = x/20$
7. $y = 10x^3$
8. $y = 100x^{-4/5}$
9. $y = 100$
10. $y = x^2 + 10x^{-1} + x + 100$
11. $y = x^{12} - x^3 + 12x + 32$
12. $y = (x^n)(e^x)$
13. $y = (e^x/x^5)$
14. $y = (\ln.x)(e^x)$
15. $y = \ln.\ x^2$
16. $x^2 + 2xy + y^2 = 10$

17. $x^2 + y^2 = 10$
18. $x^4 + x^3 + xy + y^2 = 19$
19. $x = y^2$
20. $x = y^2 + xy + y$
21. $y = \sqrt{x^2}$
22. $y = e^{x^2}$
23. $y = (\ln.x)(x^n)$
24. $y = (\ln.x)/e^x$
25. $y = \ln.x^2 e^x$

9

Chapter

APPLICATION OF DERIVATIVES: ELASTICITY

9.1 Usefulness of Elasticity

Elasticity is a measure of sensitivity or responsiveness of the dependent variable for a given small change in the independent variable in a given functional relationship of the type y = f (x). In a given range of operation if response of the dependent variable is 100% due a 10% change in the independent variable then we say that the relation is elastic in the said range of operation. Similarly, if there is a 10% response in the dependent variable for a given 10% change in the independent variable in a given range then we would say that the elasticity is unity in this range of operation. Alternatively, a given 10% change in the independent variable leads to only a 5% response in the dependent variable then we would say that this range is inelastic.

9.2 Definition of Arc and Point Elasticity

Altogether we have two distinct methods of measuring elasticity. They are:

(i) Arc Method.

(ii) Point Method.

The choice between these two methods often depends upon the nature of data available and purpose for which the elasticity is needed. If the data is discrete in nature then the right choice would be the arc method. In actual practice most of the elasticity computations use the arc method. On the other hand, if the data range is continuous then the point method is used to compute the elasticity. Point elasticities are commonly used in theoretical economics.

Definition of arc elasticity

If y = f (x) stands for the said relationship between x and y, then the arc elasticity of y with respect to x between the two points A and B, denoted by Ey/Ex, is defined as the ratio of the proportional change in the dependent variable 'y' to that of the proportional change in the independent variable 'x'.

Diagrammatic measure of arc elasticity for decreasing function

The function y = f(x) is a decreasing function provided a rise in x leads to a fall in y and vice versa as shown in Fig. 9.1. In the following example, we illustrate the method of getting the arc elasticity.

Example 1 (a): When x value rises from 10 to 15, the y value falls from 6 to 4. Obtain the arc elasticity.

Solution:

In the diagram given below when x rises from 10 to 15 the y falls from 6 to 4. Accordingly, we move from A to B on the curve in Fig. 9.1 (a).

Now by definition

$$\frac{Ey}{Ex}=\frac{\text{Proportional change in y}}{\text{Proportional change in x}}=\frac{\frac{\Delta y}{y_1}}{\frac{\Delta x}{x_1}}=\frac{x_1}{y_1}\frac{\Delta y}{\Delta x}=\frac{10}{6}\times\frac{2}{5}=0.667$$

In the above formula we use the x and y coordinates of the point A for the calculation of the proportionalities in the respective denominators on the assumption that we move from point A to point B along the curve.

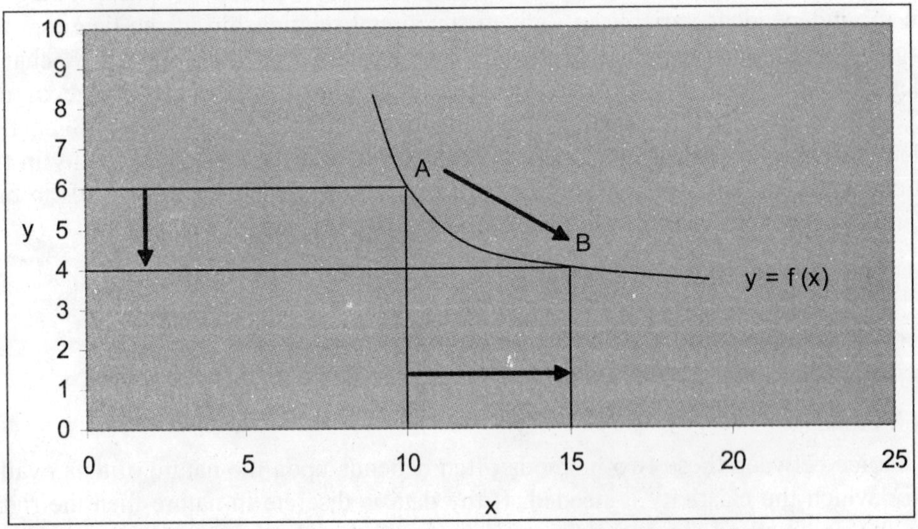

Fig. 9.1 (a) Arc elasticity for a decreasing function

Example 1 (b): When x value falls from 15 to 10, the y value rises from 4 to 6. Obtain the arc elasticity.

Solution:

$$\frac{Ey}{Ex}=\left(\frac{\Delta y}{\Delta x}\right)\left(\frac{x_2+x_1}{y_2+y_1}\right)=\left(\frac{6-4}{15-10}\right)\left(\frac{15+10}{4+6}\right)=\frac{2}{5}\times\frac{25}{10}=1.00$$

$$\frac{Ey}{Ex}=\frac{\text{Proportional change in y}}{\text{Proportional change in x}}=\frac{\frac{\Delta y}{y_2}}{\frac{\Delta x}{x_2}}=\frac{x_2}{y_2}\frac{\Delta y}{\Delta x}=\frac{15}{4}\times\frac{2}{5}=1.50$$

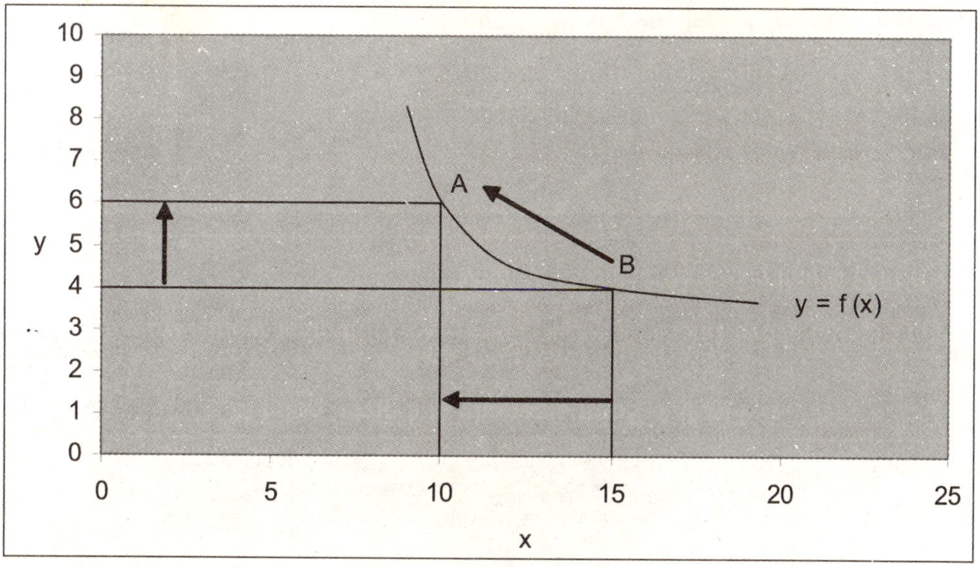

Fig. 9.1 (b) Arc elasticity for a decreasing function

Unconvincingly, both the results differ considerably though we are in the same range of operation. In fact, the first result under states the elasticity while the second result over states the same. Further, more the distance between the points A and B more will be the said difference.

A compromising formula

As a compromise to these two biased methods, the conventional approach of arc elasticity uses the average coordinate values in the respective denominators as shown below. So the modified definition is stated as

$$\frac{Ey}{Ex} = \frac{\dfrac{\Delta y}{(y_2 + y_1)/2}}{\dfrac{\Delta x}{(x_2 + x_1)/2}} = \left(\frac{\Delta y}{\Delta x}\right)\left(\frac{x_2 + x_1}{y_2 + y_1}\right)$$

Thus, the modified arc elasticity for our illustration becomes

Example 1(c): When x value falls from 15 to 10, the y value rises from 4 to 6. Obtain the arc elasticity.

Solution:

$$\frac{Ey}{Ex} = \left(\frac{\Delta y}{\Delta x}\right)\left(\frac{x_2 + x_1}{y_2 + y_1}\right) = \left(\frac{6-4}{15-10}\right)\left(\frac{15+10}{4+6}\right) = \frac{2}{5} \times \frac{25}{10} = 1.00$$

Diagrammatic measure of arc elasticity for an increasing function

The function y = f(x) is an increasing function provided a rise in x leads to a rise in y and vice versa as shown in Fig. 9.2. In the following example, we illustrate the method of getting the arc elasticity.

Definition of Arc Elasticity for increasing function:

$$\frac{Ey}{Ex} = \frac{\text{Proportional change in y}}{\text{Proportional change in x}}$$

$$= \frac{\dfrac{y_2 - y_1}{y_1 + y_2}}{\dfrac{x_2 - x_1}{x_2 + x_1}} = \frac{y_2 - y_1}{y_1 + y_2} \times \frac{x_2 + x_1}{x_2 - x_1}$$

Example 2: When x value falls from 10 to 5, the y value falls from 4 to 2. Obtain the arc elasticity by using the compromising formula.

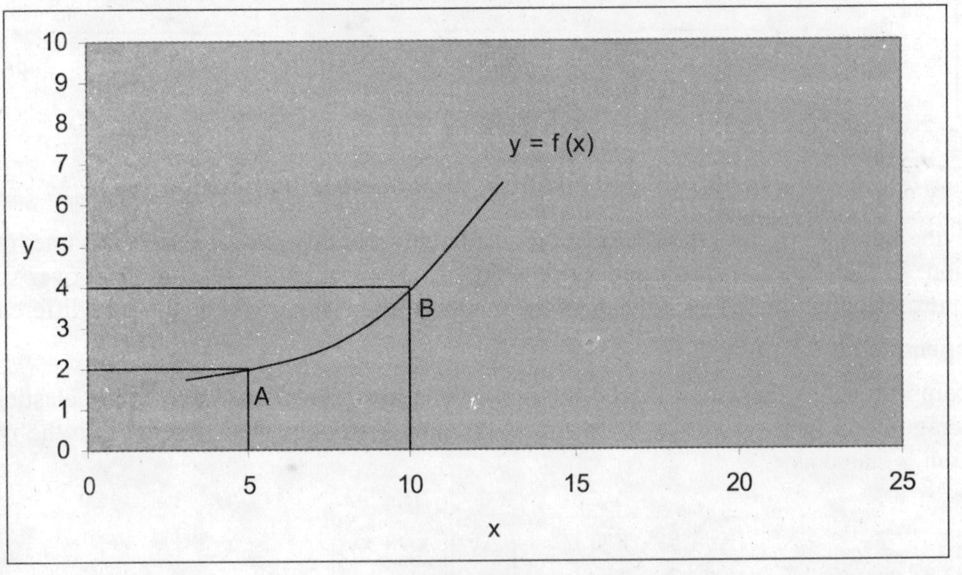

Fig. 9.2

$$\frac{Ey}{Ex} = \frac{\text{Proportional change in y}}{\text{Proportional change in x}} = \frac{\dfrac{y_2 - y_1}{y_1 + y_2}}{\dfrac{x_2 - x_1}{x_2 + x_1}}$$

$$= \frac{y_2 - y_1}{y_1 + y_2} \times \frac{x_2 + x_1}{x_2 - x_1} = \frac{4-2}{4+2} \times \frac{10+5}{10-5}$$

$$= \frac{2}{6} \times \frac{15}{5} = 1$$

Demerit of this method

Even this modified formula holds good only for a small range of the arc under reference. If the arc length becomes too large the averaging method also fails to give the correct measure of the needed sensitivity. In fact the best result could be the one in which the arc length is kept at its minimum. As a limiting case when both these points A and B coincide we get the best possible result. Such a measure is often called the point elasticity.

Definition of point elasticity

If y = f (x) stands for the said functional relationship between x and y then, the elasticity of y with respective x, denoted by $\frac{Ey}{Ex}$ is defined as the ratio of the proportional change in the dependent variable 'y' to that of the proportional change in the independent variable 'x'.

i.e.
$$\frac{Ey}{Ex} = \frac{\text{Proportional change in y}}{\text{Proportional change in x}} = \frac{\frac{dy}{y}}{\frac{dx}{x}} = \frac{x}{y}\frac{dy}{dx}$$

This method thus contains derivative in it definition. Since derivative at a given point is simply the slope of the tangent in all our elasticity calculations invariably we will be using tangents.

Diagrammatic measure of point elasticity for an increasing function

In Fig. 9.3 the relation y = f (x) is an increasing function. Now, if we want to calculate the elasticity of y with respect to x at a given point, say M, we simply draw a tangent to the curve at that point first. Let this tangent meet the x-axis at the point L as shown in the Fig. 8.1. Further, let the perpendicular drawn from M meets the x-axis at N. Now from the definition of elasticity it follows that

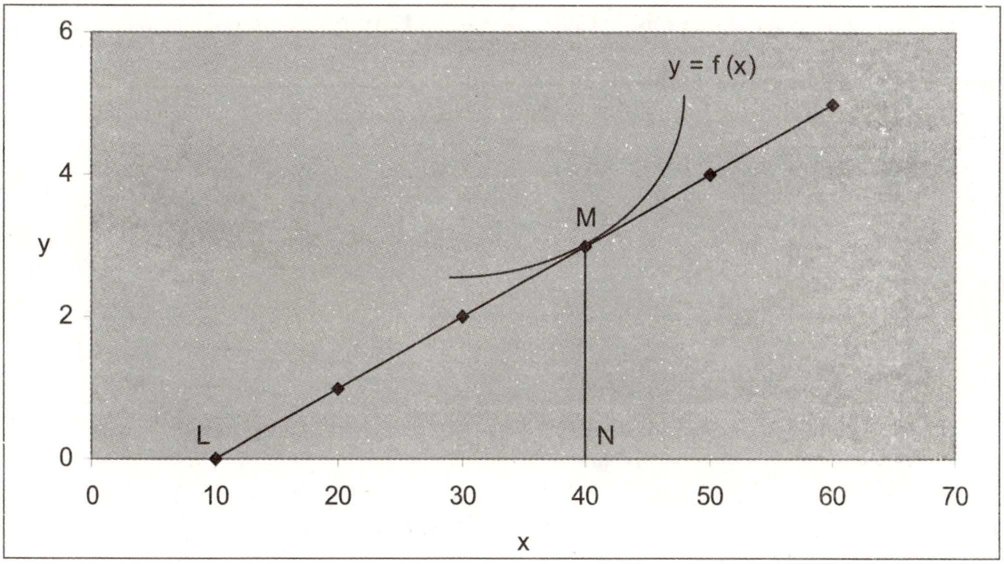

Fig. 9.3 Point elasticity at a given point M

$$\frac{Ey}{Ex} = \frac{x}{y}\frac{dy}{dx} = \frac{ON}{MN}\frac{MN}{LN} = \frac{ON}{LN}$$

Here, in Fig. 9.3 since ON > LN, $\frac{Ey}{Ex} = \frac{40}{30} = 1.3333 > 1$. The function y = f (x) is said to be elastic at neighbourhood of the given point M.

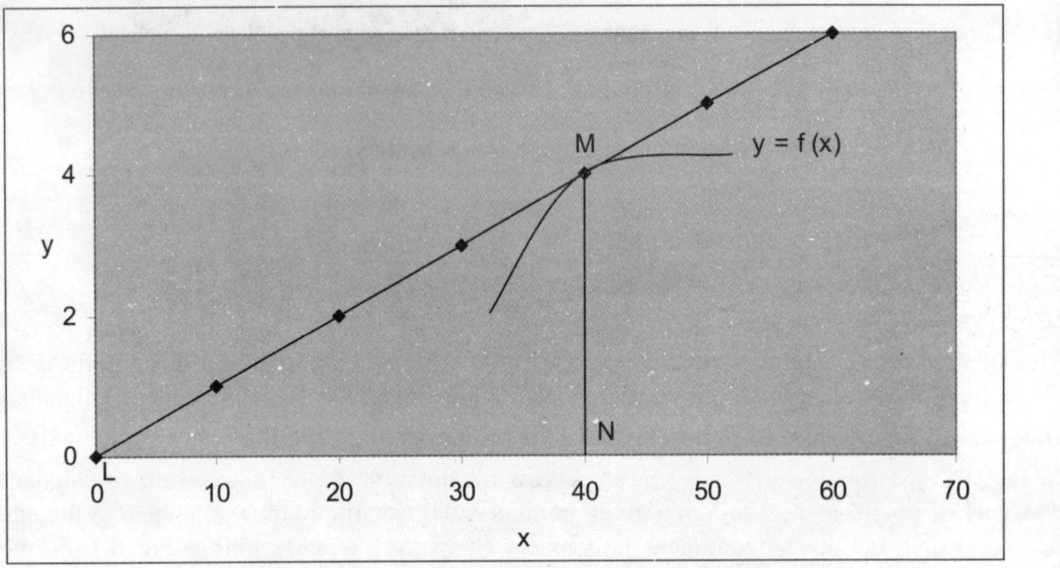

Fig. 9.4 Point elasticity at a given point M

However, in Fig. 9.4 above since ON = LN, $\frac{Ey}{Ex} = \frac{40}{40} = 1$. In other words, we would say that the function y = f (x) is unit elastic at the given point M.

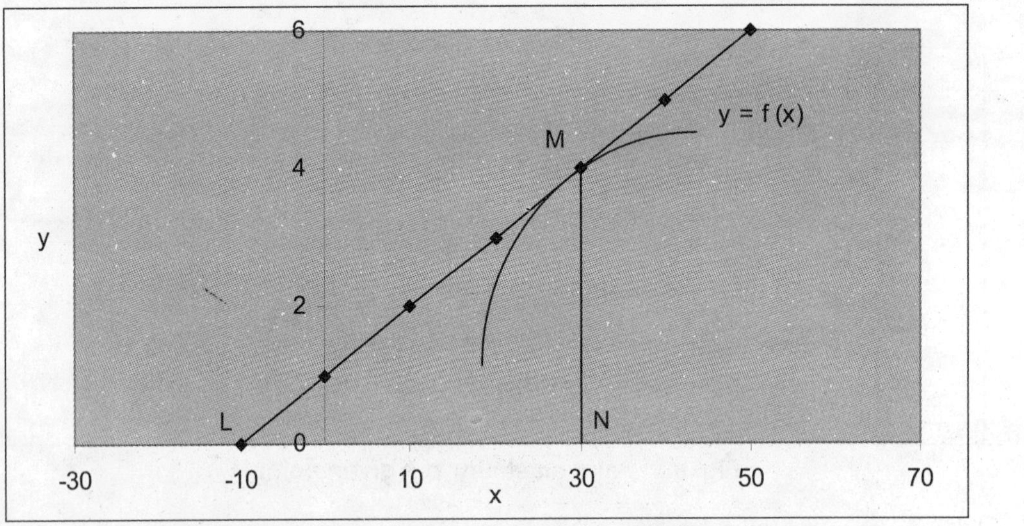

Fig. 9.5 Point elasticity at a given point M

In Fig 9.5 above since ON< LN, $\frac{Ey}{Ex} = \frac{30}{40} = 0.75 < 1$. Hence the function y = f (x) is said to be inelastic around the point M.

Diagrammatic measure of point elasticity for a decreasing function

To get the elasticity at a given point, say M, we draw a tangent at M to the given function y = f (x) first. Let this tangent meet the X-axis at L and y-axis at T as shown in Fig. 9.6. Further, let the perpendicular from M meets the x-axis at N.

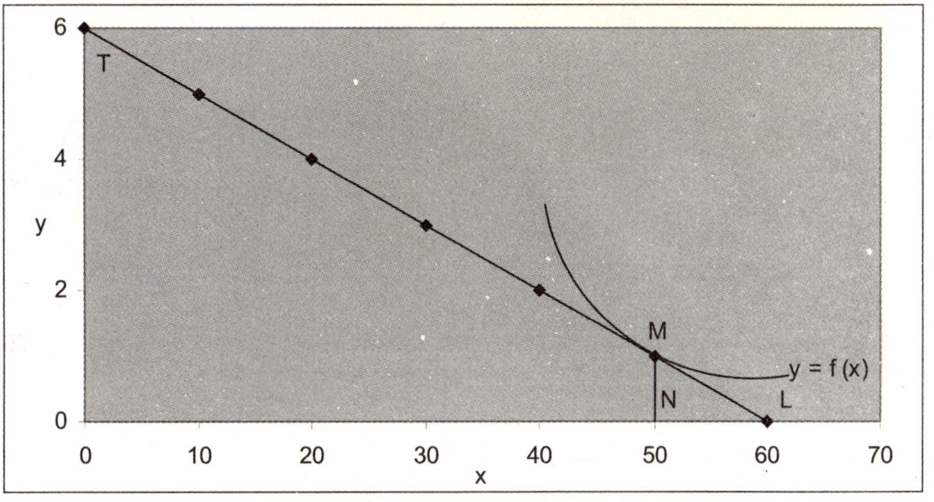

Fig. 9.6 Point elasticity at a given point M

Now by definition if M is below the mid point of LT as shown Fig 9.6 then ON > NL $\frac{Ey}{Ex} = \frac{ON}{NL} = \frac{50}{10} = \frac{TM}{ML} = \frac{5}{1} = 5$

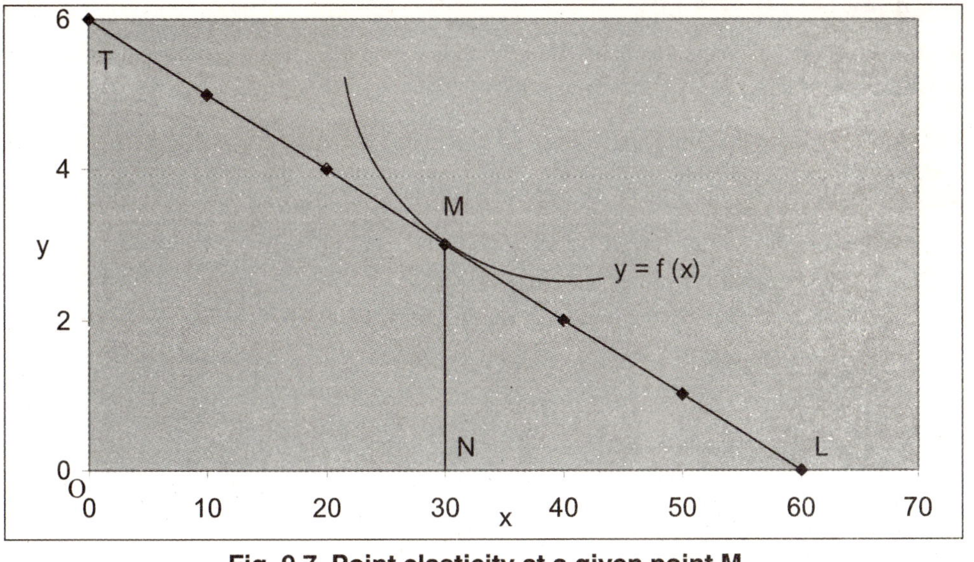

Fig. 9.7 Point elasticity at a given point M

If M is the mid point of LT as in Fig 9.7 above then ON = NL, $\eta = \frac{ON}{NL} = \frac{30}{30} = \frac{TM}{ML} = \frac{3}{3} = 1$ (Unit elastic)

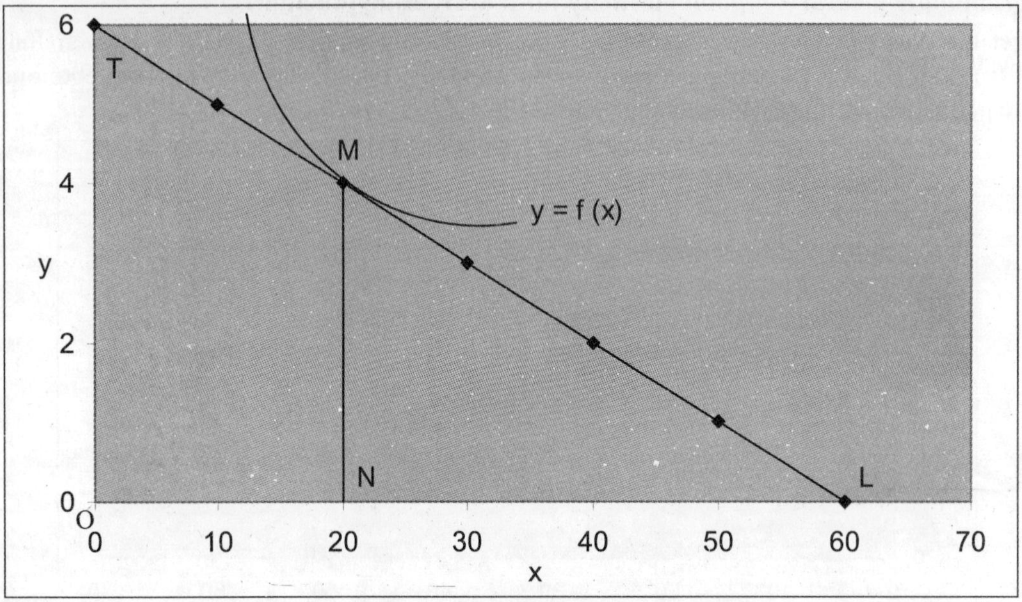

Fig. 9.8 Point elasticity at a given point M

If M is above the mid point of LT as shown Fig 9.8 then ON < NL,

$$\frac{Ey}{Ex} = \frac{ON}{NL} = \frac{20}{40} = \frac{TM}{ML} = \frac{2}{4} = 0.5$$

9.3 Elasticity is Free from the Units of Measurement

Since elasticity is a relative measure of the responsiveness of y for a given small change in x it must be free from the units of measurements of both x and y variables. As an illustration let y = f (x) stands for original function. Now $\frac{Ey}{Ex}$ measure the elasticity of y with respective to x. Now let us redefine a new variable X so that x = 100X. Similarly, let y is redefined as y so that y = 1000Y.

Now,

$$\frac{Ey}{Ex} = \frac{E(1000Y)}{E(100X)} = \frac{100X}{1000Y}\frac{d(1000Y)}{d(100X)}$$

$$= \frac{100X}{1000Y}\frac{1000dY}{100dX}$$

$$= \frac{X}{Y}\frac{dY}{dX}$$

$$\frac{Ey}{Ex} = \frac{EY}{EX}$$

In other words, this is to say that the elasticity is a relative measure and is free from the units of measurements. This is illustrated in Fig. 9.9 in old units and Fig. 9.10 in new units.

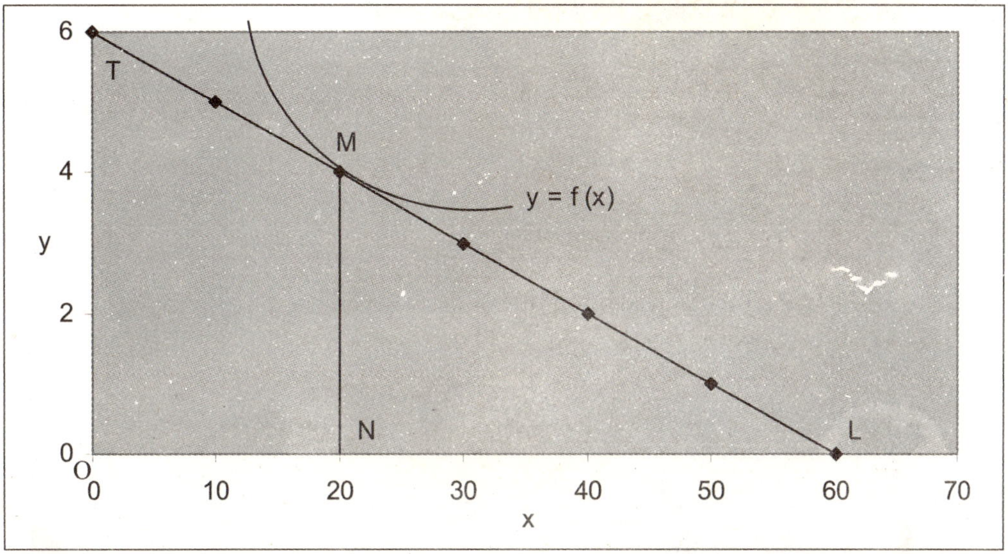

Fig. 9.9 Point elasticity at a given point M in original units.

$$\eta = \frac{ON}{NL} = \frac{20}{40} = \frac{TM}{ML} = \frac{2}{4} = 1/2$$

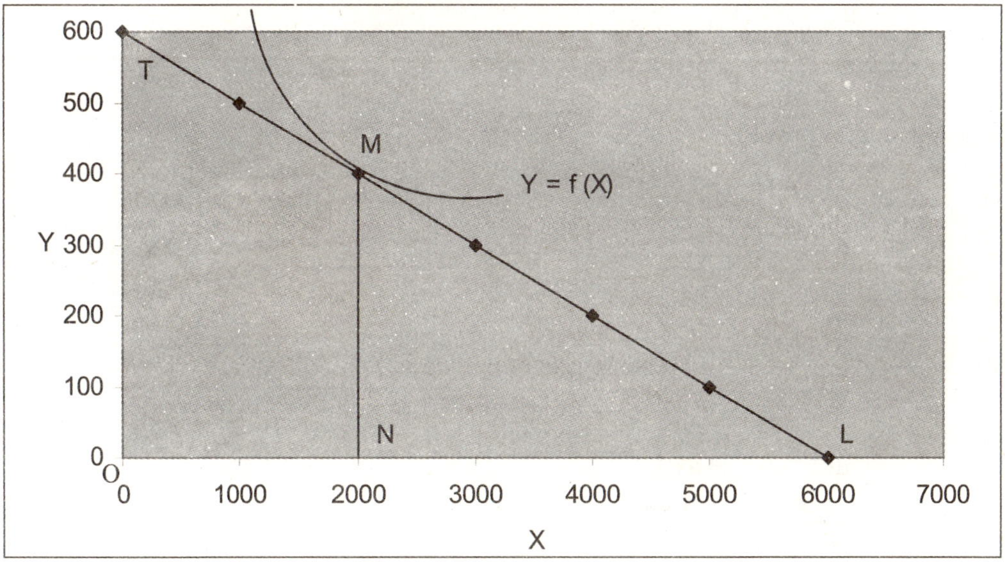

Fig. 9.10 Point elasticity at a given point M in new units.

$$\eta = \frac{ON}{NL} = \frac{2000}{4000} = \frac{TM}{ML} = \frac{2}{4} = 1/2$$

9.4 Elasticity Theorems

Theorem 1: If u = f (x) and v = g (x) then

$$\frac{E(u \pm v)}{Ex} = \frac{u\frac{Eu}{Ex} \pm v\frac{Ev}{Ex}}{u \pm v}$$

Proof:

$$\text{L.H.S.} = \frac{E(u \pm v)}{Ex}$$

$$= \frac{x}{u \pm v}\frac{d}{dx}(u \pm v) \qquad \text{(Addition rule of derivative)}$$

$$= \frac{x}{u \pm v}\left(\frac{du}{dx} \pm \frac{dv}{dx}\right)$$

$$= \frac{1}{u \pm v}\left(\frac{x\,du}{dx} \pm \frac{xdv}{dx}\right)$$

$$= \frac{1}{u \pm v}\left(u\frac{x\,du}{u\,dx} \pm v\frac{x\,dv}{v\,dx}\right)$$

$$= \frac{1}{u \pm v}\left(u\frac{Eu}{Ex} \pm v\frac{Ev}{Ex}\right)$$

$$= \frac{\left(u\frac{Eu}{Ex} \pm v\frac{Ev}{Ex}\right)}{u \pm v} = \text{R.H.S.}$$

Hence the theorem is proved.

Theorem 2: If u = f (x) and v = g (x) then

$$\frac{E(u.v)}{Ex} = \frac{Eu}{Ex} + \frac{Ev}{Ex}$$

Proof:

$$\text{L.H.S.} = \frac{E(u.v)}{Ex} = \frac{x}{uv}\frac{d(u.v)}{dx} \qquad \text{(Product rule of derivative)}$$

$$= \frac{x}{uv}\left(u\frac{dv}{dx} + v\frac{du}{dx}\right)$$

$$= \frac{x}{uv}\frac{u.dv}{dx} + \frac{x}{uv}\frac{v.du}{dx}$$

$$= \frac{x.dv}{vdx} + \frac{xdu}{udx}$$

$$= \frac{Ev}{Ex} + \frac{Eu}{Ex} = \frac{Eu}{Ex} + \frac{Ev}{Ex} = \text{R.H.S.}$$

Hence the theorem is proved.

Theorem 3: If u = f (x) and v = g (x) then

$$\frac{E\left(\frac{u}{v}\right)}{Ex} = \frac{Eu}{Ex} - \frac{Ev}{Ex}$$

Proof:

$$\text{L.H.S.} = \frac{E\left(\frac{u}{v}\right)}{Ex} = \frac{x}{\frac{u}{v}} \frac{d\left(\frac{u}{v}\right)}{dx} = \frac{xv}{u}\left(\frac{v\frac{du}{dx} - u\frac{dv}{dx}}{v^2}\right) \quad \text{(Division rule of derivative)}$$

$$= \frac{xv}{u}\frac{v}{v^2}\frac{du}{dx} - \frac{xv}{u}\frac{u}{v^2}\frac{dv}{dx}$$

$$= \frac{Eu}{Ex} - \frac{Ev}{Ex} = \text{R.H.S.}$$

Hence the theorem is proved.

Example 3: If $y = x^2$ find Ey/Ex, the elasticity of y with respect to x.

Solution:

By definition $\frac{Ey}{Ex} = \frac{E(x^2)}{Ex} = \frac{x}{x^2}\frac{d(x^2)}{dx} = \frac{x.2x}{x^2} = 2$

Note 1: In the case of the power function the constant power itself is the elasticity.

Example 4: If $y = e^x$ find Ey/Ex, the elasticity of y with respect to x.

Solution:

By definition $\frac{Ey}{Ex} = \frac{E(e^x)}{Ex} = \frac{x}{e^x}\frac{d(e^x)}{dx} = \frac{x.e^x}{e^x} = x$

Note 2: In the case of the exponential function the variable x in the power is the elasticity.

Example 5: If $y = x^n e^x$ find $\frac{Ey}{Ex}$

Solution:

$$\frac{Ey}{Ex} = \frac{E(x^n.e^x)}{Ex} = \frac{x}{x^n e^x}\frac{d(x^n.e^x)}{dx}$$

$$= \frac{x}{x^n e^x}(x^n.e^x + e^x n x^{n-1})$$

$$= \frac{x\,x^n e^x(1 + nx^{-1})}{x^n e^x}$$

$$= x + n$$

Note 3: This result directly follows from theorem No. 2 above.

Example 6: If $y = x^n/e^x$ find $\frac{Ey}{Ex}$.

Solution:

$$\frac{Ey}{Ex} = \frac{E(x^n/e^x)}{Ex} = \frac{x}{x^n/e^x} \frac{d\left(\frac{e^x}{x^n}\right)}{dx}$$

$$= \frac{xe^x}{x^n}\left[\frac{e^x nx^{n-1} - x^n e^x}{\left(e^x\right)^2}\right]$$

$$= \frac{xe^x e^x x^n}{x^n\left(e^x\right)^2}(nx^{-1} - 1)$$

$$= n - x$$

Note 4: This result directly follows from theorem No. 3 above.

9.5 The Price Elasticity of Demand

If D = f (p) is demand function then the price elasticity of demand denoted by η is defined as the ratio of proportional change in the quantity demanded to that of the proportional change in price charged. As usual both arc and point methods are commonly used in the calculation of the price elasticity.

Definition of price elasticity of demand by arc method:

If D = f (p) is the given demand law then the arc elasticity is defined as the ratio of proportional change in the quantity demanded to that of proportional change in the price charged.

$$\eta = \frac{\text{Proportional change in the quantity demanded}}{\text{Proportional change in the price charged}}$$

$$= \left(\frac{\frac{\Delta D}{D_1 + D_2}}{\frac{\Delta p}{p_2 + p_1}}\right) = \frac{\frac{D_1 - D_2}{D_1 + D_2}}{\frac{p_2 - p_1}{p_2 + p_1}} = \left(\frac{D_1 - D_2}{p_2 - p_1}\right)\left(\frac{p_2 + p_1}{D_1 + D_2}\right)$$

Example 7: The price of a commodity has fallen from Rs. 6 to Rs. 4 on a certain day. This fall has increased the demand for the product from 10 to 15 units on the same day. Calculate the arc elasticity for the said commodity in this range of operation.

Solution:

From the definition the arc elasticity

$$\eta = \frac{ED}{Ep} = \left(\frac{\Delta D}{\Delta p}\right)\left(\frac{p_2 + p_1}{q_2 + q_1}\right) = \left(\frac{5}{2}\right)\left(\frac{4+6}{10+15}\right) = \left(\frac{5}{2}\right)\left(\frac{10}{25}\right) = 1$$

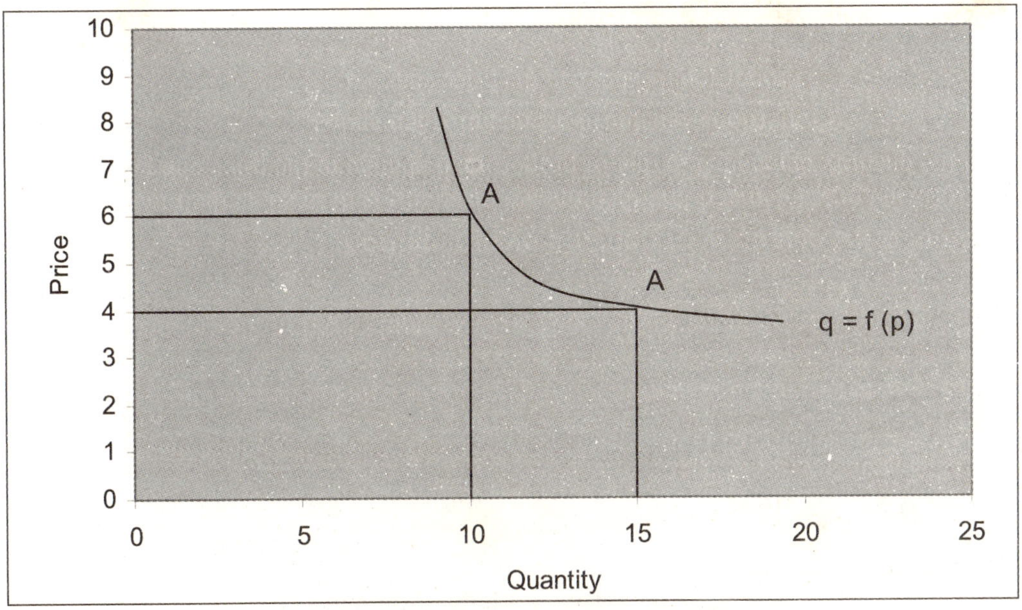

Fig. 9.11 Arc method for price elasticity of demand

Definition of price elasticity of demand by point method:

$$\eta = \frac{ED}{Ep} = \frac{\text{Proportional change in D}}{\text{Proportional change in p}}$$

$$= \frac{\frac{dD}{D}}{\frac{dp}{p}} = \frac{p}{D}\frac{dD}{dp}$$

Normally for the downward sloping demand, the derivative dD/dp in the above expression is always negative. Thus, according to the definition given above the value of η will always be negative. To avoid this problem of minus, often economists prefix a minus in the definition of η. Hence, the modified definition for η is written as

$$\eta = -\frac{ED}{Ep} = -\frac{p}{D}\frac{dD}{dp}$$

Note: Here, in this refined definition, though the elasticity is positive one must always remember the inverse relation between D and p and interpret the results accordingly. For example, if $\eta = 1$ then we would say that a 5% fall in p leads to exactly 5% rise in the quantity D and vice versa.

Diagrammatic measure of price elasticity of demand curve by point method

Let us start with an important note that in mathematics we always measure the independent variable x along the horizontal axis and the dependent variable y along the vertical axis.

However, as economists, we have a special convention of measuring the independent variable p along the vertical axis and the dependent variable D along the horizontal axis. Hence, dD/dp, the slope of function is always with respect to the vertical axis and not with respect to horizontal axis. Thus, if D = f (p) stands for the demand equation as shown in the Fig. 9.12, then

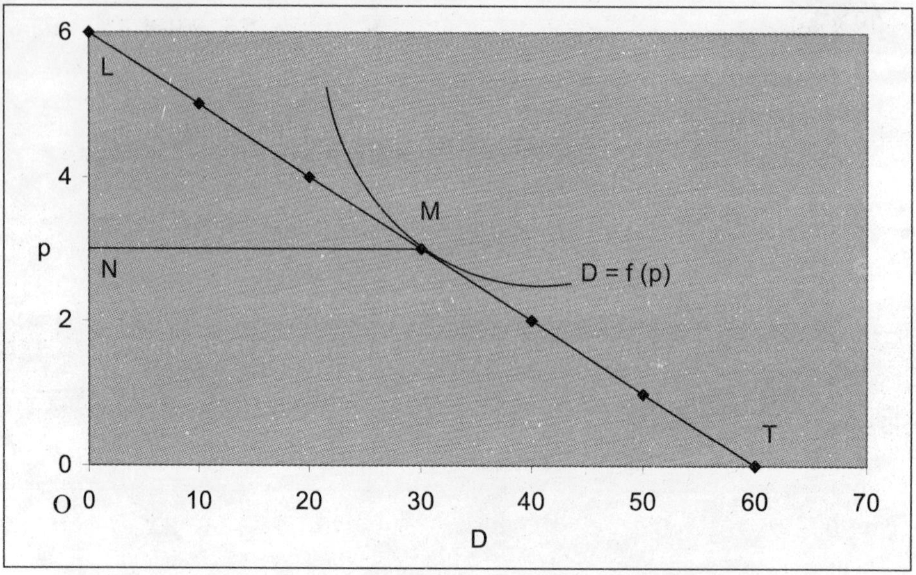

Fig. 9.12 Price elasticity of demand M

$$\eta = \frac{ED}{Ep} = \frac{p}{D}\frac{dD}{dp} = \frac{ON}{MN}\frac{MN}{LN} = \frac{ON}{LN} = \frac{TM}{ML} = \frac{\text{Length of the lower secment}}{\text{Length of the upper secment}}$$

Now depending upon the position of M on the tangent we come across three special cases.

(a) If M is the mid point of LT as in Fig. 9.12 then TM = ML and $\eta = \frac{TM}{ML} = \frac{3}{3} = 1$.

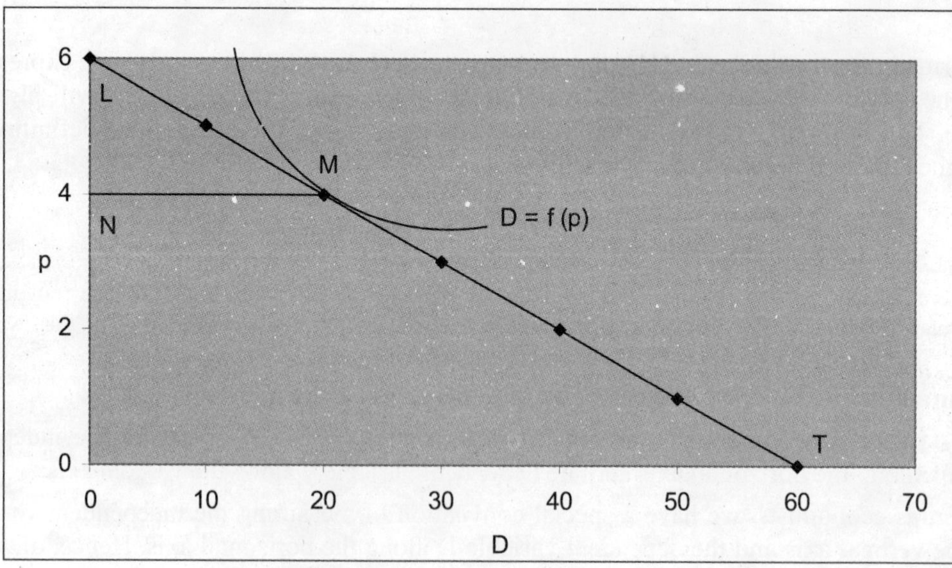

Fig. 9.13 Point elasticity at a given point M

(b) If M is above the mid point as shown in Fig. 9.13 then TM > ML. So, $\eta = \frac{TM}{ML} = \frac{4}{2} = 2$.

(c) If M is below the mid point as shown in Fig. 9.14, then TM < ML.

So $\eta = \frac{TM}{ML} = \frac{1}{4} = 0.25$

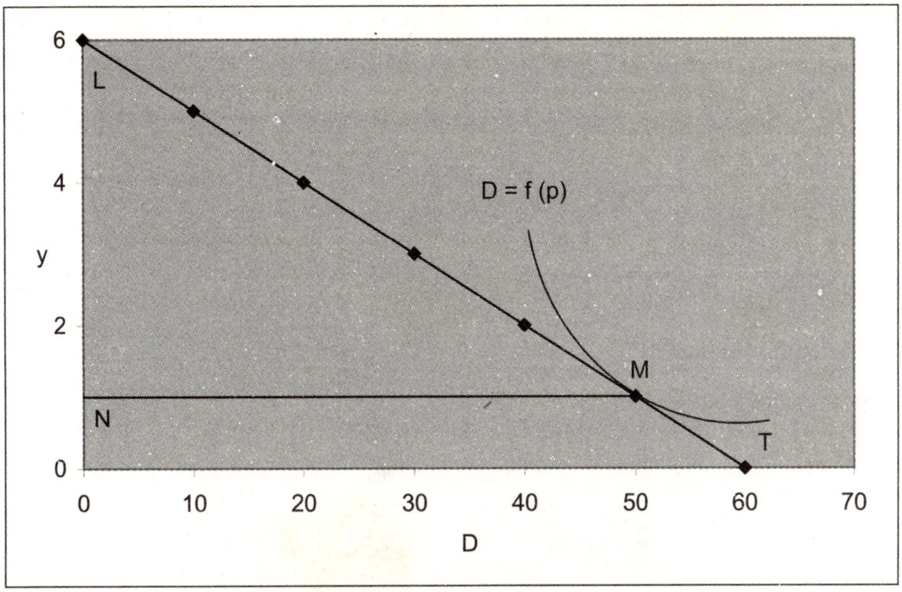

Fig. 9.14 Point elasticity at a given point M

Price elasticity of demand by point method: Numerical illustrations

Example 8: If D = 10 – 2p stands for the demand law find the point elasticity η when p = 4.

Solution:

$$\eta = -\frac{ED}{Ep} = -\frac{E(10-2p)}{Ep} = -\frac{p}{10-2p}\frac{d(10-2p)}{dp}$$

$$= -\frac{p}{10-2p} \times -2 = \frac{2p}{10-2p}$$

$$(\eta)_{p=4} = \frac{2 \times 4}{10 - 2 \times 4} = \frac{8}{2} = 4$$

Example 9: If D = 600 – 100p stands for the demand law find the point elasticity η when p = 4.
Solution:

$$\eta = -\frac{ED}{Ep} = -\frac{E(600-100p)}{Ep}$$

$$= -\frac{p}{600-100p}\frac{d(600-100p)}{dp}$$

$$= -\frac{p}{600 - 100p} \times -100$$

$$= \frac{100p}{600 - 100p}$$

$$(\eta)_{p=4} = \frac{100 \times 4}{600 - 100 \times 4} = \frac{400}{200} = 2$$

Diagrammatic measure of price elasticity of demand for a linear demand curve by point method

In the case of a straight-line demand there is no need to draw a separate tangent. In fact, the every line itself is the tangent for all points in the given straight line. In the Fig. 9.15 at mid point of the straight-line demand, since TM = ML, the price elasticity of demand is unity. For all points above mid point, since TM > ML, the price elasticity of demand $\eta > 1$. Similarly, for all points below mid point, since TM < ML, the price elasticity of demand $\eta < 1$.

Table 9.1

Linear Demand			
p	Q	R	MR
6	0	0	6
5	100	500	4
4	200	800	2
3	300	900	0
2	400	800	-2
1	500	500	-4
0	600	0	-6

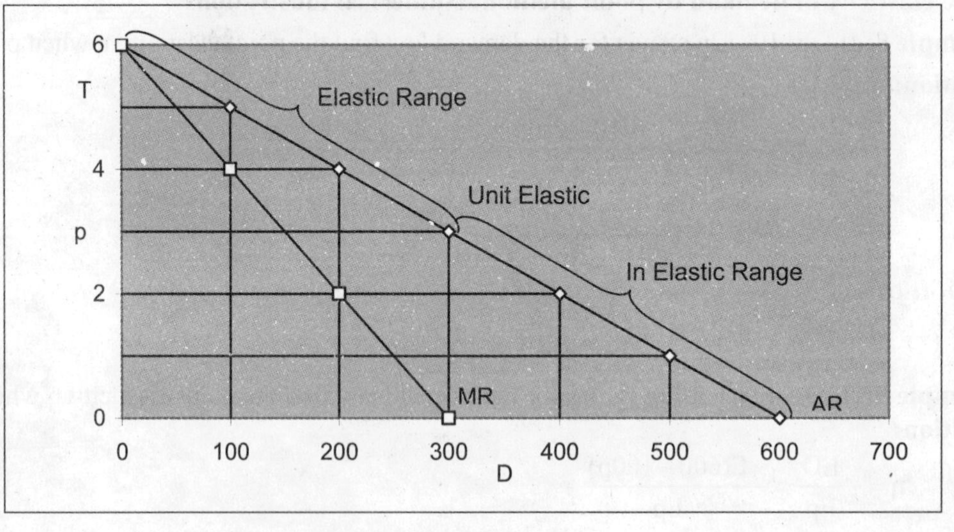

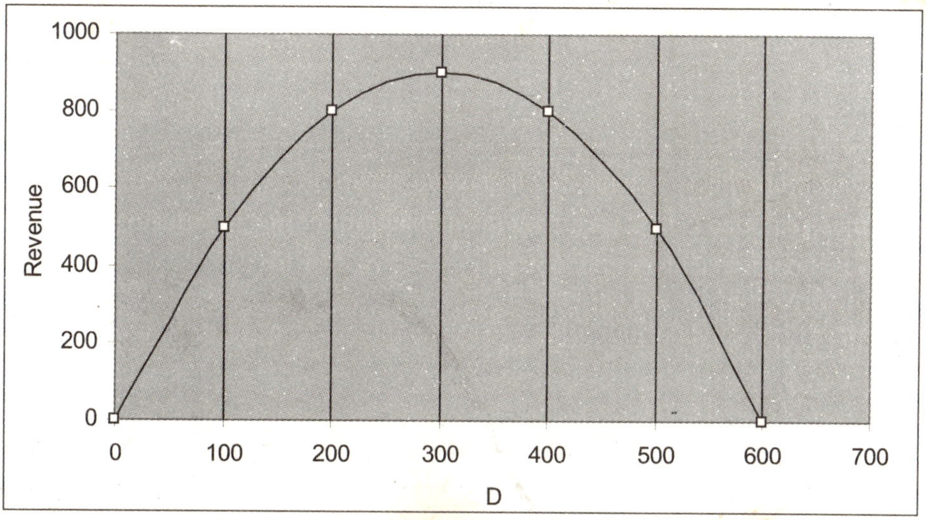

Fig. 9.15 Relation between MR, AR, R and η

In the top panel of the Fig. 9.15 we show both AR and MR functions. In the bottom panel corresponding to each and every price and quantity pairs the associated revenues (given by the area of the respective rectangles so formed in the top panel) are shown. The whole summery is given in the table 9.1. As price falls from 6 onwards the revenue rises from 0 to 500 and then to 800 and finally to 900, the maximum amount, at Rs. 3. At this point it is important to note that the price elasticity declines to 1 from infinity. Further the associated MR falls to 0. For the illustration $q = 600 - 100p$ is taken as the demand law. Thereafter, any further fall in the price reduces the total revenue to 800 and then to 500 finally to zero at zero price. In this range of operation the marginal revenue becomes negative. The respective elasticities are also less than one as shown in the table. Thus, before making a decision to alter the price to have more revenue, one must carefully study the elasticity in the relevant operational range. If you are operating in the elastic range then go for a price reduction to have more revenue. If you increase the price hoping to get more revenue you will miserably fail in your attempt. In fact such an act will bring down the revenue, because of the drastic reduction in the level of demand by the consumers. On the other hand, if you are operating in the inelastic range then opt for a price rise to have more revenue. In this range the market is inelastic and hence such an act definitely will bring down the sales, but only very little. At the same time if you opt for a price reduction the revenue will fall as shown in the diagram. Thus, the price elasticity play a very crucial role in decision making.

Relationship between R, MR, AR and η in a linear demand model: A mathematical exposition:

By definition Revenue = Price × quantity sold

i.e. $R = p.D$

Now let us differentiate the above equation with respect to D on both the sides.

$$\frac{dR}{dD} = \frac{d}{dD}(p.D)$$

$$= p\frac{dD}{dD} + D\frac{dp}{dD} \qquad \text{(Product Rule)}$$

$$= p + D\frac{dp}{dD}$$

$$= p + p\frac{D}{p}\frac{dp}{dD}$$

$$= p\left(1 + \frac{D}{p}\frac{dp}{dD}\right)$$

$$= p\left[1 - \left(-\frac{D}{p}\frac{dp}{dD}\right)\right]$$

$$= p\left[1 - \frac{1}{\left(-\frac{p}{D}\frac{dD}{dp}\right)}\right]$$

Now since, $\left(-\frac{p}{D}\frac{dD}{dp}\right) = \eta$

$$\frac{dR}{dD} = p\left[1 - \frac{1}{\eta}\right]$$

We know that AR = p

So the above relation may be written as

$$MR = AR\left(1 - \frac{1}{\eta}\right)$$

Note: If $\eta = 1$ then from the relation derived in the previous section it follows that

$$MR = AR\left(1 - \frac{1}{\eta}\right)$$

$$= AR\left(1 - \frac{1}{1}\right)$$

$$= AR(0)$$

$$= 0$$

So when $\eta = 1$, MR = 0. Hence the MR cuts the OT exactly at mid point as shown in the Fig.. Further, since MR = 0 by definition dR/dD = 0. Hence when $\eta = 1$ the total revenue will reach its maximum value as shown in the Fig.

If $\eta > 1$ then the total revenue R will keep on increasing as the demand rises (price falls). On the other hand, if $\eta < 1$ then the total revenue will fall as shown in the Fig. when the demand rises.

Thus, a fall in the price rises the total revenue when the demand is elastic. A fall in the price level leads to a fall in the revenue when the demand is inelastic.

A special result under perfect competition:

Under perfect competition since the competitive seller is a price taker and hence faces an infinitely elastic demand the above relation reduces to

$$MR = AR\left(1 - \frac{1}{\infty}\right) \quad (\infty = \text{infinity})$$

$$= AR(1-0)$$

$$= AR$$

i.e. $MR = AR$

Alternatively, since competitive seller is a price taker, p is a constant.

so, $R = pD$ and $\frac{dR}{dD} = p$ (where p is a constant)

$MR = AR$

Table 9.2

Infinitely elastic demand under perfect competition

p	Q	R	MR
10	0	0	10
10	5	50	10
10	10	100	10
10	15	150	10
10	20	200	10
10	25	250	10
10	30	300	10

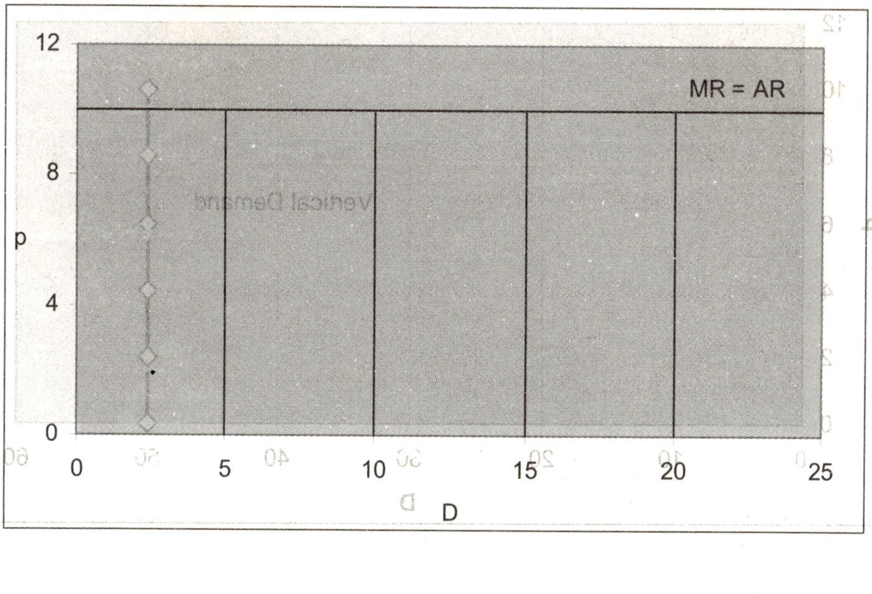

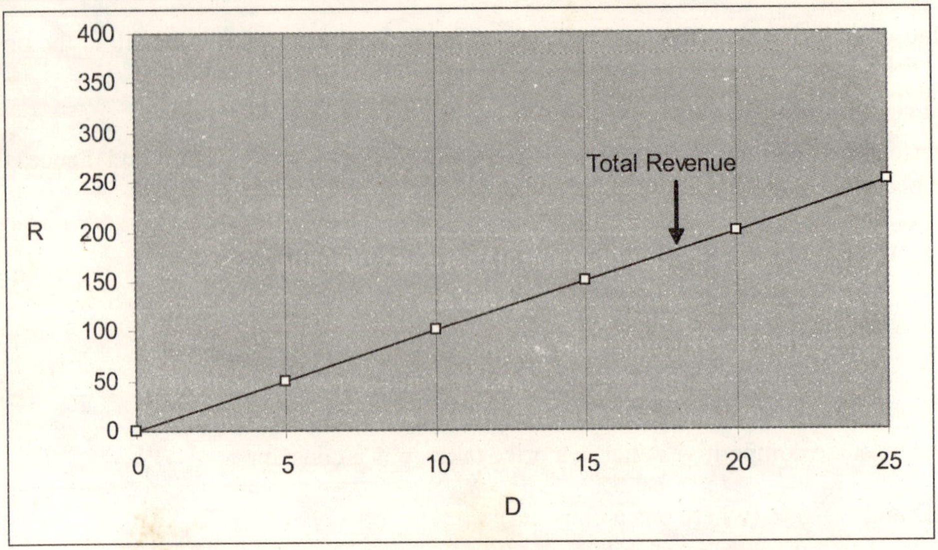

Fig. 9.16 Revenue function under perfect competition

Demand and revenue relationships of an individual seller under perfect competition is shown in Fig. 9.16.

Thus, under perfect competition by merely sales promotion methods one could increase the revenue without any limit. Price adjustment thus, is unwarranted under competition.

Zero Elastic Demand:

In this case the demand curve will be vertical. Thus, whatever the price the demand remains unaltered. For basic necessities like salt this type of demand will prevail. Thus more revenue could be earned by simply charging more price in this case. The revenue is an increasing straight-line passing through the origin as shown in the Fig. 9.17.

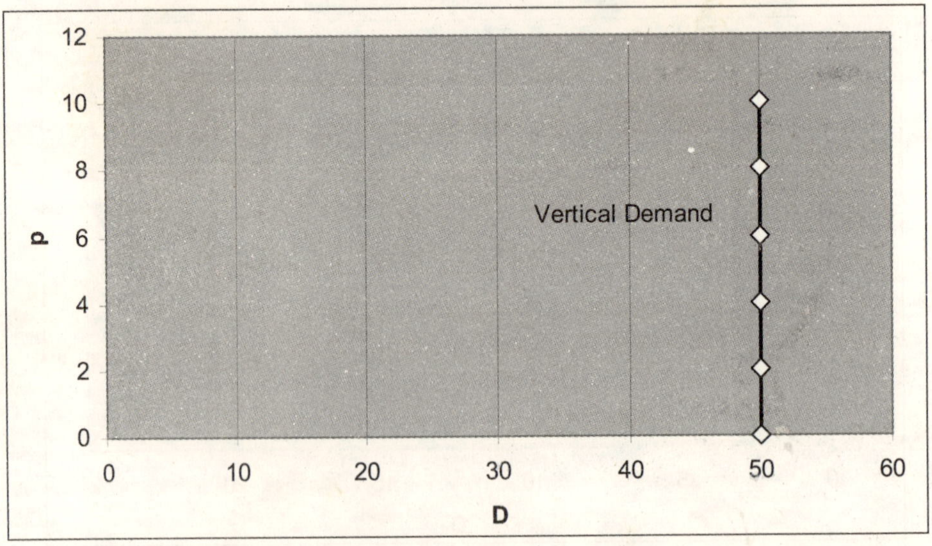

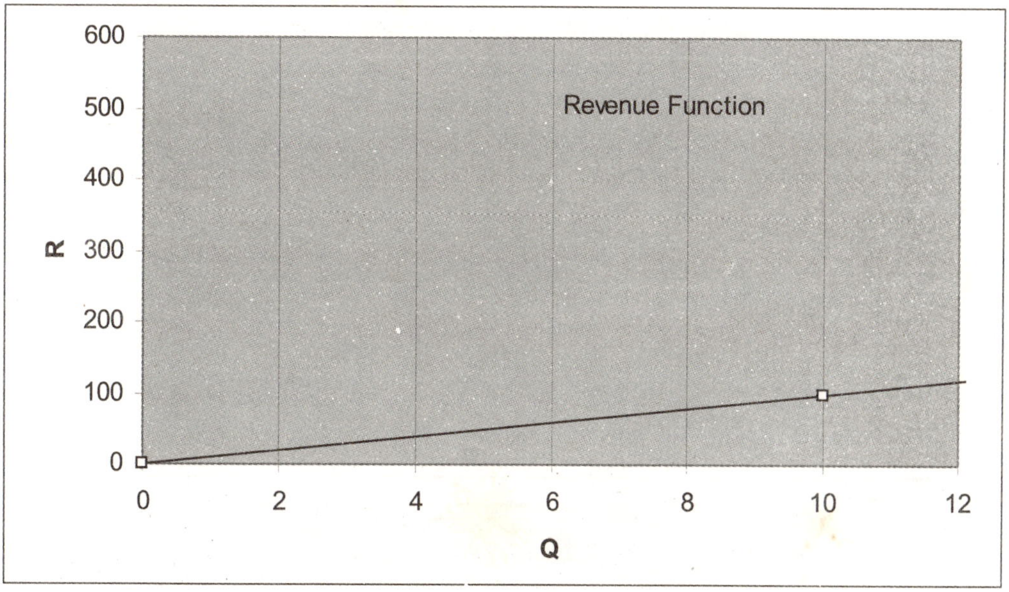

Fig. 9.17 Zero elastic demand

Constant outlay curves or unit elastic demand curve:

On this demand curve the total expenditure always will be a constant irrespective of the point chosen. Thus, a fall or a rise in the price along the curve leaves the total revenue unaltered by increasing or decreasing the quantity appropriately.

Table 9.3

Rectangular hyperbolic demand

p	Q	R	η
13	46.15	600	1
12	50.00	600	1
11	54.55	600	1
10	60.00	600	1
9	66.67	600	1
8	75.00	600	1
7	85.71	600	1
6	100.00	600	1
5	120.00	600	1
4	150.00	600	1
3	200.00	600	1
2	300.00	600	1
1	600.00	600	1

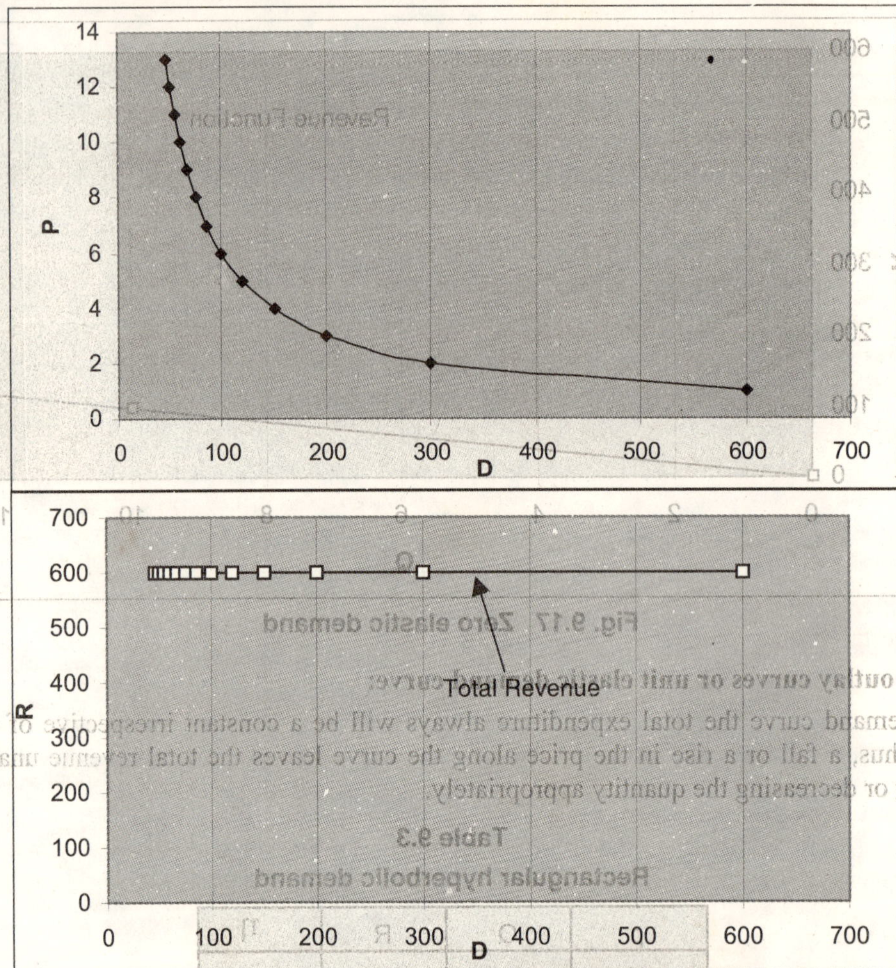

Fig. 9.18 Unit elastic demand

Such a special type of demand can always be represented by 'rectangular hyperbola'. The specialty of this curve is that at all points the tangents drawn gets bisected itself at the point of tangency. In other words, this is to say that TM = ML at all points on this demand curve so that $\eta = 1$. The Fig. 9.18 and Table 9.3 framed having the rectangular hyperbolic demand $D = 600/p$.

Constant outlay curve and unitary elasticity: A numerical illustration:

Example 10: If $p\,D = 600$ represents the demand law prove that $\eta = 1$ all through.

Solution:

The given demand law is rewritten as $D = 600p^{-1}$

Now by definition:

$$\eta = -\frac{ED}{Ep} = -\frac{E(600\,p^{-1})}{Ep}$$

$$= -\frac{p}{600p^{-1}}\frac{d(600p^{-1})}{dp}$$

$$= -\frac{p}{600p^{-1}} \times (-1)(600p^{-2})$$

$$= 1.$$

Determinants of price elasticity of demand: In real world the price elasticity of demand varies considerably from product to product. For example, the price elasticity for Maruti cars in India may be as high as 5 and the price elasticity for salt may be as low as 01. Under such diversified values one must look for the determinants of the price elasticity of demand. The following are some of the major determinants:

1. **Availability of substitutes and closeness:** More the number of substitutes available for a given product, and closer they are, more will the number of people switching over to these substitutes when the price of the product under consideration goes up. Thus, the price elasticity to the said product will be greater provided there are more number of close substitutes available.
2. **Definition of the item under reference:** Definition of the item under reference also plays important role in determining the price elasticity. If the item under reference is defined in its border sense, for example food, then clearly there is no close substitute for food. Thus the price elasticity for food must be low. On the other hand, if the defined item is rice, then price elasticity of rice must be more because rice has more number of close substitutes.
3. **The proportion of income spent on the good under consideration:** Higher the proportions of total income spend on the product under reference more will be the cut in the level consummation when its price goes up. Thus, for such products the income effect will be very high and as a result the final price elasticity also will be very high. The cut in the interest rate on housing in India is the good example for this type. We spend a lot of proportion of our earnings in house construction. A low rate thus induces more housing construction activities. However, in the case of salt since very little portion of income is spent the price elasticity is very low.
4. **The Time period:** When the price of the item under reference increases people takes little longer time to adjust themselves for the change. In other words this is to say that longer the time period given more will be the price elasticity for the said product.

9.6 Partial Price Elasticities of Demand

If $D_1 = f(p_1, p_2)$ and $D_2 = g(p_1, p_2)$ are the demand functions for two related commodities then we can define four partial elasticities in the usual manner.

$$\eta_{11} = \frac{ED_1}{Ep_1} = \frac{p_1}{D_1}\frac{\partial D_1}{\partial p_1}$$

$$\eta_{12} = \frac{ED_1}{Ep_2} = \frac{p_2}{D_1}\frac{\partial D_1}{\partial p_2}$$

$$\eta_{21} = \frac{ED_2}{Ep_1} = \frac{p_1}{D_2}\frac{\partial D_2}{\partial p_1}$$

$$\eta_{22} = \frac{ED_2}{Ep_2} = \frac{p_2}{D_2}\frac{\partial D_2}{\partial p_2}$$

Substitutes and compliments

In real world commodities are related both in production and consumption. If they are related in production then, they are called joint products. If they are related in consumption then they can be either substitutes or compliments to each other. Whenever all of them satisfy a common purpose they are called substitutes. Coffee and Tea are the familiar example for substitutes. If all of them are used in a fixed proportion in the preparation of an item they are called compliments. Milk, Coffee powder and Sugar are called compliments because these three items are combined in a fixed proportion in the preparation of wholesome coffee. Here all the time these items are jointly consumed.

When commodities are related in consumption then the demand for an item is not only a function of its own prices but also the prices of all other related commodities. For example, if D_1 and D_2 are the two related commodities then their respective demand functions are written as

$$D_1 = f(p_1, p_2)$$
$$D_2 = g(p_1, p_2)$$

Substitutes

Example 11: Let D_1 be demand for coffee and D_2 be the demand for tea. Similarly, let p_1 and p_2 are the prices of coffee and tea respectively.

Let the corresponding demand function be $D_1 = 5 - 0.5p_1 + p_2$

If the current Tea price is p_2 = Rs.5 then the demand for coffee in terms of coffee price alone is obtained by substituting $p_2 = 5$ in the given demand equation.

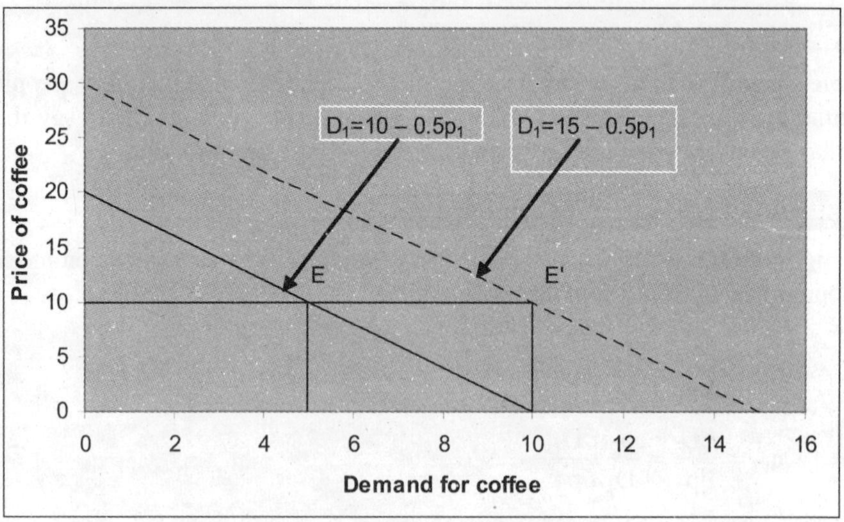

Fig. 9.19 Partial elasticity: Substitutes

$$D_1 = 5 - 0.5p_1 + 5$$

$$D_1 = 10 - 0.5p_1 \qquad \ldots(1)$$

Now let the tea price goes up from Rs.5 to Rs.10. Now the demand for coffee is rewritten as

$$D_1 = 15 - 0.5p_1 \qquad \ldots(2)$$

Assume coffee price is held constant on both the occasions at Rs.10 per 100 gram pack. Thus when coffee price is Rs.10, at a given Tea price of Rs.5, the quantity of coffee demand is obtained by substituting $p_1 = 10$ in equation (1). So obtained demand for coffee is 5 packs.

Since coffee and tea are substitutes such a drastic increase in the price of tea not only will bring down the demand for tea but also will shift the demand for coffee as shown in the Fig. 9.19. Now after the increase in Tea price the corresponding demand for coffee is obtained by substituting the unaltered coffee price of Rs.10 in equation (2) above. The corresponding new value is 10 packs. Now the arc elasticity of demand is obtained as

$$\eta_{12} = \frac{ED_1}{Ep_2} = \frac{\frac{10-5}{10+5}}{\frac{10-5}{10+5}} = 1$$

Note: Here coffee price is not taken into account in the elasticity calculation.

Example 12: Let D_1 be coffee market and D_2 the tea market for illustration

Let the demand for tea is $D_2 = 10 + p_1 - 0.5p_2$

If the coffee price is Rs.10 then the demand for tea reduces to

$$D_2 = 20 - 0.5p_2 \qquad \ldots(3)$$

Now let the coffee price goes up from Rs. 10 to Rs. 15

Now the new demand for tea is

$$D_2 = 25 - 0.5p_2 \qquad \ldots(4)$$

Now let the Tea price be Rs. 5. The associated demand for tea when coffee price is Rs.10 is obtained by substituting this price for Tea in equation (3). The demand is

$$D_2 = 20 - 0.5 \times 5 = 17.5$$

Now let the Tea price be Rs. 5. The associated demand for tea when coffee price is Rs.15 is obtained by substituting this price for Tea in equation (4). The demand is $D_2 = 25 - 0.5 \times 5 = 22.5$

$$\eta_{21} = \frac{ED_2}{Ep_1} = \frac{\frac{22.5-17.5}{22.5+17.5}}{\frac{15-10}{15+10}} = \frac{\frac{5}{40}}{\frac{5}{25}} = \frac{5}{40} \times \frac{25}{5} = \frac{25}{40} = 0.625$$

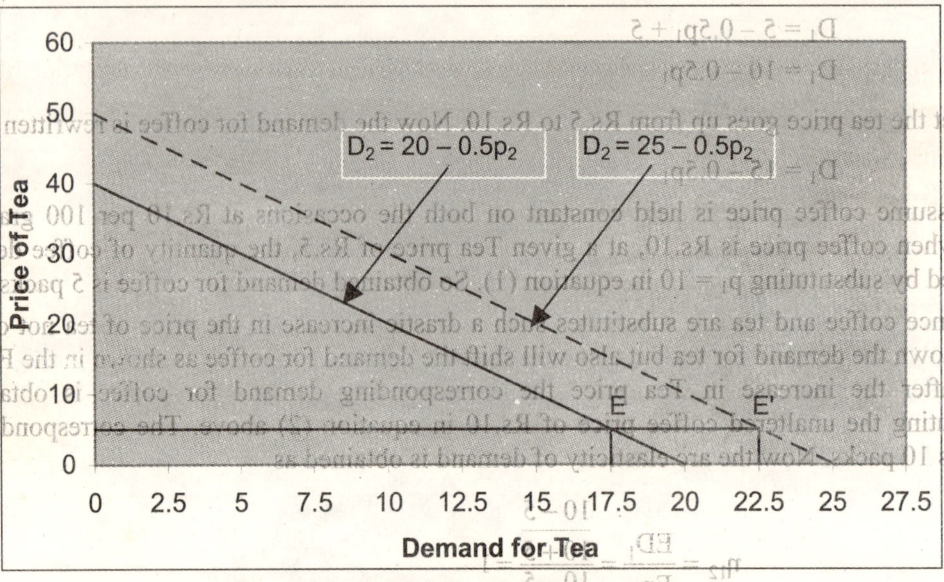

Fig. 9.20 Partial elasticity: Substitutes

Note: Here tea price is not taken into account in the calculation.

Definition of substitutes

If D_1 and D_2 are tea and coffee demands respectively then, the rise in the price of Tea led to a fal in the demand for tea and, as a result, a rise in the demand for coffee. Thus, ultimately the rise ir the price of tea leads to a rise in the quantity of coffee consumption. In other words, this is to say that in the demand law given above

$$\frac{\partial D_2}{\partial p_1} > 0$$

Now by definition

$$\eta_{21} = \frac{ED_2}{Ep_1} = \frac{p_1}{D_2}\frac{\partial D_2}{\partial p_1}$$

Since in the above expression the partial derivative of D_2 with respect to p_1 is positive for substitutes the said elasticity must be positive

$$\eta_{21} = \frac{ED_2}{Ep_1} > 0$$

By similar argument it is also true that

$$\frac{\partial D_1}{\partial p_2} > 0$$

$$\eta_{12} = \frac{ED_1}{Ep_2} > 0$$

Definition of compliments

If D_1 and D_2 are demand for milk and sugar respectively then the rise in the price of milk will reduce the demand for both milk and sugar simultaneously because these two items are consumed in a fixed proportion always. In mathematical term this is to say that

$$\frac{\partial D_1}{\partial p_2} < 0$$

$$\eta_{12} = \frac{ED_1}{Ep_2} < 0$$

Similarly,

$$\frac{\partial D_2}{\partial p_1} < 0$$

$$\eta_{21} = \frac{ED_2}{Ep_1} < 0$$

Example 13: A multi product monopolist produces two products, which are related in consumption. The demand laws for the commodities are

$$D_1 = \frac{100}{p_1 p_2}; \quad D_2 = \frac{200}{p_1 p_2}$$

Find $\eta_{11}, \eta_{12}, \eta_{21}, \eta_{22}$. Also prove that the commodities are compliments.

Solution:

$$\eta_{11} = \frac{ED_1}{Ep_1} = \frac{E(100p_1^{-1}p_2^{-1})}{Ep_1} = \frac{p_1}{100p_1^{-1}p_2^{-1}} \frac{\partial(100p_1^{-1}p_2^{-1})}{\partial p_1}$$

$$= \frac{p_1}{100p_1^{-1}p_2^{-1}} \times -100p_1^{-2}p_2^{-1}$$

$$= -1$$

$$\eta_{12} = \frac{ED_1}{Ep_2} = \frac{E(100p_1^{-1}p_2^{-1})}{Ep_2} = \frac{p_2}{100p_1^{-1}p_2^{-1}} \frac{\partial(100p_1^{-1}p_2^{-1})}{\partial p_2}$$

$$= \frac{p_2}{100p_1^{-1}p_2^{-1}} \times -100p_1^{-1}p_2^{-2}$$

$$= -1$$

$$\eta_{21} = \frac{ED_2}{Ep_1} = \frac{E(200p_1^{-1}p_2^{-1})}{Ep_1} = \frac{p_1}{200p_1^{-1}p_2^{-1}} \frac{\partial(200p_1^{-1}p_2^{-1})}{\partial p_1}$$

$$= \frac{p_1}{200p_1^{-1}p_2^{-1}} \times -100p_1^{-2}p_2^{-1}$$

$$= -1$$

$$\eta_{22} = \frac{ED_2}{Ep_2} = \frac{E(200p_1^{-1}p_2^{-1})}{Ep_2} = \frac{p_2}{100p_1^{-1}p_2^{-1}} \frac{\partial(200p_1^{-1}p_2^{-1})}{\partial p_2}$$

$$= \frac{p_2}{200p_1^{-1}p_2^{-1}} \times -200p_1^{-1}p_2^{-2}$$

$$= -1$$

Here since $\eta_{12} < 0$; $\eta_{21} < 0$ the commodities are compliments.

9.7 Income Elasticity of Demand

Income elasticities are used to measure the responsiveness of the quantity demanded in response to a given change in income of the consumer. In general the demand for a commodity, in addition to its own price, depends upon the prices of all the related commodities like substitutes, compliments, taste, income etc. Thus when other factors remain constant the demand for a commodity can always be expressed as a function of the income of the consumer.

Engel's curve: When other things remain constant then the demand curve for a commodity under consideration, expressed as a function of the income of the consumer alone is often called the Engel's curve.

Inferior goods, Necessities, and Luxuries: The income elasticity can be either positive or negative. On the basis of income elasticities, commodities are often classified into normal, inferior and superior items. Obviously, when the income elasticity is negative then a given rise in the income will lead to a fall in the demand for the said commodity. Such commodities are often called inferior. Cheap potato is often considered as poor man's meat. Those who are living on tight budget cannot afford to have meat and hence consume only potato. But as their incomes increase they give up or at least reduce the consumption of this cheap potato and go for meat. Thus an increase in income causes decrease in the demand for potato. For superior or otherwise called luxurious commodities the income elasticity is positive and often greater than unity. For basic necessitates it is moderate and hence lie in between zero and one.

If $D = f(Y)$ stands for the demand then income elasticity of demand denoted by 'm' is defined as follows.

Definition of income elasticity of demand by arc method:

$$m = \frac{\text{Proportional change in demand}}{\text{Proportional change in income}}$$

$$= \frac{\dfrac{D_2 - D_1}{D_2 + D_1}}{\dfrac{Y_2 - Y_1}{Y_2 + Y_1}} = \left(\frac{D_2 - D_1}{Y_2 - Y_1}\right)\left(\frac{Y_2 + Y_1}{D_2 + D_1}\right)$$

Example 14: When the income of a person is Rs.5,000 (in thousands) the demand for a certain product is 2 units. If the income went up to Rs.10,000 the demand went up to 4 units. Obtain the income elasticity of demand by arc method.

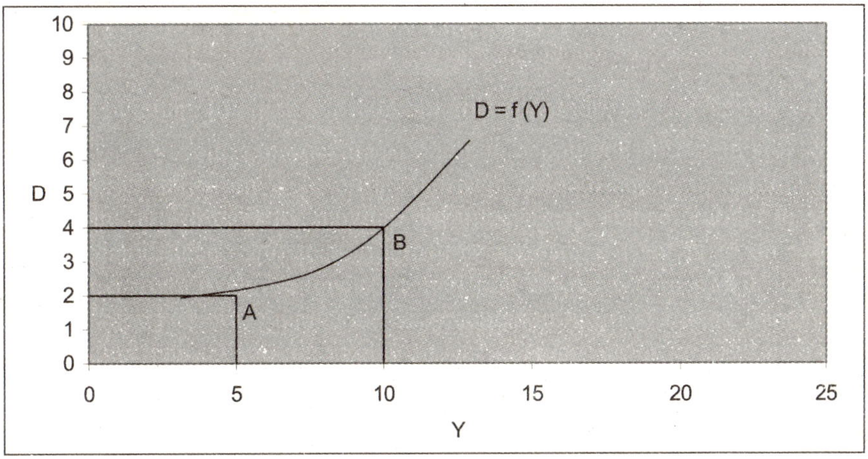

Fig. 9.21

Solution:

$$m = \left(\frac{D_2 - D_1}{Y_2 - Y_1}\right)\left(\frac{Y_2 + Y_1}{D_2 + D_1}\right)$$

$$= \frac{10 - 5}{10{,}000 - 5{,}000} \times \frac{10{,}000 + 5{,}000}{10 + 5}$$

$$= \frac{5}{5{,}000} \times \frac{15{,}000}{15}$$

$$= 1$$

Definition of income elasticity of demand by point method

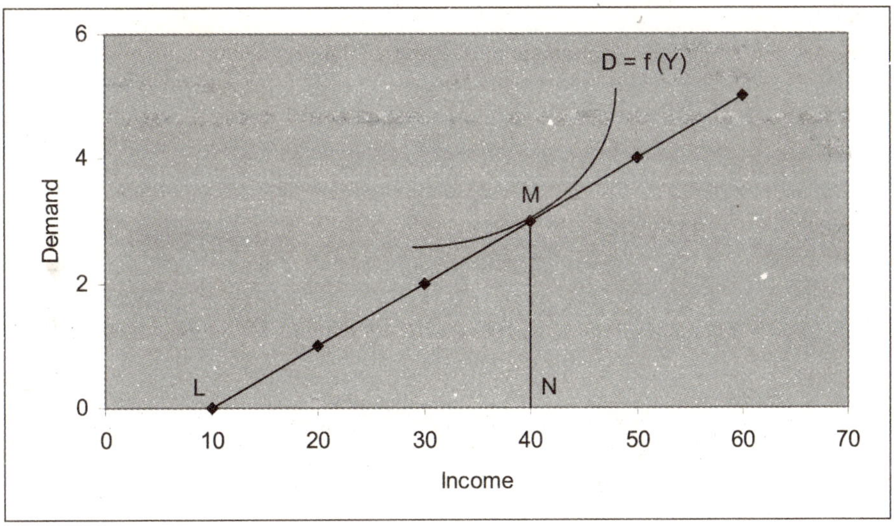

Fig. 9.22 Income elasticity: Elastic case

$$m = \frac{ED}{EY}$$

$$= \frac{\text{Proportional change in demand}}{\text{Proportional change in income}}$$

$$= \frac{Y}{D}\frac{dD}{dY} = \frac{ON}{MN} \times \frac{MN}{NL} = \frac{ON}{NL}$$

Here, in Fig 9.22 above since ON > LN, $m = \frac{ED}{EY} = \frac{ON}{NL} = \frac{40}{30} = 1.25 > 1$. In other worlds, the function D = f (Y) is said to be elastic at the neighborhood of the given point M.

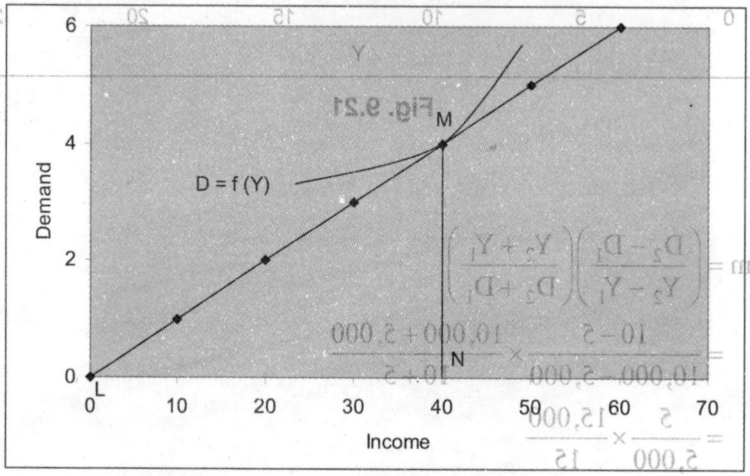

Fig. 9.23 Income elasticity: Unit elastic case

However, in Fig 9.23 above since ON = LN, $m = \frac{ED}{EY} = \frac{ON}{NL} = \frac{40}{40} = 1$. In other words, we would say that the function D = f (Y) is unit elastic at the point M.

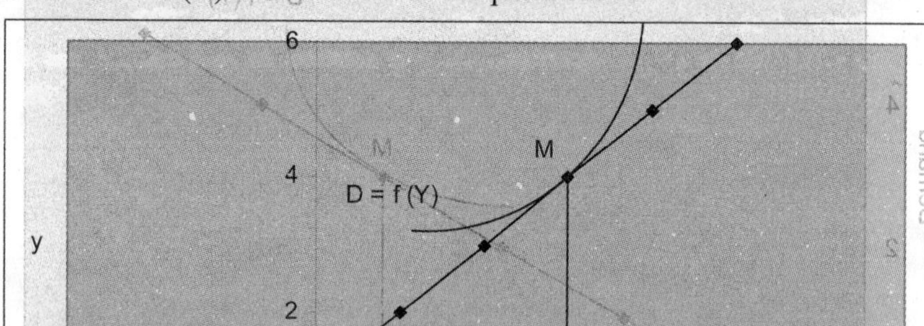

Fig. 9.24 Income elasticity: Inelastic case

In Fig 9.24 since ON < LN, $m = \frac{ED}{EY} = \frac{ON}{NL} = \frac{30}{40} = 0.75 < 1$, and hence the function D = f (Y) is said to be inelastic around the point M.

Calculation income elasticity of demand by point method in the case of linear demand

Example 15: If D = 400 + 2Y obtain the income elasticity 'm' when Y = 100.

Solution:

$$m = \frac{ED}{EY} = \frac{E(400+2Y)}{EY} = \frac{Y}{400+2Y} \frac{d(400+2Y)}{dY}$$

$$= \frac{2Y}{400+2Y} = \frac{2\times 100}{400+2\times 100}$$

$$= \frac{200}{600} = 0.3333$$

Thus, the item under reference seems to be a normal commodity.

Engel's law: In the nineteenth century, a German statistician, Ernst Engel, established his name in economic history by proposing a law commonly known as Engel's law. He studied the consumption pattern of a large number of households and concluded that the percentage of income spent on necessities like food decreases as incomes increase.

Example 16: A novel publishing company after month's hard work and exorbitant bill found out the demand law for its novel. It is estimated as $D_x = 12,000 - 5,000P_x + 5Y + 500P_s$ where P_x is the price of the novel of concerned company, Y is the per capita income and P_s is the price of the novel by competing company. Assume that the initial values of P_x, P_s, and Y are Rs.5, Rs.6 and Rs.10, 000 respectively. Based on these facts the company's manager wants to

(a) determine the effect a given price increases in the company's novel on its total revenue collection.

(b) evaluate the right price that brings maximum revenue collection to the company.

(c) evaluate the sales of the novel during the period of rising incomes.

(d) assess the probable impact when their competing novels price increase.

Solution (a):

The demand law for the novel is stated as

$$D_x = 12,000 - 5,000P_x + 5Y + 500P_s \qquad \ldots(1)$$

The effect of a given price increase in the company's novel on the company's revenue collection can be assessed by the value of the price elasticity of demand around the neighborhood of the its initial price. Before making such evaluation let us substitute the given initial values of Y and P_s into the given equation (1) and obtain the demand for the novel as a function of its own price.

$$D_x = 12,000 - 5,000P_x + 5 \times 10,000 + 500 \times 6$$

$$= 65,000 - 5,000P_x \qquad \ldots(2)$$

Now by definition

$$\eta = -\frac{ED_x}{EP_x} = -\frac{E(65,000 - 5,000P_x)}{EP_x}$$

$$= -\frac{P_x}{(65,000 - 5,000P_x)}\frac{d}{dP_x}(65,000 - 5,000P_x)$$

$$= \frac{5,000P_x}{65,000 - 5,000P_x} \qquad \text{...(3)}$$

$$= \frac{5,000 \times 5}{65,000 - 5,000 \times 5} = 0.625$$

Since the demand is inelastic in the neighborhood of 5, the initial price, a given rise in the price of its own will bring more revenue to the company. Hence the manager can go ahead with his proposal of price rise.

Solution (b):

When $\eta = 1$ then we know that the total revenue collection will be at its maximum. So from equation (2) it follows

$$\eta = \frac{5,000P_x}{65,000 - 5,000P_x}$$

$$1 = \frac{5,000P_x}{65,000 - 5,000P_x}$$

$$65,000 - 5,000P_x = 5,000P_x$$

$$-10,000P_x = -65,000$$

$$P_x = 6.5$$

Thus, when the price is Rs. 6.50 the price elasticity will be unity and the total revenue collection reaches its maximum. Hence for getting the maximum collection the manager must fix the price at Rs. 6.50.

Solution (c):

The income elasticity determines whether the novel is a basic necessity or luxury.
Now to get the Engel's curve we substitute the initial values of P_x and P_s into the equation (1) above and express demand as a function of income alone.

$$D_x = 12,000 - 5,000P_x + 5Y + 500P_s$$

$$D_x = 12,000 - 5,000 \times 5 + 5Y + 500 \times 6$$

$$= -10,000 + 5Y$$

Now by definition the income elasticity

$$m = \frac{ED_x}{EY} = \frac{E(-10,000 + 5Y)}{EY}$$

$$= \frac{Y}{(-10,000 + 5Y)}\frac{d}{dY}(-10,000 + 5Y)$$

$$= \frac{5Y}{(-10,000 + 5Y)} = \frac{5 \times 10,000}{-10,000 + 5 \times 10,000} = 1.25$$

Since the income elasticity is greater than one the novel seems to a luxury. Hence as income increases the sale should increase by more than proportionally.

Solution (d):

To answer this issue one must calculate the cross elasticity η_{xs}
Now to get the relevant demand we substitute the initial values of Y and P_x in equation (1).

$$D_x = 12{,}000 - 5{,}000P_x + 5Y + 500P_s$$
$$= 12{,}000 - 5{,}000\times 5 + 5\times 10{,}000 + 500P_s$$
$$= 37{,}000 + 500P_s$$

Now by definition the cross elasticity

$$\eta_{xs} = \frac{ED_x}{EP_s} = \frac{E(37{,}000 + 500P_s)}{P_s}$$

$$= \frac{P_s}{(37{,}000 + 500P_s)}\frac{d}{dP_s}(37{,}000 + 500P_s)$$

$$= \frac{500P_s}{(37{,}000 + 500P_s)}$$

$$= \frac{500\times 6}{37{,}000 + 500\times 6} = 0.075$$

Since the cross elasticity is positive the company's novel seems to be a close substitute to his competitor's novel. Thus, a given 1% rise in the price of the competitor's novel will increase the sale of the company's novel by 7.5%.

9.8 Price Elasticity of Supply

If S = f (p) is the given supply function then the price elasticity of supply is defined as the ratio of proportional change in the supply to that of proportional change in the price.

$$\text{The elasticity of supply s} = \frac{\text{Proportional change in supply}}{\text{Proportional change in the price}}$$

As usual one can apply arc or point method to calculate the elasticity of supply.

Definition of price elasticity of supply by arc method

$$s = \frac{\text{Proportional change in supply}}{\text{Proportional change in the price}} = \left(\frac{S_2 - S_1}{p_2 - p_1}\right)\left(\frac{p_2 + p_1}{S_2 + S_1}\right)$$

Example 17: When the price was Rs. 2 the supply of a certain product was 5 units. When the price went up to Rs. 4 the corresponding supply was 10 units. Obtain the price elasticity of supply by arc method.

Solution:

$$s = \frac{\text{Proportional change in supply}}{\text{Proportional change in the price}}$$

$$= \left(\frac{S_2 - S_1}{p_2 - p_1}\right)\left(\frac{p_2 + p_1}{S_2 + S_1}\right)$$

$$= \left(\frac{10-5}{4-2}\right)\left(\frac{4+2}{10+5}\right) = \left(\frac{5}{2}\right)\left(\frac{6}{15}\right) = 1$$

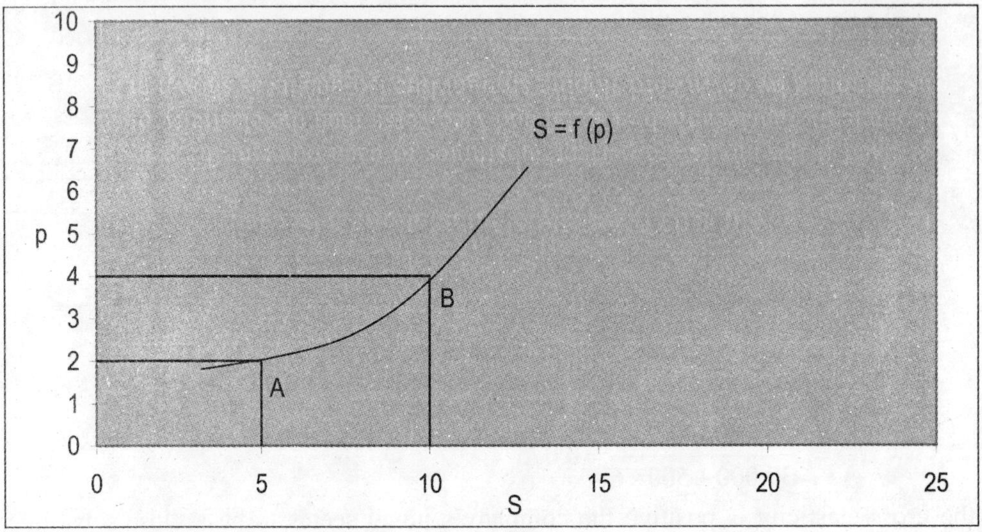

Fig. 9.25

Definition of price elasticity of supply by point method

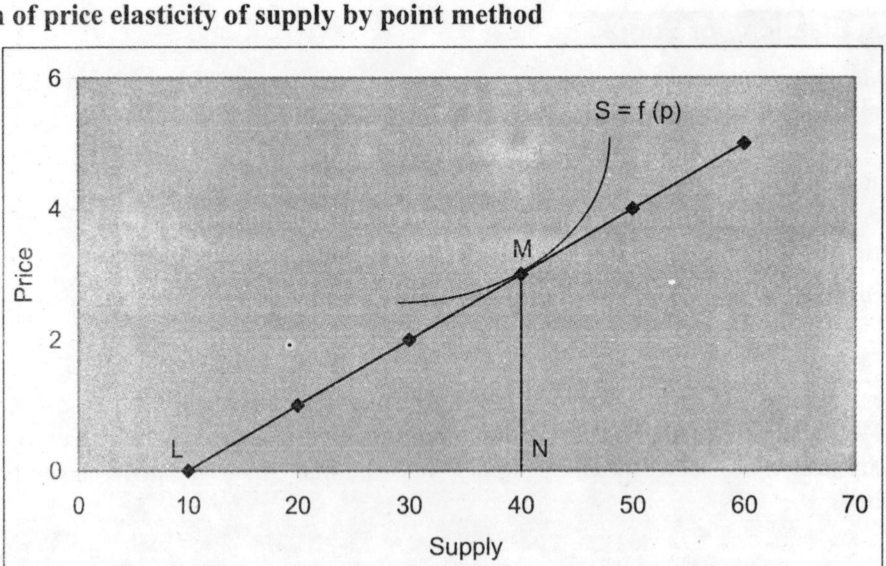

Fig. 9.26

$$s = \frac{ES}{EP} = \frac{p}{S}\frac{dS}{dP} = \frac{MN}{ON} \times \frac{LN}{MN} = \frac{LN}{ON}$$

Example 18: If S = 100 + 2p is the supply function of a certain product obtain the price elasticity. of supply when the price p = 25.

Solution:

By definition

$$s = \frac{ES}{Ep} = \frac{E(100+2P)}{Ep} = \frac{p}{(100+2P)}\frac{d}{dp}(100+2p)$$

$$= \frac{2p}{100+2p} = \frac{2 \times 25}{100+2 \times 25} = \frac{50}{150} = 0.3333$$

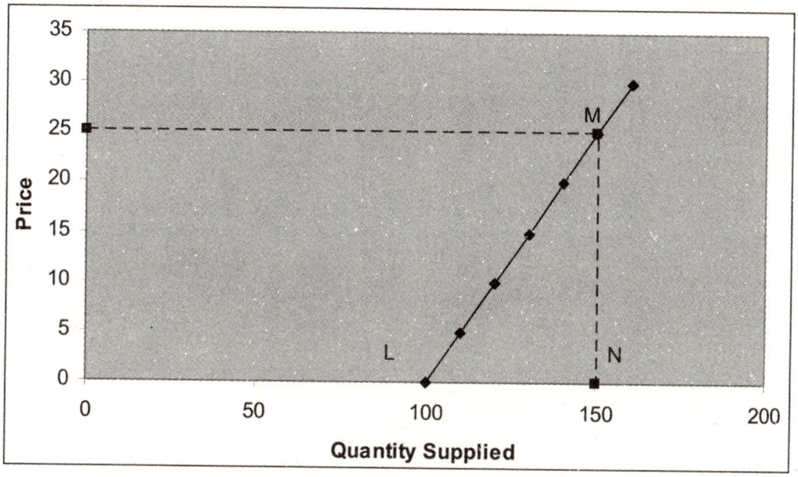

Fig. 9.27 Price elasticity of supply: Inelastic case

Example 19: If S = 2p is the supply function of a certain product obtain the price elasticity of supply when the price p = 25

Solution:

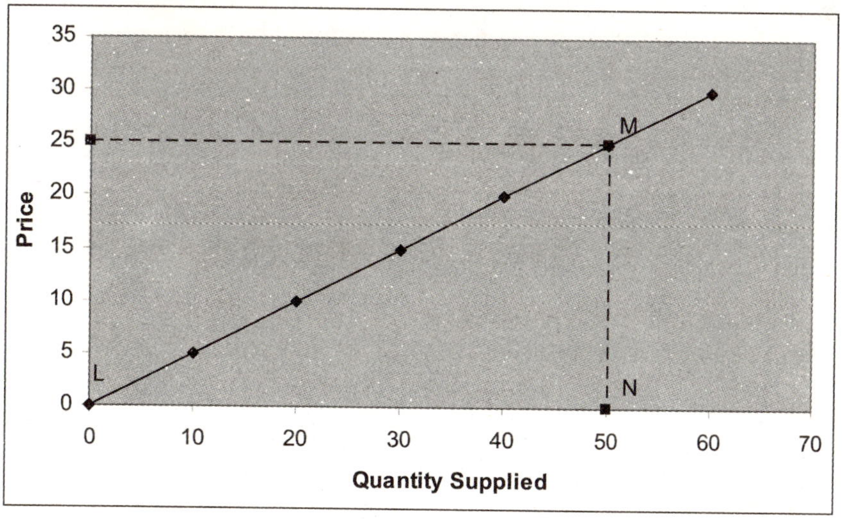

Fig. 9.28 Price elasticity of supply : Unit elastic case

By definition

$$s = \frac{ES}{Ep} = \frac{E(2p)}{Ep} = \frac{p}{(2P)}\frac{d}{dp}(2p)$$

$$= \frac{2p}{2p} = \frac{2 \times 25}{2 \times 25} = \frac{50}{50} = 1.00$$

Example 20: If S = –100 + 2p is the supply function of a certain product obtain the price elasticity of supply when the price p = 75

Solution:

By definition

$$s = \frac{ES}{EP} = \frac{E(-100+2p)}{EP} = \frac{p}{(-100+2p)}\frac{d}{dp}(-100+2p)$$

$$= \frac{2p}{-100+2p} = \frac{2 \times 75}{-100+2 \times 75} = \frac{150}{50} = 3$$

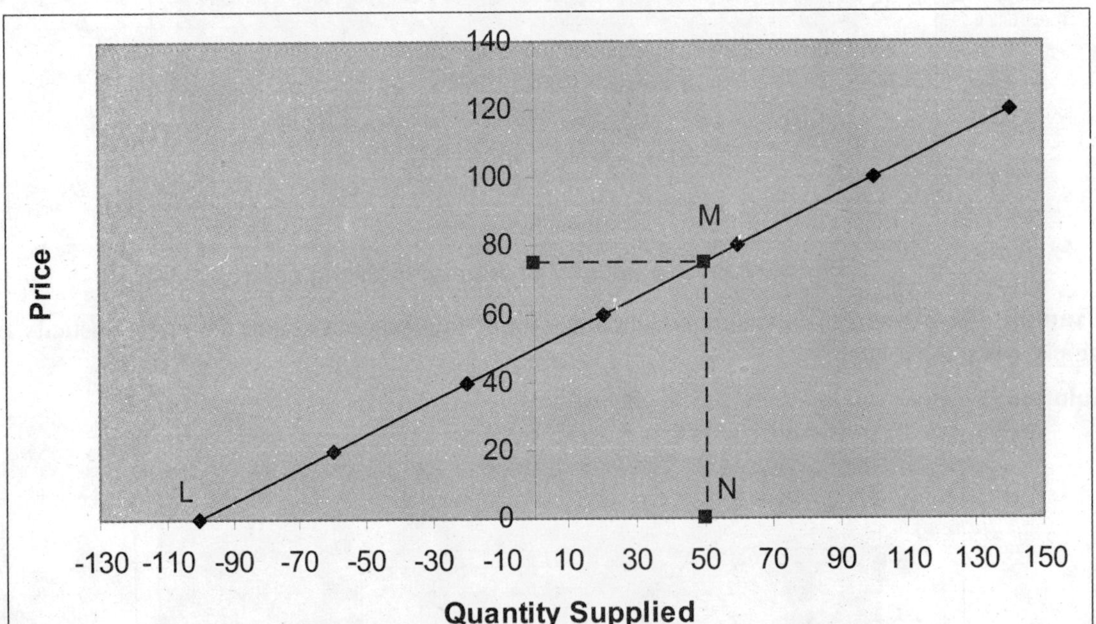

Fig. 9.29 Price elasticity of supply: Elastic case

Price elasticity of supply, infinitely elastic case:

In this case the supply function is perfectly horizontal as shown in the Fig. 9.30

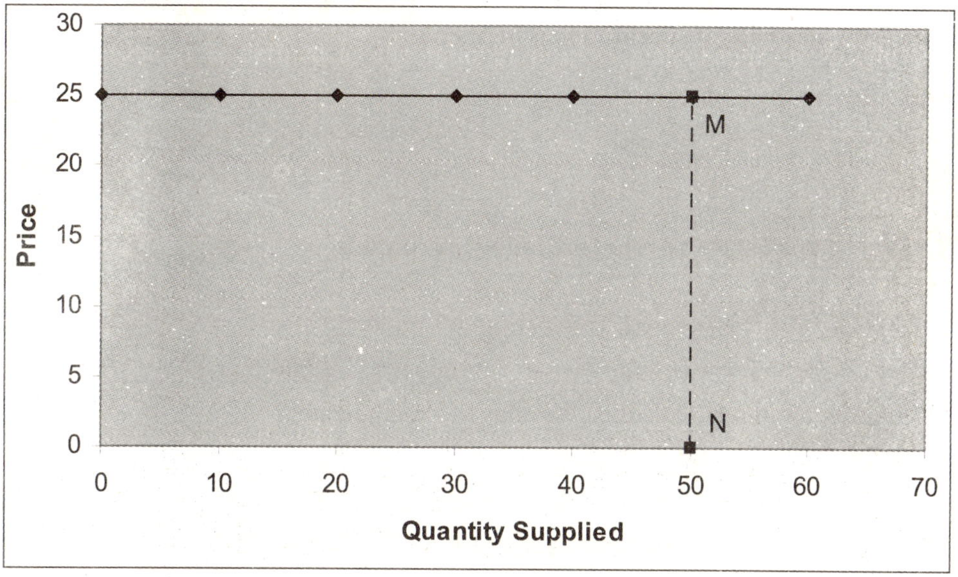

Fig. 9.30 Price elasticity of supply: Infinitely elastic case

Price elasticity of supply, zero elastic case: In this case the supply function is perfectly vertical as shown in the Fig. 9.31.

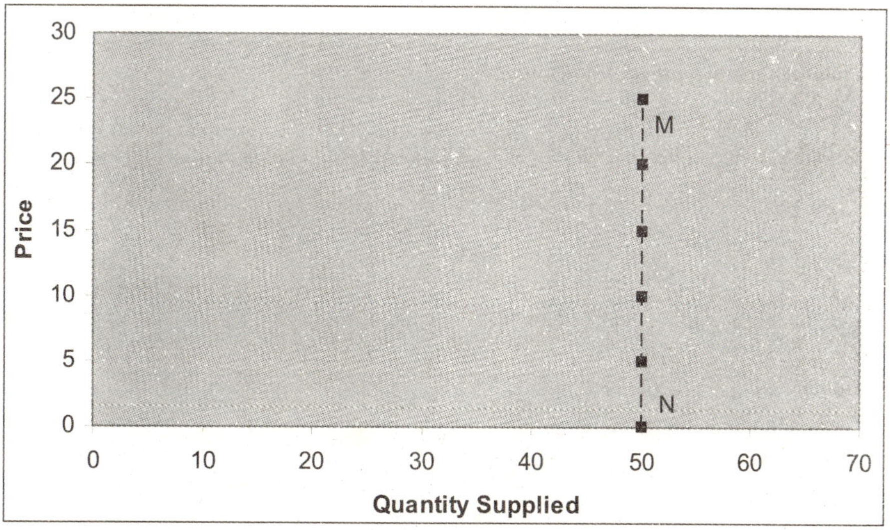

Fig. 9.31 Price elasticity of supply: Zero elastic case

9.9 Elasticity of Substitution

The elasticity of substitution denoted by 'σ' measures the substitutability of one input for the other on an iso-product curve for a given change in the input price ratio. Formally, the point elasticity of substation is defined as the ratio of proportional change in K/L to that of the proportional change in the factor price P_L/P_K. J.R. Hicks in 1932 originally introduced this concept. The point elasticity of substitution is defined as

$$\sigma = \frac{E\left(\frac{K}{L}\right)}{E\left(\frac{P_L}{P_K}\right)}$$

If Q = f (L, K) then σ is obtain by using the following formula.

$$\sigma = \frac{f_L f_K (Lf_L + Kf_K)}{LKT}$$

Where $$T = -\,(f_{LL} f_K^2 - 2f_{LK} f_L f_K + f_{KK} f_L^2)$$

If there are constant returns to scale then the above formula reduces to

$$\sigma = \frac{f_L f_K}{Q.f_{LK}}$$

Example 21: For the Cobb-Douglas production $Q = A\,L^{\alpha}K^{1-\alpha}$ prove that σ = 1

Solution:

The production function of the firm is

$$Q = A\,L^{\alpha}K^{1-\alpha} \qquad \ldots(1)$$

Since there is constant returns to scale, the formula may be written as

$$\sigma = \frac{f_L f_K}{Q.f_{LK}} \qquad \ldots(2)$$

Now from the production given in (1) above

$$f_L = \frac{\partial Q}{\partial L} = A\alpha L^{\alpha-1}K^{1-\alpha} = \frac{\alpha Q}{L}$$

Similarly,

$$f_K = \frac{\partial Q}{\partial K} = AL^{\alpha}(1-\alpha)K^{1-\alpha-1} = \frac{(1-\alpha)Q}{K}$$

$$f_{LK} = \frac{\partial}{\partial K}(f_L)$$

$$= \frac{\partial}{\partial K}(A\alpha L^{\alpha-1}K^{1-\alpha})$$

$$= A\alpha(1-\alpha)L^{-\alpha}K^{1-\alpha-1}$$

$$= \frac{\alpha(1-\alpha)}{LK}$$

$$\sigma = \frac{f_L f_K}{Q.f_{LK}} = \frac{\left(\frac{\alpha Q}{L}\right)\left(\frac{(1-\alpha)Q}{K}\right)}{Q\frac{\alpha(1-\alpha)Q}{LK}} = \left(\frac{\alpha Q}{L}\right)\left(\frac{(1-\alpha)Q}{K}\right) \times \frac{LK}{\alpha(1-\alpha)Q^2} = 1$$

The elasticity of substitution can be of either type. It is zero in the case rigidly defined production functions with fixed input output relations like H_2O with one molecule of oxygen rigidly defined two molecule of hydrogen for one molecule of water. No substitution of what so ever is possible in such cases. Thus the factor prices do not have any influence in factor use and hence output. In such cases the iso-quants will be "L" shaped as shown in Fig. 9.32.

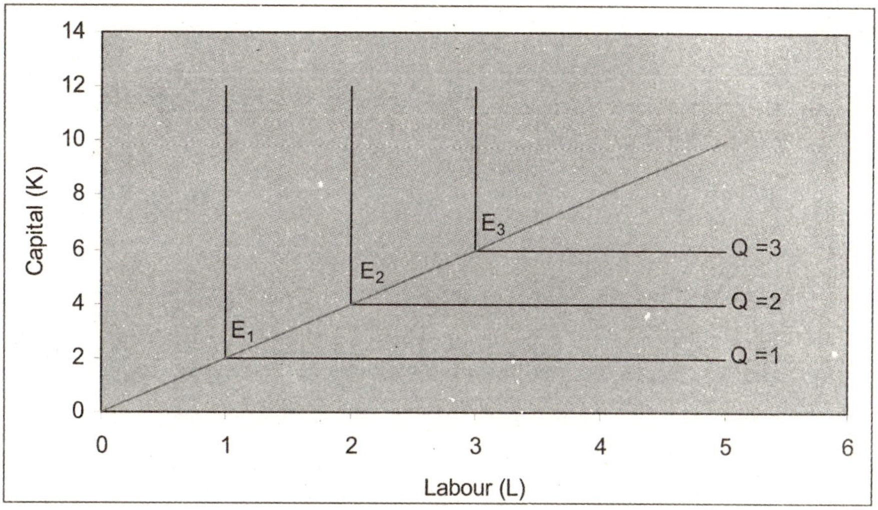

Fig. 9.32 Elasticity of substation: Zero case

On the other hand if the inputs are perfect substitutes to each other in the sense that labour for example is complexly replaceable by capital and vice versa then the elasticity of substitution will be infinity as exhibited by downward sloping straight line iso-quants as shown in Fig. 9.33.

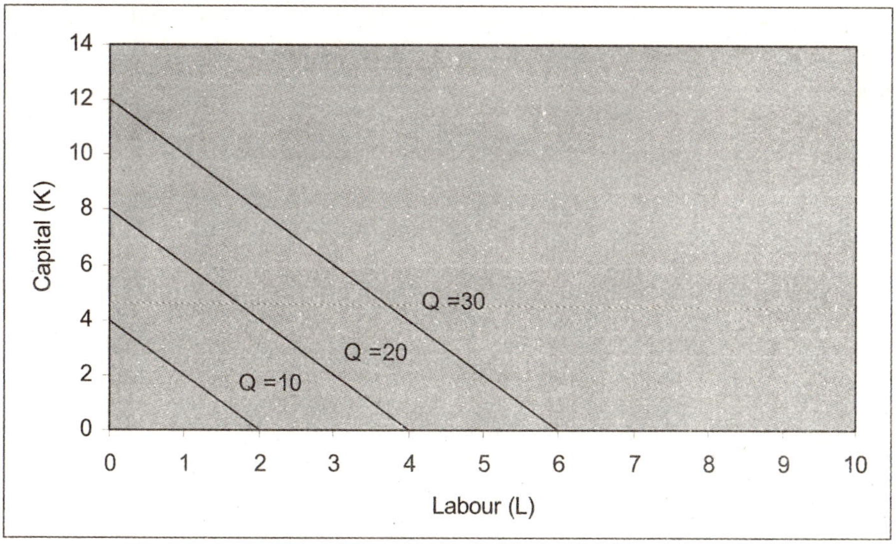

Fig. 9.33 Elasticity of substation: Infinite elastic case

If the elasticity of substitution is moderate and lie in between 0 and infinity then we will have convex iso-quants as shown in Fig. 9.34.

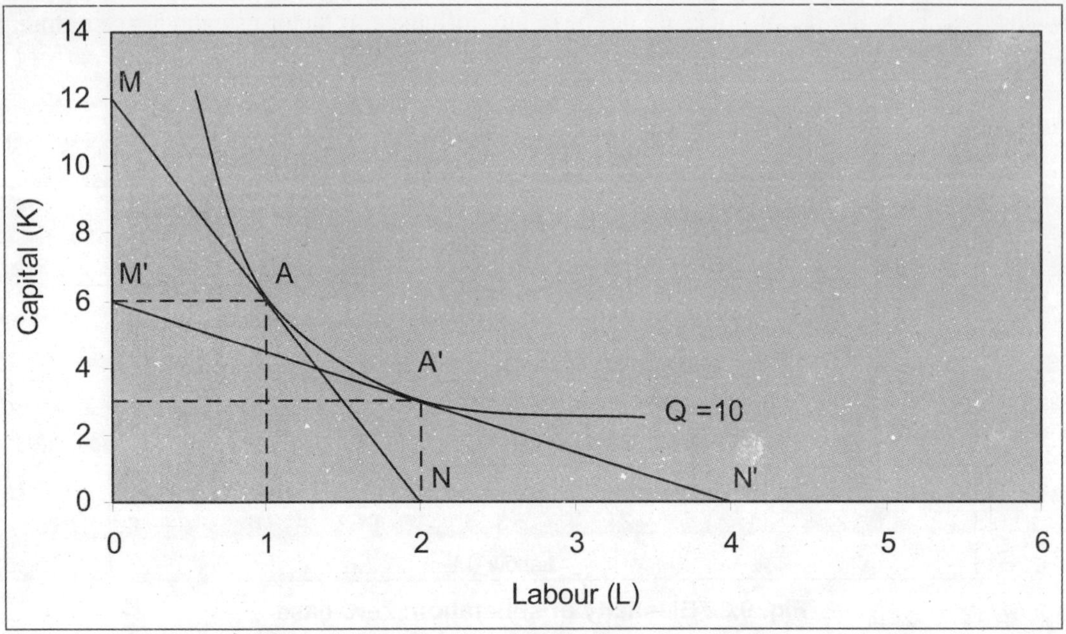

Fig. 9.34 Elasticity of substation: Positive case

9.10 Output Elasticity

The output elasticity measures the responsiveness of output for a given small change in an input when all other inputs are kept at constant levels. If Q = f (L, K) is the production function then the output elasticity of the labour denoted by O_L is defined as

$$O_L = \frac{EQ}{EL} = \frac{L}{Q}\frac{\partial Q}{\partial L} = \frac{\frac{\partial Q}{\partial L}}{\frac{Q}{L}} = \frac{MP_L}{AP_L}$$

Similarly, the output elasticity of capital denoted by O_K is defined as

$$O_K = \frac{EQ}{EK} = \frac{K}{Q}\frac{\partial Q}{\partial K} = \frac{\frac{\partial Q}{\partial K}}{\frac{Q}{K}} = \frac{MP_K}{AP_K}$$

Thus, the output elasticity is simply the ratio of marginal product to that of the average product of the concerned input.

Diagrammatic representation of the output elasticity of labour:

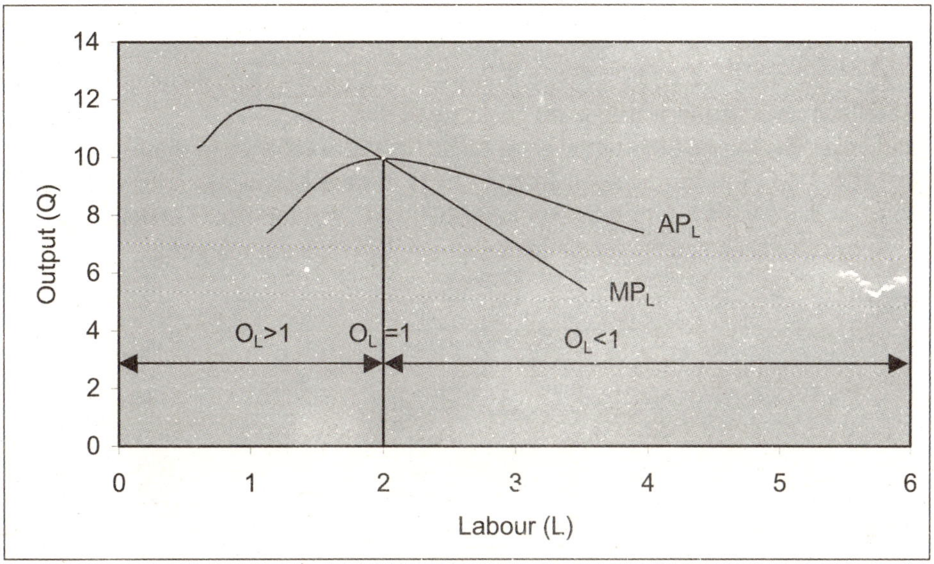

Fig. 9.35

Example 22: For the Cobb-Douglas production $Q = AL^{\alpha}K^{\beta}$ obtain the output elasticities for both labour and the capital.

Solution:

By definition

$$O_L = \frac{EQ}{EL} = \frac{E(AL^{\alpha}K^{\beta})}{EL} = \frac{L}{AL^{\alpha}K^{\beta}} \frac{\partial(AL^{\alpha}K^{\beta})}{\partial L}$$

$$= \frac{L}{AL^{\alpha}K^{\beta}} A\alpha L^{\alpha-1}K^{\beta} \quad = \alpha$$

$$O_K = \frac{EQ}{EK} = \frac{E(AL^{\alpha}K^{\beta})}{EK} = \frac{K}{AL^{\alpha}K^{\beta}} \frac{\partial(AL^{\alpha}K^{\beta})}{\partial K}$$

$$= \frac{L}{AL^{\alpha}K^{\beta}} AL^{\alpha}\beta K^{\beta-1}$$

$$= \beta$$

Thus, in the case of Cobb-Douglas Production function the respective powers of L and K represents their respective partial elasticities.

9.11 The Total Cost Elasticity

If C = f (q) stands for the total cost function of a firm then the total cost elasticity denoted by 'k' measures the response of total cost for given small change in the output. It is defined as the ratio of the proportional change in the total cost to that of the proportional change in the output.

$$\text{i.e.}\qquad k=\frac{EC}{Eq}=\frac{q}{C}\frac{dC}{dq}=\frac{\frac{dC}{dq}}{\frac{C}{q}}=\frac{MC}{AC}$$

Diagrammatic representation of the total cost elasticity:

Thus the total cost elasticity is simply the ratio of MC to AC as shown in the Fig. 9.36. In the Fig. below, since MC < AC for entire range from O to B the total cost elasticity k is less than one. Corresponding to the level of output at B since MC = AC the total cost elasticity k = 1. For all level of output beyond B since MC > AC the k value will be greater than one.

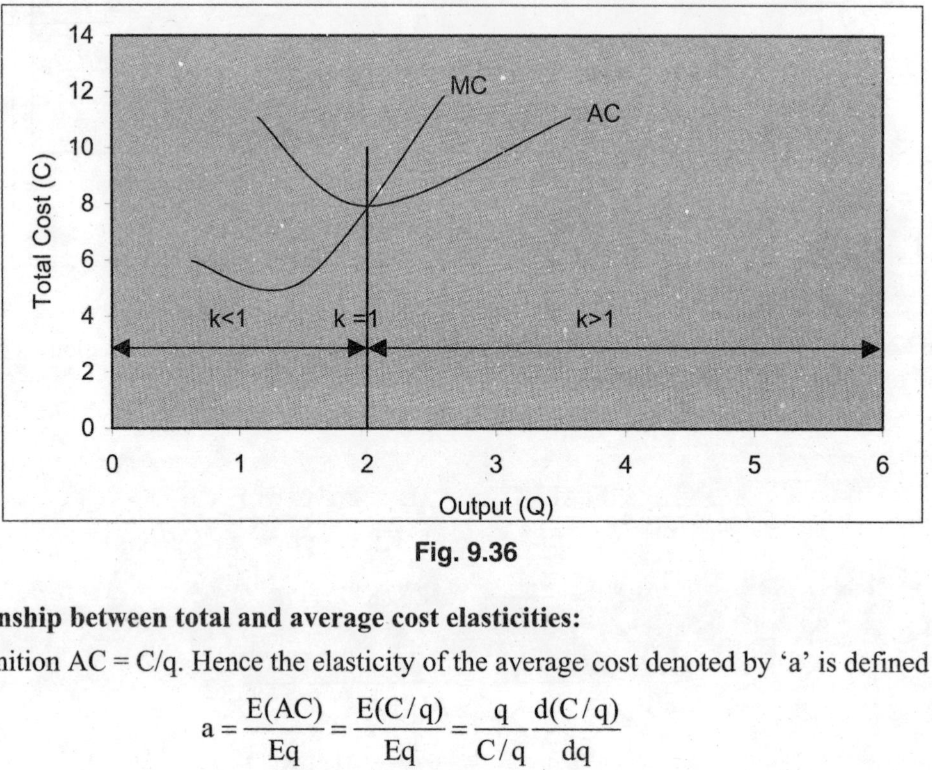

Fig. 9.36

Relationship between total and average cost elasticities:

By definition AC = C/q. Hence the elasticity of the average cost denoted by 'a' is defined as

$$a=\frac{E(AC)}{Eq}=\frac{E(C/q)}{Eq}=\frac{q}{C/q}\frac{d(C/q)}{dq}$$

$$=\frac{q^2}{C}\left[\frac{q\frac{dC}{dq}-C}{q^2}\right]$$

$$=\frac{q^2 q\, dC}{C\, q^2 dq}-\frac{q^2 C}{Cq^2}$$

$$=\frac{q}{C}\frac{dC}{dq}-1$$

$$a=k-1$$

Example 23: If $C = 20q^2 + 10q + 100$ stands for the total cost function of a firm find k, the total cost elasticity, when q = 10. Also obtain the elasticity of the average cost elasticity 'a'.

Solution:

$$k = \frac{EC}{Eq} = \frac{E(20q^2 + 10q + 100)}{Eq}$$

$$= \frac{q}{20q^2 + 10q + 100} \frac{d(20q^2 + 10q + 100)}{dq}$$

$$= \frac{q}{20q^2 + 10q + 100} \times 40q + 10$$

$$= \frac{40q^2 + 10q}{20q^2 + 10q + 100}$$

$$\text{Thus, } (k)_{q=10} = \frac{40 \times 10^2 + 10 \times 10}{20 \times 10^2 + 10 \times 10 + 100}$$

$$= \frac{4000 + 100}{2000 + 100 + 100} = 1.863$$

Now, we know that the average cost elasticity a = k–1

So, a = 1.863 – 1 = 0.865

EXERCISES

1. When the price elasticity of demand for a soft drink is less than one what action would the manager of the company will take to increase the total revenue?
2. Monopolists will never charge the profit-maximizing price in the inelastic range of the demand. Why?
3. When the income elasticity of a firm's product is greater than unity how could the manager of the firm utilize this information to forecast the future sale?
4. When the cross elasticity of demand for a soft drink is minus one how could the manager of the bottle producing company will use this information for forecasting the demand for bottles?
5. The demand laws for two related commodities are $Q_1 = \frac{200p_2}{p_1}$; $Q_2 = \frac{500p_1}{p_2}$.

   Find $\eta_{11}, \eta_{12}, \eta_{21}, \eta_{22}$. Also prove that the commodities are substitutes.
6. For two related commodities the demand laws are $Q_1 = 100 - 2p_1 + 3p_2$; $Q_2 = 200 + p_1 - 2p_2$. Find $\eta_{11}, \eta_{12}, \eta_{21}, \eta_{22}$, when $p_1 = 2$ and $p_2 = 3$. Also prove that the commodities are substitutes.

7. If $Q_1 = 400 - 3p_1 - 2p_2$ and $Q_2 = 600 - 2p_1 - 5p_2$ are the demand functions for two related commodities. Find $\eta_{11}, \eta_{12}, \eta_{21}, \eta_{22}$ when $p_1 = 4$ and $p_2 = 6$. Also prove that the commodities are compliments.
8. In 1920 the tuition fee in an institution in Bangalore was Rs. 500 per year. The enrollment in the institution was 10,275 students. In the year 2000 the tuition fee had increased to Rs.1000 and the enrollment went up to 20,587 students. Does this observation mean the demand law for tuition is upward sloping? Explain.
9. It is noticed that the quantity demanded decreases by two units for every one unit in its price. At Rs. 5 the 10 units were demanded.

   (a) Obtained a linear demand giving quantity as a function of price.

   (b) What will be the quantity when the price is Rs. 2?
10. A market consists three consumers A, B and C. Their individual demand functions are:

    $P = 35 - 0.50Q_A$

    $P = 50 - 0.25Q_B$

    $P = 40 - 2.00Q_C$

    (a) Obtain the aggregate market demand for the product.

    (b) If the aggregate supply function is $Q_S = 100 + 5p$. Determine the equilibrium price and the quantity. Also calculate the individual and aggregate market demand elasticities when $p = 4$.
11. A market consists of only two individuals A and B. The respective demand functions are; $Q_1 = 100 - 2p$, $Q_2 = 100 - 4p$.

    (a) Obtain the aggregate market demand.

    (b) Also calculate the individual and aggregate market demand elasticities when $p = 4$.
12. The demand for PC's fitted with Pentium IV processor is $P = 10{,}000 - 5Q$.

    (a) Obtain the equation for the MR.

    (b) At what price and quantity the value of MR = 0.

    (c) At what price and quantity the total revenue will be maximum.

    (d) If the price is increased from Rs. 30,000 to Rs. 40,000 what effect it will have on the total revenue. What does this imply on the elasticity?
13. The demand law of a certain product is $P = 100 - 4Q$

    (a) Calculate the arc elasticity when the price changes from Rs. 10 to Rs. 20

    (b) Calculate the arc elasticity when the price changes from Rs. 20 to Rs. 10

    (c) Account for the noticed difference between the two elasticities.

10

Chapter

MAXIMA AND MINIMA AND ITS APPLICATIONS

10.1 Types of Functions

(i) **Increasing Function:** The function y = f (x) is said to be an increasing function provided both x and y move in the same direction. In other words, this is to say that a rise in x leads to a rise in y and vice versa. In mathematical terms this is to say that dy/dx > 0. Supply functions in microeconomics and consumption function in macroeconomics are specific examples for this type of upward sloping functions.

Example 1: Keynesian consumption function C = 500 + 0.5Y.

Now $\frac{dC}{dY} = 0.5 > 0$

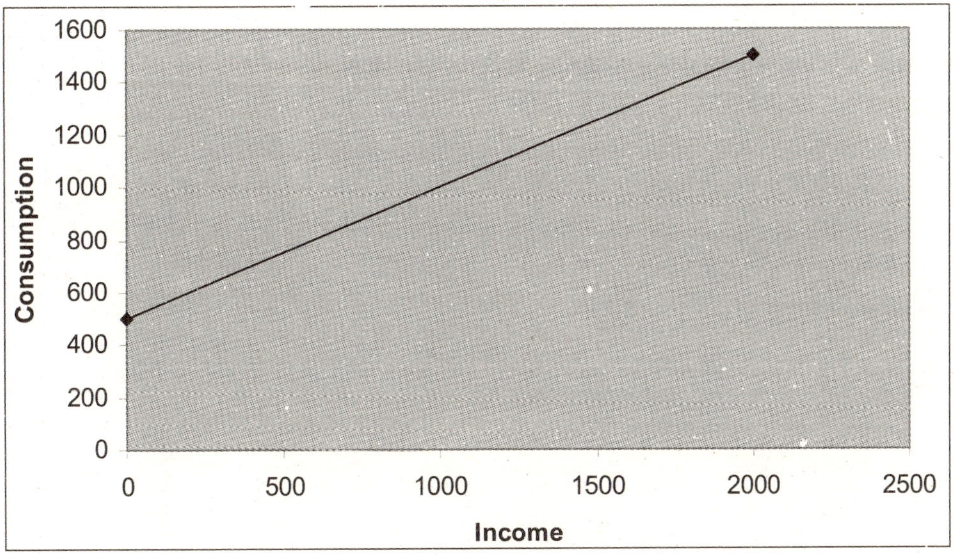

Fig. 10.1 Consumption function

Example 2: Walrasian supply function S = – 25 + 25p.

Here $\frac{dS}{dp} = 25 > 0$

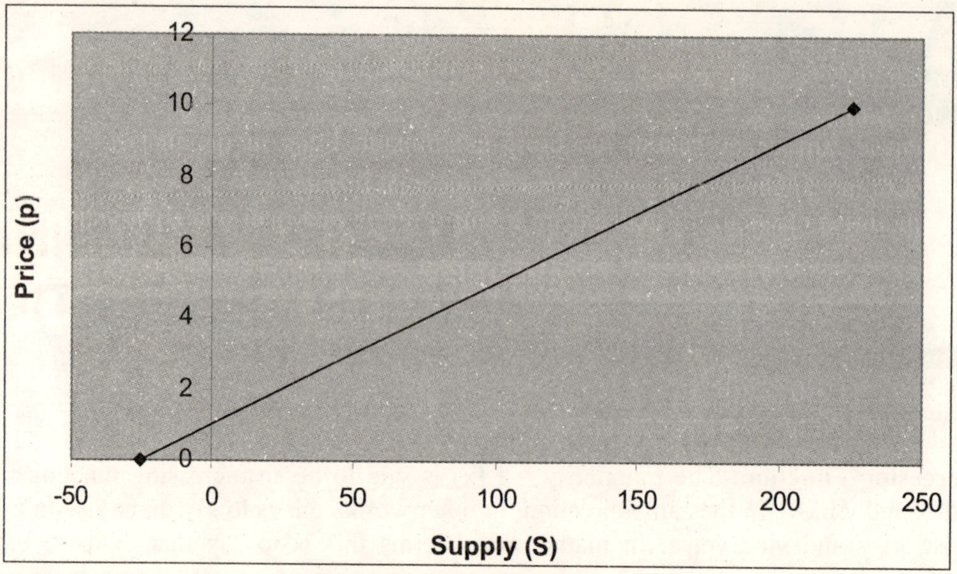

Fig. 10.2 Supply function

(ii) Decreasing Function: The function y = f (x) is said to be a decreasing function when both x and y move in the opposite direction. A rise in x leads to a fall in y and vise versa. Mathematically this is to say that dy/dx < 0 (–ve). Marshallian demand and Hicksian indifference curves are two specific illustrations for this type of decreasing functions.

Example 3: The Marshallian demand p = – 50D + 250. Here $\frac{dp}{dq} = -50 < 0$

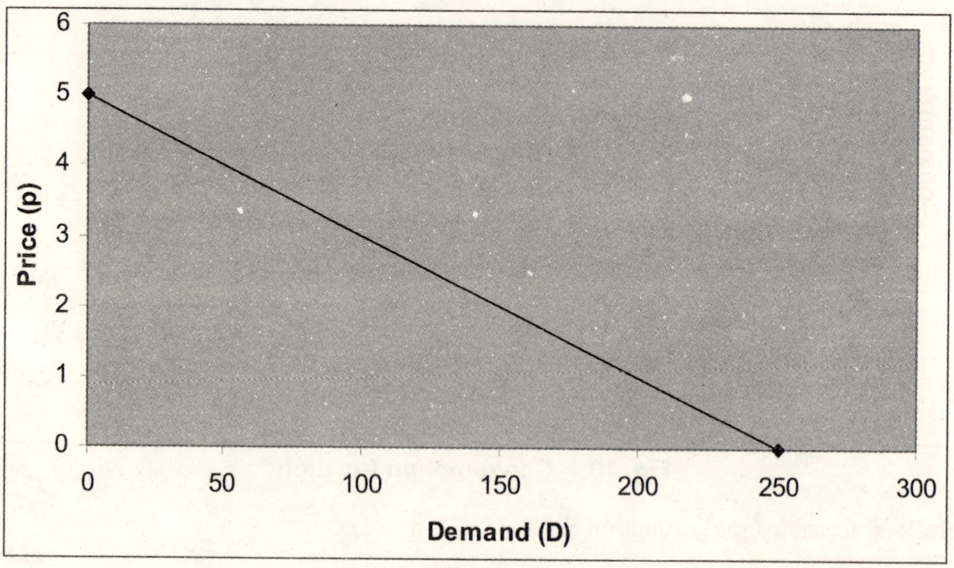

Fig. 10.3 Demand function

10.2 Shape of Functions

Convex functions

The function y = f (x) is said to be convex from below provided its second order derivative is positive i.e. $\frac{d^2y}{dx^2} > 0$. This is to say that $\frac{d}{dx}\left(\frac{dy}{dx}\right) > 0$. Since $\frac{dy}{dx}$ is nothing but the slope of the function, the above condition states that both x and $\frac{dy}{dx}$ move together as shown in the Fig. 10.4 and 10.5. From the Fig. it is clear that the slope of the tangent $\frac{dy}{dx}$ goes on increases as x increases.

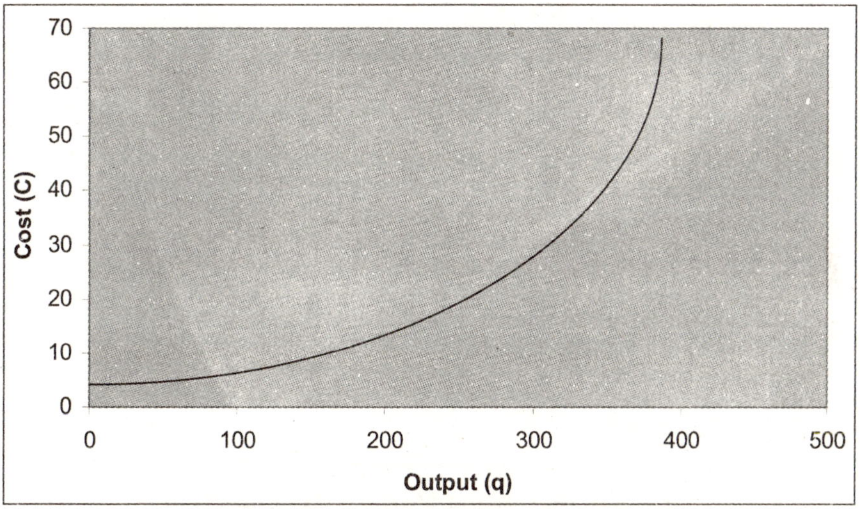

Fig. 10.4 Increasing convex cost function

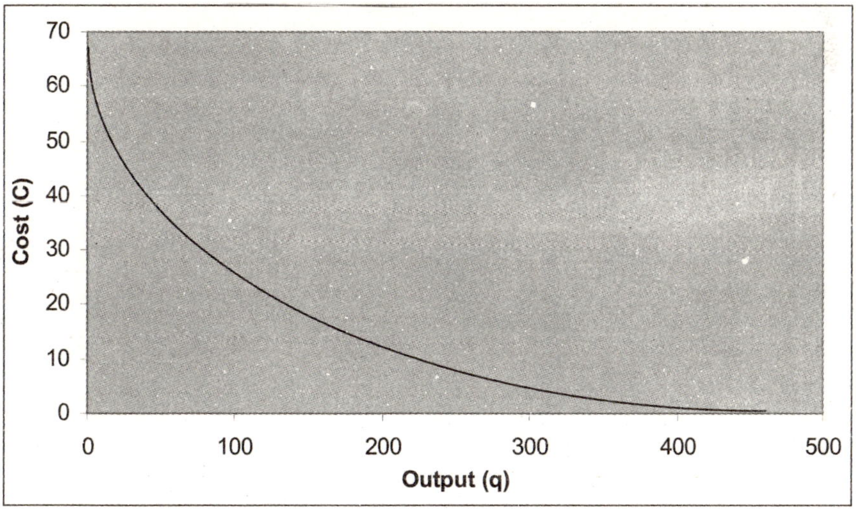

Fig. 10.5 Decreasing convex indifference curve

Concave functions

The function y = f (x) is said to be concave from below provided its second order derivative is negative i.e. $\frac{d^2y}{dx^2} < 0$. This is to say that $\frac{d}{dx}\left(\frac{dy}{dx}\right) < 0$. Since $\frac{dy}{dx}$ is nothing but the slope of the function, the above condition states that both x and $\frac{dy}{dx}$ move in the opposite direction as shown in the Fig. 10.6 and 10.7. From the Fig. it is clear that the slope of the tangent $\frac{dy}{dx}$ goes on decreases as x increases.

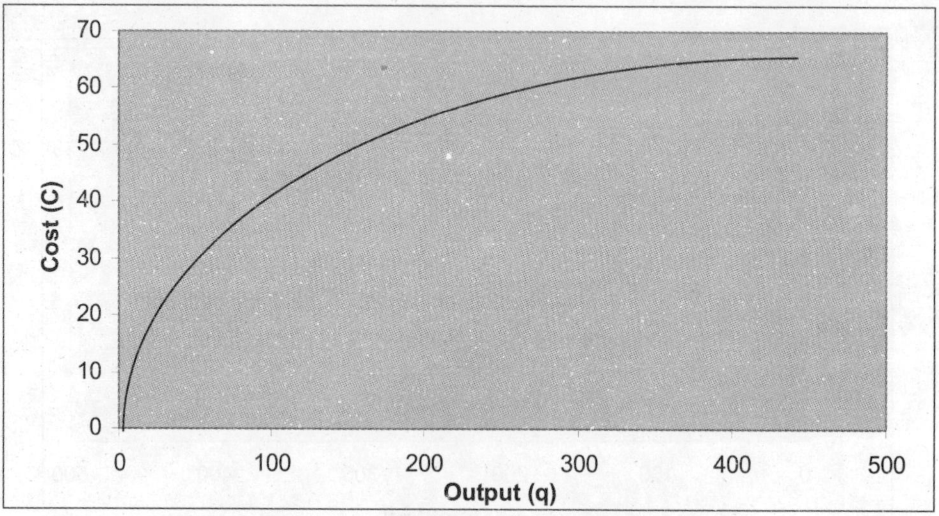

Fig. 10.6 Increasing concave cost function

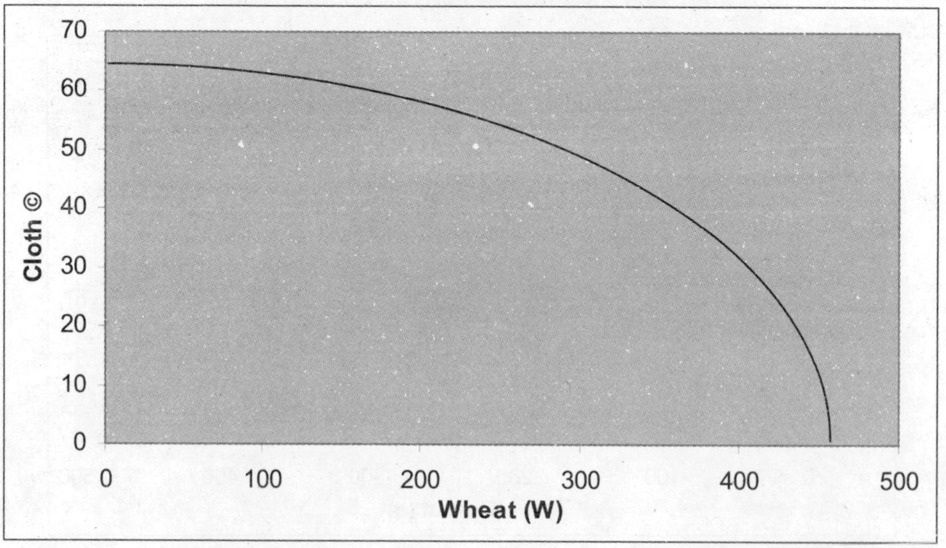

Fig. 10.7 Decreasing convex product transformation function

Use of convex and concave functions: We use these types of curves either in isolation or in combination. Decreasing convex functions are used in the theory of consumption as indifference curves and theory of production as iso-product curves otherwise called iso-quants. Increasing convex functions are used while representing the first phase of the total cost function. Decreasing concave functions are used in International economics as product transformation curves.

10.3 Maxima and Minima of Functions

(i) One Independent Variable Case

Optimization is the key concept in Economics. The consumer attains his equilibrium by maximizing his utility. The producer attains his equilibrium either by maximizing profit or minimizing cost.

In the Fig. 10.8 shown below clearly the function y = f (x) reaches its maximum at B and minimum at E in the given range of operation. At the point A the tangent drawn is upward sloping i.e.dy/dx is positive. Similarly, at point C the tangent drawn is downward sloping i.e. dy/dx is negative. Hence at the maximum point B the slope of the tangent crossing over from positive side to negative side and become horizontal and parallel to X-axis as sown in the Fig.. In mathematical terms this is to say that dy/dx = 0

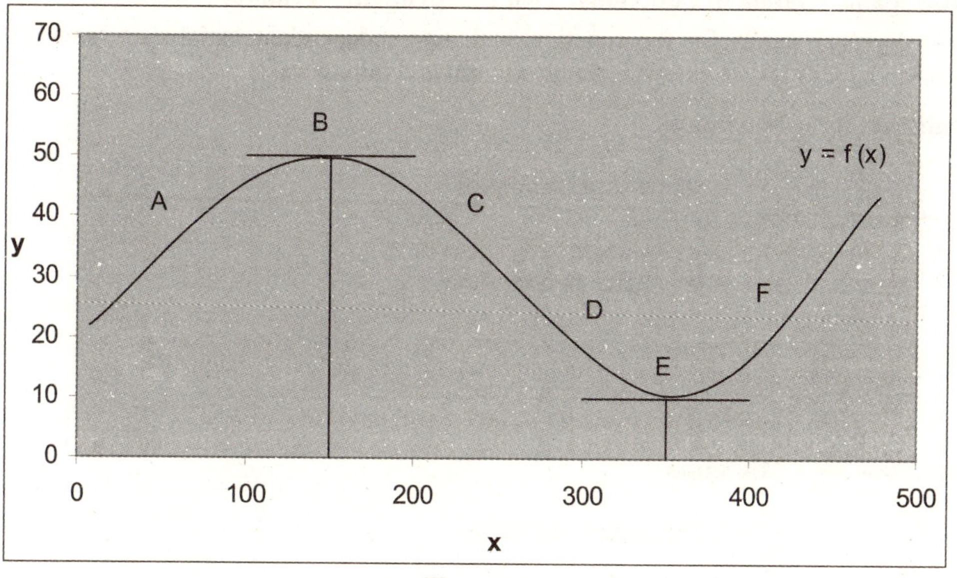

Fig. 10.8

Similarly, the slope of the tangent drawn at D is negative and drawn at F is positive. Here again at the minimum point E the slope of the tangent drawn crosses from negative side to positive side and become horizontal and parallel to the X-axis. In mathematical terms this is to say that dy/dx = 0. So we are not in a position to identify the maximum and the minimum from the first order derivative alone because at both the points dy/dx = 0.

However, luckily we notice that the function is concave around the maximum point and convex around the minimum point. For convexity of the function we know that $d^2y/dx^2 > 0$ and concavity of the function we know that $d^2y/dx^2 < 0$. Now by using both these results we are comfortable in identifying distinct conditions for maximum and minimum.

(a) Condition for a Maximum

The function y = f (x) reaches its maximum provided:

1. $\frac{dy}{dx} = 0$ (necessary condition)

2. $\frac{d^2y}{dx^2} < 0$ (sufficient condition)

(b) Condition for a Minimum

The function y = f (x) reaches its minimum provided:

1. $\frac{dy}{dx} = 0$ (necessary condition)

2. $\frac{d^2y}{dx^2} > 0$ (sufficient condition)

(ii) Maxima and Minima of Functions: Two Independent Variables

If z = f (x, y) stands for the function with two independent variables x and y then the following conditions are essential for maximum and minimum.

(a) Conditions for a Maximum

1. $\frac{\partial z}{\partial x} = 0 \ ; \ \frac{\partial z}{\partial y} = 0$ (necessary condition)

2. $\frac{\partial^2 z}{\partial x^2} < 0 \ ; \ \frac{\partial^2 z}{\partial y^2} < 0$ (sufficient conditions)

3. $\frac{\partial^2 z}{\partial x^2} \times \frac{\partial^2 z}{\partial y^2} > \left(\frac{\partial^2 z}{\partial x \partial y} \right)^2$ (saddle point condition)

(b) Conditions for a Minimum

1. $\frac{\partial z}{\partial x} = 0 \ ; \ \frac{\partial z}{\partial y} = 0$ (necessary condition)

2. $\frac{\partial^2 z}{\partial x^2} > 0 \ ; \ \frac{\partial^2 z}{\partial y^2} > 0$ (sufficient conditions)

3. $\frac{\partial^2 z}{\partial x^2} \times \frac{\partial^2 z}{\partial y^2} > \left(\frac{\partial^2 z}{\partial x \partial y} \right)^2$ (saddle point condition)

(iii) Maxima and Minima of Functions: Two Variables with Constraints

In economics very often we come across maximization and minimization problems with side relations, often called constraints. Under the circumstances the two independent variables optimization conditions discussed in the previous section obviously cannot be used. In fact these constraints restrict the process of optimization to a limit.

In the theory of consumption the utility maximization is constrained by the side relation commonly known as budget. In the theory of production either the output gets maximized having the cost constraint in mind or the cost is minimized having the targeted constant output in mind. In either case the constraint restrict the process of optimization. To handle this type of situations there are two specialized methods of optimization.

(1) **Direct elimination method:** In this method we eliminate one of the variables in the given objective function with the help of the given side relation. After eliminating one variable our objective function will have only one left out variable. Now we optimize the given function by using the one variable method outlined earlier.

(2) **The Lagrangian multiplier method:** In this alternative Lagrangian multiplier method we formulate an auxiliary equation by incorporating the both the objective and implicit form of the side relation as shown below.

$$Z = f(x, y) - \lambda [g(x, y)]$$

Once the auxiliary equation is formed we optimize this equation in the usual manner. Since this auxiliary equation involves three variables x, y and λ, for the optimum value of Z the partial derivatives of Z with respect to x, y and the multiplier λ are equated to zero.

Conditions for a Maximum

First order condition

i.e. $$\frac{\partial Z}{\partial x} = \frac{\partial Z}{\partial y} = \frac{\partial Z}{\partial \lambda} = 0$$

Second order condition

The second order condition for a constrained maximum problem is always stated in the determinant form. This determinant is often called bordered Hessian determinant.

$$\begin{vmatrix} \frac{\partial^2 Z}{\partial x^2} & \frac{\partial^2 Z}{\partial x \partial y} & \frac{\partial^2 Z}{\partial x \partial \lambda} \\ \frac{\partial^2 Z}{\partial y \partial x} & \frac{\partial^2 Z}{\partial y^2} & \frac{\partial^2 Z}{\partial y \partial \lambda} \\ \frac{\partial^2 Z}{\partial \lambda \partial x} & \frac{\partial^2 Z}{\partial \lambda \partial y} & \frac{\partial^2 Z}{\partial \lambda^2} \end{vmatrix} > 0$$

Conditions for a Minimum

First order condition

i.e. $$\frac{\partial Z}{\partial x} = \frac{\partial Z}{\partial y} = \frac{\partial Z}{\partial \lambda} = 0$$

Second order condition

$$\begin{vmatrix} \frac{\partial^2 Z}{\partial x^2} & \frac{\partial^2 Z}{\partial x \partial y} & \frac{\partial^2 Z}{\partial x \partial \lambda} \\ \frac{\partial^2 Z}{\partial y \partial x} & \frac{\partial^2 Z}{\partial y^2} & \frac{\partial^2 Z}{\partial y \partial \lambda} \\ \frac{\partial^2 Z}{\partial \lambda \partial x} & \frac{\partial^2 Z}{\partial \lambda \partial y} & \frac{\partial^2 Z}{\partial \lambda^2} \end{vmatrix} < 0$$

10.4 Applications of Maxima and Minima in the Theory of Consumption

In the theory of consumption we have two basic approaches. In the ordinal utility approach of Marshall, utility is assumed to measurable by cardinal units like kilogram that we use to measure the weight of an object, meter scale that we use to measure the length of a piece of cloth etc. He uses money as a measuring instrument. J.R. Hicks and R.G.D. Allen however, have provided an alternative theory in which the utility of various items needs only preferential ordering like first, second, third etc. However, in both the approaches consumer attains his equilibrium by maximizing his utility subject to his budget constraint otherwise called the side relation.

Derivation of both the Necessary and Sufficient Conditions for Consumer's Equilibrium

1. Elimination method

Let $$U = f(q_1, q_2) \quad \text{...(1)}$$

stands for the utility function of the consumer.

Further let $$M = p_1q_1 + p_2q_2 \quad \text{...(2)}$$

stands for the budget equation in its general form.

Now in equation (1) above the commodities q_1 and q_2 are not independent in the sense that the consumer under consideration can not have the choice of buying both q_1 and q_2 in infinite amounts, because the money income is given to the consumer. In fact, the amount of q_2 that he can buy depends upon the amount of q_1 that he has already purchased. Since the money income that he is having is restricted to M, larger the amount of q_1 already bought less will be the money leftover for the purchase of q_2 and vice versa. Thus, either q_1 can be treated as independent or q_2 can be treated independent but certainly not both at a time. Now let us treat q_1 as independent and calculate the value of q_2 from equation (2) above as follows:

$$-p_2q_2 = M - p_1q_1$$

$$q_2 = \frac{M - p_1q_1}{-p_2}$$

$$q_2 = \frac{p_1}{p_2}q_1 - \frac{M}{p_2} \quad \text{...(3)}$$

Now after substituting (3) in (1) above it becomes

$$U = f\left[q_1, \left(\frac{p_1}{p_2}q_1 - \frac{M}{p_2}\right)\right] \qquad \ldots(4)$$

Now in equation (4) U is a function of q_1 alone. So for the maximum value of U, we know that

1. Necessary condition $\frac{dU}{dq_1} = 0$
2. Sufficient condition $\frac{d^2U}{dq_1^2} < 0$

Necessary condition

So from the total derivative rule it follows that

$$\frac{dU}{dq_1} = f_1 + f_2\left(\frac{dq_2}{dq_1}\right) = 0$$

Now from (3) above $\frac{dq_2}{dq_1} = -\frac{p_1}{p_2}$

Submitting this value in the above equation it becomes

$$\frac{dU}{dq_1} = f_1 + f_2\left(-\frac{p_1}{p_2}\right) = 0$$

$$f_1 = f_2\frac{p_1}{p_2}$$

Now after dividing both the sides of the above equation by p_1 it becomes

$$\frac{f_1}{p_1} = \frac{f_2}{p_2}$$

$$\frac{MU_1}{p_1} = \frac{MU_2}{p_2}$$

The above result is often called the equi-marginal principle for consumer's equilibrium. Accordingly, the last Rupee spent on both the commodities must give equal amount of satisfaction to the consumer under equilibrium. After inter changing p_1 and f_2 the above condition may also be written as

$$\frac{f_1}{f_2} = \frac{p_1}{p_2}$$

i.e. MRCS = slope of the budget line

Sufficient condition

Now by definition

$$\frac{d^2U}{dq_1^2} = \frac{d}{dq_1}\left(\frac{dU}{dq_1}\right) < 0$$

$$= \frac{d}{dq_1}\left[f_1 + f_2\left(\frac{dq_2}{dq_1}\right)\right] < 0$$

$$= f_{11} + f_{21}\left(\frac{dq_2}{dq_1}\right) + f_{12}\left(\frac{dq_2}{dq_1}\right) + f_{22}\left(\frac{dq_2}{dq_1}\right)^2 < 0$$

$$= f_{11} + 2f_{12}\left(\frac{dq_2}{dq_1}\right) + f_{22}\left(\frac{dq_2}{dq_1}\right)^2 < 0$$

$$= f_{11} + 2f_{12}\left(\frac{-p_1}{p_2}\right) + f_{22}\left(-\frac{p_1}{p_2}\right)^2 < 0$$

$$= f_{11} - 2f_{12}\left(\frac{p_1}{p_2}\right) + f_{22}\left(\frac{p_1}{p_2}\right)^2 < 0$$

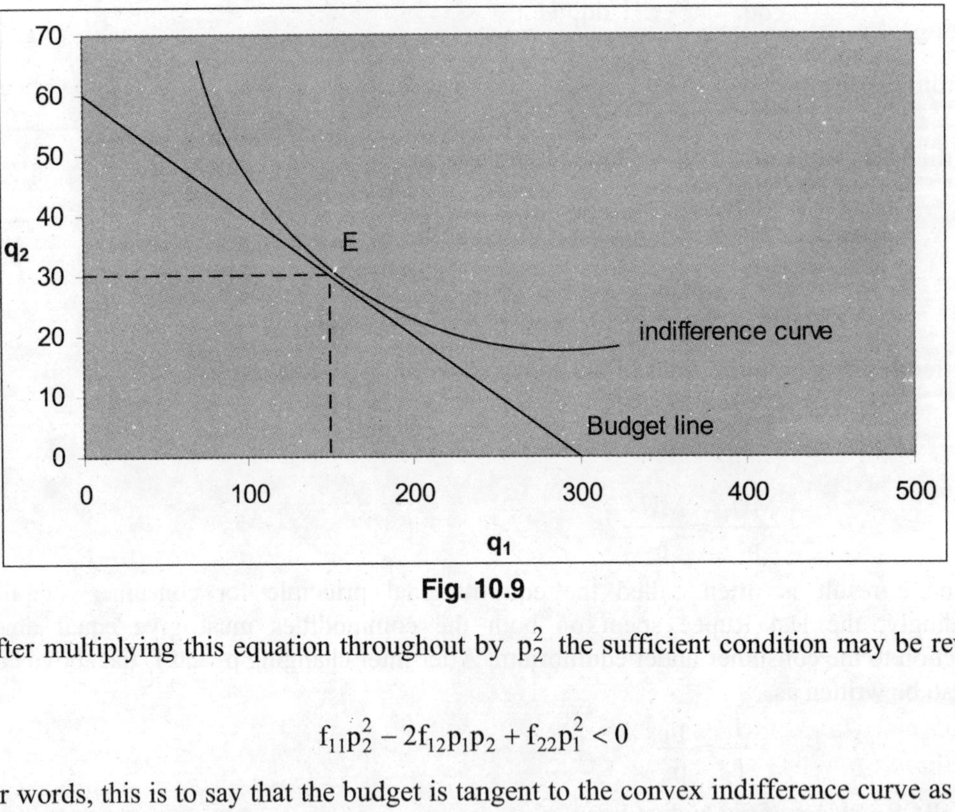

Fig. 10.9

Now after multiplying this equation throughout by p_2^2 the sufficient condition may be rewritten as

$$f_{11}p_2^2 - 2f_{12}p_1p_2 + f_{22}p_1^2 < 0$$

In other words, this is to say that the budget is tangent to the convex indifference curve as shown in the Fig. 10.9.

2. Lagrangian multiplier method

Let the utility function of the consumer be

$$U = f(q_1, q_2) \qquad \ldots(1)$$

Further, let budget equation of the consumer be

$$M = p_1q_1 + p_2q_2 \qquad \ldots(2)$$

Now to maximize (1) with respect to (2) let us rewrite equation (2) in its implicit form by moving all the RHS terms to the LHS.

i.e. $$M - p_1q_1 - p_2q_2 = 0 \qquad \ldots(3)$$

Now to maximize (1) with respect (3) the Lagrangian equation may be written as

$$Z = \text{RHS of (1)} + \lambda[\text{LHS of (3)}]$$

$$Z = f(q_1, q_2) + \lambda(M - p_1q_1 - p_2q_2) \qquad \ldots(4)$$

Now to maximize Z given in equation (4), since it involves three variables q_1, q_2 and λ, their respective partial derivatives are to be equated to zero.

i.e. $$\frac{\partial Z}{\partial q_1} = \frac{\partial Z}{\partial q_2} = \frac{\partial Z}{\partial \lambda} = 0$$

So from (4) above $$\frac{\partial Z}{\partial q_1} = f_1 - p_1\lambda = 0 \qquad \ldots(5)$$

$$\frac{\partial Z}{\partial q_2} = f_2 - p_2\lambda = 0 \qquad \ldots(6)$$

$$\frac{\partial Z}{\partial \lambda} = M - p_1q_1 - p_2q_2 = 0 \qquad \ldots(7)$$

Now from (5) above $f_1 = p_1\,\lambda$ ...(8)

(6) above $f_2 = p_2\,\lambda$ ...(9)

$$\frac{(8)}{(9)} \qquad \frac{f_1}{f_2} = \frac{p_1\lambda}{p_2\lambda}$$

$$\frac{f_1}{f_2} = \frac{p_1}{p_2}$$

$$\frac{f_1}{p_1} = \frac{f_2}{p_2}$$

$$\frac{MU_1}{p_1} = \frac{MU_2}{p_2}$$

This is called the equi-marginal principle for consumer's equilibrium. Accordingly the last Rupee spent on both the commodities must give equal amount of satisfaction to the consumer under equilibrium. After inter changing p_1 and f_2 the above condition may also be written as

$$\frac{f_1}{f_2} = \frac{p_1}{p_2}$$

i.e. MRCS = slope of the budget line

In other words, this is to say that the budget is tangent to the convex indifference curve as shown in Fig. 10.9.

Sufficient condition

The sufficient condition in this case is normally stated in terms of the bordered Hessian determinant

$$\begin{vmatrix} \frac{\partial^2 Z}{\partial q_1^2} & \frac{\partial^2 Z}{\partial q_1 \partial q_2} & \frac{\partial^2 Z}{\partial q_1 \partial \lambda} \\ \frac{\partial^2 Z}{\partial q_2 \partial q_1} & \frac{\partial^2 Z}{\partial q_2^2} & \frac{\partial^2 Z}{\partial q_2 \partial \lambda} \\ \frac{\partial^2 Z}{\partial \lambda \partial q_1} & \frac{\partial^2 Z}{\partial \lambda \partial q_2} & \frac{\partial^2 Z}{\partial \lambda^2} \end{vmatrix} > 0$$

Now from equation (5), (6) and (7) the above determinant may be written as

$$\begin{vmatrix} f_{11} & f_{12} & -p_1 \\ f_{21} & f_{22} & -p_2 \\ -p_1 & -p_2 & 0 \end{vmatrix} = f_{11}\begin{vmatrix} f_{22} & -p_2 \\ -p_2 & 0 \end{vmatrix} - f_{12}\begin{vmatrix} f_{21} & -p_2 \\ p_1 & 0 \end{vmatrix} - p_1\begin{vmatrix} f_{21} & f_{22} \\ -p_1 & -p_2 \end{vmatrix}$$

$$= -f_{11}p_2^2 + f_{12}p_1p_2 + f_{21}p_1p_2 - f_{22}p_2^2 > 0$$

Now let us multiply the above result by (– 1) throughout

$$f_{11}p_2^2 - 2f_{12}p_1p_2 + f_{22}p_2^2 < 0$$

This is exactly the same sufficient condition that we got in the elimination method.

Example 4: A student has Rs.100 per month to spend on two luxuries; the money can be spent either on clothing, which costs Rs. 50 per item or on cinema, which costs Rs.10 per visit. If q_1 is the number of items of clothing bought and q_2 is the number of visits to cinema, then the student's utility function is defined by $U = 10q_1q_2$. Show that the student will spend equal amounts of his income on each of the item under equilibrium.

Solution:

1. **Elimination method**

The Student's utility function is

$$U = q_1q_2 \qquad \ldots(1)$$

The budget constraint of the student in its general form is written as

$$M = p_1q_1 + p_2q_2$$

Now since clothing per unit costs Rs. 50, cinema costs Rs. 5 per visit and the income of the student is Rs.100 the above equation may be rewritten as

$$100 = 50\, q_1 + 10q_2. \qquad \ldots(2)$$

Now to maximize the utility given in equation (1) with respect to constraint (2) we must first eliminate either q_1 or q_2 in (1) using equation (2). Hence, let us try to eliminate q_2 in equation (1) with the help of the budget equation given in (2). To do this let us solve equation (2) for q_2 in terms of q_1 as shown below.

Equation (2) may be rewritten as

$$-10q_2 = 50q_1 - 100$$

$$q_2 = (50q_1 - 100)/-10$$

$$q_2 = 10 - 5q_1 \quad \ldots(3)$$

Now after substituting (3) in (1) our utility function may be rewritten as

$$U = q_1 (10 - 5q_1)$$

$$U = 10q_1 - 5q_1^2 \quad \ldots(4)$$

In equation (4) above the utility U is conveniently written with only one independent variable q_1.

So for the maximum value of U given in equation (4) we know that

1. $\frac{dU}{dq_1} = 0$ (Necessary condition)
2. $\frac{d^2U}{dq_1^2} < 0$ (Sufficient condition)

So from (4) above $\frac{dU}{dq_1} = 10 - 10\,q_1 = 0$

i.e. $-10q_1 = -10$

$$q_1 = 1$$

Further, from above $\frac{d^2U}{dq_1^2} = -10 < 0$

Thus $q_1 = 1$ gets confirmed as the equilibrium quantity. Now the equilibrium value of q_2 is obtained by merely substituting this value of q_1 in equation (3) above

i.e. $q_2 = 10 - (5 \times 1) = 5$

Thus under equilibrium $q_1 = 1$ and $q_2 = 5$.

Now $p_1q_1 = 1 \times 50 = 50$; $p_2q_2 = 5 \times 10 = 50$

Thus the consumer spends equal amounts of his income on each item under equilibrium.

2. Lagrangian multiplier method

The utility function of the consumer is

$$U = q_1q_2 \quad \ldots(1)$$

The budget equation of the consumer is

$$100 = 50q_1 + 10q_2 \quad \ldots(2)$$

Now to maximize (1) with respect to (2) let us rewrite equation (2) in its implicit form by moving all the RHS terms to the LHS.

i.e. $100 - 50q_1 - 10q_2 = 0 \quad \ldots(3)$

Now to maximize (1) with respect to (3) the Lagrangeian equation may be written as

$$Z = \text{RHS of (1)} + \lambda[\text{LHS of (3)}]$$

$$Z = 50q_1q_2 + \lambda(100 - 50q_1 - 10\,q_2) \qquad \ldots(4)$$

Now to maximize Z given in equation (4), since it involves three variables q_1, q_2 and λ, their respective partial derivatives are to be equated to zero.

i.e. $$\frac{\partial Z}{\partial q_1} = \frac{\partial Z}{\partial q_2} = \frac{\partial Z}{\partial q_\lambda} = 0$$

So from (4) above $$\frac{\partial Z}{\partial q_1} = 50q_2 - 50\lambda = 0 \qquad \ldots(5)$$

$$\frac{\partial Z}{\partial q_2} = 50q_1 - 10\lambda = 0 \qquad \ldots(6)$$

$$\frac{\partial Z}{\partial \lambda} = 100 - 5q_1 - 10q_2 = 0 \qquad \ldots(7)$$

Now from (5) above $50q_2 = 50\,\lambda$ ...(8)

(6) above $50q_1 = 10\lambda$ ...(9)

$$\frac{(8)}{(9)} \qquad \frac{50q_2}{50q_1} = \frac{50\lambda}{10\lambda}$$

$$\frac{q_2}{q_1} = 5$$

Now after cross multiplication this equation may be written as

$$q_2 = 5q_1 \qquad \ldots(10)$$

Now substituting this value q_2 in equation (7) above it becomes

$$100 - 5q_1 - 10(5q_1) = 0$$

$$100 = 100\,q_1$$

$$q_1 = 1$$

The equilibrium value of q_2 is obtained by merely substituting this value of q_1 in equation (10) above.

i.e. $$q_2 = 5\times 1$$

$$q_2 = 5$$

Second order condition

$$\begin{vmatrix} \dfrac{\partial^2 Z}{\partial q_1^2} & \dfrac{\partial^2 Z}{\partial q_1 \partial q_2} & \dfrac{\partial^2 Z}{\partial q_1 \partial \lambda} \\ \dfrac{\partial^2 Z}{\partial q_2 \partial q_1} & \dfrac{\partial^2 Z}{\partial q_2^2} & \dfrac{\partial^2 Z}{\partial q_2 \partial \lambda} \\ \dfrac{\partial^2 Z}{\partial \lambda \partial q_1} & \dfrac{\partial^2 Z}{\partial \lambda \partial q_2} & \dfrac{\partial^2 Z}{\partial \lambda^2} \end{vmatrix} > 0$$

Now from Equation (5), (6) and (7) the above determinant becomes

$$\begin{vmatrix} 0 & 10 & -50 \\ 10 & 0 & -10 \\ -50 & -10 & 0 \end{vmatrix} = 0\begin{vmatrix} 0 & -10 \\ -10 & 0 \end{vmatrix} - 10\begin{vmatrix} 10 & -10 \\ -50 & 0 \end{vmatrix} - 50\begin{vmatrix} 10 & 0 \\ -50 & -10 \end{vmatrix}$$

$$= 0 - 10(-500) - 50(-100) = 10000 > 0$$

Thus, $q_1 = 1$ and $q_2 = 5$ gets confirmed as the equilibrium values.

Example 5: If $U = 10q_1q_2$ derive the ordinary Marshallian demand functions for both q_1 and q_2.

Solution:

The utility function of the consumer is

$$U = 10q_1q_2 \qquad ...(1)$$

The budget equation of the consumer in its general form may be written as

$$M = p_1q_1 + p_2q_2 \qquad ...(2)$$

Now to maximize (1) with respect to (2) let us rewrite equation (2) in its implicit form by moving all the RHS terms to the LHS.

i.e. $$M - p_1q_1 - p_2q_2 = 0 \qquad ...(3)$$

Now to maximize (1) with respect (3) the Lagrangian equation may be written as

$$Z = \text{RHS of (1)} + \lambda[\text{LHS of (3)}]$$

i.e. $$Z = 10q_1q_2 - \lambda(M - p_1q_1 - p_2q_2) \qquad ...(4)$$

Now to maximize Z given in equation (4), since it involves three variables q_1, q_2 and λ, their respective partial derivatives are to be equated to zero.

i.e $$\frac{\partial Z}{\partial q_1} = \frac{\partial Z}{\partial q_1} = \frac{\partial Z}{\partial q_2} = 0$$

So from (4) above $$\frac{\partial Z}{\partial q_1} = 10q_2 - p_1\lambda = 0 \qquad ...(5)$$

$$\frac{\partial Z}{\partial q_2} = 10q_1 - p_2\lambda = 0 \qquad ...(6)$$

$$\frac{\partial Z}{\partial \lambda} = M - p_1q_1 - p_2q_2 = 0 \qquad ...(7)$$

Now from (5) above $10q_2 = p_1 \lambda$ ...(8)

(6) above $10q_1 = p_2 \lambda$ ...(9)

$$\frac{(8)}{(9)} \qquad \frac{10q_2}{10q_1} = \frac{p_1\lambda}{p_2\lambda}$$

$$\frac{q_2}{q_1} = \frac{p_1}{p_2}$$

Now after cross multiplication this equation may be written as

$$P_2q_2 = p_1q_1$$

$$q_2 = \frac{p_1}{p_2}q_1 \quad \text{...(10)}$$

Now substituting this value q_2 in equation (7) above it becomes

$$M - p_1q_1 - p_2\left(\frac{p_1}{p_2}q_1\right) = 0$$

$$M - p_1q_1 - p_1q_1 = 0$$

$$-2p_1q_1 = -M$$

$$q_1 = \frac{-M}{-2p_1} = \frac{M}{2p_1}$$

The q_2 value is obtained by substituting this value of q_1 in equation (10) above.

$$q_2 = \frac{p_1}{p_2}\frac{M}{2p_1} = \frac{M}{2p_2}$$

Thus

$$q_1 = \frac{M}{2p_1}$$

$$q_2 = \frac{M}{2p_2}$$

are the two needed ordinary demand functions.

Example 6: If $U = 10q_1q_2$ derive the compensated demand functions for both q_1 and q_2.

Solution:

The budget equation of the consumer is

$$M = p_1q_1 + p_2q_2 \quad \text{...(1)}$$

The utility function of the consumer for a given constant U^o level of utility may be written as

$$U^o = 10q_1q_2 \quad \text{...(2)}$$

Now to minimize (1) with respect to (2) let us rewrite equation (2) in its implicit form by moving all the RHS terms to the LHS.

i.e. $\quad U^o - 10q_1q_2 = 0 \quad \text{...(3)}$

Now to minimize (1) with respect to (3) the Lagrangian equation may be formulated as

$$Z = \text{RHS of (1)} + \lambda[\text{LHS of (3)}]$$

i.e. $\quad Z = p_1q_1 + p_2q_2 + \lambda(U^o - 10q_1q_2) \quad \text{...(4)}$

Now to minimize Z given in equation (4), since it involves three variables q_1, q_2 and λ, their respective partial derivatives are to be equated to zero.

i.e.
$$\frac{\partial Z}{\partial q_1} = \frac{\partial Z}{\partial q_2} = \frac{\partial Z}{\partial \lambda} = 0$$

So from (4) above $\frac{\partial Z}{\partial q_1} = p_1 - 10q_2\lambda = 0$ ...(5)

$$\frac{\partial Z}{\partial q_2} = p_2 - 10q_1\lambda = 0 \quad ...(6)$$

$$\frac{\partial Z}{\partial \lambda} = U^o - 10q_1q_2 = 0 \quad ...(7)$$

Now from (5) above $p_1 = 10q_2\,\lambda$ ...(8)

(6) above $p_2 = 10q_1\,\lambda$ ...(9)

$$\frac{(8)}{(9)} \qquad \frac{p_1}{p_2} = \frac{10q_2\lambda}{10q_1\lambda}$$

$$\frac{p_1}{p_2} = \frac{q_2}{q_1}$$

Now after cross multiplication this equation may be written as

$$p_2q_2 = p_1q_1$$

$$q_2 = \frac{p_1}{p_2}q_1 \quad ...(10)$$

Now substituting this value q_2 in equation (7) above it becomes

$$U^o - 10q_1\left(\frac{p_1}{p_2}q_1\right) = 0$$

$$-10\frac{p_1}{p_2}q_1^2 = -U^o$$

$$q_1 = \sqrt{\frac{p_2U^o}{10p_1}}$$

The equilibrium value of q_2 is obtained by merely substituting this value of q_1 in equation (10) above.

$$q_2 = \frac{p_1}{p_2}\sqrt{\frac{U^op_2}{10p_1}}$$

$$= \sqrt{\frac{p_1^2}{p_2^2}\frac{U^op_2}{10p_1}}$$

$$= \sqrt{\frac{p_1}{p_2}\frac{U^o}{10}}$$

Thus

$$q_1 = \sqrt{\frac{p_2 U^\circ}{10 p_1}}$$

$$q_2 = \sqrt{\frac{p_1 U^\circ}{10 p_2}}$$

are the needed compensated demand functions.

Example 7: The utility function U = LM of a certain consumer is solely defined in terms of daily hours of leisure 'L' and the daily income 'M'. Under equilibrium prove that the consumer will work for 12 hours in a day irrespective of the hourly wage rate r.

Solution:

The utility function of the consumer is

$$U = LM \qquad \ldots(1)$$

Let W stands for the hours of work in a day.

Hence by definition W + L = 24

Since r is the wage rate per hour by definition M = rW

Therefore $\qquad W = M/r$

Substituting this value of W in the equation given above it becomes

$$(M/r) + L = 24 \qquad \ldots(2)$$

Now to maximize (1) with respect to (2) let us rewrite equation (2) in its implicit form by moving all the RHS terms to the LHS.

i.e. $\qquad (M/r) + L - 24 = 0 \qquad \ldots(3)$

Now to maximize (1) with respect (3) the Lagrangian equation may be written as

$$Z = \text{RHS of (1)} + \lambda[\text{LHS of (3)}]$$

i.e $\qquad Z = LM + \lambda[(M/r) + L - 24] \qquad \ldots(4)$

Now to maximize Z given in equation (4), since it involves three variables L, M and λ their respective partial derivatives are to be equated to zero.

i.e. $$\frac{\partial Z}{\partial L} = \frac{\partial Z}{\partial M} = \frac{\partial Z}{\partial \lambda} = 0$$

So from (4) above $\frac{\partial Z}{\partial L} = M + \lambda = 0 \qquad \ldots(5)$

$$\frac{\partial Z}{\partial M} = L + \frac{\lambda}{r} = 0 \qquad \ldots(6)$$

$$\frac{\partial Z}{\partial \lambda} = \frac{M}{r} + L - 24 = 0 \qquad ...(7)$$

Now from (5) above $M = -\lambda$ ...(8)

(6) above $L = -\lambda/r$ ...(9)

$$\frac{(8)}{(9)} \qquad \frac{M}{L} = \frac{\lambda}{\lambda/r}$$

$$\frac{M}{L} = \frac{r}{1}$$

Now after cross multiplication this equation may be written as

$$M = r\,L \qquad ...(10)$$

Now substituting this value M in equation (7) above it becomes

$$\frac{rL}{r} + L = 24$$

$$2L = 24$$

$$L = 12$$

Therefore $W = 24 - L = 24 - 12 = 12$.

Thus the consumer will spend 12 hours irrespective of the wage rate 'r'.

EXERCISES

1. A student has Rs. 200 per month to spend on two commodity q_1 and q_2. Suppose that the price of q_1 is Rs.10 and that of q_2 is Rs. 5, calculate the equilibrium values of q_1 and q_2 given the utility function $U = q_1q_2$.
2. A consumer has Rs. 200 per month to spend on two commodity q_1 and q_2. Suppose that the price of q_1 is Rs.10 and that of q_2 is Rs. 5, calculate the equilibrium values of q_1 and q_2 given the utility function $U = 100\ q_1q$.
3. A individual has Rs. 400 per month to spend on two commodity q_1 and q_2. Suppose that the price of q_1 is Rs. 20 and that of q_2 is Rs. 10, calculate the equilibrium values of q_1 and q_2 given the utility function $U = q_1q_2$.
4. A student has Rs. 200 per month to spend on two-commodity q_1 and q_2. Suppose that the price of q_1 is Rs.10 and that of q_2 is Rs. 5, calculate the equilibrium values of q_1 and q_2 given the utility function $U = \ln q_1q_2$.
5. A student has Rs. 200 per month to spend on two commodity q_1 and q_2. Suppose that the price of q_1 is Rs.10 and that of q_2 is Rs. 5, calculate the equilibrium values of q_1 and q_2 given the utility function $U = q_1^2 q_2^2$.

6. A student has Rs. 200 per month to spend on two commodity q_1 and q_2. Suppose that the price of q_1 is Rs.10 and that of q_2 is Rs. 5, calculate the equilibrium values of q_1 and q_2 given the utility function $U=\sqrt{q_1 q_2}$

7. An individual has a utility function solely defined in terms of daily income M and daily hours of leisure L. If the individual is rational how many hours a day will he chooses to work when the utility function is U = 10LM and the wage rate is Rs. 10 per hour.

8. A consumer has Rs. M per month to spend on two commodity q_1 and q_2. If the unit price of q_1 is Rs. p_1 and that of q_2 is Rs. p_2, derive the necessary condition for consumer's equilibrium provided the utility function is $U = q_1^2 q_2^2$. Would it make any difference in the above derived equilibrium condition when the utility function is replaced by W = ln U? What conclusion about the form of the utility function does this suggest?

9. (a) Find the equilibrium values of q_1 and q_2 if the utility function is $U = 10q_1 q_2$ and the budget constraint is $100 = 5q_1 + 10 q_2$.

   (b) Would it make any difference in the equilibrium values of q_1 and q_2 when the utility function $U = 10q_1q_2$ is replaced by $W = q_1q_2$. Give reasons.

   (c) In (a) given above show that the equilibrium quantities remain unaltered when the budget constraint is doubled. What conclusion does this suggest about the form of the demand function?

10. Distinguish between ordinary and compensated demand functions. Further derive both the ordinary and compensated demand functions for both the commodities q_1 and q_2 for the utility function $U = \ln q_1q_2$.

11. If $U = q_1^2 q_2^2$ derive both the ordinary and compensated demand functions for both the commodities q_1 and q_2.

12. An individual has Rs. M available to be divided between two commodity q_1 and q_2. Suppose that the unit price of q_1 is Rs. p_1 and that of q_2 is Rs. p_2. Obtain the Marshallian demand for both q_1 and q_2 given utility function $U = q_1^{\alpha} q_2^{\beta}$.

THE THEORY OF PRODUCTION

10.5 Production Function

Production function is purely a technical relationship between inputs and outputs. The production function in its general form is normally written as Q = f (L, K), where L is the labour input, K is the capital input and Q is the output under reference. In this form the production function simply tell us that the output Q depends upon the level of utilization of both L and K. However, the production function in its specific form states the formula of the relationship itself. The Cobb-Douglas and CES production functions are the two good examples for this type specific representation. The Cobb-Douglas production function is normally written as

$$Q = AL^{\alpha}K^{\beta}$$

The CES production function is normally written as

$$Q = A[\alpha L^{-\rho} + \beta K^{-\rho}]^{-1/\rho}$$

10.6 Short-run Production Analysis

Short-run is the production period in which the input L alone is allowed to vary by keeping the capital input K as constant. Thus the general format of the short-run production with constant amount of capital is written as $Q = f(L, K_0)$, where K_0 denotes the constant amount of the capital. The short-run production function in its cubic form will have both convex and concave shapes as shown in Fig. 10.10. The corresponding Marginal and average productivities are shown in Fig. 10.11. Also note $MP_L = AP_L$ at the maximum point of AP_L. Now let us prove this simple but very useful and important result by taking an illustration.

Example 8: The production function of a firm is $Q = AL^2K^2 - BL^3K^3$.

(a) Obtain the short-run production function for labour input L when the capital input K is kept at a constant level say K_0.

(b) Calculate both the MP_L and AP_L.

(c) Prove that $MP_L = AP_L$ at the maximum point of AP_L

Solution:

(a) The production function of the firm is

$$Q = AL^2K^2 - BL^3K^3 \qquad \ldots(1)$$

Now to get at the needed shot-run production function we simply put $K = K_0$ in the production function (1) above.

i.e. $$Q = AL^2K_0^2 - BL^3K_0^3$$

After clubbing the constants together the needed short-run production function is written as

$$Q = aL^2 - bL^3 \; (a = AK_0^2 \text{ and } b = BK_0^3) \qquad \ldots(2)$$

(b) Now by definition

$$AP_L = \frac{Q}{L} = \frac{aL^2 - bL^3}{L} = aL - bL^2 \qquad \ldots(3)$$

$$MP_L = \frac{dQ}{dL} = 2aL - 3bL^2 \qquad \ldots(4)$$

(c) Now for the maximum value of AP_L we know that

(1) Necessary condition $\frac{d}{dL}(AP_L) = 0$

(2) Sufficient condition $\frac{d^2}{dL^2}(AP_L) < 0$

So from (4) above $\frac{d}{dL}(AP_L) = a - 2bL = 0$

$$L = \frac{a}{2b} \quad \ldots(5)$$

Further, $\frac{d^2}{dL^2}(AP_L) = -2b < 0$

Thus AP_L reaches its maximum when $L = \frac{a}{2b}$. Now the actual maximum value of AP_L is obtained by merely substituting this value of L in the AP_L given in (3) above

i.e. $(AP_L)_{L=a/2b} = a\left(\frac{a}{2b}\right) - b\left(\frac{a}{2b}\right)^2 = \frac{a^2}{2b} - \frac{a^2}{4b} = \frac{2a^2 - a^2}{4b} = \frac{a^2}{4b}$

Thus the maximum value of $AP_L = \frac{a^2}{4b}$ ...(6)

At this point the value of the MP_L is obtained by putting $L = \frac{a}{2b}$ in equation (4) above.

i.e. $(MP_L)_{L=a/2b} = 2a\frac{a}{2b} - 3b\left(\frac{a}{2b}\right)^2$

$$= \frac{2a^2}{2b} - \frac{3a^2}{4b}$$

$$= \frac{4a^2 - 3a^2}{4b} = \frac{a^2}{4b}$$

Thus the $MP_L = \frac{a^2}{4b}$ ...(7)

Thus from (6) and (7) it is true that $MP_L = AP_L$ at the maximum point of AP_L.

A numerical illustration

If A = 5, B = 2, K= 2 then $a = AK^2 = 5 \times 2^2 = 20$, $b = BK^3 = 0.25 \times 2^3 = 2$. So our production function reduces to $Q = 20L^2 - 2L^3$. The following table and the associate chart illustrate the interrelationship between relevant functions.

Table 10.1 A Numerical Illustration

K	L	TP_L	MP_L	AP_L
2	0	0	-	-
2	1	18	34	18
2	2	64	56	32
2	3	126	66	42
2	4	192	64	48
2	5	250	50	50
2	6	288	24	48
2	7	294	-14	42
2	8	256	-64	32

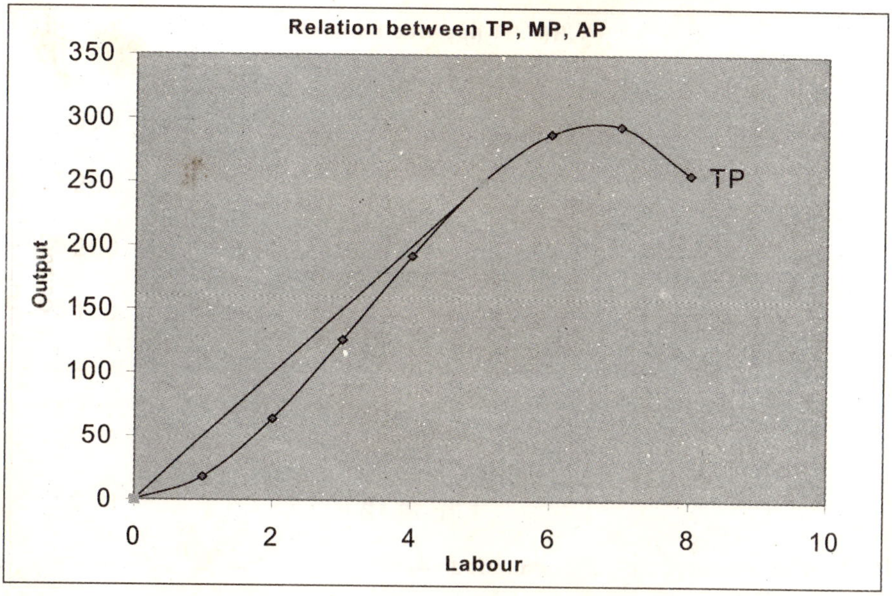

Fig. 10.10

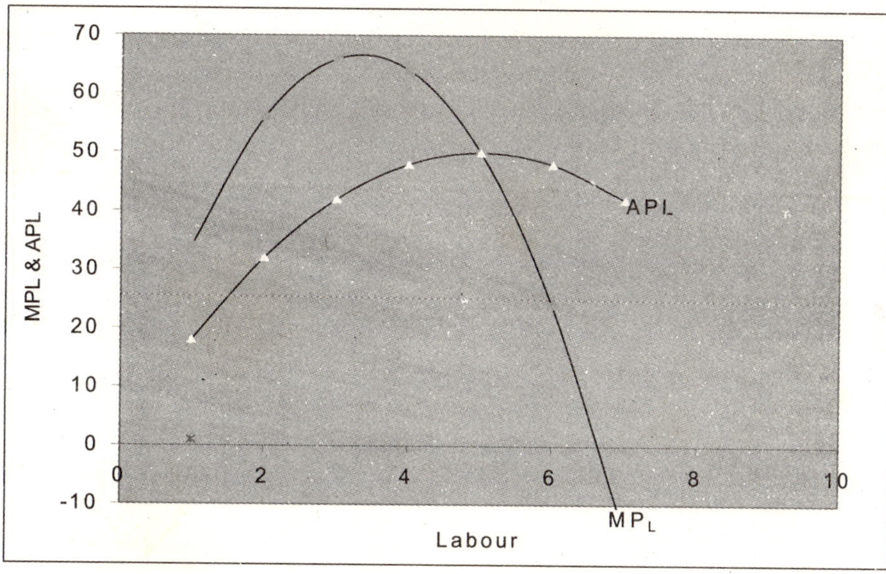

Fig. 10.11

10.7 Long-run Production Analysis

n the long-run both the inputs are allowed to vary in order to have the optimum utilization of oth the resources. However, to make the analysis manageable often Q, the output, is treated as onstant. Such an approach is often called the iso-quant approach to the theory of production. The quation of the iso-quant is normally written as $Q_o = f(L, K)$. These iso-quants are convex to the rigin as shown in Fig. 10.12.

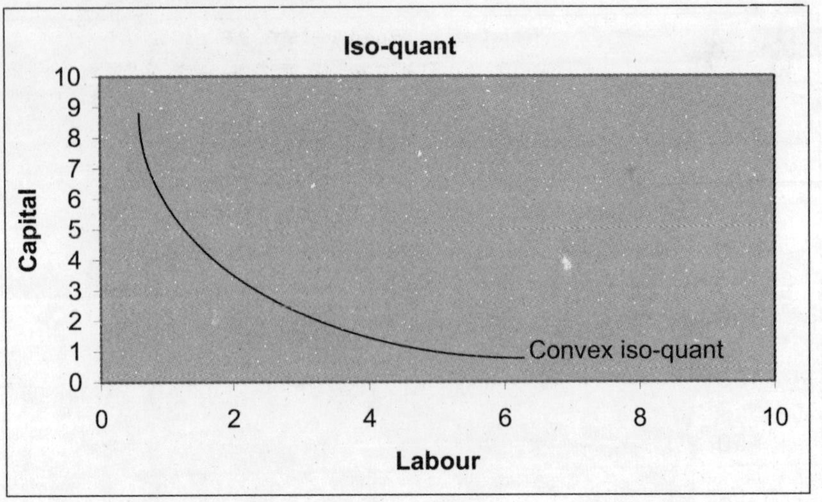

Fig. 10.12

Example 9: The production function of a firm is $Q = AL^{\alpha}K^{\beta}$. Given the output Q = $\alpha = 0.5$, $\beta = 0.5$ and A = 100 obtain the equation of the iso-quant and prove that it is convex.

Solution:

The production function of the firm is $Q = AL^{\alpha}K^{\beta}$.

Now the equation of the iso-quant is obtained by merely substituting Q = 400 in the production

So $$400 = 100\,L^{0.5}K^{0.5}.$$

$$\therefore \quad K^{0.5} = \frac{400}{100L^{0.5}} = \frac{400}{100}L^{-0.5}$$

$$K = \left(\frac{400}{100}\right)^{1/0.5}\left(L^{-0.5}\right)^{1/0.5}$$

$$\therefore \quad K = 4^{0.5}L^{-1}$$

$$KL = 2$$

Thus, KL = 2 is the needed iso-quant.

Now $$\frac{dK}{dL} = -2L^{-2}$$

$$\frac{d^2K}{dL^2} = 4L^{-3}$$

$$\frac{d^2K}{dL^2} > 0$$

Thus, the iso-quant is convex to the origin.

(i) Derivation of the necessary and sufficient condition for producer's equilibrium output maximization:

lution:

t the production function of the firm may be written as

$$Q = f(L, K) \quad \ldots(1)$$

e cost equation in its general form is written as

$$C = p_L L + p_K K \quad \ldots(2)$$

w to maximize (1) with respect to (2) let us rewrite equation (2) in its implicit form by moving the RHS terms to the LHS.

$$C - p_L L - p_K K = 0 \quad \ldots(3)$$

w to maximize (1) with respect to (3) the Lagrangian equation may be written as

$$Z = \text{RHS of (1)} + \lambda[\text{LHS of (3)}]$$

$$Z = f(L,K) + \lambda(C - p_L L - p_K K) \quad \ldots(4)$$

w to maximize Z given in equation (4), since it involves three variables L, K and λ, their pective partial derivatives are to be equated to zero.

$$\frac{\partial Z}{\partial L} = \frac{\partial Z}{\partial K} = \frac{\partial Z}{\partial \lambda} = 0$$

from (4) above

$$\frac{\partial Z}{\partial L} = f_L - \lambda p_L = 0 \quad \ldots(5)$$

$$\frac{\partial Z}{\partial K} = f_K - \lambda p_K = 0 \quad \ldots(6)$$

$$\frac{\partial Z}{\partial \lambda} = C - p_L L - p_K K = 0 \quad \ldots(7)$$

w from (5) $\quad f_L = \lambda p_L \quad \ldots(8)$

(6) $\quad f_K = \lambda p_k \quad \ldots(9)$

$\frac{(8)}{(9)} \quad \frac{f_L}{f_K} = \frac{p_L \lambda}{p_K \lambda}$

$$\frac{f_L}{f_K} = \frac{p_L}{p_K}$$

$$\frac{f_L}{p_L} = \frac{f_K}{p_K}$$

$$\frac{Mp_L}{p_L} = \frac{Mp_K}{p_K}$$

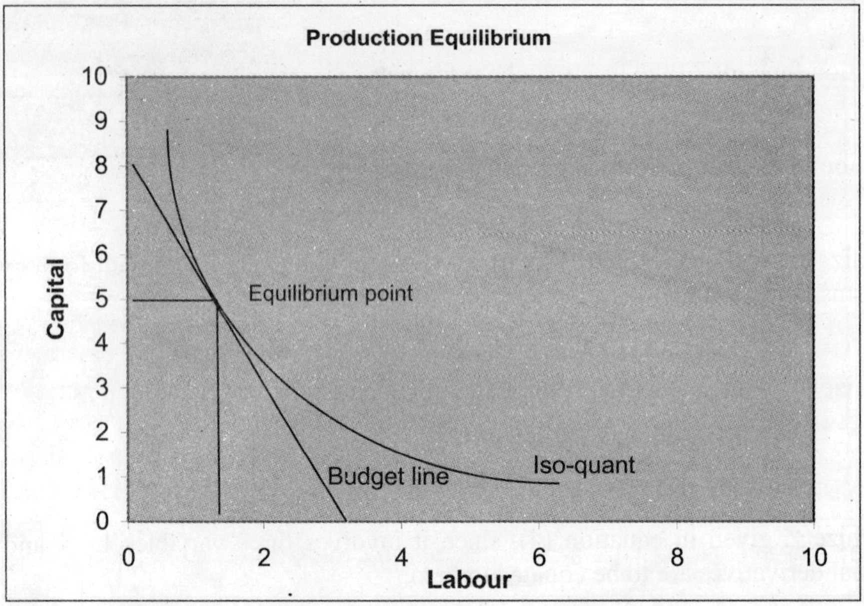

Fig. 10.13

This condition is satisfied if and only the budget lines is tangent to the iso-quant as shown in the Fig. 10.13.

Sufficient condition

The sufficient condition can be stated in terms of the bordered Hessian determinant as usual.

$$\begin{vmatrix} \dfrac{\partial^2 Z}{\partial L^2} & \dfrac{\partial^2 Z}{\partial L \partial K} & \dfrac{\partial^2 Z}{\partial L \partial \lambda} \\ \dfrac{\partial^2 Z}{\partial K \partial L} & \dfrac{\partial^2 Z}{\partial K^2} & \dfrac{\partial^2 Z}{\partial K \partial \lambda} \\ \dfrac{\partial^2 Z}{\partial \lambda \partial L} & \dfrac{\partial^2 Z}{\partial \lambda \partial K} & \dfrac{\partial^2 Z}{\partial \lambda^2} \end{vmatrix} > 0$$

from equations (5), (6) and (7) the above determinant becomes

$$\begin{vmatrix} f_{LL} & f_{LK} & -p_L \\ f_{KL} & f_{KK} & -p_K \\ -p_L & -p_K & 0 \end{vmatrix} > 0$$

$$= f_{LL}\begin{vmatrix} f_{KK} & -p_K \\ -p_K & 0 \end{vmatrix} - f_{LK}\begin{vmatrix} f_{KL} & -p_K \\ -p_L & 0 \end{vmatrix} - p_L\begin{vmatrix} f_{KL} & f_{KK} \\ -p_L & -p_K \end{vmatrix}$$

$$= -f_{LL}p_K^2 + f_{LK}p_Lp_K + f_{KL}p_Lp_K - f_{KK}p_L^2 > 0$$

$$= f_{LL}p_K^2 - 2f_{LK}p_Lp_K + f_{KK}p_L^2 < 0$$

This condition is satisfied provided the iso-quant is convex to the origin as shown above.

Example 10: An entrepreneur has 100 thousand Rupees to spend on labour and raw materials. He hires L quantity of labour at an annual price of Rs. 2 per unit and buys K quantity of raw material at price of Rs. 1 per unit (both prices are in terms of thousand Rupees). Find L and K if he wants to get as much output as possible when the production function is given by Q = 10LK.

Solution:

The production function of the firm is

$$Q = 10\,LK \qquad \ldots(1)$$

From the given data the cost equation is written as

$$100 = 2L + K \qquad \ldots(2)$$

Now to maximize (1) with respect to (2) let us rewrite equation (2) in its implicit form by moving all the RHS terms to the LHS.

i.e. $$100 - 2L - K = 0 \qquad \ldots(3)$$

Now to maximize (1) with respect to (3) the Lagrangian equation may be written as

$$Z = \text{RHS of (1)} + \lambda[\text{LHS of (3)}]$$

i.e. $$Z = 10LK + \lambda(100 - 2L - K) \qquad \ldots(4)$$

Now to maximize Z given in equation (4), since it involves three variables L, M and λ, their respective partial derivatives are to be equated to zero.

i.e. $$\frac{\partial Z}{\partial L} = \frac{\partial Z}{\partial K} = \frac{\partial Z}{\partial \lambda} = 0$$

So from (4) above

$$\frac{\partial Z}{\partial L} = 10K - 2\lambda = 0 \qquad \ldots(5)$$

$$\frac{\partial Z}{\partial K} = 10L - \lambda = 0 \qquad \ldots(6)$$

$$\frac{\partial Z}{\partial \lambda} = 100 - 2L - K = 0 \qquad \ldots(7)$$

Now from (5) $10K = 2\lambda \qquad \ldots(8)$

(6) $10L = \lambda \qquad \ldots(9)$

$\frac{(8)}{(9)}$ $$\frac{10K}{10L} = \frac{2\lambda}{\lambda}$$

$$\frac{K}{L} = \frac{2}{1}$$

$$K = 2L \qquad \ldots(10)$$

Substituting this value of K in (7) above it becomes

$$100 - 2L - 2L = 0$$

$$-4L = -100$$

$$L = 25$$

Now substituting this value of L in (10) above

$$K = 2 \times 25 = 50$$

Thus, under equilibrium L = 25 and K = 50

Sufficient condition

The sufficient condition can be stated in terms of the bordered Hessian determinant.

$$\begin{vmatrix} \frac{\partial^2 Z}{\partial L^2} & \frac{\partial^2 Z}{\partial L \partial K} & \frac{\partial^2 Z}{\partial L \partial \lambda} \\ \frac{\partial^2 Z}{\partial K \partial L} & \frac{\partial^2 Z}{\partial K^2} & \frac{\partial^2 Z}{\partial K \partial \lambda} \\ \frac{\partial^2 Z}{\partial \lambda \partial L} & \frac{\partial^2 Z}{\partial \lambda \partial K} & \frac{\partial^2 Z}{\partial \lambda^2} \end{vmatrix} > 0$$

Now from equations (5), (6) and (7) the above determinant becomes

$$\begin{vmatrix} 0 & 10 & -2 \\ 10 & 0 & -1 \\ -2 & -1 & 0 \end{vmatrix} = 0\begin{vmatrix} 0 & -1 \\ -1 & 0 \end{vmatrix} - 10\begin{vmatrix} 10 & -1 \\ -2 & 0 \end{vmatrix} - 2\begin{vmatrix} 10 & 0 \\ -2 & -1 \end{vmatrix}$$

$$= 0 - 10(-2) - 2(-10) = 40 > 0$$

Thus L = 25 and K = 50 gets confirmed as the equilibrium quantities. The corresponding maximum output is obtained by merely substituting these values of L and K in the production function given in equation (1) above.

i.e. $Q = 10LK = 10 \times 25 \times 50 = 12{,}500$.

(ii) Derivation of the necessary and sufficient condition for producer's equilibrium by cost minimization:

Solution:

The cost equation that is to be minimized in its general form is written as

$$C = P_L L + P_K K \qquad \ldots(1)$$

Let the production constraint of the firm be

$$Q_0 = f(L, K) \qquad \ldots(2)$$

Now to minimize (1) with respect to (2) let us rewrite equation (2) in its implicit form by moving all the RHS terms to the LHS.

i.e. $$Q_0 - f(L, K) = 0 \qquad \ldots(3)$$

Now to minimize (1) with respect to (3) the Lagrangian equation may be written as

$$Z = \text{RHS of (1)} + \lambda[\text{LHS of (3)}]$$

i.e. $$Z = P_L L + P_K K + \lambda[Q_0 - f(L, K)] \qquad \ldots(4)$$

Now to minimize Z given in equation (4), since it involves three variables L, K and λ, their respective partial derivatives are to be equated to zero.

i.e. $$\frac{\partial Z}{\partial L} = \frac{\partial Z}{\partial K} = \frac{\partial Z}{\partial \lambda} = 0$$

from (4) above

$$\frac{\partial Z}{\partial L} = P_L - \lambda f_L = 0 \qquad \ldots(5)$$

$$\frac{\partial Z}{\partial K} = P_K - \lambda f_K = 0 \qquad \ldots(6)$$

$$\frac{\partial Z}{\partial \lambda} = Q - f(L, K) = 0 \qquad \ldots(7)$$

w from (5) $\quad P_L = \lambda f_L \qquad \ldots(8)$

.. (6) $\quad P_K = \lambda f_K \qquad \ldots(9)$

$\frac{(8)}{(9)} \quad \frac{P_L}{P_K} = \frac{f_L \lambda}{f_K \lambda}$

$$\frac{P_L}{P_K} = \frac{f_L}{f_K}$$

$$\frac{f_L}{P_L} = \frac{f_K}{P_K}$$

$$\frac{MP_L}{P_L} = \frac{MP_K}{P_K}$$

s condition will be satisfied provided the budget line is tangent to the iso-quant as shown in Fig. 10.13.

fficient condition

e sufficient condition can be stated in terms of the bordered Hessian determinant.

$$\begin{vmatrix} \frac{\partial^2 Z}{\partial L^2} & \frac{\partial^2 Z}{\partial L \partial K} & \frac{\partial^2 Z}{\partial L \partial \lambda} \\ \frac{\partial^2 Z}{\partial K \partial L} & \frac{\partial^2 Z}{\partial K^2} & \frac{\partial^2 Z}{\partial K \partial \lambda} \\ \frac{\partial^2 Z}{\partial \lambda \partial K} & \frac{\partial^2 Z}{\partial \lambda \partial L} & \frac{\partial^2 Z}{\partial \lambda^2} \end{vmatrix} > 0$$

w from equations (5), (6) and (7) the above determinant becomes

$$\begin{vmatrix} -\lambda f_{LL} & -\lambda f_{LK} & -f_L \\ -\lambda f_{KL} & -\lambda f_{KK} & -f_K \\ -f_L & -f_K & 0 \end{vmatrix} > 0$$

$$= -\lambda f_{LL} \begin{vmatrix} -\lambda f_{KK} & -f_K \\ -f_K & 0 \end{vmatrix} + \lambda f_{LK} \begin{vmatrix} -\lambda f_{KL} & -f_K \\ -f_L & 0 \end{vmatrix} - f_L \begin{vmatrix} -\lambda f_{KL} & -\lambda f_{KK} \\ -f_L & -f_K \end{vmatrix} > 0$$

$$= -\lambda \left(f_{LL} f_K^2 - f_{LK} f_L f_K - f_{KL} f_L f_K + f_{KK} f_L^2 \right) > 0$$

$$= -\lambda\left(f_{LL}f_K^2 - 2f_{LK}f_Lf_K + f_{KK}f_L^2\right) > 0$$

$$= f_{LL}f_K^2 - 2f_{LK}f_Lf_K + f_{KK}f_L^2 < 0$$

$$= f_{LL}P_K^2 - 2f_{LK}P_LP_K + f_{KK}P_L^2 < 0$$

Example 11: An entrepreneur has a target of 12,500 units of output per production period. He hires L quantity of labour at an annual price 2 per unit and buys K quantity of raw materials at price 1 per unit. Calculate the least cost budget given the production function Q = 10LK.

Solution:

Let the objective function that is to be minimized is written as

$$C = P_L \cdot L + P_K \cdot K$$

i.e. $C = 2L + 1K$ ...(1)

The constraint to the problem is the production function.

$$Q = 10\,LK$$

i.e. $12{,}500 = 10LK$ ...(2)

Now to minimize (1) with respect to (2), the equation (2) may be rewritten in its implicit from by bringing all the RHS terms to the LHS.

i.e. $12{,}500 - 10LK = 0$ ...(3)

Now to minimize (1) with respect to (3) the Lagrangian formulation may be written as

$$Z = \text{RHS of (1)} + \lambda\{\text{LHS of (3)}\}$$

$$Z = 2L + K + \lambda\,(12{,}500 - 10LK) \quad ...(4)$$

Now for the minimum value of Z, since it involves three variables namely L, K, and λ, their respective partial derivatives are to be equated to zero.

$$\frac{\partial Z}{\partial L} = \frac{\partial Z}{\partial K} = \frac{\partial Z}{\partial \lambda} = 0$$

So from (4)

$$\frac{\partial Z}{\partial L} = 2 + \lambda\,(-10K) = 0 \quad ...(5)$$

$$\frac{\partial Z}{\partial K} = 1 - 10\lambda L = 0 \quad ...(6)$$

$$\frac{\partial Z}{\partial \lambda} = 12{,}500 - 10LK = 0 \quad ...(7)$$

Now from (5) $2 = 10\lambda K$ ...(8)

Now from (6) $1 = 10\lambda L$ ...(9)

Now

$$\frac{(8)}{(9)} = \frac{2}{1} = \frac{10\lambda K}{10\lambda L}$$

$$\frac{2}{1} = \frac{K}{L}$$

On cross multiplication this may by written

$$K = 2L \qquad \ldots(10)$$

Substituting this value of K in (7) above it becomes

$$12{,}500 - 10\,L\,(2L) = 0$$

$$20L^2 = 12{,}500$$

i.e. $L^2 = 625$

$$L = 25$$

Now the equilibrium value of K is obtained by substituting this value of L in (10) above

i.e. $K = 2(25) = 50.$

Now for the minimum value of (4) the second order Hessian bordered determinant may by written as

$$\begin{vmatrix} \frac{\partial^2 Z}{\partial L^2} & \frac{\partial^2 Z}{\partial L \partial K} & \frac{\partial^2 Z}{\partial L \partial \lambda} \\ \frac{\partial^2 Z}{\partial K \partial L} & \frac{\partial^2 Z}{\partial K} & \frac{\partial^2 Z}{\partial K \partial \lambda} \\ \frac{\partial^2 Z}{\partial \lambda \partial L} & \frac{\partial^2 Z}{\partial \lambda \partial K} & \frac{\partial^2 Z}{\partial \lambda^2} \end{vmatrix} < 0$$

Now from equations (5), (6) and (7)

$$= \begin{vmatrix} 0 & -10\lambda & -10K \\ -10\lambda & 0 & -10L \\ -10K & -10L & 0 \end{vmatrix} < 0$$

$$= 0[0 - 100L^2] + 10\lambda\,[0 - 100LK] - 10K\,[100\lambda\,L - 0]$$

$$= -\,1000\,\lambda\,LK - 1000\,\lambda\,LK$$

$$= -\,\lambda\,[1000LK]$$

$$= -\,\lambda\,[1000 \times 25 \times 50] \qquad [\text{because } L = 25, K = 50]$$

Since λ is positive the value of the above determinant is clearly negative. Hence L = 25 and K = 50 get confirmed as the equilibrium values. Now the least cost budget is obtained by substituting these values in equation (1) above.

i.e. $C = 2L + K$

$$= 2 \times 25 + 50$$

$$C = 100$$

10.8 Producers Equilibrium under Profit Maximization

Example 12: The production function of a firm is $Q = 10 - 6/L - 3/K$. Calculate the equilibrium values of L, K, Q and the profit Π when $P_L = 2$, $P_K = 1$ and $P_Q = 3$.

Solution:

By definition Profit = Revenue – Cost

$$\Pi = R - C$$
$$= PQ - C$$
$$= P\,(10 - 6/L - 3/K) - (P_L L + P_K K)$$
$$= 3\,(10 - 6/L - 3/K) - (2L + K)$$
$$= 30 - 18/L - 9/K - 2L - K \qquad \ldots(1)$$

Now for the Maximum value of profit Π we know that

1. Necessary condition $\dfrac{\partial \Pi}{\partial L} = 0, \; \dfrac{\partial \Pi}{\partial K} = 0$

2. Sufficient condition $\dfrac{\partial^2 \Pi}{\partial L^2} = 0, \; \dfrac{\partial^2 \Pi}{\partial K^2} = 0$

2. Saddle point condition $\dfrac{\partial^2 \Pi}{\partial L^2} \times \dfrac{\partial^2 \Pi}{\partial K^2} > \left(\dfrac{\partial^2 \Pi}{\partial L \partial K}\right)^2$

So from (1) above

$$\frac{\partial \Pi}{\partial L} = \frac{18}{L^2} - 2 = 0$$
$$\frac{18}{L^2} = 2$$
$$2L^2 = 18$$
$$L^2 = 9$$
$$L = 3$$
$$\frac{\partial \Pi}{\partial K} = \frac{9}{K^2} - 1 = 0$$
$$\frac{9}{K^2} = 1$$
$$K^2 = 9$$
$$K = 3$$

Further,

$$\frac{\partial^2 \Pi}{\partial L^2} = \frac{-36}{L^3} = \frac{-36}{27} = -1.33 < 0$$
$$\frac{\partial^2 \Pi}{\partial K^2} = \frac{-18}{K^3} = \frac{-18}{27} = -0.67 < 0$$

$$\left(\frac{\partial^2 \Pi}{\partial L \partial K}\right)^2 = 0$$

$$\frac{\partial^2 \Pi}{\partial L^2} \times \frac{\partial^2 \Pi}{\partial K^2} > \left(\frac{\partial^2 \Pi}{\partial L \partial K}\right)^2$$

$$-1.33 \times -0.67 > 0^2$$

$$0.89 > 0$$

Thus L = 3 and K = 3 get confirmed as the equilibrium values. Now the equilibrium level of output is obtained by substituting these values in the given production function

$$Q = 10 - 6/L - 3/K$$

$$Q = 10 - 6/3 - 3/3$$

$$Q = 10 - 3 = 7$$

Similarly,

$$\Pi = 30 - 18/L - 9/K - 2L - K$$

$$\Pi = 30 - 18/3 - 9/3 - 2 \times 3 - 3$$

$$\Pi = 30 - 6 - 3 - 6 - 3$$

$$\Pi = 30 - 18 = 12$$

Thus under equilibrium

$$L = 3, K = 3, Q = 7, \Pi = 12$$

10.9 Derived Demand Functions

The demand functions for the inputs like labour and capital are often called the derived demands. Really they are derived from the demand for the output that they produce. More the demand for the product more will be the demand for these inputs. Normally, these demand functions are expressed as a function of the output price. These input demands are obtained by maximizing the profit of the firm under consideration.

Example 13: A firm has the production function $Q = \ln L + 2 \ln K$. Derive the input demand laws for both L and K in terms of the product price p when the factor prices are P_L = Rs. 2 and P_K = Rs. 8. Hence derive the supply function for the firm's product giving the output as a function of the product price p.

Solution:

Now by definition Profit = Revenue – Cost

$$\Pi = R - C$$

$$= PQ - C$$

$$= P(\ln L + 2 \ln K) - (P_L L + P_K K)$$

$$= P \ln L + 2P \ln K - 2L - 8K \quad \ldots(1)$$

Now for the maximum value of Π given above we know that

1. Necessary condition $\dfrac{\partial \Pi}{\partial L} = 0, \dfrac{\partial \Pi}{\partial K} = 0$

2. Sufficient condition $\dfrac{\partial^2 \Pi}{\partial L^2} = 0, \dfrac{\partial^2 \Pi}{\partial K^2} = 0$

2. Saddle Point condition $\dfrac{\partial^2 \Pi}{\partial L^2} \times \dfrac{\partial^2 \Pi}{\partial K^2} > \left(\dfrac{\partial^2 \Pi}{\partial L \partial K}\right)^2$

So from (1) above

$$\frac{\partial \Pi}{\partial L} = \frac{P}{L} - 2 = 0$$

$$\frac{P}{L} = 2$$

$$2L = P$$

$$L = P/2$$

$$= 0.5P$$

$$\frac{\partial \Pi}{\partial K} = \frac{2P}{K} - 8 = 0$$

$$\frac{2P}{K} = 8$$

$$8K = 2P$$

$$K = 0.25P$$

Further,

$$\frac{\partial^2 \Pi}{\partial L^2} = \frac{-P}{L^2} < 0$$

$$\frac{\partial^2 \Pi}{\partial K^2} = \frac{-2P}{K^2} < 0$$

$$\left(\frac{\partial^2 \Pi}{\partial L \partial K}\right) = 0$$

$$\frac{\partial^2 \Pi}{\partial L^2} \times \frac{\partial^2 \Pi}{\partial K^2} > \left(\frac{\partial^2 \Pi}{\partial L \partial K}\right)^2$$

$$\left(\frac{-P}{L^2}\right)\left(\frac{-2P}{K^2}\right) > 0$$

$$\frac{2P^2}{L^2K^2} > 0$$

Thus L = 0.5 P and K = 0.25 P are the derived demand functions for L and K respectively. Now the needed supply function of the firm is obtained by simply eliminating L and K from the given production functions using the derived demand functions given above.

$Q = \ln L + 2\ln K$

$S = \ln 0.5P + \ln 0.25P$ (Q is renamed as S to reflect the supply function)

10.10 Expansion Path

The expansion path is nothing but the collection of all equilibrium points of the producer for varying levels of his budget with constant factor prices as shown in the following Fig. 10.14. It is obtained by maximizing the output with respect to the budget line.

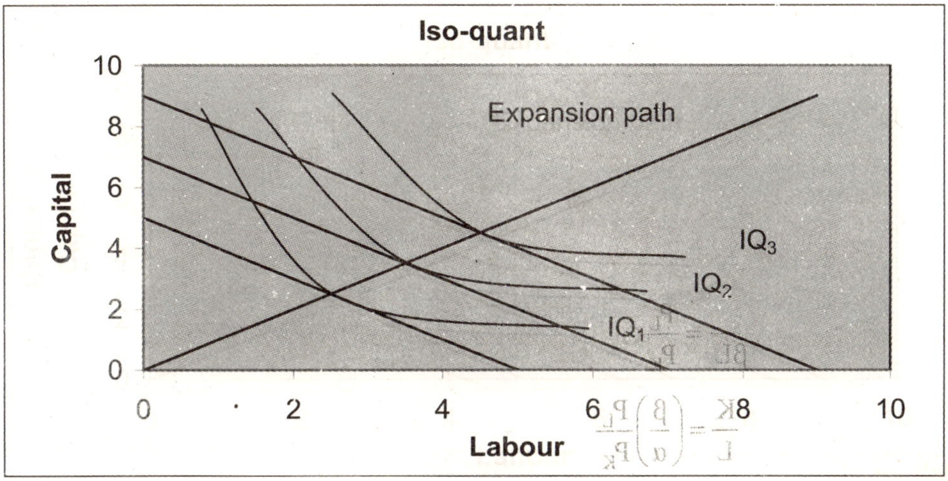

Fig. 10.14

Example 14: The production function of a firm is $Q = AL^{\alpha}K^{\beta}$. Prove that the equation of the expansion path is linear.

Solution:

The production function of the firm is

$$Q = AL^{\alpha}K^{\beta} \quad \ldots(1)$$

The cost equation in its general form is written as

$$C = P_L L + P_K K \quad \ldots(2)$$

Now to maximize (1) with respect to (2) let us rewrite equation (2) in its implicit form by moving all the RHS terms to the LHS.

i.e. $$C - P_L L - P_K K = 0 \quad \ldots(3)$$

Now to maximize (1) with respect to (3) the Lagrangian equation may be written as

$$Z = \text{RHS of (1)} + \lambda\,[\text{LHS of (3)}]$$

i.e. $$Z = AL^{\alpha}K^{\beta} + \lambda(C - P_L L - P_K K) \quad \ldots(4)$$

Now to maximize Z given in equation (4), since it involves three variables L, K and λ the respective partial derivatives are to be equated to zero.

i.e. $$\frac{\partial Z}{\partial L} = \frac{\partial Z}{\partial K} = \frac{\partial Z}{\partial \lambda} = 0$$

So from (4) above

$$\frac{\partial Z}{\partial L} = A\alpha L^{\alpha-1}K^{\beta} - \lambda P_L = 0 \quad \text{...(5)}$$

$$\frac{\partial Z}{\partial K} = AL^{\alpha}\beta K^{\beta-1} - \lambda P_K = 0 \quad \text{...(6)}$$

$$\frac{\partial Z}{\partial \lambda} = C - P_L L - P_K K = 0 \quad \text{...(7)}$$

Now from (5) $A\alpha L^{\alpha-1}K^{\beta} = \lambda P_L$ ...(8)

(6) $AL^{\alpha}\beta K^{\beta-1} = \lambda P_L$ ...(9)

$$\frac{(8)}{(9)} \; \frac{A\alpha L^{\alpha-1}K^{\beta}}{AL^{\alpha}\beta K^{\beta-1}} = \frac{P_L\lambda}{P_K\lambda}$$

$$\frac{\alpha K}{\beta L} = \frac{P_L}{P_K}$$

$$\therefore \quad \frac{K}{L} = \left(\frac{\beta}{\alpha}\right)\frac{P_L}{P_K}$$

Now let $\left(\frac{\beta}{\alpha}\right)\frac{P_L}{P_K} = a$

Now $\frac{K}{L} = a$

i.e. $K = aL$

This is of the standard straighty line form y = mx + c with c value zero and the slope 'm'. Thus the equation of the expansion path is a straight line passing through the origin as shown in Fig. 10.14.

Example 15: For the CES production $Q = A\left[\alpha L^{-\rho} + \beta K^{-\rho}\right]^{-1/\rho}$ prove that the equation of the expansion path is linear.

Solution:

The production of the firm is

$$Q = A\left[\alpha L^{-\rho} + \beta K^{-\rho}\right]^{-1/\rho} \quad \text{...(1)}$$

The cost equation in its general form is written as

$$C = P_L L + P_K K \quad \text{...(2)}$$

Now to maximize (1) with respect to (2) let us rewrite equation (2) in its implicit form by moving all the RHS terms to the LHS.

i.e. $$C - P_L L - P_K K = 0 \quad \ldots(3)$$

Now to maximize (1) with respect to (3) the Lagrangian equation may be written as

$$Z = \text{RHS of}(1) + \lambda[\text{LHS of } (3)]$$

i.e. $$Z = A\left[\alpha L^{-\rho} + \beta K^{-\rho}\right]^{-1/\rho} + \lambda(C - P_L L - P_K K) \quad \ldots(4)$$

Now to maximize Z given in equation (4), since it involves three variables L, K and λ, their respective partial derivatives are to be equated to zero.

i.e. $$\frac{\partial Z}{\partial L} = \frac{\partial Z}{\partial K} = \frac{\partial Z}{\partial \lambda} = 0$$

So from (4) above

$$\frac{\partial Z}{\partial L} = A\left(\frac{-1}{\rho}\right)\left[\alpha L^{-\rho} + \beta K^{-\rho}\right]^{-\frac{1}{\rho}-1} \times \alpha(-\rho)L^{-\rho-1} - \lambda P_L = 0 \quad \ldots(5)$$

$$\frac{\partial Z}{\partial K} = A\left(\frac{-1}{\rho}\right)\left[\alpha L^{-\rho} + \beta K^{-\rho}\right]^{-\frac{1}{\rho}-1} \times \beta(-\rho)K^{-\rho-1} - \lambda P_K = 0 \quad \ldots(6)$$

$$\frac{\partial Z}{\partial \lambda} = C - P_L L - P_K K = 0 \quad \ldots(7)$$

Now from (5)

$$A\left(\frac{-1}{\rho}\right)\left[\alpha L^{-\rho} + \beta K^{-\rho}\right]^{-\frac{1}{\rho}-1} \times \alpha(-\rho)L^{-\rho-1} = \lambda P_L \quad \ldots(8)$$

From (6) $$A\left(\frac{-1}{\rho}\right)\left[\alpha L^{-\rho} + \beta K^{-\rho}\right]^{-\frac{1}{\rho}-1} \times \alpha(-\rho)L^{-\rho-1} = \lambda P_K \quad \ldots(9)$$

$\frac{(8)}{(9)}$ $$\frac{A\left(\frac{-1}{\rho}\right)\left[\alpha L^{-\rho} + \beta K^{-\rho}\right]^{-\frac{1}{\rho}-1} \times \alpha(-\rho)L^{-\rho-1}}{A\left(\frac{-1}{\rho}\right)\left[\alpha L^{-\rho} + \beta K^{-\rho}\right]^{-\frac{1}{\rho}-1} \times \beta(-\rho)K^{-\rho-1}} = \frac{\lambda P_L}{\lambda P_K}$$

$$\left(\frac{\alpha}{\beta}\right)\left(\frac{K}{L}\right)^{\rho+1} = \frac{P_L}{P_K}$$

$\therefore$ $$\left(\frac{K}{L}\right)^{\rho+1} = \left(\frac{\beta}{\alpha}\right)\left(\frac{P_L}{P_K}\right)$$

$$\frac{K}{L}=\left[\left(\frac{\beta}{\alpha}\right)\left(\frac{P_L}{P_K}\right)\right]^{\frac{1}{\rho+1}}$$

Now let $\left[\left(\frac{\beta}{\alpha}\right)\left(\frac{P_L}{P_K}\right)\right]^{\frac{1}{\rho+1}}=a$

So $\frac{K}{L}=a$

i.e. $K=aL$

This is of the standard straight line form y = m x + c with c value zero and the slope m. Thus the equation of the expansion path is a straight line passing through the origin as shown in Fig. 10.14.

10.11 Elasticity of Substation

Like any other elasticity, the elasticity of substation, denoted by σ, plays a very important role in the theory of production, specially in the determination of both absolute and relative shares to the factor inputs. It is defined as the ratio of proportional change in K/L to that of proportional change in P_L/P_K.

So in our usual notation $\sigma=\frac{E(K/L)}{E(P_L/P_K)}$

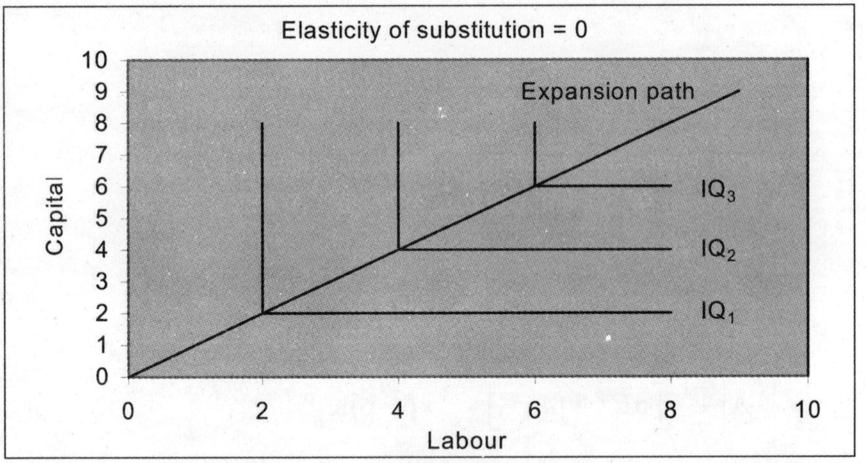

Fig. 10.15

Depending upon the value of the elasticity of substitution we will have three different iso-quants. If σ = 0 then, there is no possibility of substitution between capital and labour. Hence, the iso-quants take the 'L' shape as shown in the Fig. 10.15. On the other hand if $\sigma=\infty$ (infinity), exhibiting the possibility infinite substitution between the inputs, the iso-quants take the downward sloping straight-line shape as shown in the Fig. 10.16. As a third case, if $0<\sigma<\infty$, exhibiting the moderate substitution possibility, the iso-quants take the familiar convex shape as shown in the Fig. 10.17.

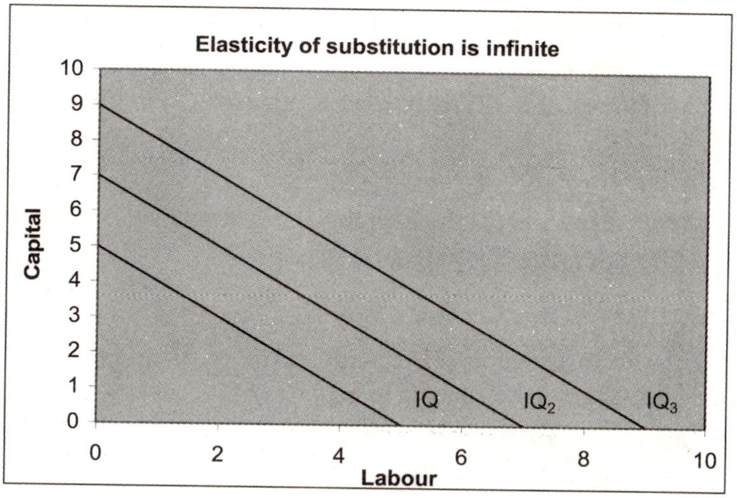

Fig. 10.16

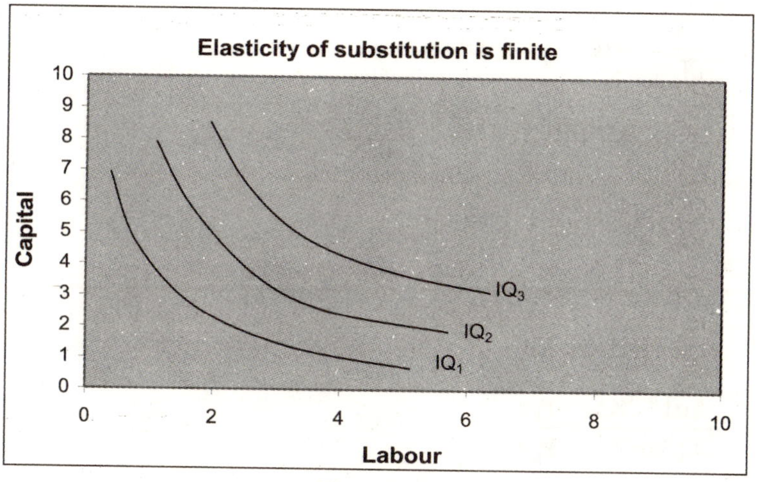

Fig. 10.17

Example 16: The production function of a firm is $Q = AL^{\alpha}K^{\beta}$. Prove that the elasticity of substitution is equal to unity.

Solution:

By definition the elasticity of substitution

$$\sigma = \frac{E(K/L)}{E(P_L/P_K)}$$

So let us try to get the equilibrium relation between K/L and P_L/P_K by using Lagrangian multiplier method.

The production function of the firm is

$$Q = AL^{\alpha}K^{\beta} \qquad \ldots(1)$$

The cost equation in its general form is written as

$$C = P_L L + P_K K \qquad \ldots(2)$$

Now to maximize (1) with respect to (2) let us rewrite equation (2) in its implicit form by moving all the RHS terms to the LHS.

i.e. $$C - P_L L - P_K K = 0 \qquad \ldots(3)$$

Now to maximize (1) with respect to (3) the Lagrangian equation may be written as

$$Z = \text{RHS of (1)} + \lambda[\text{LHS of (3)}]$$

i.e. $$Z = AL^{\alpha}K^{\beta} + \lambda(C - P_L L - P_K K) \qquad \ldots(4)$$

Now to maximize Z given in equation (4), since it involves three variables L, K and λ, their respective partial derivatives are to be equated to zero.

i.e. $$\frac{\partial Z}{\partial L} = \frac{\partial Z}{\partial K} = \frac{\partial Z}{\partial \lambda} = 0$$

So from (4) above

$$\frac{\partial Z}{\partial L} = A\alpha L^{\alpha-1}K^{\beta} - \lambda P_L = 0 \qquad \ldots(5)$$

$$\frac{\partial Z}{\partial K} = AL^{\alpha}\beta K^{\beta-1} - \lambda P_K = 0 \qquad \ldots(6)$$

$$\frac{\partial Z}{\partial \lambda} = C - P_L L - P_K K = 0 \qquad \ldots(7)$$

Now from (5) $$A\alpha L^{\alpha-1}K^{\beta} = \lambda P_L \qquad \ldots(8)$$

(6) $$AL^{\alpha}\beta K^{\beta-1} = \lambda P_K \qquad \ldots(9)$$

$\frac{(8)}{(9)}$ $$\frac{A\alpha L^{\alpha-1}K^{\beta}}{AL^{\alpha}\beta K^{\beta-1}} = \frac{P_L \lambda}{P_K \lambda}$$

$$\frac{\alpha K}{\beta L} = \frac{P_L}{P_K}$$

$$\therefore \quad \frac{K}{L} = \left(\frac{\beta}{\alpha}\right)\frac{P_L}{P_K}$$

Now let $\left(\frac{\beta}{\alpha}\right) = a$, $\frac{K}{L} = y$ and $\frac{P_L}{P_K} = x$

So the above equation becomes $y = a\,x$

Now by definition

$$\sigma = \frac{E(K/L)}{E(P_L/P_K)} = \frac{Ey}{Ex} = \frac{Eax}{Ex} = \frac{x}{ax}\frac{d}{dx}(ax)$$

$$= \frac{x}{ax} \times a = 1$$

Example 17: For the CES production $Q = A\left[\alpha L^{-\rho} + \beta K^{-\rho}\right]^{-1/\rho}$ prove that the Elasticity is $\frac{1}{1+\rho}$.

Solution:

The production of the firm is

$$Q = A\left[\alpha L^{-\rho} + \beta K^{-\rho}\right]^{-1/\rho} \quad ...(1)$$

The cost equation in its general form is written as

$$C = P_L L + P_K K \quad ...(2)$$

Now to maximize (1) with respect to (2) let us rewrite equation (2) in its implicit form by moving all the RHS terms to the LHS.

i.e. $$C - P_L L - P_K K = 0 \quad ...(3)$$

Now to maximize (1) with respect to (3) the Lagrangian equation may be written as

$$Z = \text{RHS of}(1) + \lambda[\text{LHS of } (3)]$$

i.e. $$Z = A\left[\alpha L^{-\rho} + \beta K^{-\rho}\right]^{-1/\rho} + \lambda(C - P_L L - P_K K) \quad ...(4)$$

Now to maximize Z given in equation (4), since it involves three variables L, K and λ, their respective partial derivatives are to be equated to zero.

i.e. $$\frac{\partial Z}{\partial L} = \frac{\partial Z}{\partial K} = \frac{\partial Z}{\partial \lambda} = 0$$

So from (4) above

$$\frac{\partial Z}{\partial L} = A\left(\frac{-1}{\rho}\right)\left[\alpha L^{-\rho} + \beta K^{-\rho}\right]^{-\frac{1}{\rho}-1} \times \alpha(-\rho)L^{-\rho-1} - \lambda P_L = 0 \quad ...(5)$$

$$\frac{\partial Z}{\partial K} = A\left(\frac{-1}{\rho}\right)\left[\alpha L^{-\rho} + \beta K^{-\rho}\right]^{-\frac{1}{\rho}-1} \times \beta(-\rho)K^{-\rho-1} - \lambda P_K = 0 \quad ...(6)$$

$$\frac{\partial Z}{\partial \lambda} = C - P_L L - P_K K = 0 \quad ...(7)$$

Now from (5)

$$A\left(\frac{-1}{\rho}\right)\left[\alpha L^{-\rho} + \beta K^{-\rho}\right]^{-\frac{1}{\rho}-1} \times \alpha(-\rho)L^{-\rho-1} = \lambda P_L \quad ...(8)$$

From (6) $$A\left(\frac{-1}{\rho}\right)\left[\alpha L^{-\rho} + \beta K^{-\rho}\right]^{-\frac{1}{\rho}-1} \times \beta(-\rho)K^{-\rho-1} = \lambda P_K \quad ...(9)$$

$$\frac{(8)}{(9)} \quad \frac{A\left(\frac{-1}{\rho}\right)\left[\alpha L^{-\rho}+\beta K^{-\rho}\right]^{-\frac{1}{\rho}-1} \times \alpha(-\rho)L^{-\rho-1}}{A\left(\frac{-1}{\rho}\right)\left[\alpha L^{-\rho}+\beta K^{-\rho}\right]^{-\frac{1}{\rho}-1} \times \beta(-\rho)K^{-\rho-1}} = \frac{\lambda P_L}{\lambda P_K}$$

$$\left(\frac{\alpha}{\beta}\right)\left(\frac{K}{L}\right)^{\rho+1} = \frac{P_L}{P_K}$$

$$\therefore \quad \left(\frac{K}{L}\right)^{\rho+1} = \left(\frac{\beta}{\alpha}\right)\left(\frac{P_L}{P_K}\right)$$

$$\frac{K}{L} = \left(\frac{\beta}{\alpha}\right)^{\frac{1}{\rho+1}}\left(\frac{P_L}{P_K}\right)^{\frac{1}{\rho+1}}$$

Now let $\left(\frac{\beta}{\alpha}\right)^{\frac{1}{\rho+1}} = a$

$$\left(\frac{P_L}{P_K}\right) = x \quad \text{and} \quad \frac{K}{L} = y$$

Now the above equation may be rewritten as $y = ax^{\frac{1}{\rho+1}}$

Now by definition:

$$\sigma = \frac{E(K/L)}{E(P_L/P_K)} = \frac{Ey}{Ex} = \frac{Eax^{\frac{1}{\rho+1}}}{Ex}$$

$$= \frac{x}{ax^{\frac{1}{\rho+1}}}\frac{d}{dx}\left(ax^{\frac{1}{\rho+1}}\right)$$

$$= \frac{x}{ax^{\frac{1}{\rho+1}}} \times a\frac{1}{\rho+1} \times x^{\frac{1}{\rho+1}-1}$$

$$= \frac{1}{\rho+1}$$

10.12 Homogeneous Functions

The homogeneous functions are special type of functions used in economics mostly in explaining returns to scales.

Definition: The function Q = f (L, K) is said to be homogeneous in degree 'h' provided a given 't' fold increase in both L and K leads to a t^h fold rise in the output Q. In other words this to say that

$$f(tL, tK) = t^h Q \qquad \text{...(A)}$$

Depending upon the value of 'h' we come across three special cases:

Case No.1: If h = 1 then homogeneity condition stated in equation (A) above reduces to

$$f(tL, tK) = t\,Q \qquad \text{...(1)}$$

A 't' fold rises in both L and K leads to exactly a 't' fold rise in the output Q. Such a situation in economics is called constant returns to scale. In particular if t = 2, then the equation (1) above further reduces to

$$f(2L, 2K) = 2Q \qquad \text{...(1a)}$$

A given two-fold rise in both L and K exhibits exactly a two-fold rise in the output Q.

A numerical illustration

Table 10.2

K	L	K/L	Q
20	10	2	100
40	20	2	200
60	30	2	300

In the above table row No. 2 exhibits a two fold rise in both L and K and the associated two fold rise in the output Q. Similarly, row No. 3 exhibits a three fold rise in both L and K and the associated three fold rise in the output Q.

A diagrammatic representation

In Fig. 10.18 the constant returns to scale is illustrated by using equi-distant iso-quants. It is simply the diagrammatic reproduction of the table given above.

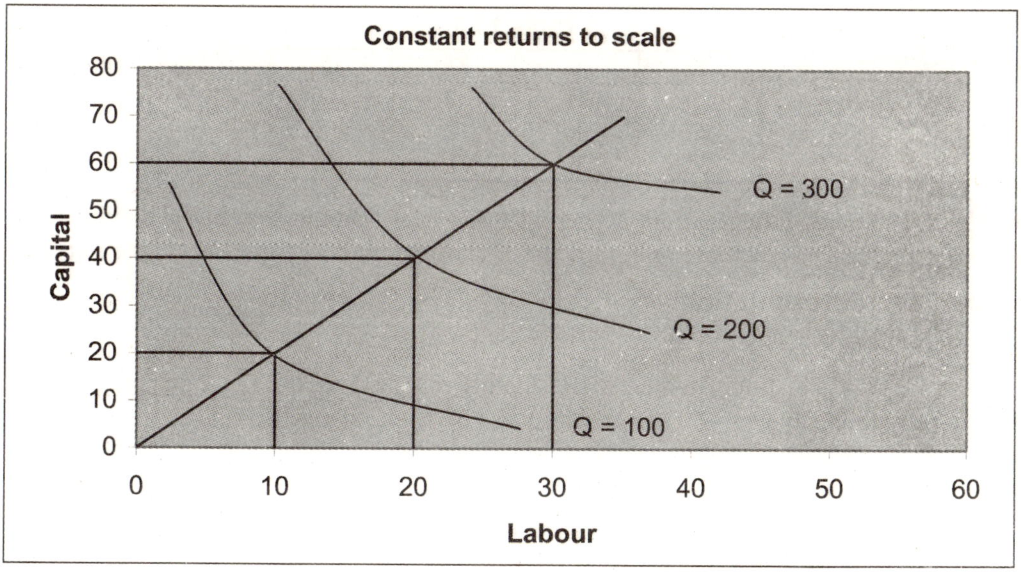

Fig. 10.18

A mathematical illustration

Let the production of the firm be $Q = AL^{\alpha}K^{1-\alpha}$

Now to see the homogeneity let us increase both L and K by a constant proportion say 't' times. The new level of output is obtained by simply replacing L by tL and K by tK in the original production function given above.

i.e. $$\begin{aligned} f(tL, tK) &= A(tL)^{\alpha}(tK)^{1-\alpha} \\ &= At^{\alpha}L^{\alpha}t^{1-\alpha}K^{1-\alpha} \\ &= t^{\alpha+1-\alpha}AL^{\alpha}K^{1-\alpha} \\ &= tQ \end{aligned}$$

Thus a 't' fold rises in both L and K leads to exactly a 't' fold rise in Q.

In particular If t = 2 then from above it follows that f (2L, 2K) = 2Q. Here a mere doubling of both L and K show an exactly doubling in the output.

Case No. 2: If 'h' is greater than one, say two, then the homogeneity definition given in above equation (A) above reduces to

$$f(tL, tK) = t^2Q \qquad \ldots(2)$$

Here a 't' fold rise in both L and K leads to a t^2 fold rise in the output exhibiting increasing returns to scale.

In particular if t = 2 then the equation (2) above reduces to

$$f(2L, 2K) = 2^2Q = 4Q \qquad \ldots(2a)$$

A two-fold increase in both L and K leads to a four-fold increase in the output Q

A numerical example

Table 10.3

K	L	K/L	Q
20	10	2	100
40	20	2	400
60	30	2	900

In row No. 2, a mere doubling in both L and K show a four-fold increase in the output. Similarly, in row No. 3 a three folds increase in both L and K shows a nine-fold increase in the output Q.

Diagrammatic representation

In the Fig. 10.19 increasing returns to scale is being illustrated by equi-distant iso-quants. The only difference now is that the iso-quants are suitably renamed i.e. the first one being named as Q = 100. The second one by Q = 400 and the third one by Q = 900 and so on.

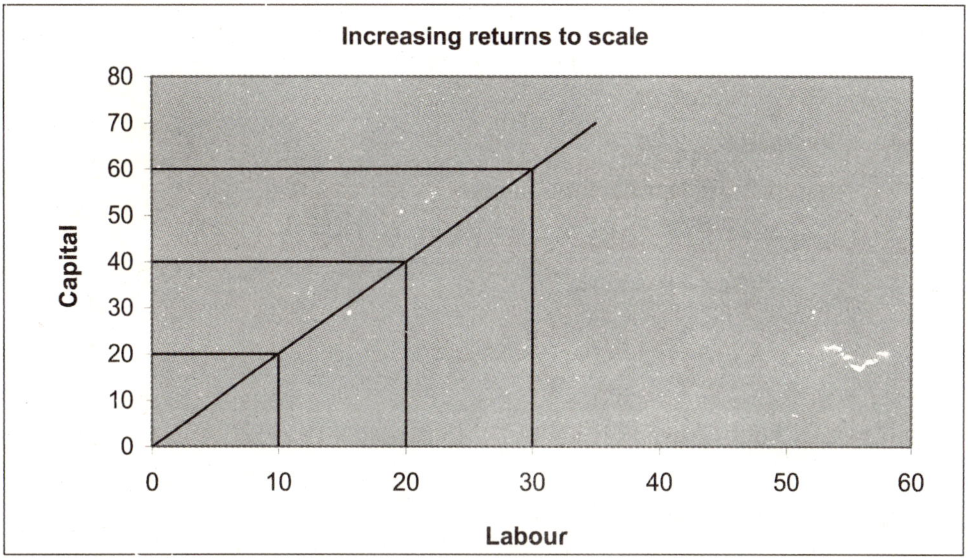

Fig. 10.19

A mathematical illustration

Let $Q = A\,L^{3/4}K^{3/4}$. Now let K is increased to tK and L is increased to tL.

Then $f(tL, tK) = A\,(tL)^{3/4}(tK)^{3/4}$

$$= A\,t^{3/4}L^{3/4}t^{3/4}K^{3/4}$$
$$= t^{1.5}A\,L^{3/4}K^{3/4}$$
$$= t^{1.5}Q$$

Here a given t fold rise in both L and K leads to a $t^{1.5}$ fold rise in the output Q exhibiting increasing returns to scale.

Case No. 3: If h is less than one, say h = ½, then the homogeneity definition given in equation (A) above reduces to

$$f(tL, tK) = t^{1/2}\,Q \qquad \ldots(3)$$

In (3) above a given t fold rise in both L and K leads to only a $t^{1/2}$ fold rise in the output exhibiting decreasing returns to scale.

In particular if h = 4 then the equation (3) above reduces to

$$f(4L, 4K) = 4^{1/2}Q = 2Q$$

Here a 4 fold rise in both L and K show only a 2 fold rise in the output Q exhibiting decreasing returns to scale.

A numerical illustration

Table 10.4

K	L	K/L	Q
20	10	2	100
40	20	2	$\sqrt{2}\times100$
60	30	2	$\sqrt{3}\times100$

In the Fig. 10.20 once again we show the decreasing returns by equi-distinct iso-quants. However, they are named differently. The second one is being named as $Q = \sqrt{2} \times 100$ and the third one is named as $Q = \sqrt{3} \times 100$.

A mathematical illustration

Let $Q = AL^{1/4}K^{1/4}$ stands for the production function.

Now $$f(tL, tK) = A\,(tL)^{1/4}(tK)^{1/4}$$

$$= A\,t^{1/4}\,L^{1/4}\,t^{1/4}\,K^{1/4}$$

$$= t^{1/2}\,AL^{1/4}K^{1/4}$$

$$= t^{1/2}\,Q$$

A given t fold rise in both L and K leads to $t^{1/2}$ fold rise in Q exhibiting decreasing returns to scale.

A diagrammatic representation

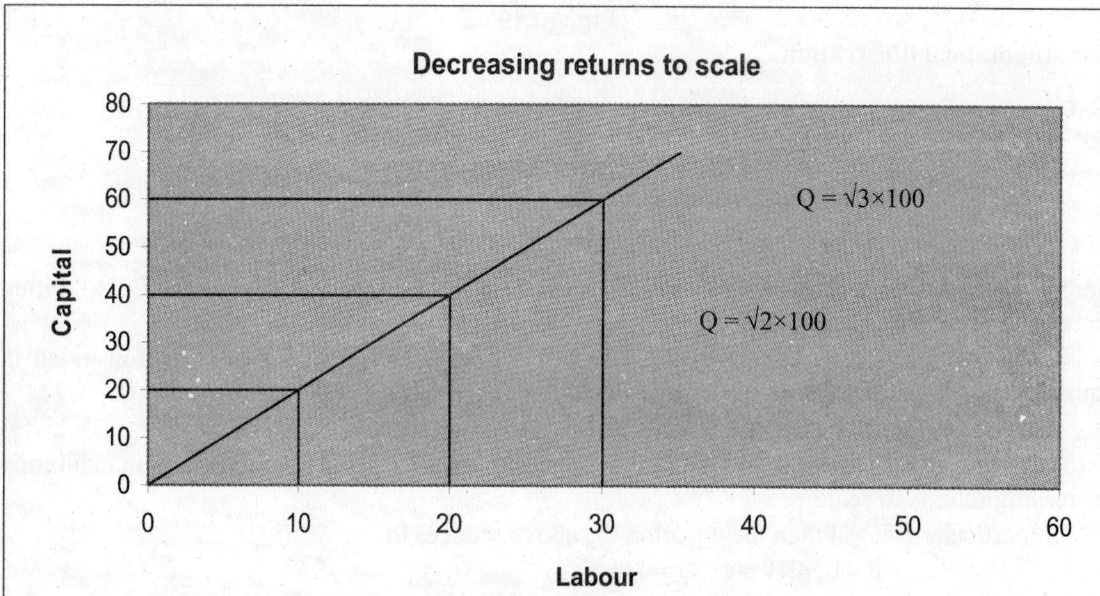

Fig. 10.20

10.13 Euler's Theorem and Adding up Controversy

A mathematical result relating to homogeneous functions with several independent variables, developed by a Swedish Mathematician Euler, is effectively utilized by economists in explaining distribution of output to the factor inputs on the basis of the neo classical marginal productivity payment rule.

Statement of the Euler's theorem

If Q = f (L, K) is homogeneous in degree 'h'

[i.e. (tL, tK) = t^hQ] then f_L. L + f_K. K = h. Q ...(A)

In the above result f_L and f_K are the marginal productivities of the two inputs namely L and K respectively. Thus, if the factor inputs are paid in accordance with their respective marginal productivities then f_L.L is simply labour's absolute share in the total output. Similarly, f_K.K is the absolute payment that is due to the capital input K. Therefore, the sum shown in the LHS of equation (A) above show the total output that is needed for both L and K whenever these factors are paid in accordance with their respective marginal productivity rates.

Adding up controversy

Euler's theorem plays a major role in the development of marginal productivity theory of distribution. Here we come across three special cases depending upon the value of 'h', the degree of homogeneity.

Case No.1: h = 1: Constant returns to scale

If h = 1 then we know that there is constant returns to scale. Further, when h = 1 the Euler's theorem statement stated in equation (A) above reduces to

$$f_L.\ L + f_K.\ K = Q \qquad ...(1)$$

The left-hand side of the above statement gives us the sum of the payments made to the factor inputs, paid at the respective marginal productivity rates. As per the theorem this total is equal to Q.

$$Q = f\,(L, K)$$

The total output obtained by using L units of labour and K units of capital is also equal to Q. Thus when the factors are paid in accordance with their respective marginal productivity rates then the total payments made to the factor inputs will always be equal to the total output that is being produced. Thus, under constant returns to scale there is no controversy regarding the payments. In fact, no factor input is under paid or over paid.

Diagrammatic representation

In Fig. 10.21 we show both MP_L and AP_L. In the case of homogeneous functions of the Cobb-Douglas type both MP_L and AP_L will slope downwards in the entire range of operation exhibiting only the presence of stage two of the short-run production process. With a given amount of fixed capital, if we use OB amount of the variable input namely labour L then the total output produced is given by the area of the rectangle ABEO (Q = AP_L.L). In it, the area of the rectangle DCEO refers the total payment made to the labour input L that too paid at the marginal productivity rate (i.e. f_L. L). Since there is exact adding up, the left over output given by the area of the rectangle ABCD will be just enough to meet the capital payments that too at its marginal productivity rate (f_K. K).

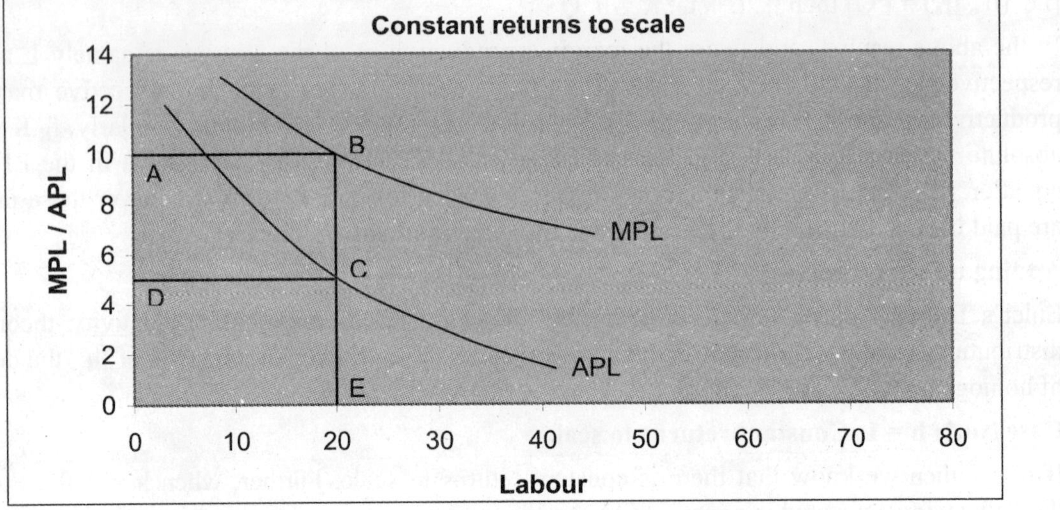

Fig. 10.21

A mathematical illustration

If $Q = A L^{\alpha} K^{1-\alpha}$ stands for the production function then prove that there is exact adding up.

$$f_L = \frac{\partial Q}{\partial L} = A\alpha L^{\alpha-1} K^{1-\alpha} = \frac{\alpha Q}{L}$$

$$f_K = \frac{\partial Q}{\partial K} = A L^{\alpha}(1-\alpha) K^{1-\alpha-1} = \frac{(1-\alpha)Q}{K}$$

$$\therefore \quad f_L.L + f_K.K = \frac{\alpha Q}{L}.L + \frac{(1-\alpha)Q}{K}.K = Q$$

Case No. 2: h > 1: say h = 1.5: Increasing returns to scale

If h = 1.5 then we know that there is increasing returns to scale. Hence the Euler's theorem statement given in equation (A) above reduces to

$$f_L.\, L + f_K.\, K = 1.5\, Q \qquad \ldots(2)$$

Thus the total payment to the factors in this case will become 1.5Q,

Hence, there will be a deficit of 0.5Q in this case. Here deficit does not mean that some of the factors are over paid. In fact, they are paid in accordance with their respective marginal productivity rates only. Thus, following are the controversial unsettled issues.

(1) How does this deficit occur?

(2) Who should bear this deficit?

(3) If so, under what rationality?

Diagrammatic representation

In Fig. 10.22 the area of the rectangle DCEO = f_L. L. However, the left out area given by the rectangle ABCD < f_K. K. Thus there will be a deficit of 0.5Q ultimately.

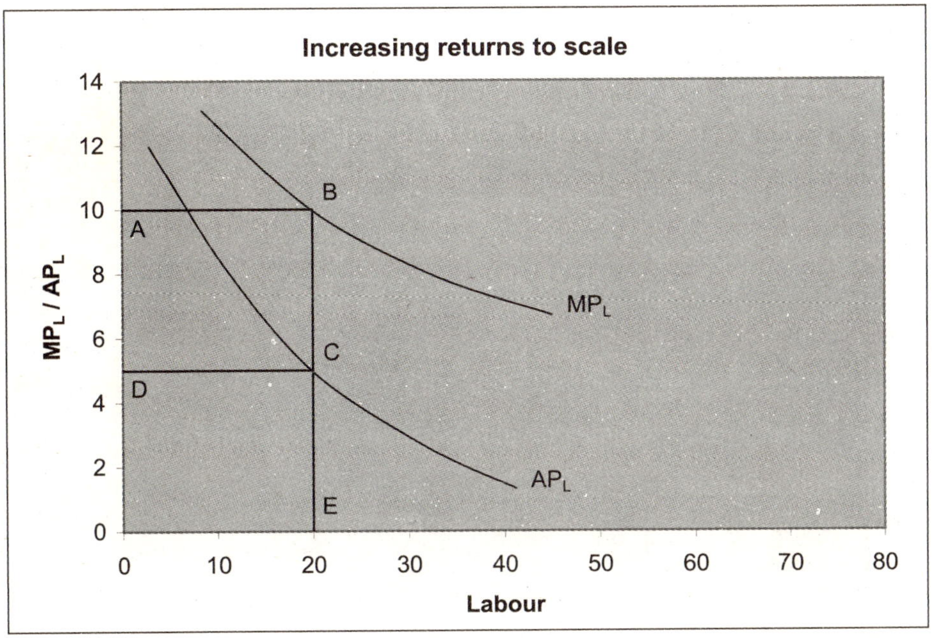

Fig. 10.22

A mathematical representation

Let $$Q = AL^{0.75}K^{0.75}$$

$$f_L = A \times 0.75 \times L^{0.75-1}K^{0.75} = \frac{0.75Q}{L}$$

$$f_L = A \times L^{0.75} \times 0.75 \times K^{0.75-1} = \frac{0.75Q}{K}$$

so $$f_L L + f_k K = \frac{0.75Q}{L}L + \frac{0.75Q}{K}K = 1.5Q$$

Hence there will be a deficit of 0.5Q

Case No. 3: h < 1 say h =1/2: Decreasing returns to scale

If h = ½ then, we now that there is decreasing returns to scale. Further when h = ½ the Euler's theorem statement given in equation (A) above reduces to

$$f_L . L + f_K . K = ½ Q.$$

Thus, when the total payment is equal to ½ Q and the total output is Q, there will be a surplus of ½ Q in this case. Here surplus does not mean that some of the factors are under paid. In fact, they are all fairly paid in accordance with their respective marginal productivity rates. Thus, once again the following are the unsettled and controversial issues. (1) How the surplus occur? (2) Who should enjoy the surplus? (3) If so under what rationality?

Diagrammatic representation

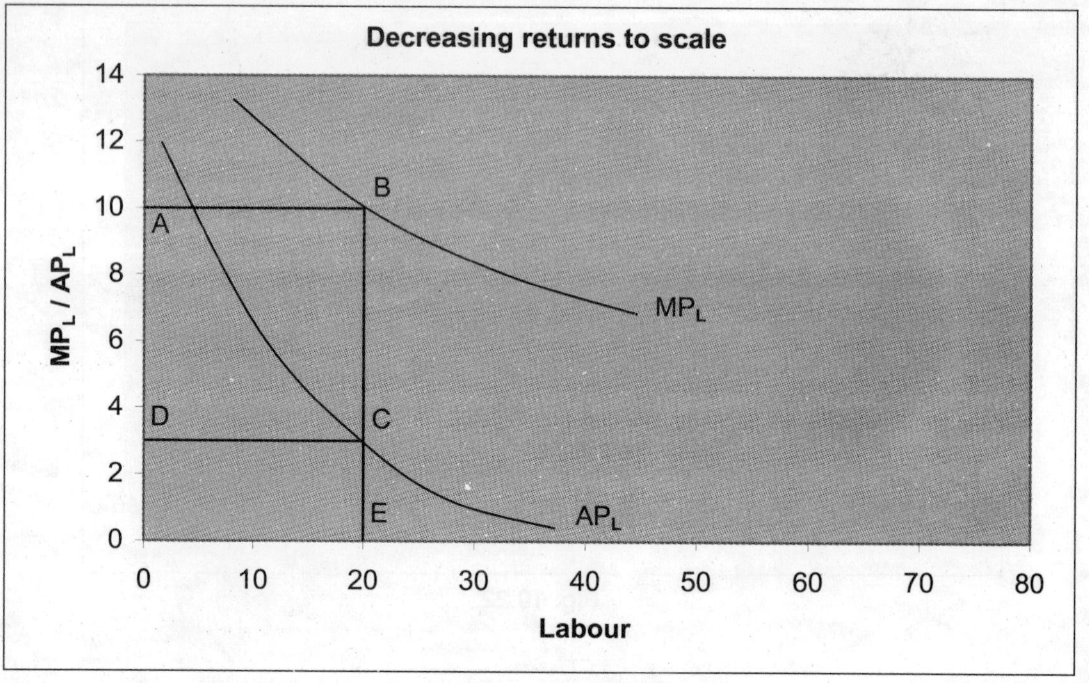

Fig. 10.23

In the diagram given above the area of the rectangle DCEO = f_L.L once again. However, the left out area of the rectangle ABCD> f_K. K. Thus, there will be a surplus in this case to the extend of 0.5Q.

A mathematical representation

Let
$$Q = AL^{0.25}K^{0.25}$$

$$f_L = A \times 0.25 \times L^{0.25-1}K^{0.25} = \frac{0.25Q}{L}$$

$$f_L = A \times L^{0.25} \times 0.25 \times K^{0.25-1} = \frac{0.25Q}{K}$$

so
$$f_L L + f_k K = \frac{0.25Q}{L}L + \frac{0.25Q}{K}K = 0.5Q$$

Thus there will be 0.5Q amount of surplus in this case.

10.14 Production Possibility Curve

Although, we were discussing the production with one output and two inputs namely labour and capital. In reality a given resource can be used in many ways. For example, a certain amount of labour and capital can be used either in the production of wheat completely, or in the production of cloth completely, or in the production both wheat and cloth in a certain proportion. The production possibility curve is the locus of the output combinations of these two commodities that can be produced from a fixed supply of a certain resource. At constant cost conditions, as envisaged by classical economists, the product transformation curve will be a downward slopping straight line as shown in Fig. 10.24. Under increasing cost conditions, it takes the concave shape as shown in Fig. 10.25. Under decreasing cost conditions it takes the convex shape as shown in Fig. 10.26.

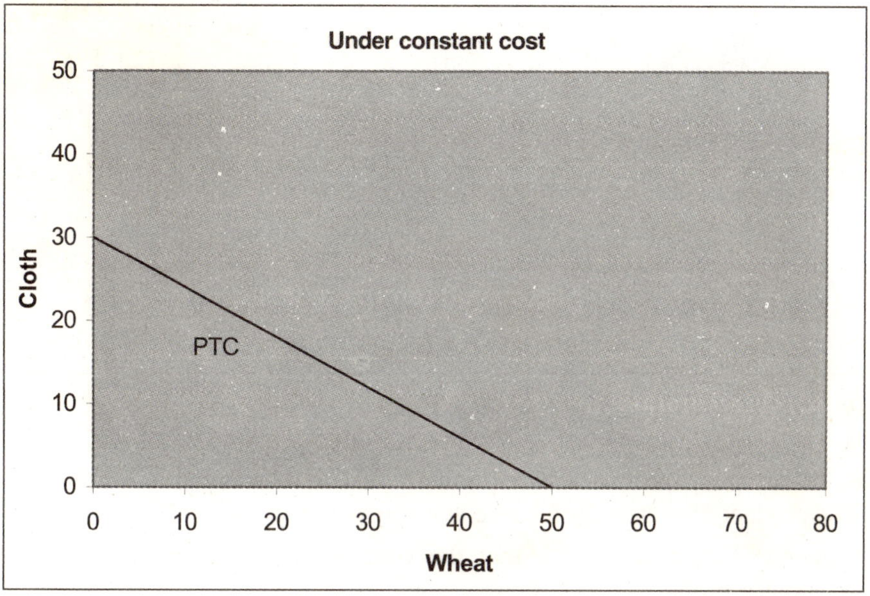

Fig. 10.24

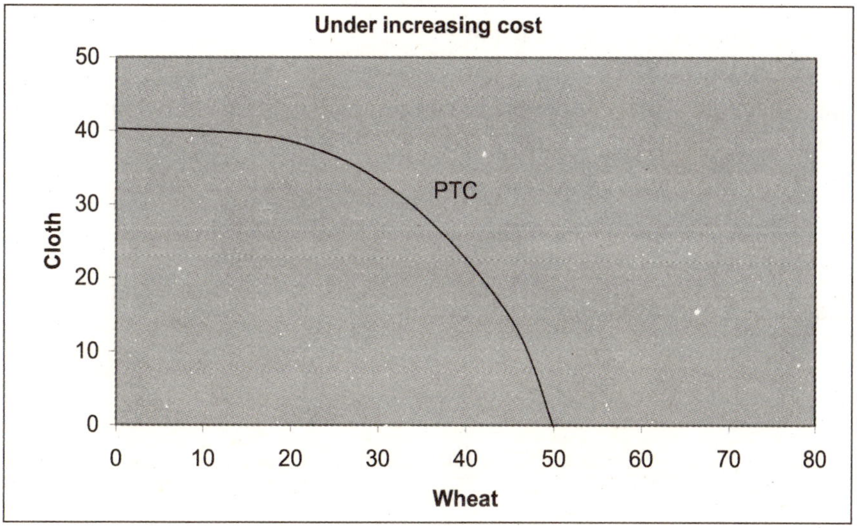

Fig. 10.25

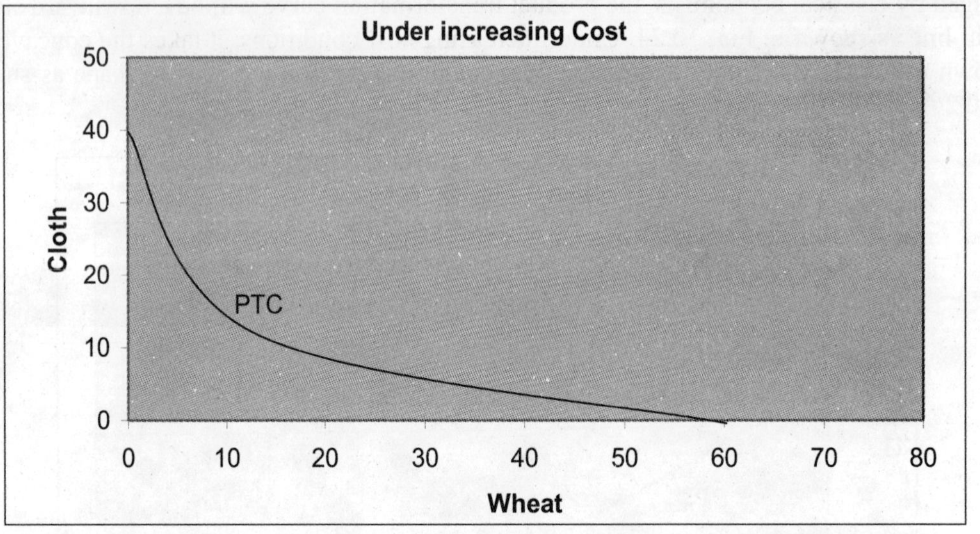

Fig. 10.26

Example 18: A company produces two products x, and y using fixed amount of a certain resource A. The product transformation curve is given by $x + y^2 + 4y = 20$.

(a) Find out the largest amount x that the company can produce by using all its fixed resource in the production of x alone.

(b) Find out the largest amount y that the company can produce by using all its fixed resource in the production of y alone.

(c) What an amount of x and y should be produced in order to have $x = 4y$?

(d) Draw the graph and confirm the results.

Solution:

(a) The largest amount of x that the company can produce is obtained by simply putting $y = 0$ in the given product transformation curve.

i.e.,
$$x + 0^2 + 4 \times 0 = 20$$
$$x = 20$$

(b) Similarly, the largest amount of y that the company can produce is obtained by simply putting $x = 0$ in the given product transformation curve.

i.e.,
$$0 + y^2 + 4.y = 20$$
$$y^2 + 4.y - 20 = 0 \text{ This is quadratic equation in y}$$
$$y = \frac{-b \pm \sqrt{b^2 - 4ac}}{2a}$$
$$= \frac{-4 \pm \sqrt{(-4)^2 - 4(1)(-20)}}{(2)(1)}$$

$$= \frac{-4 \pm \sqrt{16+80}}{2}$$

$$y = \frac{-4 \pm 0.797}{2}$$

$$= \frac{-13.8}{2} = -6.9 \quad \text{or}$$

$$= \frac{5.8}{2} = 2.9$$

Since negative output has no relevance in economics we take only the positive output namely y = 2.9 as the maximum output.

(c) To answer this part we simply put x = 4y in the given product transformation curve.

i.e.,
$$4y + y^2 + 4y - 20 = 0$$
$$y^2 + 8y - 20 = 0$$

This is a quadratic equation again in y. So let us get the solution by factorizing the equation.

$$y^2 + 10\,y - 2\,y - 20 = 0$$
$$y(y + 10) - 2(y + 10) = 0$$
$$(y + 10)(y - 2) = 0$$

So, y = – 10 or y = 2 are the two solutions for our equation. Once again since negative values has no relevance in economics we take only the positive value namely y = 2 as the right level of output. The appropriate x value is obtained by substituting this value of y in the given condition.

$$x = 4\,y$$
$$x = (4)\,.\,(2) = 8$$

Therefore, x = 8 and y = 2 are the needed values.

(d) Graphical solution

Table 10.5

$x = -y^2-4y+20$		$x = 4y$	
x	y	x	y
20	0	0	0
17.75	0.5	2	0.5
15	1	4	1
11.75	1.5	6	1.5
8	**2**	**8**	**2**
3.75	2.5	10	2.5
2.84	2.6	10.4	2.6
1.91	2.7	10.8	2.7
0.96	2.8	11.2	2.8
–0.01	2.9	11.6	2.9

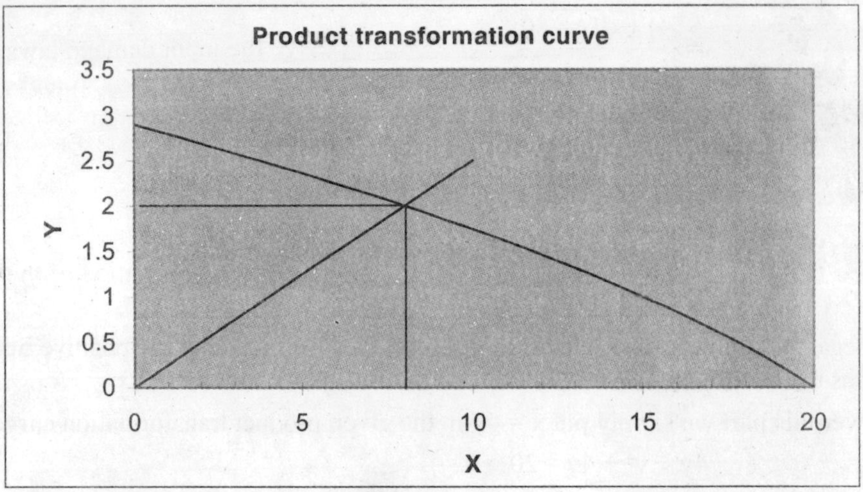

Fig. 10.27

EXERCISES

1. An entrepreneur has Rs.100 to spend on two inputs namely labour and raw material. He hires L quantity of labour at an annual price Rs. 2 per unit and buys M quantity of raw material at price Re. 1 per unit. Find L and M if he wants to get as much output as possible given the production function $Q = LM$.
2. An entrepreneur has Rs. 100 to spend on labour and raw materials. He hires L quantity of labour at an annual price Rs. 2 per unit and buys M quantity of raw material at price Re.1 per unit. Find L and M if he wants to get as much output as possible, given the production function $Q = 100LM$.
3. An entrepreneur has Rs. 1000 to spend on labour and raw materials. He hires L quantity of labour at an annual price Rs. 20 per unit and buys M quantity of raw material at price Rs.10 per unit. Find L and M if he wants to get as much output as possible, when the production function is given by $Q = LM$.
4. An entrepreneur has Rs. 100 to spend on labour and raw materials. He hires L quantity of labour at an annual price Rs. 2 per unit and buys M quantity of raw material at price Re. 1 per unit. Find L and M if he wants to get as much output as possible, given the production function $Q = L^2 M^2$.
5. An entrepreneur has target of 12500 units of output for the current year. He hires L quantity of labour at an annual price Rs. 2 per unit and buys M quantity of raw material at price Rs. 1 per unit. Find the least cost output when the production function is given by $Q = LM$.
6. Given the production $Q = 10K^{0.4} L^{0.6}$. Find the maximum output subject to the constraint $6K + 2L = 384$.
7. A firm has the production function $Q = \ln L^4K^3$. Derive the input demand laws for both L and K in terms of the product price P when the factor prices are P_L = Rs. 2 and P_K = Rs. 8. Hence derive the supply function for the firm's product giving the output as a function of the product price P.

8. The production function of a firm is $Q = A\,L^{1/2}K^{1/2}$. Derive the input demand laws for both L and K in terms of the product price P when the factor prices are P_L = Rs. 5 and P_K = Rs. 6. Hence derive the supply function for the firm's product giving the output as a function of the product price P.
9. A firm has the production $Q = A\,L^2\,K^2 - B\,L^3\,K^3$. Obtain the equation of the expansion path and prove that it is linear.
10. The production function of a firm is $Q = A\,L^{1/2}K^{1/2}$. Prove that the equation of the expansion path is linear.
11. The production function of a firm is $Q = 100\ L^{1/4}\ K^{1/2}$. Prove that the equation of the expansion path is linear.
12. The production function of a firm is $Q = 25\ L^{3/4}K^{1/2}$. Prove that the equation of the expansion path is linear.
13. The production function of a firm is $Q = A\left[\alpha L^{-\rho} + (1-\alpha)^{-\rho}\right]^{-1/\rho}$. Prove that the equation of the expansion path is linear.
14. The production function of a firm is $Q = 100\ L^{3/4}K^{1/2}$. Prove that the elasticity of substitution is unity.
15. $Q = A\left[0.25L^{-1} + 0.75)^{-1}\right]^{-1}$. Prove that the elasticity of substitution is 1/2.
16. $Q = A\left[0.5L^{-0.5} + 0.5)^{-0.5}\right]^{-1/0.5}$. Prove that the elasticity of substitution is 2/3.
17. The production function of a firm is $Q = 10\ L^{1/2}K^{1/2}$. Prove that there is a constant return to scale.
18. The production function of a firm is $Q = 50\ L^{1/4}K^{1/2}$. Prove that there is diminishing return to scale.
19. The production function of a firm is $Q = 200\ L^{3/4}K^{3/4}$. Prove that there is increasing return to scale.
20. The production function of a firm is $Q = A\,L^{1/2}K^{1/2}$. If the factors are paid in accordance with their respective marginal productivities, prove that there is exact adding up.
21. The production function of a firm is $Q = A\,L^{1/4}K^{1/2}$. If the factors are paid in accordance with their respective marginal productivities, prove that there will be surplus 1/4 units of the output.
22. The production function of a firm is $Q = A\,L^{3/4}K^{1/2}$. If the factors are paid in accordance with their respective marginal productivities, prove that there will be deficit 1/4 units of the output.
23. A firm has the production function

$$Q = A\left[0.5L^{-\rho} + 0.75K^{-\rho}\right]^{-1/\rho}.$$

If the factors are paid in accordance with their respective marginal productivities then prove that there is exact adding up.

24. A company produces two products x, and y by using fixed amount of a certain resource A. The product transformation curve is given by $(x - 24)(y - 36) = 240$ and $x < 24$.

   (a) Find out the largest amount x that the company can produce by using all its fixed resource in the production of x alone.

   (b) Find out the largest amount y that the company can produce by using all its fixed resource in the production of y alone.

   (c) What an amount of x and y should be produced in order to have $x = 2y$.

25. A company produces two products x, and y by using fixed amount of a certain resource A. The product transformation curve is given by $y = \frac{300}{30 - x}$ and $x < 30$.

   (a) Find out the largest amount x that the company can produce by using all its fixed resource in the production of x alone.

   (b) Find out the largest amount y that the company can produce by using all its fixed resource in the production of y alone.

   (c) What an amount of x and y should be produced in order to have $x = y$.

26. A company produces two products x, and y by using fixed amount of a certain resource A. The product transformation curve is given by $y = 20 - \frac{x^2}{5}$.

   (a) Find out the largest amount x that the company can produce by using all its fixed resource in the production of x alone.

   (b) Find out the largest amount y that the company can produce by using all its fixed resource in the production of y alone.

   (c) What an amount of x and y should be produced in order to have $x = 5y$.

10.15 Cost Analysis

Normally we derive both the long-run and the short-run cost functions from the given production and cost equations. The cost analysis in a way provides an alternative approach to the theory of production. The cost behaviour is normally analyzed in two distinct ways. The short-run cost involves two components namely the total fixed cost and total variable cost. The total fixed cost by definition does not vary with the level of output. In fact, it is a constant amount for all levels of output including zero. Such fixed cost is always shown by horizontal straight line above the X-axis as shown in the Fig. 10.28. The variable cost on the other hand, varies with the level of output. In particular, when nothing is produced the variable cost is zero. Thus in diagrammatic terms the total variable cost starts from the origin and takes the upward sloping convex shape first then upward sloping concave shape later as shown in the Fig.27. The average and marginal costs take the familiar 'U' shape as shown in Fig. 10.29. Moreover, MC = AC only at the minimum point of AC. The following Table 10.6 and the Figs. are based on the numerical cost function $C = 0.04q^3 - 0.9q^2 + 10q + 100$.

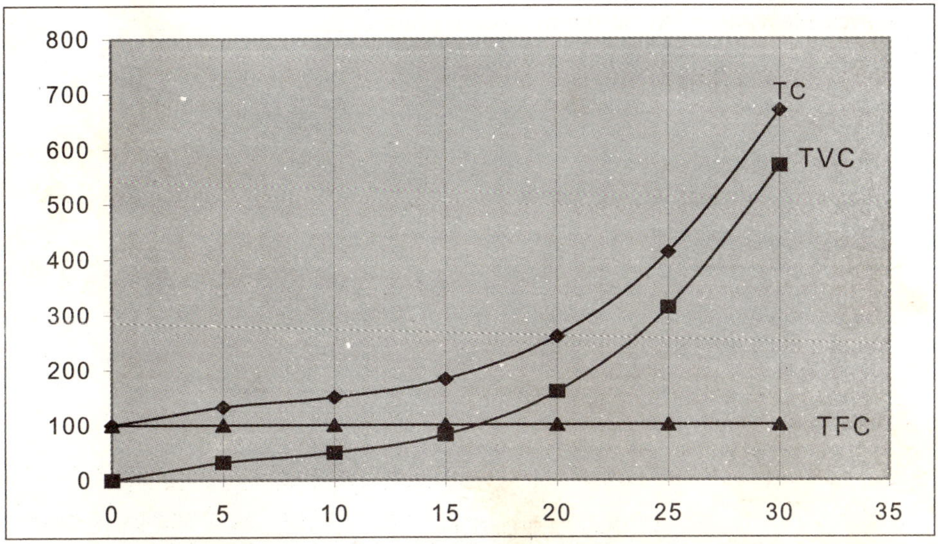

Fig. 10.28

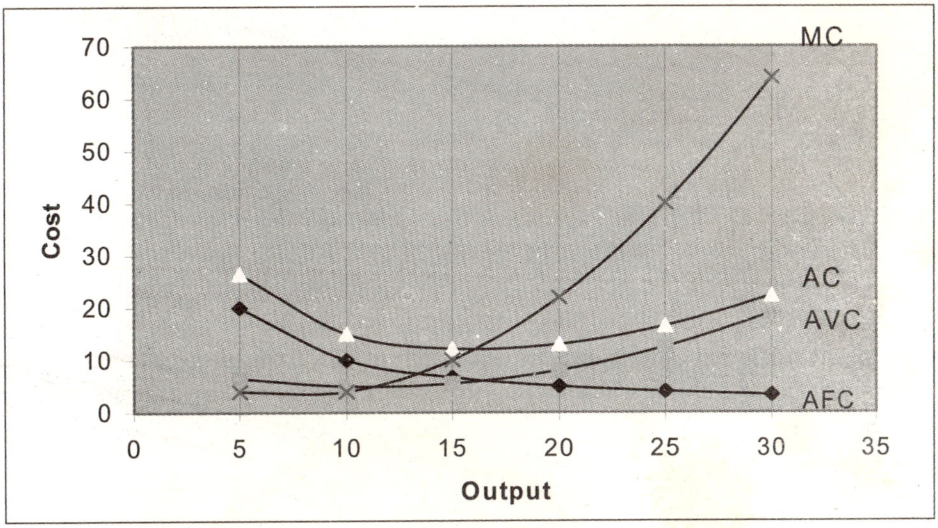

Fig. 10.29

Table 10.6

Q	TC	TVC	TFC	AFC	AVC	AC	MC
0	100.00	0.00	100.00	-	-	-	0.00
5	132.50	32.50	100.00	20.00	6.50	26.50	4.00
10	150.00	50.00	100.00	10.00	5.00	15.00	4.00
15	182.50	82.50	100.00	6.67	5.50	12.17	10.00
20	260.00	160.00	100.00	5.00	8.00	13.00	22.00
25	412.50	312.50	100.00	4.00	12.50	16.50	40.00
30	670.00	570.00	100.00	3.33	19.00	22.33	64.00

Example 19: Prove that MC = AC at the minimum point of AC.

Solution:

By definition $AC = \frac{C}{q}$

Now for the minimum value of AC we know that:

1. $$\frac{d}{dq}(AC) = 0$$

2. $$\frac{d^2}{dq^2}(AC) > 0$$

So $$\frac{d}{dq}(AC) = \frac{d}{dq}\left(\frac{C}{q}\right)$$

$$= \frac{q \times \frac{dC}{dq} - C\frac{dq}{dq}}{q^2}$$

$$= \frac{\frac{dC}{dq} - C = 0}{q}$$

i.e., $$\frac{dC}{dq} = \frac{C}{q}$$

$$MC = AC$$

Thus MC = AC only at the minimum point of AC.

(a) Necessary and sufficient conditions for equilibrium of a firm under perfect competition: The firm under perfect competition attains its equilibrium by maximizing its profit. Now by definition

Profit = Revenue – Cost

$$\Pi = R - C \qquad \ldots(1)$$

In equation (1) the profit is a function of the output q. So for the maximum value of the profit Π the appropriate conditions are as follows.

1. $\frac{d\Pi}{dq} = 0$ [Necessary condition]

2. $\frac{d^2\Pi}{dq^2} < 0$ [Sufficient condition]

Necessary condition

Now from equation (1) above

$$\frac{d\Pi}{dq} = \frac{d}{dq}(R - C) = 0$$

$$= \frac{dR}{dq} - \frac{dC}{dq} = 0$$

Now since by definition $\frac{dR}{dq}$ = MR, the marginal revenue, and $\frac{dC}{dq}$ = MC, marginal cost, the above condition may be rewritten as

$$MR - MC = 0$$

or $$MC = MR \qquad ...(2)$$

Under perfect competition the individual competitive seller is a price taker. Hence in the revenue function R = Pq, the price P is a constant.

Therefore $\frac{dR}{dq} = P = AR$

i.e. $$MR = AR \qquad ...(3)$$

Since AR = P is a constant under perfect competition MR = AR is a horizontal straight line.

Now from (2) and (3) the necessary condition for the equilibrium of a firm under competition is restated as

$$MC = MR = AR \qquad ...(4)$$

Second order condition

Further, from the above

$$\frac{d^2\Pi}{dq^2} = \frac{d}{dq}(MR) - \frac{d}{dq}(MC) < 0$$

Since by definition $\frac{d}{dq}$ (MR) = slope of MR and $\frac{d}{dq}$ (MC) = slope of MC, the above condition may be rewritten as

$$\text{Slope of MR} - \text{Slope of MC} < 0$$

This condition will be satisfied if and only if the MC cuts MR from below Fig.10.30.

Since MR = AR = P is a constant under perfect competition the sufficient condition may also deserves a special extension. Now under perfect competition since MR = AR = P, a constant it follows that:

$$\frac{d}{dq}(MR) = \frac{d}{dq}(AR) = \frac{d}{dq}(P) = 0$$

Hence, the above result may by rewritten as $\frac{d}{dq}(MC) > 0$

In other words, this is to say that slope of MC > 0. Thus under perfect competition in the neighbourhood of the equilibrium the MC must be upward sloping Fig. 10.31.

Example 20: The short-run cost function of the firm is $C = 0.04q^3 - 0.9q^2 + 10q + 5$. Given the competitive price p = 22 obtain the equilibrium quantity q and the equilibrium profit Π.

Solution:

We know that under equilibrium, the perfectly competitive firm will maximize its profit by appropriately choosing level of its output. Hence by definition:

Profit = Revenue – Cost

i.e.

$$\begin{aligned}\Pi &= R - C\\ &= pq - C\\ &= 22q - (0.04q^3 - 0.9q^2 + 10q + 5)\\ &= 22q - 0.04q^3 + 0.9q^2 - 10q - 5\\ \Pi &= -0.04q^3 + 0.9q^2 + 12q - 5 \qquad \text{...(1)}\end{aligned}$$

Now in equation (1) above the profit Π is a function of the quantity q that is being produced. So for the maximum profit we know that

1. $\frac{d\Pi}{dq} = 0$ (Necessary condition)
2. $\frac{d^2\Pi}{dq^2} < 0$ (Sufficient condition)

So from (1) above $\frac{d\Pi}{dq} = -0.12q^2 + 1.8q + 12 = 0$ ...(2)

Now

$$\begin{aligned}q &= \frac{-b \pm \sqrt{b^2 - 4ac}}{2a}\\ &= \frac{-(1.8) \pm \sqrt{(1.8)^2 - (4)(-0.12)(12)}}{2(-0.12)}\\ &= \frac{-1.8 \pm \sqrt{3.24 + 5.76}}{-0.24}\\ &= \frac{-1.8 \pm \sqrt{9}}{-0.24}\\ &= \frac{-1.8 \pm 3}{-0.24}\\ &= 5, \text{or } 20\end{aligned}$$

Therefore, q = 5 and q = 20 are the two solutions to the given quadratic equation. Now to confirm one among the two let us use the second order condition.

From (2) above

Diagrammatic representation of equilibrium under competition

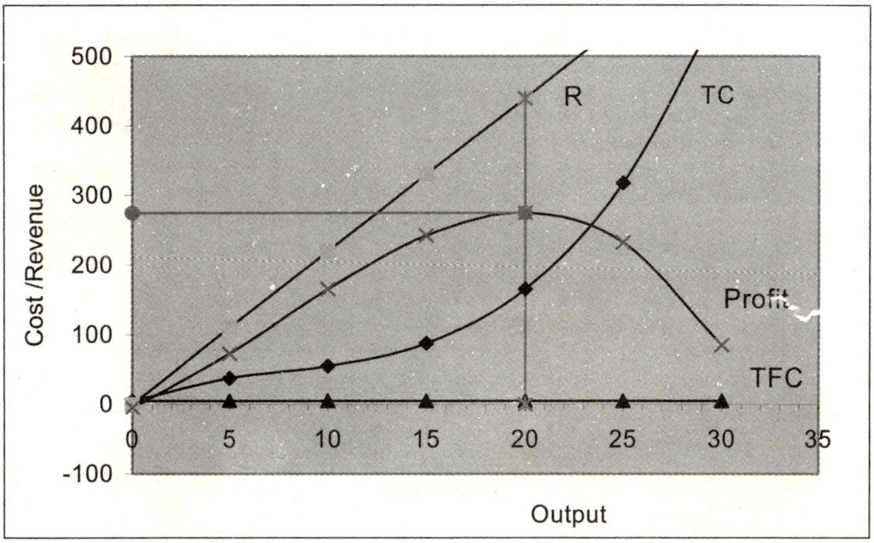

Fig. 10.30

$$\frac{d^2\Pi}{dq^2} = -0.24q + 1.8$$

$$\left(\frac{d^2\Pi}{dq^2}\right)_{q=5} = -0.24 \times 5 + 1.8$$

$$= -1.2 + 1.8$$

$$= 0.6 > 0$$

$$\left(\frac{d^2\Pi}{dq_2}\right)_{q=20} = -0.24 \times 20 + 1.8$$

$$= -4.8 + 1.8$$

$$= -3 < 0$$

Thus q = 20 gets confirmed as the equilibrium quantity. Now the equilibrium profit is obtained by merely substituting q = 20 in the profit function given in equation (1) above.

$$\Pi = -0.04q^3 + 0.9q^2 + 12q - 5$$

$$= -0.04 \times 20^3 + 0.9 \times 20^2 + 12 \times 20 - 5$$

$$= -320 + 360 + 240 - 5$$

$$= 280 - 5$$

$$= 275$$

Thus under equilibrium q = 20 and Π = 275. Figure 10.30 and 10.31 describe this situation.

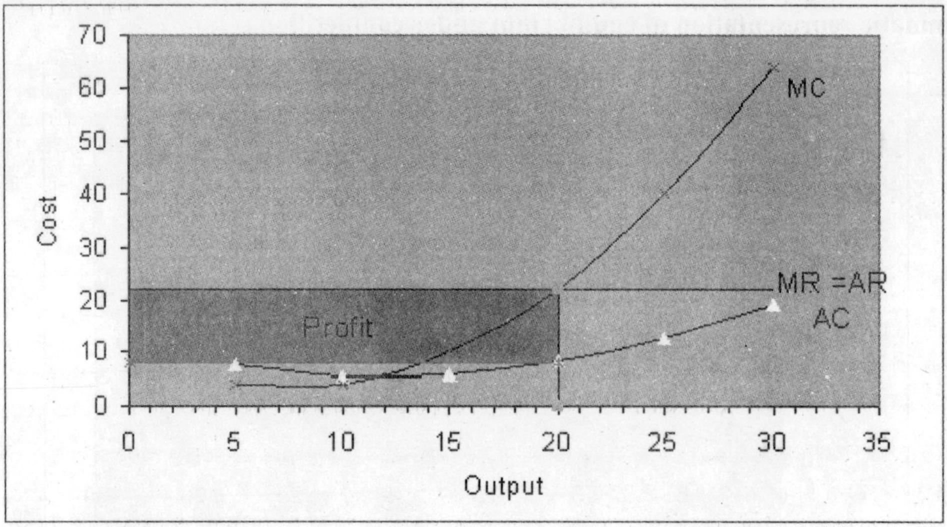

Fig. 10.31

Example 21: The short-run cost function of the firm is $C = 0.04q^3 - 0.9q^2 + 10q + 5$. Given the competitive price $p = 5.35$ obtain the equilibrium quantity q and the equilibrium profit Π.

Solution:

We know that under equilibrium, the perfectly competitive firm will maximize its profit by appropriately choosing level of its output. Hence by definition:

Profit = Revenue – Cost

$$\Pi = R - C$$

$$= pq - C$$

$$= 5.35q - (0.04q^3 - 0.9q^2 + 10q + 5)$$

$$= -0.04q^3 + 0.9q^2 - 4.65q - 5 \qquad ...(1)$$

Now in equation (1) above the profit Π is a function of the output q that is being produced. So for the maximum profit we know that

1. $\frac{d\Pi}{dq} = 0$ (Necessary condition)

2. $\frac{d^2\Pi}{dq^2} < 0$ (Sufficient condition)

So from (1) above $\frac{d\Pi}{dq} = -0.12q^2 + 1.8q - 4.65 = 0 \qquad ...(2)$

This is a quadratic equation in q.

Now $\qquad q = \frac{-b \pm \sqrt{b^2 - 4ac}}{2a}$

$$= \frac{-(1.8) \pm \sqrt{(1.8)^2 - (4)(-0.12)(-4.56)}}{2(-0.12)}$$

$$= \frac{-1.8 \pm \sqrt{3.24 - 2.1889}}{-0.24}$$

$$= \frac{-1.8 \pm \sqrt{1.0911}}{-0.24}$$

$$= \frac{-1.8 \pm 1.2523}{-0.24} = 12.7, \text{ or } 2.3$$

Therefore, q = 12.7 and q = 2.3 are the two solutions to the given quadratic equation. Now to confirm one among the two let us use the second order condition.

From (2) above

$$\frac{d^2\Pi}{dq^2} = -0.24q + 1.8$$

$$\left(\frac{d^2\Pi}{dq^2}\right)_{q=2.3} = -0.24 \times 2.3 + 1.8$$

$$= 1.248 > 0$$

$$\left(\frac{d^2\Pi}{dq^2}\right)_{q=12.7} = -0.24 \times 12.7 + 1.8$$

$$= -3.048 + 1.8 = -1.248 < 0$$

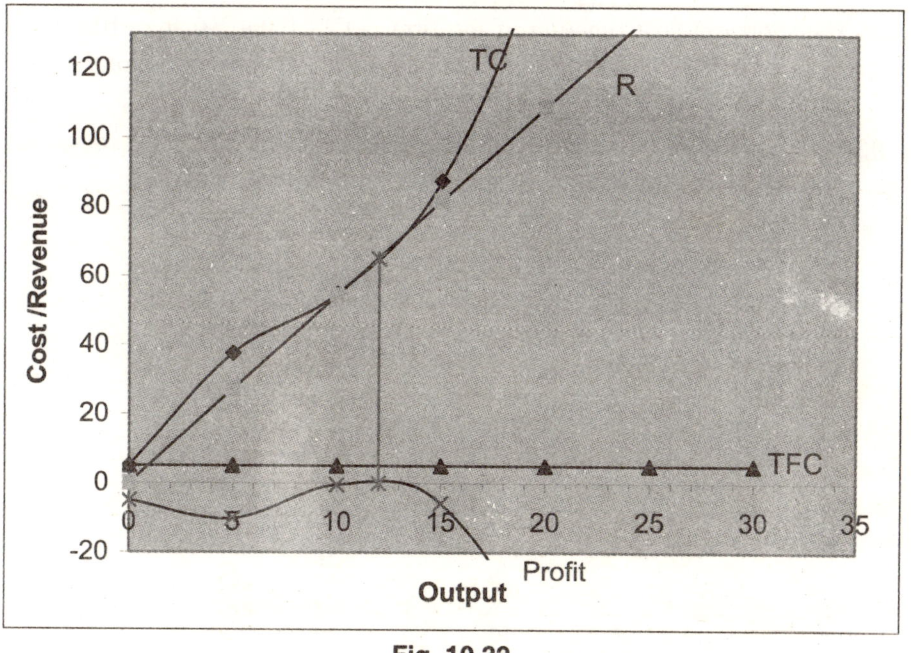

Fig. 10.32

Thus q = 12.7 gets confirmed as the equilibrium quantity. Now the equilibrium profit is obtained by merely substituting q = 12.7 in the profit function given in equation (1) above.

$$\Pi = -0.04q^3 + 0.9q^2 - 4.65q - 5$$
$$= -0.04 \times 12.7^3 + 0.9 \times 12.7^2 - 6 \times 12.7 - 5$$
$$= 0$$

Thus under equilibrium q =12.7 and Π = 0. Fig. 10.32 and Fig. 10.33 describe this situation.

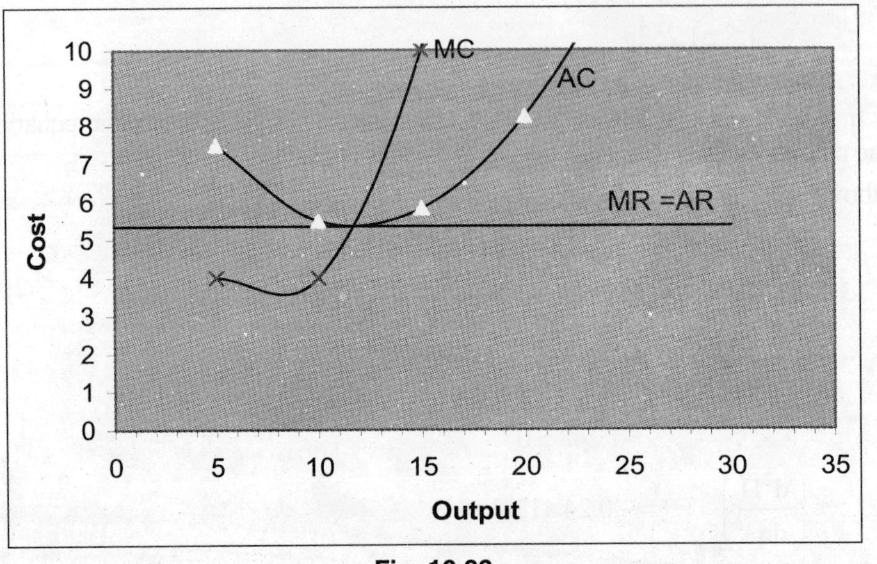

Fig. 10.33

Example 22: The short run cost function of the firm is C = $0.04q^3-0.9q^2+10q+5$. Given the competitive price p = 4 obtain the equilibrium quantity q and the equilibrium profit Π.

Solution:

We know that under equilibrium, the perfectly competitive firm will maximize its profit by appropriately choosing level of its output. Hence by definition:

Profit = Revenue – Cost

i.e.
$$\Pi = R - C$$
$$= pq - C$$
$$= 4q - (0.04q^3 - 0.9q^2 + 10q + 5)$$
$$= 4q - 0.04q^3 + 0.9q^2 - 10q - 5$$
$$\Pi = -0.04q^3 + 0.9q^2 - 6q - 5 \qquad ...(1)$$

Now in equation (1) above the profit Π is a function of the output q that is being produced. So for the maximum profit we know that

1. $\frac{d\Pi}{dq} = 0$ (Necessary condition) 2. $\frac{d^2\Pi}{dq^2} < 0$ (Sufficient condition)

So from (1) above $\frac{d\Pi}{dq} = -0.12q^2 + 1.8q - 6 = 0$ ...(2)

This is a quadratic equation in q. So let use the factorization method to obtain its solutions. To make the task simple let us multiply equation (2) by –100 and eliminate the decimals.

i.e. $12q^2 - 180q + 600 = 0.$

Now since it is divisible by 12 let us divide it by 12.

i.e $q^2 - 15q + 50 = 0$

$q^2 - 10q - 5q + 50 = 0$

$q(q - 10) - 5(q - 10) = 0$

$(q -- 10)(q - 5) = 0$

Therefore, q = 10 and q = 5 are the two solutions to the given quadratic equation. Now to confirm one among the two let us use the second order condition.

From (2) above

$$\frac{d^2\Pi}{dq^2} = -0.24q + 1.8$$

$$\left(\frac{d^2\Pi}{dq^2}\right)_{q=5} = -0.24 \times 5 + 1.8$$

$$= -1.2 + 1.8$$

$$= 0.6 > 0$$

$$\left(\frac{d^2\Pi}{dq_2}\right)_{q=10} = -0.24 \times 10 + 1.8$$

$$= -2.4 + 1.8$$

$$= -0.6 < 0$$

Thus q = 10 gets confirmed as the equilibrium quantity. Now the equilibrium profit is obtained by merely substituting q = 10 in the profit function given in equation (1) above.

$$\Pi = -0.04q^3 + 0.9q^2 - 6q - 5$$

$$= -0.04 \times 10^3 + 0.9 \times 10^2 - 6 \times 10 - 5$$

$$= -40 + 90 - 60 - 5$$

$$= -105 + 90$$

$$= -15$$

Thus under equilibrium q = 10 and Π = – 15. Figures 10.34 and 10.35 describe this situation.

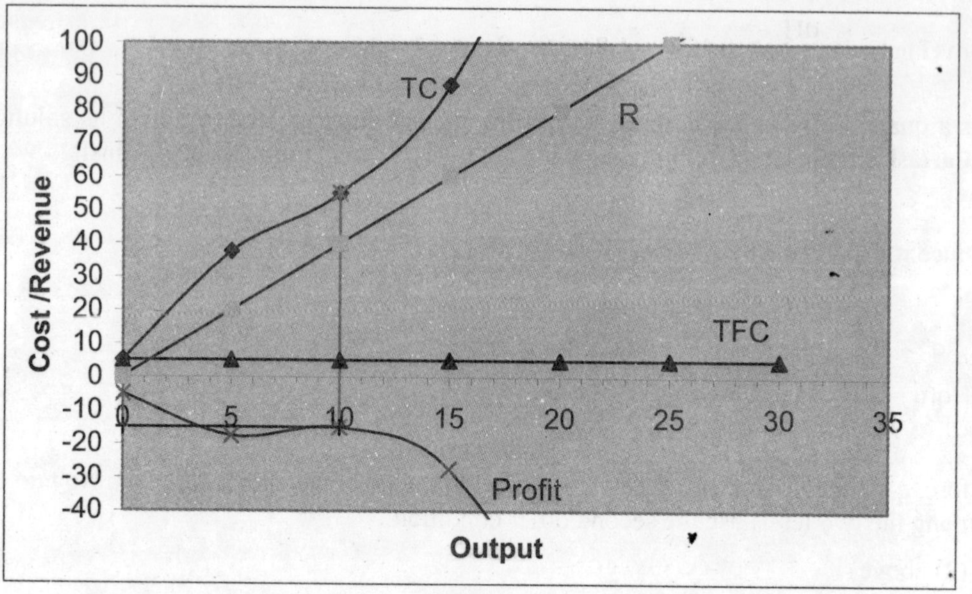

Fig. 10.34

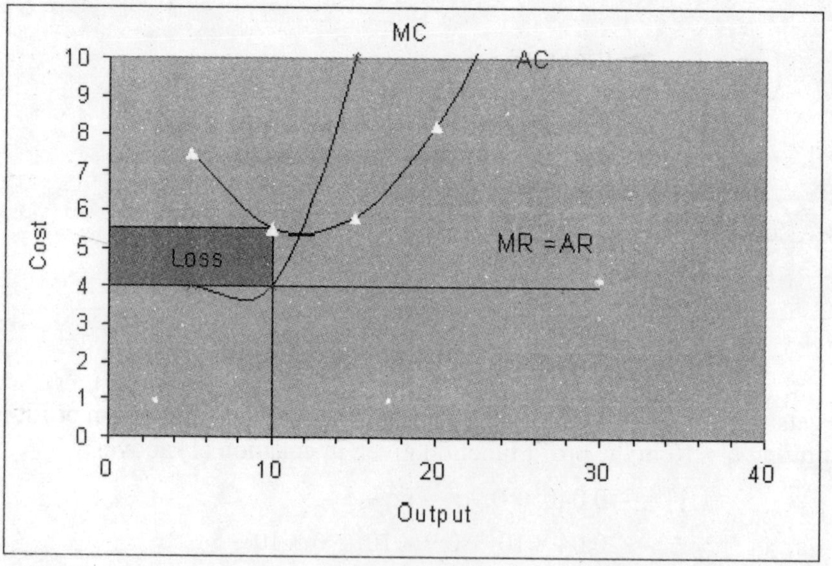

Fig. 10.35

Note: Here the profit –15 really means a loss of 15 in the short-run. Though the firm incurs a loss in the short-run it will continue its production, provided it earns enough revenue to cover at least the total variable cost, having the long-run hopes of earning positive profit in mind. However, even in the long-run if this situation continues to prevail then definitely the firm will have to discontinue its production at the earliest.

Example 23: The short-run cost function of a firm is $C = q^3 - 15q^2 + 80q + 10$. Calculate the equilibrium quantity q and the maximum profit Π when the competitive price for the product is given by p = Rs. 8 per unit.

Solution:

We know that under equilibrium, the perfectly competitive firm will maximize its profit by appropriately choosing level of its output. Hence by definition:

Profit = Revenue – Cost

i.e.
$$\begin{aligned}\Pi &= R - C\\ &= pq - C\\ &= 8q - (q^3 - 15q^2 + 80q + 10)\\ &= 8q - q^3 + 15q^2 - 80q - 10\\ &= -q^3 + 15q^2 - 72q - 10 \qquad \ldots(1)\end{aligned}$$

Now for the maximum value Π we know that

1. $\dfrac{d\Pi}{dq} = 0$ (Necessary condition)

2. $\dfrac{d^2\Pi}{dq^2} < 0$ (Sufficient condition)

So from equation No. (1)

$$\frac{d\Pi}{dq} = -3q^2 + 30q - 72 = 0 \qquad \ldots(2)$$

This is clearly a quadratic equation in q. So to get at the solutions let us divide the above equation by – 3 first to make the equation simple for further manipulation.

i.e.
$$\begin{aligned}q^2 - 10q + 24 &= 0\\ q^2 - 6q - 4q + 24 &= 0\\ q(q-6) - 4(q-6) &= 0\\ (q-6)(q-4) &= 0\end{aligned}$$

i.e. $(q - 6) = 0$ or $q = 6$

$(q - 4) = 0$ or $q = 4$

Now to confirm one among the two results we must go for the sufficient condition. So from equation (2) above

$$\frac{d^2\Pi}{dq^2} = -6q + 30$$

Now
$$\left(\frac{d^2\Pi}{dq^2}\right)_{q=4} = -6 \times 4 + 30 = 6 > 0$$

$$\left(\frac{d^2\Pi}{dq^2}\right)_{q=6} = -6 \times 6 + 30 = -6 < 0$$

Thus, among the two results obtained q = 6 gets confirmed as the equilibrium quantity. Now the equilibrium profit is obtained by merely substituting this equilibrium value of q (q = 6) in the profit equation (1) above.

i.e.
$$\Pi = -q^3 + 15^2 - 72q - 10$$
$$(\Pi)_{q=6} = (-6)^3 + 15 \times 6^2 - 72 \times 6 - 10$$
$$= -216 + 540 - 432 - 10 = -118$$

So under equilibrium

$p = 8$, $q = 6$, and $\Pi = -118$

Example 24: If $C = 0.04q^3 - 0.9q^2 + (11 - k)\,q + 5k^2$ represents the family of short-run cost curves for varying values of the firm size k, obtained the long-run cost function. Also calculate the equilibrium quantity and the profit in the long-run when the competitive price is p = 4.

Solution:

The family of short-run cost functions is given here as

$$C = 0.04q^3 - 0.9q^2 + (11 - k)\,q + 5k^2 \qquad \ldots(1)$$

Now let 'q' stands for the long-run targeted level of output. The appropriate optimum plant size k for the output level q is obtained by equating the partial derivative of C with respect to k to zero.

So
$$\frac{\partial C}{\partial k} = -q + 10k = 0$$
$$10k = q$$
$$k = 0.1q \qquad \ldots(2)$$

Equation (2) above give us the relationship between the long-run output q and the correct size of the plant k. Now the needed long-run cost function is obtained by simply eliminating k from equation (1) using equation (2)

$$C = 0.04q^3 - 0.9q^2 + (11 - 0.1q)\,q + 5(0.1q)^2$$
$$C = 0.04q^3 - 0.9q^2 + 11q - 0.1q^2 + 0.05q^2$$
$$C = 0.04q^3 - 0.95q^2 + 11q \qquad \ldots(3)$$

This is the needed long run cost function. Now by definition

Profit = Revenue - Cost

i.e.
$$\Pi = R - C$$
$$= pq - (0.04q^3 - 0.95q^2 + 11q)$$
$$= 4q - 0.04q^3 + 0.95q^2 - 11q$$
$$= -0.04q^3 + 0.95q^2 - 7q \qquad \ldots(4)$$

Now for the maximum value of Π in (4) above

1. $\frac{d\Pi}{dq} = 0$ (Necessary condition)

2. $\frac{d^2\Pi}{dq^2} < 0$ (Sufficient condition)

So from (4) $\frac{d\Pi}{dq} = -0.12q^2 + 1.9q - 7 = 0$

This is a quadratic equation in q

$$\therefore \quad q = \frac{-b \pm \sqrt{b^2 - 4ac}}{2a}$$

$$q = \frac{-1.9 \pm \sqrt{(-1.9)^2 - 4(-0.12)(-7)}}{-0.24}$$

$$= \frac{-1.9 \pm \sqrt{3.61 - 3.36}}{-0.24}$$

$$= \frac{-1.9 \pm \sqrt{0.25}}{-0.24}$$

$$= \frac{-1.9 \pm 0.5}{-0.24}$$

$$= \frac{-2.4}{-0.24} = 10 \quad \text{or}$$

$$= \frac{-1.4}{-0.24} = 5.833$$

Now to confirm one among the two results we use our second order condition.

$$\left(\frac{d^2\Pi}{dq^2}\right)_{q=10} = -0.24 \times 10 + 1.9$$

$$= -2.4 + 1.9 = -0.5 < 0$$

$$\left(\frac{d^2\Pi}{dq^2}\right)_{q=5.83} = -0.24 \times 5.83 + 1.9$$

$$= -1.4 + 1.9 = 0.5 > 0$$

Thus q =10 gets confirmed as the equilibrium quantity.

The equilibrium profit is obtained by substituting q = 10 in the long-run profit function given in equation (4) above

$$\Pi = -0.04q^3 + 0.95q^2 - 7q$$

$$= -0.04 \times 10^3 + 0.95 \times 10^2 - 7 \times 10$$

$$= -40 + 95 - 70$$

$$= -110 + 95$$

$$= -15$$

Since the long-run profit is –15 (loss of 15) the firm will have to discontinue its production as early as possible to avoid further loss.

Note: When q =10 then from equation (2) above it follows that the size of the firm is k =1. Substituting this value of k in (1) above it becomes $C = 0.04q^3 - 0.9q^2 + 10q + 5$. This is exactly the short-run cost function problem discussed in the previous section with – 15 as the short-run profit.

10.16 Short-run Supply Function

The short-run supply function of a firm is simply the MC function above the minimum AVC. Thus, for all prices equal or above the minimum AVC, thc producer will supply the product to market. For example, if the price is Rs. 22 then the producer will make a positive profit (AR > AC) and hence will supply the product to the market.

For the price 12 since AC = AR the profit will become zero. Since it is short-run once again he will supply the product having the hope of getting a positive profit in the long-run. For the price Rs. 8 since AC >AR >AVC, the whole of the variable cost is covered at this price. However, here the price is enough to cover a part of the fixed cost in addition to the whole of the variable cost. Thus, hc will supply the product to the market though there is a loss. At Rs. 5 the whole of the variable cost is being covered leaving the total fixed cost fully uncovered. The supply will continue even now, because the revenue earned is enough to run the day-to-day business. For all prices below the minimum AVC, for example Rs. 4 the supply will cease, because the revenue receipt at this price is not enough to meet the day-to-day expenses. Thus MC above the minimum AVC represents the short-run supply function of the firm under consideration. The aggregate market supply function is thus obtained by summing all the individual supply functions horizontally.

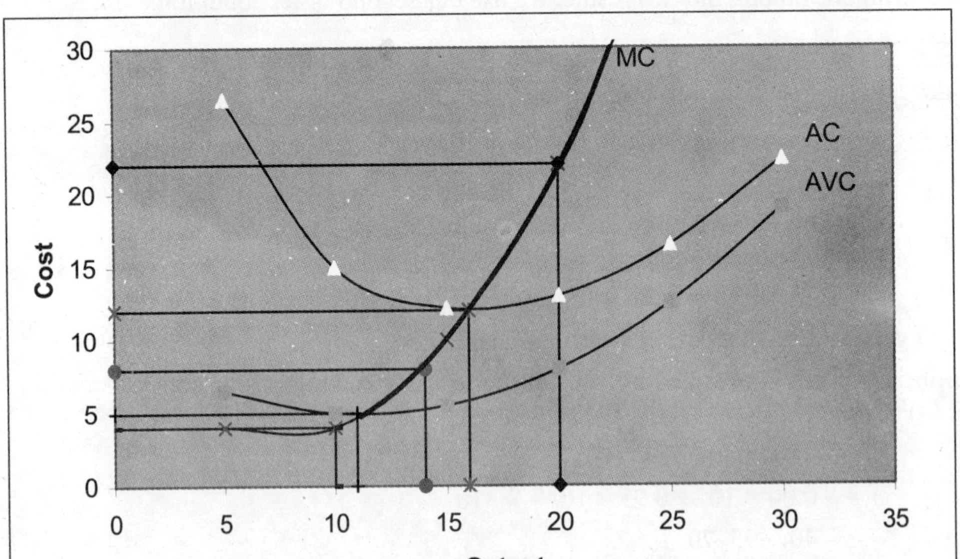

Fig. 10.36

Example 25: The short-run cost function of the representative firm in an industry is $C = 0.04\, q^3 - 0.9q^2 + 10q + 5$. Obtain the aggregate supply function when there are 100 firms in the industry.

Solution:

The short-run cost function of a representative firm is

$$C = 0.04q^3 - 0.9q^2 + 10q + 5 \qquad \ldots(1)$$

Now the supply function is obtained by equating the MC to the price p.

So $\qquad MC = 0.12q^2 - 1.8q + 10 = p$

i.e. $\qquad 0.12q^2 - 1.8q + (10 - p) = 0 \qquad \ldots(2)$

This is a quadratic equation in q

$$q = \frac{-b \pm \sqrt{b^2 - 4ac}}{2a}$$

$$= \frac{-(-1.8) \pm \sqrt{(-1.8)^2 - 4 \times 0.12 \times (10 - p)}}{2 \times 0.12}$$

$$= 1.8 \pm \frac{\sqrt{3.24 - 4.8 + 0.48p}}{0.24}$$

$$= 1.8 \pm \frac{\sqrt{0.48p - 1.56}}{0.24}$$

$$s = 1.8 + \frac{\sqrt{0.48p - 1.56}}{0.24}$$

Now after deleting minus and renaming q as 's' the short run supply function of the representative firm may be written as

$$s = \left[1.8 \pm \frac{\sqrt{0.48p - 1.56}}{0.24}\right]$$

Therefore, the aggregate supply function of the industry is written as

$$S = 100 \times s = 100\left[1.8 \pm \frac{\sqrt{0.48p - 1.56}}{0.24}\right] \qquad \ldots(3)$$

Now by minimizing the AVC function we can identify the relevant portion of the MC above the AVC. So from (1) above $TVC = 0.04q^3 - 0.9q^2 + 10q$

Hence $\qquad AVC = 0.04q^2 - 0.9q + 10 \qquad \ldots(4)$

Now for the minimum value of AVC we know that

(1) $\frac{d}{dq}(AVC) = 0$ Necessary condition

(2) $\frac{d^2}{dq^2}(AVC) > 0$ Sufficient condition

So from (4) above

$$\frac{d}{dq}(AVC) = 0.08q - 0.9 = 0$$

$$= 0.08q = 0.9$$

$$q = \frac{0.9}{0.08} = 11.25$$

Further $\frac{d^2}{dq^2}(AVC) = 0.08 > 0$

Hence AVC is minimum when q = 11.25

Now the actual minimum value of AVC is obtained by substituting this value of q in AVC itself.

$$\begin{aligned} AVC &= 0.04q^2 - 0.9q + 10 \\ &= 0.04(11.25)^2 - 0.9(11.25) + 10 \\ &= 4.9375 \\ &= 5 \end{aligned}$$

Now the complete form of the aggregate supply function is written as

$$S = 100 \times s = 100\left[1.8 \pm \frac{\sqrt{0.48p - 1.56}}{0.24}\right] \quad \text{when} \quad p \geq 5$$

$$S = 0 \quad \text{when} \quad p < 0$$

Figure 10.36 describe the situation graphically.

10.17 Long-run Equilibrium: Equilibrium of an Industry

An industry is nothing but the collection of firms that all produce a homogeneous product. The industry as a whole is said to be in equilibrium provided all the member firms are in equilibrium. The member firms are in equilibrium provided they all earn only the normal profit. If they all earn super normal profits, then under the free entry and free exit assumption new firm will start entering into the industry in order to avail of the situation. Such an entry will continue till the super normal profit of the old and new entrants' ceases. Similarly, if all the existing firms earn less than the normal profit some of the firms will start leaving the industry until all the remaining firms start earning their normal profit once again. Similar to the subsistence wage in the theory of wages here by normal profit we mean a mere profit that is just enough for the firm to be there in the industry. However, since it is customary to include these normal profits into the very cost function, a zero profit in diagrammatic terms always refer a normal profit situation. In the below Fig. 10.37 at OP price all the member firms produce Oq units each and earn only the normal profit. The point of intersection between the demand DD and the supply S, as shown in the right side diagram, determines equilibrium price and the individual firms take this price and determine their level of output. The aggregate supply in this case is simply OQ. By definition OQ = n × OQ. Now let us assume that the demand DD shifts to D'D' as shown in the diagram due to some exogenous reasons.

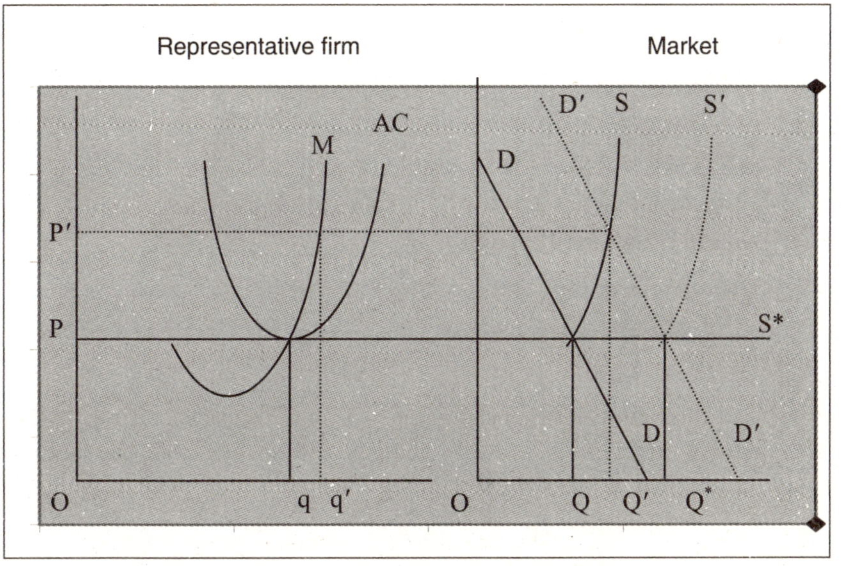

Fig. 10.37

Such a shift will increase the price from OP to OP' immediately in the very short run. At OP' price all the existing firms will start earning super normal profit by supplying Oq' units of output each leading to an increase in the aggregate market supply to OQ'. This inducement will attract new firms into the industry. The new entry will continue till the old and the new firms start earning only the normal profit and supply OQ units each at OP price once again. By this time the short run supply shifts from S to S'. The corresponding aggregate supply to the market is given by OQ^*. In other words, this is equivalent to say that the old customers are taken care of by the old firms and the new firms take care of the new customers. Thus for the long run equilibrium of the industry the appropriate condition would be MR = MC = AC = AR revealing a zero profit situation diagrammatically and a normal profit to all the existing firms.

Example 26: The long-run cost function of a representative firm in an industry is $C = q^3 - 10q^2 + 50q$. Determine the equilibrium price, aggregate quantity supplied and the number of firms in the industry when demand law for the product is $D = 100 - 2p$.

Solution:

The long-run cost function of the representative firm is

$$C = q^3 - 10\,q^2 + 50q \qquad \ldots(1)$$

For long-run equilibrium of the industry as a whole we know that

$$MR = MC = AC = AR \qquad \ldots(2)$$

Now from (1) above $MC = 3q^2 - 20\,q + 50 \qquad \ldots(3)$

$$AC = q^2 - 10\,q + 50 \qquad \ldots(4)$$

So from (2) above MC = AC

i.e. $3q^2 - 20\,q + 50 = q^2 - 10\,q + 50$

$$3q^2 - q^2 - 20\,q + 10q + 50 - 50 = 0$$

$$2q^2 - 10q = 0$$

$$2q(q-5) = 0$$

i.e. $q = 0$ or $q = 5$

Thus when q = 5, MR = MC = AC = AR is satisfied.

Now the actual value of AC = AR = P is obtained by merely substituting this value of q in the AC function given in equation (4) above

$$AC = AR = P = q^2 - 10\,q + 50$$

$$= 5^2 - 10 \times 5 + 50$$

$$= 25$$

Thus when P = 25 all the member firms will supply 5 units each and earn only the normal profit. Now since the demand function is known we can always calculate the equilibrium quantity demanded as well as supplied by merely substituting the equilibrium price in the given demand law.

i.e. $D = 100 - 2p$

$$= 100 - 2\times 25$$

$$= 50$$

Now by definition since $S = n \times s$

$$n = S/s$$

$$= 50/5 = 10$$

Thus under equilibrium S = D = 50

$$s = 5$$

$$P = 25$$

$$n = 10$$

Example 27: The long-run cost function of a firm is $C = q^3 - 8q^2 + 20\,q$. Prove that MC = AC at the minimum point of AC.

Solution:

The long-run cost function of a firm is $C = q^3 - 8q^2 + 20q$

By definition $MC = \dfrac{dC}{dq} = 3q^2 - 16q + 20$ ...(1)

$$AC = q^2 - 8q + 20 \quad ...(2)$$

Now for the minimum value of AC we know that

1. $\dfrac{d}{dq}(AC) = 0$ (Necessary condition)

2. $\frac{d^2}{dq^2}$ (AC) > 0 (Sufficient condition)

So from equation (2) above $\frac{d}{dq}$ (AC) = 2q – 8 = 0 ...(3)

$$2q = 8$$
$$q = 4$$

Further from equation (3) above $\frac{d^2}{dq^2}$ (AC) = 2 > 0

So when q = 4 the function reaches its minimum. The actual minimum is obtained by substituting this value of q in the AC function given in equation No. (2) above.

$$\begin{aligned}(AC)_{q=4} &= q^2 - 8q + 20 \\ &= 4^2 - 8 \times 4 + 20 \\ &= 16 - 32 + 20 \\ &= 4 \qquad ...(4)\end{aligned}$$

Similarly,

$$\begin{aligned}(MC)_{q=4} &= 3 \times 4^2 - 16 \times 4 + 20 \\ &= 48 - 64 + 20 \\ &= 4 \qquad ...(5)\end{aligned}$$

Now from (4) and (5) we confirm that MC = AC = 4 at the minimum point of AC.

10.18 Joint Production

Commodities are often related in production. For such commodities it is not possible to separate the cost of production item-wise. We know only the joint cost of production for all the commodities. Cotton and cotton seeds are jointly produced goods. The farmer can state only the total cost of production for both cotton and cotton seed. Similarly petrol, diesel, tar etc. are jointly produced from crude oil. Hence, in the case of joint production we can not get the item-wise cost of production. Under such conditions the producer will maximize only the joint profit.

Example 28: Under perfect competition, a firm sells two chocolates lines q_1 and q_2 at prices Rs. 12 and Rs. 18 respectively per kg. The joint cost function of the firm $C = 2q_1^2 + 2q_2^2 + q_1 q_2$. Find the equilibrium values of q_1, q_2 and Π.

Solution:

By definition, Profit = R – C

i.e.

$$\begin{aligned}\Pi &= R - C = R_1 + R_2 - C \\ &= p_1q_1 + p_2 q_2 - C \\ \Pi &= 12q_1 + 18q_2 - 2q_1^2 - q_1q_2 - 2q_2^2 \qquad ...(1)\end{aligned}$$

Now for the maximum value of Π we know that

1. $\dfrac{\partial \Pi}{\partial q_1} = 0$; $\dfrac{\partial \Pi}{\partial q_2} = 0$ (Necessary condition)

2. $\dfrac{\partial^2 \Pi}{\partial q_1^2} < 0$; $\dfrac{\partial^2 \Pi}{\partial q_2^2} < 0$ (Sufficient condition)

3. $\dfrac{\partial^2 \Pi}{\partial q_1^2} \times \dfrac{\partial^2 \Pi}{\partial q_2^2} > \left(\dfrac{\partial^2 \Pi}{\partial q_1 \partial q_2}\right)^2$ (Saddle point condition)

1. Necessary condition

Now from equation (1) above

$$\frac{\partial \Pi}{\partial q_1} = 12 - 4q_1 - q_2 = 0$$

i.e. $$12 = 4q_1 + q_2 \qquad \ldots(2)$$

$$\frac{\partial \Pi}{\partial q_2} = 18 - q_1 - 4q_2 = 0$$

i.e. $$18 = q_1 + 4q_2 \qquad \ldots(3)$$

Now in equation (2) and (3) we are having two equations in two unknowns.

$$q_1 = \frac{\begin{vmatrix} 12 & 1 \\ 18 & 4 \end{vmatrix}}{\begin{vmatrix} 4 & 1 \\ 1 & 4 \end{vmatrix}} = \frac{48 - 18}{16 - 1} = \frac{30}{15} = 2$$

$$q_2 = \frac{\begin{vmatrix} 4 & 12 \\ 1 & 18 \end{vmatrix}}{\begin{vmatrix} 4 & 1 \\ 1 & 4 \end{vmatrix}} = \frac{72 - 12}{15} = \frac{60}{15} = 4$$

2. Sufficient condition

$$\frac{\partial^2 \Pi}{\partial q_1^2} = -4 < 0$$

$$\frac{\partial^2 \Pi}{\partial q_2^2} = -4 < 0$$

$$\frac{\partial^2 \Pi}{\partial q_1 \partial q_2} = -1$$

So $$\frac{\partial^2 \Pi}{\partial q_1^{\,2}} \times \frac{\partial^2 \Pi}{\partial q_2^{\,2}} > \left(\frac{\partial^2 \Pi}{\partial q_1 \partial q_2}\right)^2$$

i.e. $(-4)(-4) > (-1)^2$ i.e. $16 > 1$

Thus $q_1 = 2$ and $q_2 = 4$ get confirmed as the equilibrium quantities.

The equilibrium profit is obtained by merely substituting these equilibrium values in the profit function given in equation (1) above.

i.e., $$\Pi = 12q_1 + 18q_2 - 2q_1^{\,2} - q_1q_2 - 2q_2^{\,2} \qquad \ldots(1)$$
$$= (12 \times 2) + (18 \times 4) - (2 \times 2^2) - (2 \times 4) - (2 \times 4^2)$$
$$= 24 + 72 - 8 - 8 - 32$$
$$= 96 - 48 = 48$$

So under equilibrium $q_1 = 2$; $q_2 = 4$; $\Pi = 48$

EXERCISES

1. The shor-trun cost function of the firm is $C = 0.04q^3 - 0.9q^2 + 10q + 5$. Given the competitive price p = Rs. 10, obtain the equilibrium quantity q and the equilibrium profit Π.
2. A firm has the short-run cost function $C = q^3 - 12q^2 + 50q + 100$. Determine the equilibrium output q and the profit Π given the competitive price for the product p = Rs. 5.
3. The short-run cost function of a firm is $C = q^3 - 15q^2 + 80q + 10$. Calculate the equilibrium quantity q and the maximum profit Π when the competitive price for the product is given by p = Rs. 6 per unit.
4. A firm has the short-run cost function $C = q^3 - 12q^2 + 50q + 100$. Derive the supply curve. At what price will 50 tons are produced?
5. A manufacturing concern has the short-run total cost $C = q^2 + 5q + 200$. What is the supply curve of the firm? At what price will 100 tons are produced?
6. The family of short-run cost functions are given by $C = q^3 - 15q^2 + (10 - k)\,q + 10k^2$ for varying values of the firm size k. Obtained the long-run cost function. Also calculate the equilibrium quantity and the profit in the long-run when the competitive price p = Rs. 6.
7. The long-run cost function of a representative firm in an industry is $C = q^3 - 4q^2 + 4q$. Calculate the equilibrium price, aggregate quantity supplied as well as demanded and the number of firms in the industry when demand law for the product is $D = 1000 - 20p$.
8. Under joint production, a perfect competitive firm sells two products q_1 and q_2 at prices Rs. 20 and Rs. 25 respectively per kg. The joint cost function of the firm is $C = 4q_1^{\,2} + 2q_2^{\,2} + 4\,q_1 q_2$. Find the equilibrium values of q_1, q_2 and Π.

THEORY OF IMPERFECT COMPETITION

10.19 Monopoly

Monopolist by definition is a price maker. However, if he wants to sell a larger output then he will have to reduce the price of the product concerned. Hence the demand function under monopoly slopes downwards as shown in the Fig. 10.38. The corresponding MR function also slopes downwards and lies completely below the AR function. In particular, if the AR is linear, then the slope of MR is twice the slope of AR. Further MR meets the x-axis at the mid point.

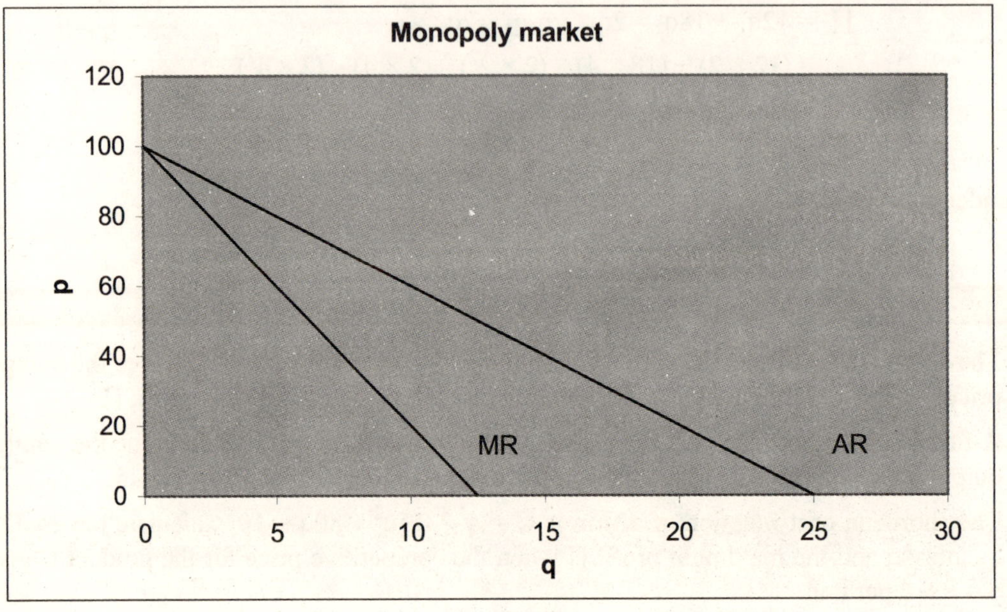

Fig. 10.38

Example 29: A monopolist is facing a linear demand $p = 100 - 4q$. His linear cost function is given by $C = 50 + 20q$. Calculate the equilibrium price, equilibrium quantity, and the maximum profit.

Solution:

Since the under equilibrium the monopolists profit is maximum let us write the profit function first.

By definition, Profit = Revenue – Cost

i.e.
$$\begin{aligned}\Pi &= R - C \\ &= pq - C \\ &= (100 - 4q)\, q - (50 + 20q) \\ &= 100q - 4q^2 - 50 - 20q \\ &= -4q^2 + 80q - 50 \qquad \ldots(1)\end{aligned}$$

Now in equation (1) Π is a function of the output q. Hence for the maximum value of Π we know that

1. $\frac{d\Pi}{dq} = 0$ (Necessary condition)

2. $\frac{d^2\Pi}{dq^2} < 0$ (Sufficient condition)

So from (1) $$\frac{d\Pi}{dq} = 80 - 8q = 0 \quad \text{...(2)}$$

i.e. $$-8q = -80$$

Therefore $$q = -(80)/-8$$
$$= 10$$

Now to confirm this result let us go back to our second order condition.

From equation (2) above $\frac{d^2\Pi}{dq^2} = -8 < 0$

Hence the monopolist maximizes the profit when the output q = 10. Now the equilibrium price is obtained by merely substituting this value of q in the demand law given.

i.e. $$p = 100 - 4q$$
$$p = 100 - 4 \times 10$$
$$p = 60$$

Similarly, the equilibrium profit is obtained by substituting q = 10 in the profit function given in equation (1).

$$\Pi = -4q^2 + 80q - 50 \quad \text{...(1)}$$
$$= -4 \times 10 \times 10 + 80 \times 10 - 50$$
$$= -400 + 800 - 50$$
$$= 350$$

Thus under equilibrium p = 60; q = 10; and $\Pi = 350$.

Diagrammatic solution: In the Fig. 10.39 we show the equilibrium by using total revenue and the total cost. In Fig. 10.40, we use MR = MC condition to get the equilibrium.

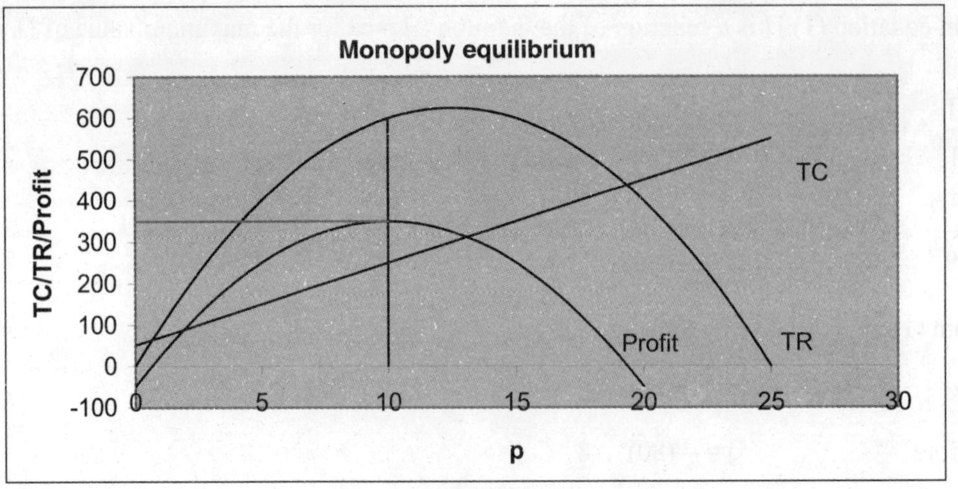

Fig. 10.39

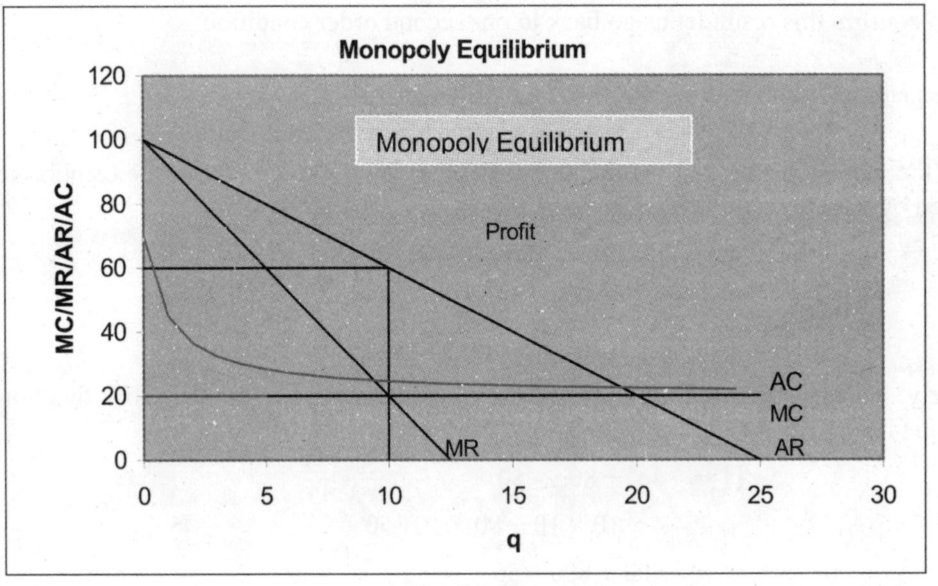

Fig. 10.40

Effect of Taxation on Monopoly: Tax either can be specific or advaloram. A specific tax is a tax levied as a fixed sum per unit of the output irrespective of the attributes like brand, price, size etc.

An advaloram tax on the other hand is a tax levied as a percentage of the value of the commodity irrespective of other attributes.

Example 30: In example 29 above when a specific tax of 8 per unit is levied on the monopoly output find the new equilibrium values.

Solution:

Effect of a Specific Tax

Now after taxation

$$\Pi = R - C - T$$

$$= pq - C - tq$$
$$= (100 - 4q)\,q - (50 + 20q) - 8q.$$
$$= 100q - 4q^2 - 50 - 20q - 8q$$
$$= 72q - 4q^2 - 50 \qquad ...(1)$$

Now in equation (1) Π is a function of q. Hence for the maximum value of Π we know that

1. $\dfrac{d\Pi}{dq} = 0$ (Necessary condition)

2. $\dfrac{d^2\Pi}{dq^2} < 0$ (Sufficient condition)

$$\frac{d\Pi}{dq} = 72 - 8q = 0$$
$$-8q = -72$$
$$q = 9$$

Further $\dfrac{d^2\Pi}{dq^2} = -8 < 0$

Thus q = 9 gets confirmed as the equilibrium output.

Now the equilibrium price

$$p = 100 - 4q$$
$$= 100 - 4 \times 9$$
$$= 100 - 36$$
$$= 64.$$

Similarly,

$$\Pi = 72\,q - 4q^2 - 50$$
$$= 72 \times 9 - 4 \times 9^2 - 50$$
$$= 648 - 324 - 50$$
$$= 274.$$
$$T = tq = 8 \times 9 = 72$$

Thus after the specific tax; $q = 9$, $p = 64$, $\Pi = 274$, $T = 72$ are the equilibrium values.

Example 31: If the monopolist in example 1 above is levied a lump sum tax by an amount equivalent to the specific tax collection in example 2 above, calculate the new equilibrium values. Hence prove that the lump sum tax is preferable both from consumer and producer points of view.

Solution:

Effect of a lump sum tax

By definition

$$\Pi = R - C - T$$
$$= (100 - 4q)q - (50 + 20q) - 72$$
$$= 100q - 4q^2 - 50 - 20q - 72$$
$$\Pi = 80q - 4q^2 - 122 \qquad ...(1)$$

Now in equation (1) Π is a function of q. Hence for the maximum value of Π we know that

1. $\frac{d\Pi}{dq} = 0$ (Necessary condition)

2. $\frac{d^2\Pi}{dq^2} < 0$ (Sufficient condition)

$$\frac{d\Pi}{dq} = 80 - 8q = 0$$

$$-8q = -80$$

$$q = 10$$

$$\frac{d^2\Pi}{dq^2} = -8 < 0$$

So

$$\begin{aligned} p &= 100 - 4q \\ &= 100 - 4 \times 10 \\ &= 60 \\ \Pi &= 80q - 4q^2 - 122 \\ &= 80 \times 10 - 4 \times 10^2 - 122 \\ &= 800 - 400 - 122 \\ &= 278. \end{aligned}$$

Table 10.7

	q	p	Π	T
Monopoly	10	60	350	-
A. L. Tax	10	60	278	72
A. S. Tax	9	64	274	72

From the table it is clear that the lump sum tax is preferable than the specific tax because under lump sum tax the consumer pay only Rs. 60 per unit. Similarly it is again preferable from producer's point of view also because the profit after the lump sum tax is larger by Rs. 4.

Optimum tax rate

Example 32: For the monopoly in example 1 above if a specific tax of 't' per unit is levied on the monopoly output find the equilibrium output in terms of the specific tax rate 't'. What tax rate do you suggest for maximum total collection?

Solution:

Effect of specific tax at 't' rate

Now by definition

$$\begin{aligned} \Pi &= R - C - T \\ &= pq - C - tq \\ &= (100 - 4q)q - (50 + 20q) - tq \\ &= 100q - 4q^2 - 50 - 20q - tq \\ &= 80\,q - 4q^2 - 50 - tq \qquad \text{...(1)} \end{aligned}$$

Now in equation (1) Π is a function of q. Hence for the maximum value of Π we know that

1. $\dfrac{d\Pi}{dq} = 0$ (Necessary condition)

2. $\dfrac{d^2\Pi}{dq^2} < 0$ (Sufficient condition)

$$\frac{d\Pi}{dq} = 80 - 8q - t = 0$$

$$-8q = -80 + t$$

$$q = 10 - 0.125\,t$$

$$\frac{d^2\Pi}{dq^2} = -8 < 0$$

Thus q = 10 – 0.125 t gets confirmed as the equilibrium quantity.

Hence p = 100 – 4 (0.125t)

= 100 – 0.5t

Now by definition T = tq

$$= t\,(10 - 0.125t)$$

$$= 10\,t - 0.125t^2$$

So for the maximum value of T we know that

1. $\dfrac{dT}{dt} = 0$ Necessary condition

2. $\dfrac{d^2T}{dt^2} < 0$ Sufficient condition

$$\frac{dT}{dt} = 10 - 0.25t = 0$$

$$-0.25t = -10$$

$$t = 40$$

$$\frac{d^2T}{dt^2} = -0.25 < 0$$

Thus t = 40 maximizes the total tax collection in this case

So $T = 10t - 0.125t^2$

$$= 10 \times 40 - 0.125 \times 40^2$$

$$= 400 - 200$$

$$= 200$$

Thus t = 40 is the optimum tax rate and T = 200 is the associated maximum collection.

10.20 Discriminating Monopolist

Monopolist often finds it more profitable by discriminating his customers. For this purpose he divides the market into many more sub-markets on the basis of price elasticities. After having done this successfully he will charge more price in the less elastic market and less price in more elastic market. By doing so his monopoly profit gets improved further.

Example 33:

(a) Given two isolated markets supplied by a single monopolist, let the corresponding demand functions be $p_1 = 12 - q_1$, $p_2 = 20 - q_2$. The monopolist's cost function is $C = 3 + 2q$ where $q = q_1 + q_2$. What will be prices and sales in the two markets under a regime of price discrimination?

(b) Also obtain the price elasticities for both the markets and prove that the monopolist will charge a low price in the high elastic market and high price in the low elastic market.

(c) If the monopolist is not in a position to discriminate calculate the simple monopoly output, price and the maximum profit.

Solution:

(a) By definition, Profit = Revenue – Cost

i.e.

$$\begin{aligned} \Pi &= R - C \\ &= R_1 + R_2 - C \\ &= p_1q_1 + p_2q_2 - C \\ &= (12 - q_1)\, q_1 + (20 - q_2)q_2 - [(3 + 2(q_1 + q_2)] \\ &= 12q_1 - q_1^2 + 20q_2 - q_2^2 - 3 - 2q_1 - 2q_2 \\ &= 10q_1 - q_1^2 + 18q_2 - q_2^2 - 3 \end{aligned} \qquad \ldots(1)$$

Now for the maximum value of Π in (1) above we know that

1. $\dfrac{\partial \Pi}{\partial q_1} = 0$; $\dfrac{\partial \Pi}{\partial q_2} = 0$ (Necessary condition)

2. $\dfrac{\partial^2 \Pi}{\partial q_1^2} < 0$; $\dfrac{\partial^2 \Pi}{\partial q_2^2} < 0$ (Sufficient condition)

3. $\dfrac{\partial^2 \Pi}{\partial q_1^2} \times \dfrac{\partial^2 \Pi}{\partial q_2^2} > \left(\dfrac{\partial^2 \Pi}{\partial q_1 \partial q_2}\right)^2$ (Saddle point condition)

So from (1) above

$$\frac{\partial \Pi}{\partial q_1} = 10 - 2q_1 = 0$$

$$-2q_1 = -10$$

$$q_1 = 5$$

$$\frac{\partial \Pi}{\partial q_2} = 18 - 2q_2 = 0$$

$$-2q_2 = -18$$

$$q_2 = 9$$

$$\frac{\partial^2 \Pi}{\partial q_1^2} = -2 < 0 \;;\; \frac{\partial^2 \Pi}{\partial q_2^2} = -2 < 0$$

$$\left(\frac{\partial^2 \Pi}{\partial q_1 \partial q_2}\right)^2 = 0$$

$$\frac{\partial^2 \Pi}{\partial q_1^2} \times \frac{\partial^2 \Pi}{\partial q_2^2} > \left(\frac{\partial^2 \Pi}{\partial q_1 \partial q_2}\right)^2$$

$$-2 \times -2 > 0$$

$$4 > 0$$

Thus $q_1 = 5$ and $q_2 = 9$ get confirmed as the equilibrium quantities.

Now the equilibrium prices are obtained by merely substituting these values in the given demand equations.

Thus $p_1 = 12 - 5 = 7$, $p_2 = 20 - 9 = 11$

Similarly the equilibrium profit is obtained by substituting these values in the profit function given in equation (1)

$$\Pi = 10q_1 - q_1^2 + 18q_2 - q_2^2 - 3$$

$$= 10 \times 5 - 5^2 + 18 \times 9 - 9^2 - 3$$

$$= 50 - 25 + 162 - 81 - 3$$

$$= 103$$

(b) Elasticity for the first market: $q_1 = 12 - p_1$

So by definition

$$\eta_1 = -\frac{Eq_1}{Ep_1} = -\frac{E(12 - p_1)}{Ep_1} = -\frac{p_1}{12 - p_1}\frac{d(12 - p_1)}{dp_1}$$

$$= \frac{p_1}{12 - p_1}$$

$$\frac{7}{12 - 7} = \frac{7}{5} = 1.4$$

Elasticity for the second market: $q_2 = 20 - p_2$

$$\eta_2 = -\frac{Eq_2}{Ep_2} = -\frac{E(20 - p_2)}{Ep_2} = -\frac{p_2}{20 - p_2}\frac{d(20 - p_2)}{dp_2}$$

$$= \frac{p_2}{20 - p_2}$$

$$= \frac{11}{20\text{-}11} = \frac{11}{9} = 1.22$$

So $\quad \eta_1 = 1.4; \quad p_1 = 7$

$\quad \eta_2 = 1.22; \quad p_2 = 11$

Thus the monopolist is charging low price in high elastic and high price in low elastic market.

(c) If the monopolist is not in a position to discriminate then the prices in both the markets must be equal to one another

So $\quad p_1 = p_2 = p$ (say)

Now from the first market

$$p_1 = 12 - q_1$$

$$q_1 = 12 - p \; (p_1 = p)$$

Similarly from the second market

$$p_2 = 20 - q_1$$

$$q_2 = 20 - p \;\; (p_2 = p)$$

So the aggregate market $q = q_1 + q_2$

$$q = 12 - p + 20 - p$$

$$q = 32 - 2p$$

$$2p = 32 - q$$

$$p = 16 - 0.5q$$

Now $\quad \Pi = R - C$

$$= pq - C$$

$$= (16 - 0.5q)\, q - (3 + 2q)$$

$$= 16q - 0.5q^2 - 3 - 2q$$

$$= 14q - 0.5q^2 - 3 \quad \ldots(1)$$

Now for the maximum value of Π in (1) above we know that

(1) $\frac{d\Pi}{dq} = 0$ Necessary condition

(2) $\frac{d^2\Pi}{dq^2} < 0$ Sufficient condition

$$\frac{d\Pi}{dq} = 14 - q = 0$$

$$q = 14$$

$$\frac{d^2\Pi}{dq^2} = -1 < 0$$

Thus q = 14 is the simple monopolist output

The equilibrium price is obtained by substituting this value of q in the demand law

$$p = 16 - 0.5q$$
$$= 16 - 0.5 \times 14$$
$$p = 16 - 7 = 9$$

Similarly $\Pi = 14q - 0.5q^2 - 3$

$$\Pi = 14 \times 14 - 0.5 \times 14^2 - 3$$
$$\Pi = 196 - 98 - 3 = 95$$

Thus under equilibrium q = 14, p = 9, Π = 95.

10.21 Multi-Product Monopolist

A multi-product monopolist is one who produces a variety of products jointly using a single plant. Such commodities are called joint products. Under such circumstances the monopolist will be interested in the total profit irrespective of the number of units of the individual items. Under equilibrium the marginal revenues from each item must be equal to the combined marginal cost.

Example 34: A multi-product monopolist produces two commodities, which are technically related in production. The joint cost function of the firm is $C = q_1^2 + 2q_1q_2 + q_2^2$. Find the equilibrium values of q_1, q_2, p_1, p_2 and the profit Π. The demand laws of the products are $p_1 = 10 - q_1$ and $p_2 = 20 - 2q_2$.

Solution:

(a) By definition, Profit = Revenue – Cost

i.e. $\Pi = R - C$

$$= R_1 + R_2 - C$$
$$= p_1q_1 + p_2q_2 - C$$
$$= (10 - q_1)\, q_1 + (20 - 2q_2)\, q_2 - (q_1^2 + 2q_1q_2 + q_2^2)$$
$$= 10q_1 - q_1^2 + 20q_2 - 2q_2^2 - q_1^2 - 2q_1q_2 - q_2^2$$
$$= 10q_1 - 2q_1^2 + 20q_2 - 3q_2^2 - 2q_1q_2 \qquad \ldots(1)$$

Now for the maximum value of Π in (1) above we know that

1. $\dfrac{\partial \Pi}{\partial q_1} = 0;\quad \dfrac{\partial \Pi}{\partial q_2} = 0$ (Necessary condition)

2. $\dfrac{\partial^2 \Pi}{\partial q_1^2} < 0;\quad \dfrac{\partial^2 \Pi}{\partial q_2^2} < 0$ (Sufficient conditions)

3. $\dfrac{\partial^2 \Pi}{\partial q_1^2} \times \dfrac{\partial^2 \Pi}{\partial q_2^2} > \left(\dfrac{\partial^2 \Pi}{\partial q_1 \partial q_2}\right)^2$ (Saddle point condition)

So from (1) above

$$\frac{\partial \Pi}{\partial q_1} = 10 - 4q_1 - 2q_2 = 0$$

So $10 = 4q_1 + 2q_2$ ...(2)

$$\frac{\partial \Pi}{\partial q_2} = 20 - 6q_2 - 2q_1 = 0$$

So $20 = 2q_1 + 6q_2$ ...(3)

Now from (2) and (3) as per Cramer's rule

$$q_1 = \frac{\begin{vmatrix} 10 & 2 \\ 20 & 6 \end{vmatrix}}{\begin{vmatrix} 4 & 2 \\ 2 & 6 \end{vmatrix}} = \frac{60-40}{24-4} = \frac{20}{20} = 1$$

$$q_2 = \frac{\begin{vmatrix} 4 & 10 \\ 2 & 20 \end{vmatrix}}{\begin{vmatrix} 4 & 2 \\ 2 & 6 \end{vmatrix}} = \frac{80-20}{20-4} = \frac{60}{20} = 3$$

$$\frac{\partial^2 \Pi}{\partial q_1} = -4 < 0 \;;\; \frac{\partial^2 \Pi}{\partial q_2{}^2} = -6 < 0$$

$$\left(\frac{\partial^2 \Pi}{\partial q_1 \partial q_2}\right)^2 = -2$$

$$\frac{\partial^2 \Pi}{\partial q_1{}^2} \times \frac{\partial^2 \Pi}{\partial q_2{}^2} > \left(\frac{\partial^2 \Pi}{\partial q_1 \partial q_2}\right)^2$$

$$-4 \times -6 > (-2)^2$$

$$24 > 4$$

Thus $q_1 = 1$ and $q_2 = 3$ gets confirmed as the equilibrium values. Now the equilibrium prices and the maximum profit are obtained by substituting these values in the respective functions.

$$\begin{aligned} p_1 &= 10 - q_1 \\ &= 10 - 1 \\ &= 9 \\ p_2 &= 20 - 2q_2 \\ &= 20 - 2 \times 3 \\ &= 14 \end{aligned}$$

Similarly,

$$\begin{aligned} \Pi &= 10q_1 - 2q_1{}^2 + 20q_2 - 3q_2{}^2 - 2q_1q_2 \\ &= 10 \times 1 - 2 \times 1^2 + 20 \times 3 - 3 \times 3^2 - 2 \times 1 \times 3 \\ &= 10 - 2 + 60 - 27 - 6 \\ &= 70 - 35 \\ &= 35. \end{aligned}$$

Thus under equilibrium; $q_1 = 1$, $q_2 = 3$, $p_1 = 9$, $p_2 = 14$, $\Pi = 35$.

10.22 Baumol's Sales Maximization

In a firm not only the share holders, managers, employees but also the consumers of the product, society in general and government in particular normally will have their claims with special interest of their own. The group interest of all these units often proved to be conflicting to each other. The neo-classical theory however treats all these units as single entity and advocates its common goal of profit maximization. In actual practice, especially in the case of large corporations there is a split between the shareholding owners and the managers in particular, as far as their goals are concerned. According to W.J Baumol, managers get salaries plus other allowances, power and prestige. They would like to maximize the sale and hence the total revenue rather than the profit. Thus the typical oligopolist objective accordingly would be the sale maximization subject a certain minimum profit constraint for the sake of shareholders.

Example 35: For the monopoly problem given in example 1 above obtain the Baumol's sale maximizing output, price and the profit.

Solution:

Baumol's revenue or sale maximizing

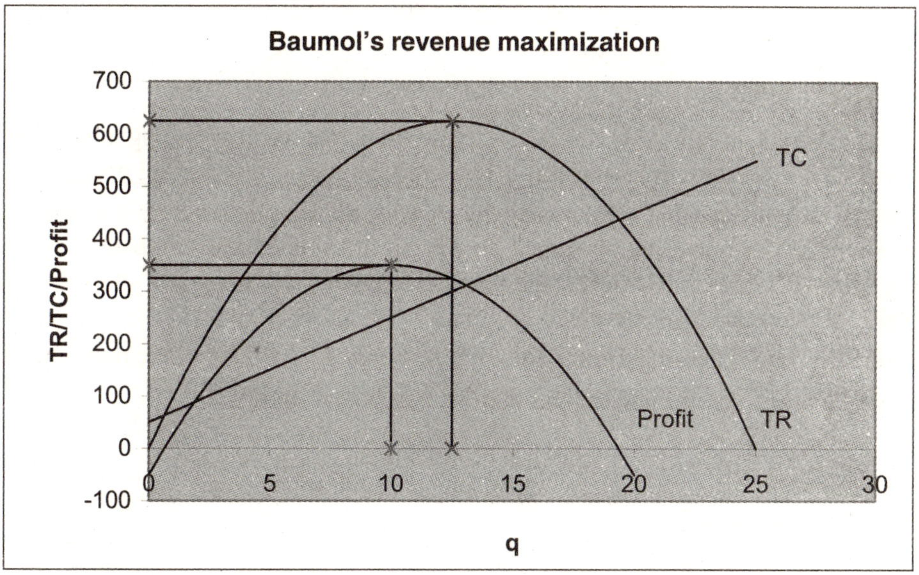

Fig. 10.41

By definition $R = pq$

$$= (100 - 4q)q$$

$$= 100q - 4q^2 \quad \ldots(1)$$

Now in equation (1) R is a function of q, hence for the maximum value of Π we know that

1. $\dfrac{dR}{dq} = 0$ (Necessary condition)

2. $\frac{d^2R}{dq^2} < 0$ (Sufficient condition)

So from (1) $\frac{dR}{dq} = 100 - 8q = 0$

$$-8q = -100$$

$$q = 12.5$$

Further, $\frac{d^2R}{dq^2} = -8 < 0$

Thus q = 12.5 gets confirmed as the revenue maximizing output.

Now the maximum revenue is obtained by simply substituting this equilibrium output in the revenue function given in equilibrium (1) above

$$R = 100 \times 12.5 - 4 \times 12.5^2$$

$$= 1250 - 625 = 625$$

The associated revenue maximizing profit is obtained as

$$\Pi = -4q^2 + 80q - 50$$

$$= -4 \times 12.5 \times 12.5 + 80 \times 12.5 - 50$$

$$= -625 + 1000 - 50$$

$$= 325$$

Note that the revenue maximizing output is more than the corresponding profit maximizing output. Also the revenue maximizing profit is less than the profit maximizing profit.

Example 36: A famous novelist wants a royalty of 15% on the sale revenue and insists the price fixation that maximizes the total revenue. However, the publishing company is interested in mâximizing the profit. If $R = 10{,}000Q - 10Q^2$ and $C = 1000 + 2500Q + 5Q^2$ are the total revenue and the total cost functions respectively

(a) Determine the output that maximizes the total revenue. Also obtained the maximum royalty.

(b) Calculate the profit maximizing output and the associated royalty.

Solution:

Revenue maximization

The total revenue function is

$$R = 10{,}000Q - 10Q^2$$

Now for the maximum value of R in (1) above we know that

1. $\frac{dR}{dQ} = 0$ Necessary condition

2. $\frac{d^2R}{dR^2} < 0$ Sufficient condition

So from (1) above

$$\frac{dR}{dQ} = 10,000 - 20Q = 0$$

$$-20Q = -10,000$$

$$Q = 500$$

Further $\frac{d^2R}{dR^2} = -20 < 0$

Thus when Q = 500 gets confirmed as the revenue maximizing output.

Now the maximum revenue is obtained by substituting this equilibrium output in the revenue function given in (1) above

$$R = 10,000Q - 10Q^2 = 10,000 \times 500 - 10 \times 500^2 = \text{Rs. } 25,00,000$$

The maximum royalty that the novelist can get

$$\text{Royalty} = R \times \frac{15}{100} = 25,00,000 \times \frac{15}{100} = \text{Rs. } 3,75,000$$

Profit maximization

By definition

Profit = Revenue – Cost

$$\Pi = R - C$$
$$= 10,000Q - 10Q^2 - (1000 + 2500Q + 5Q^2)$$
$$= 10000Q - 10Q^2 - 1000 - 2500Q - 5Q^2$$
$$= -15Q^2 + 7500Q - 1000 \quad \text{...(1)}$$

Now for the maximum value of Π in (1) above we know that

3. $\frac{d\Pi}{dq} = 0$ Necessary condition

4. $\frac{d^2\Pi}{dq^2} < 0$ Sufficient condition

$$\frac{d\Pi}{dq} = -30Q + 75000 = 0$$

So $-30Q = -75000$

$$Q = 2500$$

$$\frac{d^2\Pi}{dq^2} = -30 < 0$$

Thus Q = 2500 gets confirmed as the profit maximizing output

So $R = 10,000Q - 10Q^2 = 10,000 \times 300 - 10 \times 300^2 = \text{Rs. } 21,00,000$

$$\text{Royalty} = R \times \frac{15}{100} = 21,00,000 \times \frac{15}{100} = \text{Rs. } 3,15,000$$

10.23 Duopoly

Duopoly is a special market situation in which two producers, with the plants of their own supply a homogeneous product to a common market at a single common price. Here we come-across a variety of equilibrium situations depending upon the type of behaviouristic pattern that is being assumed among the two participating duopolists.

1. **Cournot solution:** In the Cournot model, because of the interdependency, the profit functions of each duopolist not only depends upon his own output but also the level of output of his rival.

i.e. $$\Pi_1 = f(q_1, q_2)$$
$$\Pi_2 = g\,(q_1, q_2)$$

However, the first duopolist assumes the second duopolist as his business leader and decides not to intertwine. So he treats his boss's output as uninfluensable and hence constant. As a last resort he maximizes his profit Π_1 with respect to his output q_1 after treating q_2 as constant. In other words this is to say that

$$\frac{\partial \Pi_1}{\partial q_1} = 0 \qquad \ldots(1)$$

This equation gives the level of output that the first duopolist is suppose to produce for any given output level of the second. This is called the reaction function of the first duopolist. In a similar fashion the second duopolist consider the first duopolist as his business leader and maximizes his profit Π_2 with respect to his output q_2 after treating q_1 as constant. In other words this is to say that

$$\frac{\partial \Pi_2}{\partial q_2} = 0 \qquad \ldots(2)$$

This equation gives the level of output that the second duopolist is suppose to produce for any given output level of the first. This gives the reaction function of the second duopolist. Ultimately the Cournot solution is obtained by solving these two reaction functions simultaneously.

2. **Collusion solution:** Under Collusion the colluding duopolists after making a collusive agreement maximize the joint profit function. Such an objective function is obtained by merely adding their individual duopoly profit functions.

3. **Stackelberg solution:** Stackelberg model is based on leadership and followership behaviours of the participating duopolists. The profit functions of both the duopolists are interdependent. By this we mean that the profit function of the first duopolist is a function of the level of output of his rival as well in addition to his own output. Similarly the profit function of the second duopolist is a function of the level of output of his rival also in addition to his own output. So

$$\Pi_1 = f\,(q_1, q_2)$$
$$\Pi_2 = g\,(q_1, q_2)$$

(i) **Definition of a leader:** A leader by definition does not go by his own reaction function. Instead he assumes himself as the business leader and uses the reaction function of his rival to eliminate his rival's output from his own profit function. After such elimination he maximizes his profit with respect to his output in the usual manner by following both the first and the second order conditions. For example if the first duopolist wants to be a leader then he uses the reaction function of the second duopolist and eliminates q_2 in Π_1. After such elimination Π_1 becomes a function of q_1 alone. Now Π_1 is maximized in the usual manner.

(ii) Definition of a follower: A follower by definition accepts the leadership of his rival. Accordingly, he takes the leadership output as uninfluensable. So he substitutes this leadership output into his own reaction function and calculates the residual leftover for his own production. Thus here the question optimization does not arise. Once such a leftover is obtained he readily calculates his level of profit. In particular for example if the first duopolist wants to be a mere follower then he simply substitutes the leadership output of the second into his own reaction function and calculates the leftover q_1. Once this is done he substitutes both q_1 and q_2 and gets his own residual leftover profit.

Example 37: Two duopolists draw q_1 and q_2 quantities of a certain mineral water from a common spring. The demand law for the spring water is $p = 1200 - 20q$ (where $q = q_1 + q_2$) under equilibrium show that the water will be drawn equally when the cost of production is nil for both. If a single monopolist were to supply the water by himself at zero cost of production, show that the monopolist will restrict the outflow and charge a higher price that too for a larger total profit.

Solution:

Duopoly solution:

Profit maximization of the first duopolist

By definition

$$\begin{aligned}\Pi_1 &= R_1 - C_1 \\ &= pq_1 - C_1 \\ &= [1200 - 20(q_1 + q_2)]\, q_1 - 0 \\ &= 1200q_1 - 20\, q_1^2 - 20\, q_1q_2 \qquad \text{...(1)}\end{aligned}$$

Now according to Cournot we know that

$$\frac{\partial \Pi_1}{\partial q_1} = 0$$

$$\frac{\partial^2 \Pi_1}{\partial q_1^2} < 0$$

So from (1) above

$$\frac{\partial \Pi_1}{\partial q_1} = 1200 - 40q_1 - 20q_2 = 0$$

i.e. $$1200 = 40q_1 + 20q_2 \qquad \text{...(2)}$$

$$q_1 = 30 - 0.5q_2 \qquad \text{...(3)}$$

This is the reaction function of the first duopolist.

$$\frac{\partial^2 \Pi_1}{\partial q_1^2} = -40 < 0$$

Profit maximization of the second duopolist

Similarly

$$\Pi_2 = R_2 - C_2$$
$$= pq_2 - C_2$$
$$= [1200 - 20(q_1 + q_2)]\, q_2 - 0$$
$$= 1200q_2 - 20\, q_2^2 - 20\, q_1q_2 \qquad \ldots(4)$$

Now according to Cournot we know that

$$\frac{\partial \Pi_2}{\partial q_2} = 0$$

$$\frac{\partial^2 \Pi_2}{\partial q_2^2} < 0$$

So from (4) above

$$\frac{\partial \Pi_2}{\partial q_2} = 1200 - 20q_1 - 40q_2 = 0$$

i.e. $$1200 = 20q_1 + 40q_2 \qquad \ldots(5)$$

$$q_2 = 30 - 0.5q_1 \qquad \ldots(6)$$

This is the reaction function of the second duopolist.

Now from (2) and (5) as per Cramer's rule

$$q_1 = \frac{\begin{vmatrix} 1200 & 20 \\ 1200 & 40 \end{vmatrix}}{\begin{vmatrix} 40 & 20 \\ 20 & 40 \end{vmatrix}} = \frac{48000 - 24000}{1600 - 400} = \frac{24000}{1200} = 20$$

$$q_2 = \frac{\begin{vmatrix} 40 & 1200 \\ 20 & 1200 \end{vmatrix}}{\begin{vmatrix} 40 & 20 \\ 20 & 40 \end{vmatrix}} = \frac{48000 - 24000}{1600 - 400} = \frac{24000}{1200} = 20$$

Thus the deposits share 20 units each under equilibrium.

Now $$p = 1200 - 20(q_1 + q_2)$$
$$= 1200 - 20 \times 40$$
$$= 1200 - 800$$
$$= 400$$

$$\Pi_1 = 1200q_1 - 20q_1^2 - 20q_1q_2$$
$$= 1200 \times 20 - 20 \times 20^2 - 20 \times 20 \times 20$$
$$= 24000 - 8000 - 8000$$
$$= 8000$$

$$\Pi_1 = 1200q_2 - 20\,q_2^2 - 20\,q_1q_2$$
$$= 1200 \times 20 - 20 \times 20^2 - 20 \times 20 \times 20$$
$$= 24000 - 8000 - 8000$$
$$= 8000$$

Monopoly solution:

If a single monopolist is to supply the water by himself then

$$\Pi = R - C$$
$$= pq - C$$
$$= (1200 - 20q)q - 0$$
$$= 1200q - 20q^2 \qquad ...(1)$$

Now for the maximum value of Π we know that

1. $\dfrac{d\Pi}{dq} = 0$
2. $\dfrac{d^2\Pi}{dq^2} < 0$

$$\frac{d\Pi}{dq} = 1200 - 40q = 0$$
$$-40q = -1200$$
$$q = 30$$
$$\frac{d^2\Pi}{dq^2} = -40 < 0$$

Thus q = 30 is the simple monopolist output.

Now $p = 1200 - 20q$
$$= 1200 - 20 \times 30$$
$$= 600$$
$$\Pi = 1200q - 20q^2$$
$$= 1200 \times 30 - 20 \times 30^2$$
$$= 36000 - 18000$$
$$= 18000$$

Table 10.8

	q_1	q_2	Q	Π_1	Π_2	Π	p
Duopoly	20	20	40	8000	8000	16000	400
Monopoly	-	-	30	-	-	18000	600

From the table given above it is very much clear that the monopoly restricts the water, and charge more price that too for a larger total profit.

Example 38: Two duopolists produce q_1 and q_2 quantities of a homogeneous product q. The market demand for the product is given by $p = 100 - 0.5q$, where $q = q_1 + q_2$. The cost functions of the duopolist are $C_1 = 5q_1$ and $C_2 = 0.5q_2^2$. Find the equilibrium values of q_1, q_2, p and the profits Π_1 and Π_2 according to Cournot.

Solution:

Cournot Solution:

Profit maximization of the first duopolist

$$\begin{aligned}\Pi_1 &= R_1 - C_1 \\ &= pq_1 - 5q_1 \\ &= [100 - 0.5(q_1 + q_2)]q_1 - 5q_1 \\ &= 100q_1 - 0.5q_1^2 - 0.5q_1q_2 - 5q_1 \\ &= 95q_1 - 0.5q_1^2 - 0.5q_1q_2 \quad \text{...(1)}\end{aligned}$$

Now according to Cournot we know that

$$\frac{\partial \Pi_1}{\partial q_1} = 0$$

$$\frac{\partial^2 \Pi_1}{\partial q_1^2} < 0$$

So from (1) above

$$\frac{\partial \Pi_1}{\partial q_1} = 95 - q_1 - 0.5q_2 = 0$$

i.e. $95 = q_1 + 0.5q_2$ ...(2)

or $q_1 = 95 - 0.5q_2$ ...(3)

This is the reaction function of the first duopolist.

$$\frac{\partial^2 \Pi_1}{\partial q_1^2} = -1 < 0$$

Profit maximization of the second duopolist

$$\begin{aligned}\Pi_2 &= R_2 - C_2 \\ &= pq_2 - 0.5q_2^2 \\ &= [100 - 0.5(q_1 + q_2)]q_2 - 0.5q_2^2 \\ &= 100q_2 - 0.5q_2^2 - 0.5q_1q_2 - 0.5q_2^2 \\ &= 100q_2 - q_2^2 - 0.5q_1q_2 \quad \text{...(4)}\end{aligned}$$

Now according to Cournot we know that

$$\frac{\partial \Pi_2}{\partial q_2} = 0$$

$$\frac{\partial^2 \Pi_2}{\partial q_2^2} < 0$$

So from (1) above

$$\frac{\partial \Pi_2}{\partial q_2} = 100 - 0.5q_1 - 2q_2 = 0$$

i.e. $100 = 0.5q_1 + 2q_2$ ...(5)

or $q_2 = 50 - 0.25q_1$ ...(6)

This is the reaction function of the second duopolist.

$$\frac{\partial^2 \Pi_2}{\partial q_2^2} = -2 < 0$$

Now from (2) and (5) as per Cramer's rule

$$q_1 = \frac{\begin{vmatrix} 95 & 0.5 \\ 100 & 2 \end{vmatrix}}{\begin{vmatrix} 1 & 0.5 \\ 0.5 & 2 \end{vmatrix}} = \frac{190 - 50}{2 - 0.25} = \frac{140}{1.75} = 80$$

$$q_2 = \frac{\begin{vmatrix} 1 & 95 \\ 0.5 & 100 \end{vmatrix}}{\begin{vmatrix} 1 & 0.5 \\ 0.5 & 2 \end{vmatrix}} = \frac{100 - 47.5}{1.75} = \frac{52.5}{1.75} = 30$$

Now the equilibrium price is obtained by substituting these values in the given demand law.

i.e.
$$\begin{aligned} p &= 100 - 0.5\,(q_1 + q_2) \\ &= 100 - 0.5\,(80 + 30) \\ &= 100 - 55 \\ &= 45. \end{aligned}$$

Similarly,

$$\begin{aligned} \Pi_1 &= 95q_1 - 0.5q_1^2 - 0.5q_1q_2 \\ &= 95 \times 80 - 0.5 \times 80^2 - 0.5 \times 80 \times 30 \\ &= 7600 - 3200 - 1200 \\ &= 7600 - 4400 \\ &= 3200 \end{aligned}$$

$$\begin{aligned} \Pi_2 &= 100q_2 - q_2^2 - 0.5q_1q_2 \\ &= 100 \times 30 - 30^2 - 0.5 \times 80 \times 30 \\ &= 3000 - 900 - 1200 \\ &= 3000 - 2100 \\ &= 900 \end{aligned}$$

Thus under equilibrium $q_1 = 80$, $q_2 = 30$, $p = 45$, $\Pi_1 = 3200$, $\Pi_2 = 900$

Example 39: For the duopoly problem given in example 10 above obtained the collusion solution.

Collusion solution:

Under collusion we know that

$$\begin{aligned}\Pi &= \Pi_1 + \Pi_2 \\ &= 95q_1 - 0.5q_1^2 - 0.5q_1q_2 + 100q_2 - q_2^2 - 0.5q_1q_2 \\ &= 95q_1 - 0.5q_1^2 + 100q_2 - q_2^2 - q_1q_2 \qquad \text{...(1)}\end{aligned}$$

Now for the maximum value of Π in (1) above we know that

1. $\dfrac{\partial \Pi}{\partial q_1} = 0;\quad \dfrac{\partial \Pi}{\partial q_2} = 0$ (Necessary condition)

2. $\dfrac{\partial^2 \Pi}{\partial q_1^2} < 0;\quad \dfrac{\partial^2 \Pi}{\partial q_2^2} < 0$ (Sufficient condition)

3. $\dfrac{\partial^2 \Pi}{\partial q_1^2} \times \dfrac{\partial^2 \Pi}{\partial q_2^2} > \left(\dfrac{\partial^2 \Pi}{\partial q_1 \partial q_2}\right)^2$ (Saddle point condition)

$$\frac{\partial \Pi}{\partial q_1} = 95 - q_1 - q_2 = 0$$

$$95 = q_1 + q_2 \qquad \text{...(2)}$$

$$\frac{\partial \Pi}{\partial q_2} = 100 - q_1 - 2q_2 = 0$$

$$100 = q_1 + 2q_2 \qquad \text{...(3)}$$

Now from (2) and (3) as per Cramer's rule

$$q_1 = \frac{\begin{vmatrix} 95 & 1 \\ 100 & 2 \end{vmatrix}}{\begin{vmatrix} 1 & 1 \\ 1 & 2 \end{vmatrix}} = \frac{190 - 100}{2 - 1} = \frac{90}{1} = 90$$

$$q_2 = \frac{\begin{vmatrix} 1 & 95 \\ 1 & 100 \end{vmatrix}}{\begin{vmatrix} 1 & 1 \\ 1 & 2 \end{vmatrix}} = \frac{100 - 95}{2 - 1} = \frac{5}{1} = 5$$

$$\frac{\partial^2 \Pi}{\partial q_1^2} = -1 < 0 \ ; \quad \frac{\partial^2 \Pi}{\partial q_2^2} = -2 < 0; \quad \left(\frac{\partial^2 \Pi}{\partial q_1 \partial q_2}\right)^2 = -1$$

$$\frac{\partial^2 \Pi}{\partial q_1^2} \times \frac{\partial^2 \Pi}{\partial q_2^2} > \left(\frac{\partial^2 \Pi}{\partial q_1 \partial q_2}\right)^2$$

$$= -1 \times -2 > (-1)^2$$

$$= 2 > 1$$

Thus $q_1 = 90$ and $q_2 = 5$ get confirmed as the equilibrium values.

$$\Pi = \Pi_1 + \Pi_2$$

$$= (95q_1 - 0.5q_1^2 - 0.5q_1q_2) + (100q_2 - q_2^2 - 0.5q_1q_2)$$

$$= (95 \times 90 - 0.5 \times 90^2 - 0.5 \times 90 \times 5) + (100 \times 5 - 5^2 - 0.5 \times 90 \times 5)$$

$$= (8550 - 4050 - 225) + (500 - 25 - 225)$$

$$= 4275 + 250$$

Thus $\Pi_1 = 4275$ and $\Pi_2 = 250$

$$p = 100 - 0.5\,(q_1 + q_2)$$

$$= 100 - 0.5\,(95)$$

$$= 100 - 47.5$$

$$= 52.5$$

Table 10.9

	q_1	q_2	q	Π_1	Π_2	Π	p
Cournot	80	30	110	3200	900	4100	45
Collusion	90	5	95	4275	250	4525	52.5

From the table it is very much clear that the colluding duopolists produce less and charge more price that too for a larger total profit. However the first monopolist is better of after the collusion. His profit has gone up by Rs.1075. At the same time the profit of the second duopolist has come down to just Rs. 250. Such is the case the collusion definitely will not materialize because even otherwise the first duopolist can get his higher duopoly profit of Rs. 900. Thus to make the collusion viable the first duopolist will have to make a minimum side payment of Rs. 650. Such a payment will bring back the profit of the first to his pre collusion level. However this is not the end of the story, even after such a side payment, the first duopolists profit is more by Rs. 450. Thus, here the maximum side payment that the first duopolist can make is Rs.1075. It is also important to note the output level after collusion has gone up from 80 to 90 in the case of the first and came down from 30 to just 5 in the case of the second. The logical reason that one could find is that the first duopolist's plant seems to be more efficient and modern than the second.

Stackelberg solution:

Example 40: For the duopoly problem given in example 10 above obtained the collusion and Stackelberg solution.

Solution:

Calculation of the leadership profit of the first duopolist

From the Cournot model discussed above the profit function of the first duopolist is obtained as

$$\Pi_1 = 95q_1 - 0.5q_1^2 - 0.5q_1q_2 \quad ...(1)$$

If the first duopolist wants to be a business leader then according to Stackelberg he will eliminates the output level of his rival by using rival's reaction function. The reaction function of the second duopolist is given by

$$q_2 = 50 - 0.25q_1 \quad ...(2)$$

Now after substituting (2) in (1) above it reduces to

$$\begin{aligned}\Pi_1 &= 95q_1 - 0.5q_1^2 - 0.5q_1q_2\\ &= 95q_1 - 0.5q_1^2 - 0.5q_1(50 - 0.25q_1)\\ &= 95q_1 - 0.5q_1^2 - 25q_1 + 0.125q_1^2\\ &= 70q_1 - 0.375q_1^2 \quad ...(3)\end{aligned}$$

Now for the maximum value of Π_1 we know that

1. $\dfrac{d\Pi_1}{dq_1} = 0$

2. $\dfrac{d^2\Pi_1}{dq_1^2} < 0$

So from (3)

1. $\dfrac{d\Pi_1}{dq_1} = 70 - 0.75q_1 = 0$

$$-0.75q_1 = -70$$

$$q_1 = 93.33$$

2. $\dfrac{d^2\Pi_1}{dq_1^2} = -0.75 < 0$

Thus $q_1 = 93.33$ gets confirmed as the leadership output of the first duopolist. Now the leadership profit is obtained by merely substituting this leadership output into the profit function given in equation (1) above

$$\begin{aligned}\Pi_1 &= 75q_1 - 0.375q_1^2\\ &= 75 \times 93.33 - 0.375 \times 93.33^2\\ &= 3266.67\end{aligned}$$

Calculation of the leadership profit of the second duopolist

From the Cournot model discussed above the profit function of the second duopolist is obtained as

$$\Pi_2 = 100q_2 - q_2^2 - 0.5q_1q_2 \quad ...(4)$$

If the second duopolist wants to be a business leader the according to Stackelberg he will eliminates the output level of his rival by using his reaction function. The reaction function of the first duopolist is given by

$$q_1 = 95 - 0.5q_2 \quad ...(5)$$

Now after substituting (5) in (4) above it reduces to

$$\Pi_2 = 100q_2 - q_2^2 - 0.5q_1q_2$$
$$= 100q_2 - q_2^2 - 0.5q_2(95 - 0.5q_2)$$
$$= 100q_2 - q_2^2 - 47.5q_2 + 0.25q_2^2$$
$$= 52.5q_2 - 0.75q_2^2 \quad \ldots(6)$$

Now for the maximum value of Π_2 we know that

1. $\frac{d\Pi_2}{dq_2} = 0$

2. $\frac{d^2\Pi_2}{dq_2^2} < 0$

So from (6)

1. $\frac{d\Pi_2}{dq_2} = 52.5 - 1.5q_2 = 0$

$$-1.5q_2 = -52.5$$
$$q_2 = 35$$

2. $\frac{d^2\Pi_2}{dq^2} = -1.5 < 0$

Thus $q_2 = 35$ gets confirmed as the leadership output of the second duopolist. Now his leadership profit is obtained by merely substituting this leadership output into the profit function given in equation (6) above

$$\Pi_2 = 52.5q_2 - 0.75q_2^2$$
$$= 52.5 \times 35 - 0.75 \times 35^2$$
$$= 918.75$$

Calculation of the followership profit of the first duopolist

A follower by definition assumes his rival as his business leader. Thus, he treats his rivals output as a constant and hence substitutes it into his own reaction function and calculates the leftovers as his level of output. Once this is done his followership profit is obtained by substituting the leadership output of his rival and the followership output of his own into his own profit function given in equation (1) above

$$q_1 = 95 - 0.5\,q_2$$
$$= 95 - 0.5 \times 35$$
$$= 77.5$$

$$\Pi_1 = 95q_1 - 0.5q_1^2 - 0.5q_1q_2$$
$$= 95 \times 77.5 - 0.5 \times 77.5^2 - 0.5 \times 77.5 \times 35$$
$$= 3003.125$$

Calculation of the followership profit of the second duopolist

$$q_2 = 50 - 0.25q_1$$
$$= 50 - 0.25 \times 93.33$$
$$= 26.67$$
$$\Pi_2 = 100q_2 - q_2^2 - 0.5q_1q_2$$
$$= 100 \times 26.27 - 26.67^2 - 0.5 \times 93.33 \times 26.67$$
$$= 711.11$$

Here it is important to note that the leadership profits are more than the corresponding followership profits for both the duopolists. Hence both the duopolists want to be leaders in the business. However, such a conflicting case is not possible in reality. Under Cournot model we were able to get a consistent solution. The real problem in this case is the typical behaviour about the duopolists that is being assumed.

10.24 Oligopolist Market

By definition by oligopoly we mean few sellers market. In fact duopoly is a special case of oligopoly. Here the oligopolist differentiates their product from the rest and charge different prices by adopting techniques like advertisement, trademark etc. Often they try their best to keep a certain portion of the market intact, having the long run prospects in mind irrespective of the short run profit considerations. Such a solution is often called the market share models.

Example 41: Under product differentiation two duopolist produce q_1 and q_2 quantities of a differentiated product q. If $p_1 = 250 - 5(q_1 + q_2)$ and $C_1 = 50\ q_1$ are the demand and the cost functions of the first duopolist respectively find the equilibrium values of q_1 and q_2 when the second duopolist wants to have ¾th of the market share all the time regardless of his short-run profit.

Solution:

Now by definition

$$\Pi_1 = R - C$$
$$= p_1q_1 - C$$
$$= [250 - 5(q_1 + q_2)]q_1 - 50\ q_1$$
$$= 250q_1 - 5q_1^2 - 5q_1q_2 - 50q_1$$
$$= 200q_1 - 5q_1^2 - 5q_1q_2 \qquad \ldots(1)$$

Since the second duopolist wants to have ¾th of the market by definition

$$\frac{3}{4} = \frac{q_2}{q_1 + q_2}$$

$$\therefore \quad 3q_1 + 3q_2 = 4q_2$$
$$3q_2 - 4q_2 = -3q_1$$
$$\therefore \quad q_2 = 3q_1 \qquad \ldots(2)$$

Now substituting this value of q_2 in equation (1) above it becomes

$$\Pi_1 = 200q_1 - 5q_1^2 - 5q_1q_2$$
$$= 200q_1 - 5q_1^2 - 5q_1(3q_1)$$
$$= 200q_1 - 20q_1^2 \qquad \ldots(3)$$

Now for the maximum value of Π we know that

1. $\frac{d\Pi_1}{dq_1} = 0$ Necessary condition

2. $\frac{d^2\Pi_1}{dq^2} < 0$ Sufficient condition

So from (3) above

$$\frac{d\Pi_1}{dq_1} = 200 - 40q_1 = 0$$

$$-40q_1 = -200$$
$$q_1 = 5$$

Further, $\frac{d^2\Pi}{dq^2} = -40 < 0$

Thus, $q_1 = 5$ gets confirmed as the equilibrium value. Now the equilibrium value of q_2 is obtained by substituting this value in equation (2) above.

$$q_2 = 3q_1$$
$$= 3 \times 5$$
$$= 15$$

Thus, $q_1 = 5$ and $q_2 = 15$ are the equilibrium values.

Now the equilibrium price is obtained by substituting these values in the given demand law

$$p_1 = 250 - 5(q_1 + q_2)$$
$$= 250 - 5 \times 20$$
$$= 150$$

Similarly $\Pi_1 = 200q_1 - 20q_1^2$

$$= 200 \times 5 - 20 \times 5^2$$
$$= 1000 - 500$$
$$= 500$$

Thus under equilibrium $q_1 = 5$, $q_2 = 15$, $p = 150$, $\Pi_1 = 500$.

EXERCISES

1. A monopolist is facing a linear demand $p = 200 - 6q$. His linear cost function is given by $C = 100 + 10q$. Calculate the equilibrium price, equilibrium quantity, and the profit.

(a) A specific tax of 4 per unit is levied on the monopoly output find the new equilibrium values.

(b) If the monopolist is levied a lump sum tax by an amount equivalent to the specific tax collection in above calculate the new equilibrium values. Hence prove that the lump sum tax is preferable both from consumer and producer points of view.

(c) A specific tax of 't' per unit is levied on the monopoly output find the equilibrium output in terms of the specific tax rate 't'. What tax rate do you suggest for maximum total tax collection.

2. Given two isolated markets supplied by a single monopolist, let the corresponding demand functions be $p_1 = 10 - q_1$, $p_2 = 20 - q_2$. The monopolist's cost function is $C = 50 + 20q$ where $q = q_1 + q_2$. What will prices and sales be in the two markets under a regime of price discrimination?

   (a) Also obtain the price elasticities for both the markets and prove that the monopolist will charge a low price in the high elastic market and high price in the low elastic market.

   (b) If the monopolist is not in a position to discriminate calculate the simple monopoly output, price and the maximum profit.

3. A multi-product monopolist produces two commodities, which are technically related in production. The joint cost function of the firm is $C = 4q_1^2 + 2q_1q_2 + 4q_2^2$. Find the equilibrium values of q_1, q_2, p_1, p_2 and the profit Π. The demand laws of the products are $p_1 = 20 - q_1$ and $p_2 = 10 - 2q_2$.

4. A monopolist is facing a linear demand $p = 200 - 4q$. His linear cost function is given by $C = 60 + 20q$. Calculate the equilibrium price, equilibrium quantity, and the profit. Also obtain the Baumol's sale maximizing output, price and the profit.

5. A famous author wants a royalty of 10% on the sales revenue and insists the price fixation that maximizes the total revenue. However the publishing company is interested in maximizing the profit. If $R = 1000Q - 10Q^2$ and $C = 100 + 20Q + Q^2$ are the total revenue and the total cost functions respectively.

6. (a) Two duopolists draw q_1 and q_2 quantities of a certain mineral water from a common spring. The demand law for the spring water is $p = 100 - 0.5q$ (where $q = q_1+q_2$) under equilibrium show that the water will be drawn equally when the cost of production is nil for both. Also prove that under equilibrium both the duopolist's will produce 1/3 rd of the market observing capacity.

   (b) If a single monopolist were to supply the water by himself at zero cost of production, show that the monopolist will restrict the outflow and charge a higher price.

7. Two duopolists produce q_1 and q_2 quantities of a homogeneous product q. The market demand for the product is given by $D = 2000 - 0.5q$, where $q = q_1 + q_2$. The cost functions of the duopolist are $C_1 = 10q_1$ and $C_2 = q_2^2$. Find the equilibrium values of q_1, q_2, p and the profits Π_1 and Π_2 according to Cournet.

   (a) For the above problem obtained the collusion solution.

   (b) For the above problem calculate the Stackelberg solution and list out your observations.

8. Under product differentiation two duopolist produce q_1 and q_2 quantities of a differentiated product q. If $p_1 = 500 - 2(q_1 + q_2)$ and $C_1 = 40\, q_1$ are the demand and the cost functions of the

first duopolist respectively find the equilibrium values of q_1 and q_2 when the second duopolist wants to have 1/2th of the market share regardless of his short-run profit.

9. (a) A monopolist faces a linear demand law $p = 50 - 2q$. His total cost function is $C = q^2 + 10q + 50$. Find the values p, q and the profit when the monopolist maximizes his profit.

   (b) A specific tax of 't' per unit is levied on the monopoly output find the equilibrium output in terms of the specific tax rate 't'.

   What tax rate do you suggest for maximum total tax collection.

10. Under duopoly, suppose the total cost of each firm are $C_1 = 10q_1$; $C_2 = q_2^2$. Suppose the market price is determined by $p = 100 - q_1 - q_2$. Find the equilibrium values of q_1, q_2, p and profits Π_1 and Π_2 when there is no conjectural variation.

❍ ❍

11

Chapter

INTEGRAL CALCULUS AND ITS APPLICATIONS

11.1 Introduction

Integration is the reverse process of differentiation in which we will be finding the original function from its given derivative. It is simply the process of finding the anti-derivative from a given derivative, similar to anti-log for a given log value. Hence, the integral of a function f(x) is another function F(x) for which f(x) is the derivative. For example, for the function f(x) = 2x, the function $F(x) = x^2$ is one such integral. The other one could be $F(x) = x^2 + 4$ because for this function also the derivative is 2x. This is not the end of the story. One can have as many integrals as possible by keep on changing the constant 4 to some other constant. This is all due to the vanishing nature of the constant while differentiation. Hence, if c stands for the unspecified constant to take care of all possibilities then the integral $x^2 + c$ is defined as the infinite integral for the function 2x and is normally denoted by $\int 2x.\, dx = x^2 + c$.

Note: For a given function the derivative is unique, but for a given derivative the integral need not be unique.

11.2 Some Important Basic Rules of Integration

1. $\int x^n dx = \dfrac{x^{n+1}}{n+1} + c$
2. $\int e^x dx = e^x + c$
3. $\int (1/x)dx = \ln x + c$
4. $\int a\, x^n\, dx = a \int x^n dx$
5. $\int [g(x) + h(x)]dx = \int g(x)\, dx + \int h(x)\, dx$

Applications of infinite integrals

Example 1: If MR = 100 – 8q obtain the equation of the total revenue. Also calculate the R corresponding to the output level q = 10.

Solution:

By definition

$$R = \int MR\,dq$$

$$R = \int (100 - 8q)\,dq$$

$$= 100\int dq - 8\int q\,dq$$

$$= 100q - 8\frac{q^2}{2} + c$$

$$= 100q - 4q^2 + c$$

Now, from economics we know that R = 0 when q = 0. So this could be taken as the needed initial condition in getting the value of c, the constant of integration.

$$0 = 100 \times 0 - 8 \times 0 \times 0 + c$$

$$c = 0$$

So our final result is written as

$$R = 100q - 4q^2$$

Now, the needed R when q = 10 is obtained by simply substituting this value in the above obtained revenue function.

$$R = 100 \times 10 - 4 \times 10 \times 10$$

$$R = 600$$

Thus, when q = 10 the revenue R = 600 in our problem as highlighted in Fig. 11.1.

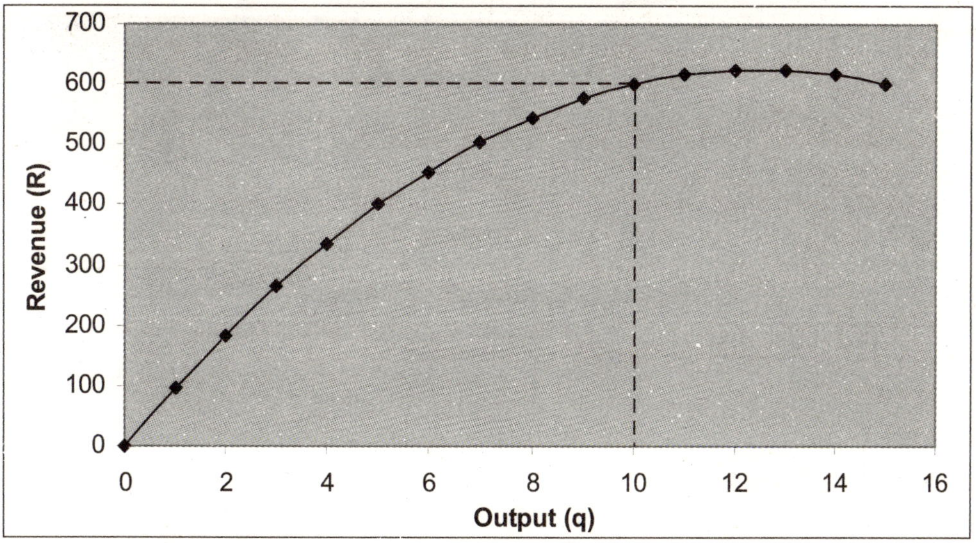

Fig. 11.1 Calculation of total revenue from the marginal revenue

Example 2: If dC/dY, the marginal propensity consume, is equal to ½ obtain the consumption function, given initial condition C = Rs. 200 when Y = Rs. 0.

Solution:

By definition

$$C = \int MPC\,dY$$

$$C = \int 0.5\,dY$$

$$= 0.5 \int dY$$

$$= 0.5Y + c$$

Now we know that C = 200 when Y = 0. So this can be taken as the needed initial condition

$$200 = 0.5 \times 0 + c$$

$$c = 200$$

So our final result is written as $C = 200 + 0.5Y$. Figure 11.2 highlights this consumption function.

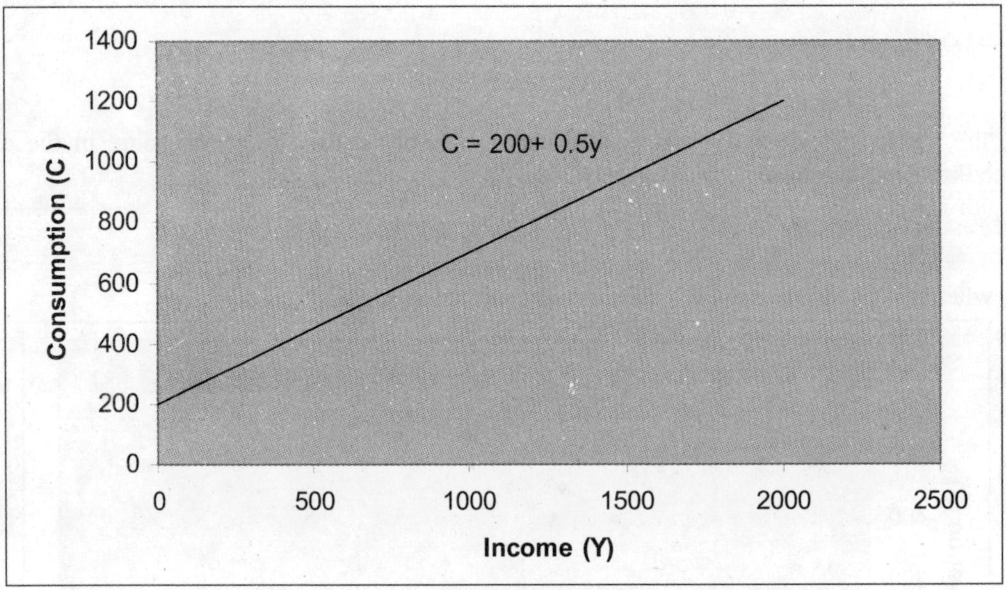

Fig. 11.2 Consumption function

Example 3: If MPC= 0.5 find the savings function given C = 200 when Y = 0.

Solution:

By definition

$$C = \int MPC\,dY$$

$$C = \int 0.5\,dY$$

$$= 0.5 \int dY$$

$$= 0.5Y + c$$

Consumption function:

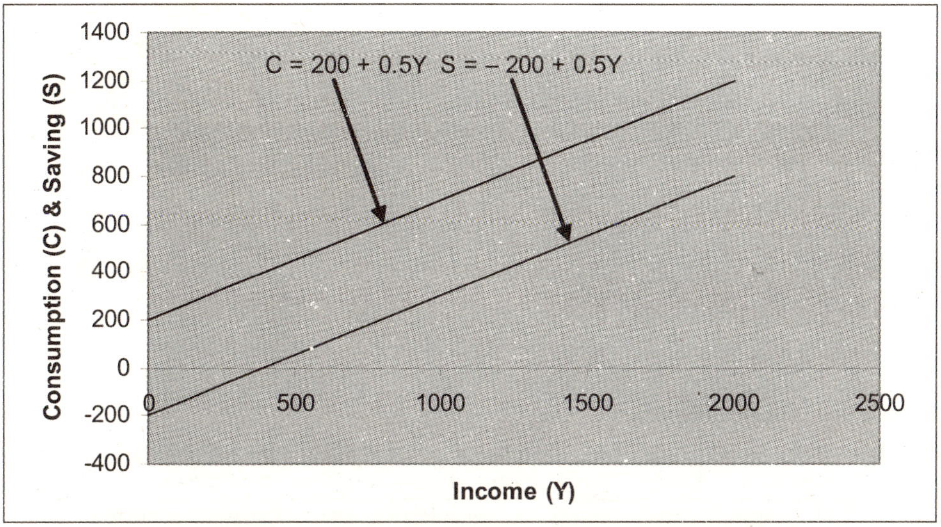

Fig. 11.3 Saving and consumption functions

Now we know that C = 200 when Y = 0. So this can be taken as the needed initial condition

$$200 = 0.5 \times 0 + c$$

$$c = 200$$

So our final result is written as

$$C = 200 + 0.5Y$$

By Definition $\quad Y = C + S$

So $\quad S = Y - C$

$$S = Y - (200 + 0.5Y)$$

$$S = -200 + 0.5Y$$

Figure 11.3 highlights both consumption and savings function.

Example 4: Given the MC = $0.12q^2 - 1.8q + 10$

(a) Obtain the total variable cost.

(b) If TFC = 100 find TC

Solution:

(a) By definition

$$TVC = \int MC dq$$

$$TVC = \int (0.12q^2 - 1.8 + 10) dq$$

$$= 0.12\frac{q^3}{3} - 1.8\frac{q^2}{2} + 10q + c$$

From economics we know that TVC = 0 when q = 0. So the constant of integration c = 0 in our problem

$$TVC = 0.04q^3 - 0.9q^2 + 10q$$

(b) By definition

$$TC = \int MC dq$$

$$TC = \int (0.12q^2 - 1.8q + 10)dq$$

$$= 0.12\frac{q^3}{3} - 1.8\frac{q^2}{2} + 10q + c$$

$$= 0.04q^3 - 0.9q^2 + 10q + c$$

It is given here that TFC = 100 when q = 0

So TC = $0.04q^3 - 0.9q^2 + 10q + 5$. The following Fig. 11.4 highlights all the cost functions.

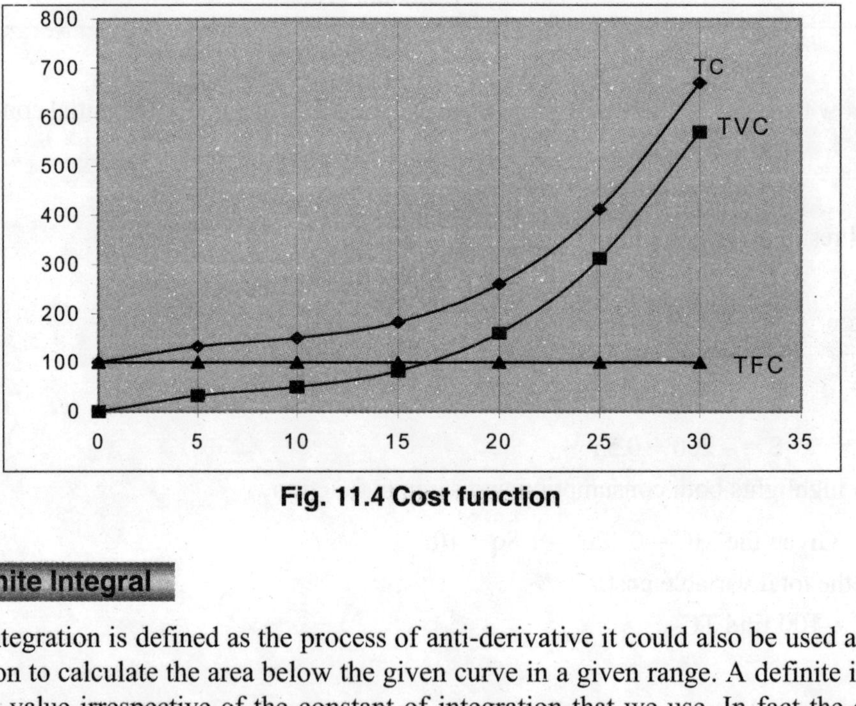

Fig. 11.4 Cost function

11.3 Definite Integral

Although integration is defined as the process of anti-derivative it could also be used as a process of summation to calculate the area below the given curve in a given range. A definite integral has a numerical value irrespective of the constant of integration that we use. In fact the constant of integration gets canceled during the process integration. An infinite integral on the other hand possesses no definite numerical value.

Example 5:

$$\int_1^2 x^3 dx = \left[\frac{x^4}{4} + c\right]_1^2 = \left[\frac{2^4}{4} + c\right] - \left[\frac{1^4}{4} + c\right] = 4 - \frac{1}{4} = 3.75$$

11.4 Area Under a Curve as a Definite Integral

Integration can be used to calculate the area under the given curve. For this task the function $y = f(x)$ is plotted in Fig 11.5. Now to calculate the area that lies in between the curve and the x-axis within the interval (a, b) let us subdivide the distance (b – a) into segments of width x_i and then construct rectangles of heights $f(x_i)$ over each segment as shown in the figure. The required area A is approximately equal to the sum of the areas of these small rectangles i.e., $A = \sum f(x_i).\Delta x_i$. Now to make the measure more accurate let us make the interval Δx_i as small as possible by increasing the number of rectangles.

i.e. $A = \sum_{\Delta x \to 0} f(x_i).\Delta x_i$

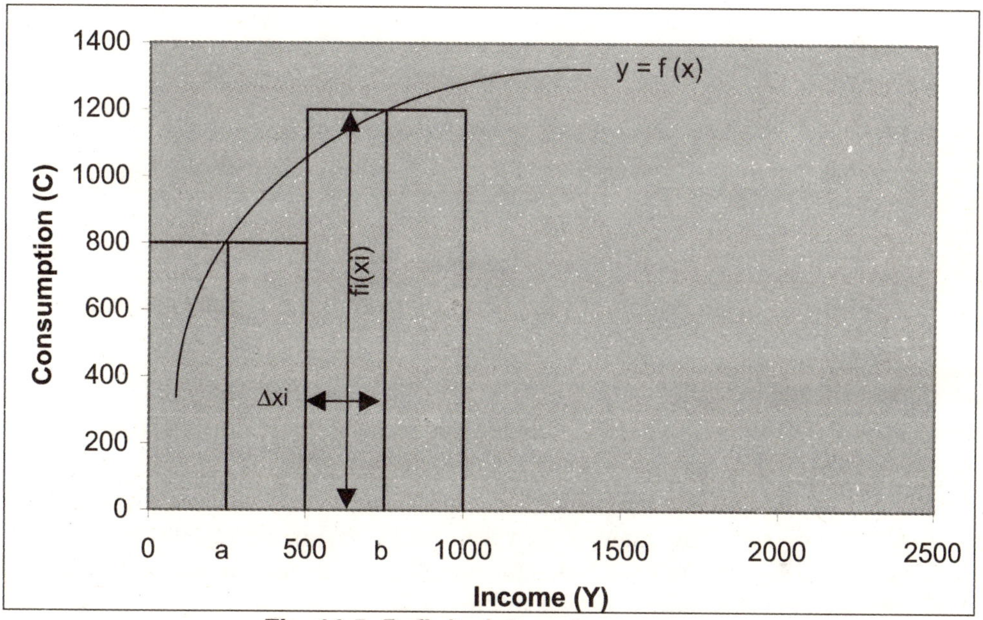

Fig. 11.5 Definite integral as area

To represent this measure more accurate and continuous, the Greek Symbol • which stands for discrete summation is replaced by the Old-style English long S i.e. ∫. The whole notation of summing the area thus with the new notation may be written as

$$A = \int_a^b f(x) \cdot dx$$

Example: 6 If MR = 100 – 8q calculate the total revenue as a sum of the area below the MR when the demand for the product is q = 10.

Solution: The total revenue, when q = 10 is obtained by integrating the MR function within the interval (0, 10).

$$R = \int_0^{10} (100 - 8q)dq = \left[100q - \frac{8q^2}{2} + c\right]_0^{10}$$

$$= \left[100 \times 10 - \frac{8 \times 10^2}{2} + c\right] - \left[100 \times 0 - \frac{8 \times 0^2}{2} - c\right]$$

$$= (1000 - 400) = 600$$

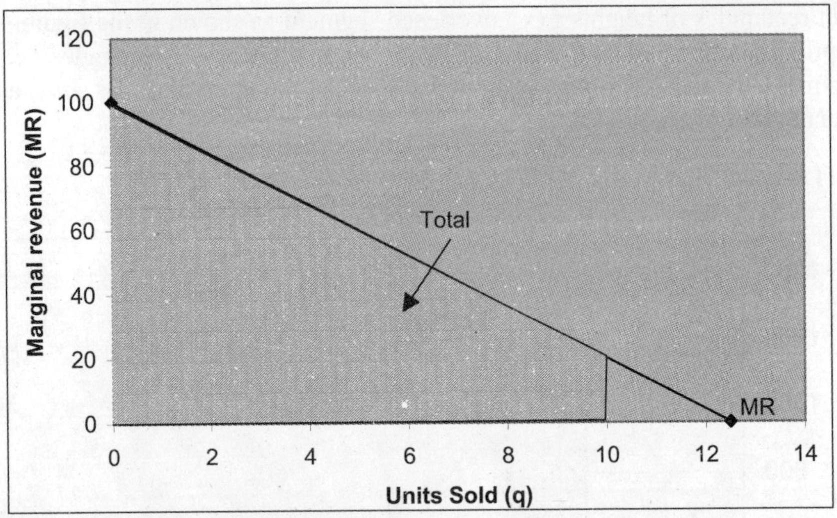

Fig. 11.6 Calculation of total revenue from the marginal revenue

11.5 Consumer's Surplus

Consumer's surplus is defined as the difference between the price that a consumer is willing to pay for a commodity rather than go without it and the actual price that he pays.

In the Fig. 11.7 the line AE represents the demand law. If p_0 is the ongoing market price and q_0 represents the corresponding quantity then the area OABD is the amount that the consumer is willing to pay. Similarly, the area OCBD is the actual payment the consumer is making. Thus the area ABC represent the consumer's surplus in Fig. 11.7.

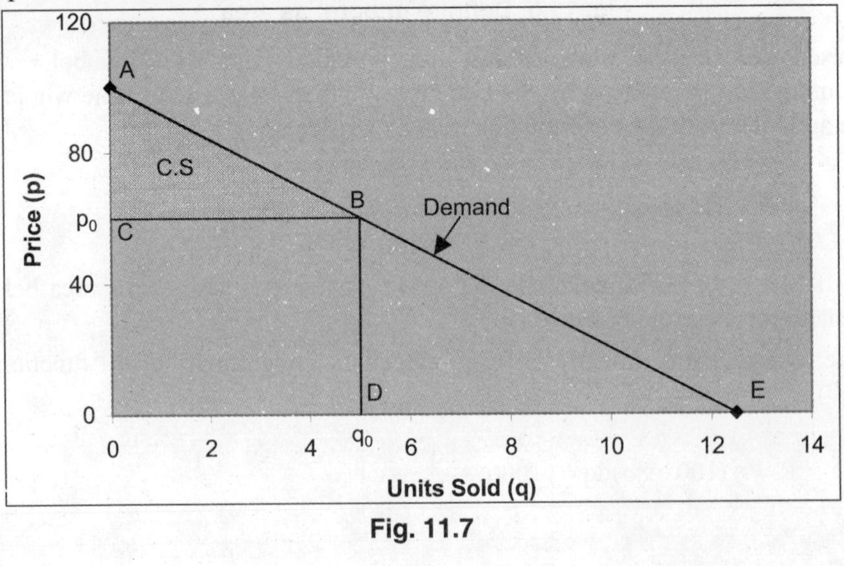

Fig. 11.7

So by definition consumer's surplus = area $OABq_0$ – area Op_0Bq_0

$$C.S. = \int_0^{q_0} f(q)\,dq - p_0 q_0$$

Example 7: The demand law of a certain product is p = 25 – 2q. Calculate the consumer's surplus when the equilibrium price for the product is Rs. 5.

Solution:

Since the equilibrium price for the product is Rs. 5 the equilibrium quantity is obtained by substituting this equilibrium price in the demand law given

i.e. $5 = 25 - 2q$

$2q = 25 - 5 = 20$

$q_0 = 10$

Now by definition the consumer's surplus

$$C.S = \int_0^{10} (25 - 2q)\,dq - p_0 q_0$$

$$= \left[25q - \frac{2q^2}{2}\right]_0^{10} - 5 \times 10$$

$= \{(25 \times 10) - (10 \times 10)\} - 50$

$= (250 - 100) - 50$

$= 100$

Alternative method as the area of the triangle in Fig. 11.8

$$C.S = \frac{1}{2} \times \text{base} \times \text{height} = \frac{1}{2} \times 10 \times 20 = 100$$

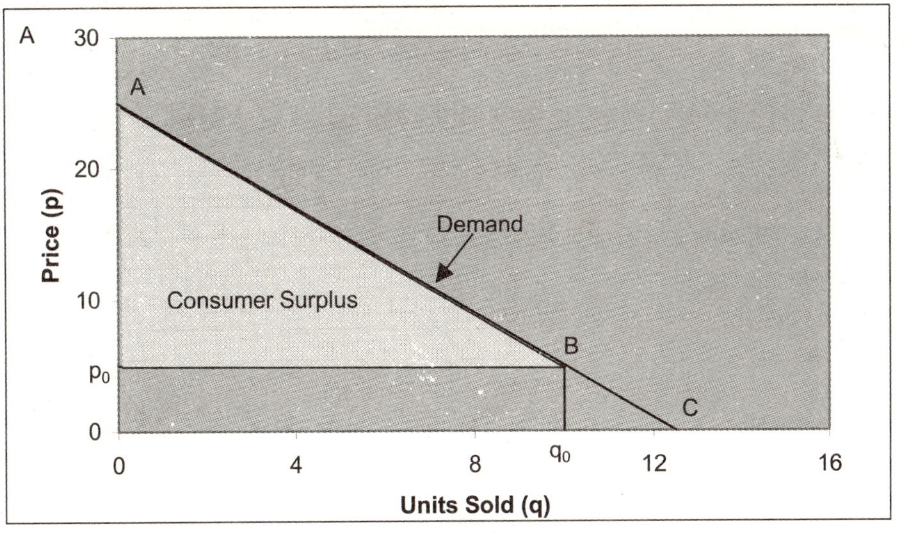

Fig. 11.8

11.6 Producer's Surplus

The producer's surplus on a given unit is defined as the difference between the actual price that the seller is getting and the expected price by the seller for that unit.

If SS stands for the market supply function, then the producer's surplus corresponding to the equilibrium supply q_0 is defined as

In Fig. 11.9, P.S. = area $p_0 A q_0 O$ – area O BAq_0 i.e. $P.S = p_0 \cdot q_0 - \int_0^{q_0} g[q].dq$

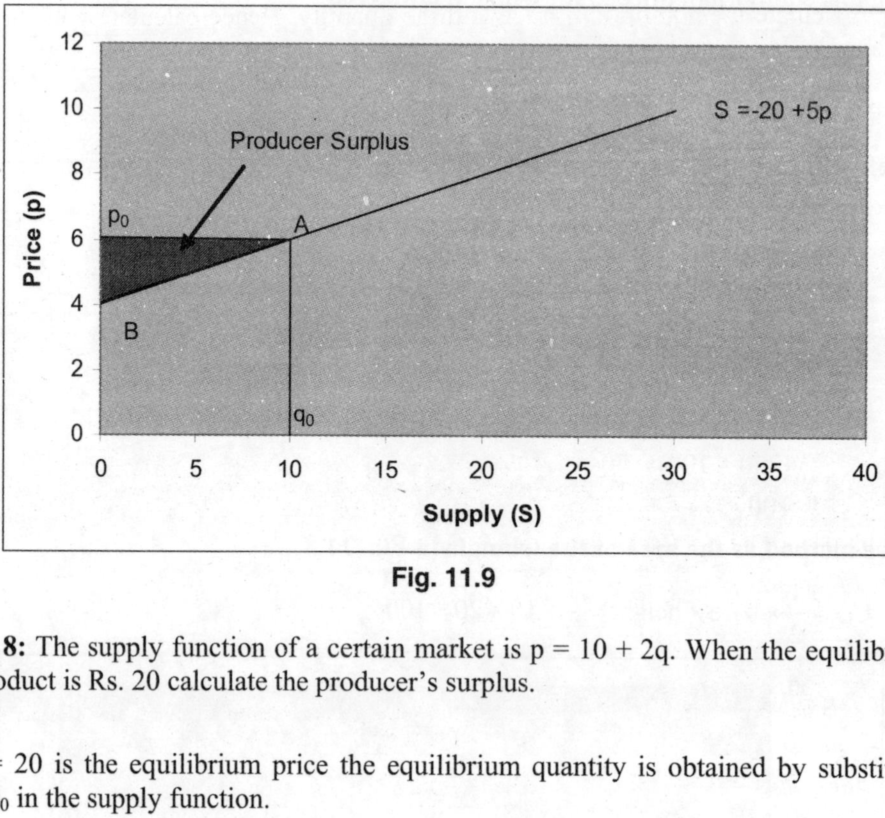

Fig. 11.9

Example 8: The supply function of a certain market is p = 10 + 2q. When the equilibrium price for the product is Rs. 20 calculate the producer's surplus.

Solution:

Since p = 20 is the equilibrium price the equilibrium quantity is obtained by substituting this value of p_0 in the supply function.

i.e.
$$20 = 10 + 2q$$
$$-2q = 10 - 20$$
$$= -10$$

$$\therefore \quad q_0 = \frac{-10}{-2} = 5$$

Now the producer's surplus

$$= p_0 q_0 - \int_0^5 [10 + 2q]\, dq$$

$$= 20 \times 5 - \left[10q + \frac{2q^2}{2}\right]_0^5$$

$$= 100 - [(10 \times 5) + (5 \times 5)]$$

$$= 25.$$

$$\text{P.S.} = \frac{1}{2} \times \text{base} \times \text{height} = \frac{1}{2} \times 5 \times 10 = 25$$

Example 9: If D = 250 – 50p and S = 25p + 25 are the demand and the supply functions respectively. Calculate the equilibrium price and the quantity. Hence calculate both consumer's and producer's surpluses under equilibrium.

Solution:

Under equilibrium we know that D = S

i.e. $250 - 50p = 25p + 25$

$$-50p - 25p = -250 + 25$$

$$-75p = -225$$

$$p = 3$$

The equilibrium quantity is obtained by substituting this value of p either in the supply or in the demand.

i.e. $D = 250 - 50 \times 3$

$$= 250 - 150$$

$$= 100$$

So under equilibrium D = S = 100

Calculation of consumer's surplus:

The demand law for the product is

$$D = 250 - 50p$$

Now to calculate the consumer's surplus we must express the demand law in its inverse form i.e. the price as a function of the quantity.

$$50p = 250 - D$$

$$p = (250 - D)/50$$

$$p = 5 - 0.02D$$

Now by definition consumer's surplus

$$\text{C.S.} = \int_0^{100} \left(5 - \frac{D}{50}\right) dD - p_0 q_0$$

$$= \left[5D - \frac{D^2}{2 \times 50}\right]_0^{100} - 3 \times 100$$

$$= \left[5 \times 100 - \frac{100^2}{2 \times 50}\right]_0^{100} - 300$$

$$= (500 - 100) - 300$$

$$= 100$$

Calculation of producer's surplus

The supply function for the product is S = 25p + 25

Now to calculate the producer's surplus we must express this supply function in its inverse form, expressing price as a function of the quantity supplied.

i.e. $-25p = 25 - S$

$$p = -1 + 0.04\,S$$

Now by definition producer's surplus

$$\text{P.S.} = p_0 q_0 - \int_0^{100} (-1 + S/25)\, dS$$

$$= 3 \times 100 - \left(-S + \frac{S^2}{2 \times 25}\right)_0^{100}$$

$$= 300 - \left(-100 + \frac{100^2}{50}\right)$$

$$= 300 - 100$$

$$= 200$$

Figure 11.10 depicts this situation.

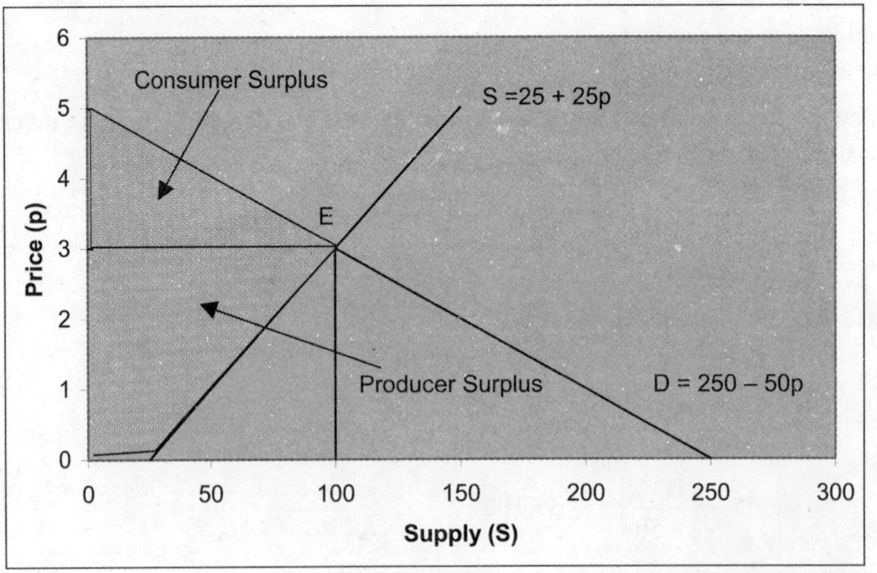

Fig. 11.10

EXERCISES

1. The marginal cost function of a firm is $5 + q^2$. Calculate the total cost when the fixed cost of production is Rs. 50.
2. If dC/dY, the marginal propensity consume is equal to 0.75 find the consumption function, given that consumption Rs. 100 when income is zero.
3. If MPS = 0.25, find the savings function when S = – 100 when Y = 0. Hence or otherwise calculate the consumption function and prove that MPS + MPC = 1.
4. If $MR = 5 + 3q - q^2$ calculate the total revenue given that R = 100 when q = 5.
5. If for 4 units of output the sales revenue is R = 400 find the total revenue function given $MR = 10 + 20q - 3q^2$.
6. If MR = 5 find the total revenue function. Further prove that the market is competitive.
7. If MR = 100 – 8q calculate the AR function.
8. The demand law of a certain product is 3p = 36 – 6q. Find the consumer's surplus when the equilibrium price p = 2.
9. If $p = 64 - q^3$ stands for the demand law of a free good calculate the consumer's surplus.

12

Chapter

MARKOV PROCESS AND ITS APPLICATIONS

12.1 Introduction

On several occasions, we will be interested in knowing the time path of a given random variable overtime. For example, the manager concern may be interested in knowing the way in which the market share of the Maruti cars will change overtime. Similarly, an investor in capital market may be interested in knowing the behaviour of the price of a certain share that he is having. Such a time path of the random variables overtime is often called the *stochastic process*. In this section we plan to introduce one such stochastic process often called Markov process in analyzing the evolution of a given system overtime, by using repeated trials. In such an evolution process, the state of the system at a particular period on a future date is obtained by using initial otherwise called transition probabilities. Markov process could be used to identify the probability that a machine which is functioning well in the current period will continue to do so in the next period. Similarly, it can also be used to find the probability that a particular customer shopping at Food World currently will switch over to Big Bazaar in the subsequent period.

12.2 Markov Process

State of the system

Suppose we are interested in analyzing the customer's loyalty to the Food World and Big Bazaar in Bangalore city. In this illustration we propose to analysis the sequence of shopping patterns by a customer who normally goes for shopping once in a week regularly. Given the choice, in a weekly trip, he can shop either at Food World or at Big Bazaar. A particular store selected in a given week is often refereed as the ***state of the system.*** In the illustration, because our typical customer has two alternatives at each trial, at a given point of time he may either be in state 1 or 2

State 1: The customer shops at Food World.

State 2: The customer shops at Big Bazaar.

With this state of the system definition, if we say that the system is in state 1 in trip two, we simply say that our customer shops at Food World in the second trip. Given the initial state (state 1 or state 2) in period 0, by using Markov Chain process we can find the probability of his shopping either at Big Bazaar or at Food World on any future date. To find the probability of the various states at successive trips by using Markov process, we need the probability that a customer remains with the same shop in the subsequent trip.

Transitional probability

Suppose that the market research study reveals that out of 100 customers' shops at Food World during the current trip, only 90 comes for Food World in the subsequent trip. This amounts to a shift over of 10 customers from Food World to Big Bazaar in the subsequent trip. Similarly, suppose that the same market research study reveals that out of 100 customers' shops at Big Bazaar during the current trip, only 80 comes for Big Bazaar again for shopping in the subsequent trip. This amounts to a shift of 20 customers from Big Bazaar to Food World in the subsequent trip. Thus, among the current Food World Customers 90% are loyal to Food World and come again to Food World in the subsequent trips. Only 10% of current Food World customers go for Big Bazaar in the subsequent trips. In a similar way, among the current Big Bazaar customers, only 80% come again to Big Bazaar in the subsequent trip and 20% move to Food World in the subsequent trip. These probabilities observed in the beginning are only transitional in character and hence called transitional probabilities. For developing the Markov process we assume that these transitional probabilities are contents for all the trips to come. The following Table 12.1 gives the whole summary of this discussion.

Table 12.1

Transitional Probabilities

Current week shopping	Next week shopping	
	Food World	Big Bazaar
Food World	0.9	0.1
Big Bazaar	0.2	0.8

Since in the above table, there are two rows and two columns it is common practice to represent these transitional probabilities in a matrix form as shown below.

$$P = \begin{bmatrix} P_{11} & P_{12} \\ P_{21} & P_{22} \end{bmatrix} = \begin{bmatrix} 0.9 & 0.1 \\ 0.2 & 0.8 \end{bmatrix}$$

where P_{ij} = Probability of making transition from state i in a given trip to state j in the subsequent trip. In Fig. 12.1 we show the corresponding brand switching transition diagram.

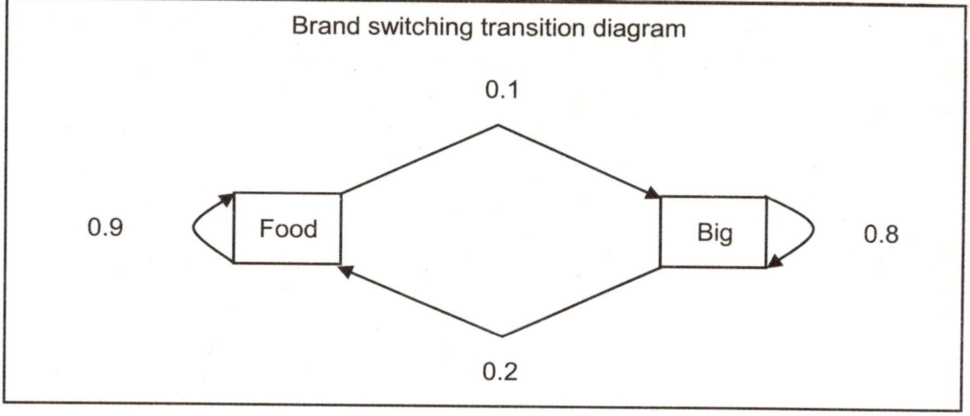

Fig. 12.1

State and steady state probabilities

By *state probability* we refer the probability of our Food World customer at different future states under reference, like the first trip, second trip etc. After crossing several such states these state probabilities themselves remain unaltered in all the future trips. Such an altered state probabilities are called *steady state probabilities*. In the following Fig. 12.2 we illustrate the method of calculating the state 1 and state 2 probabilities of our Food World customer by using tree diagram approach.

Assumptions underlying Markov chain process

1. **First order condition:** In our loyalty switching problem, the customer's shopping choice for any given future trip depends up on his choice in the just preceding trip and the associated transition probability matrix. The process with this assumed first order characteristic is often called *first order Markov process*. If the customer's current shopping choice depends up on two just consecutive preceding shopping choices then it is called *second order Markov process*. In this text only the *first order Markov* models are being addressed.
2. **Stationary or homogeneous models:** The transitional probabilities remain unaltered from time to time for the entire sequence in Markov process. Thus, such models are often called *stationary or homogenous* Markov chain models. In addition if it satisfies the first order condition as well then it is called *first order stationary* Markov chain process.
3. **Uniform time period models:** The change from one state to another takes place only once during the given time period. Thus the time intervals are equal for all periods. The uniform time could be one week or one month or one year depending upon the situation.

12.3 Tree Diagram Approach for Calculation of State Probabilities

Given the constant transitional probabilities and the initial shopping state (Food World or Big Bazaar) one can find the probability of his being with the initial shop as well his being in the alternative shop at any given future week. To illustrate this process let our customer's current shopping is in Food World (state 1) in week 0 as shown in the tree diagram in Fig. 12.2.

Now for our customer, the probability visiting Food World in the first week is given here as $P_{11} = 0.9$. Thus, given this probability, the probability of restoring our customer at Food World (state1) in second week is obtained as $(0.9) \times (0.9) = 0.81$.

In a similar way, the probability of our customer switching over to Big Bazaar in the first week is given in the table 12.1 as $P_{12} = 0.1$. So, the probability of this customer who has switched over to Big Bazaar in the first week, coming back to Food World in the second week is given by $(0.1) \times (0.2) = 0.02$. So in week 2, the probability of our customer being with Food World is obtained as $(0.81) + (0.02) = 0.83$.

Similarly, the probability our customer who has switched over to Big Bazaar in week 1 and continue to be there in the second week is given by $(0.1) \times (0.8) = 0.08$. The probability of the customer who was loyal to Food World in the first week but loyal to Big Bazaar in the second week is given by $(0.9) \times (0.1) = 0.09$. Thus, the probability of customer being with Big Bazaar at the second week is given by $(0.08) + (0.09) = 0.17$.

Thus, ultimately the probability of our typical customer, who was fond in the Food World in the zero week, to be seen in the Food World again for the second week purchase is only 0.83. The probability of his being in the Big Bazaar during the second week is 0.17. Thus, it is important to note that the probability of our customer being in Food World and being in Big Bazaar in week 2 is = 0.83 + 0.17 = 1.00.

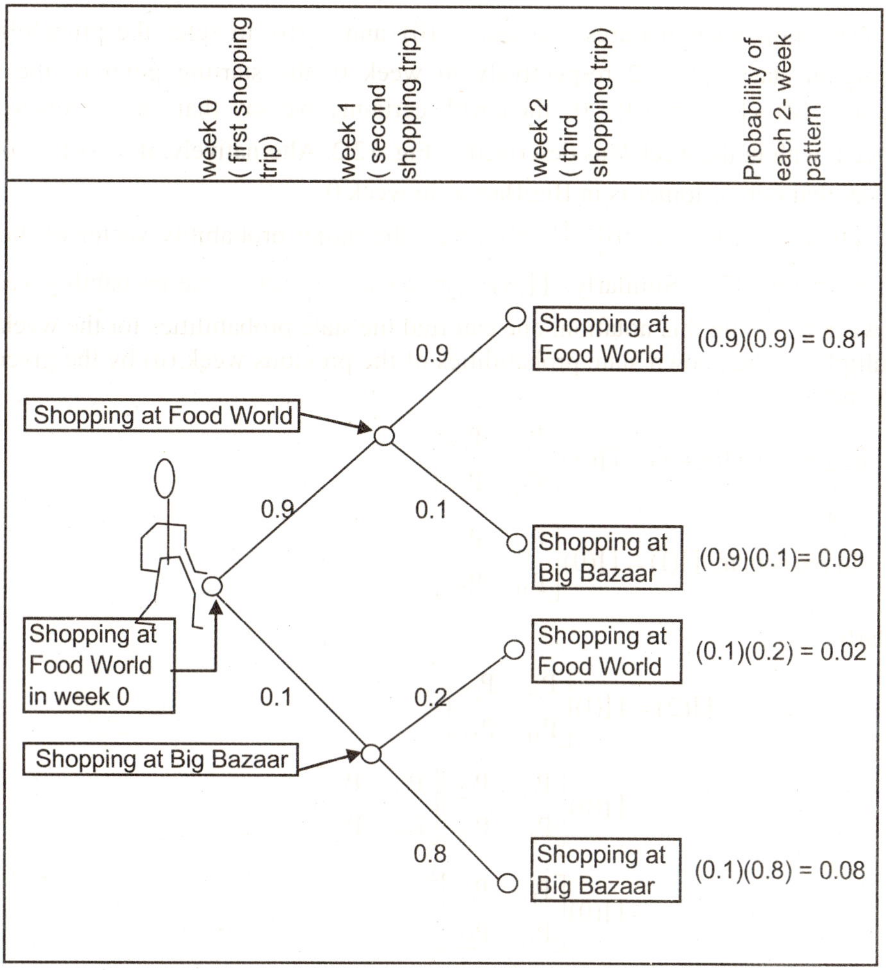

Fig. 12.2

In this way, given the initial shopping information of our typical customer, one can find the probability of being with Food World as well as with Big Bazaar on any future date by merely repeating these calculations up to the concerned week. Such probabilities are called state probabilities because they keep on changing during the period under reference.

12.4 Systematic Approach for Calculation of State Probabilities

Whatever may be the desirability and simplicity, the tree diagram approach is cumbersome and time consuming if we are interested in many more such calculations with longer week under reference. To make the task simple, let us proceed in a systematic way as shown below.

Let $\pi_i(n)$ = the probability that our system is in state i (1, or 2) in week n. For example, $\pi_1(1)$ denotes the probability of the system under consideration in state 1 (Food World) in week 1. Similarly, $\pi_2(1)$ refers the probability of the system in state 2 (Big Bazaar) in week 1.

With these notational features, we use $\pi_1(0)$ and $\pi_2(0)$ to refer the probabilities of the system being in state 1 and 2 respectively in week 0, the starting point of the system. In particular, if $\pi_1(0)=1$ or $\pi_2(0)=0$, then with certainty we say that our customer is in Food World to begin with in the week 0 as described in Fig. 12.2. Alternatively, if $\pi_2(0)=1$ or $\pi_1(0)=0$ we would say that our customer is in Big Bazaar in week 0.

Thus, $\Pi(0)=[\pi_1(0) \quad \pi_2(0)]=[1 \quad 0]$ refers the initial probability vector of the system in week zero as in Fig. 12.2. Similarly, $\Pi(n)=[\pi_1(n)\ \pi_2(n)]$ refers the probability vector of this system in week n. Using this notation, one can find the state probabilities for the week (n + 1) by merely multiplying the known state probabilities of the previous week (n) by the given transition probability matrix.

Thus, in general $\Pi(n+1)=\Pi(n)\begin{bmatrix} P_{11} & P_{12} \\ P_{21} & P_{22} \end{bmatrix}$

In particular, $\Pi(1)=\Pi(0)\begin{bmatrix} P_{11} & P_{12} \\ P_{21} & P_{22} \end{bmatrix}$

Similarly,

$$\Pi(2)=\Pi(1)\begin{bmatrix} P_{11} & P_{12} \\ P_{21} & P_{22} \end{bmatrix}$$

$$=\Pi(0)\begin{bmatrix} P_{11} & P_{12} \\ P_{21} & P_{22} \end{bmatrix}\begin{bmatrix} P_{11} & P_{12} \\ P_{21} & P_{22} \end{bmatrix}$$

$$=\Pi(0)\begin{bmatrix} P_{11} & P_{12} \\ P_{21} & P_{22} \end{bmatrix}^2$$

$$\Pi(3)=\Pi(2)\begin{bmatrix} P_{11} & P_{12} \\ P_{21} & P_{22} \end{bmatrix}$$

$$=\Pi(0)\begin{bmatrix} P_{11} & P_{12} \\ P_{21} & P_{22} \end{bmatrix}^2\begin{bmatrix} P_{11} & P_{12} \\ P_{21} & P_{22} \end{bmatrix}$$

$$=\Pi(0)\begin{bmatrix} P_{11} & P_{12} \\ P_{21} & P_{22} \end{bmatrix}^3$$

$$\Pi(n) = \Pi(n-1)\begin{bmatrix} P_{11} & P_{12} \\ P_{21} & P_{22} \end{bmatrix}$$

$$= \Pi(0)\begin{bmatrix} P_{11} & P_{12} \\ P_{21} & P_{22} \end{bmatrix}^{n-1}\begin{bmatrix} P_{11} & P_{12} \\ P_{21} & P_{22} \end{bmatrix}$$

$$= \Pi(0)\begin{bmatrix} P_{11} & P_{12} \\ P_{21} & P_{22} \end{bmatrix}^{n}$$

Calculation of state probabilities for week 1

To begin with let our system is in state 1 in week 0 as in Fig. 12.2. So $\Pi(0) = [1 \quad 0]$ follows from Fig. 12.2. Now we can compute the probabilities for week 1 as follows

$$\Pi(1) = \Pi(0)\begin{bmatrix} P_{11} & P_{12} \\ P_{21} & P_{22} \end{bmatrix}$$

$$[\pi_1(1) \quad \pi_2(1)] = [\pi_1(0) \quad \pi_2(0)]\begin{bmatrix} P_{11} & P_{12} \\ P_{21} & P_{22} \end{bmatrix}$$

$$= [1 \quad 0]\begin{bmatrix} 0.9 & 0.1 \\ 0.2 & 0.8 \end{bmatrix}$$

$$= [1 \times 0.9 + 0 \times 0.2 \quad 1 \times 0.1 + 0 \times 0.8]$$

$$= [0.9 \quad 0.1]$$

Calculation of state probabilities for week 2

The stated probabilities $\pi_1(1) = 0.9$ and $\pi_2(1) = 0.1$ are the state probabilities for week 1 of our customer who was shopping at Food World during the 0 week. Here $\pi_1(1) = 0.9$ refers the state probability of our Food World customer shopping at Food World again in week 1. Similarly, $\pi_2(1) = 0.1$ refers the state probability of our Food World customer in week 0 found in Big Bazaar in week 1.

Similarly,

$$\Pi(2) = \Pi(1)\begin{bmatrix} P_{11} & P_{12} \\ P_{21} & P_{22} \end{bmatrix}$$

$$[\pi_1(2) \quad \pi_2(2)] = [\pi_1(1) \quad \pi_2(1)]\begin{bmatrix} P_{11} & P_{12} \\ P_{21} & P_{22} \end{bmatrix}$$

$$= [0.9 \quad 0.1]\begin{bmatrix} 0.9 & 0.1 \\ 0.2 & 0.8 \end{bmatrix}$$

$$= [0.9 \times 0.9 + 0.1 \times 0.2 \quad 0.9 \times 0.1 + 0.1 \times 0.8]$$

$$= [0.83 \quad 0.17]$$

(Note that the same values are obtained in tree diagram approach as well.)

12.5 Systematic Approach for Calculation of Steady State Probabilities

From the preceding discussions, we know that

$$\prod(n+1) = \prod(n)\begin{bmatrix} P_{11} & P_{12} \\ P_{21} & P_{22} \end{bmatrix}$$

$$\begin{bmatrix}\pi_1(n+1) & \pi_2(n+1)\end{bmatrix} = \begin{bmatrix}\pi_1(n) & \pi_2(n)\end{bmatrix}\begin{bmatrix} P_{11} & P_{12} \\ P_{21} & P_{22} \end{bmatrix}$$

Because of the steady and constant probabilities in the long run, the time reference 'n' could conveniently be omitted while representing the steady state probabilities. So let us rename the associated steady state probabilities merely by π_1 and π_2 for state 1 and 2 respectively without any time reference.

$$\pi_1(n+1) = \pi_1(n) = \pi_1$$

$$\pi_2(n+1) = \pi_2(n) = \pi_2$$

So the above equation may be rewritten as

$$\begin{bmatrix}\pi_1 & \pi_2\end{bmatrix} = \begin{bmatrix}\pi_1 & \pi_2\end{bmatrix}\begin{bmatrix} P_{11} & P_{12} \\ P_{21} & P_{22} \end{bmatrix}$$

$$= \begin{bmatrix}\pi_1 & \pi_2\end{bmatrix}\begin{bmatrix} 0.9 & 0.1 \\ 0.2 & 0.8 \end{bmatrix}$$

$$= \begin{bmatrix}\pi_1 \times 0.9 + \pi_2 \times 0.2 & \pi_1 \times 0.1 + \pi_2 \times 0.8\end{bmatrix}$$

Thus

$$\pi_1 = 0.9\pi_1 + 0.2\pi_2$$

$$\pi_2 = 0.1\pi_1 + 0.8\pi_2$$

Further we also know that the sum of these two steady state probabilities always equal to one. So

$$\pi_1 + \pi_2 = 1$$

$$\pi_2 = 1 - \pi_1$$

Substituting this value of π_2 in the above equation it becomes

$$\pi_1 = 0.9\pi_1 + 0.2(1 - \pi_1)$$

$$\pi_1 = 0.9\pi_1 + 0.2 - 0.2\pi_1$$

$$\pi_1 - 0.7\pi_1 = 0.2$$

$$0.3\pi_1 = 0.2$$

$$\pi_1 = 2/3$$

$$\pi_2 = 1 - \pi_1 = 1 - 2/3 = 1/3$$

12.6 Calculation of State and Steady Probabilities using Excel Worksheet Template

The vectors $\Pi(1), \Pi(2), \Pi(3), \ldots\ldots\ldots$ show the *state* probabilities that our Food World customer with Food World or Big Bazaar overtime. In table 12.2 we generate 30 sets of state probabilities of our Food World customer in week 0. To prepare the work sheet and type the formula in Cell B6 =B5*\$E\$6+C5*\$E\$8 and C6 = B5*\$F\$6+C5*\$F\$8 and copy the formulas down the line up to 35th row as shown in table 12.2. The resulting result is displayed in table 12.3.

In table 12.3, from week 17 onwards we notice that these state probabilities do not change and become stationary. These stationary probabilities are often called ***steady-state probabilities.*** Accordingly, if there were 1000 customers to begin with in 0 week with Food World then there will be only 667 customers left with Food World after 17th week and there after. The remaining 333 of our original Food World customers by now have already moved to Big Bazaar.

Table 12.2: Excel template

	A	B	C	D	E	F	G
1							
2							
3		Initial Shopping at Food World					
4	Week	$\pi_1(n)$	$\pi_2(n)$				
5	0	1	0				
6	1	=B5*$E$6+C5*$E$8	=B5*$F$6+C5*$F$8		0.9	0.1	
7	2	=B6*$E$6+C6*$E$8	=B6*$F$6+C6*$F$8	P =			
8	3	=B7*$E$6+C7*$E$8	=B7*$F$6+C7*$F$8		0.2	0.8	
9	4	=B8*$E$6+C8*$E$8	=B8*$F$6+C8*$F$8				
10	5	=B9*$E$6+C9*$E$8	=B9*$F$6+C9*$F$8				
11	6	=B10*$E$6+C10*$E$8	=B10*$F$6+C10*$F$8				
12	7	=B11*$E$6+C11*$E$8	=B11*$F$6+C11*$F$8				
13	8	=B12*$E$6+C12*$E$8	=B12*$F$6+C12*$F$8				
14	9	=B13*$E$6+C13*$E$8	=B13*$F$6+C13*$F$8				
15	10	=B14*$E$6+C14*$E$8	=B14*$F$6+C14*$F$8				
16	11	=B15*$E$6+C15*$E$8	=B15*$F$6+C15*$F$8				
17	12	=B16*$E$6+C16*$E$8	=B16*$F$6+C16*$F$8				
18	13	=B17*$E$6+C17*$E$8	=B17*$F$6+C17*$F$8				
19	14	=B18*$E$6+C18*$E$8	=B18*$F$6+C18*$F$8				
20	15	=B19*$E$6+C19*$E$8	=B19*$F$6+C19*$F$8				
21	16	=B20*$E$6+C20*$E$8	=B20*$F$6+C20*$F$8				
22	17	=B21*$E$6+C21*$E$8	=B21*$F$6+C21*$F$8				
23	18	=B22*$E$6+C22*$E$8	=B22*$F$6+C22*$F$8				
24	19	=B23*$E$6+C23*$E$8	=B23*$F$6+C23*$F$8				
25	20	=B24*$E$6+C24*$E$8	=B24*$F$6+C24*$F$8				
26	21	=B25*$E$6+C25*$E$8	=B25*$F$6+C25*$F$8				
27	22	=B26*$E$6+C26*$E$8	=B26*$F$6+C26*$F$8				
28	23	=B27*$E$6+C27*$E$8	=B27*$F$6+C27*$F$8				
29	24	=B28*$E$6+C28*$E$8	=B28*$F$6+C28*$F$8				
30	25	=B29*$E$6+C29*$E$8	=B29*$F$6+C29*$F$8				
31	26	=B30*$E$6+C30*$E$8	=B30*$F$6+C30*$F$8				
32	27	=B31*$E$6+C31*$E$8	=B31*$F$6+C31*$F$8				
33	28	=B32*$E$6+C32*$E$8	=B32*$F$6+C32*$F$8				
34	29	=B33*$E$6+C33*$E$8	=B33*$F$6+C33*$F$8				
35	30	=B34*$E$6+C34*$E$8	=B34*$F$6+C34*$F$8				

Table 12.3: Excel solution

Week	Initial Shopping at Food World $\pi_1(n)$	$\pi_2(n)$	
0	1	0	
1	0.900	0.100	$P = \begin{vmatrix} 0.9 & 0.1 \\ 0.2 & 0.8 \end{vmatrix}$
2	0.830	0.170	
3	0.781	0.219	
4	0.747	0.253	
5	0.723	0.277	
6	0.706	0.294	
7	0.694	0.306	
8	0.686	0.314	
9	0.680	0.320	
10	0.676	0.324	
11	0.673	0.327	
12	0.671	0.329	
13	0.670	0.330	
14	0.669	0.331	
15	0.668	0.332	
16	0.668	0.332	
17	0.667	0.333	
18	0.667	0.333	
19	0.667	0.333	
20	0.667	0.333	
21	0.667	0.333	
22	0.667	0.333	
23	0.667	0.333	
24	0.667	0.333	
25	0.667	0.333	
26	0.667	0.333	
27	0.667	0.333	
28	0.667	0.333	
29	0.667	0.333	
30	0.667	0.333	

These steady state probabilities highlighted in the table are in conformity with the steady state probabilities obtained in the previous section.

Example 1: Given the transitional matrix

$$P = \begin{bmatrix} P_{11} & P_{12} \\ P_{21} & P_{22} \end{bmatrix} = \begin{bmatrix} 0.9 & 0.1 \\ 0.2 & 0.8 \end{bmatrix}$$

Obtain the state and steady state probabilities by using excel worksheet, given initial condition that this time our customer is seen in Big Bazaar in week 0.

Solution:

Table 12.4: Excel solution

Week	Initial Shopping at Big bazzar $\pi_1(n)$	$\pi_2(n)$	
0	0	1	
1	0.200	0.800	P = | 0.9 0.1 |
2	0.340	0.660	| 0.2 0.8 |
3	0.438	0.562	
4	0.507	0.493	
5	0.555	0.445	
6	0.588	0.412	
7	0.612	0.388	
8	0.628	0.372	
9	0.640	0.360	
10	0.648	0.352	
11	0.653	0.347	
12	0.657	0.343	
13	0.660	0.340	
14	0.662	0.338	
15	0.664	0.336	
16	0.664	0.336	
17	0.665	0.335	
18	0.666	0.334	
19	0.666	0.334	
20	0.666	0.334	
21	0.666	0.334	
22	0.666	0.334	
23	0.666	0.334	
24	0.667	0.333	
25	0.667	0.333	
26	0.667	0.333	
27	0.667	0.333	
28	0.667	0.333	
29	0.667	0.333	
30	0.667	0.333	

The table 12.4 shows the state probability calculations for 30 weeks for our Big Bazaar customer. This time note that the probabilities 0 and 1 are suitably interchanged in zero week in the table 12.4.

This time the steady state is reached from 24th week onwards. Accordingly, out of 1000 Big Bazaar customers after 24th week only 667 will be with the Big Bazaar. The remaining 333 will have a switch over to Food World by this time.

Note: Observation of steady state probabilities in table 12.3 and 12.4 tell us that the steady state probabilities remain unaltered irrespective of our customer's shopping in the zero week.

Example 2: Suppose Big Bazaar is initiating an advertising program to attract customers from Food World. Such a program is expected to increase the probability of Food World customers switching over to Big Bazaar from the present 0.1 to 0.15. Obtain the revised steady state probabilities.

Solution:

The revised transient matrix is obtained as

Table 12.5

Current Week Shopping	Next Week Shopping	
	Food World	Big Bazaar
Food World	0.85	0.15
Big Bazaar	0.2	0.8

Table 12.6: Excel solution

Week	Initial Shopping at Food World $\pi_1(n)$	$\pi_2(n)$
0	1	0
1	0.850	0.150
2	0.753	0.248
3	0.689	0.311
4	0.648	0.352
5	0.621	0.379
6	0.604	0.396
7	0.592	0.408
8	0.585	0.415
9	0.580	0.420
10	0.577	0.423
11	0.575	0.425
12	0.574	0.426
13	0.573	0.427
14	0.572	0.428
15	0.572	0.428
16	0.572	0.428
17	0.572	0.428
18	0.572	0.428
19	0.572	0.428
20	0.572	0.428
21	0.571	0.429
22	0.571	0.429
23	0.571	0.429
24	0.571	0.429
25	0.571	0.429

$$P = \begin{vmatrix} 0.85 & 0.15 \\ 0.2 & 0.8 \end{vmatrix}$$

(Contd...)

26	0.571	0.429	
27	0.571	0.429	
28	0.571	0.429	
29	0.571	0.429	
30	0.571	0.429	

With these new transitional probability matrix we repeat the calculation using the excel template and report result in table 12.6. To achieve this result copy the worksheet template and change the probabilities in the matrix as shown table 12.5. The result will be automatically displayed as shown in table 12.6.

From the resulting table 12.6 the steady state probabilities are obtained as

$$\pi_1 = 0.571 \text{ and } \pi_2 = 0.429$$

Alternatively, we recalculate the steady state probabilities once again under the new circumstances in the usual manner.

$$\pi_1 = 0.85\pi_1 + 0.2\pi_2$$
$$\pi_2 = 0.15\pi_1 + 0.8\pi_2$$

Further we also know that the sum of these two steady state probabilities always equal to one. So

$$\pi_1 + \pi_2 = 1$$
$$\pi_2 = 1 - \pi_1$$

Substituting this value of π_2 in the above equation it becomes

$$\pi_1 = 0.85\pi_1 + 0.2(1 - \pi_1)$$
$$\pi_1 = 0.85\pi_1 + 0.2 - 0.2\pi_1$$
$$\pi_1 - 0.65\pi_1 = 0.2$$
$$0.35\pi_1 = 0.2$$
$$\pi_1 = 0.571$$

$\pi_2 = 1 - \pi_1 = 1 - 0.571 = 0.429$. These values π_1 and π_2 are in conformity with the steady state probabilities obtained in the table 12.6 after week 21 onwards.

Example 3: Instead of advertisement let this time the Big Bazaar initiates a gift program to all its loyal customers to prevent switching over to Food World. Given the new transition matrix, obtain the revised steady state probabilities.

Table 12.7

Current Week Shopping	Next Week Shopping	
	Food World	Big Bazaar
Food World	0.9	0.1
Big Bazaar	0.15	0.85

Now let us recalculate the state and steady state probabilities once again under the new circumstances and find the resulting steady state as usual.

Table 12.8: Excel solution

Week	Initial Shopping at Food World $\pi_1(n)$	$\pi_2(n)$		
0	1	0		
1	0.900	0.100		0.9 0.1
2	0.825	0.175	P =	
3	0.769	0.231		0.15 0.85
4	0.727	0.273		
5	0.695	0.305		
6	0.671	0.329		
7	0.653	0.347		
8	0.640	0.360		
9	0.630	0.370		
10	0.623	0.377		
11	0.617	0.383		
12	0.613	0.387		
13	0.610	0.390		
14	0.607	0.393		
15	0.605	0.395		
16	0.604	0.396		
17	0.603	0.397		
18	0.602	0.398		
19	0.602	0.398		
20	0.601	0.399		
21	0.601	0.399		
22	0.601	0.399		
23	0.601	0.399		
24	0.600	0.400		
25	0.600	0.400		
26	0.600	0.400		
27	0.600	0.400		
28	0.600	0.400		
29	0.600	0.400		
30	0.600	0.400		

From the resulting table 12.8 the steady state probabilities are obtained as

$$\pi_1 = 0.600 \text{ and } \pi_2 = 0.400$$

Alternatively, the result is also obtained as follows:

$$\pi_1 = 0.9\pi_1 + 0.15\pi_2$$

$$\pi_2 = 0.1\pi_1 + 0.85\pi_2$$

Further we also know that the sum of these two steady state probabilities always equal to one. So

$$\pi_1 + \pi_2 = 1$$

$$\pi_2 = 1 - \pi_1$$

Substituting this value of π_2 in the above equation it becomes

$$\pi_1 = 0.9\pi_1 + 0.15(1 - \pi_1)$$

$$\pi_1 = 0.9\pi_1 + 0.15 - 0.15\pi_1$$

$$\pi_1 - 0.75\pi_1 = 0.15$$

$$0.25\pi_1 = 0.15$$

$$\pi_1 = 0.600$$

$\pi_2 = 1 - \pi_1 = 1 - 0.600 = 0.400$. These values π_1 and π_2 are in conformity with the steady state probabilities obtained in the table 12.8 after 24 week. Out of 1000 customers only 600 will be with the Food World leaving 400 to Big Bazaar by this time. In table 12.8 the same result is achieved using the excel template.

Example 4: In a certain market only two brands of soaps A and B are available. A consumer was found to purchase A brand last month. There is 80% chance that he will buy the same brand this month also. Similarly, the customer who purchased B brand last month, there is 90% for restoring it now also.

(a) Calculate the probability for a currently A brand purchaser moving to B brand after two purchases from now.

(b) Calculate the probability for a currently B brand purchaser moving to A brand after two purchases from now.

(c) Calculate the steady state probability for a currently A brand purchaser.

(d) Calculate the steady state probability for a currently B brand purchaser.

Solution: (a)

Table 12.9

From Brand (this month)	To Brand (next month)	
	A	B
A	0.80	0.20
B	0.10	0.90

$$P = \begin{bmatrix} P_{11} & P_{12} \\ P_{21} & P_{22} \end{bmatrix} = \begin{bmatrix} 0.8 & 0.2 \\ 0.1 & 0.9 \end{bmatrix}$$

To begin with our system is in state 1 (brand A) in month 0. So $\Pi(0) = \begin{bmatrix} 1 & 0 \end{bmatrix}$ follows from the definition. Now we can compute the probabilities for month 1 as follows

$$\Pi(1) = \Pi(0) \begin{bmatrix} P_{11} & P_{12} \\ P_{21} & P_{22} \end{bmatrix}$$

$$\begin{bmatrix} \pi_1(1) & \pi_2(1) \end{bmatrix} = \begin{bmatrix} \pi_1(0) & \pi_2(0) \end{bmatrix} \begin{bmatrix} P_{11} & P_{12} \\ P_{21} & P_{22} \end{bmatrix}$$

$$= \begin{bmatrix} 1 & 0 \end{bmatrix} \begin{bmatrix} 0.8 & 0.2 \\ 0.1 & 0.9 \end{bmatrix}$$

$$= \begin{bmatrix} 1 \times 0.8 + 0 \times 0.1 & 1 \times 0.2 + 0 \times 0.9 \end{bmatrix}$$

$$= \begin{bmatrix} 0.8 & 0.2 \end{bmatrix}$$

The state probabilities $\pi_1(1) = 0.8$ and $\pi_2(1) = 0.2$ are the state probabilities of our customer who was buying brand A during the 0 month. Here $\pi_1(1) = 0.8$ refers the state probability of our brand A customer buying brand A again in month 1. Similarly, $\pi_2(1) = 0.2$ refers the state probability of our brand A customer moving to brand B in month 1.

Now,

$$\prod(2) = \prod(1) \begin{bmatrix} P_{11} & P_{12} \\ P_{21} & P_{22} \end{bmatrix}$$

$$\begin{bmatrix} \pi_1(2) & \pi_2(2) \end{bmatrix} = \begin{bmatrix} \pi_1(1) & \pi_2(1) \end{bmatrix} \begin{bmatrix} P_{11} & P_{12} \\ P_{21} & P_{22} \end{bmatrix}$$

$$= \begin{bmatrix} 0.8 & 0.2 \end{bmatrix} \begin{bmatrix} 0.8 & 0.2 \\ 0.1 & 0.9 \end{bmatrix}$$

$$= \begin{bmatrix} 0.8 \times 0.8 + 0.2 \times 0.1 & 0.8 \times 0.2 + 0.2 \times 0.9 \end{bmatrix}$$

$$= \begin{bmatrix} 0.66 & 0.34 \end{bmatrix}$$

So the probability for a currently A brand purchaser moving to B brand after two purchases from now is 0.34.

Excel Solution

Table 12.10: Excel solution

Month	Initial Shopping Brand A $\pi_1(n)$	$\pi_2(n)$			
0	1	0			
1	0.800	0.200		0.8	0.2
2	0.660	0.340	P =		
3	0.562	0.438		0.1	0.9
4	0.493	0.507			

Solution: (b)

To begin with our system is in state 2 (B Brand) in month 0. So $\prod(0) = \begin{bmatrix} 0 & 1 \end{bmatrix}$ follows from the definition. Now we can compute the probabilities for month 1 as follows:

$$\prod(1) = \prod(0) \begin{bmatrix} P_{11} & P_{12} \\ P_{21} & P_{22} \end{bmatrix}$$

$$\begin{bmatrix} \pi_1(1) & \pi_2(1) \end{bmatrix} = \begin{bmatrix} \pi_1(0) & \pi_2(0) \end{bmatrix} \begin{bmatrix} P_{11} & P_{12} \\ P_{21} & P_{22} \end{bmatrix}$$

$$= [0 \quad 1] \begin{bmatrix} 0.8 & 0.2 \\ 0.1 & 0.9 \end{bmatrix}$$

$$= [0 \times 0.8 + 1 \times 0.1 \quad 0 \times 0.2 + 1 \times 0.9]$$

$$= [0.1 \quad 0.9]$$

The state probabilities $\pi_1(1) = 0.9$ and $\pi_2(1) = 0.1$ are the transitional probabilities of our customer who was buying brand A during the month 0. Here $\pi_1(1) = 0.9$ refers the transitional probability of our brand B customer buying brand B again in month 1. Similarly, $\pi_2(1) = 0.2$ refers the transitional probability of our brand B customer moving to brand A in period 1.

Now,

$$\Pi(2) = \Pi(1) \begin{bmatrix} P_{11} & P_{12} \\ P_{21} & P_{22} \end{bmatrix}$$

$$[\pi_1(2) \quad \pi_2(2)] = [\pi_1(1) \quad \pi_2(1)] \begin{bmatrix} P_{11} & P_{12} \\ P_{21} & P_{22} \end{bmatrix}$$

$$= [0.1 \quad 0.9] \begin{bmatrix} 0.8 & 0.2 \\ 0.1 & 0.9 \end{bmatrix}$$

$$= [0.1 \times 0.8 + 0.9 \times 0.1 \quad 0.1 \times 0.2 + 0.9 \times 0.9]$$

$$= [0.17 \quad 0.83]$$

Table 12.11: Excel solution

Month	Initial Shopping Brand B $\pi_1(n)$	 $\pi_2(n)$			
0	0	1			
1	0.100	0.900		0.8	0.2
2	0.170	0.830	P =		
3	0.219	0.781		0.1	0.9
4	0.253	0.747			

So the probability for a currently B brand purchaser moving to A brand after two purchases from now is 0.17

Solution: (c)

Steady state probability of currently A brand purchaser

From the preceding discussion we know that

$$[\pi_1(n+1) \quad \pi_2(n+1)] = [\pi_1(n) \quad \pi_2(n)] \begin{bmatrix} P_{11} & P_{12} \\ P_{21} & P_{22} \end{bmatrix}$$

Now because of the observed steady state property

$$\pi_1(n+1) = \pi_1(n) = \pi_1$$
$$\pi_2(n+1) = \pi_2(n) = \pi_2$$

So the above equation may be rewritten as

$$\begin{bmatrix}\pi_1 & \pi_2\end{bmatrix} = \begin{bmatrix}\pi_1 & \pi_2\end{bmatrix}\begin{bmatrix}P_{11} & P_{12}\\ P_{21} & P_{22}\end{bmatrix}$$
$$= \begin{bmatrix}\pi_1 & \pi_2\end{bmatrix}\begin{bmatrix}0.8 & 0.2\\ 0.1 & 0.9\end{bmatrix}$$
$$= \begin{bmatrix}\pi_1 \times 0.8 + \pi_2 \times 0.1 & \pi_1 \times 0.2 + \pi_2 \times 0.9\end{bmatrix}$$

Thus

$$\pi_1 = 0.8\pi_1 + 0.1\pi_2$$
$$\pi_2 = 0.2\pi_1 + 0.9\pi_2$$

Further we also know that the sum of these two steady state probabilities always equal to one. So

$$\pi_1 + \pi_2 = 1$$
$$\pi_2 = 1 - \pi_1$$

Table 12.12: Excel solution

Month	Initial Shopping Brand A $\pi_1(n)$	$\pi_2(n)$	
0	1	0	
1	0.800	0.200	0.8 0.2
2	0.660	0.340	P =
3	0.562	0.438	0.1 0.9
4	0.493	0.507	
5	0.445	0.555	
6	0.412	0.588	
7	0.388	0.612	
8	0.372	0.628	
9	0.360	0.640	
10	0.352	0.648	
11	0.347	0.653	
12	0.343	0.657	
13	0.340	0.660	
14	0.338	0.662	
15	0.336	0.664	
16	0.336	0.664	
17	0.335	0.665	
18	0.334	0.666	

(Contd...)

19	0.334	0.666	
20	0.334	0.666	
21	0.334	0.666	
22	0.334	0.666	
23	0.334	0.666	
24	0.333	0.667	
25	0.333	0.667	
26	0.333	0.667	
27	0.333	0.667	
28	0.333	0.667	
29	0.333	0.667	
30	0.333	0.667	

Substituting this value of π_2 in the above equation it becomes

$$\pi_1 = 0.8\pi_1 + 0.1(1 - \pi_1)$$
$$\pi_1 = 0.8\pi_1 + 0.1 - 0.1\pi_1$$
$$\pi_1 - 0.7\pi_1 = 0.1$$
$$0.3\pi_1 = 0.1$$
$$\pi_1 = 1/3$$
$$\pi_2 = 1 - \pi_1 = 1 - 1/3 = 2/3$$

These highlighted values π_1 and π_2 in excel table are in conformity with the steady state probabilities obtained by calculation. Also note that this steady state probability is obtained irrespective of the start of our customer either with brand A or brand B.

Solution: (d)

Steady state probability of a customer currently buying B brand

From the preceding discussion we know that

$$\begin{bmatrix}\pi_1(n+1) & \pi_2(n+1)\end{bmatrix} = \begin{bmatrix}\pi_1(n) & \pi_2(n)\end{bmatrix}\begin{bmatrix}P_{11} & P_{12}\\ P_{21} & P_{22}\end{bmatrix}$$

Now because of the observed steady state property

$$\pi_1(n+1) = \pi_1(n) = \pi_1$$
$$\pi_2(n+1) = \pi_2(n) = \pi_2$$

So the above equation may be rewritten as

$$\begin{bmatrix}\pi_1 & \pi_2\end{bmatrix} = \begin{bmatrix}\pi_1 & \pi_2\end{bmatrix}\begin{bmatrix}P_{11} & P_{12}\\ P_{21} & P_{22}\end{bmatrix}$$
$$= \begin{bmatrix}\pi_1 & \pi_2\end{bmatrix}\begin{bmatrix}0.8 & 0.2\\ 0.1 & 0.9\end{bmatrix}$$
$$= \begin{bmatrix}\pi_1 \times 0.8 + \pi_2 \times 0.1 & \pi_1 \times 0.2 + \pi_2 \times 0.9\end{bmatrix}$$

Thus

$$\pi_1 = 0.8\pi_1 + 0.1\pi_2$$
$$\pi_2 = 0.2\pi_1 + 0.9\pi_2$$

Further we also know that the sum of these two steady state probabilities always equal to one. So

$$\pi_1 + \pi_2 = 1$$
$$\pi_2 = 1 - \pi_1$$

Substituting this value of π_2 in the above equation it becomes

$$\pi_1 = 0.8\pi_1 + 0.1(1 - \pi_1)$$
$$\pi_1 = 0.8\pi_1 + 0.1 - 0.1\pi_1$$
$$\pi_1 - 0.7\pi_1 = 0.1$$
$$0.3\pi_1 = 0.1$$
$$\pi_1 = 1/3$$
$$\pi_2 = 1 - \pi_1 = 1 - 1/3 = 2/3$$

Table 12.13: Excel solution

Month	Initial Shopping Brand A $\pi_1(n)$	$\pi_2(n)$	
0	0	1	
1	0.100	0.900	P = | 0.8 0.2 |
2	0.170	0.830	| 0.1 0.9 |
3	0.219	0.781	
4	0.253	0.747	
5	0.277	0.723	
6	0.294	0.706	
7	0.306	0.694	
8	0.314	0.686	
9	0.320	0.680	
10	0.324	0.676	
11	0.327	0.673	
12	0.329	0.671	
13	0.330	0.670	
14	0.331	0.669	
15	0.332	0.668	
16	0.332	0.668	
17	0.333	0.667	
18	0.333	0.667	
19	0.333	0.667	
20	0.333	0.667	
21	0.333	0.667	
22	0.333	0.667	

(Contd...)

23	0.333	0.667	
24	0.333	0.667	
25	0.333	0.667	
26	0.333	0.667	
27	0.333	0.667	
28	0.333	0.667	
29	0.333	0.667	
30	0.333	0.667	

Note: table 12.12 and 12.13 observations confirm once again that the steady state probabilities are independent of states in the zero month.

Example 5: Suppose that there are three brands of detergents D_1, D_2, and D_3. It is observed that every month customers are being drawn from brand D_1 to brand D_2 to the extent of 30%; another 10% drawn to D_3 brand and as a result only 40% is restored by the brand D_1. Similarly, 20% of those using D_2 brand in a given month, 20% are found to move to D_1 brand, another 30% move to brand D_3. Only 50% are loyal to D_2 brand. Moreover, as far as D_3 is concerned only 80% are loyal to D_3, 15% move to D_1 and another 5% move to D_2.

(a) Formulate a suitable transitional probability matrix and interpret the result.

(b) Calculate the steady state for a currently D_1 brand purchaser.

(c) Calculate the probability for a currently D_1 brand purchaser restores to D_1 brand after two purchases from now.

(d) Calculate the probability for a currently D_1 brand purchaser moving to D_2 brand after two purchases from now.

(e) Calculate the probability for a currently D_1 brand purchaser moving to D_3 brand after two purchases from now.

Solution: (a)

Table 12.14: Transition probability matrix

From Brand (this month)	To Brand (next month)		
	D_1	D_2	D_3
D_1	0.60	0.30	0.10
D_2	0.20	0.50	0.30
D_3	0.15	0.05	0.80

Alternatively, $$P = \begin{bmatrix} 0.60 & 0.30 & 0.10 \\ 0.20 & 0.50 & 0.30 \\ 0.15 & 0.05 & 0.80 \end{bmatrix}$$

The rows of this matrix tell us the restoration as well as lose of market to other brands. For example the first row convey the message that as far as D_1 is concerned 60% is restored, 30% move to D_2 and 10% move to D_3.

Similarly, the columns tell us the respective restoration and gain from others, for example the first column show a 60% of it own, 20% from D_2 and 15% from D_3. Note that the sums of the row probabilities are always equal to unity.

Solution: (b)

We know that

$$[\pi_1 \quad \pi_2 \quad \pi_3] = [\pi_1 \quad \pi_2 \quad \pi_3] \begin{bmatrix} P_{11} & P_{12} & P_{13} \\ P_{21} & P_{22} & P_{23} \\ P_{31} & P_{32} & P_{33} \end{bmatrix}$$

$$= [\pi_1 \quad \pi_2 \quad \pi_3] \begin{bmatrix} 0.60 & 0.30 & 0.10 \\ 0.20 & 0.50 & 0.30 \\ 0.15 & 0.05 & 0.80 \end{bmatrix}$$

$$\pi_1 = 0.60\pi_1 + 0.20\pi_2 + 0.15\pi_3$$

$$\pi_2 = 0.30\pi_1 + 0.50\pi_2 + 0.05\pi_3$$

$$\pi_3 = 0.10\pi_1 + 0.30\pi_2 + 0.80\pi_3$$

$$0 = -0.40\pi_1 + 0.20\pi_2 + 0.15\pi_3$$

$$0 = 0.30\pi_1 - 0.50\pi_2 + 0.05\pi_3$$

$$0 = 0.10\pi_1 + 0.30\pi_2 - 0.20\pi_3$$

Further we know that $\pi_1 + \pi_2 + \pi_3 = 1$

So to get the solution we take the first two equations in addition to the probability conditions stated above. Now by using the Cramer's Rule the results are obtained reported below

$$A = \begin{vmatrix} -0.4 & 0.2 & 0.15 \\ 0.3 & -0.5 & 0.05 \\ 1 & 1 & 1 \end{vmatrix} = 0.29$$

$$A1 = \begin{vmatrix} 0 & 0.2 & 0.15 \\ 0 & -0.5 & 0.05 \\ 1 & 1 & 1 \end{vmatrix} = 0.085 \qquad \pi_1 = A1/A = 0.2931034$$

$$A2 = \begin{vmatrix} -0.4 & 0 & 0.15 \\ 0.3 & 0 & 0.05 \\ 1 & 1 & 1 \end{vmatrix} = 0.065 \qquad \pi_2 = A2/A = 0.2241379$$

$$A3 = \begin{vmatrix} -0.4 & 0.2 & 0 \\ 0.3 & -0.5 & 0 \\ 1 & 1 & 1 \end{vmatrix} = 0.14 \qquad \pi_3 = A3/A = 0.4827586$$

Thus in the long run the steady state market shares will be as follows

$$\pi_1 = 0.2931; \quad \pi_2 = 0.2241; \quad \pi_3 = 0.4828$$

Excel template

This time since there are three brands one must follow, the following excel template for ready use

Table 12.15: Excel template

	A	B	C	D
1				
2				
3			Initial purchase D1	
4	Month	$\pi_1(n)$	$\pi_2(n)$	$\pi_3(n)$
5	0	1	0	0
6	1	=B5*$B$38+C5*$B$39+D5*$B$40	=B5*$C$38+C5*$C$39+D5*$C$40	=B5*$D$38+C5*$D$39+D5*$D$40
7	2	=B6*$B$38+C6*$B$39+D6*$B$40	=B6*$C$38+C6*$C$39+D6*$C$40	=B6*$D$38+C6*$D$39+D6*$D$40
8	3	=B7*$B$38+C7*$B$39+D7*$B$40	=B7*$C$38+C7*$C$39+D7*$C$40	=B7*$D$38+C7*$D$39+D7*$D$40
9	4	=B8*$B$38+C8*$B$39+D8*$B$40	=B8*$C$38+C8*$C$39+D8*$C$40	=B8*$D$38+C8*$D$39+D8*$D$40
10	5	=B9*$B$38+C9*$B$39+D9*$B$40	=B9*$C$38+C9*$C$39+D9*$C$40	=B9*$D$38+C9*$D$39+D9*$D$40
11	6	=B10*$B$38+C10*$B$39+D10*$B$40	=B10*$C$38+C10*$C$39+D10*$C$40	=B10*$D$38+C10*$D$39+D10*$D$40
12	7	=B11*$B$38+C11*$B$39+D11*$B$40	=B11*$C$38+C11*$C$39+D11*$C$40	=B11*$D$38+C11*$D$39+D11*$D$40
13	8	=B12*$B$38+C12*$B$39+D12*$B$40	=B12*$C$38+C12*$C$39+D12*$C$40	=B12*$D$38+C12*$D$39+D12*$D$40
14	9	=B13*$B$38+C13*$B$39+D13*$B$40	=B13*$C$38+C13*$C$39+D13*$C$40	=B13*$D$38+C13*$D$39+D13*$D$40
15	10	=B14*$B$38+C14*$B$39+D14*$B$40	=B14*$C$38+C14*$C$39+D14*$C$40	=B14*$D$38+C14*$D$39+D14*$D$40
16	11	=B15*$B$38+C15*$B$39+D15*$B$40	=B15*$C$38+C15*$C$39+D15*$C$40	=B15*$D$38+C15*$D$39+D15*$D$40
17	12	=B16*$B$38+C16*$B$39+D16*$B$40	=B16*$C$38+C16*$C$39+D16*$C$40	=B16*$D$38+C16*$D$39+D16*$D$40
18	13	=B17*$B$38+C17*$B$39+D17*$B$40	=B17*$C$38+C17*$C$39+D17*$C$40	=B17*$D$38+C17*$D$39+D17*$D$40
19	14	=B18*$B$38+C18*$B$39+D18*$B$40	=B18*$C$38+C18*$C$39+D18*$C$40	=B18*$D$38+C18*$D$39+D18*$D$40
20	15	=B19*$B$38+C19*$B$39+D19*$B$40	=B19*$C$38+C19*$C$39+D19*$C$40	=B19*$D$38+C19*$D$39+D19*$D$40
21	16	=B20*$B$38+C20*$B$39+D20*$B$40	=B20*$C$38+C20*$C$39+D20*$C$40	=B20*$D$38+C20*$D$39+D20*$D$40
22	17	=B21*$B$38+C21*$B$39+D21*$B$40	=B21*$C$38+C21*$C$39+D21*$C$40	=B21*$D$38+C21*$D$39+D21*$D$40
23	18	=B22*$B$38+C22*$B$39+D22*$B$40	=B22*$C$38+C22*$C$39+D22*$C$40	=B22*$D$38+C22*$D$39+D22*$D$40
24	19	=B23*$B$38+C23*$B$39+D23*$B$40	=B23*$C$38+C23*$C$39+D23*$C$40	=B23*$D$38+C23*$D$39+D23*$D$40
25	20	=B24*$B$38+C24*$B$39+D24*$B$40	=B24*$C$38+C24*$C$39+D24*$C$40	=B24*$D$38+C24*$D$39+D24*$D$40
26	21	=B25*$B$38+C25*$B$39+D25*$B$40	=B25*$C$38+C25*$C$39+D25*$C$40	=B25*$D$38+C25*$D$39+D25*$D$40
27	22	=B26*$B$38+C26*$B$39+D26*$B$40	=B26*$C$38+C26*$C$39+D26*$C$40	=B26*$D$38+C26*$D$39+D26*$D$40
28	23	=B27*$B$38+C27*$B$39+D27*$B$40	=B27*$C$38+C27*$C$39+D27*$C$40	=B27*$D$38+C27*$D$39+D27*$D$40
29	24	=B28*$B$38+C28*$B$39+D28*$B$40	=B28*$C$38+C28*$C$39+D28*$C$40	=B28*$D$38+C28*$D$39+D28*$D$40
30	25	=B29*$B$38+C29*$B$39+D29*$B$40	=B29*$C$38+C29*$C$39+D29*$C$40	=B29*$D$38+C29*$D$39+D29*$D$40
31	26	=B30*$B$38+C30*$B$39+D30*$B$40	=B30*$C$38+C30*$C$39+D30*$C$40	=B30*$D$38+C30*$D$39+D30*$D$40
32	27	=B31*$B$38+C31*$B$39+D31*$B$40	=B31*$C$38+C31*$C$39+D31*$C$40	=B31*$D$38+C31*$D$39+D31*$D$40
33	28	=B32*$B$38+C32*$B$39+D32*$B$40	=B32*$C$38+C32*$C$39+D32*$C$40	=B32*$D$38+C32*$D$39+D32*$D$40
34	29	=B33*$B$38+C33*$B$39+D33*$B$40	=B33*$C$38+C33*$C$39+D33*$C$40	=B33*$D$38+C33*$D$39+D33*$D$40
35	30	=B34*$B$38+C34*$B$39+D34*$B$40	=B34*$C$38+C34*$C$39+D34*$C$40	=B34*$D$38+C34*$D$39+D34*$D$40
36				
37				
38		0.6	0.3	0.1
39	P =	0.2	0.5	0.3
40		0.15	0.05	0.8
41				

Excel result sheet

Table 12.16: Excel solution

Month	Initial Shopping Brand D1 $\pi_1(n)$	$\pi_2(n)$	$\pi_3(n)$
0	1	0	0
1	0.600	0.300	0.100
2	0.435	0.335	0.230
3	0.363	0.310	0.328
4	0.329	0.280	0.392
5	0.312	0.258	0.430
6	0.303	0.244	0.453
7	0.299	0.236	0.466
8	0.296	0.231	0.473
9	0.295	0.228	0.477
10	0.294	0.226	0.480
11	0.294	0.225	0.481
12	0.293	0.225	0.482
13	0.293	0.225	0.482
14	0.293	0.224	0.482
15	0.293	0.224	0.483
16	0.293	0.224	0.483
17	0.293	0.224	0.483
18	0.293	0.224	0.483
19	0.293	0.224	0.483
20	0.293	0.224	0.483
21	0.293	0.224	0.483
22	0.293	0.224	0.483
23	0.293	0.224	0.483
24	0.293	0.224	0.483
25	0.293	0.224	0.483
26	0.293	0.224	0.483
27	0.293	0.224	0.483
28	0.293	0.224	0.483
29	0.293	0.224	0.483
30	0.293	0.224	0.483

$$P = \begin{vmatrix} 0.6 & 0.3 & 0.1 \\ 0.2 & 0.5 & 0.3 \\ 0.15 & 0.05 & 0.8 \end{vmatrix}$$

Solution: (c, d, e)

$$\Pi(2) = \Pi(0)P^2$$

$$= \begin{bmatrix} 1 & 0 & 0 \end{bmatrix} \begin{bmatrix} 0.60 & 0.30 & 0.10 \\ 0.20 & 0.50 & 0.30 \\ 0.15 & 0.05 & 0.80 \end{bmatrix}^2$$

$$= \begin{bmatrix} 1 & 0 & 0 \end{bmatrix} \begin{bmatrix} 0.60 & 0.30 & 0.10 \\ 0.20 & 0.50 & 0.30 \\ 0.15 & 0.05 & 0.80 \end{bmatrix} \begin{bmatrix} 0.60 & 0.30 & 0.10 \\ 0.20 & 0.50 & 0.30 \\ 0.15 & 0.05 & 0.80 \end{bmatrix}$$

$$= \begin{bmatrix} 1 & 0 & 0 \end{bmatrix} \begin{bmatrix} 0.435 & 0.335 & 0.235 \\ 0.265 & 0.325 & 0.410 \\ 0.220 & 0.110 & 0.670 \end{bmatrix}$$

$$\begin{bmatrix} \pi_1(2) & \pi_2(2) & \pi_3(2) \end{bmatrix} = \begin{bmatrix} 0.435 & 0.335 & 0.230 \end{bmatrix}$$

(c) $\pi_1(2) = 0.435$

(d) $\pi_2(2) = 0.335$

(e) $\pi_3(2) = 0.230$

Table 12.17: Excel solution

Trip	Initial Shopping Brand D1 $\pi_1(n)$	$\pi_2(n)$	$\pi_3(n)$
0	1	0	0
1	0.600	0.300	0.100
2	0.435	0.335	0.230
3	0.363	0.310	0.328
4	0.329	0.280	0.392
P =	0.6	0.3	0.1
	0.2	0.5	0.3
	0.15	0.05	0.8

Example 6: Recently, a market research unit has conducted a survey of customers buying habits three brands of toothpastes in Bangalore. It estimates that, at present, 20% of the customers buy brand A, 50% of the customers buy brand B and 30% of the customers buy brand C. In addition the research unit reported the following switching brand matrix.

Table 12.18

Brand just bought	Brand next bought		
	A	B	C
A	0.6	0.3	0.1
B	0.4	0.5	0.1
C	0.2	0.1	0.7

(a) What will be the expected distribution market shares in two time periods latter?

Solution:

The initial condition indicates the present market share.

$$\Pi(0) = [\pi_1(0) \quad \pi_2(0) \quad \pi_3(0)] = [0.20 \quad 0.50 \quad 0.30]$$

Further from the table given above the transitional probability matrix is obtain as

$$P = \begin{bmatrix} 0.6 & 0.3 & 0.1 \\ 0.4 & 0.5 & 0.1 \\ 0.2 & 0.1 & 0.7 \end{bmatrix}$$

The expected distribution of market share after 2 periods from now Q(2) is obtained as $Q(0) \times P^2$.

$$\begin{aligned} \Pi(2) &= [\pi_1(2) \quad \pi_2(2) \quad \pi_3(2)] \\ &= [\pi_1(0) \quad \pi_2(0) \quad \pi_3(0)]\ P^2 \\ &= [\pi_1(0) \quad \pi_2(0) \quad \pi_3(0)] \begin{bmatrix} 0.6 & 0.3 & 0.1 \\ 0.4 & 0.5 & 0.1 \\ 0.2 & 0.1 & 0.7 \end{bmatrix}^2 \\ &= [0.20 \quad 0.50 \quad 0.30] \begin{bmatrix} 0.6 & 0.3 & 0.1 \\ 0.4 & 0.5 & 0.1 \\ 0.2 & 0.1 & 0.7 \end{bmatrix}^2 \\ &= [0.420 \quad 0.312 \quad 0.268] \end{aligned}$$

Thus, after 2 periods the expected market shares will be 42%, 31.2%, 26.8% respectively for three brands A, B, and C.

Table 12.19: Excel solution

Trip	Initial Shopping Brand D1		
	$\pi_1(n)$	$\pi_2(n)$	$\pi_3(n)$
0	0.2	0.5	0.3
1	0.380	0.340	0.280
2	0.420	0.312	0.268
3	0.430	0.309	0.261
4	0.434	0.310	0.256
P =	0.6	0.3	0.1
	0.4	0.5	0.1
	0.2	0.1	0.7

Example 7: A research team surveyed the shoppers in an area to discover the brand switching habits among customers in three brands A, B, and C type of detergents. Finally they were able to get the following information from the shoppers.

Table 12.20

Current Purchase	Previous Purchase	Number
A	A	200
B	B	150
C	C	100
B	A	50
C	A	25
A	B	80
C	b	45
A	C	130
B	C	20

(a) By using the given data obtain the transition matrix.

(b) Calculate the market share for each of the brands after two periods from now.

Solution:

Let us tabulate the given data first as shown below.

Table 12.21

From Brand	To Brand			
	A	B	C	Total
A	200	50	25	275
B	80	150	45	275
C	130	20	100	250
Total	410	220	170	800

(a) Now the needed transition matrix is obtained by dividing each element in the above table by the respective row total.

$$P = \begin{bmatrix} 8/11 & 2/11 & 1/11 \\ 16/55 & 30/55 & 9/55 \\ 13/25 & 2/25 & 10/25 \end{bmatrix}$$

(b) The current market share vector is obtained by dividing the column total by the grand total in the data summary table given above.

$$\Pi(0) = [410/800 \quad 220/800 \quad 170/800]$$

Now the needed $\Pi(2)$ is obtained as

$$\Pi(2) = \Pi(0) \times P^2$$

$$= [41/80 \quad 22/80 \quad 17/80] \begin{bmatrix} 8/11 & 2/11 & 1/11 \\ 16/55 & 30/55 & 9/55 \\ 13/25 & 2/25 & 10/25 \end{bmatrix}^2$$

$$= [0.577 \quad 0.258 \quad 0.164]$$

Thus the expected market shares after 2 periods latter will be: 57.7 %, 25.8%, and 16.4% respectively for A, B, and C brands.

Table 12.22: Excel solution

Trip	Initial Shopping Brand D1 $\pi_1(n)$	$\pi_2(n)$	$\pi_3(n)$
0	0.5125	0.275	0.2125
1	0.563	0.260	0.177
2	0.577	0.258	0.164
3	0.580	0.259	0.161
4	0.581	0.260	0.159
P =	0.73	0.18	0.09
	0.29	0.55	0.16
	0.52	0.08	0.40

Example 8: Suppose that new razor blades were introduced in the market by three companies at the same time. When they were introduced, each company had an equal share of the market, but during the first year the following changes took place.

(i) Company A retained 90% of its customers, lost 3% to B and 7% to C

(ii) Company B retained 70% of the customers, lost 10% to A and 20% to C

(iii) Company C retained 80% of the customers, lost 10% to A and 10% to B

Assume that no changes in the buying habits of the consumer occur.

1. What are the market shares of these companies at the end of the second year?
2. What are the long run market shares of these three companies?

Solution 1:

From the data given we obtain the initial condition and the transition matrix obtained as

$$\Pi(0) = [\pi_1(0) \quad \pi_2(0) \quad \pi_3(0)] = [0.333 \quad 0.333 \quad 0.333]$$

$$P = \begin{bmatrix} 0.90 & 0.03 & 0.07 \\ 0.10 & 0.70 & 0.20 \\ 0.10 & 0.10 & 0.80 \end{bmatrix}$$

$$\Pi(1) = \Pi(0) \times P$$

$$= [0.333 \quad 0.333 \quad 0.333] \begin{bmatrix} 0.90 & 0.03 & 0.07 \\ 0.10 & 0.70 & 0.20 \\ 0.10 & 0.10 & 0.80 \end{bmatrix}$$

$$= [0.367 \quad 0.277 \quad 0.356]$$

Market share after one year will be: 36.7%, 27.7%, and 35.6% respectively.

$$\Pi(1) = \Pi(0) \times P^2$$

$$= \begin{bmatrix} 0.333 & 0.333 & 0.333 \end{bmatrix} \begin{bmatrix} 0.90 & 0.03 & 0.07 \\ 0.10 & 0.70 & 0.20 \\ 0.10 & 0.10 & 0.80 \end{bmatrix} \begin{bmatrix} 0.90 & 0.03 & 0.07 \\ 0.10 & 0.70 & 0.20 \\ 0.10 & 0.10 & 0.80 \end{bmatrix}$$

$$= \begin{bmatrix} 0.3933 & 0.2403 & 0.3663 \end{bmatrix}$$

Market share at the end of second year: 39.33%, 24.03%, and 36.64% respectively.

Table 12.23: Excel solution

Trip	Initial Shopping Brand D1 $\pi_1(n)$	$\pi_2(n)$	$\pi_3(n)$
0	0.3333	0.3333	0.3333
1	0.3667	0.2767	0.3567
2	0.3933	0.2403	0.3663
3	0.4147	0.2167	0.3687
4	0.4317	0.2010	0.3673
	0.90	0.03	0.07
P =	0.10	0.70	0.20
	0.10	0.10	0.80

Solution 2:

Let π_1, π_2 and π_3 are the expected market shares in the long run.

$$\begin{bmatrix} \pi_1 & \pi_2 & \pi_3 \end{bmatrix} = \begin{bmatrix} \pi_1 & \pi_2 & \pi_3 \end{bmatrix} \begin{bmatrix} P \end{bmatrix}$$

$$= \begin{bmatrix} \pi_1 & \pi_2 & \pi_3 \end{bmatrix} \begin{bmatrix} 0.90 & 0.03 & 0.07 \\ 0.10 & 0.70 & 0.20 \\ 0.10 & 0.10 & 0.80 \end{bmatrix}$$

$$\pi_1 = 0.90\pi_1 + 0.10\pi_2 + 0.10\pi_3$$

$$\pi_2 = 0.03\pi_1 + 0.07\pi_2 + 0.10\pi_3$$

$$\pi_3 = 0.07\pi_1 + 0.20\pi_2 + 0.80\pi_3$$

Now from the first two equations and the probability condition we obtain

$$0.10\pi_1 - 0.10\pi_2 - 0.10\pi_3 = 0 \quad \text{... (1)}$$

$$-0.03\pi_1 + 0.3\pi_2 - 0.10\pi_3 = 0 \quad \text{... (2)}$$

$$\pi_1 + \pi_2 + \pi_3 = 1 \quad \text{... (3)}$$

Now as Cramer's rule we obtain the results as shown below

Table 12.24

Trip	Initial Shopping Brand D1		
	$\pi_1(n)$	$\pi_2(n)$	$\pi_3(n)$
0	0.3333	0.3333	0.3333
1	0.3666	0.2766	0.3566
2	0.3933	0.2403	0.3663
3	0.4146	0.2166	0.3686
4	0.4317	0.2010	0.3673
5	0.4453	0.1903	0.3642
6	0.4563	0.1830	0.3606
7	0.4650	0.1779	0.3570
8	0.4720	0.1742	0.3538
9	0.4776	0.1714	0.3509
10	0.4821	0.1694	0.3484
11	0.4856	0.1679	0.3464
12	0.4885	0.1667	0.3447
13	0.4908	0.1658	0.3433
14	0.4926	0.1651	0.3421
15	0.4941	0.1646	0.3412
16	0.4953	0.1642	0.3405
17	0.4962	0.1638	0.3399
18	0.4969	0.1635	0.3394
19	0.4975	0.1633	0.3390
20	0.4980	0.1632	0.3387
21	0.4984	0.1630	0.3385
22	0.4987	0.1629	0.3383
23	0.4990	0.1628	0.3381
24	0.4992	0.1628	0.3380
25	0.4993	0.1627	0.3379
26	0.4994	0.1627	0.3378
27	0.4995	0.1626	0.3377
28	0.4996	0.1626	0.3377
29	0.4997	0.1626	0.3376
30	0.4997	0.1626	0.3376

$$P = \begin{vmatrix} 0.90 & 0.03 & 0.07 \\ 0.10 & 0.70 & 0.20 \\ 0.10 & 0.10 & 0.80 \end{vmatrix}$$

$$A = \begin{vmatrix} 0.1 & -0.1 & -0.1 \\ -0.03 & 0.3 & -0.1 \\ 1 & 1 & 1 \end{vmatrix} = 0.08$$

$$A1 = \begin{vmatrix} 0 & -0.1 & -0.1 \\ 0 & 0.3 & -0.1 \\ 1 & 1 & 1 \end{vmatrix} = 0.04 \qquad \pi_1 = \text{A1/A} = 0.5$$

$$A2 = \begin{vmatrix} 0.1 & 0 & -0.1 \\ -0.03 & 0 & -0.1 \\ 1 & 1 & 1 \end{vmatrix} = 0.013 \qquad \pi_2 = \text{A2/A} = 0.1625$$

$$A3 = \begin{vmatrix} 0.1 & -0.1 & 0 \\ -0.03 & 0.3 & 0 \\ 1 & 1 & 1 \end{vmatrix} = 0.027 \qquad \pi_1 = \text{A3/A} = 0.3375$$

So in the long run the steady equilibrium market shares will be: 50%, 16% and 34% respectively.

12.7 Finite and Absorbing States

In our illustrative example of three detergents there are only three finite numbers of states in the sense that the customer under reference must be using either D_1 or D_2 or D_3 and no other brands. Note that all the 100% of the customers are absorbed by any of the three states.

Further, none of the states are completely absorbing in the sense having the probability of 1.00, such states are called non-observing states. For such non-observing states the following properties hold good.

- For two states i and j, the sequence of transition that begins at i and ends at j is called a *path* from i to j.
- A state j is *reachable* from the state i provided there is a defined path from i to j
- The states i and j are said to be *communicative* provided there exists a path form i to j
- A state i is known as *transient* state if there exists a state j reachable from i, and at the same time i is not reachable from j. Thus, a state i is transient provided there is a way to leave i and joint j but no way to come back from j to i again.
- If a state is not transient then it is called a recurrent state.

In Fig. 12.3 it could be seen that each of the three stages are reachable from all others and hence become commutative as well. Also none of these three states are in absorbing stage and hence become recurrent and suitable for Markov process analysis.

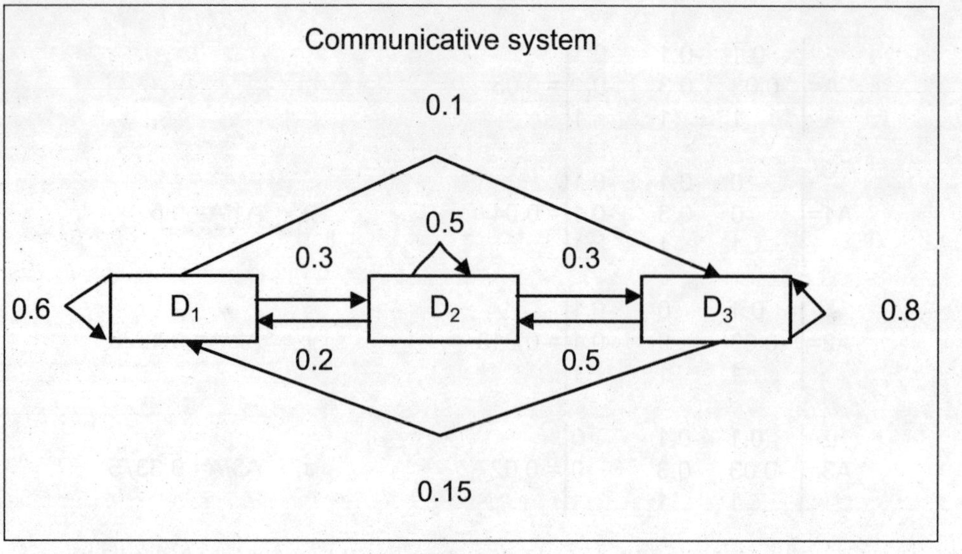

Fig. 12.3

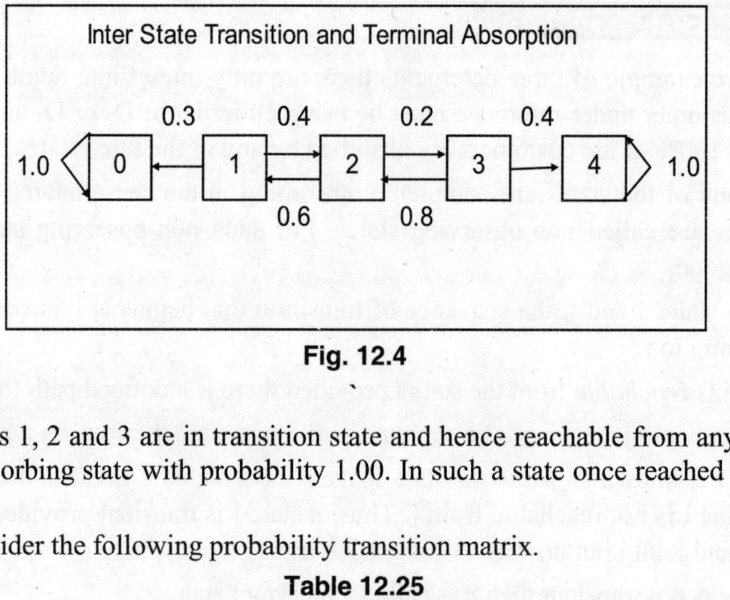

Fig. 12.4

In Fig. 12.4, states 1, 2 and 3 are in transition state and hence reachable from any other, but state 0 and 4 are in absorbing state with probability 1.00. In such a state once reached no way to come out it.

Example 9: Consider the following probability transition matrix.

Table 12.25

From State	To State				
	1	2	3	4	5
1	0.3	0.5	0	0	0
2	0.7	0.5	0	0	0
3	0	0	0.8	0.2	0
4	0	0	0.4	0.3	0.3
5	0	0	0	0.3	0.9

(a) Provide an example of a path in it.`

(b) Give an example of states which communicate.

(c) Provide an example of recurrent state.

(d) Identify the transient states if any.

(e) Identify the absorbing sates if any.

Solution:

Figure 12.5 and 12.6 illustrates the whole situation diagrammatically.

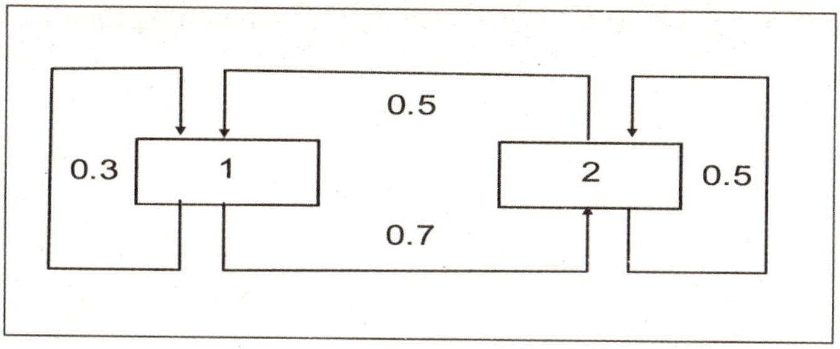

Fig. 12.5

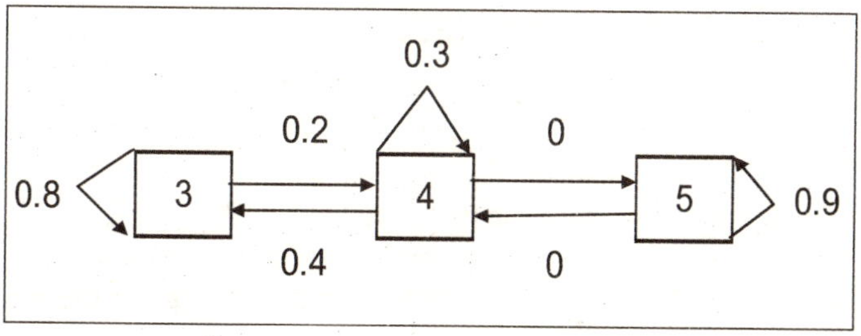

Fig. 12.6

(a) A path could be seen from state 3 to state 5 via state 4. Similarly, a path could be traced from state 1 to 2 also.

(b) The state i and j are communicative provided from state i, one can reach state j and from state j, one can reach i. For example, state 1 and 2 are communicative because stare 1 is reachable from state 2 and vice versa.

(c) Each state in this matrix is recurrent, because each i there exist a state j that is reachable from it.

(d) None of the state is transient because all of them are recurrent.

(e) None of the state is absorbing because no state is having probability 1.

12.8 Absorbing Chain and Its Application in Accounts

Till now in all our problems none of the states were found to be absorbing. In this section we consider an application of Markov process with two observing states. In accounting related problems an amount receivable is either received within the over due time of 90 days or written off as bad dept beyond 90 days. Thus, whatever may be the transient state, finally the said account ends either as paid category or written off category. These two categories often called observing category. Any account beyond 90 days default is definitely going to be written off with the probability of 1. Similarly, even the paid category within 90 days will not be considered again. Thus the fully paid and fully written cases are not at all in the preview of our analysis. Further, for absorbing type of problems there is no long run steady state probability as such, in the sense that no account will prolong after 90 days. All probability calculations are state probabilities only in this section.

Given this scenario, let us illustrate the Food World's accounting department for illustration. Food World departmental store has two aging categories for its amount receivable: (1) accounts that are classified as 0 – 30 days old and (2) accounts that are classified as 31–90 days old. If any portion of an account exceeds 90 days, is written off as bad dept. To illustrate this method of classification let us concentrate on Mr. A's account. Suppose customer Mr. A's balance as on April 30 is as follows:

Table 12.26

Date of purchase	Amount billed
August 15	Rs.25
September 18	Rs.10
September 28	Rs.50
Total balance to be paid	Rs.85

An aging account receivable on September 30 would assign the balance of Rs. 85 to 31 to 90 days category because the oldest unpaid bill of August 15 is 46 days old. Suppose our customer pays the August 15th bill of Rs. 25 on October 7. Now on this day the remaining balance of Rs.60 deserves a 0–30 day category and will be recorded accordingly, because the oldest unpaid September 18th bill is only 12 days old on September 30. This method of obtaining aging account receivable is called total balance method because the total balance till the aging day is placed in this account. Note that in this illustration the balance portion of Rs. 60 will be shifted from 31–90 days category to 0–30 day's category once the August bill of Rs. 25 is paid on October 7.

Let, on December 31 the departmental store show a total of Rs. 3000 in its accounts receivable from all the customers. Out of this due amount how much the Food World will eventually collect and how much will eventually treated, as bad dept on December 31 while submitting the year ending financial statement for notification is the real problem.

Now let us see how we can evaluate the account receivable using Markov process. First let us concentrate on imaginary amount 1 rupee which is there on the account receivable account instead of the actual amount of Rs.3000. As the business concern the manager would be interested in monitoring the situation on weekly basis. At a given point of time the said one rupee will lie in any one of the following four mutually exhaustive states of the system.

1. Paid category
2. Bad dept and hence written off category
3. 0–30 Days category
4. 31–90 Days Category

Now let us check track record of the said one Rupee account on weekly basis by using Markov process.

Let p_{ij} = the probability of a Rupee in state i in current week moving to the state j in the next week. Based on historical data let the obtained transition probability matrix by Food World be

$$P = \begin{bmatrix} p_{11} & p_{12} & p_{13} & p_{14} \\ p_{21} & p_{22} & p_{23} & p_{24} \\ p_{31} & p_{32} & p_{33} & p_{34} \\ p_{41} & p_{42} & p_{43} & p_{44} \end{bmatrix} = \begin{bmatrix} 1.0 & 0.0 & 0.0 & 0.0 \\ 0.0 & 1.0 & 0.0 & 0.0 \\ 0.4 & 0.0 & 0.3 & 0.3 \\ 0.4 & 0.2 & 0.3 & 0.1 \end{bmatrix}$$

Now let us interpret the entries in the transition matrix by taking the third row as example. From the transaction matrix third row it is clear that the probability of a rupee moving from state 3 (0–30 days) to state 1 (paid category) in the next week is 0.4. Also notice that the probability of this rupee to be there in state 3 itself (0–30 days) in the next week is 0.3, and moving to category 4 (31–90 days) in the next week is also 0.3. But definitely this Rupee cannot become a bad dept in the next week because of the zero state in the matrix. Once a Rupee is moved into paid category (state 1) the probability of moving to any other state in latter weeks is invariably shown by zero entries as shown in the first row of the matrix

Similarly, once the Rupee enters into state 2 (bad dept will not be converted into any other state in latter weeks as reveled by the second row. Here state 1 and 2 are called absorbing states since once the rupee moves into these states it gets absorbed and hence will not move to any other state. Also note, in the above table the sum of all the probabilities added up to unity for all the four rows as expected.

In Markov process, since we have two definite paid up and bad dept observing states we do not go for the calculation of steady state probability as stated earlier. Irrespective of the states they belong in the transitory period they all ultimately end up in any one of these two observing states.

We will be interested only in

1. Getting the probabilities of a 0–30 age category ending with the paid category as well as bad dept category.
2. Getting the probabilities of a 31–90 age category ending with the paid category as well as bad dept category.

The computation of the said absorbing state probabilities requires the use of what is called *fundamental matrix* the mathematical logic underling the fundamental matrix is beyond the scope of this text. However, we derive the fundamental matrix from the transition probability matrix. To do the task we begin the computation by partitioning the given transition matrix as shown below.

$$P = \left[\begin{array}{c} \left\langle\begin{array}{cc|cc} 1.0 & 0.0 & 0.0 & 0.0 \\ 0.0 & 1.0 & 0.0 & 0.0 \end{array}\right\rangle \\ \hline \left\langle\begin{array}{cc|cc} 0.4 & 0.0 & 0.3 & 0.3 \\ 0.4 & 0.2 & 0.3 & 0.1 \end{array}\right\rangle \end{array}\right] = \left[\begin{array}{c} \left\langle\begin{array}{cc|cc} 1.0 & 0.0 & 0.0 & 0.0 \\ 0.0 & 1.0 & 0.0 & 0.0 \end{array}\right\rangle \\ \hline \langle R|Q \rangle \end{array}\right]$$

where $R = \begin{bmatrix} 0.4 & 0.0 \\ 0.4 & 0.2 \end{bmatrix}$ $\quad Q = \begin{bmatrix} 0.3 & 0.3 \\ 0.3 & 0.1 \end{bmatrix}$

Now the needed fundamental matrix is defined as

$$N = (I - Q)^{-1}$$

$$I-Q = \begin{bmatrix} 1 & 0 \\ 0 & 1 \end{bmatrix} - \begin{bmatrix} 0.3 & 0.3 \\ 0.3 & 0.1 \end{bmatrix} = \begin{bmatrix} 0.7 & -0.3 \\ -0.3 & 0.9 \end{bmatrix}$$

$$I-Q = \begin{bmatrix} 0.7 & -0.3 \\ -0.3 & 0.9 \end{bmatrix}$$

$$\text{Cofactor of } I-Q = \begin{bmatrix} 0.9 & 0.3 \\ 0.3 & 0.7 \end{bmatrix}$$

$$\text{adj of } I-Q = \begin{bmatrix} 0.9 & 0.3 \\ 0.3 & 0.7 \end{bmatrix}$$

$$\text{Determinant } I-Q = 0.54$$

$$N = (I-Q)^{-1} = \begin{bmatrix} 1.667 & 0.56 \\ 0.556 & 1.3 \end{bmatrix}$$

$$N \times R = \begin{bmatrix} 1.667 & 0.56 \\ 0.556 & 1.3 \end{bmatrix} \times \begin{bmatrix} 0.4 & 0 \\ 0.4 & 0.2 \end{bmatrix} = \begin{bmatrix} 0.889 & 0.11 \\ 0.741 & 0.26 \end{bmatrix}$$

The first row in NR above gives us the probabilities of a 0–30 category will end up with respective observing states. With probability of 0.89 this category will end with paid state. Similarly, with probability of 0.11 this category will end with bad debt state. The second row in NR give us the probabilities of a 31–90 category will end up with respective observing states. With probability of 0.74 this category will end with paid state. Similarly, with probability of 0.26 this category will end with bad debt state.

Example 10: Consider the receivable account of a firm. Suppose that, for this firm, amounts receivable turns into a bad dept provided the account is more than three months old. Now at the beginning of each month, each of the accounts may be classified into one of the following states.

1. New Account
2. Account is one month over due for payment
3. Account is two month over due for payment.
4. Account is three month over due for payment.
5. Account has been paid.
6. Account is written off as bad debt.

Suppose further that on the basis of past experience, the bank evaluated the following transition matrix for the six states stated.

Table 12.27

State	State					
	1	2	3	4	5	6
1	0	0.7	0	0	0.3	0
2	0	0	0.6	0	0.4	0
3	0	0	0	0.4	0.6	0
4	0	0	0	0	0.8	0.2
5	0	0	0	0	1	0
6	0	0	0	0	0	1

(i) What is the probability of a new account shall eventually be paid?

(ii) What is the probability that a new account shall be written off as bad debt?

(iii) What is the probability that a one month overdue account shall eventually be paid?

(iv) What is the probability that a one month overdue account shall eventually written off?

(v) What is the probability that a two month overdue account shall eventually be paid?

(vi) What is the probability that a two month overdue account shall eventually written off?

(vii) If the bank makes a credit sale of Rs.4,00,000 per month then what amount it can expect to lose per annum by way bad debt.

To answer these questions let us we first partition the given transition matrix as shown below with the states listed as transient states as one part and absorbing states as another part.

Table 12.28

State	State					
	t_1	t_2	t_3	t_4	a_1	a_2
t_1	0	0.7	0	0	0.3	0
t_2	0	0	0.6	0	0.4	0
t_3	0	0	0	0.4	0.6	0
t_4	0	0	0	0	0.8	0.2
a_1	0	0	0	0	1	0
a_2	0	0	0	0	0	1

$$\text{Now let } Q = \begin{bmatrix} 0 & 0.7 & 0 & 0 \\ 0 & 0 & 0.6 & 0 \\ 0 & 0 & 0 & 0.4 \\ 0 & 0 & 0 & 0 \end{bmatrix} \quad R = \begin{bmatrix} 0.3 & 0 \\ 0.4 & 0 \\ 0.6 & 0 \\ 0.8 & 0.2 \end{bmatrix}$$

Now the needed fundamental matrix is defined as

$$NR = (I - Q)^{-1} R$$

$$I - Q = \begin{bmatrix} 1 & 0 & 0 & 0 \\ 0 & 1 & 0 & 0 \\ 0 & 0 & 1 & 0 \\ 0 & 0 & 0 & 1 \end{bmatrix} - \begin{bmatrix} 0 & 0.7 & 0 & 0 \\ 0 & 0 & 0.6 & 0 \\ 0 & 0 & 0 & 0.4 \\ 0 & 0 & 0 & 0 \end{bmatrix}$$

$$= \begin{bmatrix} 1 & -0.7 & 0 & 0 \\ 0 & 1 & -0.6 & 0 \\ 0 & 0 & 1 & -0.4 \\ 0 & 0 & 0 & 1 \end{bmatrix}$$

$$(I-Q)^{-1} = \begin{bmatrix} 1 & 0.7 & 0.42 & 0.168 \\ 0 & 1 & 0.6 & 0.24 \\ 0 & 0 & 1 & 0.4 \\ 0 & 0 & 0 & 1 \end{bmatrix}$$

$$(I-Q)^{-1}R = \begin{bmatrix} 1 & 0.7 & 0.42 & 0.168 \\ 0 & 1 & 0.6 & 0.24 \\ 0 & 0 & 1 & 0.4 \\ 0 & 0 & 0 & 1 \end{bmatrix} \times \begin{bmatrix} 0.3 & 0 \\ 0.4 & 0 \\ 0.6 & 0 \\ 0.8 & 0.2 \end{bmatrix}$$

$$= \begin{bmatrix} 0.9664 & 0.0336 \\ 0.9520 & 0.0480 \\ 0.9200 & 0.0800 \\ 0.8000 & 0.2000 \end{bmatrix}$$

The ij^{th} element of this fundamental matrix gives the expected number of periods that will have to be spent in the transient state before reaching any one of the absorbing sates. Similarly, if the chain begins in a transient state say t_i then the probability that it shall eventually absorbed in absorbing state a_j is given by the ij^{th} element of the matrix $(I - Q)^{-1}R$.

(i) The probability of a new account holder (t_1) shall eventually make payment (a_1) = 0.9664.

(ii) The probability that a new account holder (t_1) shall be written off (a_2) as bad debt = 0.0336.

(iii) The probability that a one month overdue account holder (t_2) shall eventually make payment (a_1) = 0.9520.

(iv) The probability that a one month overdue account holder (t_2) shall eventually written off (a_2) = 0.0480.

(v) The probability that a two month overdue account holder (t_3) shall eventually make payment (a_1) = 0.9200.

(vi) What is the probability that a two month overdue account holder (t_3) shall eventually written off (a_2) = 0.0800.

(vii) For a credit sale of Rs.4,00,000 per month the corresponding annual sales will by $12 \times 4,00,000$ = Rs.48,00,000. Thus the amount that the bank is likely to loose as bad debt $= 48,00,000 \times 0.0336$ = Rs.1,61,280.

EXERCISES

1. What do you understand by Markov process? In what areas of management can they be applied?
2. What do you understand by transition probabilities? Is the assumption of stationary transition probabilities realistic, in your opinion? Why or Why are not?
3. Distinguish between recurrent and an absorbing state.

4. Discuss the importance of the following assumption in Markov chain:
   (a) Finite state
   (b) First- order process
   (c) Stationary and transition probabilities
   (d) Uniform time period
5. How do we calculate the steady state probabilities? Do you think they are independent of initial conditions?
6. Explain the use of probability tree in Markov process with suitable illustration.
7. (a) The purchase patterns of two brands of toothpaste can be expressed as a Markov process with the following probabilities:

	Brand X	Brand Y
Brand X	0.90	0.10
Brand Y	0.05	0.95

   (i) Which brand appears to have more loyal customers?
   (ii) What are the projected market shares for the two brands?

   (b) Suppose that in part (a) a new toothpaste brand enters the market such that the following transitional probabilities exist

	Brand X	Brand Y	Brand Z
Brand X	0.80	0.10	0.10
Brand Y	0.05	0.75	0.20
Brand Z	0.40	0.30	0.30

   What ate the new long run market shares? Which brand will suffer from introduction of the new brand of toothpaste?
8. A market survey is made on three brands of breakfast foods X, Y and Z. Every time the customer purchases a new package, he may buy the same brand or switch over to other brands. The following estimates are obtained, expressed as decimal fractions:

$$\begin{array}{c} \text{Next Brand} \\ \begin{array}{cc} & \begin{array}{ccc} X & Y & Z \end{array} \\ \text{Present Brand} \begin{array}{c} X \\ Y \\ Z \end{array} & \begin{pmatrix} 0.7 & 0.2 & 0.1 \\ 0.3 & 0.5 & 0.2 \\ 0.3 & 0.3 & 0.4 \end{pmatrix} \end{array} \end{array}$$

   At this time, it is estimated that 30 per cent of the people buy brand X, 20 per cent brand Y and 50 per cent brand Z. What will the distribution of customers be two times periods later and at equilibrium? *(Delhi University, M.B.A , Dec. 1984)*
9. On January 1, (this year), Bakery A had 40% of its market share while the other two bakeries B and C has 40% and 20% respectively of the market share. Based upon a study by a marketing research firm, the following facts were compiled. Bakery A retains 90% of its own customers while gaining 5% of B's customers and 10% of C's customers. Bakery B retains 85% of its own customers while gaining 5% of A's customers and 7% of C's customers. Bakery C retains 83% of its own customers and gains 5% of A's

customers and 10% of B's customers. What will each firm share be on January 1, next year and what will each firm's market share be at equilibrium?

(Delhi University, M.B.A., Nov. 1996)

10. A manufacturing company has a certain piece of equipment that is inspected at the end of each day and classified as overhauled, good, fair or inoperative. If the piece is inoperative, it is overhauled, a procedure that takes one day. Assume that the working condition of the equipment follows a Markov process with the following transitional matrix.

From State	To State			
	1	2	3	4
1	0.00	0.75	0.25	0.00
2	0.00	0.50	0.50	0.00
3	0.00	0.00	0.50	0.50
4	1.00	0.00	0.00	0.00

It costs Rs.125 a machine (including last time) on the average and Rs.75 in production is in lost if the machine is found inoperative. Using the steady state probability, compute the expected per day cost of maintenance.

11. A credit card company is attempting to determine a more effective set of credit control policies. It has traditionally classified all its accounts receivable into five distinct categories listed below:

Account receivable category	Status of account receivable
1	0–30 days late
2	31–90 days late
3	91 plus date late
4	Paid in full
5	Defaulted

Based on the research, the company has derived the following transition matrix describing the behaviour of various categories on a weekly basis.

From Category	To Category				
	1.00	2.00	3.00	4.00	5.00
1.00	0.40	0.20	0.10	0.20	0.10
2.00	0.30	0.40	0.10	0.10	0.10
3.00	0.20	0.40	0.10	0.10	0.20
4.00	0.00	0.00	0.00	1.00	0.00
5.00	0.00	0.00	0.00	0.00	1.00

Currently the company has the following accounts in various categories.

Category	Amount
1	Rs.2 Million
2	Rs.4 Million
3	Rs.3 Million

You are required to calculate the expected amounts which may eventually be (i) collected, and (ii) defaulted.

OO

13

Chapter

DECISION THEORY

13.1 Introduction

In business when a decision-maker faces several alternatives, the decision analysis helps him to take appropriate decisions. For example, a global manufacturer might be interested in identifying the best location for his new plant. Suppose our manufacturer has identified six plant locations for his business in four different countries. Choosing one among the six locations is a difficult task indeed. The choice often depends upon factors like the political stability of the country concerned, extent of market, availability raw material, its cost and so on. Under such circumstances, several scenarios could emerge by way of combining various factors. Accordingly, every scenario will have a probability of its own. Using profit or cost consequence in mind attempt will be made to identify the best possible plant location. With all due care often uncertain future complicates the selection process. In certain cases, the selected decision alternative may yield very good unexpected result even. In other cases it might be very fatal for the survival. Thus, the risk associated with any final decision is the directly related to the risk associated with the respective individual factors taken into consideration. A good decision theory therefore should invariably relate to the theory of probability.

Let us begin the study of decision theory by considering problem having reasonably few decision alternatives and reasonably few possible future events. To make a simple beginning let us introduce ourselves to influence diagrams and the concept of the associated payoff tables. In the second stage we propose to introduce decision trees that will simplify even more complex real World problems.

13.2 Formulation of the Problem

As usual, in any other research, the first step in the decision analysis is problem formulation. We begin with the verbal statement of the problem as follows. The Bangalore Development Authority, in its Civic Amenities site at HSR layout decides to construct a commercial complex. This location provides a spectacular view of the project. The BDA had preliminary architectural design for three alternative-sized projects. The alternatives are

d_1 = a small complex with 100 shops
d_2 = a medium sized complex with 300 shops
d_3 = a large complex with 500 shops

Given these three alternatives, the BDA want to identify the appropriate size that gives the maximum profit. A factor that affects the selection of the best alternative project is the uncertainty associated the chance event otherwise called the demand for the shops in the proposed complex. In the decision analysis, the possible outcomes of a chance event are often referred as ***states of nature.*** The chance events are defined so that at a given point of time only one of the possible states of nature will occur. For the BDA problem let the two chance events are

s_1 = Strong demand for the shops
s_2 = Weak demand for the shops

Thus, under the given circumstances, the BDA must select the complex size having the state of nature that is going to follow in future in mind. Once the selection is made, depending upon the chance event that follows a final consequence will result.

13.3 Influence Diagram

An influence diagram is a special graphical device describing the relationship between the decision variable, the chance events and the final consequence. In this presentation it is a common practice to use squares to represent decision ***nodes***. Circles or ovals are used to depict the ***chance nodes,*** and diamonds are used to represent ***consequence nodes***. The lines connecting these nodes are called ***arcs.*** These lines show the direction of influence that is being exerted.

Influence diagram for the BDA problem

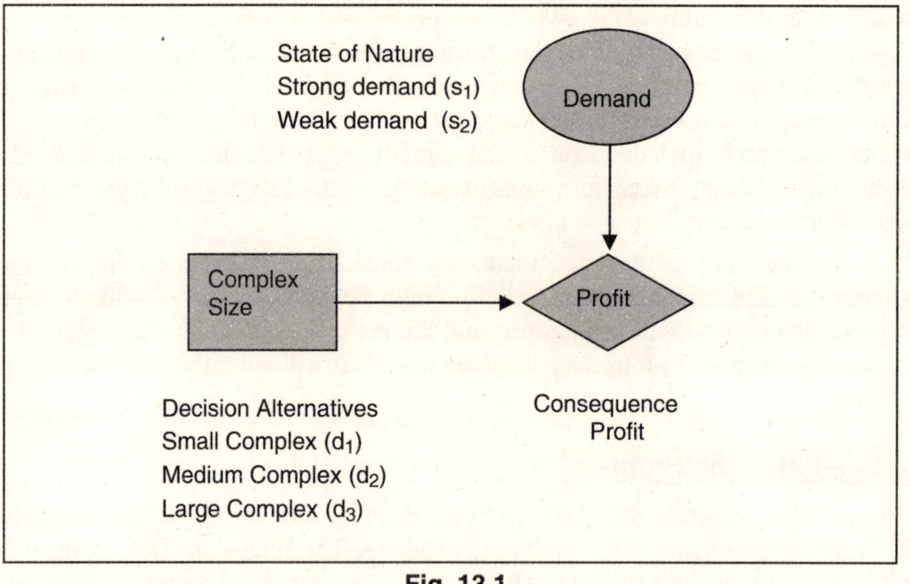

Fig. 13.1

Payoff Table

Given the three decision alternatives and two states of nature, what size the BDA would choose? To arrive at an appropriate answer BDA must know the consequence associated with each decision alternative and each state on nature. In decision theory, we express the consequence resulting from a particular combination of a decision alternative and the state of nature as payoff.

Table 13.1

Payoff Table for BDA		
	State of Nature	
Decision Alternatives	Strong Demand (s_1)	Weak Demand (s_2)
Small Complex (d_1)	8	7
Median Complex (d_2)	14	5
Large Complex (d_3)	20	–9

From the table 13.1 for example, if a medium complex is build and demand turns out to be weak then our BDA would receive a profit (payoff) of Rs. 5 Crores. On the other hand, the same complex would fetch Rs. 14 Crores provided the demand is strong. Thus, in general V_{ij} refers the payoff for i^{th} complex size and j^{th} demand pattern.

Decision Tree

Decision tree is a novel diagrammatic representation of the decision problem. It is designed to enhance the logical sequence of the given problem. In our BDA problem since there are three decision

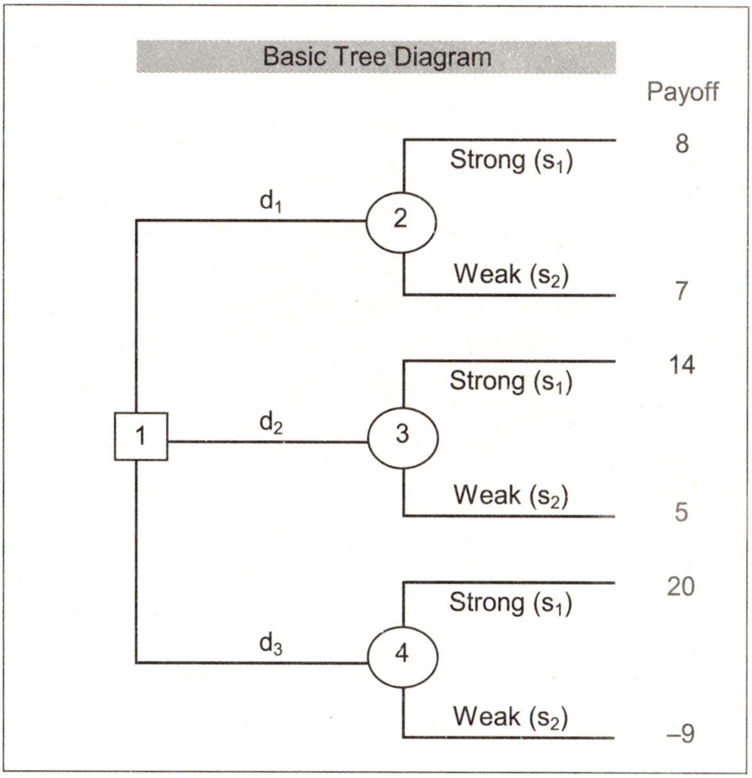

Fig. 13.2

alternatives, our decision tree will have three mutually exclusive branches as shown in the diagram to begin with. Further, since there are two states of nature associated, each branch drawn in the first step is further sub-divided into two minor branches leading to a total of six (3 × 2) branches finally. Once this is done we finally write the respective payoffs against their respective tree branches at the tail end as shown in the Fig.. For example, if BDA wants to have the big complex and the associated demand turns out to be large, then it will receive a payoff of Rs. 20 Crores, big boom indeed. On the other hand the demand turns out to be small then the same old big complex decision will end up with a loss of Rs.9 Crores (– 9).

In the diagram there are four junctions from which the branches emerge. Such points are called nodes and they are numbered from 1 to 4 as shown in the Fig. 13.2. However, to distinguish between decision nodes and chance nodes we use squares for decision nodes and circles or ovals for state of nature otherwise called chance nodes. Thus, in our diagram there is only one decision node [1] and three chance nodes from (2) to (4).

13.4 Decision Making under Uncertainty

Under uncertain situations there is no way for the decision maker to assess the probabilities of the various states of nature. Now given the tree diagram the real problem is to identify one best decision alternative among the three. To begin with, to have a simple model, we assume that our DBA do not posses any probability statistics relating to the two chance events namely strong and weak demand. Under the circumstances to arrive at a decision alternative normally five basic approaches are being discussed in this section.

1. The Optimistic Approach: Maximum among Maximums

In this approach, as the name suggests, we propose to identify the best payoffs for all the three decision alternatives. Once this is done we chose the best among the best as the final solution. Such an optimistic decision is often called maximum of the maximum payoffs. To illustrate this approach let us go back to our BDA illustration once again.

(i) If BDA constructs a small complex and the demand turns out to be weak then the corresponding payoff is Rs. 7 Crores. On the other hand, if the demand is strong then our BDA will get Rs. 8 Crores. Between the two payoffs since Rs. 8 Crores is more, our BDA would construct small complex assuming a strong demand for it.

(ii) If BDA constructs a medium complex and the demand turns out to be weak then the corresponding payoff is Rs. 5 Crores. On the other hand, if the demand is strong then our BDA will get Rs. 14 Crores. Between the two Figs. since Rs. 14 Crores is more, our BDA would construct medium complex assuming a strong demand for it.

(iii) If BDA constructs a large complex and the demand turns out to be weak then the corresponding payoff is Rs. –9 Crores. On the other hand, if the demand is strong then our BDA will get Rs. 20 Crores. Between the two Figs. since Rs. 20 Crores is more, our BDA would construct large complex assuming a strong demand for it.

(a) Tabular Method: The following table 13.2 gives the summery statement of all the three discussions alternatives discussed so far. The last column in the table gives the payoffs for all the three alternative decisions.

Table 13.2

	Optimistic Solution		
	State of Nature		
Decision Alternatives	Strong Demand s_1	Weak Demand s_2	Maximum Payoff
Small Complex d_1	18	7	18
Medium Complex d_2	14	5	14
Large Complex d_3	20	–9	20
	Maximum of Maximum Payoff =		20
	Optimistic Solution =		d_3

Since we are interested in maximum of all these three maximums, the maximum value of Rs. 20 Crores is reported in the last but one row in the table. The associated decision namely d_3 (large complex) is reported in the last row. Thus, the final solution to this approach is to go for a large complex with full expectation of strong demand in future.

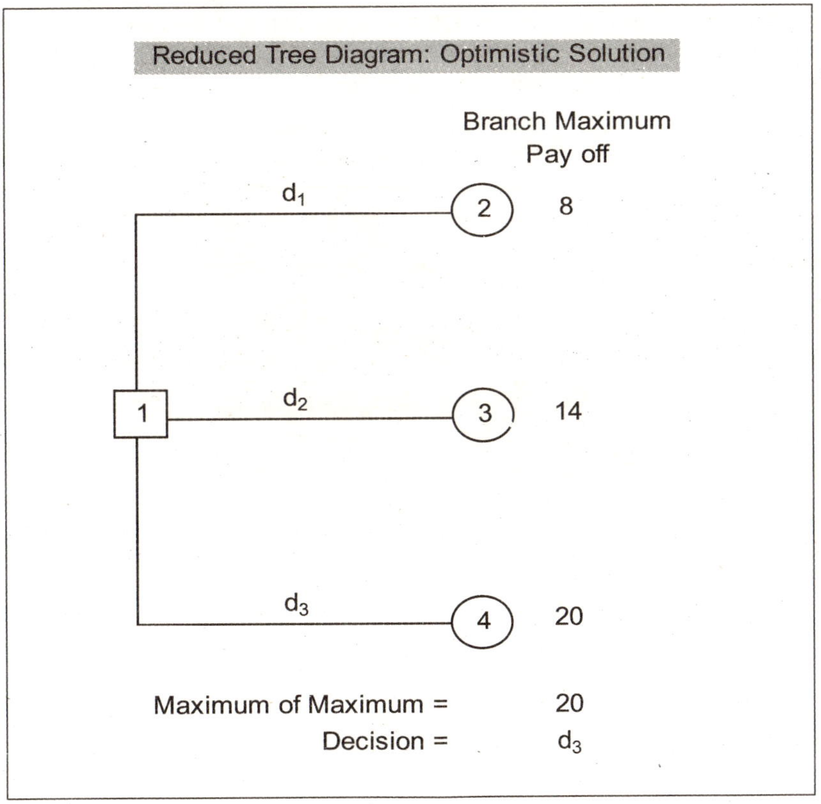

Fig. 13.3

(b) Decision Tree Method: In this method we take only the branch maximum payoffs and report against their respective chance nodes. For example, for the top most branch pertaing to small complex given in Fig. 13.2 above, the branch payoffs are 8 (for strong demand) and 7 (for weak demand).

Among the two since the payoff 8 is the maximum, we report this probability against the corresponding chance node (2) in Fig. 13.3. In a similar way the branch maximum payoffs are obtained and reported against node (3) and (4) in the Fig. 13.3. Among the three maximums reported since 20 is 'the best' it is selected as the maximum of maximum and reported at the bottom of the Fig. 13.3. Since 20 is the payoff related to large complex we conclude that our BDA would go for the large complex (d_3) hopping to get Rs. 20 Crores as the profit on completion.

2. Conservative Approach: Maximum among Minimums

This is indeed a defensive approach in the sense that our decision maker will try his best to avoid the worst thing that can happen to him in the business. Accordingly, he will obtain the minimum payoffs for all the three decision alternatives first. In the second stage he will chose the maximum among the three minimums obtained in the first stage.

(i) To illustrate the approach, we go back to our BDA example. If BDA constructs a small complex and the demand turns out to be weak then the corresponding payoff is Rs. 7 Crores. On the other hand, if the demand is strong, then our BDA will get Rs. 8 Crores. Among the two figures since Rs. 7 Crores is the minimum our BDA would construct small complex assuming a weak demand.

(ii) If BDA constructs a medium complex and the demand turns out to be weak then the corresponding payoff is Rs. 5 Crores. On the other hand, if the demand is strong, then our BDA will get Rs. 14 Crores. Among the two figures since Rs. 5 Crores is the minimum our BDA would construct medium complex assuming a weak demand.

(iii) If BDA constructs a large complex and the demand turns out to be weak then the corresponding payoff is Rs. –9 Crores. On the other hand, if the demand is strong, then our BDA will get Rs. 20 Crores. Among the two figures since Rs. –9 Crores is the minimum our BDA would construct large complex assuming a weak demand.

(a) Tabular Method: The following table gives the summery statement of all the three discussions.

Table 13.3

	Conservative Solution		
	State of Nature		
Decision Alternatives	Strong Demand s_1	Weak Demand s_2	Minimum Payoff
Small Complex d_1	18	7	7
Medium Complex d_2	14	5	5
Large Complex d_3	20	–9	–9
	Maximum of Minimum Payoff =		7
	Conservative Solution =		d_1

Thus, the final solution to this approach is to go for a small complex with full expectation of weak demand in future.

(b) Decision Tree Method: In this method we take only the branch minimum payoffs and report against their respective chance nodes. For example, for the top most branch pertaing to small complex given in Fig. 13.2 above, the branch payoffs are 8 (for strong demand) and 7 (for weak demand).

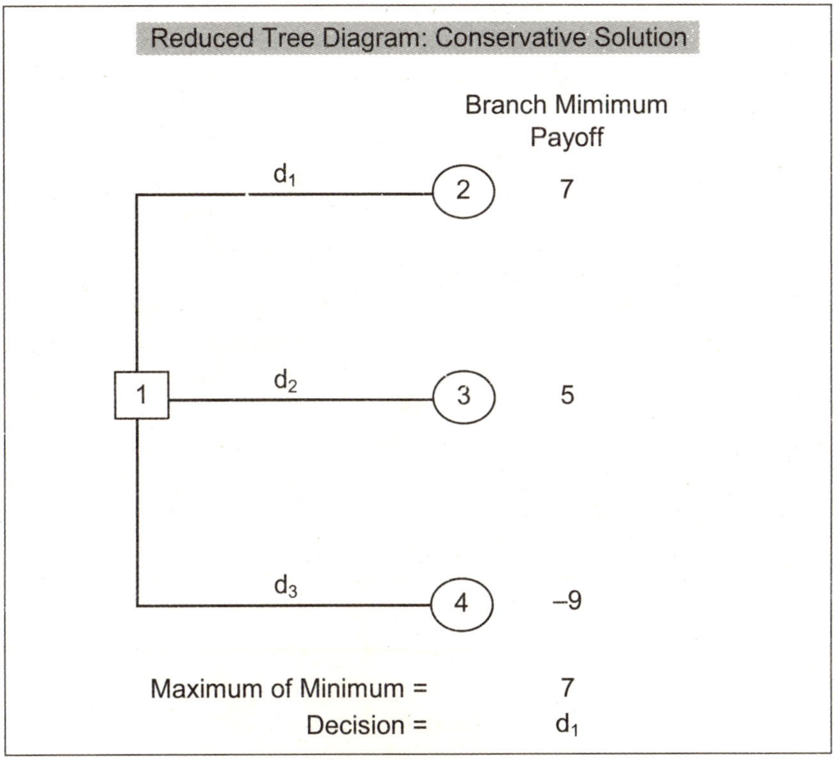

Fig. 13.4

Among the, two since the payoff 7 is the minimum we report this probability against the corresponding chance node (2) in Fig. 13.4. In a similar way the branch minimum payoffs are obtained and reported against node (3) and (4) in the Fig. 13.4. Among the three minimums reported, since 7 is 'the best' it is selected as the maximum of minimum and reported at the bottom of the Fig. 13.4. Since 7 is the payoff related to small complex we conclude that our BDA would go for the small complex (d_1) hopping to get at least Rs. 7 Crores as the profit on completion.

3. Regret Approach or Savage Approach: Minimum among Maximums

In this approach when every time the BDA calculates the payoff, the opportunity cost otherwise called the best alternative foregone is also obtained. This payoff due to foregone alternative is often called regret payoff.

(i) To illustrate the approach, we go back to our BDA example. If BDA constructs a small complex and the demand turns out to be weak then the corresponding payoff is Rs. 7 Crores.

Under the circumstances (weak demand) the best alternative is going for the small complex yielding a payoff of Rs. 7 Crores. Thus, the regret amount turns out to be (7 – 7) Rs. 0 Crores

(ii) If BDA constructs a medium complex and the demand turns out to be weak then the corresponding payoff is Rs. 5 Crores. Under the circumstances (weak demand) the best alternative is going for a small complex yielding a payoff of Rs. 7 Crores. Thus, the regret amount turns out to be (7 – 5) Rs.2 Crores.

(iii) If BDA constructs a large complex and the demand turns out to be weak then the corresponding payoff is Rs. –9 Crores. Under the circumstances (weak demand) the best alternative is going for the small complex yielding a payoff of Rs. 7 Crores. Thus, the regret amount turns out to be {7 – (– 9)} Rs.16 Crores.

(iv) If BDA constructs a small complex and the demand turns out to be strong then the corresponding payoff is Rs.8 Crores. Under the circumstances (strong demand) the best alternative is going for large complex yielding a payoff of Rs. 20 Crores. Thus, the regret amount turns out to be (20 – 8) Rs.12 Crores.

(v) If BDA constructs a medium complex and the demand turns out to be strong then the corresponding payoff is Rs.14 Crores. Under the circumstances (strong demand) the best alternative is going for large complex yielding a payoff of Rs. 20 Crores. Thus, the regret amount turns out to be (20 – 14) Rs. 6 Crores.

(vi) If BDA constructs a large complex and the demand turns out to be strong then the corresponding payoff is Rs. 20 Crores. Under the circumstances (strong demand) the best alternative is going for large complex yielding a payoff of Rs. 20 Crores. Thus, the regret amount turns out to be (20 – 20) Rs.0 Crores.

(a) Tabular Method: All the six calculations stated above are reported in the regret payoff column in table 13.4. Among the regrets the maximum regrets are reported in the last column. Since the minimum of all maximums regrets is our target it is reported in the last but one column.

Table 13.4

	Mini Max Regret Solution				
	State of Nature		Regret Payoff		
Decision Alternatives	Strong Demand s_1	Weak Demand s_2	Strong Demand s_1	Weak Demand s_2	Maximum Regret Payoff
Small Complex d_1	8	7	12	0	12
Medium Complex d_2	14	5	6	2	6
Large Complex d_3	20	–9	0	16	16
			Minimum of Maximum Regrets =		6
			Minimum Regret Decision =		d_2

Finally the decision-maker will minimize the maximum regrets. Thus, the final solution to this approach is to go for a medium complex with full expectation of strong demand in future.

(b) Decision Tree Method:

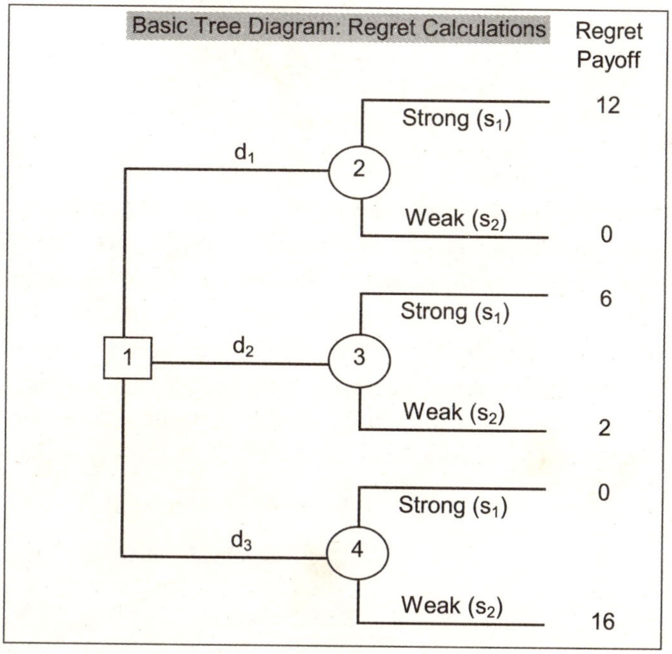

Fig. 13.5

In this method all the associated six regret payoffs discussed earlier are written against the respective branches as shown in Fig. 13.5.

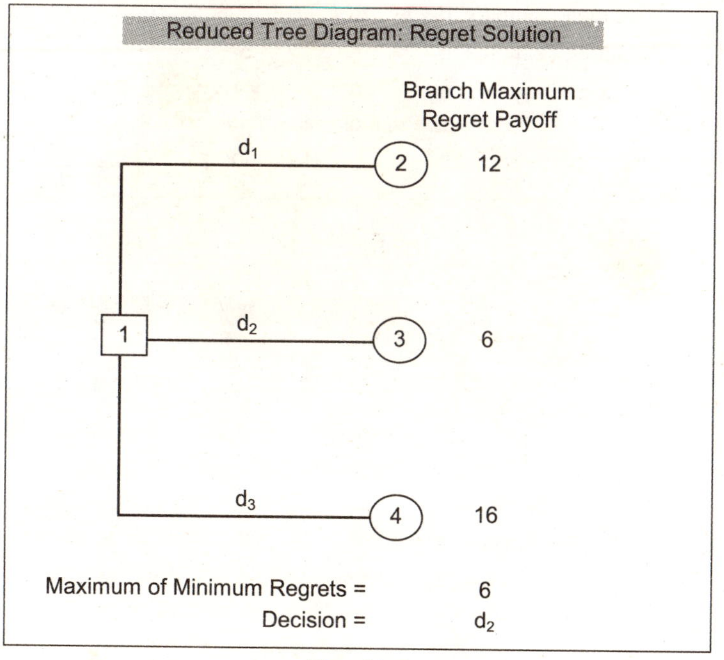

Fig. 13.6

The maximum regrets of the concerned branches are obtained and reported against their respective chance nodes in Fig. 13.6. The minimum of all these three regrets is the final solution to the problem. Since 6 is the minimum regret the associated decision is going for a medium complex.

4. Hurwicz Principle

In this method the needed optimum solution is obtained somewhere in between the optimistic Maximaxi principle and the conservative Maximini principle. Accordingly, the needed decision result is obtained as the weighted average of these two results. For this purpose a weight α is defined in the interval 0 to 1 both inclusive. According to this principle, for each decision alternative the weighted average is obtained as the sum of the maximum payoff multiplied by α and the minimum payoff multiplied by $(1-\alpha)$. Once such calculations are made, the best decision is taken based on the highest value among the values obtained. If α is 1 clearly our optimistic result will be the result this time also. If it is 0 then the resulting result will be our conservative solution obtained in the previous section. The following table 13.5, 13.6 and 13.7 illustrates this method.

Table 13.5

Hurwicz Solution			
	State of Nature		$\alpha = 0.4$
	Strong Demand	Weak Demand	Weighted Average
Decision Alternatives	s_1	s_2	
Small Complex d_1	8	7	7.4
Medium Complex d_2	14	5	8.6
Large Complex d_3	20	–9	2.6
	Hurwicz Principle Maximum =		8.6
		Decision =	d_2

Table 13.6

Hurwicz Solution			
	State of Nature		$\alpha = 1$
	Strong Demand	Weak Demand	Weighted Average
Decision Alternatives	s_1	s_2	
Small Complex d_1	8	7	8
Medium Complex d_2	14	5	14
Large Complex d_3	20	–9	20
	Hurwicz Principle Maximum =		20
		Decision =	d_3

Table 13.7

Hurwicz Solution			
	State of Nature		$\alpha = 0$
	Strong Demand	Weak Demand	Weighted Average
Decision Alternatives	s_1	s_2	
Small Complex d_1	8	7	7
Medium Complex d_2	14	5	5
Large Complex d_3	20	–9	–9
		Hurwicz Principle Maximum =	7
		Decision =	d_1

5. Laplace Principle

This principle is based on the simple philosophy that the uncertain events are equally likely. Thus, it is again a weighted average with equal weights for all the uncertain events. In terms of our BDA it is simply $\alpha = 0.5$ case as illustrated in tables.

Table 13.8

Laplace Solution			
	State of Nature		$\alpha = 0.5$
	Strong Demand	Weak Demand	Weighted Average
Decision Alternatives	s_1	s_2	
Small Complex d_1	8	7	7.5
Medium Complex d_2	14	5	9.5
Large Complex d_3	20	–9	5.5
		Laplace Principle Maximum =	9.5
		Decision =	d_2

13.5 Decision Making Under Risk

The decision making situation wherein the decision maker knows the probability of each event is often called decision making under risk. Such probabilities are obtained from the past data in the said business. Even in the absence of past data, on the basis of experience and judgment he can work out reasonably good probabilities. This additional information guides the decision maker to make a more accurate decision.

(a) Reduced tree diagram method for optimum decision by expected value approach

The expected value concept developed in the probability theory is very handy in this context. Accordingly, the decision-maker calculates the expected value for all the possibilities and finalizes the decision on the basis of largest expected payoff. So let the subjective probability of relishing the strong demand is P $(s_1) = 0.8$ and weak demand is P $(s_2) = 0.2$. The calculations of expected payoffs could conveniently be done with the tree diagram. Accordingly we redraw the tree diagram with the subjective branch probabilities as shown in Fig. 13.7. Working backward through the tree, we compute the expected payoff values at each chance node as shown in Fig. 13.8.

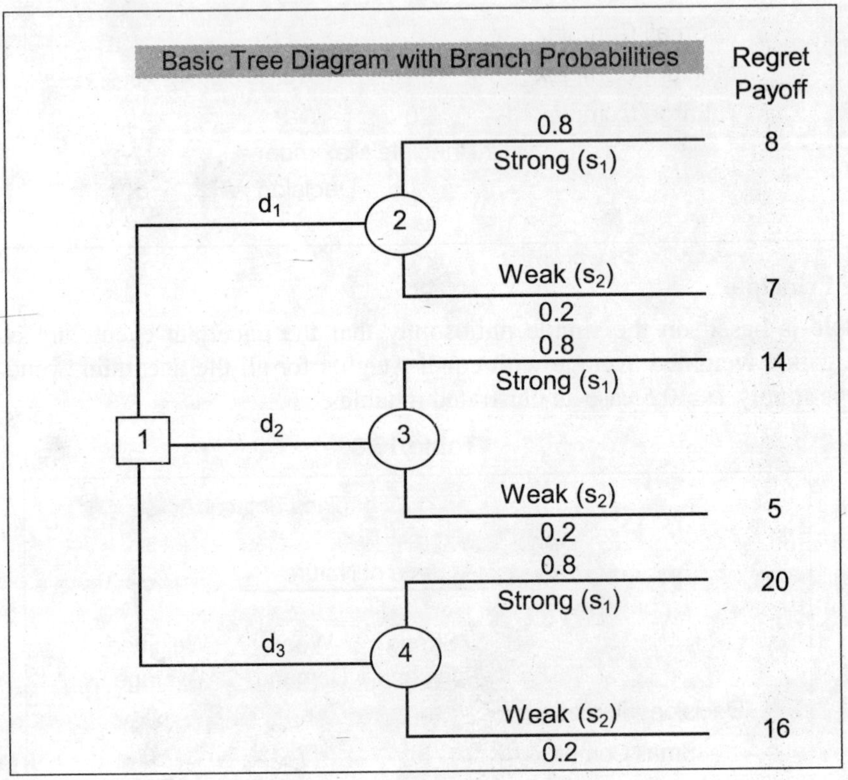

Fig. 13.7

For example, at node (2) the branch expected value is obtained as EV $(d_1) = 0.8(8) + 0.2(7) = 7.8$. In the same way the expected values at node (3) and (4) are obtained and reported in the reduced tree diagram. In Fig. 13.8, the profit of Rs.14.2 is the highest expected value. Thus, the best alternative at decision node [r] is d_3, the large complex.

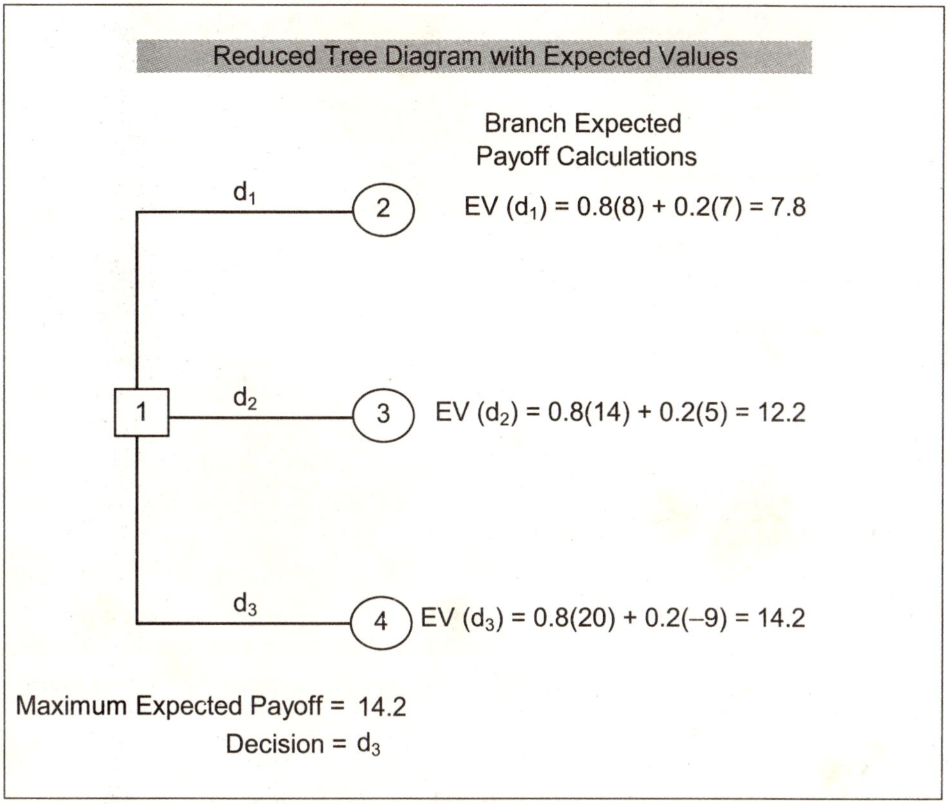

Fig. 13.8

(b) Tabular method for optimum decision by expected value approach

Table 13.9

Maximum Expected Value Solution

	State of Nature		Prior Probabilities		
	Strong Demand	Weak Demand	Strong Demand	Weak Demand	Expected value
Decision Alternatives	s_1	s_2	s_1	s_2	Payoff
Small Complex d_1	8	7	0.8	0.2	7.8
Medium Complex d_2	14	5	0.8	0.2	12.2
Large Complex d_3	20	-9	0.8	0.2	14.2
			Maximum Expected Value =		14.2
			Decision =		d_3

From table 13.9, the profit of Rs. 14.2 is the highest expected value. Thus, the best decision is d_3, the large complex.

13.6 Expected Payoff Calculations with Perfect Information

Suppose BDA had the opportunity to conduct market research regarding the customer's tastes, the management could use this additional information for its advantage. Under the circumstances, BDA could determine with certainty, prior to making decision, which state of nature is going to occur in the future. From payoff table discussed earlier note that,

(i) If BDA knew with certainty that state of nature s_1 would occur, it would venture for large complex and knockout a hefty profit of Rs. 20 Crores.

(ii) If BDA knew with certainty that state of nature s_2 would occur, it would venture for small complex and earn a profit of Rs. 7 Crores.

Now to compute the expected payoffs with perfect information, let us restore the probabilities 0.8 and 0.2 respectively for strong and weak demands respectively. Thus, there is a probability of 0.8 that this perfect information will indicate the state of nature s_1 and the resulting decision alternative d_3 will provide Rs. 20 Crores profit. Similarly, with a probability of 0.2 for the state of nature s_2, the optimal decision d_1 will provide Rs. 7 Crores profit. Thus, with perfect information the expected value is obtained as

$(EV)_{W.P.I.} = 0.8(20) + 0.2(7) = 17.4$ where $(EV)_{W.P.I}$ refers expected value with perfect information.

In our earlier discussion without such perfect information the expected value was obtained as Rs.14.2 Crores. So here after we refer this value as the expected value without perfect information and denote it as $(EV)_{W.O.P.I}$

Thus, $(EV)_{W.O.P.I.} = 14.2$

It is worth to note that with perfect information our BDA could earn an additional profit of Rs. 3.2 Crores (17.4 – 14.2). Thus, to get this type of perfect market information, any market research costs less than or equal to Rs. 3.2 Crores is rewarding to undertake.

The expected value of perfect information is given by

$$\begin{aligned}(EV)_{P.I} &= |(EV)_{W.P.I} - (EV)_{W.O.P.I}| \\ &= |17.4 - 14.2| \\ &= \text{Rs. } 3.2 \text{ Crores}\end{aligned}$$

Since the expected value of the perfect information is Rs. 3.2 Crores the final decision is to go for a market research and to assertion the nature of the demand in future provided the market research cost anything less than Rs. 3.2 Crores.

13.7 Risk Profiles

The risk profile for a decision alternative shows the payoffs and their associated probabilities. In our illustrative example the expected value of Rs.14.2 Crores for the decision alternative d_3 is based on a 0.8 probability of getting Rs. 20 Crores and a 0.2 probability of involving a loss of Rs. 9 Crores. Here the 0.8 for Rs. 20 Crores and 0.2 for Rs. −9 Crores constitutes the needed risk profile. The following diagrams illustrate the risk profiles for all the three decision alternatives.

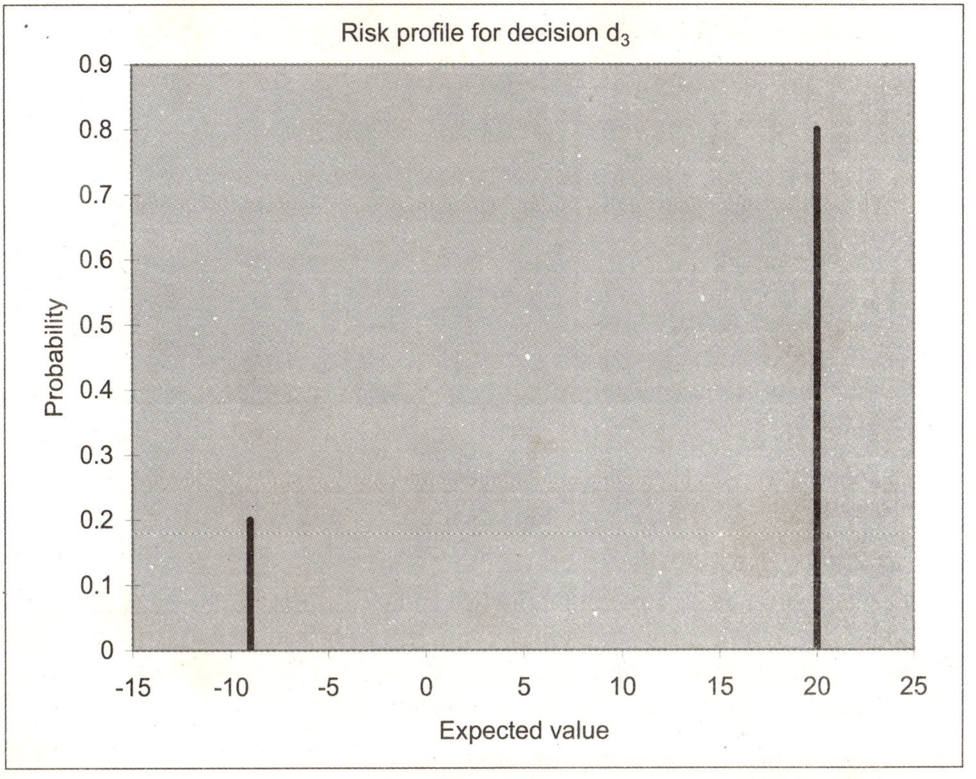

Fig. 13.9

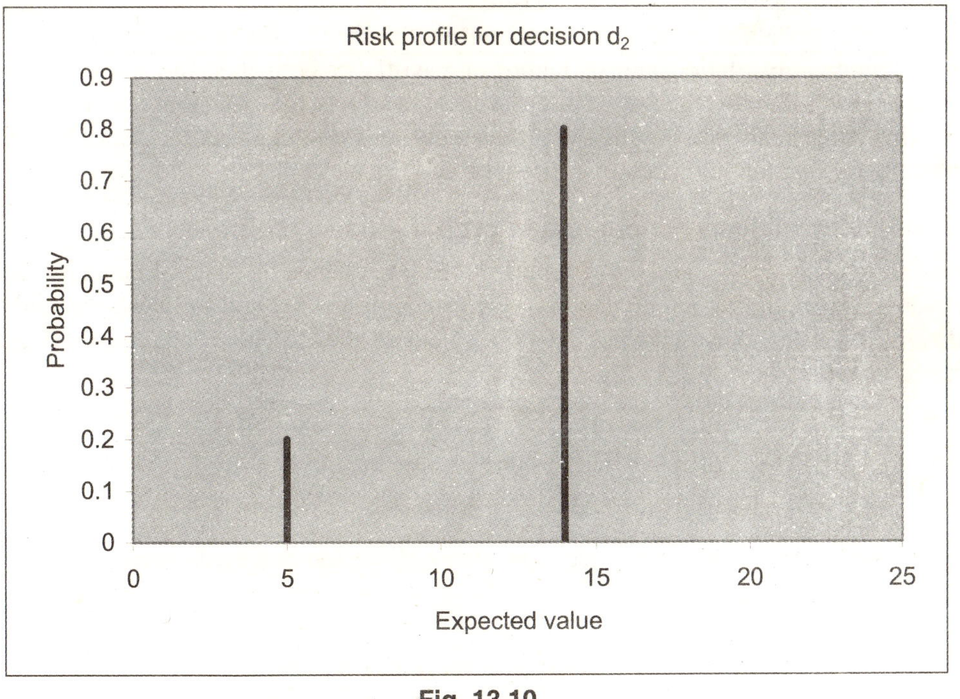

Fig. 13.10

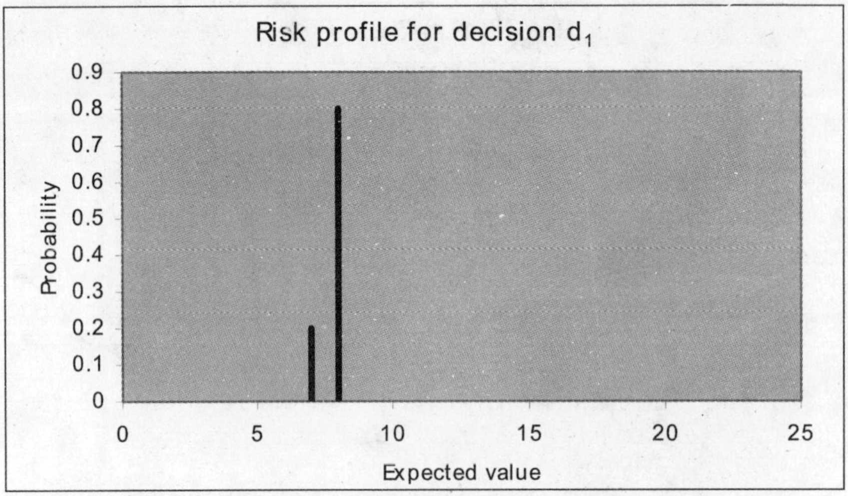

Fig. 13.11

Remember that the highest expected value decision need not be the final solution all the time. To avoid the risk one may go even for inferior expected payoffs. In our illustrative examples, option d_2 and d_3 does not have any risk of getting into the trap of loss. So, often person wants to avoid risk of loss go for such inferior decisions as well.

13.8 Sensitivity Analysis for Expected Value Criteria

Sensitivity analysis is a devise to test the sensitivity of the decision alternative taken already due to changes in the probabilities of state of nature and/or changes in the payoffs. If any change either in the probability of the state of nature or payoffs or both then the associated decision alternative may or may not change. If such a change affects the decision alternative then we would say that the said change is sensitive. If such changes do not affect the decision alternative then we would say that the said change is insensitive.

13.8.1 Sensitivity analysis for change in probabilities

To illustrate the sensitivity of our BDA problem let us interchange the state of nature probabilities for a moment. Assume for strong demand (s_1) the probability is 0.2 and for weak demand (s_2) the probability is 0.8. With these changes let us recalculate the expected values for all the three decision alternatives

$$EV(d_1) = 0.2(8) + 0.8(7) = 7.2$$

$$EV(d_2) = .02(14) + 0.8(5) = 6.8$$

$$EV(d_3) = 0.2(20) + .08(-9) = -3.2$$

The above calculations reveal that under the changed circumstances d_1 seems to be the best decision with the highest expected value. Thus, this change in the probability is very much sensitive in this case.

To through some more light on this issue, let us restate the said probability in general as p so that $P(s_1) = p$. Further, since $P(s_1) + P(s_2) = 1$ the probability of weak demand may be restated as

$P(s_2) = 1 - P(s_1) = 1 - p$. Now with these new algebraic probabilities let us recalculate the expected values once again.

$$\begin{aligned} EV(d_1) &= p(8) + (1-p)(7) \\ &= 8p - 7p + 7 \\ &= p + 7 \\ EV(d_2) &= p(14) + (1-p)(5) \\ &= 14p + 5 - 5p \\ &= 9p + 5 \\ EV(d_3) &= p(20) + (1-p)(-9) \\ &= 20p - 9 + 9p \\ &= 29p - 9 \end{aligned}$$

Thus, we are having three straight-line equations with the expected value as the dependent variable and the probability p as the independent variable. The following Fig. 13.12 shows all the three straight lines and the range in which the decision operates.

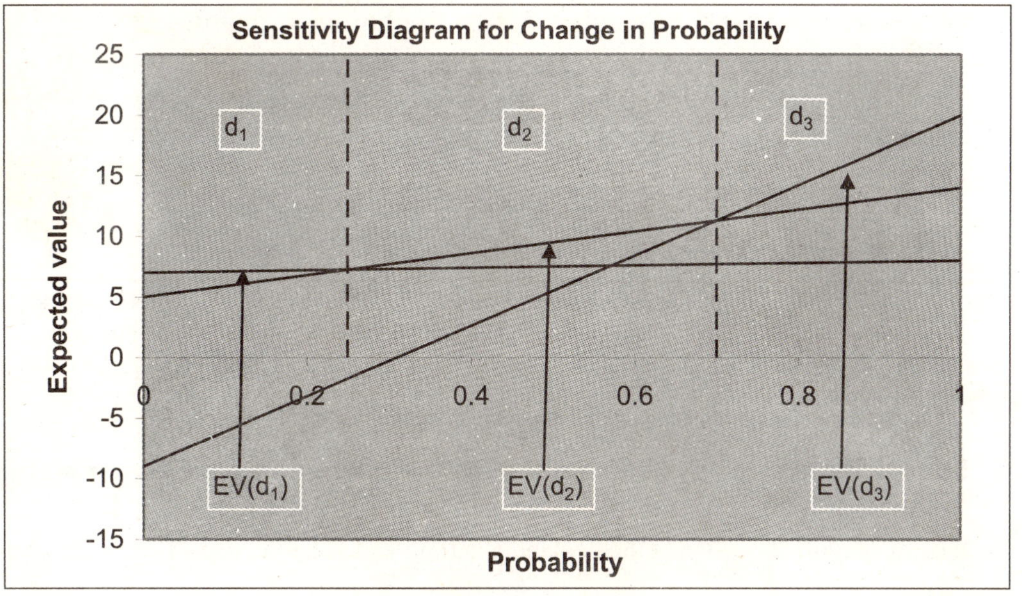

Fig. 13.12

The diagram shows how the probability change affects the decision. On the vertical axis we measure the expected payoffs and on the horizontal axis we measure the probability p. Let us calculate the point of intersection of EV (d_1) and EV (d_2)

$$\begin{aligned} p + 7 &= 9p + 5 \\ 8p &= 2 \\ p &= 2/8 = 0.25 \end{aligned}$$

Similarly, the point of intersection between EV (d_2) and EV (d_3) is obtained as

$$29p - 9 = 9p + 5$$
$$20p = 14$$
$$p = 14/20 = 0.7$$

Now from the graph one can get the following five special results

(i) If $p < 0.25$ then since EV (d_1) > EV (d_2) > EV (d_3) d_1 is the right choice. Thus, such a change in the probability is sensitive on d_3 decision taken already.

(ii) If p = 0.25, then EV (d_1) = EV (d_2) > EV (d_3). So one can chose either d_1 or d_2. Thus, such a change in the probability is sensitive on d_3 decision taken already.

(iii) If $0 < p < 0.7$ then since EV (d_2) > EV (d_1) > EV (d_3). d_2 choice is the right decision. Thus, such a change in the probability is sensitive on d_3 decision taken already.

(iv) If p = 0.7 then since EV (d_2) = EV (d_3) > E (d_1) one can chose either d_2 or d_3. Thus, such a change in the probability is insensitive on d_3 decision taken already.

(v) If $p > 0.7$ then since EV (d_3) > EV (d_2) > E (d_1) d_3 is the right choice. Thus, such a change in the probability is insensitive on d_3 decision taken already.

13.8.2 Sensitivity analysis for decision d_3 due to change in payoffs

In this section we analyze the sensitivity by changing the payoffs rather than probability. Let once again p = 0.8 and (1 – p) = 0.2 for s_1 and s_2 respectively. Corresponding to these probabilities from the earlier section we know that

$$EV\,(d_1) = 7.8$$
$$EV\,(d_2) = 12.2$$
$$EV\,(d_3) = 14.2$$

Since the expected value is high for d_3 we recommended large complex construction as the final decision alternative. Accordingly, d_2 is the second best decision alternative yielding a payoff or Rs.12.2 Crores. Thus, it is a simple logic that d_3 will be the decision alternative provided $EV(d_3) \geq 12.2$.

13.8.3 Sensitivity test for d_3 decision due to the change in payoffs pertaining to d_3 one at a time

Now let A be the payoff for d_3 when the demand is strong and B be the payoff when the demand is weak.

So, $$EV\,(d_3) = 0.8A + 0.2B$$

(i) Assume that the payoff B is restored at the same old level of Rs. – 9. Now let us try to calculate the minimum payoff A to restore the decision d_3.

Now d_3 holds good as the best payoff alternative provided

$$EV(d_3) = 0.8A + 0.2(-9) \geq 12.2$$
$$0.8A \geq 14$$
$$A \geq 17.5$$

Recall that when demand is strong, d_3 has an estimated payoff of Rs. 20 Crores. The preceding calculation shows that the decision alternative d_3 will holds good with strong demand provided the payoff is at least Rs. 17.5 Crores.

(ii) Assume that the payoff A is restored at the same old level of Rs. 20. Let us try to calculate the minimum payoff B to restore the decision d_3.

Now d_3 holds good as the best payoff alternative provided

$$EV(d_3) = 0.8(20) + 0.2B \geq 12.2$$

$$0.2B \geq -3.8$$

$$B \geq -19$$

Recall that when demand was weak, d_3 has an estimated payoff of Rs. – 9 Crores. The preceding calculation shows that the decision alternative d_3 with weak demand will holds good provided the payoff $B \geq$ Rs. – 19 Crores.

However, in these cases decision alternative d_3 remains optimal only the chances in the expected payoffs for d_1 and d_2 meet the requirements $EV(d_1) \leq 14.2$ and $EV(d_2) \leq 14.2$.

13.8.4 Sensitivity test for d_3 decision due to the change in payoffs pertaining to d_1 one at a time

Now let C be the payoff for d_1 when the demand is strong and D be the payoff when the demand is weak.

So, $$EV(d_1) = 0.8C + 0.2D$$

(i) Assume that the payoff D is restored at the same old level of Rs.7. Now let us try to calculate the minimum payoff C to restore the decision d_3.

Now d_3 holds good as the best payoff alternative provided

$$EV(d_1) = 0.8C + 0.2(7) \leq 14.2$$

$$0.8C \leq 14.2 - 1.4$$

$$C \leq \frac{12.8}{0.8}$$

$$C \leq 16$$

(ii) Assume that the payoff C is restored at the same old level of Rs.8. Let us try to calculate the minimum payoff D to restore the decision d_3.

$$EV(d_1) = 0.8(8) + 0.2D \leq 14.2$$

$$0.2D \leq 14.2 - 6.4$$

$$D \leq \frac{7.8}{0.2}$$

$$D \leq 39$$

13.8.5 Sensitivity test for d_3 decision due to the change in payoffs pertaining to d_2 one at a time

Now let E be the payoff for d_2 when the demand is strong and F be the payoff when the demand is weak.

So, $EV(d_2) = 0.8E + 0.2F$

(i) Assume that the payoff F is restored at the same old level of Rs. 5. Now let us try to calculate the minimum payoff E to restore the decision d_3.

Now d_3 holds good as the best payoff alternative provided

$$EV(d_2) = 0.8E + 0.2(5) \leq 14.2$$

$$0.8E \leq 14.2 - 1.0$$

$$E \leq \frac{13.2}{0.8}$$

$$E \leq 16.5$$

(ii)Assume that the payoff E is restored at the same old level of Rs.14. Let us try to calculate the minimum payoff F to restore the decision d_3.

$$EV(d_2) = 0.8(14) + 0.2F \leq 14.2$$

$$0.2F \leq 14.2 - 11.2$$

$$F \leq \frac{3}{0.8}$$

$$F \leq 15$$

Table 13.10: Sensitivity analysis summary table

	State of Nature			
	Strong Demand s_1		Weak Demand s_2	
Decision Alternatives	Original	Permisable change	Original	Permisable change
Small Complex d_1	8	$\leq$ 16	7	$\leq$ 39
Medium Complex d_2	14	$\leq$ 16.5	5	$\leq$ 15
Large Complex d_3	20	$\geq$ 17.5	–9	$\geq$ –9

13.9 Decision Analysis with Sample Information

In the expected value approach discussed in the previous section we utilized the prior probability information at every stage. However, the decision-maker often wants to improve the prior probability information on the basis of actual field experiments. The revised posterior probabilities often change the decision alternatives already taken.

Let the BDA is considering a six-month market research to learn more about the acceptance of its customers for the complex project. On the basis of the study the BDA can expect any one of the following two results.

1. **Favourable report:** A significant number of customers contacted show interest in complex purchase.
2. **Unfavourable report:** Only very few contacted individuals show interest in complex purchase.

13.9.1 The influence diagram

After introducing the market research, our BDA problem become more complex. Note that, now we have two decision nodes one for research study and another for complex size. The chance node has also gone up to two one for market research and another for market demand. Finally, the consequence node is the profit as in the previous case. Figure 13.13 is the new extended influence diagram.

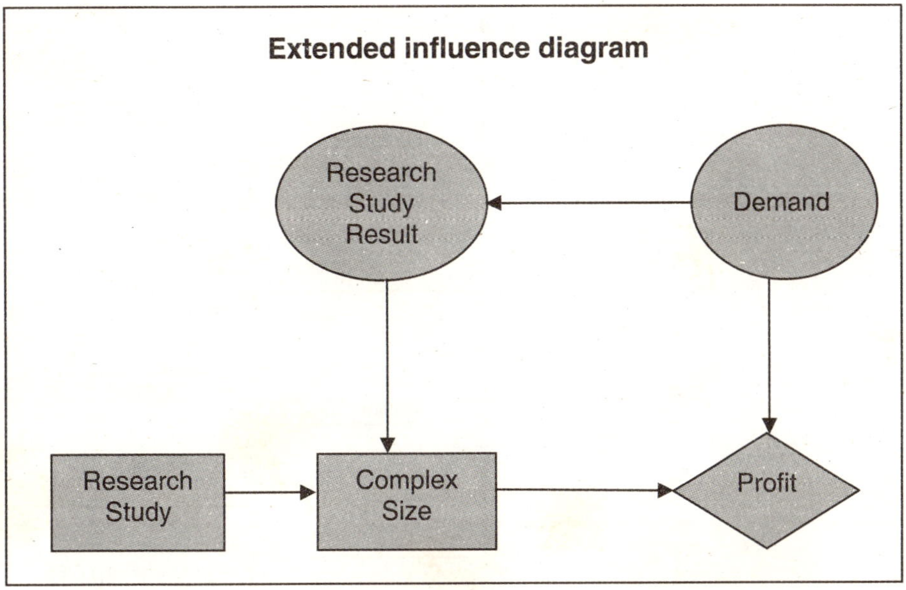

Fig. 13.13

13.9.2 Tree diagram with market research study

The tree diagram with the market study information given in Fig. 13.14 illustrates the logical sequence for the decision and associated chance nodes. First BDA must decide whether to have the market study or not. Thus, at decision node [1] we have two branches, one for going to market research {chance node (2)} and another for not going for market research {decision node [5]}.

Once decision is taken to have the market study, the result may either be favourable or not. Thus, our chance node (2) will have two branches once again, one for favourable market report {decision node [3] and another for unfavourable market report {decision node [4]}.

If the report is favourable then again at decision node [3] we have three branches one for large size complex {chance node (6)} another for the medium size complex {chance node (7)} and a third one for the small size complex {chance node (8)}.

In this logical fashion the rest of the diagram is constructed and completed in Fig. 13.14. Note that, here the squares are used for decision nodes and circles or ovals are used for chance nodes.

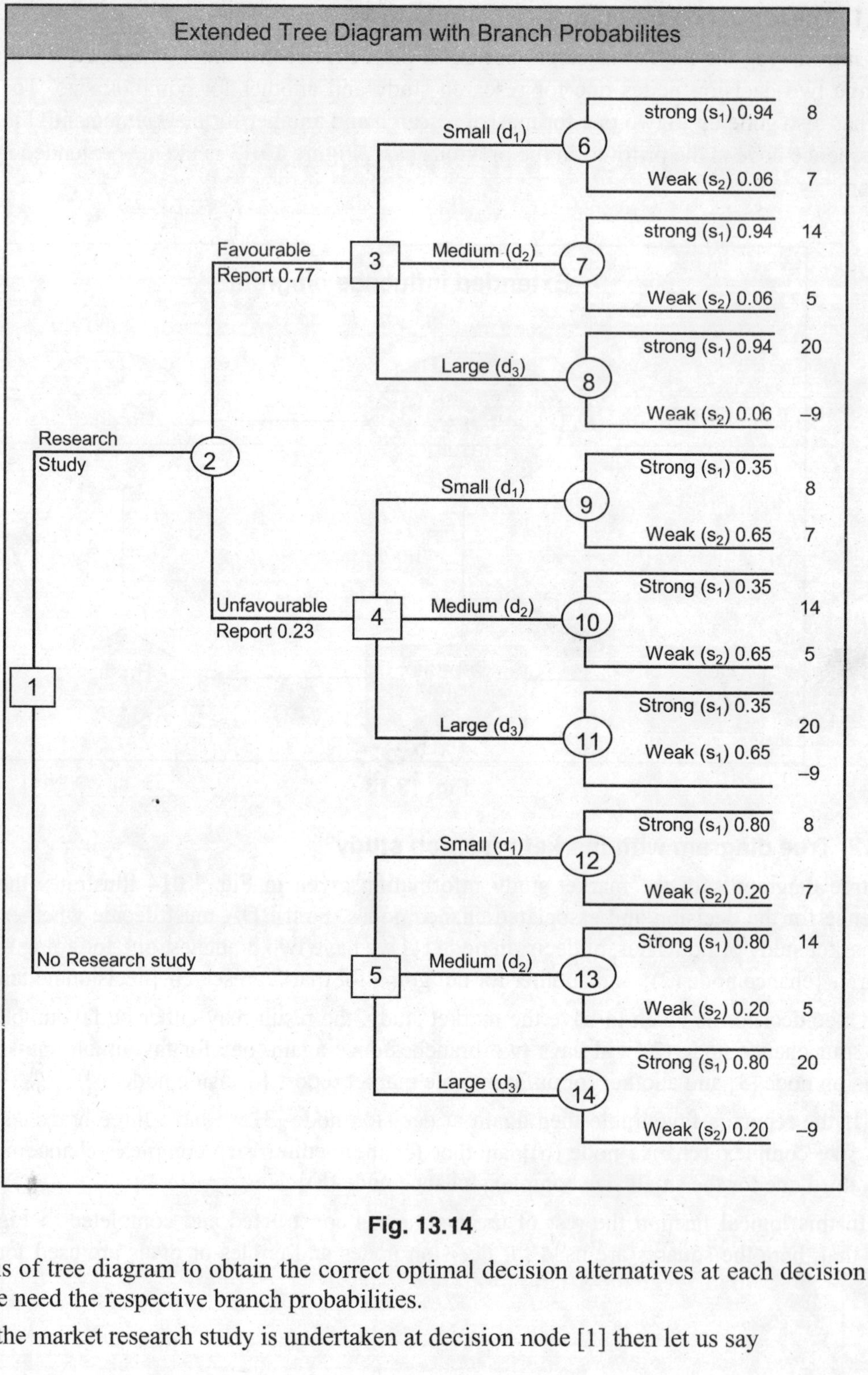

Fig. 13.14

Analysis of tree diagram to obtain the correct optimal decision alternatives at each decision node level we need the respective branch probabilities.

If the market research study is undertaken at decision node [1] then let us say

P (Favourable report) = 0.77

P (Unfavourable report) = 0.23

If market research report is favourable at decision node [3] then again let us say

P (Strong demand given a favourable report) = 0.94

P (Weak demand given a favourable report) = 0.06

If market research report is unfavourable at decision node [4] then again let us say

P (Strong demand given a unfavourable report) = 0.35

P (Weak demand given a unfavourable report) = 0.65

If market research is not taken then at decision node [5] we will have the associated prior probabilities discussed in the previous section.

P (strong demand) = 0.8

P (weak demand) = 0.2

A decision strategy is a sequence of decisions taken at decision node on the basis of the yet to take place outcomes of the chance nodes. Here we propose to get the optimum strategy at each nodal level by using backward pass rule as usual.

First Reduction Tree Diagram Showing the Expected Values

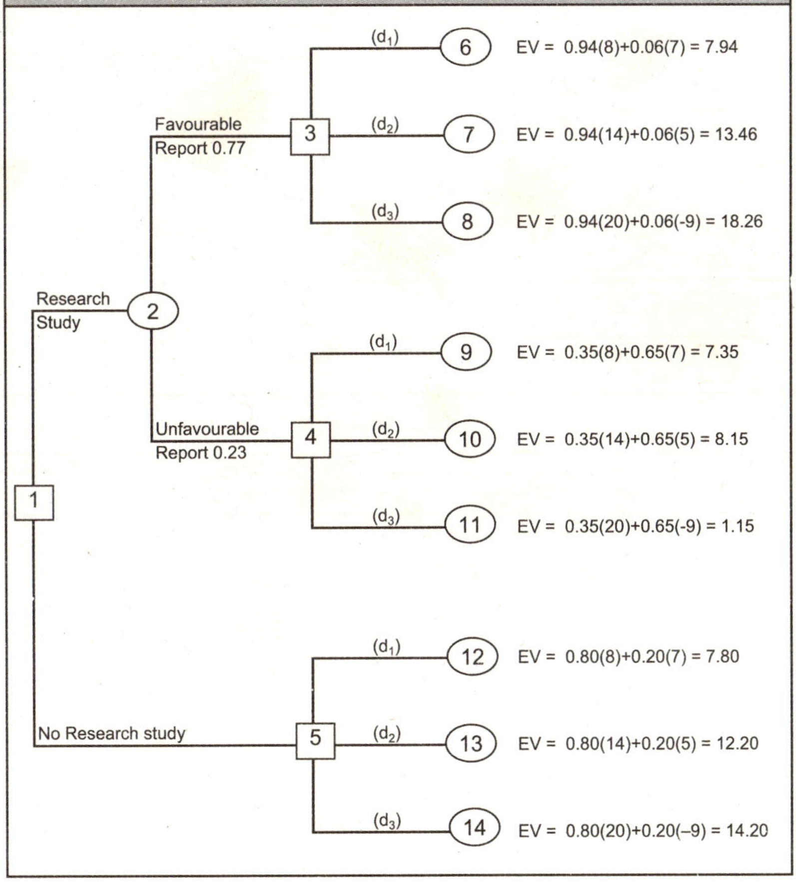

Fig. 13.15

13.9.3 Rules

1. If you are at chance node, obtain the expected value by multiplying the payoff at the tail end by the respective probabilities and add the results, obtained. Write these expected values against the respective nodal levels after rolling back the relevant branches.
2. If you are at the decision node, select the branch corresponds to the highest expected value and leaves the other branches. Write the so obtained branch expected value against the decision node.
   (i) In Fig. 13.15 after first stage of reduction the expected values for chance node [6] to [14] are reported.
   (ii) In Fig. 13.16 after the second stage of reduction the best expected values for decision node [3] to [5] are reported.
   (iii) In Fig. 13.17 after third stage of reduction the best expected values are reported for chance node (2) and decision node [5].

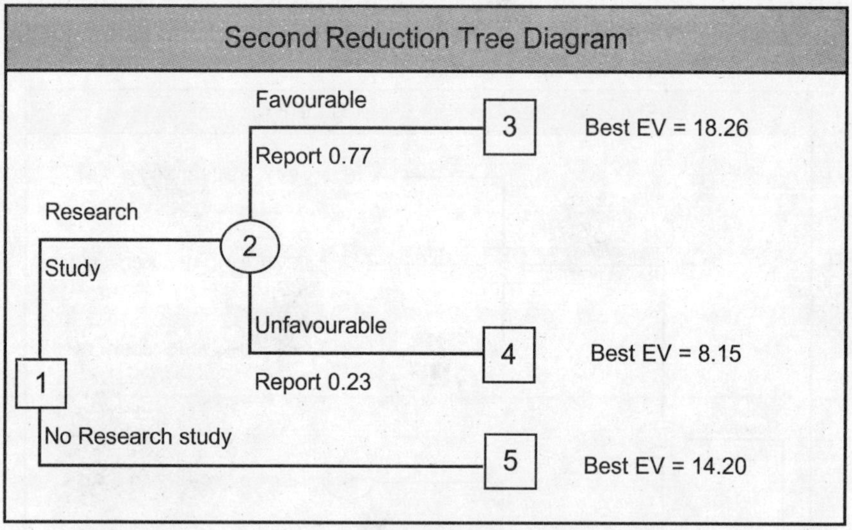

Fig. 13.16

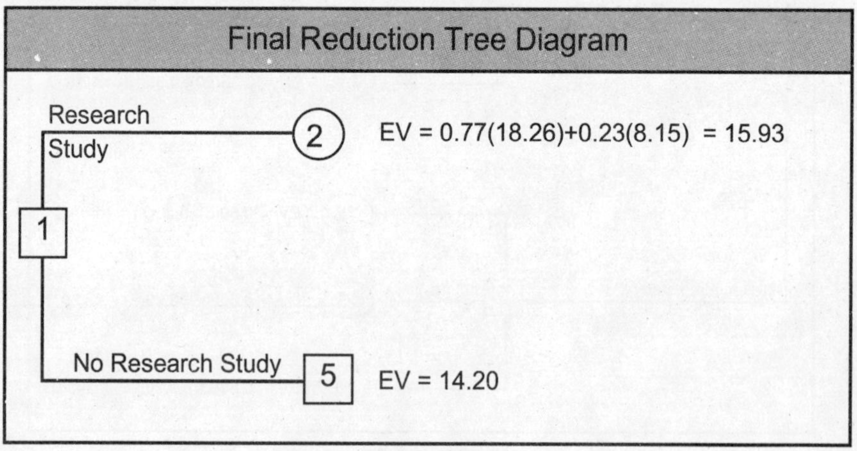

Fig. 13.17

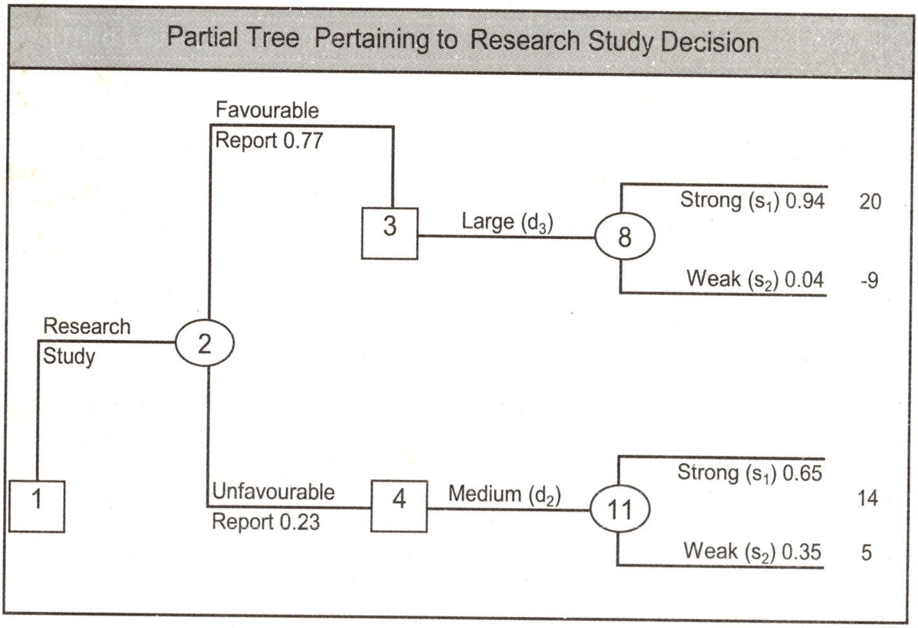

Fig. 13.18

In Fig. 13.17 since the expected value at chance node (2) is greater than the expected value t decision node number [5], Our BDA would go for market research study finally. Once decision s taken for market research study the relevant part of the decision tree is reported in Fig. 13.18 or ready reference.

Table 13.11

Expected Value Solution Under Market Research					
Decision Alternative	State of Nature		Market Research EV		EV
	s_1	s_2	MRF	MRU	NMR
d_1	8	7	7.94	7.35	7.8
d_2	14	5	13.46	8.15	12.2
d_3	20	-9	18.26	1.15	14.2
$P(s_j)$	0.8	0.2			
$P(s_j/F)$	0.94	0.06			
$P(s_j/U)$	0.35	0.65			
P(F)	0.77				
P(U)	0.23				
Maximum Branch Expected Values			18.26	8.15	14.2
Reduced Expected values (MR & NMR)			15.93		14.2
First Leval Decision			MR		
Second Level Decision (MRF)			d_3		
Third Level Decision (MRU)			d_2		

Note:

MRF = Market Research Favourable

MRU = Market Research Unfavourable

NMR = No Market Research

(i) If market research study is favourable, as per partial decision tree Fig. 13.18 it will go for a large complex.

(ii) If market the study is unfavourable then as per the partial decision tree Fig. 13.18 it will go for medium complex.

13.10 Risk Profile for the Decision to Take-up Research Study

Figure 13.18 above show the partial decision tree pertaining to the decision alternative for the market research study. Accordingly, BDA will get one of the payoffs depending upon the result of the research and the size of the demand shown at the terminal branches of the decision tree. Recall that a risk profile shows the possible payoffs with their associated probabilities.

(i) The BDA will get Rs. 20 Crores and go for large complex (d_3) provided the research study is favourable and the associated demand is strong. So the probability of getting Rs. 20 Crores = 0.77 × 0.94 = 0.72.

(ii) The BDA will get Rs. – 9 Crores and go for large complex (d_3) provided the research study is favourable and the associated demand is weak. So the probability of getting Rs. –9 Crores = 0.77 × 0.06 = 0.05.

(iii) The BDA will get Rs.14 Crores and go for medium complex (d_2) provided the research study is unfavourable and the associated demand is strong. So the probability of getting Rs.14 Crores = 0.23 × 0.35 = 0.08.

(iv) The BDA will get Rs.5 Crores and go for large complex (d_2) provided the research study is favourable and the associated demand is weak. So the probability of getting Rs. 20 Crores = 0.23 × 0.65 = 0.15.

The following table 13.12 and the associated Fig. 13.19 show the risk profile for taking up the market research study.

Table 13.12

Risk Profile for Market Research	
Payoffs	Probability
–9	0.05
5	0.15
14	0.08
20	0.72
Total	1.00

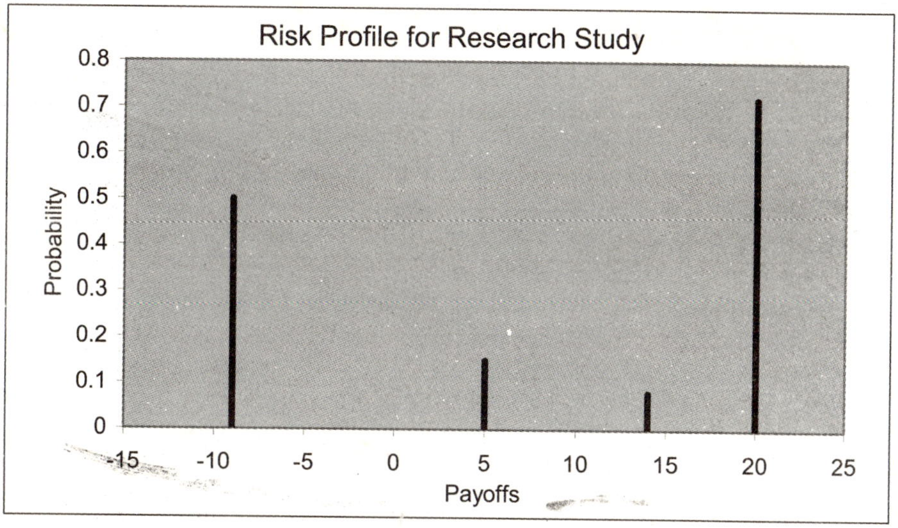

Fig. 13.19

The above table 13.12 and the associated Fig. 13.19 reveal that the probability getting Rs.20 Crores is very high at 72%.

Expected value of the sample information

The expected payoff when market research study is not undertaken is obtained as Rs.14.2 Crores in the previous section. Now with the market research, the expected value is Rs.15.93 Crores. Thus, Rs.1.73 Crores, the difference between the expected value with market research and without market research, is often called the expected value of the market research sample information. In other words, this is to say that the conducting the market research study adds Rs.1.73 Crores to the BDA. In general this calculation is represented by

$$EV_{SI} = |EV_{WSI} - EV_{WOSI}|$$

EV_{SI} = Expected value of the sample information.

EV_{WSI} = Expected value with the sample information.

EV_{WOSI} = Expected value without the sample information.

Efficiency of the sample information

The percentage of EV_{SI} to EV_{PI} is defined as the measure of efficiency for the market research study.

$$E = \frac{EV_{SI}}{EV_{PI}} \times 100$$

In our BDA problem $E = \dfrac{1.73}{3.2} \times 100 = 54.1\%$

This is to say that the market research information is 54.1% efficient than the perfect information discussed in the beginning. Low efficiency often leads to search for better information by some other means. High efficiency information is as good as that of the perfect information.

13.11 Computing the Branch Probabilities by Using Baye's Theorem

In the BDA problem discussed in Fig. 13.14 the branch probabilities were specified in advance. No attempt was made to calculate these probabilities. In this section we propose to use Baye's theorem to compute these branch probabilities. To highlight the decision tree, let F stand for favourable market research report and U stands for unfavourable market research report.

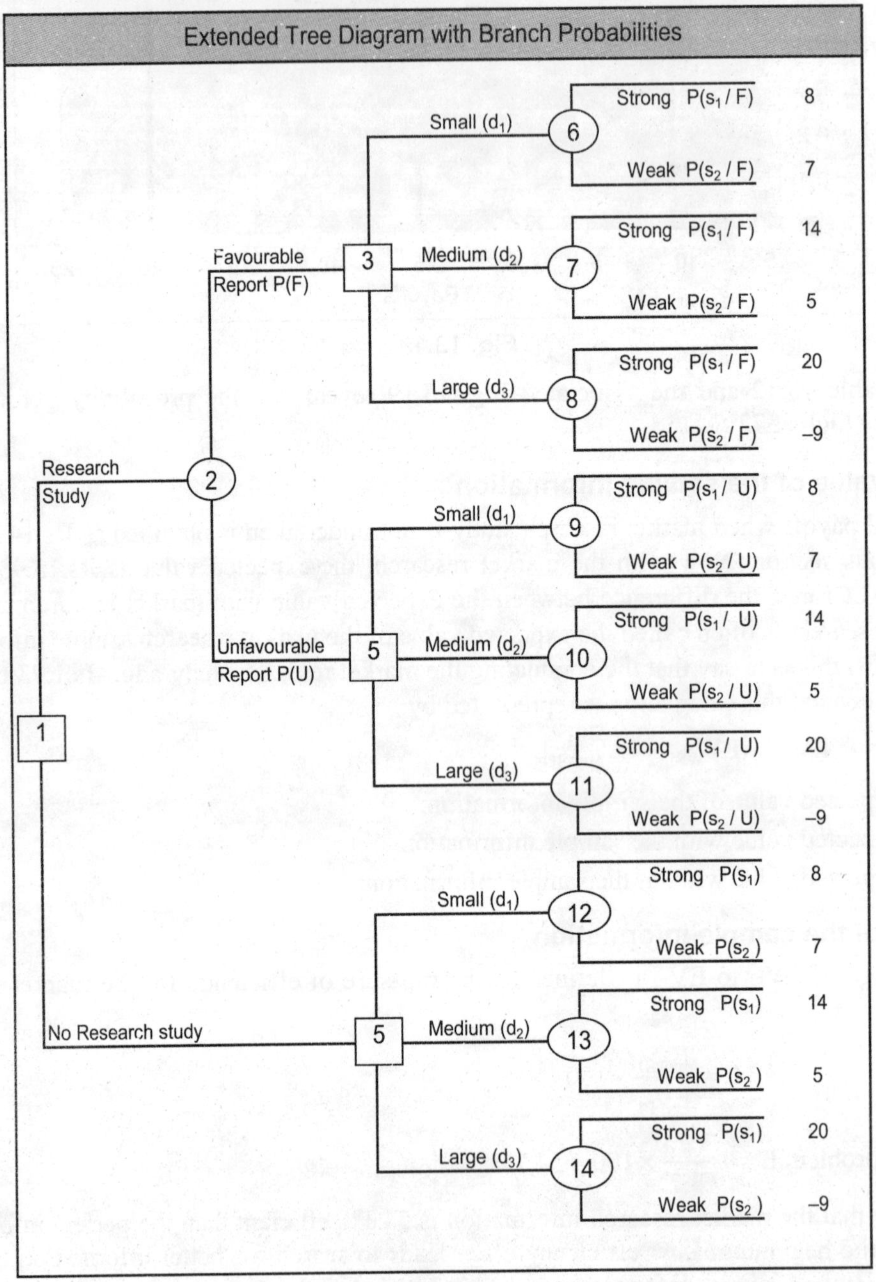

Fig. 13.20

In the tree diagram in Fig. 13.20, at chance node (2) we need to now the branch probabilities P(F) and P(U). At chance node (6), (7), (8) we are in need of $P(s_1/F)$, the probability of strong demand given a favourable market report, and $P(s_2/F)$, the probability of weak demand given a favourable market report. At chance node (9), (10), (11) we are in need of $P(s_1/U)$, the probability of strong demand given an unfavourable market report, and $P(s_2/U)$, the probability of weak demand given an unfavourable market report. These probabilities are often called posterior probabilities because they all conditional probabilities based on the outcome of the sample market research. At chance nodes (12), (13), (14) we want to know $P(s_1)$ and $P(s_2)$, if the market research is not under taken. These are the prior probabilities discussed in the very first section. All these probabilities are obtainable provided we know conditional probabilities $P(F/s_1)$, $P(F/s_2)$, $P(U/s_1)$, and $P(U/s_2)$. The market research out comes including the original data are listed below in table 13.13 and 13.14.

Table 13.13

Payoff Data		
	States of Nature	
Decision Alternatives	s_1	s_2
d_1	8	7
d_2	14	5

Table 13.14

Probability Data			
State of Nature s_j	Prior Probabilities $P(s_j)$	Conditional Probabilities $P(F/s_j)$	Conditional Probabilities $P(U/s_j)$
s_1	0.8	0.9	0.1
s_2	0.2	0.25	0.75

With this original and market research information, to get the needed branch probabilities follow the following steps

1. In column 1 in the table 13.15 enter the states of nature s_1 and s_2.
2. In column two enter the prior probabilities for s_1 and s_2.
3. In column three enter the given conditional probabilities of the favourable market report.
4. In column four calculate the joint probabilities by merely multiplying the conditional probability and the corresponding prior probabilities.
5. Add the probabilities in column 4 and obtain the needed probability of the favourable market research P(F).
6. Divide the respective joint probabilities by the P(F) = 0.77 and obtain the needed posterior probabilities, $P(s_1/F)$ and $P(s_2/F)$ in the last column table 13.15.

Similarly, to get the branch probabilities for the unfavourable market research, replace the conditional probabilities in column 3 for unfavourable market research probabilities in table 13.16.

Repeat all the steps listed above and get the needed probabilities as shown in table 13.16 The associated summary results are highlighted in table 13.17.

Table 13.15

Calculation of Posterior Probabilities (F)				
State of Nature s_j	Prior Probabilities	Conditional Probabilities P(F/sj)	Joint Probabilities $(P(F \cap s_j)$	Posterior Probabilities $P(s_j/F)$
s_1	0.8	0.9	0.72	0.94
s_2	0.2	0.25	0.05	0.06
		P(F) =	0.77	1.00

Table 13.16

Calculation of Posterior Probabilities (U)				
State of Nature s_j	Prior Probabilities $P(s_j)$	Conditional Probabilities $P(U/s_j)$	Joint Probabilities $P(U \cap s_j)$	Posterior Probabilities $P(s_j/U)$
Strong, s_1	0.8	0.1	0.08	0.35
Weak , s_2	0.2	0.75	0.15	0.65
		P(U) =	0.23	1.00

Table 13.17

Summary of all the Needed Probabilites		
Probabilites	States of Nature	
	s_1	s_2
$P(s_j)$	0.8	0.2
$P(s_j/F)$	0.94	0.06
$P(s_j/U)$	0.35	0.65
P(F)	0.77	
P(U)	0.23	

13.12 Decision Making with Expected Utility

In the preceding section, we expressed the expected values although in money terms to arrive at the needed optimum profit solution. Often the decision alternative with best-expected money value need not necessarily be the best. In certain special cases one will have to go beyond the mere expected value to arrive at the correct optimum solution. Certainly the decision to go for fire insurance policy for our house does not provide a high money expected value than for not going for insurance. Similarly people go for state lotteries even though the expected money is very small. If we go by the rule of high expected money value no one will buy the state lotteries because not going for lottery certainly gives a high positive expected value always. Thus, the expected monetary value is not the only comfortable measure of the optimum decision under all circumstances. Often people find more joy in taking risks then avoiding it. Under such circumstances, one should go invariably for the highest expected utility rather than the mere highest expected money value.

13.13 The Concept Utility

Utility by definition is a measure of the wants satisfying capacity of the commodity when it is consumed. In this context we propose to construct utility numbers for all the payoffs expressed in money terms first. Once this is done we calculate the expected utility rather than the expected money value in the usual manner to arrive at the needed optimum solution. As an example, let us consider the problems faced by the Prestige group, relatively a new real estate firm, in Bangalore. The cash available with the firm currently is so meager that it cannot even think of investing more than one project at a time, though it is having two projects in hand. Under the circumstances, it can think of the following three decision alternatives.

d_1 = Make investment in the project A.

d_2 = Make investment in the project B.

d_3 = Do not invest in either.

In Bangalore though the real estate is flourishing currently, the price of the real estate in future is very much uncertain, it may either go up, or come down or stable. Thus, the states of nature faced by the company are:

s_1 = Real estate prices go up in future.

s_2 = Real estate prices stay stable in future.

s_3 = Real estate prices come down in future.

With the best of information available the associated payoffs in money terms and their prior probabilities are reported in the summary table 13.18.

Table 13.18

Money Payoffs			
	State of Nature		
Decision Alternative	Prices up, s_1	Prices stable, s_2	Prices down, s_3
Invest in A, d_1	30000	20000	–50000
Invest in B, d_2	50000	–20000	–30000
Do not Invest, d_3	0	0	0
Probability	0.3	0.5	0.2

From the table information given above we calculate the expected money values for all the three decision alternatives first.

$$EV(d_1) = 0.3(30000) + 0.5(20000) + 0.2(-50000) = 9000$$
$$EV(d_2) = 0.3(50000) + 0.5(-20000) + 0.2(-30000) = -1000$$
$$EV(d_3) = 0.3(0) + 0.5(0) + 0.2(0) = 0$$

The above calculations reveal that the expected money value is high in the case of d_1. So the optimum decision of the company is to go for the project A. However, it is high time to go for the risk profile before making such a decision.

Though the expected value is high for d_1 it is very risky to take this venture. According to this decision the company will earn a profit of 30,000 provided price goes up in future. It will

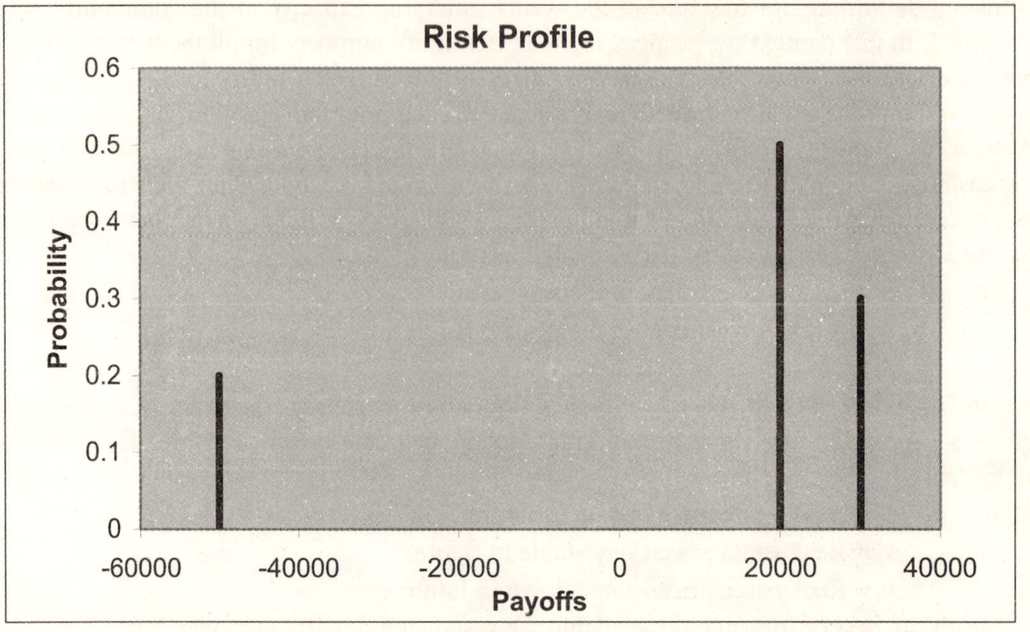

Fig. 13.21

earn a profit of Rs. 20,000 if price level is going to be stable in future. If any of these two happens it is well and good for the new company. Unfortunately, if prices of the real estate comes down in future (0.2 probability) the company will eventually incur a loss of Rs. 50,000, which is totally unacceptable at this stage take off. If it happens, it will have to shut down its operation in Bangalore once for all. The second best solution of Project B also leads to a similar situation with a lose of Rs. 30,000, which is again unbearable for the firm. The best decision that the Manager could take under the risky circumstances is to opt for d_3 and avoid the dear consequence of quitting the business.

The only way out to this tricky problem is to calculate the expected utility values rather than the expected money values. Such an optimum utility is capable of considering the risk factor as well into the analysis. If we succeed in getting such an optimum utility package the decision-making problem gets solved automatically.

13.14 Assignment of Utility Index for Payoffs

The Neumann and Morgenstern utility analysis is very much handy in solving this conflict. So let us assign two arbitrary utility levels to the highest and lowest payoffs given in the payoff table 13.18.

Let

Utility of the lowest payoff of Rs. –50,000 = 0

Utility of the highest payoffs of Rs. 50,000 = 10

With the help of these two arbitrary utility numbers we can readily calculate the utility numbers for all the in between payoffs given in the table 13.18 by using Neumann Morgensten method.

Standard Lottery: Let us introduce a lottery, which fetches the highest payoff of Rs.50, 000 with winning probability of p and the lowest payoff of Rs. –50,000 with the losing probability of (1 – p).

(a) Calculation of utility for Rs. 30,000 payoff

Now when p is equal or at least very close to one say for example, 0.98 clearly the Chairman of the Prestige group will opt for the lottery rather than the guaranteed payoff of Rs. 30,000 for the decision d_1 combined with the increasing price of the estates in future, because the firm is virtually ensured itself a payoff Rs. 50,000 by winning the lottery. On the other hand, if the probability of winning the lottery is very meager say 0.001, then clearly our manger will be comfortable in having Rs. 30,000, rather than going for the lottery and loosing it (Rs. –50,000). Thus, in any event, the probability p changes from 1 to 0, the Chairman's preference over the lottery goes on diminishing. Certainly at a point between 0 and 1, the manager will be in a confusing state of affair as whether to have the lottery or the ready cash payoff of Rs. 30,000. At this point the expected utility of the lottery must invariably equal to that of the ready cash payoff of Rs. 30,000. Let this critical probability be 0.9 as per the Chairman's opinion.

$$\begin{aligned} U(30{,}000) &= p[U(50{,}000)] + (1-p)[U(-50{,}000)] \\ &= 0.9(10) + 0.1(0) \\ &= 9 \end{aligned}$$

(b) Calculation of utility for Rs. 20,000 payoff

Now since the guaranteed payoff is only Rs. 20,000 the Chairman will be indifferent between the lottery and the guaranteed payoff for a low probability only. Let this probability be p = 0.8

$$\begin{aligned} U(20{,}000) &= p[U(50{,}000)] + (1-p)[U(-50{,}000)] \\ &= 0.8(10) + 0.2(0) \\ &= 8 \end{aligned}$$

(c) Calculation of utility for Rs. 0 payoff

Now since the guaranteed payoff only Rs. 0 the Chairman will be indifferent between the lottery and the guaranteed payoff for a still low probability only. Let this probability be p = 0.7

$$\begin{aligned} U(20{,}000) &= p[U(50{,}000)] + (1-p)[U(-50{,}000)] \\ &= 0.7(10) + 0.3(0) \\ &= 7 \end{aligned}$$

(d) Calculation of utility for Rs. 20,000 payoff

Now since the guaranteed payoff only Rs. 20.000 the Chairman will be indifferent between the lottery and the guaranteed payoff for a still low probability only. Let this probability be p = 0.5

$$U(-20{,}000) = p[U(50{,}000)] + (1-p)[U(-50{,}000)]$$
$$= 0.5(10) + 0.5(0)$$
$$= 5$$

(e) Calculation of utility for Rs. 30,000 payoff

Now since the guaranteed payoff only Rs. –30,000 the Chairman will be indifferent between the lottery and the guaranteed payoff for a still low probability only. Let this probability be p = 0.4

$$U(-30{,}000) = p[U(50{,}000)] + (1-p)[U(-50{,}000)]$$
$$= 0.4(10) + 0.6(0)$$
$$= 4$$

The summary results of all these calculations are reported in table 13.19.

Table 13.19

Utility Payoffs

Decision Alternative	State of Nature: Prices up, s_1	Prices stable, s_2	Prices down, s_3
Invest in A, d_1	9	8	0
Invest in B, d_2	10	5	4
Do not invest, d_3	7	7	7
Probability	0.3	0.5	0.2

Now from the table 13.19 let us calculate the expected utility in the usual manner

$$EU(d_1) = 0.3(9) + 0.5(8) + 0.2(0) = 6.7$$
$$EU(d_2) = 0.3(10) + 0.5(5) + 0.2(4) = 6.3$$
$$EU(d_3) = 0.3(7) + 0.5(7) + 0.2(7) = 7$$

Note that the optimum decision with highest utility value is d_3, not to invest. The ranking assignment of the Chairman's utility index and the associated expected money payoffs are presented in table 13.20.

Table 13.20

Expeted Utility and Money Values

Decision Alternatives Ranking	Expected Utility	Expected Money Value
Do not invest, d_3	7	0
Invest in A, d_1	6.7	9000
Invest in B, d_2	6.3	–1000

Note: That even though the money expected value is high for d_1, the project A, the Chairman's decision is d_3, not to invest. The rationality behind the decision for not going for A is that the probability 0.2 for a loss of Rs. 50,000 is considered as a very risky involvement. The seriousness of this risk is not brought out by the high-expected money value criterion.

Review Problems:

Example 1: A Philanthropist wants to build a hospital in his village. He can build 100, 200, or 300 bed hospital, depending upon the anticipated low, medium or high demand. The expected net profits and the prior probability probabilities regarding the states of nature is given in the following table 13.21.

Table 13.21

State of nature	Decision Nodes			Prior Probability
	100 bed (d_1)	200 bed (d_2)	300 bed (d_3)	
Low (s_1)	20,000	-10,000	-30,000	0.2
Medium (s_2)	25,000	30,000	-5,000	0.3
High (s_3)	30,000	50,000	60,000	0.5

(i) Compute EMV_{WOPI}, EMV_{WPI}, and EMV_{PI}

(ii) A researcher agrees to conduct a survey for Rs.1500 for the Philanthropist and provide him with information regarding the states of nature. Should the survey be conducted?

Solution:

The following tree diagram exhibits the given problem.

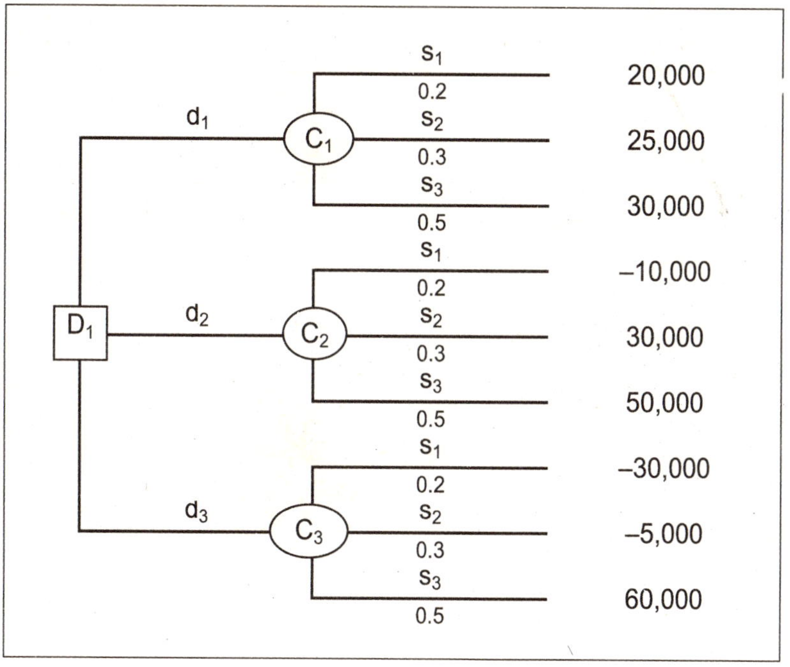

Fig. 13.22

Let us first calculate the expected money values for all the nodes stated in the tree diagram by using the backward rolling principle.

$$EMV(C_1) = 20,000 \times 0.2 + 25,000 \times 0.3 + 30,000 \times 0.5 = 26,500$$

$$EMV(C_2) = -10,000 \times 0.2 + 30,000 \times 0.3 + 50,000 \times 0.5 = 32,000$$

$$EMV(C_3) = -30,000 \times 0.2 + -5,000 \times 0.3 + 60,000 \times 0.5 = 22,500$$

$$EMV[D_1] = MAX(26,500, \quad 32,000, \quad 22,500] = 32,000$$

From the above computations it is clear that the highest expected payoff or profit is associated to decision node C_2. Thus $EMV_{W.O.P.I}$ = Rs.32.000 and the associated decision is d_2.

For the calculation of $EMV_{PI,}$ we will have to calculate the highest payoff for each actio under certainty. Therefore, for certainty of d_1 to occur the highest payoff is Rs. 20,000. Fc certainty of d_2 to occur, the highest payoff is Rs. 50,000. For certainty of d_3 to occur, the highe: payoff is Rs.60, 000. Thus, the expected pay off with perfect information is obtained as

$$EMV_{WPI} = 20,000 \times 0.2 + 30,000 \times 0.3 + 60,000 \times 0.5 = \text{Rs. } 43,000$$

$$EVM_{PI} = EMV_{WPI} - EMV_{WOPI} = \text{Rs.}43,000 - 32,000 = \text{Rs. } 11,000$$

Since EMV_{PI} is larger than the cost of conducting the survey the Philanthropist is advised to g for the survey.

Example 2: A daily newspaper vender out of past experience assigns probabilities to the demanc for newspaper as follows:

Table 13.22

No. of copies demanded per day	1	2	3	4
Probability	0.4	0.3	0.2	0.1

A copy of the newspaper costs Rs. 6 is sold at Rs.7 per copy. The unsold copies in the sam evening are returned to the agent at the rate of Rs.5 per copy. Formulate a suitable payoff matri and obtain the optimum number of copies to be purchased for sale on the basis of highe expected money (EMV) value principle.

Solution:

Profit per copy = Rs.7 – Rs. 6 = Re. 1.

Loss per unsold copy = Rs. 6 – Rs. 5 = Re. 1.

If he orders only one copy per day and the same one copy sold in a day then there is n excess supply to return. Thus, he will make a profit of Re.1 on that day as stated in the table c the top most corner corresponding to one copy order and one copy demand. Similarly, if th demand is one copy and he orders for two copies then the net gain is Rs. 2 – Re. 1 = Re. 1. This stated in the table in the right place. If he orders for 4 copies and the demand is only one cop then after returning three copies the net profit = Re.1 – Rs. 3 = Rs. –2. This figure is entered i the correct place in the table 13.23. In a similar way all the entries are made in the table.

Table 13.23

Copies demanded	Copies Ordered 1	2	3	4	Probability
1	1	0	-1	-2	0.4
2	1	2	1	0	0.3
3	1	2	3	2	0.2
4	1	2	3	4	0.1
EMV	1	1.2	0.8	0	

Given the probabilities in the last column the expected values are calculated and reported in the last row. For example, for the 2 copies order case the expected money value is obtained as:

EMV (2) $= 0 \times 0.4 + 2 \times 0.3 + 2 \times 0.2 + 2 \times 0.1 = 1.2$

In a similar way all other expected values are calculated and reported in the last row.

The maximum EMV = Rs. 1.2. Thus, the vender should order for 2 copies per day.

Example 3: A printing company has two machines new and old. The new machine gives good printing only when the paper quality is good, if the paper quality is bad then it gives only bad prints. Irrespective of the quality of the paper the slow going old machine gives good quality print all the time. The company is having 80% good quality and 20% of poor quality papers in its stock room. The good quality print in good quality paper gives him a net profit of Rs. 2000, at the same time the good print in bad quality paper gives him only Rs. 1600 profit. With new machine and good print the profit is Rs. 2400 and poor print it is Rs. 800. Suggest a suitable printing policy to earn more money as profit.

Solution:

Figure 13.23 shows the associated tree diagram

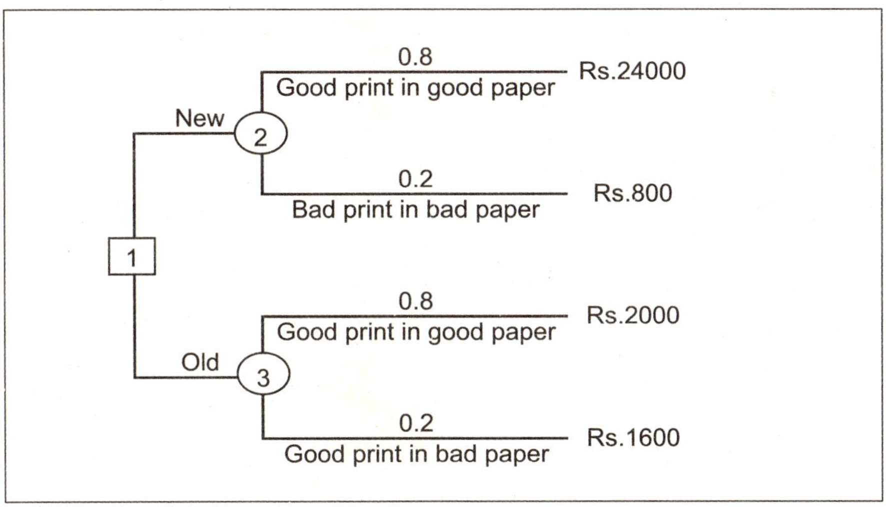

Fig. 13.23

Expected profit at chance node (2) $= 0.8 \times 2400 + 0.2 \times 800 =$ Rs. 2080

Expected profit at chance node (3) $= 0.8 \times 2000 + 0.2 \times 1600 =$ Rs. 1920

Since the expected profit is high in the case of new machine at decision node [1] the printer should go for the new machine for printing.

Example 4: The XYZ investment bank is considering four options for investment; shares, bonds, real estate and saving certificates. The past data regarding the performance of the four options are given below.

Shares: There is 25% chance that these shares will decline by 10% of its value, a 30% chance that they will remain stable and a 45% chance that they will increase by 15%. The shares under consideration pay no dividends.

Bonds: The bond stand a 40% chance of increase in value by 5% and 60% chance of remaining stable. It's yield is at 12% per annum.

Real estate: This proposal has a 20% chance of increasing the value by 30%, a 25% chance of increasing the value by 20%, a 40% chance of increasing the value by 10% a 10% chance of being stable and a 5% chance of losing the value by 5%.

Saving certificates: These certificates yield 8.5% per annum with certainty.

Draw a suitable tree diagram and obtain the best possible investment option.

Solution:

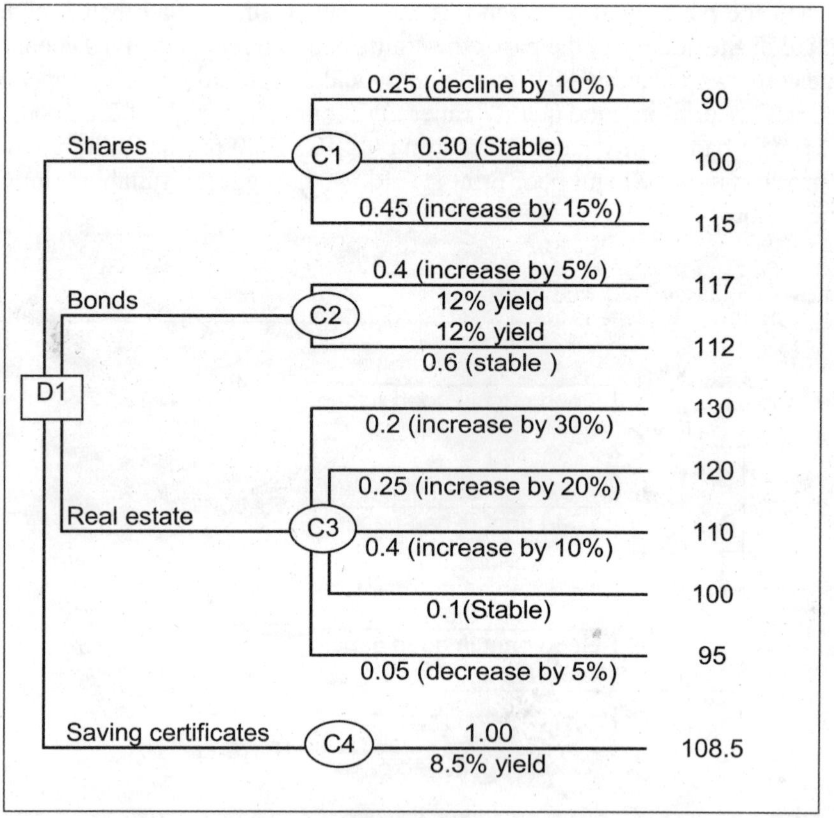

Fig. 13.24

Assume that we have Rs.100 to invest. The relevant decision tree is shown above in Fig. 13.24.

EMV at the chance node $(C_1) = 0.25 \times 90 + 0.30 \times 100 + 0.45 \times 115 =$ Rs. 104.25

EMV at the chance node $(C_2) = 0.4 \times 117 + 0.60 \times 112 =$ Rs. 114

EMV at the chance node (C_3) $= 0.2 \times 130 + 0.25 \times 120 + 0.40 \times 110 + 0.1\times 100 + 0.05 \times 95 = 114.75$

EMV at chance node (C_4) $= 1 \times 108.50 = 108.50$

EMV at decision node [D_1] $= \text{MAX}\{104.25, 114, 114.75, 108.50] = 114.75$

The real estate alternative gives the highest EMV. Thus, real estate investment is correct solution.

Example 5: A new product is being at the introductory stage. In this context the company has three options for introducing the product. The company can manufacture the product by itself or collect royalty and allow others to produce or sell the right absolutely for a lump sum payment. The following table gives the payoffs over and above the cost for all the three options under three states of nature. Construct a suitable tree diagram and obtain the optimum solution:

Table 13.24

Event	Probability	Manufacture itself Rs. '000	Collect Royalty Rs.'000	Sell the rights Rs.'000
High Demand	0.2	100	40	20
Medium Demand	0.3	30	25	20
Low Demand	0.5	–10	15	20

Extend the diagram on the basis of the following additional information and obtain the optimum decision rule.

(i) If the company opts to manufacture itself and sales are either medium or high, the company has the opportunity for developing a new version of its product.

(ii) From the past experience, it estimates that there is 60% chance of successful development of this new venture.

(iii) If the cost of development is Rs. 20,000 and return (after deducting the development cost) are Rs.35,000 and Rs.10,000 for high and medium demand respectively.

Solution:

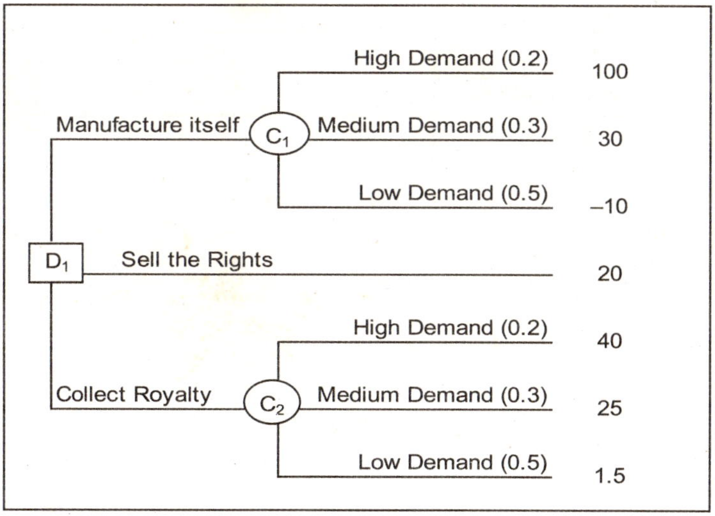

Fig. 13.25

From Fig. 13.25 we calculate the expected money values by backward rolling as follows

EVM at chance node (C_1) = {1000(0.2 × 100) + (0.3 × 30) + (0.5 × –10)} = Rs. 24,000

EVM at chance node (C_2) = {1000(0.2 × 40) + (0.3 × 25) + (0.5 × 1.5)} = Rs. 23,000

Decision at decision node D_1 = Max (Rs. 24,000, Rs. 20,000, Rs. 23,000) = Rs. 24,000.

Thus the correct decision is to manufacture the product by itself and make the expected profit of Rs. 24,000.

Solution for the Extended Tree Diagram Shown

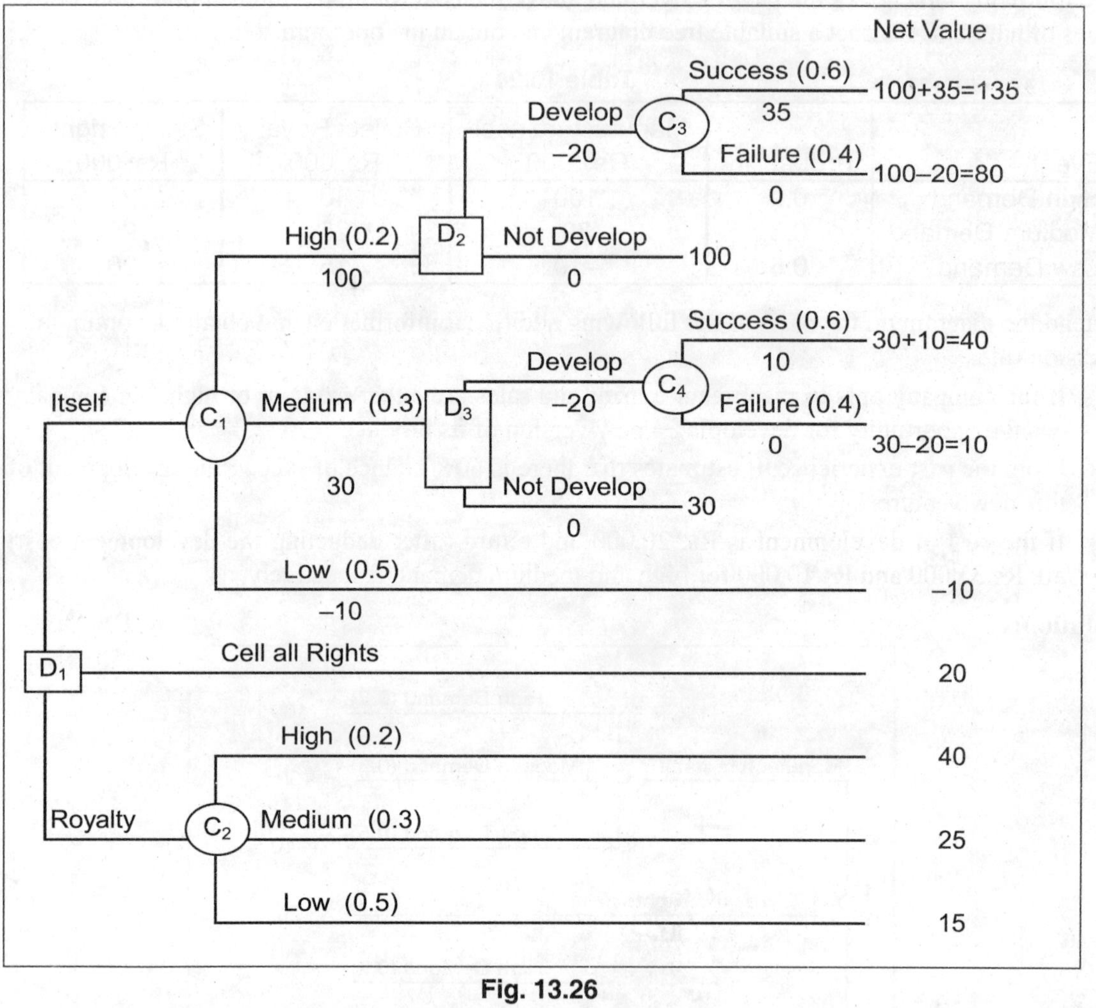

Fig. 13.26

Note that in this diagram the tail end values are net pays values calculated from the bottom of the tree after making all necessary adjustments.

From Fig. 13.26 we calculate the expected money values by backward rolling as follows

EMV at chance node (C_3) = 1000{{0.6 × 135) + (0.4 × 80)} =1,13,000

EMV at Decision node $[D_2]$ = Max (1,13,000, 1,00,000) = 1,13,000

EMV at chance node (C_4) = 1000{0.6 × 40) + (0.4 × 10)} = 28,000

EMV at Decision node $[D_3]$ = Max (28,,000, 30,000) = 30,000

EMV at chance node (C_1) = (0.2 × 1,13,000 + 0.3 × 30,000 + 0.5 × –10,000 = 26,000

EMV at chance node (C_2) = (0.2 × 40,000 + 0.3 × 25,000 + 0.5 × 15,000) = 23,000

EMV at Decision node $[D_1]$ = Max (26,000, 20,000, 23,000) = 26,000

Thus, the optimum expected profit is Rs. 26, 000. To have such a profit the company under reference should manufacture the device by itself. Further it should develop the new version if the demand is high or should not develop if the demand is medium.

Example 6: A farmer is considering drilling a well in his farmland. In the past only 70% well drilled were successful at 20 meters depth. Moreover on failure up to 20 meters he prefers to go for another 25 meters. The probability of success this time is 20%. The prevailing cost of drilling is Rs. 500 per meter. In case if he does not succeed he will have to by water from his neighbor by paying Rs.15000 for the same period. Draw appropriate tree diagram and suggest the best decision for the farmer.

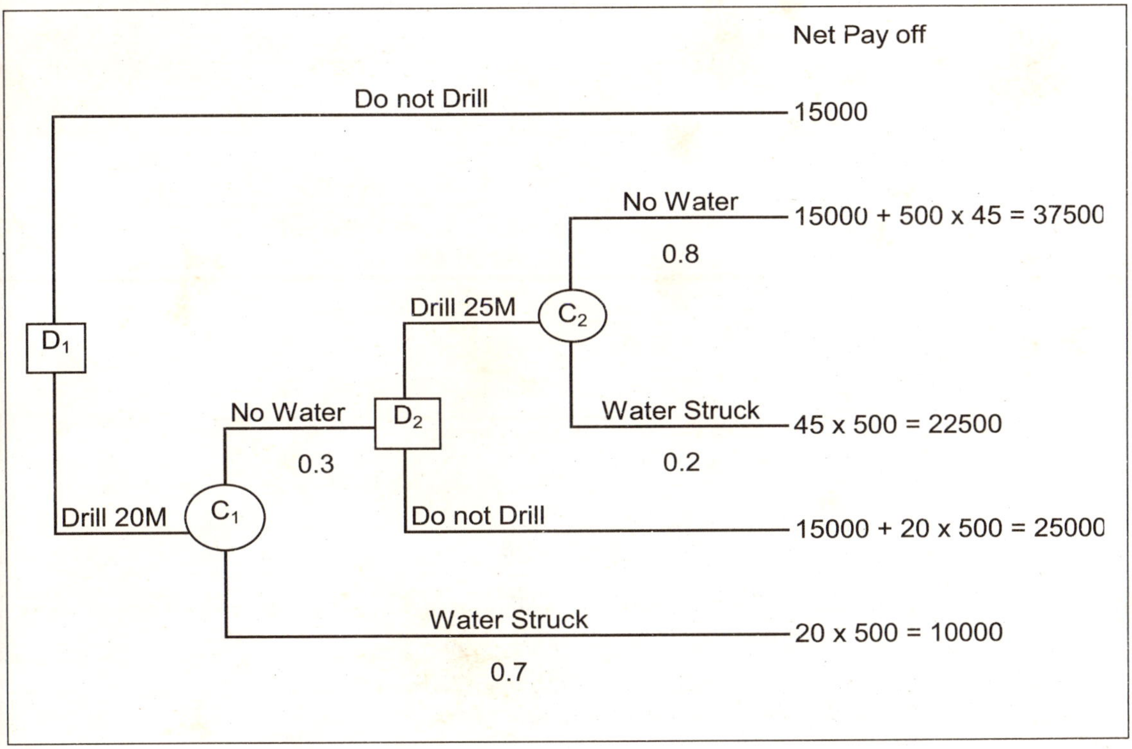

Fig. 13.27

Solution by backward rolling from tree diagram in Fig. 13.27:

EMV (C_2) = 0.8 × 37500 + 0.2 × 22500 = 34500

EMV $[D_2]$ = MIN [25000, 34500] = 25000

$$EMV\ (C_1) - 0.3 \times 25000 + 0.7 \times 10000 = 14500$$
$$EMV\ [D_1] = MIN[14500,15000]=14500$$

Since the expected cost of drilling at both the stages is less than buying water the correct decision could be drill 20M if no water struck then drill up to 25 M.

Example 7: A businessman from Chennai wishes to sell his products in Bangalore, he can set up a show room in the city or can sell through a wholesaler. Setting up a show room will entail a cost of Rs. 6,00,000 with a 0.55 probability of success. If the showroom succeeds, he can gain a net profit of 10,00,000 per year. If it fails, he can either shutdown the showroom or rent it out for an annual rent of Rs. 3,60,000 (for the rest of the year). The probability that he gets rent for the showroom is 40%. If he sells through a wholesaler, he incurs Rs. 3,00,000 initial cost. If he succeeds in whole sales he will get a net profit of Rs. 5,50,000. The associated probability of success is 0.45. Advise the executive on the best decision.

Solution:

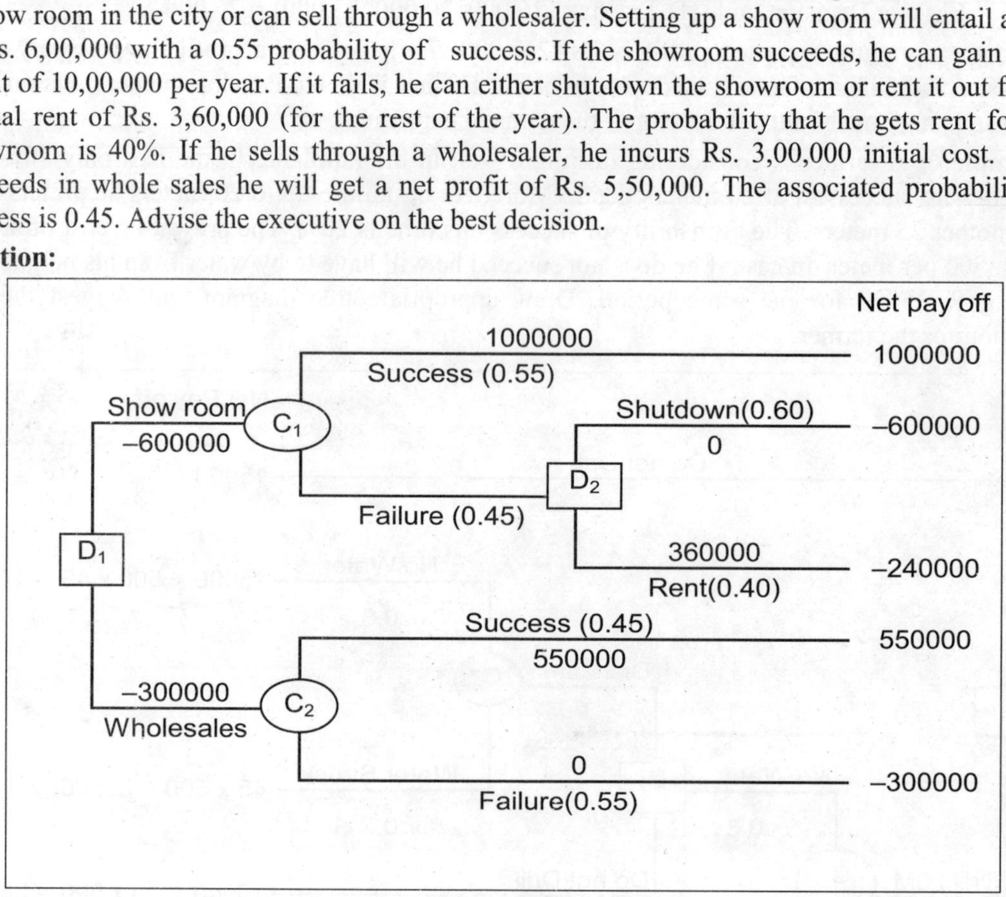

Fig. 13.28

$$EMV[D_2] = MAX(0.6 \times -6,00,000\ ;\ 0.4 \times -2,40,000) = MAX(-3,60,000\ ;\ -96,000) = -96,000$$
$$EMV\ (C_1) = 0.55 \times 10,00,000 + 0.45 \times - 96,000 = 5,06,800$$
$$EMV\ (C_2) = 0.45 \times 5,50,000 + 0.55 \times - 3,00,000 = 82,500$$
$$EMV\ [D_1] = MAX(82,500\ ;\ 5,06,800) = 5,06800$$

Thus the businessman must opt for showroom at the first stage decision making.

Example: 8 An organization has 3 alternative projects A, B and C under consideration. Which one it should choose based on decision tree approach. The data are given below for all the three projects.

Project A: For project A a capital investment of Rs.60, 000 is required. If the project is completed on time, then the organization will receive reward of Rs.1,00,000 as revenue. If not completed on ime, a penalty of Rs. 5000 per day will be deducted from assured reward of 1,00,000 with a naximum penalty of Rs.15,000. The following table gives the probabilities of delay.

Table 13.25

0 day	0.75
1 day	0.10
2 days	0.10
3 or more days	0.05
Total	1.00

roject B: Project B needs an initial investment of Rs.75, 000. After completion the company vill get a reward of Rs.75, 000. If the said project is completed in 2 days the organization will get follow up project that will require an expenditure of Rs. 20, 000 and revenue reward of Rs. 50, 00 with 70% chance and Rs.75, 000 with 30% chance. If more than 2 days are required for the irst project, the follow up project will not be available. They have equal chance of completing he first project in two days.

roject C: Project C needs an initial investment of Rs.1,00,000. A chance of success for this roject is 70% the associated revenue reward will be 1,80,000. If the project fails then no revenue vill be received. Suggest suitable optimum decision for the said investor.

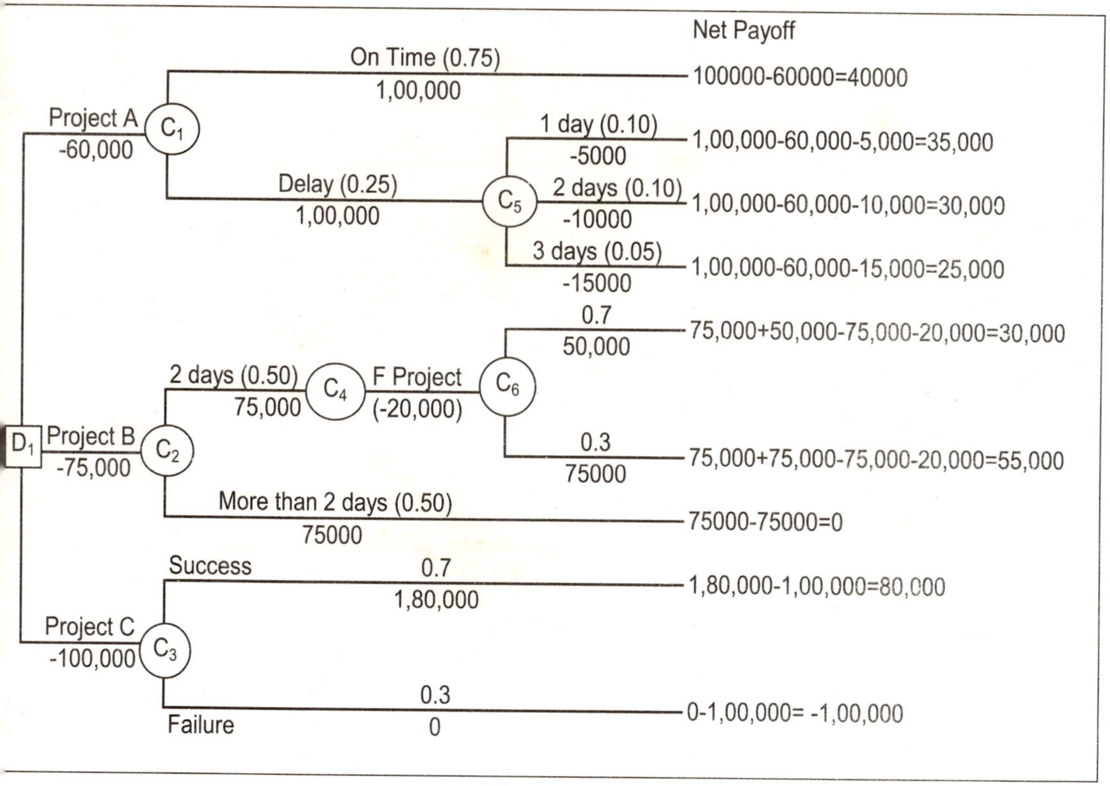

Fig. 13.29

Solution:

$$EMV\ (C_5) = 0.1 \times 35000 + 0.1 \times 30000 + 0.05 \times 25 = 7750$$
$$EMV\ (C_1) = 0.75 \times 40000 + 7750 = 37750$$
$$EMV\ (C_6) = 0.7 \times 30000 + 0.3 \times 55000 = 37500$$
$$EMV\ (C_2) = 0.5 \times 37500 + 0.5 \times 0 = 18750$$
$$EMV\ (C_3) = 0.7 \times 80000 + 0.3 \times -100000 = 26000$$
$$EMV\ [D_1] = MAX\ [37750, 18750, 26000] = 37500$$

Since EMV is high in the case of Project A the company should go for project A—

Example 9: A company is considering whether to go for the new product or not. If it decides to go further in producing the new product, it must either install a new division, which cost Rs. 4 Crores or work overtime with existing division at an additional cost of Rs. 1.5 Crores Further in the case of new division before proceeding further it will have to get an approval from the government. It is believed that there is 70% chance of getting it approved from the government. The market survey has revealed the following facts regarding the quantity of sales.

Table 13.26

Amount of sales	Probability	Resulting Profit
High	0.45	15
Medium	0.30	7
Low	0.20	3
Nil	0.05	–5

However, by overtime option the company knew that it will be able to meet up to the level of medium magnitude only. Suggest a suitable optimum decision.

Solution:

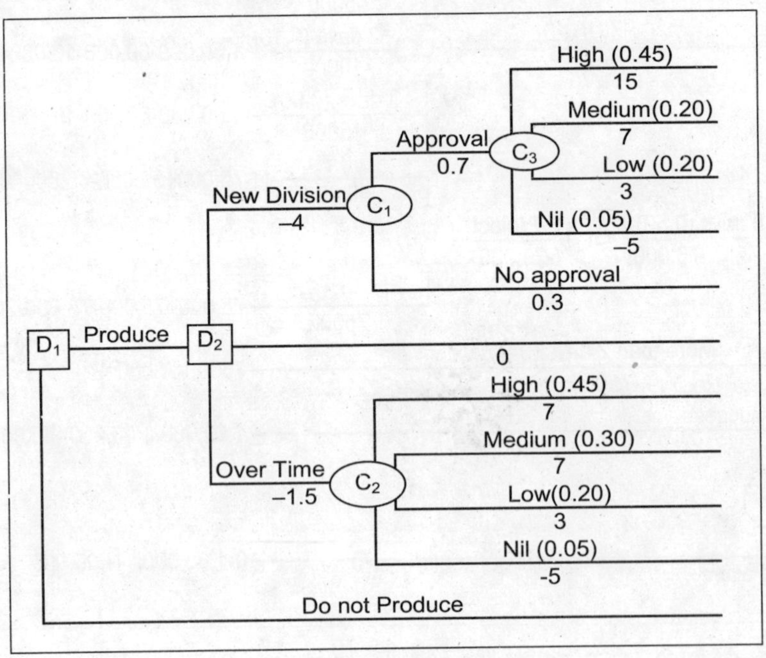

Fig. 13.30

$$EMV(C_3) = 0.45 \times 15 + 0.2 \times 7 + 0.2 \times 3 + 0.05 \times -5 = 9.2$$
$$EMV(C_1) = 0.7 \times 9.2 + 0.3 \times 0 = 6.44.$$
$$EMV(C_2) = 0.45 \times 7 + 0.3 \times 7 + 0.2 \times 3 + 0.05 \times -5 = 5.6$$
$$EMV[D_2] = MAX[6.44 - 4; 5.6 - 1.5] = MAX[2.44; 4.1] = 4.1$$
$$EMV[D_1] = 4.1$$

Thus the company must go for the new product by utilizing the over time.

Example 10: A businessman has two independent invest options A and B. However, he lacks funds for undertaking both simultaneously. He can undertake investment A and then stop or go for B on the event success in A. Alternatively, he can opt for B first and then stop or go for A provided he succeeds in B. The probability of success for A is 0.7 while for B it is 0.4. Both the investments needs Rs. 2,000 each and both pay back nothing when they fail. Successful completion of A will pay Rs. 3000 over cost, and successful completion of B will pay Rs. 5000 over cost. Draw a suitable tree diagram and option the optimum solution.

Solution:

In the tree diagram the tail end values are only conditional at the stage when move backward values are taken care off.

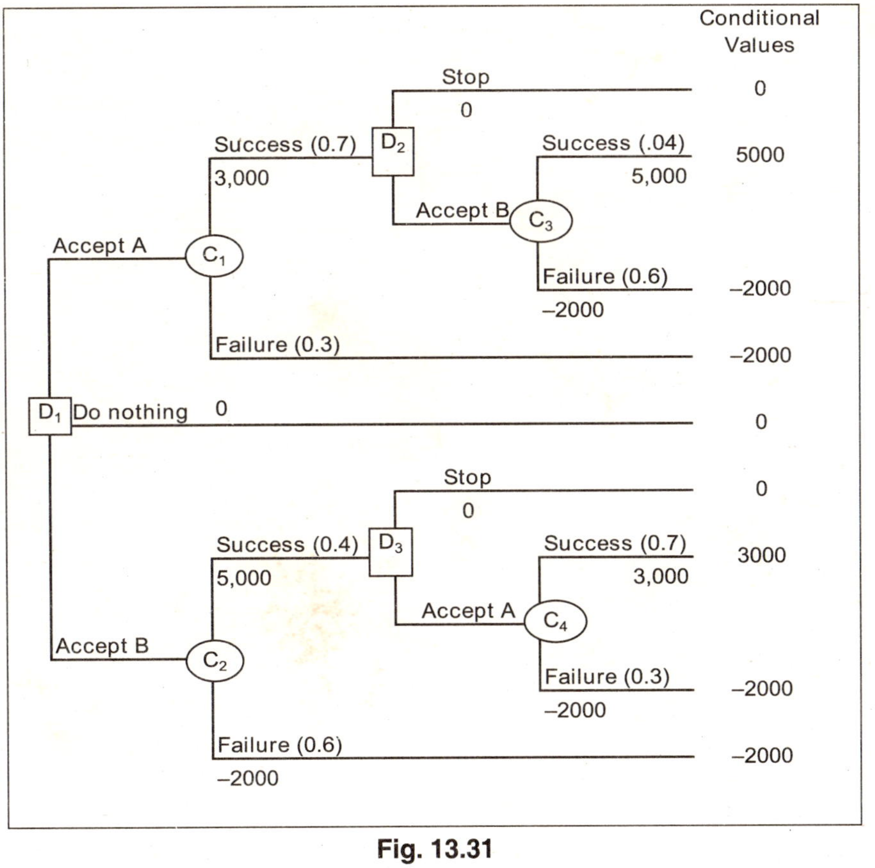

Fig. 13.31

Evaluation of tree diagram by backward rolling

$$\text{EMV}(C_3) = 0.4 \times 5000 + 0.6 \times -2000 = 800$$

$$\text{EMV}([D_2] = \text{Max}(800,0) = 800$$

$$\text{EMV}(C_4) = 0.7 \times 3000 + 0.3 \times -2000 = 1500$$

$$\text{EMV}[D_3] = \text{MAX}(1500,0] = 1500$$

$$\text{EMV}(C_1) = 0.7(3000 + 800) + 0.3 \times -2000 = -1200$$

$$\text{EMV}(C_2) = 0.4(1500 + 5000) + 0.6 \times -2000 = 1400$$

$$\text{EMV}[D_1] = \text{MAX}(-1200, 0, 1400] = 1400$$

Thus, the best strategy is to accept the investment B first and if it is successful then accept investment A.

Example 11: There is 40% chance that a patient admitted to the hospital is suffering from cancer. The doctor has to decide whether a serious operation should be performed or not. If the patient is suffering from cancer and the serious operation is performed, the chance that he will recover is 70%. Otherwise, it is 35%. On the other hand, if the patient is not suffering from cancer and the serious operation is performed the chance that he will recover is only 29% otherwise, it is 100%. Assume that recovery and death are the only two alternatives. Construct an appropriate decision tree and find the best possible decision.

Solution:

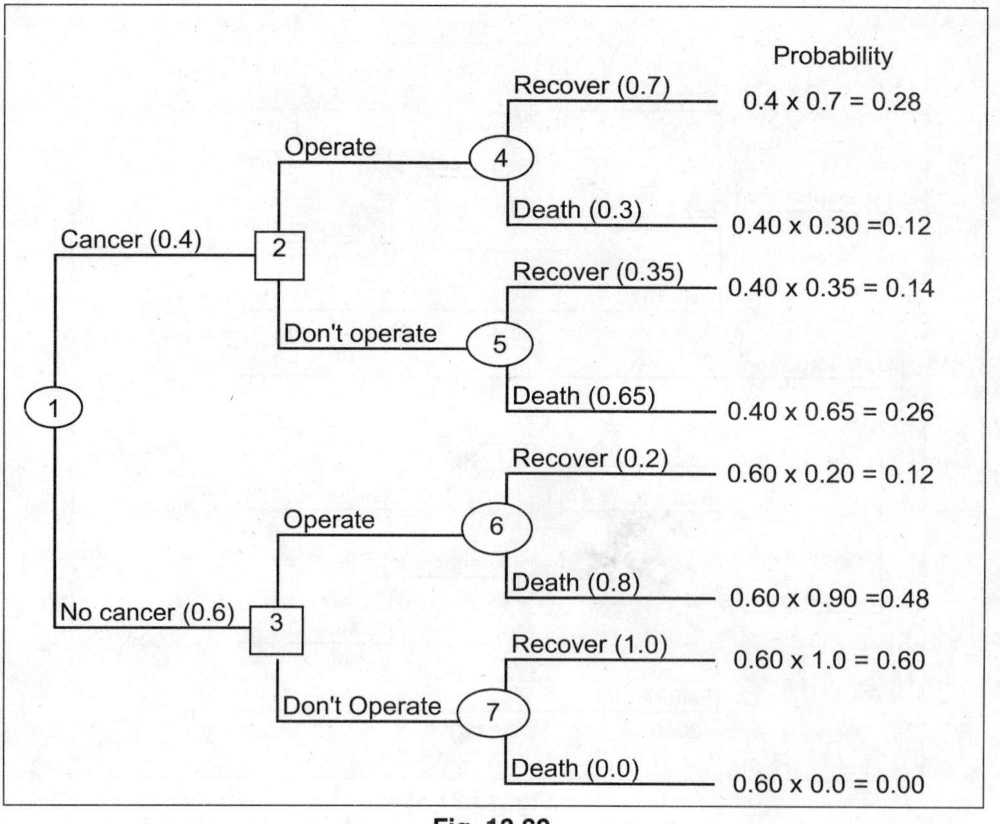

Fig. 13.32

From the decision tree 13.32, we find that

Patient recovers when operation is done = 0.28 + 0.12 = 0.40

Patient recovers when no operation is done = 0.14 + 0.602 = 0.74

Since 0.74 is grater than 0.40 we conclude that doctor should not operate such a patient.

EXERCISES

1. Under an employment promotion program, it is proposed to allow sales of newspapers on the buses during off-peak hours. The vendor can purchase the newspaper at a special discounted rate of 25 paise per copy against the selling price of 40 paise. Any unsold copies are, however a dead loss. A vendor has estimated the following probability distribution for the number of copies demanded.

No.of copies demanded	15	16	17	18	19	20
Probability	0.04	0.19	0.33	0.26	0.11	0.07

How many copies should he order so that his expected profit is maximum?

2. A food company is contemplating the introduction of a revolutionary new product with new packaging to replace the existing product at same price (S_1) or a moderate change in the composition of the existing product with a new packing at a small increase in price (S_2) or a small change in the composition of the existing except the word (new) with a negligible change in the price (S_3). The three possible states of nature of events are (i) high increase in sales (N_1) (ii) no change in sales (N_2) (iii) decrease in sales (N_3). The marketing department of the company worked out the payoffs in terms of yearly net profit for each course of action for these events (expected sales). This is represented in the following table.

States of Nature	S_1	S_2	S_3
N_1	7,00,000	5,00,000	30,000
N_2	3,00,000	4,50,000	3,00,000
N_3	1,50,000	0	3,00,000

Which strategy should the company choose on the basis of (a) Maximin criterion? (b) Maximaxi criterion (c) Minimum regret criterion (d) Laplace criterion

3. A person has two independent investment options A and B available to him but he can undertake only one at a time due to certain constraints. He can choose a first and then stop, or if A is successful then take B and vice versa. The probability of success of A is 0.6, while for B it is 0.4. Both the investments require an initial capital outlay of Rs.10,000 and both returns nothing, if the venture is unsuccessful. Successful completion of A will return Rs. 20,000 (over cost) and successful completion of B will return Rs. 24,000 (over cost). Draw decision tree and determine the best strategy. *(C.A., May 1988)*

4. Matrix Company is planning to launch a new product, which can be introduced initially in Western India or in the entire country. If the product is introduced only in Western India, the investment outlay will be Rs.12 million. After two years, matrix can evaluate the project to determine, whether it should cover the entire country. For such expansion, it will have to

incur an additional investment of Rs.10 million. To introduce the product in the entire country right in the beginning would involve an outlay of Rs.20 million. The product, in any case, will have a life of 5 years, after which the plant will have zero net value.

If the product is introduced only in the Western India, demand would be high or low with the probabilities of 0.8 and 0.2 respectively and annual cash inflow of Rs. 4 million and Rs. 2.5 million respectively.

If the product is introduced in the entire country right from the beginning, the demand would be high or low with probabilities of 0.6 and 0.4 respectively and annual cash inflow of Rs. 5 million respectively.

Based on the observed demand in the Western India , if the product is introduced in the entire country, the following probabilities would exist for high and low demand on an all India basis.

	Whole country	
Western India	High demand	Low demand
High demand	0.9	0.1
Low demand	0.4	0.6

The hurdle rate applicable to this problem is 12 per cent.

(a) Set up a decision tree for the investment situation

(b) Advice the matrix company on the investment policy it should follow. Support your advice with appropriate reasoning.

(ICWA, June 1990)

5. A company which operates a chain of lunch rooms, plan to install a unit in either of the two locations. The company feels that the probability of a unit being successful in location X is 3/4 and that, if it is successful it will make an annual profit of Rs. 4,00,000. If it is not successful, the company will lose Rs.1,00,000 per year. The probability of a unit making success in location Y is only 1/2, but if it does succeed, the annual profit will be Rs. 6,00,000. If it does not succeed in location Y, the annual lose will be Rs.1,20,000. Where should the company locate the new unit so as to maximize its expected gain?

(Banaras University, M.M.S., 1984)

6. The demand for cakes made in a bakery is as follows:

No. of Cakes	0	1	2	3	4	5
Probability	0.05	0.1	0.25	0.3	0.2	0.1

If the preparation cost is Rs. 2 and selling price is Rs. 4 per unit, how many should the baker make to maximize his profit?

7. A manager has a choice between (i) a risky contract promising Rs.7 lakhs with probability 0.6 and Rs. 4 lakhs with probability 0.4 and (ii) a diversified portfolio consisting of two contracts with independent outcomes and each promising Rs.3.5 lakhs with probability 0.6 and Rs. 2 lakhs with probability 0.4. Construct a decision tree using EMV criteria. Can you arrive at the decision using EMV criteria.

(Poona University, M.B.A., 1982)

8. You have a new furnace installed. The dealer offers to sell you spare fuel pumps at Rs. 200 each, if you buy them during installation the pumps sell for Rs. 500 in retail. These pumps cannot be repaired if they fail. Manufacturer's records indicate the following probability of fuel pumps failures during the furnaces life time.

Failure	0	1	2	3	4
Probability	0.01	0.3	0.4	0.1	0.1

Ignoring installation and holding costs, how many spare fuel pumps should be purchased during installation? *(Delhi University, M.B.A., 1987)*

9. A modern home appliances dealer finds that the cost of holding a mini cooking range in stock for a month is Rs. 200 (insurance, minor deterioration, interest on browed capital etc.). Customers who cannot obtain a cooking range immediately go to other dealers and he estimates that for every customer, who cannot get immediate delivery, he loses an average of Rs. 500. the probabilities of demand for 0, 1, 2, 3, 4, 5 mini cooking ranges in a month are 0.05, 0.1, 0.2, 0.3, 0.2 and 0.15 respectively. Determine the optimal stock level of cooking ranges. Also fin EVPI. *(Delhi University, M.B.A 1990)*

10. A businessman has two independent investments A and B available to him, but he lacks the capital to undertake both of them simultaneously. He can choose to take A first and then stop, or if A is successful, then take B or viceversa. The probability of success on A is 0.7, while for B, it is 0.4. Both investments require an initial capital outlay of Rs. 2,000 and both return nothing, if the venture is unsuccessful. Successful completion of A will return Rs. 3,000(over cost) whereas successful completion of B will return Rs. 5,000 (over cost). Draw the decision tree and determine the best strategy. *(C.A., May 1985)*

11. The owner of a boat has estimated the following distribution of demand for a particular kind of boat.

No. of boat demanded	0	1	2	3	4	5	6
Probability:	0.14	0.27	0.27	0.18	0.09	0.04	0.01

Each boat costs him Rs 7,000 and he sells them for Rs. 10,000 each. Boats that are left unsold at the end of the season must be disposed off for Rs. 6,000 each. How many should be stocked so as to maximize his expected profit? *(Delhi University, M.Com., 1988)*

12. A mineral processing company wants to decide about the number of spare gear trains it has to order out at the time of placing order for a high horsepower gear box connected to a grinding unit. Although the life of a gear can be as high as 30 years and more, sudden failures cannot be ruled out. In case of failure, it would be expensive and time consuming to get a spare gear-train. The cost would be Rs. 2,00,000 including the loss of production due to down time of the equipment. If ordered-out with gear box, a gear train would cost only Rs. 10,000 per unit. The following data is based on an analysis of past experience of 100 gear boxes.

Number of spare gear trains required	0	1	2	3	4
Number of gear boxes requiring the spares:	93	4	2	1	0

You are expected to advice the optimal order size. *(Poona University, M.B.A., 1982)*

13. A milkman buys milk at Rs. 2 and sells it for Rs. 2.5 per litre. Unsold milk has to be thrown away. The daily demand litres has the following probabilistic distribution.

Litres	46	48	50	52	54	58	60	62	64
Probability	0.01	0.03	0.06	0.1	0.2	0.25	0.15	0.1	0.1

If each day's demand is independent of the previous day's demand, how many litres should he order every day? *(Rajasthan University, M.B.A., 1982)*